The Phenomenon of Religious Faith

Edited by

Terrence Reynolds
Georgetown University

PEARSON
Prentice
Hall

Upper Saddle River, New Jersey 07458

Library of Congress Cataloging-in-Publication Data

The phenomenon of religious faith   /   edited by Terrence Reynolds. — 1st ed.
       p. cm.
Includes bibliographical references.
   ISBN 0-13-048115-7
   1. God.   2. God—Proof, Ontological.   3. Philosophical theology.   I. Reynolds, Terrence Paul

   BT103 .P48 2005
   210—dc22

                                              2003026358

Editorial Director: Charlyce Jones-Owen
Senior Acquisitions Editor: Ross Miller
Assistant Editor: Wendy Yurash
Managing Editor: Joanne Riker
Production Liaison: Joanne Hakim
Production Editor: Bruce Hobart
Editorial Assistant: Carla Worner
Senior Marketing Manager: Chris Ruel
Manufacturing Buyer: Christina Helder
Cover Art Director: Jayne Conte
Cover Design: Bruce Kenselaar
Composition/Full-Service Project Management: Pine Tree Composition
Printer/Binder: Courier Companies, Inc.

Pearson Education Ltd., London
Pearson Education Singapore, Pte. Ltd
Pearson Education, Canada, Ltd
Pearson Education—Japan
Pearson Education Australia PTY, Limited

Pearson Education North Asia Ltd
Pearson Educación de Mexico, S.A. de C.V.
Pearson Education Malaysia, Pte. Ltd
Pearson Education, Upper Saddle River, New Jersey

10 9 8 7 6 5 4 3 2 1
0-13-048115-7

Contents

Preface vii
Introduction ix

PART ONE   Preliminary Questions on Religious Faith. 1

1. Theology and Falsification
    ANTONY FLEW, R.M. HARE, BASIL MITCHELL 2

2. The Creed of a Savoyard Priest
    JEAN JACQUES ROUSSEAU 8

3. A Free Man's Worship
    BERTRAND RUSSELL 25

4. The Meaning of Life
    A.J. AYER 31

PART TWO   Arguments for God's Existence 47

5. The Cosmological Argument: A Defense
    RICHARD TAYLOR 47

6. The Watch and the Watchmaker
    WILLIAM PALEY 56

7. The Classical Ontological Argument
    ST. ANSELM OF CANTERBURY 59

8. The Cosmological Argument
    DAVID HUME 61

9. Against Revelation and Deism
    PERCY BYSSHE SHELLEY 64

10. Existence, Predication, and the Ontological Argument
    JEROME SHAFFER 83

PART THREE   Models of Religious Faith. 99

A.   St. Thomas Aquinas: Faith, Belief, and Intellectual Assent 99

11.   On Faith
        St. Thomas Aquinas 100

12.   Of God and His Creatures
        St. Thomas Aquinas 116

13.   The Thomist-Catholic View of Faith
        John Hick 125

14.   The Agnostic's Dilemma
        Norwood Russell Hanson 136

B.   Blaise Pascal and William James: Faith, Will,
       and Prudential Options 140

15.   The Wager
        Blaise Pascal 141

16.   Pascal's Wager
        James Cargile 144

17.   Pascalian Wagering
        Thomas V. Morris. 151

18.   The Ethics of Belief
        W.K. Clifford. 163

19.   The Will to Believe
        William James. 168

20.   Passion and Suspicion: Religious Affections in "The Will to Believe"
        D. M. Yeager 183

C.   Søren Kierkegaard: Faith, Subjectivity,
       and Religious Possibility. 197

21.   Truth Is Subjectivity
        Søren Kierkegaard. 197

22.   Selections from *Fear and Trembling:*
        Eulogy on Abraham and Epilogue
        Søren Kierkegaard. 205

23.   The Strategy of the Authorship
        Mark C. Taylor 214

24.   Faith Against Reason: Kierkegaard
      C. STEPHEN EVANS 223

D.   John Hick: Faith, Language, and Experience of God 240

25.   The Nature of Faith
      JOHN HICK 241

26.   Faith and the Logic of Seeing-As
      JAMES HEANEY 254

27.   John Hick on Religious Experience and Perception
      J. WESLEY ROBBINS 261

PART FOUR   The Rationality of Religious Faith 269

28.   Lectures on Religious Belief
      LUDWIG WITTGENSTEIN 270

29.   The Groundlessness of Belief
      NORMAN MALCOLM 283

30.   Knowledge, Belief, and Reformed Epistemology
      JAY VAN HOOK 293

31.   Is Reason Enough?
      NICHOLAS WOLTERSTORFF 300

32.   Is Belief in God Properly Basic?
      ALVIN PLANTINGA 308

33.   A Critique of Plantinga's Religious Epistemology
      MICHAEL MARTIN 317

PART FIVE   Religious Faith and the Issue of Pluralism 327

34.   Religious Pluralism and Ultimate Reality
      JOHN HICK 328

35.   The Philosophy of Religious Pluralism: A Critical Appraisal of Hick
      and His Critics
      SUMNER B. TWISS 338

36.   Atheism and Implicit Christianity
      KARL RAHNER 368

37. Theology and the World's Religious History
     WILFRED CANTWELL SMITH 383

PART SIX   The Experience of the Divine. 403

38. Mysticism
     WILLIAM JAMES. 404

39. Contemplation
     THOMAS MERTON. 422

40. Religious Experience and Religious Belief
     WILLIAM P. ALSTON. 430

41. Religious Experience and Religious Belief
     WAYNE PROUDFOOT 438

42. Mysticism and Philosophy
     RICHARD M. GALE 460

Preface

The idea for this anthology was generated by a course for which I served as a graduate teaching assistant some years ago at Brown University. Taught by Sumner Twiss, the course was entitled "Faith and Reason," and it exposed the diverse student population at Brown to the rich complexity of issues surrounding the phenomenon of religious faith. At the time, I thought the course was extremely well conceived and hoped one day to teach a course like it myself. When I came to Georgetown some twelve years ago, I was asked to teach *The Problem of God*, a required course for all first-year students, and I immediately decided that I would approach the course as we had at Brown, as an introduction to the philosophy of religion with an emphasis on the phenomenon of religious faith and its implications. Over time, the course has evolved into an examination of any number of foundational questions of religious epistemology, including the relationship of faith to reason, belief, knowledge, and will, and the meaning, truth, and justification of religious claims. In addition, the readings pose related questions in the philosophy of religion such as the nature and implications of religious pluralism, religious experience, the relationship between religion and morality, miracle claims, inclusive and exclusive notions of salvation, and the nature of religious language. At Georgetown, as at Brown, the course has been very well received by the students. Unfortunately, in order to teach the course effectively, I have had to require students to purchase four or five texts and augment these with additional readings. This collection is designed to enable others to teach a comparable course with greater convenience.

As in any project that assumes a great deal of time and care, thanks are in order to many who have been of invaluable assistance. I wish first to thank Barney Twiss for his initial design of the course; its essential structure has endured over time and proved the wisdom of his pedagogical insight. I also wish to thank Ross Miller, the philosophy and religion editor at Prentice-Hall, for his openness to my proposal and for his generosity and patience as the process of assembling the collected readings slowly drew to a close. His support was all that one could ask for in an editor, and I'm very grateful for his kindness. I also owe a word of thanks to all the publishers who responded swiftly and professionally to my permission requests; I can assure them that what may seem at times like thankless work is profoundly appreciated. A very special word of thanks is also owed to Linda Ferneyhough, the Executive Assistant for the Theology Department at Georgetown, who assisted enormously in the permission process, and without whose support this collection may not have come into being. Britt Borgstrom is also deserving of thanks for her goodwill, and her devotion to the compiling of materials, copying of articles, and other organizational tasks without which such a volume could not be produced. Thanks are also much in order to Diane Yeager, my colleague in the Theology Department at Georgetown, who offered characteristically incisive suggestions that improved my Introduction and the ordering of the essays immensely. Many thanks also to the following reviewers of this project: Wallace A. Murphy, Mississippi State University and Karen Bell, California State University, Fresno. Most of all, thanks are due to my wife, Lyn, and my children, Marie, Heather, and Colin, for their never-ending patience with my eccentricities. Finally, I dedicate this collection to my late parents, Edward and Ruth Reynolds, who wondered what generated my interest in these matters, but who were always supportive and convinced that the issues were well worth the attention I gave to them.

Great thinkers pondering great themes provide a never-ending source of nourishment for the mind and the imagination. My hope is that the efforts that went into the making of this volume will bear fruit in the classrooms, offices, and homes in which this collection is put to use and that the essays collected here will prove as provocative to others as they have to my students.

Terrence Reynolds
Georgetown University
Washington, D.C.

Introduction

The constellation of issues that surround the beliefs and practices associated with religious faith have prompted any number of volumes. Most of these collections are admirably broad in scope, including issues as diverse as the arguments for the existence of God, the attributes of God, the problem of evil, rebuttals to theism, the relationship of religious faith to morality, the nature of miracles, religious or mystical experience, death and immortality, religion and science, faith and reason, religious epistemology, the problem of religious pluralism, the relationship of language to religious faith, particular doctrinal formulations, as well as other areas of inquiry. Such volumes offer a comprehensive, albeit brief, introduction to the philosophical issues that are generated by religious faith. In this volume, however, the focus has deliberately been more limited. The emphasis has been placed on the phenomenon of religious faith itself, exploring the relationship of faith to reason, belief, knowledge, will, and language, and examining the meaning, truth, and justification of its claims. It has been my experience that such an approach makes possible a more concentrated examination of the issues addressed, and also engages students of all religious and nonreligious convictions.

Although religious traditions vary immensely in the ways they conceive of the transcendent, of evil, of the miraculous, of the relationship between belief and one's life in the world, and of the faiths of others, the one thing that all believers share is a faith that there is something Real beyond the range of the senses that is worthy of their deepest devotion. Faith itself, whatever the categories through which it becomes explicit, has shaped and continues to shape the lives of countless numbers of persons across boundaries of time and space, and has exerted an influence on human affairs that is beyond measure.

I would anticipate that one familiar with the issues that have risen to forefront in the study of the philosophy of religion might wonder why I would choose to focus on the relationship between faith and reason. For many, the parameters of the debate were established in the early decades of the previous century, and were clearly set forth by Antony Flew, Basil Mitchell, and R. M. Hare in their Oxford Symposium of 1955. In that debate, the position that claims require verification or falsification is argued by Flew, and religious faith is found wanting. Mitchell and Hare appear to grant Flew's premises about the nature of rationality, and they attempt to justify faith convictions on other grounds. Mitchell suggests that faith rests on an encounter with the Divine, a rational experience for the believer but one that is not verifiable to others. Hare, taking a different approach, argues that faith is built upon "bliks," or assumptions that shape one's interpretation of subsequent experiences. While Hare's suggestion protects the believer against the verificationist objection, it offers no clear guidelines for adjudicating the truth or falsity of bliks themselves.

For many, this symposium largely delineated and, in effect, closed the faith and reason conversation. However, it is my conviction that the renewed interest in the work of

Ludwig Wittgenstein in the latter part of the last century reopened the discussion, throwing into uncertainty many of the received assumptions about the nature and function of rationality itself. Wittgenstein posed the question whether our rationality was shaped by cultural-linguistic factors arising out of distinctive forms of life. If this were so, then our claims themselves and their justification would arise out of distinctive communities and traditions to which others would be outsiders. No longer could we look with confidence on a single, objective notion of human rationality. Instead, we would find ourselves in a world in which persons could not hold others to uniform standards for the justification of claims, such as the verification/falsification criterion, for such universal standards would not exist. In fact, it may be the case, Wittgenstein suggested, that believers and unbelievers have no way of understanding or ultimately assessing the claims of one another.

In my view, the renewed appreciation for the work of Wittgenstein has invigorated the interest in questions long ago thought to have been answered. This volume is designed to trace the relationship of faith and reason, through a discussion of the arguments for God's existence, and an assessment of four models of faith which move progressively in the direction described by Wittgenstein. It continues with a discussion of the meaning of religious pluralism in light of this conversation, a look at Wittgenstein and the debate over the nature of rationality, and concludes with an examination of the claims of religious mystics to have experienced the Divine. The sections in this volume attempt to address a number of fundamental questions to which faith gives rise:

- Is the Real to which faith clings available, in whole or in part, to human reason?
- On what epistemic grounds are religious claims based?
- What, precisely, is the origin of religious faith, and in what ways is it related to reason, will, belief, knowledge, and language?
- If one lacks religious faith, is there a path or process by which one can attain it?
- How do believers come to hold the convictions of their faith, and how can they be assured that they are justified?
- How can conflicting religious claims be adjudicated?
- Are religious claims true or false at all, and on what basis could one resolve such a question?
- Is religious faith ultimately rational or irrational?
- How is faith to be distinguished from madness?
- What is one to make of the great diversity of religious convictions?
- In what ways are believers and unbelievers different, and can believers and unbelievers truly understand one another?
- Can there be a direct experience of the Real, and how ought claims to such experience be assessed?

The essays included in this volume are both classical and contemporary, and are accessible to undergraduates as well as graduate students. It has been my experience that the rich complexity of arguments at work in this collection assist students immensely in understanding, adapting, defending, and articulating the core beliefs that structure their lives, whether those beliefs are best described as theistic or atheistic.

Further, it has been my experience that students are genuinely engaged by the subtlety and existential significance of the discussion. Whether believers or not, they acknowledge the influence of religious sentiment in those around them and wish to understand more clearly what gives shape to the mind and heart of the believer. In the many years that this subject has been explored with my students, it has never failed to excite their imaginations, engage their intellects, and leave them grateful for the experience. It is hoped that a similar journey awaits all who choose to employ this volume.

PART ONE

Preliminary Questions on Religious Faith: How Is Faith Related to Reason, Trust, Will, Experience, and Language?

Part I introduces a number of perspectives on religious faith, including differing notions of its character, along with negative observations that faith violates reason and subverts the human quest for the discovery of authenticity and meaning in life. The classic discussion between Antony Flew, R. M. Hare, and Basil Mitchell (1955) presents three widely divergent notions of faith. Mitchell and Hare defend faith, though on different grounds, whereas Flew counters with the skeptical assertion that such faith violates the canons of verifiability and falsifiability. Jean Jacques Rousseau, in "The Creed of a Savoyard Priest" (1762), argues that a commonsense appraisal of the world around us, conducted solely by reason, demonstrates clearly the providential oversight of a loving God to whom we owe our gratitude and a life's pursuit of the good. According to Rousseau, only an obstinate refusal to appreciate the order and loveliness of the world would allow one to deny the existence of a God. Also relying solely upon reason, Bertrand Russell (1903) comes to a quite different conclusion. Russell describes the world as fundamentally chaotic and senseless, an arena for ongoing suffering in which the positing of an all-powerful and benevolent Creator would be nonsensical. A. J. Ayer (1988) concludes this introductory section with a lucid discussion of the meaning of life, as it is discovered in the absence of the Divine.

1. Theology and Falsification

ANTONY FLEW

Let us begin with a parable. It is a parable developed from a tale told by John Wisdom in his haunting and revelatory article "Gods." Once upon a time two explorers came upon a clearing in the jungle. In the clearing were growing many flowers and many weeds. One explorer says, "Some gardener must tend this plot." The other disagrees, "There is no gardener." So they pitch their tents and set a watch. No gardener is ever seen. "But perhaps he is an invisible gardener." So they set up a barbed-wire fence. They electrify it. They patrol with bloodhounds. (For they remember how H. G. Wells's *The Invisible Man* could be both smelt and touched though he could not be seen.) But no shrieks ever suggest that some intruder has received a shock. No movements of the wire ever betray an invisible climber. The bloodhounds never give cry. Yet still the Believer is not convinced. "But there is a gardener, invisible, intangible, insensible to electric shocks, a gardener who has no scent and makes no sound, a gardener who comes secretly to look after the garden which he loves." At last the Sceptic despairs, "But what remains of your original assertion? Just how does what you call an invisible, intangible, eternally elusive gardener differ from an imaginary gardener or even from no gardener at all?"

In this parable we can see how what starts as an assertion, that something exists or that there is some analogy between certain complexes of phenomena, may be reduced step by step to an altogether different status, to an expression perhaps of a "picture preference." The Sceptic says there is no gardener. The Believer says there is a gardener (but invisible, etc.). One man talks about sexual behaviour. Another man prefers to talk of Aphrodite (but knows that there is not really a superhuman person additional to, and somehow responsible for, all sexual phenomena). The process of qualification may be checked at any point before the original assertion is completely withdrawn and something of that first assertion will remain (Tautology). Mr. Wells's invisible man could not, admittedly, be seen, but in all other respects he was a man like the rest of us. But though the process of qualification may be, and of course usually is checked in time, it is not always judiciously so halted. Someone may dissipate his assertion completely

Source: From *New Essays in Philosophical Theology,* edited by Antony Flew and Alasdair MacIntyre (London: SCM Press, 1955), pp. 96–108. Copyright © 1953 by SCM Press Ltd. Reprinted by permission of Macmillan Publishing Company. Footnotes omitted.

without noticing that he has done so. A fine brash hypothesis may thus be killed by inches, the death by a thousand qualifications.

And in this, it seems to me, lies the peculiar danger, the endemic evil, of theological utterance. Take such utterances as "God has a plan," "God created the world," "God loves us as a father loves his children." They look at first sight very much like assertions, vast cosmological assertions. Of course, this is no sure sign that they either are, or are intended to be, assertions. But let us confine ourselves to the cases where those who utter such sentences intend them to express assertions. (Merely remarking parenthetically that those who intend or interpret such utterances as crypto-commands, expressions of wishes, disguised ejaculations, concealed ethics, or as anything else but assertions, are unlikely to succeed in making them either properly orthodox or practically effective).

Now to assert that such and such is the case is necessarily equivalent to denying that such and such is not the case. Suppose then that we are in doubt as to what someone who gives vent to an utterance is asserting, or suppose that, more radically, we are sceptical as to whether he is really asserting anything at all, one way of trying to understand (or perhaps it will be to expose) his utterance is to attempt to find what he would regard as counting against, or as being incompatible with, its truth. For if the utterance is indeed an assertion, it will necessarily be equivalent to a denial of the negation of that assertion. And anything which would count against the assertion, or which would induce the speaker to withdraw it and to admit that it had been mistaken, must be part of (or the whole of) the meaning of the negation of that assertion. And to know the meaning of the negation of an assertion, is as near as makes no matter, to know the meaning of that assertion. And if there is nothing which a putative assertion denies then there is nothing which it asserts either: and so it is not really an assertion. When the Sceptic in the parable asked the Believer, "Just how does what you call an invisible, intangible, eternally elusive gardener differ from an imaginary gardener or even from no gardener at all?" he was suggesting that the Believer's earlier statement had been so eroded by qualification that it was no longer an assertion at all.

Now it often seems to people who are not religious as if there was no conceivable event or series of events the occurrence of which would be admitted by sophisticated religious people to be a sufficient reason for conceding "There wasn't a God after all" or "God does not really love us then." Someone tells us that God loves us as a father loves his children. We are reassured. But then we see a child dying of inoperable cancer of the throat. His earthly father is driven frantic in his efforts to help, but his Heavenly Father reveals no obvious sign of concern. Some qualification is made—God's love is "not a merely human love" or it is "an inscrutable love," perhaps—and we realize that such sufferings are quite compatible with the truth of the assertion that "God loves us as a father (but, of course, . . .)." We are reassured again. But then perhaps we ask: what is this assurance of God's (appropriately qualified) love worth, what is this apparent guarantee really a guarantee against? Just what would have to happen not merely (morally and wrongly) to tempt but also (logically and rightly) to entitle us to say "God does not love us" or even "God does not exist?" I therefore put to the succeeding symposiasts the simple central question, "What would have to occur or to have occurred to constitute for you a disproof of the love of, or of the existence of, God?"

R. M. HARE

I wish to make it clear that I shall not try to defend Christianity in particular, but re-ligion in general—not because I do not believe in Christianity, but because you can-not understand what Christianity is, until you have understood what religion is.

I must begin by confessing that, on the ground marked out by Flew, he seems to me to be completely victorious. I therefore shift my ground by relating another parable. A certain lunatic is convinced that all dons want to murder him. His friends introduce him to all the mildest and most respectable dons that they can find, and after each of them has retired, they say, "You see, he doesn't really want to murder you; he spoke to you in a most cordial manner; surely you are convinced now?" But the lunatic replies "Yes, but that was only his diabolical cunning; he's really plotting against me the whole time, like the rest of them; I know it I tell you." However many kindly dons are pro-duced, the reaction is still the same.

Now we say that such a person is deluded. But what is he deluded about? About the truth or falsity of an assertion? Let us apply Flew's test to him. There is no behav-iour of dons that can be enacted which he will accept as counting against his theory; and therefore his theory, on this test, asserts nothing. But it does not follow that there is no difference between what he thinks about dons and what most of us think about them—otherwise we should not call him a lunatic and ourselves sane, and dons would have no reason to feel uneasy about his presence in Oxford.

Let us call that in which we differ from this lunatic, our respective *bliks*. He has an insane *blik* about dons; we have a sane one. It is important to realize that we have a sane one, not no *blik* at all; for there must be two sides to any argument—if he has a wrong *blik*, then those who are right about dons must have a right one. Flew has shown that a *blik* does not consist in an assertion or system of them; but nevertheless it is very important to have the right *blik*.

Let us try to imagine what it would be like to have different *bliks* about other things than dons. When I am driving my car, it sometimes occurs to me to wonder whether my movements of the steering-wheel will always continue to be followed by corresponding alterations in the direction of the car. I have never had a steering failure, though I have had skids, which must be similar. Moreover, I know enough about how the steering of my car is made, to know the sort of thing that would have to go wrong for the steering to fail—steel joints would have to part, or steel rods break, or some-thing—but how do I know that this won't happen? The truth is, I don't know; I just have a *blik* about steel and its properties, so that normally I trust the steering of my car; but I find it not at all difficult to imagine what it would be like to lose this *blik* and ac-quire the opposite one. People would say I was silly about steel; but there would be no mistaking the reality of the difference between our respective *bliks*—for example, I should never go in a motor-car. Yet I should hesitate to say that the difference between us was the difference between contradictory assertions. No amount of safe arrivals or bench-tests will remove my *blik* and restore the normal one: for my *blik* is compatible with any finite number of such tests.

It was Hume who taught us that our whole commerce with the world depends upon our *blik* about the world; and that differences between *bliks* about the world cannot be settled by observation of what happens in the world. That was why, having performed the interesting experiment of doubting the ordinary man's *blik* about the world, and showing that no proof could be given to make us adopt one *blik* rather than another, he turned to backgammon to take his mind off the problem. It seems, indeed, to be impossible even to formulate as an assertion the normal *blik* about the world which makes me put my confidence in the future reliability of steel joints, in the continued ability of the road to support my car, and not gape beneath it revealing nothing below; in the general nonhomicidal tendencies of dons; in my own continued well-being (in some sense of that word that I may not now fully understand) if I continue to do what is right according to my lights; in the general likelihood of people like Hitler coming to a bad end. But perhaps a formulation less inadequate than most is to be found in the Psalms: "The earth is weak and all the inhabiters thereof: I bear up the pillars of it."

The mistake of the position which Flew selects for attack is to regard this kind of talk as some sort of *explanation*, as scientists are accustomed to use the word. As such, it would obviously be ludicrous. We no longer believe in God as an Atlas—*nous n'avons pas besoin de cette hypothese.* But it is nevertheless true to say that, as Hume saw, without a *blik* there can be no explanation; for it is by our *bliks* that we decide what is and what is not an explanation. Suppose we believed that everything that happened, happened by pure chance. This would not of course be an assertion; for it is compatible with anything happening or not happening, and so, incidentally, is its contradictory. But if we had this belief, we should not be able to explain or predict or plan anything. Thus, although we should not be asserting anything different from those of a more normal belief, there would be a great difference between us; and this is the sort of difference that there is between those who really believe in God and those who really disbelieve in him.

The word "really" is important, and may excite suspicion. I put it in, because when people have had a good Christian upbringing, as have most of those who now profess not to believe in any sort of religion, it is very hard to discover what they really believe. The reason why they find it so easy to think that they are not religious, is that they have never got into the frame of mind of one who suffers from the doubts to which religion is the answer. Not for them the terrors of the primitive jungle. Having abandoned some of the more picturesque fringes of religion, they think that they have abandoned the whole thing—whereas in fact they still have got, and could not live without, a religion of a comfortably substantial, albeit highly sophisticated, kind, which differs from that of many "religious people" in little more than this, that "religious people" like to sing Psalms about theirs—a very natural and proper thing to do. But nevertheless there may be a big difference lying behind—the difference between two people who, though side by side, are walking in different directions. I do not know in what direction Flew is walking; perhaps he does not know either. But we have had some examples recently of various ways in which one can walk away from Christianity, and there are any number of possibilities. After all, man has not changed biologically since primitive times; it is his religion that has changed, and it can easily change again. And if you do not think that such changes make a difference, get acquainted with some Sikhs and some Mussulmans of the same Punjabi stock; you will find them quite different sorts of people.

There is an important difference between Flew's parable and my own which we have not yet noticed. The explorers do not *mind* about their garden; they discuss it with interest, but not with concern. But my lunatic, poor fellow, minds about dons; and I mind about the steering of my car; it often has people in it that I care for. It is because I mind very much about what goes on in the garden in which I find myself, that I am unable to share the explorers' detachment.

BASIL MITCHELL

Flew's article is searching and perceptive, but there is, I think, something odd about his conduct of the theologian's case. The theologian surely would not deny that the fact of pain counts against the assertion that God loves men. This very incompatibility generates the most intractable of theological problems—the problem of evil. So the theologian *does* recognize the fact of pain as counting against Christian doctrine. But it is true that he will not allow it—or anything—to count decisively against it; for he is committed by his faith to trust in God. His attitude is not that of the detached observer, but of the believer.

Perhaps this can be brought out by yet another parable. In time of war in an occupied country, a member of the resistance meets one night a stranger who deeply impresses him. They spend that night together in conversation. The Stranger tells the partisan that he himself is on the side of the resistance—indeed that he is in command of it, and urges the partisan to have faith in him no matter what happens. The partisan is utterly convinced at that meeting of the Stranger's sincerity and constancy and undertakes to trust him.

They never meet in conditions of intimacy again. But sometimes the Stranger is seen helping members of the resistance, and the partisan is grateful and says to his friends, "He is on our side."

Sometimes he is seen in the uniform of the police handing over patriots to the occupying power. On these occasions his friends murmur against him; but the partisan still says, "He is on our side." He still believes that, in spite of appearances, the Stranger did not deceive him. Sometimes he asks the Stranger for help and receives it. He is then thankful. Sometimes he asks and does not receive it. Then he says, "The Stranger knows best." Sometimes his friends, in exasperation, say "Well, what *would* he have to do for you to admit that you were wrong and that he is not on our side?" But the partisan refuses to answer. He will not consent to put the Stranger to the test. And sometimes his friends complain, "Well, if *that's* what you mean by his being on our side, the sooner he goes over to the other side the better."

The partisan of the parable does not allow anything to count decisively against the proposition "The Stranger is on our side." This is because he has committed himself to trust the Stranger. But he of course recognizes that the Stranger's ambiguous behaviour *does* count against what he believes about him. It is precisely this situation which constitutes the trial of his faith.

When the partisan asks for help and doesn't get it, what can he do? He can (a) conclude that the stranger is not on our side or, (b) maintain that he is on our side, but that he has reasons for withholding help.

The first he will refuse to do. How long can he uphold the second position without its becoming just silly?

I don't think one can say in advance. It will depend on the nature of the impression created by the Stranger in the first place. It will depend, too, on the manner in which he takes the Stranger's behaviour. If he blandly dismisses it as of no consequence, as having no bearing upon his belief, it will be assumed that he is thoughtless or insane. And it quite obviously won't do for him to say easily, "Oh, when used of the Stranger the phrase 'is on our side' means ambiguous behavior of this sort." In that case he would be like the religious man who says blandly of a terrible disaster, "It is God's will." No, he will only be regarded as sane and reasonable in his belief, if he experiences in himself the full force of the conflict.

It is here that my parable differs from Hare's. The partisan admits that many things may and do count against his belief; whereas Hare's lunatic who has a *blik* about dons doesn't admit that anything counts against his *blik*. Nothing can count against *bliks*. Also the partisan has a reason for having in the first instance committed himself, viz. the character of the Stranger; whereas the lunatic has no reason for his *blik* about dons—because, of course, you can't have reasons for *bliks*.

This means that I agree with Flew that theological utterances must be assertions. The partisan is making an assertion when he says, "The Stranger is on our side."

Do I want to say that the partisan's belief about the Stranger is, in any sense, an explanation? I think I do. It explains and makes sense of the Stranger's behaviour; it helps to explain also the resistance movement in the context of which he appears. In each case it differs from the interpretation which the others put upon the same facts.

"God loves men" resembles "the Stranger is on our side" (and many other significant statements, e.g. historical ones) in not being conclusively falsifiable. They can both be treated in at least three different ways: (1) As provisional hypotheses to be discarded if experience tells against them; (2) As significant articles of faith; (3) As vacuous formulae (expressing, perhaps, a desire for reassurance) to which experience makes no difference and which make no difference to life.

The Christian, once he has committed himself, is precluded by his faith from taking up the first attitude: "Thou shalt not tempt the Lord thy God." He is in constant danger, as Flew has observed, of slipping into the third. But he need not; and, if he does, it is a failure in faith as well as in logic.

2. The Creed of a Savoyard Priest*

Jean Jacques Rousseau

My son, do not expect learned discourse or profound reasoning from me. I am not a great philosopher, and I have little desire to be one. But I sometimes have common sense, and I always love truth. I do not wish to argue with you, or even to try to convince you; it will be enough for me to tell you what I think in the simplicity of my heart. Consult your own while I speak; that is all I ask of you. If I am mistaken, it is in good faith, and my error therefore cannot be charged to me as a crime. If you are mistaken in the same way, you can be accused of no great wrong. I believe I am right in assuming that you and I are both endowed with reason, and have the same interest in listening to it. Why should you not think as I do?

I was born poor and a peasant, destined by my condition to till the soil, but my parents felt that it would be better for me to make my living as a priest, and they succeeded in enabling me to have the necessary education. Neither they nor I had any concern for my learning what was good, true, or useful, but only what was needed for me to be ordained. I learned what I was expected to learn, I said what I was expected to say, I assumed the required obligations, and I was made a priest. But I soon became aware that in committing myself to not being a man, I had promised more than I could fulfill. . . .

Such experiences have a profound effect on a thoughtful mind. My melancholy reflections overturned my former concepts of justice, honesty, and all the duties of man. Each day I lost another of the opinions I had accepted. Those that remained were not enough to form a body of ideas that could stand alone. I felt the self-evidence of my principles being gradually obscured in my mind, and finally, when I had been reduced to no longer knowing what to think, I reached the point where you are now, with this difference: that since my unbelief had developed with greater difficulty and at a later age, it would be all the harder to destroy.

I was in the state of uncertainty and doubt that Descartes considers essential to the search for truth. It is not likely to be lasting, because it is disquieting and painful. Only

---

The Creed of a Savoyard Priest is a section of Rousseau's *Emile*. In it, the priest is speaking to a young man whom he is in the process of saving from cynicism and despair. (Translator's note.)

a lazy mind or the interest of vice can keep us in it. My heart had not been corrupted enough to make me willing to remain in it, and nothing maintains the habit of reflection better than being more satisfied with oneself than with one's situation.

I meditated on the sad fate of mortals adrift on that sea of human opinions, without rudder or compass, at the mercy of their stormy passions, with no other guide than an inexperienced pilot who knows neither from where he has come nor where he is going. I said to myself, "I love truth, I seek it, and cannot find it. Show me where it is and I will hold fast to it. Why must it hide from a heart that is eager to worship it?"

Although I have often experienced greater suffering, I have never led such a constantly unpleasant life as during that time of confusion and anxiety when I was incessantly wandering from one doubt to another, and gaining nothing from my long meditations but uncertainty, obscurity, and contradictions with regard to the cause of my being and the rule of my duties.

How can anyone be a systematic and sincere skeptic? I do not understand it. Either there really are no such philosophers, or they are the unhappiest of men. Doubt concerning the things most important for us to know is a stress too great for the human mind to endure very long. We cannot help putting an end to our doubt in one way or another, because we would rather be mistaken than believe nothing.

My perplexity was made still worse by the fact that since I had been born into a Church that decides everything and permits no doubt, rejecting one of its tenets made me reject all the rest, and my inability to accept its many absurd decisions turned me against those that were not absurd. Having been told to believe everything prevented me from believing anything, and I did not know where to stop.

I turned to the philosophers: I studied their books and examined their various opinions. I found them all to be proud, assertive, and dogmatic, even in their supposed skepticism. They know everything, prove nothing, and ridicule each other; only on this last point do I feel that all of them are right. They are triumphant when they attack, and feeble when they defend themselves. If you weigh their arguments, they all prove to be destructive; if you examine their doctrines, you find that each man is limited to his own; they agree only in wrangling with each other. Listening to them was not the way for me to cast off my uncertainty.

It became clear to me that the inadequacy of the human mind is the first cause of that prodigious diversity of views, and that pride is the second. The vast mechanism of the world is beyond our grasp. We cannot calculate its ratios; we know neither its first laws nor its final cause. We do not know ourselves; we know neither our nature nor the primary force that moves us; we scarcely know whether man is a simple or a composite being. We are surrounded by impenetrable mysteries that lie beyond the realm of perception. We believe that we have the intelligence needed to fathom them, but we can use only our imagination. Through this imaginary world, each man clears a path which he believes to be the right one, but he cannot determine whether or not it leads toward the goal. Yet we want to know and understand everything. We are unable to accept our ignorance of what we cannot know. We prefer to choose our certainties at random and believe in illusions, rather than admit that none of us can perceive reality. We are small parts of a great whole whose limits we cannot see and whose Maker leaves us to our foolish disputes, yet we are vain enough to want to decide what that whole is in itself, and what we are in relation to it. . . .

The first benefit I derived from these reflections was learning to limit my inquiries to what concerned me directly, to be willing to remain in profound ignorance of everything else, and to trouble myself to the point of doubt only with regard to things that were important for me to know.

I also realized that, far from ridding me of my useless doubts, the philosophers would only multiply those that tormented me, without resolving any of them. I therefore took another guide. "I must follow the inner light," I told myself. "It will mislead me less than they do, or at least my error will be my own, and I shall be less perverted if I follow my illusions than if I believe their lies." . . .

Thus, with love of truth as my only philosophy, and as my only method a simple and easy rule that enabled me to dispense with vain and subtle arguments, I resumed my examination, with the help of that rule, of the knowledge that concerned me. I resolved to accept as self-evident all propositions that I could not sincerely refuse to believe, to regard as true all those that seemed to follow necessarily from them, and to leave all others in uncertainty, neither rejecting nor accepting them, without bothering to clarify them if they had no bearing on practical reality.

But who am I? What right do I have to judge things, and what determines my judgments? If they are forced upon me by the impressions I receive, it is futile for me to expend any energy in such inquiry, because they will either occur or not occur, without any effort on my part to direct them. First, therefore, I must examine myself, to become acquainted with the instrument I intend to use and learn the extent to which I can rely on it.

I exist, and I have senses by which I am affected. That is the first truth which strikes me and forces me to accept it. Do I have an independent feeling of my existence, or do I feel it only by means of my sensations? That is my first doubt. For the present, I cannot resolve it: Since I am continually affected by sensations, either immediately or in memory, how can I know if the feeling of my *self* is something outside those sensations and if it can be independent of them?

My sensations take place within me, since they make me aware of my existence; but their cause is external to me, since they affect me whether I am willing or not, and I can neither produce nor abolish them of my own volition. I therefore clearly understand that a sensation, which is inside me, and its cause or object, which is outside of me, are not the same thing.

Thus, not only do I exist, but other entities exist also, namely, the objects of my sensations; and even if those objects are only ideas, it is still truth that they are distinct from me.

Everything which I feel to be outside of me, and which acts on my senses, I call matter; and all particles of matter which I perceive as being combined into separate entities, I call bodies. Thus all the disputes between idealists and materialists mean nothing to me: Their distinctions between the appearance and the reality of bodies are idle fancies.

I am now already as sure of the existence of the universe as I am of my own. Next I consider the objects of my sensations, and finding in myself the ability to compare them, I discover that I am endowed with an active force which I previously did not know I possessed.

To perceive is to feel; to compare is to judge; judging and feeling are not the same. By sensation, objects are presented to me as separate, isolated, as they are in nature; in comparing them, I move and rearrange them, so to speak, I place one over another to see whether they are alike or different and to ascertain, in general, all their relations. In my opinion, the distinctive faculty of an active or intelligent being is the ability to give meaning to the word "is." In purely sentient beings I fail to find that intelligent force which superposes and then judges; I cannot see it in nature. Such a passive being will feel each object separately, or will even feel a total object formed by two together, but having no power to place one upon the other, it will never compare them, it will not judge them. . . .

Let any name be given to the power of my mind which brings together my sensations and compares them, let it be called attention, meditation, reflection, or whatever you like; it is still true that it is in me and not in things, that it is I alone who produce it, even though I produce it only when I receive impressions from objects. Though I have no control over whether I feel or not, I do control the extent to which I examine what I feel.

I am therefore not merely a passive sentient being, but an active and intelligent being, and no matter what philosophy may say, I dare to claim the honor of thinking. I know only that truth is in things, not in the mind that judges them, and that the less of myself I put into my judgments of them, the surer I am to approach truth; thus my rule of relying more on feeling than on reason is confirmed by reason itself.

Having made sure of myself, so to speak, I begin looking outside myself, and I consider myself with a kind of shudder, cast into this vast universe, lost in the immense number of entities without knowing what they are, either among themselves or in relation to me. I study them, I observe them; and the first object that presents itself to me as a basis for comparison is myself.

Everything that I perceive through my senses is matter, and I deduce all the essential properties of matter from the sensory qualities that make me perceive it and are inseparable from it. I see it sometimes in motion and sometimes at rest, from which I infer that neither rest nor motion is essential to it; but motion, being an action, is the effect of a cause of which rest is only the absence. Therefore, when nothing acts on matter it does not move, and for the very reason that it can be either in motion or at rest, indifferently, its natural state is the state of rest.

I perceive in bodies two kinds of motion: imparted motion and spontaneous or voluntary motion. In the first, the cause of motion is external to the body that moves, and in the second it is in the body itself. I do not conclude from this that the motion of a watch, for example, is spontaneous; for if nothing external to the spring acted on it, it would not tend to straighten itself and would not pull the chain. For the same reason, I do not attribute spontaneity to fluids, or even to the fire that causes their fluidity.

If you ask me if the movements of animals are spontaneous, I will answer that I do not know, but that analogy would seem to indicate that they are. If you ask me how I know that there are spontaneous movements, I will answer that I know it because I feel it. If I will to move my arm, I move it, and its movement has no other immediate cause than my will. It would be futile for anyone to try to destroy that feeling in me by reasoning, because it is stronger than any logic he could use; he might as well try to prove to me that I do not exist.

If there were no spontaneity in men's actions, or in anything that happens on earth, it would be all the more difficult to imagine the first cause of all motion. For my part, I am so thoroughly convinced that matter is at rest in its natural state, and has no power to move of itself, that whenever I see a body in motion I immediately judge that either it is a living body or its motion was imparted to it. My mind rejects the idea of inorganic matter moving of itself, or producing any action.

Yet this visible universe consists of matter, scattered and dead matter, which as a whole has none of the cohesion, organization, or common feeling of the parts of a living body, for it is certain that we, who are parts, have no feeling of ourselves in the whole. This same universe is in motion, and in its movements, which are ordered, uniform, and subject to fixed laws, it has none of the freedom that appears in the movements of men and animals. The world is therefore not a great animal that moves of itself; its movements have a cause external to it, which I do not perceive. But inner conviction makes that cause so real to me that I cannot see the sun moving across the sky without imagining a force that drives it, and when I think of the earth turning I seem to feel a hand that makes it turn. . . .

The first causes of motion are not in matter; it receives motion and transmits it, but does not produce it. The more I observe the action and reaction of natural forces acting on one another, the more I see that, going from effect to effect, we must always arrive at some will as a first cause, for to suppose an infinite regression of causes is to suppose none at all. In short, any movement that is not caused by another movement can come only from a spontaneous, voluntary act; inanimate bodies act only by motion, and there is no real action without will. This is my first principle. I believe that a will moves the universe and animates nature. This is my first dogma, or my first article of faith. . . .

If moving matter shows me a will, matter moving in accordance with certain laws shows me an intelligence: that is my second article of faith. Acting, comparing, and choosing are operations of an active and thinking being; therefore that being exists. You may ask me where I see him existing. I see him not only in the revolving heavens and in the sun that gives us light, not only in myself, but also in a grazing sheep, a flying bird, a falling stone, a windblown leaf.

I judge the order of the world even though I do not know its purpose, because to judge it I have only to compare its parts with one another, to study their connections and relations, and to observe how they work together. I do not know why the universe exists, but that does not prevent me from seeing how it is modified, or from perceiving the close interconnections by which the entities that compose it aid one another. I am like a man who, seeing an open watch for the first time, admires its mechanism even though he does not know its function and has not seen its dial. "I do not know what the whole machine is designed to do," he might say, "but I see that each part of it is made for the others, I admire its maker in the details of his work, and I am sure that its parts all move together in this way for some common purpose which I cannot perceive."

Let us compare the particular ends, the means, the ordered relations of every kind, and then listen to our inner feeling. What healthy mind can reject its testimony? What unprejudiced eye can fail to see the obvious order of the universe as evidence of a supreme intelligence? How many sophistries must a man amass before he becomes blind to the harmony of all parts of that universe and the admirable way in which each works to preserve the others? Anyone may speak to me of combinations and chances as much as he likes, but what good will it do him to reduce me to silence if he cannot convince me? And how can he deprive me of the involuntary feeling that continues to deny what he says? If organized bodies came together in countless fortuitous ways before taking on stable forms, if there were first stomachs without mouths, feet without heads, hands without arms, and imperfect organs of all kinds which perished because they were unable to preserve themselves, why are none of those imperfect attempts still to be seen in the world? Why did nature finally lay down laws for herself to which she was not subject before? I grant that I ought not to be surprised if something that is possible actually happens, and if the number of attempts compensates for the improbability of the event. But if I were told that printer's type had been thrown at random and the letters had fallen in such a way as to spell out the entire *Aeneid*, I would not deign to take one step to investigate that falsehood. "You are overlooking the number of throws," I might be told. But how many throws must I assume in order to make the combination plausible? Since I see the result of only one, to me the odds are infinity to one that it was not the effect of chance. Furthermore, since combinations and chances never yield anything but products of the same nature as the elements combined, the organization of life cannot result from a random aggregation of atoms, and a chemist making compounds will never cause them to feel and think in his crucible. . . .

I therefore believe that the world is governed by a wise and powerful will; I see that, or rather I feel it, and it is important for me to know it. But is the world eternal or created? Is there a single source of all things? Are there two, or more? And what is their nature? I do not know, and what does it matter to me? When knowledge of those things becomes important to me, I will try to acquire it; until then, I will refrain from speculating on idle questions, which, though they may trouble my vanity, are irrelevant to my conduct and beyond my reason.

Always remember that I am not urging you to accept my views: I am simply presenting them to you. Whether matter is eternal or created, whether there is a passive source or not, it is still certain that the whole is one, and proclaims a single intelligence, for I see nothing that is not ordered within the same system and does not work toward the same end, namely, maintaining the whole in the established order. The being who has both will and power, who is active of himself, who moves the universe and orders all things—that being, whatever he may be, I call God. I add to that name the ideas of intelligence, power, and will, which I have assembled, and that of goodness, which necessarily follows from them; but in attributing that idea to him, I have no better knowledge of him. He remains beyond the reach of both my senses and my understanding. The more I think about him, the more perplexed I am; I know with certainty that he exists, and that he exists of himself; I know that my existence is subordinate to his, and that the same is true of all things known to me. I perceive God everywhere in his works, I feel him within myself, I see him all around me; but as soon as I try to contemplate him in himself, as soon as I try to discover where he is, what he is, what his substance is, he eludes me, and my troubled mind no longer perceives anything.

Deeply aware of my inadequacy, I will never reason about the nature of God unless I am forced to do so by the feeling of his relation to me. Such reasoning is always rash; a wise man should engage in it only with trepidation and the conviction that he is incapable of attaining ultimate truth, for what is most insulting to God is not refraining from thinking about him at all, but thinking about him wrongly.

After having discovered those of his attributes by which I conceive his existence, I return to myself and try to ascertain the rank I occupy in the order of things which he governs and which I can examine. I find that I an incontestably in the foremost rank because of the species to which I belong, for by my will and the means of executing it that I have at my disposal, I have more power to act on all things around me, or to accept or avoid their action as I choose, than any of them has to act on me against my will by mere physical impulsion; and by my intelligence, I am the only one able to examine the whole. What earthly entity except man can observe all others, measure, calculate, and foresee their movements and effects, and join, so to speak, the feeling of common existence to that of his individual existence? What is so ridiculous in thinking that all things were made for me, if I alone am able to relate them to myself?

It is therefore true that man is lord of the earth on which he lives, for not only does he subdue all animals, not only does he control the elements by his skills and industry, but he alone on earth is able to control them, and in contemplation he even takes possession of the heavenly bodies that are beyond his physical grasp. Show me another animal on earth that can make use of fire and admire the sun. What! I can observe and know the parts of the world and their relations; I can comprehend the meaning of order, beauty, and virtue; I can contemplate the universe and raise myself toward the hand that governs it; I can love good and do it—and yet I should compare myself to an animal? Abject soul, it is your wretched philosophy that makes you resemble an animal; or rather, you try in vain to degrade yourself, but your spirit testifies against your principles, your charitable heart belies your doctrine, and the very misuse of your faculties proves their excellence in spite of you.

I have no system to uphold; I am a simple and honest man, unaffected by the jealous spirit of any faction and with no aspiration to the honor of being the head of a sect. I am content with the place assigned to me by God. After God, I see nothing better than my species. If I had to choose my place in the order of existence, what more could I choose than to be a man?

I am deeply moved by this thought, rather than being made proud by it, for my state did not result from my own choice; it could not have been determined by the merit of a being who did not yet exist. Can I see myself thus distinguished without being thankful that I hold this honorable position, and without blessing the hand that placed me in it? My first return to self-contemplation gives rise in my heart to a feeling of gratitude and exaltation toward the Creator of my species, and from this feeling comes my first homage to the benevolent Divinity. I worship his supreme power and I am touched by his kindness. This worship is not something that must be taught to me: it is dictated to me by nature herself. Is it not a natural consequence of our self-love to honor what protects us and to love what is benevolently inclined toward us?

But when, seeking to learn my individual place in my species, I consider the various ranks in it and the men who occupy them, what am I to think? What a spectacle! Where is the order I had observed? The panorama of nature showed me only harmony and proportion; that of the human race now shows me only confusion and disorder! Concord reigns among the elements, and men are in chaos! The animals are happy, and their lord is miserable! O Wisdom, where are your laws? O Providence, is this how you order the world? O Benevolent Being, what has become of your power? I see evil on earth.

Would you believe, my dear friend, that it was from these sad thoughts and apparent contradictions that my mind conceived the sublime idea of the soul, to which my reflections had not yet led me? As I meditated on the nature of man, I seemed to discover two distinct principles in him. The first elevated him to the study of eternal truths, to love of justice and moral beauty, to those realms of the intellectual world that the wise delight in contemplating. The second drew him downward into himself, subjected him to the power of his senses and the passions that are their ministers, and counteracted, through them, everything inspired in him by the first principle. Feeling myself swayed and torn by those two conflicting tendencies, I said to myself, "No, man is not one: I both exert my will and fail to exert it; I feel both enslaved and free; I see what is good, I love it, and I do evil; I am active when I listen to my reason and passive when I am carried away by my passions; and when I give in to them, my worst torment is the feeling that I could have resisted them."...

If men are active and free, they act of themselves. What they do freely is not part of the system ordained by God, and cannot be imputed to him. He does not will the evil they do when they misuse the freedom he has given them, but neither does he prevent them from doing it, whether because the evil done by such weak beings is as nothing in his eyes, or because he cannot prevent it without restricting their freedom and doing a greater evil by degrading their nature. He has made them free not in order that they may do evil, but that they may do good by choice. He has given them the ability to make that choice by rightly using the faculties with which he has endowed them, but he has so limited their powers that misuse of their freedom cannot disrupt the general order. The evil that they do falls back upon them without changing anything in the system of the world, without preventing the human race from being preserved in spite of itself. To complain that he does not prevent them from doing evil is to complain that he has given them an excellent nature, that he has endowed their acts with the morality that ennobles them, that he has given them a right to virtue. Supreme happiness lies in being content with oneself; it is in order to deserve that contentment that we are placed on earth and endowed with freedom, that we are tempted by the passions and restrained by conscience.

What more could divine power itself have done for us? Could it have placed contradiction in our nature and given the reward for having done good to a man who was incapable of doing evil? What! To prevent man from being wicked, should he have been limited to instinct and made an animal? No, God of my soul, I will never reproach you for having made me in your image, so that I may be free, good, and happy, like you. . . .

Man, look no farther for the author of evil: that author is yourself. There is no evil but the evil you do and the evil you suffer, and both come from yourself. Evil in general can arise only from disorder, and in the system of the world I see only unfailing order. Particular evil is only in the feeling of the suffering being; man did not receive that feeling from nature: he gave it to himself. Pain has little power over someone who, having thought little, has neither memory nor foresight. Take away our baneful progress, take away our errors and vices, take away the work of man, and all is well.

Where all is well, nothing is unjust. Justice is inseparable from goodness, and goodness is the necessary effect of boundless power and the self-love that is an essential attribute of all sentient beings. The all-powerful Being extends his existence, so to speak, with that of others. Producing and preserving are the everlasting work of power; it does not act on what does not exist. God is not the God of the dead; he could not be destructive and wicked without harming himself. The all-powerful Being can will only what is good. Therefore the Being who is supremely good because he is supremely powerful must also be supremely just; otherwise he would contradict himself, for the love of order that produces order is called goodness, and the love of order that preserves order is called justice.

It is sometimes said that God owes nothing to his creatures. I believe that he owes them everything he promised them when he brought them into being; and in giving them the idea of good and making them feel the need of it, he promised it to them. The more I turn inward and reflect on myself, the more clearly I read these words written in my soul: "Be just and you will be happy." Yet, considering the present state of things, this is not true: The wicked prosper and the just are oppressed. And what indignation flares up in us when that expectation is disappointed! Conscience rebels and protests against its Author; it groans and cries out to him, "You have deceived me!"

"I have deceived you, rash creature? Who told you that? Has your soul been destroyed? Have you ceased to exist? O Brutus, O my son, do not sully your noble life in ending it; do not leave your hope and glory with your body in the fields of Philippi. Why do you say, 'Virtue is nothing,' when you are about to enjoy the reward of your own? You are about to die, you think; no, you will live, and then I will keep all my promises to you."

From the complaints of impatient mortals, one might think that God owed them a reward before they earned it, that he was obliged to pay them for their virtue in advance. No! Let us first be good, and then we shall be happy. Let us not demand our prize before our victory, or our wages before our work. "It is not while they are on the racetrack that the winners in our sacred games are crowned," says Plutarch, "but after they have run their course."

If the soul is immaterial, it may survive the body; and if it does so, Providence is justified. If I had no other proof of the immateriality of the soul than the triumph of the wicked and the oppression of the just in this world, that alone would prevent me from doubting it. Such a flagrant discord in the universal harmony would make me seek to resolve it. I would say to myself, "Everything does not end for us when life ends; death puts everything back in order." I would have to ask myself, it is true, what becomes of a man when all his perceptible aspects have been destroyed, but that question ceases to be a difficulty for me as soon as I recognize the existence of two substances. It is quite simple that during my bodily life, when I perceive only through my senses, everything that lies beyond them escapes me. I can understand that when the union of the body and the soul has been broken, one may be dissolved and the other preserved. Why should the destruction of one cause the destruction of the other? Being so different in nature, they are in an unstable condition during their union; when that union ceases, each returns to its natural state: The active, living substance regains all the force it used in moving the passive, dead substance. Alas, my vices make it all too clear to me that man is only half alive during his life: The life of the soul begins only with the death of the body.

But what is that life? Is the soul immortal by nature? My limited mind cannot grasp anything limitless: everything that is called infinite escapes me. What can I deny or affirm? How can I reason with regard to what I cannot conceive? I believe that the soul survives the body long enough to assure the maintenance of order; who knows if that is enough to make it endure forever? But although I understand how the body is worn out and destroyed by the division of its parts, I cannot conceive such a destruction of a thinking being; and unable to imagine how it could die, I assume that it does not die. Since that assumption is comforting and not unreasonable, why should I fear to accept it? . . .

Do not ask me if the torments of the wicked will be everlasting, if the goodness of the Author of their being can condemn them to suffer forever; I do not know that, either, and I have no vain curiosity about such useless questions. Is it important for me to know what will become of the wicked? I have little interest in their fate. It is difficult for me to believe, however, that they are condemned to endless torments. If supreme justice takes vengeance, it does so in this life. O nations, you and your errors are its ministers! It uses the evils you inflict on yourselves to punish the crimes that cause them. It is in your insatiable hearts, consumed with envy, greed, and ambition, that the avenging passions punish your iniquities in the midst of your false prosperity. What need is there to look for hell in another life? It is here, in this life, in the hearts of the wicked. . . .

Having thus deduced the main truths that it concerns me to know, from the impressions of perceptible objects and the inner awareness that leads me to judge causes in accordance with my natural understanding, it remains for me to determine the principles of conduct I must derive from them, and what rules I must lay down for myself in order to fulfill my destiny on earth, according to the intention of the Being who placed me here. Still following my method, I do not draw those rules from the principles of a lofty philosophy: I find them in the depths of my heart, indelibly written there by nature. I have only to consult myself about what I want to do: What I feel to be right is right, what I feel to be wrong is wrong. Conscience is the best of all casuists; only when we bargain with it do we resort to the subtleties of reasoning. Our first concern is for ourselves, yet how often the inner voice tells us that in seeking our own good at the expense of others we are doing wrong! We believe that we are following the impulsion of nature when we are actually resisting her; listening to what she says to our senses, we despise what she says to our hearts; the active being obeys, the passive being commands. Conscience is the voice of the soul, the passions are the voice of the body. Is it surprising that these two voices often contradict each other? To which must we listen? Reason deceives us all too often, and we have acquired all too good a right to disregard it, but conscience never deceives us. It is man's true guide; it is to the soul what instinct is to the body; whoever follows it obeys nature, and has no fear of going astray. This is an important point; let me dwell on it awhile, to make it clearer. . . .

Look at all modern nations and read the histories of ancient ones. Among all those strange and harsh cults, amid that prodigious diversity of customs and behavior, you will find everywhere the same ideas of justice and integrity, the same principles of morality, the same notions of good and evil. Ancient paganism engendered abominable gods who, had they been mortals, would have been punished as scoundrels. But even though vice descended from the immortal realm armed with sacred authority, the moral instinct repulsed it from the hearts of men. While Jupiter's debauchery was celebrated, Xenocrates' continence was admired; chaste Lucretia worshiped shameless Venus; the dauntless Romans offered sacrifices to Fear; they invoked the god who mutilated his father, and died without a murmur at the hands of their own fathers. The most despicable divinities were served by the greatest men. The holy voice of nature, stronger than that of the gods, was respected on earth and seemed to relegate both crime and criminals to heaven.

There is thus within our souls an innate principle of justice and virtue by which, in spite of our maxims, we judge our acts and those of others as good or bad, and it is this principle that I call conscience. . . .

For us, to exist is to feel; our sensitivity unquestionably preceded our intelligence: we had feelings before ideas. Whatever the cause of our existence may be, it has provided for our preservation by giving us feelings suited to our nature, and it cannot be denied that those feelings, at least, are innate. They are, so far as the individual is concerned, self-love, fear of pain, horror of death, and desire for well-being. But if, as cannot be doubted, man is sociable by nature, or at least capable of becoming so, he can be sociable only by other innate feelings, relative to his species, for if physical need were the only consideration, it would surely disperse men rather than bring them together. The impulsion of conscience arises from the moral system formed by the individual's double relation between himself and his fellow men. To know good is not to love it; man has no innate knowledge of it, but as soon as his reason leads him to know it, his conscience impels him to love it: it is this feeling that is innate. . . .

Conscience! Conscience! Divine instinct, immortal and celestial voice! You are the sure guide of a being who is ignorant and limited, but intelligent and free. You are the infallible judge of good and evil; it is through you that man resembles God; it is to you that he owes the excellence of his nature and the morality of his acts. Aside from you, I feel nothing in me that raises me above the level of the beasts, except the sad privilege of wandering from error to error by means of understanding without rules and reason without principles. . . .

There is an age when the heart, still free, but ardent, anxious, and eager for a happiness that it does not know, seeks it with curious uncertainty, and deceived by the senses, finally fixes on a vain image of it and believes it has found it where it is not. In my case, those illusions lasted too long. Alas, I knew them too late, and I have not been able to destroy them completely; they will endure as long as the mortal body that causes them. But although they entice me, they at least do not deceive me; I know them for what they are, and I despise them even when I follow them. Far from seeing them as the object of my happiness, I see them as an obstacle to it. I long for the time when, freed from the shackles of the body, I shall be *myself*, without conflict or division; I shall then need only myself in order to be happy. Meanwhile I am happy even in this life, because I attach little importance to all its ills and regard it as almost foreign to my being, and I know that all the real good I can draw from it depends on me.

By means of lofty meditation I approach that future state of happiness, strength, and freedom as closely as it is now possible for me to do. I contemplate the order of the universe, not to explain it with vain systems, but to admire it unceasingly and worship the wise Maker whose presence I feel in it. I converse with him, I impregnate all my faculties with his divine essence, I am deeply moved by his kindness, and I give thanks to him for his gifts; but I do not pray to him. What could I ask of him? That he change the course of the world for me, that he perform miracles in my favor? Knowing that I must love above all else the order established by his wisdom and maintained by his providence, shall I ask him to disrupt that order for my sake? No, that audacious wish would deserve to be punished rather than granted. Neither do I ask him for the power to act rightly—why should I ask him for what he has already given me? Has he not given me conscience to love the good, reason to know it, and freedom to choose it? If I do evil, I have no excuse; I do it willingly, and asking him to change my will would be asking of him what he asks of me; it would be wanting him to do my work and let me reap the reward for it. To be dissatisfied with my state would be to wish to cease being a man, to want something other than what is, to desire disorder and evil. Good and merciful God, source of all justice and truth, I trust in you, and the supreme wish of my heart is that your will be done. When I join my own will to yours, I do as you do, I acquiesce in your goodness; I feel that I share in advance the supreme happiness that is its reward.

In my justified mistrust of myself, all that I ask of God, or rather what I expect of his justice, is to correct my error if I go astray and if that error is dangerous to me. I do not believe that my good faith makes me infallible; the opinions that seem truest to me may be so many falsehoods, for what man does not cling to his own opinions, and how many men are in agreement on everything? Although the illusion that misleads me comes from myself, only God can cure me of it. I have done all I can to reach truth, but its source is too high for me. If I lack the strength to go farther, am I at fault? I can now only wait for truth to come to me.

The good priest had been speaking fervently; he was deeply moved, and so was I.*
I felt as if I had been hearing the divine Orpheus singing the first hymns and teaching

---

*In this section the speaker is the young man who has been listening to the priest. (Translator's note.)

men to worship the gods. Yet I saw many objections that I could have raised; I raised none of them, however, because they were less solid than perplexing, and I was basically persuaded in his favor. As he spoke according to his conscience, my own seemed to confirm what he said.

"The views you have just expressed to me," I said, "seem more unusual to me because of what you admit you do not know than because of what you say you believe. I see in them something very close to theism or natural religion, which Christians profess to equate with atheism or irreligion, though it is actually the exact opposite. But in the present state of my faith I would have to ascend, rather than descend, to adopt your opinions, and it would be difficult for me to remain precisely where you are, unless I were as wise as you. To be at least as sincere as you, I want to take counsel with myself. It is the inner voice that must lead me to follow your example, and you yourself have told me that after it has been silenced for a long time it cannot be quickly called back. What you have said will remain in my heart; I must meditate on it. If, after careful reflection, I am as convinced as you, you will be my last teacher, and I will be your disciple till death. But continue your teaching now; you have told me only half of what I need to know. Speak to me of revelation, of the Scriptures, of those obscure dogmas about which I have been undecided since my childhood, unable either to understand or believe them, to accept or reject them."

He embraced me and said:

Yes, my son, I will finish telling you what I think. I do not want to open my heart to you only halfway; but the desire you have expressed was necessary to make me feel justified in speaking to you without reserve. Till now I have told you nothing which I did not think would be of use to you, and of which I was not firmly convinced. The inquiry that remains to be made is quite different; I see in it only perplexity, mystery, and obscurity; I approach it with uncertainty and misgiving. I tremble at the thought of it, and I shall be telling you of my doubts, rather than of my opinions. If your views were more settled, I would hesitate to give you mine; but in your present condition it will be better for you if you think as I do. Give my words only the authority of reason, however; I do not know if I am in error. In discussion it is sometimes difficult to avoid taking a decisive tone, but remember that all my assertions will be only reasons for doubt. Seek truth for yourself; as for me, I promise you only sincerity.

In the statement of my opinions you you see only natural religion; it is strange that another kind should be required. If so, how am I to know it? Of what am I guilty if I serve God in accordance with the understanding he has given to my mind and the feelings he has aroused in my heart? Is there any moral purity, any dogma that will help man and honor his Maker, which I can derive from a formal doctrine but cannot derive without such a doctrine by the right use of my faculties? Show me what can be added, for the glory of God, the good of society, and my own advantage, to the duties of natural law, and how a new form of worship could produce a virtue that would not be a consequence of mine. The greatest ideas of the Divinity come to us through reason alone. Look at the spectacle of nature, listen to the inner voice. Has not God presented everything to our eyes, our conscience, our judgment? What more can we learn from men? Their revelations only degrade God by attributing human passions to him. Far from elucidating our ideas of the great Being, specific dogmas seem to me to confuse them; far from ennobling them, they debase them; to the inconceivable mysteries that surround God, they add absurd contradictions; they make man haughty, intolerant, and cruel; instead of assuring peace on earth, they bring fire and the sword. I ask myself what is the good of all that, and I cannot answer. I see in it only the crimes of men and the misery of the human race.

I am told that a revelation was needed to teach men the way in which God wanted to be served; the diversity of strange cults that they have instituted is given as proof of this, but what is overlooked is that this very diversity comes from the vagaries of revelations. When nations began making God speak, each one made him speak in its own manner, and say what it wanted to hear. If men had listened only to what God says in their hearts, there would always have been only one religion on earth. . . .

Assuming that the Almighty had condescended to make a man the medium for communicating his sacred will, would it be reasonable and just to demand that the whole human race obey that spokesman's voice without making him known as such? Would it be fair to give him no credentials but a few special signs that were witnessed only by a small number of obscure people and could never be known to the rest of mankind except by hearsay? If we were to believe all the miracles that simple and uneducated people all over the world claim to have seen, each sect would be the right one; there would be more miracles than natural events, and the greatest of all miracles would be that there were no miracles where fanatics were persecuted. It is the immutable order of nature that best shows the wise hand that guides it. If there were many exceptions to it, I would no longer know what to think of it. For my part, I believe in God too firmly to believe in all those miracles that are so little worthy of him.

Suppose a man were to say to us, "Mortals, I proclaim to you the will of the Almighty. Recognize, by my voice, him who has sent me. I order the sun to change its course, the stars to form another arrangement, the mountains to become flat, the waves to rise, and the face of the earth to take on a new appearance." Seeing such miracles, who would not immediately recognize the master of nature? She does not obey impostors; they work their miracles on street corners, in deserts, or behind closed doors, and there they easily take in a small number of specators already disposed to believe anything. Who will venture to tell me how many eyewitnesses are required to make a miracle worthy of belief? If miracles performed to prove a doctrine must themselves be proved, they are useless, and performing them is a waste of time.

The most important question with regard to the proclaimed doctrine still remains to be examined. Since those who say that God works miracles on earth maintain that the devil sometimes imitates them, even the best-attested miracles leave us no better off than before; and since Pharaoh's magicians dared, in Moses' presence, to produce the same signs that he produced at God's command, why, in his absence, should they not have claimed the same authority, with the same justification? Thus, after the doctrine has been proved by miracles, the miracles must be proved by the doctrine, lest we mistake the work of the devil for the work of God. What do you think of that way of begging the question?

If a doctrine comes from God, it must bear the sacred stamp of the Divinity; not only must it elucidate the confused ideas that reasoning sketches in our minds, but it must also offer us a form of worship, a morality, and guiding principles that are compatible with the attributes by which we conceive God's essence. If, then, it taught us only absurd and unreasonable things, if it aroused in us only feelings of aversion of our fellow men and fear for ourselves, and if it depicted only a wrathful, jealous, vengeful, and partial God who hates men, a God of war and combat, always ready to strike and destroy, always speaking of torments and penalties, and boasting of punishing even the innocent, my heart would not be drawn to that God, and I would certainly not give up natural religion to embrace that doctrine; for, as you can see, a choice would have to be made. "Your God is not ours," I would say to his followers. "A God who begins by choosing a single people for himself, and proscribing the rest of mankind, is not the common father of men; a God who dooms most of his creatures to eternal suffering is not the good and merciful God whom my reason has shown to me."

With regard to dogmas, my reason tells me that they must be clear, illuminating, and strikingly self-evident. If natural religion is inadequate, it is because of the obscurity it leaves in the great truths it teaches us; it is for revelation to teach us those truths in a way that the human mind can grasp, to bring them within our reach, to make us comprehend them so that we can believe them. Faith is made strong and firm by understanding; the best of all religions is necessarily the clearest. A religion that preaches a doctrine laden with mysteries and contradictions tells me by that very fact that I must mistrust it. The God I worship is not a God of darkness, he has not given me understanding so that he can forbid me to use it; to tell me to subdue my reason is to insult its Author. The minister of truth does not tyrannize my reason: he enlightens it. . . .

As for revelation, if I were a better reasoner or more erudite, I might perceive its truth and its usefulness for those who are fortunate enough to recognize it; but if I see evidence in its favor which I cannot oppose, I also see objections against it which I cannot resolve. There are so many solid arguments for and against it that, not knowing what to decide, I neither accept nor reject it. I reject only the obligation to recognize it, because that supposed obligation is incompatible with God's justice; far from removing obstacles to salvation, it would multiply them and make them insurmountable for most of mankind. With that exception, I remain in respectful doubt concerning the matter. I do not presume to think myself infallible. Other men have been able to reach a decision on what seems to me uncertain; I reason for myself, not for them; I neither blame nor imitate them; their judgment may be better than mine, but it is not my fault if mine is not the same as theirs. . . .

Such is the involuntary skepticism in which I have remained; but it is by no means painful to me, because it does not extend to essential matters of practice, and I am firmly convinced with regard to the principles of all my duties. I serve God in the simplicity of my heart. I seek to know only what concerns my conduct. Unlike so many others, I do not trouble myself about dogmas that have no bearing on action or morality. I regard all particular religions as so many salutary institutions which in each country prescribe a uniform manner of honoring God in public worship, and which may all have been shaped by climate, government, the spirit of the people, or other local conditions that make one religion preferable to another in specific times and places. I believe that they are all good when God is properly served in them. The essential worship comes from the heart. God rejects no homage, in whatever form it may be offered to him, if it is sincere. Called to the service of the Church in the religion that I profess, I fulfill as scrupulously as possible all the duties that it prescribes for me, and my conscience would reproach me if I deliberately neglected them in any way. . . .

Honored by the sacred ministry, even though I am in its lowest rank, I will never do or say anything that will make me unworthy of fulfilling its sublime duties. I will always preach virtue to men, I will always exhort them to do what is right; and so far as I am able, I will always set an example for them. It is not within my power to make religion attractive to them or to strengthen their faith in the truly useful dogmas that every man is obliged to believe; but God grant that I may never preach the cruel dogma of intolerance to them, that I may never teach them to hate their neighbors or say to other men, "You will be damned. There is no salvation outside the Church." If I were in a more conspicuous position, my unwillingness to do those things might bring me into difficulties, but I am too obscure to have much to fear, and I can hardly fall any lower than I am. Come what may, I will never blaspheme against divine justice, or tell lies against the Holy Ghost. . . .

My young friend, I have now stated my creed to you as God reads it in my heart; you are the first to hear it, and you will perhaps be the last. As long as any good belief remains among men, we must not trouble peaceful souls or alarm the faith of simple people with difficulties which they could not resolve and which would only distress them without enlightening them. But when everything is shaken, the trunk must be preserved at the cost of the branches. Consciences that are agitated, uncertain, and almost stifled, as I saw yours to be, need to be strengthened and aroused; and to reestablish them on the foundation of eternal truth, one must pull down the tottering pillars by which they think they are still supported.

You are at that critical age when the mind opens to certainty, when the heart receives its form and character, and when each of us becomes what he will be for the rest of his life, for better or worse. Later, the substance is hardened and new impressions no longer leave their mark. Young man, receive the imprint of truth in your soul while it is still malleable. If I were surer of myself, I would have spoken to you dogmatically and decisively, but I am a man, ignorant and subject to error: What could I do? I have opened my heart to you without reserve; what I consider certain, I have given you as such; I have given you my doubts as doubts, my opinions as opinions; I have told you my reasons for doubting and believing. It is now for you to judge. You have said that you want to take time; that is a wise precaution which makes me think well of you. Begin by making your conscience willing to be enlightened. Be honest with yourself. Take from my views whatever has convinced you, and discard the rest. You have not yet been so perverted by vice as to be in danger of making a bad choice. I would offer to discuss the choice with you, but as soon as a dispute arises, tempers flare, vanity and stubbornness intervene, and sincerity vanishes. Never argue, my friend, because argument enlightens neither oneself nor others. As for myself, I came to my conclusions only after many years of meditation; I will continue to accept them; my conscience is at peace and my heart is content. If I were to decide to reexamine my views, I could not do so with a purer love of truth, and my mind, already less active, would be less capable of perceiving it. I will remain as I am, for fear that love of meditation might become an idle passion and gradually make me apathetic toward the fulfillment of my duties, and for fear that I might fall back into my former skepticism without having the strength to bring myself out of it. More than half my life is over; I now have time only to make good use of what is left, and to efface my errors by my virtues. If I am mistaken, it is in spite of myself. He who sees into the depths of my heart knows that I do not love my blindness. Since I am powerless to overcome it by my own understanding, my only means of freeing myself from it is to lead a good life; and if God is able to make children for Abraham out of stones,* every man has a right to hope for enlightenment when he makes himself worthy of it.

If my reflections lead you to think as I do, if my views are yours, and if we have the same creed, I give you this advice: Cease exposing your life to the temptations of misery and despair; cease leading it ignominiously at the mercy of strangers; and cease abjectly eating the bread of charity. Go back to your country, return to the religion of your fathers, follow it in the sincerity of your heart, and never forsake it: It is very simple and very holy; I believe that of all religions on earth it is the one whose morality is purest and most acceptable to reason. As for the expenses of the journey, do not trouble yourself about them: they will be provided for. And do not fear the false shame of a humiliating return; we should be ashamed of making a mistake, not of repairing it. You are still at the age when everything is forgiven, but when one can no longer sin with impunity. If you are willing to listen to your conscience, countless empty objections will vanish at the sound of its voice. You will realize that in our state of uncertainty it is an inexcusable presumption to profess a religion other than the one into which we were born, and that it is duplicity not to practice sincerely the one we profess. If we stray from it, we deprive ourselves of a great excuse before the tribunal of the Sovereign Judge. Will he not be more inclined to forgive an error in which we were brought up than one which we dared to choose for ourselves?

My son, keep your soul in the state of always desiring God's existence, and you will never doubt it. Moreover, whatever your final decision may be, remember that the true duties of religion are independent of human institutions; that a righteous heart is the true temple of the Divinity; that in all countries and all sects, the epitome of the law is to love God above all else and one's neighbor as oneself; that there is no religion which absolves man from the duties of morality, and that they alone are truly essential; that inner worship is the first of those duties; and that without faith there can be no real virtue. . . .

My good young man, be sincere and truthful without arrogance; know how to be ignorant: you will deceive neither yourself nor others. If cultivation of your talents should ever enable you to speak to men, always speak to them only in accordance with your conscience, without caring whether or not they applaud you. Misuse of knowledge causes incredulity. Learned men always scorn common opinions; each wants to

*A reference to Matthew 3:9, in the New Testament. (Translator's note.)

have his own. Haughty philosophy leads to irreligion, as blind devotion leads to fanaticism. Avoid those extremes; always hold fast to the path of truth, or what appears to you as such in the simplicity of your heart, without ever letting yourself be turned away from it by vanity or weakness. Dare to confess God to philosophers; dare to preach humanity to the intolerant. You may have to stand alone, but you will have within you a testimony in your favor that will free you from dependence on the judgments of men. It will not matter whether they love or hate you, whether they read or disdain your writings. Say what is true, do what is right; what matters is to fulfill our duties on earth, and it is by forgetting ourselves that we work for ourselves. My son, self-interest deludes us; only the hope of the righteous man is never deceptive.

———————————————————— ■ ————————————————————

3. A Free Man's Worship

BERTRAND RUSSELL

To Dr. Faustus in his study Mephistopheles told the history of the Creation, saying:

"The endless praises of the choirs of angels had begun to grow wearisome; for, after all, did he not deserve their praise? Had he not given them endless joy? Would it not be more amusing to obtain undeserved praise, to be worshipped by beings whom he tortured? He smiled inwardly, and resolved that the great drama should be performed.

"For countless ages the hot nebula whirled aimlessly through space. At length it began to take shape, the central mass threw off planets, the planets cooled, boiling seas and burning mountains heaved and tossed, from black masses of cloud hot sheets of rain deluged the barely solid crust. And now the first germ of life grew in the depths of the ocean, and developed rapidly in the fructifying warmth into vast forest trees, huge ferns springing from the damp mould, sea monsters breeding, fighting, devouring, and passing away. And from the monsters, as the play unfolded itself, Man was born, with the power of thought, the knowledge of good and evil, and the cruel thirst for worship. And Man saw that all is passing in this mad, monstrous world, that all is struggling to snatch, at any cost, a few brief moments of life before Death's inexorable decree. And Man said: 'There is a hidden purpose, could we but fathom it, and the purpose is good; for we must reverence something, and in the visible world there is nothing worthy of

Source: From Bertrand Russell, *Mysticism and Logic.* Copyright © George Allen and Unwin 1917, pp. 46–57.

reverence.' And Man stood aside from the struggle, resolving that God intended harmony to come out of chaos by human efforts. And when he followed the instincts which God had transmitted to him from his ancestry of beasts of prey, he called it Sin, and asked God to forgive him. But he doubted whether he could be justly forgiven, until he invented a divine Plan by which God's wrath was to have been appeased. And seeing the present was bad, he made it yet worse, that thereby the future might be better. And he gave God thanks for the strength that enabled him to forgo even the joys that were possible. And God smiled; and when he saw that Man had become perfect in renunciation and worship, he sent another sun through the sky, which crashed into Man's sun; and all returned again to nebula.

" 'Yes,' he murmured, 'it was a good play; I will have it performed again.' "

Such, in outline, but even more purposeless, more void of meaning, is the world which Science presents for our belief. Amid such a world, if anywhere, our ideals henceforward must find a home. That Man is the product of causes which had no prevision of the end they were achieving; that his origin, his growth, his hopes and fears, his loves and his beliefs, are but the outcome of accidental collocations of atoms; that no fire, no heroism, no intensity of thought and feeling, can preserve an individual life beyond the grave; that all the labours of the ages, all the devotion, all the inspiration, all the noonday brightness of human genius, are destined to extinction in the vast death of the solar system, and that the whole temple of Man's achievement must inevitably be buried beneath the débris of a universe in ruins—all these things, if not quite beyond dispute, are yet so nearly certain, that no philosophy which rejects them can hope to stand. Only within the scaffolding of these truths, only on the firm foundation of unyielding despair, can the soul's habitation henceforth be safely built.

How, in such an alien and inhuman world, can so powerless a creature as Man preserve his aspirations untarnished? A strange mystery it is that Nature, omnipotent but blind, in the revolutions of her secular hurryings through the abysses of space, has brought forth at last a child, subject still to her power, but gifted with sight, with knowledge of good and evil, with the capacity of judging all the works of his unthinking Mother. In spite of Death, the mark and seal of the parental control, Man is yet free, during his brief years, to examine, to criticise, to know, and in imagination to create. To him alone, in the world with which he is acquainted, this freedom belongs; and in this lies his superiority to the resistless forces that control his outward life.

The savage, like ourselves, feels the oppression of his impotence before the powers of Nature; but having in himself nothing that he respects more than Power, he is willing to prostrate himself before his gods, without inquiring whether they are worthy of his worship. Pathetic and very terrible is the long history of cruelty and torture, of degradation and human sacrifice, endured in the hope of placating the jealous gods: surely, the trembling believer thinks, when what is most precious has been freely given, their lust for blood must be appeased, and more will not be required. The religion of Moloch—as such creeds may be generically called—is in essence the cringing submission of the slave, who dare not, even in his heart, allow the thought that his master deserves no adulation. Since the independence of ideals is not yet acknowledged, Power may be freely worshipped, and receive an unlimited respect, despite its wanton infliction of pain.

But gradually, as morality grows bolder, the claim of the ideal world begins to be felt; and worship, if it is not to cease, must be given to gods of another kind than those created by the savage. Some, though they feel the demands of the ideal, will still consciously reject them, still urging that naked Power is worthy of worship. Such is the attitude inculcated in God's answer to Job out of the whirlwind: the divine power and knowledge are paraded, but of the divine goodness there is no hint. Such also is the attitude of those who, in our own day, base their morality upon the struggle for survival, maintaining that the survivors are necessarily the fittest. But others, not content with an answer so repugnant to the moral sense, will adopt the position which we have become accustomed to regard as specially religious, maintaining that, in some hidden manner, the world of fact is really harmonious with the world of ideals. Thus Man creates God, all-powerful and all-good, the mystic unity of what is and what should be.

But the world of fact, after all, is not good; and, in submitting our judgment to it, there is an element of slavishness from which our thoughts must be purged. For in all things it is well to exalt the dignity of Man, by freeing him as far as possible from the tyranny of non-human Power. When we have realised that Power is largely bad, that man, with his knowledge of good and evil, is but a helpless atom in a world which has no such knowledge, the choice is again presented to us: Shall we worship Force, or shall we worship Goodness? Shall our God exist and be evil, or shall he be recognised as the creation of our own conscience?

The answer to this question is very momentous, and affects profoundly our whole morality. The worship of Force, to which Carlyle and Nietzsche and the creed of Militarism have accustomed us, is the result of failure to maintain our own ideals against a hostile universe: it is itself a prostrate submission to evil, a sacrifice of our best to Moloch. If strength indeed is to be respected, let us respect rather the strength of those who refuse that false "recognition of facts" which fails to recognise that facts are often bad. Let us admit that, in the world we know, there are many things that would be better otherwise, and that the ideals to which we do and must adhere are not realised in the realm of matter. Let us preserve our respect for truth, for beauty, for the ideal of perfection which life does not permit us to attain, though none of these things meet with the approval of the unconscious universe. If Power is bad, as it seems to be, let us reject it from our hearts. In this lies Man's true freedom: in determination to worship only the God created by our own love of the good, to respect only the heaven which inspires the insight of our best moments. In action, in desire, we must submit perpetually to the tyranny of outside forces; but in thought, in aspiration, we are free, free from our fellowmen, free from the petty planet on which our bodies impotently crawl, free even, while we live, from the tyranny of death. Let us learn, then, that energy of faith which enables us to live constantly in the vision of the good; and let us descend, in action, into the world of fact, with that vision always before us.

When first the opposition of fact and ideal grows fully visible, a spirit of fiery revolt, of fierce hatred of the gods, seems necessary to the assertion of freedom. To defy with Promethean constancy a hostile universe, to keep its evil always in view, always actively hated, to refuse no pain that the malice of Power can invent, appears to be the duty of all who will not bow before the inevitable. But indignation is still a bondage, for it compels our thoughts to be occupied with an evil world; and in the fierceness of desire from which rebellion springs there is a kind of self-assertion which it is necessary for the wise to overcome. Indignation is a submission of our thoughts, but not of our desires; the Stoic freedom in which wisdom consists is found in the submission of our desires, but not of our thoughts. From the submission of our desires springs the virtue of resignation; from the freedom of our thoughts springs the whole world of art and philosophy, and the vision of beauty by which, at last, we half reconquer the reluctant world. But the vision of beauty is possible only to unfettered contemplation, to thoughts not weighted by the load of eager wishes; and thus Freedom comes only to those who no longer ask of life that it shall yield them any of those personal goods that are subject to the mutations of Time.

Although the necessity of renunciation is evidence of the existence of evil, yet Christianity, in preaching it, has shown a wisdom exceeding that of the Promethean philosophy of rebellion. It must be admitted that, of the things we desire, some, though they prove impossible, are yet real goods; others, however, as ardently longed for, do not form part of a fully purified ideal. The belief that what must be renounced is bad, though sometimes false, is far less often false than untamed passion supposes; and the creed of religion, by providing a reason for proving that it is never false, has been the means of purifying our hopes by the discovery of many austere truths.

But there is in resignation a further good element: even real goods, when they are un-attainable, ought not to be fretfully desired. To every man comes, sooner or later, the great renunciation. For the young, there is nothing unattainable; a good thing desired with the whole force of a passionate will, and yet impossible, is to them not credible. Yet, by death, by illness, by poverty, or by the voice of duty, we must learn, each one of us, that the world was not made for us, and that, however beautiful may be the things we crave, Fate may nevertheless forbid them. It is the part of courage, when misfortune comes, to bear without repining the ruin of our hopes, to turn away our thoughts from vain regrets. This degree of submission to Power is not only just and right: it is the very gate of wisdom.

But passive renunciation is not the whole of wisdom; for not by renunciation alone can we build a temple for the worship of our own ideals. Haunting foreshadow-ings of the temple appear in the realm of imagination, in music, in architecture, in the untroubled kingdom of reason, and in the golden sunset magic of lyrics, where beauty shines and glows, remote from the touch of sorrow, remote from the fear of change, re-mote from the failures and disenchantments of the world of fact. In the contemplation of these things the vision of heaven will shape itself in our hearts, giving at once a touchstone to judge the world about us, and an inspiration by which to fashion to our needs whatever is not incapable of serving as a stone in the sacred temple.

Except for those rare spirits that are born without sin, there is a cavern of darkness to be traversed before that temple can be entered. The gate of the cavern is despair, and its floor is paved with the gravestones of abandoned hopes. There Self must die; there the eagerness, the greed of untamed desire must be slain, for only so can the soul be freed from the empire of Fate. But out of the cavern the Gate of Renunciation leads again to the daylight of wisdom, by whose radiance a new insight, a new joy, a new ten-derness, shine forth to gladden the pilgrim's heart.

When, without the bitterness of impotent rebellion, we have learnt both to resign ourselves to the outward rule of Fate and to recognise that the non-human world is unworthy of our worship, it becomes possible at last so to transform and refashion the unconscious universe, so to transmute it in the crucible of imagination, that a new image of shining gold replaces the old idol of clay. In all the multiform facts of the world—in the visual shapes of trees and mountains and clouds, in the events of the life of man, even in the very omnipotence of Death—the insight of creative idealism can find the reflection of a beauty which its own thoughts first made. In this way mind asserts its subtle mastery over the thoughtless forces of Nature. The more evil the material with which it deals, the more thwarting to untrained desire, the greater is its achievement in inducing the reluctant rock to yield up its hidden treasures, the prouder its victory in compelling the opposing forces to swell the pageant of its triumph. Of all the arts, Tragedy is the proudest, the most triumphant; for it builds its shining citadel in the very centre of the enemy's country, on the very summit of his highest mountain; from its impregnable watch-towers, his camps and arsenals, his columns and forts, are all revealed; within its walls the free life continues, while the legions of Death and Pain and Despair, and all the servile captains of tyrant Fate, afford the burghers of that dauntless city new spectacles of beauty. Happy those sacred ramparts, thrice happy the dwellers on that all-seeing eminence. Honour to those brave warriors who, through countless ages of warfare, have preserved for us the priceless heritage of liberty, and have kept undefiled by sacrilegious invaders the home of the unsubdued.

But the beauty of Tragedy does but make visible a quality which, in more or less obvious shapes, is present always and everywhere in life. In the spectacle of Death, in the endurance of intolerable pain, and in the irrevocableness of a vanished past, there is a sacredness, an overpowering awe, a feeling of the vastness, the depth, the inexhaustible mystery of existence, in which, as by some strange marriage of pain, the sufferer is bound to the world by bonds of sorrow. In these moments of insight, we lose all eagerness of temporary desire, all struggling and striving for petty ends, all care for the little trivial things that, to a superficial view, make up the common life of day by day; we see, surrounding the narrow raft illumined by the flickering light of human comradeship, the dark ocean on whose rolling waves we toss for a brief hour; from the great night without, a chill blast breaks in upon our refuge; all the loneliness of humanity amid hostile forces is concentrated upon the individual soul, which must struggle alone, with what of courage it can command, against the whole weight of a universe that cares nothing for its hopes and fears. Victory, in this struggle with the powers of darkness, is the true baptism into the glorious company of heroes, the true initiation into the overmastering beauty of human existence. From that awful encounter of the soul with the outer world, enunciation, wisdom, and charity are born; and with their birth a new life begins. To take into the inmost shrine of the soul the irresistible forces whose puppets we seem to be—Death and change, the irrevocableness of the past, and the powerlessness of man before the blind hurry of the universe from vanity to vanity— to feel these things and know them is to conquer them.

This is the reason why the Past has such magical power. The beauty of its motionless and silent pictures is like the enchanted purity of late autumn, when the leaves, though one breath would make them fall, still glow against the sky in golden glory. The Past does not change or strive; like Duncan, after life's fitful fever it sleeps well; what was eager and grasping, what was petty and transitory, has faded away, the things that were beautiful and eternal shine out of it like stars in the night. Its beauty, to a soul not worthy of it, is unendurable; but to a soul which has conquered Fate it is the key of religion.

The life of Man, viewed outwardly, is but a small thing in comparison with the forces of Nature. The slave is doomed to worship Time and Fate and Death, because they are greater than anything he finds in himself, and because all his thoughts are of things which they devour. But, great as they are, to think of them greatly, to feel their passionless splendour, is greater still. And such thought makes us free men; we no longer bow before the inevitable in Oriental subjection, but we absorb it, and make it a part of ourselves. To abandon the struggle for private happiness, to expel all eagerness of temporary desire, to burn with passion for eternal things—this is emancipation, and this is the free man's worship. And this liberation is effected by a contemplation of Fate; for Fate itself is subdued by the mind which leaves nothing to be purged by the purifying fire of Time.

United with his fellow-men by the strongest of all ties, the tie of a common doom, the free man finds that a new vision is with him always, shedding over every daily task the light of love. The life of Man is a long march through the night, surrounded by invisible foes, tortured by weariness and pain, towards a goal that few can hope to reach, and where none may tarry long. One by one, as they march, our comrades vanish from our sight, seized by the silent orders of omnipotent Death. Very brief is the time which we can help them, in which their happiness or misery is decided. Be it ours to shed sunshine on their path, to lighten their sorrows by the balm of sympathy, to give them the pure joy of a never-tiring affection, to strengthen failing courage, to instil faith in hours of despair. Let us not weigh in grudging scales their merits and demerits, but let us think only of their need—of the sorrows, the difficulties, perhaps the blindnesses, that make the misery of their lives; let us remember that they are fellow-sufferers in the same darkness, actors in the same tragedy with ourselves. And so, when their day is over, when their good and their evil have become eternal by the immortality of the past, be it ours to feel that, where they suffered, where they failed, no deed of ours was the cause; but wherever a spark of the divine fire kindled in their hearts, we were ready with encouragement, with sympathy, with brave words in which high courage glowed.

Brief and powerless is Man's life; on him and all his race the slow, sure doom falls pitiless and dark. Blind to good and evil, reckless of destruction, omnipotent matter rolls on its relentless way; for Man, condemned to-day to lose his dearest, to-morrow himself to pass through the gate of darkness, it remains only to cherish, ere yet the blow falls, the lofty thoughts that ennoble his little day; disdaining the coward terrors of the slave of Fate, to worship at the shrine that his own hands have built; undismayed by the empire of chance, to preserve a mind free from the wanton tyranny that rules his outward life; proudly defiant of the irresistible forces that tolerate, for a moment, his knowledge and his condemnation, to sustain alone, a weary but unyielding Atlas, the world that his own ideals have fashioned despite the trampling march of unconscious power.

4. The Meaning of Life

A. J. AYER

A saying attributed to Nietzsche is that since God is dead everything is permitted. I suppose that the assertion that God is dead is not to be taken literally. There have, indeed, been philosophers, as good as A. N. Whitehead and Samuel Alexander, who held that God did not yet exist. In their evolutionary metaphysics, the universe was represented as progressing towards the emergence of a deity. Anthropologists have also described religious rites, supposed by them to be connected with harvests, in which gods are slain, annually, only to be replaced or in some instances reborn. I do not, however, know of any instance in which a deity, conceived as supernatural, is thought simply to have perished, without surviving or reappearing in any form, or leaving a successor.

I may be mistaken on this point and do not attach much importance to it, since its implications do not significantly differ from those of a theory which is known to have been held, that of the Epicureans, who did believe that there were gods but thought of them as having something better to do than fuss about human beings. They were credited with living lives of unalloyed pleasure somewhere far out in space, without exercising any control over our world or anything within it. The behaviour of the material atoms by which the course of nature was regulated was not of their contriving and to take any notice of the vicissitudes of human life would only cause them pain.

I shall address myself later on to the general topic of religious belief, in very many of its aspects. The question which I first wish to eliminate is that of the connection, suggested by Nietzsche and still very widely thought to obtain, between religious belief and moral conduct. If what Nietzsche meant by speaking of the death of God was that his audience had mostly ceased to believe in the creation of the world by an omnipotent, omniscient, supremely benevolent, necessary being, his assertion was probably false at the time at which he made it. If he meant that there was no good reason to believe in the existence of any such being, I shall in due course be arguing that he was right. That is not, however, the point at issue here. The point is that even if there were such a being as Nietzsche may be thought to have envisaged, or indeed a deity of any kind, his will could not supply a basis for morality. The reason, which is purely logical, was pointed out by Plato, in his dialogue *Euthyphro,* and has been restated by a series of philosophers down to the present day. It is simply that while moral rules may be propounded by authority the fact that these were so propounded would not validate them. For let us suppose that it is possible for there to be a God and possible that he be good.

Source: A. J. Ayer, *The Meaning of Life* (New York: Charles Scribner's Sons, 1990), pages 178–97. Reprinted with the permission of Orion Books.

Even so his goodness could not simply consist of his divinity. For if it did, then in saying that he willed what was good, his votaries would be asserting no more than the tautology that he willed what he willed. They count themselves fortunate in his goodness and regard it as warranting their gratitude, but if all that they meant by ascribing goodness to him was that his wishes were what they were, they would have nothing to be grateful for. If it were the devil that was in supreme power, what he willed, however diabolical, would have to be reckoned good.

It is no answer to this argument to protest, as some do, that God's goodness issues from his nature. For exactly the same considerations apply. A theist is at liberty to include the notion of goodness in the concept of his deity, thereby making it necessary that if there were a God he would be good, but this very manoeuvre illustrates the point that I am making. If our theist did not possess a concept of goodness, which was logically independent of the other predicates which he conjoined with it to identify his deity, the inclusion of it would add nothing to them. From the supposition that an intelligent being created the universe and continues to rule over it, nothing whatsoever follows about his moral character. In supposing this being also to be benevolent, his devotees are assuming that he satisfies their own moral standards. They can indeed argue that he is responsible for their possession of these standards, as he is, in their view, for everything else. The fact remains that the verdicts which they reach in accordance with these standards have no logical connection with the existence or character of the source from which their acceptance of the standards proceeded. To take a less dubious example, those whom we regard as well-brought up children learn from their parents and schoolteachers how they should behave. It does not follow that their moral sentiments are validated by the fact that they acquired them in this way. Nor does it follow that the teachers are necessarily protected from the moral appraisal of those whom they have taught. The children may find reasons to adopt different standards. More pertinently, they may retain the standards in question and judge that their parents and teachers do not always measure up to them.

I should think myself guilty of labouring the obvious, were it not that the simple point at issue has had such difficulty in gaining general acceptance, especially when religion is brought into the picture. Put succinctly, the point is that morals cannot be founded on authority, and here it makes no difference whether the authority be supposed human or divine.

To say that authority, whether secular or religious, supplies no ground for morality is not to deny the obvious fact that it supplies a sanction. There is a great deal to be said about the justification and efficacy of rewards and punishments, but a thorough examination of this topic would take me too far afield, and I shall limit myself, in this context, to a few remarks about the factor of religious belief. My principal reason for singling out religious belief is that it is intimately connected not logically, as we shall discover, but historically, with a question which has a strong bearing upon what I have chosen to call the meaning of life, namely that of the possibility of the continuance of one's existence, in one form or another, after death.

Both the importance attached to the concept of survival and the manner of conceiving it vary to a great extent in different religions. For instance, with the possible exception of some initiates into mystery cults, the worshippers of the Homeric gods, and indeed their Latin counterparts, took little stock of an afterlife. If they believed that their souls were destined for Hades, it was an abode of shadows, and the prospect of inhabiting it appears to have had next to no effect upon the way they lived. The remark attributed to Achilles that it was preferable to be a slave on earth than a king in the underworld might be taken to suggest that the afterlife figures in Greek mythology as something to be feared, but I think that its implication is not that a shadowy future is unpleasant in itself, but rather that it is not worth considering because of its inferiority in status to even the meanest condition of bodily human life.

The Christian religion, with its view of man's life on earth as principally a prelude to the life to come, lies at the opposite extreme, but even in Christianity as I have just described it, after the abandonment of the belief in the millennium, inaugurated by the second coming of Christ, as the triumph of Christians on earth, the differences at different periods and among different sects in conceptions of the afterlife and their effects upon conduct are very great. A striking example is the threat of hell. Nowadays, the belief that those who are divinely adjudged to have been sinners are fated to undergo an eternity of physical torment has been generally abandoned by Anglicans and to a lesser extent by Roman Catholics. Hellfire has been replaced by the mental frustration of being deprived of the sight of God, and even more mildly by the mere lack of this privilege. Nevertheless, I am given to understand that the literal conception of hellfire is still entertained by the growing number of Protestants who answer to the description of born-again Christians and there is no doubt that throughout the Christian era, at least until the present century, it was universally orthodox, promulgated with varying degrees of eloquence by the preachers adhering to different sects and at least nominally accepted by their congregations.

But can the acceptance have been more than nominal in the general run of cases? There is a distinction to be drawn here between applying the doctrine to others and applying it to oneself. The early Christian fathers applied it to Pagans: there is a passage in Tertullian in which he looks forward to the pleasure of occupying a front seat in heaven, enjoying the spectacle of his opponents suffering in hell. Are we to assume that it never occurred to him that he himself might be adjudged a sinner?

Evangelical parents tortured their children to rid them of their innate propensities to sin. Were they quite certain that all such propensities had been beaten out of themselves? Yet, if they were uncertain, how could they have faced the future with any equanimity? Dr Johnson, for all his virtues, was a Christian who believed that he stood a serious risk of being sent to hell. There were times when the fear of death brought him very close to madness. Romantic love is a strong passion and usually represented, except in American films, as being incompatible with marriage. Consequently, its physical consummation is most frequently a sin. In James Elroy Flecker's play *Hassan,* the lovers are offered a night of love at the cost of being tortured to death in the morning. They choose the night of love. Would any remotely rational couple, however enamoured, make such a choice, at the cost of being tortured for eternity?

What I am suggesting is that there has often been a discrepancy between the conscious acceptance of the Christian doctrine of eternal damnation and the conduct which such a belief might be expected to cause if it were seriously held. This is not to say that the doctrine was wholly inoperative. In the case of Roman Catholics its force was diminished by the liberating practice of confession and the power ascribed to remit the penalties for sin. There is, however, evidence that men were afraid of dying in circumstances which denied them the opportunity of receiving absolution, even if this fear did not deter them from committing the offences for which absolution was required.

The Christians for whom the prospect of incurring the rewards and penalties of a posthumous judgment ought rationally to have the strongest effect upon their conduct are the Protestants who believe that they are protected by nothing except God's mercy. For some reason which has never been made clear, they have tended to assume that their chances of prospering in the next world were inversely proportionate to their enjoyment of pleasure, especially sensual pleasure, on earth. I should add that this view did not originate with the Reformation. The earliest Christians were also apt to take the view that extreme asceticism, often carried to the point of causing oneself physical injury, found favour with their God.

Even less intelligible is the behaviour of Calvinists who have subscribed to the doctrine of predestination, according to which salvation does not depend upon one's conduct. Whatever one does, one's eventual fate is preordained from eternity. It might have been expected that persons who subscribed to this doctrine would be disposed towards hedonism. On the contrary with a very few exceptions, such as the first Lord Beaverbrook, they have been among the foremost enemies of pleasure. I suppose the explanation to be that, sharing the Puritan belief that God was in favour of asceticism, and not being entirely confident that they were among the elect, they refrained from the pursuit of pleasure as a means of bolstering their confidence. An alternative explanation which I have frivolously put forward, although it would show them to be more ingenious, and would not, in my unorthodox view, convict them of absurdity, is that they believed in backward causation. They conducted themselves as Puritans in order to have been saved.

Before I leave the topic of the effect on moral conduct of Christian belief, I ought to say that I am not suggesting that it has been wholly or even primarily utilitarian. No doubt the hope of future reward or the fear of future punishment has had some influence, if only temporarily, and especially on the behaviour of children, but I believe that this influence has been much smaller than those hostile to Christianity generally suppose. Very often people have behaved well, and badly also, as in the persecution of so-called heretics, because they believed that they were fulfilling God's intentions, irrespective of any advantage to themselves. Whether the worth of their lives is affected by the fact, if it is one, as I hope to show, that their motivation is delusive is a difficult question to which I shall return.

At this point it needs to be remarked that by no means all believers in the future life situate it in another world. There are very many persons, especially in the East, who subscribe to a theory of reincarnation, according to which one has led and will lead an indefinite series of lives on earth. Belief in this theory may well have more influence on conduct than the Christian conceptions of an afterlife, since the level at which one is incarnated in one's next life is believed to depend on one's behaviour in one's present existence. I have been told that some sects admit the possibility of one's returning to

earth in something other than a human form, but as I have no idea what moral standards could be thought to govern the behaviour of what are popularly known as the higher nonhuman organisms, let alone fish or insects, I shall confine myself to the cases where the one who is reincarnated always reappears as a human being, the value of each of his successive lives, whether measured in terms of happiness, or honour, or moral worth, being determined by the character of its predecessors.

But now we confront the objection that, even in this restricted form, the doctrine is not intelligible. It might seem strange that millions of people should believe what is unintelligible but however strange it may seem, there is no doubt that it frequently happens. The Christian doctrine of the trinity affords another example. In the case which we are considering, the difficulty is to give a sense to saying that anyone is identical with a single person, let alone a series of persons, who died before he was born. One could perhaps just imagine a person's living discontinuously. He might perhaps vanish for a period and then reappear, perhaps with no consciousness of where he had been, but not greatly changed in appearance, retaining his old memories, recognizing his surroundings and the persons that he had known. But this would be a strange mode of persistence, not reincarnation.

It is indeed possible to imagine circumstances in which it would be possible to give a sense to saying that one was same person as someone who had lived and died long ago. To revive an example that I used in an earlier work,[1] suppose that someone now living claimed to have been Julius Caesar and supported his claim by asserting that he remembered Caesar's experiences: and suppose that not only did his description of the experiences agree with all the known facts, but new discoveries were made which confirmed his account of events in Caesar's life that were hitherto unknown to us. In that case, we should probably adjust our concept of memory in such a way as to allow for the possibility of one's 'remembering' experiences that one never had. It would, however, also be open to us to alter our concept of personal identity, dispensing with the requirement of physical continuity, and putting the onus on memory, supported perhaps by the possession of similar talents or a similar character. It is important to realize that this would simply be a question of a linguistic distinction. To borrow Quine's useful phrase, there is no 'fact of the matter' in such a case.

If we enter into the realm of science fiction, allowing the possibility of brain transplants, teletransportation, fusion and so forth, we are likely to attach less weight to spatiotemporal continuity, and more to memory and similarity of character. The far-reaching implications of such thought experiments have been brilliantly developed by Derek Parfit in his book *Reasons and Persons*. Parfit is reductionist, in the sense of insisting that the ascription of personal identity over time must depend entirely upon the character of the experiences which form the links in the chain. There is no call, and no warrant, for a substance, a soul, to be the owner of the experiences. It is worth noting that Buddha, who is widely regarded as the foremost authority for the doctrine of reincarnation, also took this view. What is not so clear is that Buddha always insisted that there had to be criteria for determining that series of experiences which were separated in place and time belonged to the same self. Yet this was essential for his theory to be intelligible. Someone who says 'I used to be Julius Caesar' or 'Florence Nightingale' or

both, without establishing any connection between her present experiences, and those, is literally talking nonsense.

An oddity of Buddhism at least is that one would expect its doctrine of reincarnation to be allied with a sense of the value of life. And indeed, as we have remarked, the quality of one segment of a person's life is believed to determine the value of the starting point of the segment which succeeds it. Nevertheless, life as such, at least as experienced by a self-conscious being, is regarded as being at best a necessary evil. The summit of moral achievement is admission to Nirvana; implying, both in Buddhism and Hinduism, release from the cycle of reincarnation, with a consequent loss of the sense of self-identity and of all desire. In Buddhism this is supposed to yield 'absolute blessedness': in Hinduism, absorption into Brahman, the impersonal divine reality of the universe. I confess that I cannot conceive what a state of absolute blessedness would be like if one had no desires to be satisfied and no awareness that one had attained it. So far as the reality of the universe goes, I suppose that I already form part of it, inasmuch as I exist; and I have no objection to its being called impersonal, if this means that it is not a person, though I balk at calling it divine. I have no trouble at all with the notion of the loss of the sense of self-identity. On the contrary it is something that I expect to occur to me, if not within the next decade, at least not very long after that.

Notice that I have avoided speaking of the loss of the sense of self-identity as something that I am due to suffer. This could, indeed, happen, if my mental condition were sufficiently abnormal. This loss of the sense of self-identity is that which results from being dead, and being dead is not something that one suffers, because one is no longer there to enjoy or suffer anything. As Wittgenstein expressed it, in one of his best sayings 'Death is not an event in life: we do not live to experience death.'[2]

Is it because they fail to take this into account that many people who do not expect to survive, and therefore are not affected by the fear of having to atone for their sins, or merely passing into a worse state of existence, are nevertheless afraid of death. They regard it as somehow terrible to cease to exist. I was tempted to quote Claudio's famous speech from *Measure for Measure,* but with the possible exception of the line 'To lie in cold obstruction and to rot' it is too strongly infected with the fallacy that death is a state of wretchedness that one undergoes.

The rational attitude is that attributed by Boswell to David Hume, whom Boswell reports as saying to him 'that he was no more uneasy to think that he should *not be* after his life, than that he *had not been* before he began to exist,' prompting Dr Johnson to exclaim that Hume was either mad or insincere. Yet, if one comes to consider it, why should it worry me more, if at all, that I shall not be alive in the year 2050 than that I was not alive in the year 1850. The way things are going indeed, the latter, at least for Englishmen in comfortable circumstances, might well prove the better time to have lived. In the very long, perhaps infinite history of the universe, there is a relatively minute period that contains my life. Apart from the character of the experiences that I undergo, which are of course affected by the nature of my material and social environment, why should it matter to me at what points in the four-dimensional continuum this minute stretch begins and ceases?

I have to confess that when I have put this argument to my friends, they have tended not to find it convincing. They may be willing to admit that for some people at least, and in certain moods even for themselves, it would not have been a misfortune never to have been born, but having embarked on life, they take it almost as a grievance that they are going to be deprived of it. The prevalence of this attitude is borne out by the fact that the death penalty has generally been considered the most severe of punishments, a view commonly though not universally shared by those who are in danger of having it inflicted on them. Yet is it obviously preferable to spend many years, perhaps the rest of one's days, in prison, under conditions which are almost certain to cause more pain than pleasure, than to be freed of the possibility of continuing to experience one or the other?

A similar peculiarity is that murder should be reckoned the most heinous of crimes. Is it always the case that the murderer, even if he is not caught, comes off better than his victim? Even though it is partly fiction, I think it fair to take the play of *Macbeth* as an example. Would any rational assessor prefer Macbeth's fate to Duncan's? 'Thou hast it now: King, Cawdor, Glamis, all . . .' and much good did it do him. And what about Duncan? 'After life's fitful fever, he sleeps well.'

Macbeth died too, eventually. So do we all, though nowadays few of us in battle. And this is a relevant fact, that we all do die. A feature of the general attitude to murder and to capital punishment appears to me to be the universal assumption, manifestly untenable when it is brought to light, that in putting an end to a man's life, one is taking something away from him that he would possess for as long as he pleased, if not for ever. It is as though we believed ourselves to be robbing him of immortality. What we are doing is shortening his life. And how much harm does this do him, if it does him any harm at all? Clearly there is no general answer to this question. It depends on his mental and physical condition, the type of society in which he lives, and his position within it, the work, if any, in which he is employed, the range of his desires and his capacity for satisfying them, his vitality, his age. It is not only for personal reasons that I consider this last factor to be important. I quote three stanzas of a well-known poem by A. E. Housman, who in fact lived to the age of seventy-seven, just the age that I am now.

> Loveliest of trees, the cherry now
> Is hung with bloom along the bough,
> And stands about the woodland ride
> Wearing white for Eastertide.
>
> Now, of my threescore years and ten,
> Twenty will not come again,
> And take from seventy springs a score,
> It only leaves me fifty more.
>
> And since to look at things in bloom
> Fifty springs are little room,
> About the woodlands I will go,
> To see the cherry hung with snow.

I cannot claim that I have spent more than a negligible fraction of my last fifty-seven springs going out of my way to look at things in bloom. I am not even sure that I should immediately recognize a cherry tree if I saw one. Nevertheless, the moral of the poem is one that I can appreciate. I am not a stranger to the feeling that the average span of life is too short to allow one to do all the things that one wants to do, to visit all the places that one wants to visit, or the same places often enough, to saturate oneself sufficiently in painting, or music, or literature, if they are where one's enjoyments lie, perhaps even to complete the work that one feels oneself capable of doing.

But now I must enter two caveats. The first is that my last paragraph was written from the point of view of a member of a privileged minority. Opportunities for travel, for acquiring pictorial skills and visiting galleries, for making and listening to music, for reading a wide variety of books have indeed increased very markedly in many Western countries in the last thirty years, but they are still rather narrowly circumscribed. Not many people can afford to take long holidays and the majority of holiday-makers are reported to prefer taking their own culture with them to enlarging their view of life. Not many people receive the education which disposes them to attach value to the arts. Not that they are the only domain in which one might reasonably ask for more. Anyone who takes an interest in anything at all, in science at any level, even if he only reads about it, in sport as a player or observer, in gardening, in social life, even like the speaker in Housman's poem, in nothing more than the passage of the seasons, may complain that life is too short for his interest to be exhausted.

But, even with this addition I maintain that we are still talking about a privileged minority. The vast majority of the human race, in Asia, in Latin America, in Africa, in the so-called underclasses of the more affluent Western societies, are far too fully occupied in waging a losing struggle to achieve a tolerable standard of living for it to be rational for them to wish their miseries prolonged. Perhaps they do wish it, nevertheless. Perhaps they never lose the hope that things will take a turn for the better. In some cases the myth of reincarnation may play a role. I claim only that they can have no good reason to wish that life were longer than it is.

> The trivial round, the common task
> would furnish all we ought to ask;
> Room to deny ourselves; a road
> To bring us, daily, nearer God.

This quotation from John Keble's hymn 'The Christian Year' was intended to assure its readers or performers that they were not required to retire to a 'cloistered-cell.' What is interesting is the implication, persisting in mid-nineteenth century High Anglicanism, that life should not be altogether pleasurable. There has to be some self-denial, apparently for its own sake, or perhaps because it is what God requires. Here there is indeed a suggestion that a reward lies in store, though it is left unclear what relation the certainty or quality of the reward bears to the length of the trivial round. What is implied is that once the end is secured, the sooner the trivial round stops the better. I think that this is a pervasive feature of mid-Victorian piety, though not often made explicit. If that is so, it is odd that they seemed never quite to make up their minds whether death was

a blessing or a misfortune. In either case, they clothed it with ritual trappings, which on the whole have not persisted.

I come now belatedly to the second of my two caveats and that is the onset of age. Obviously I am not concerned with the truism that people grow older as the years pass, but the fact that they almost inevitably deteriorate, both physically and mentally. There are indeed societies where the aged are honoured. It is, or used to be, preferable in old age to be a Chinese than a French peasant, underfed by your daughter-in-law and entrusted with the care of the geese. Still even the Chinese patriarch was not protected from 'grey hairs and the loosening of teeth,' let alone more serious physical disabilities. There are those, presumably enjoying some financial security and not in any fear of lacking warmth or nourishment, who profess to value the calm and detachment of old age. I think that it was Sophocles who is said to have congratulated himself on outgrowing sexual desire. This is not an attitude that I should wish to share. From my own experiences I judge it to be true that as one gets older, one tends to live with less intensity. One is more prone to the mood of Mallarmé's 'La chair est triste, hélas, et j'ai lu tous les livres': even one's aesthetic sensibilities become less keen. It seems to me absurd, however, to regard these as compensations of age.

Are we then to welcome the fact that doctors are said to be on the verge of finding ways of combating the hardening of the arteries, so that the average expectation of life is likely to be increased? Is this desirable? Not if it amounts to no more than an addition to the number of decrepit centenarians. It would be different if some method were found of arresting the process of ageing. If my condition remained what it was in the prime of my life, I should have no objection to living a greater number of years. Perhaps this would be true of most people, at any rate those whom I have described as belonging to the privileged minority. In the case of those for whom life at its best is disagreeable I can see no reason why they should wish it prolonged.

If the average expectation of life were markedly increased, it would be necessary to limit the number of new births. The general opinion is that life is a good in itself but it is a good which is dependent on the possession of it being fairly strictly rationed. Otherwise Malthus comes into his own and the value of life is swamped by the misery of living.

There are many ways in which a person's life may come to have a meaning for him in itself. He may find fulfilment in his work, though this cannot be guaranteed to last until old age. The same is true of the satisfaction which some people find in their domestic lives, with the factor of children and grandchildren playing its part. The English, of all classes, have not been noted in the past for the affection which they have commonly shown towards their children, or indeed received from them, but there have been exceptions and they may be on the increase. There are hobbies, like chess or stamp collecting, which may become a passion. I am not suggesting that these activities are of equal worth but only that they may be equally absorbing. Some people are absorbed in making money, presumably in most cases for the sake of the luxury, prestige, or power that the possession of it brings, but in some cases simply for its own sake; I know of a man who having set himself the goal of making a million pounds by the time he had attained a relatively youthful age could think of nothing better to do than set out to make another. His life might have been more interesting if he had been less sure of success. It lacked the spice which the fear of ruin gives to the life of the gambler. Again, I am not saying that the life of a gambler is morally preferable to that of a shrewd investor but only that it may be a life of greater intensity.

One of the most conspicuous elements in what counts and has long counted in many societies for most people as a meaningful life is the pursuit and still more the acquisition of fame. This has increased its importance in the present century because the improvement of communication, the diffusion throughout the world of many of the same programmes on television and the cinema, has spread fame much more widely. It is also ephemeral. Pop stars drop out of fashion and questionnaires reveal a surprising ignorance of what one might have thought were household names. I wonder, for example, what percentage of Asians could name either the Prime Minister of England, or the President of the United States. I think it might turn out to be surprisingly small.

In general, people who desire fame also wish to be thought to deserve it. They wish that their work should be esteemed by those whom they regard as persons best qualified to judge it, preferably in their lifetime when they can be awarded honour and gratified by praise, but also after their death. Sometimes those who are neglected in their lifetime take consolation in the thought that its merits will eventually be recognized. 'On me lira vers 1880,' said Stendhal in the 1830s and how right he was. Of those who are recognized in their lifetime, I think many attach more importance to the hope that their work will endure and their names be honoured as the authors of it.

Yet there is something irrational about this. It is comprehensible that if one has created an outstanding work of art, of whatever kind, or hit upon an original scientific theory, or written good poetry, or a novel of unusual depth, or even made some contribution to philosophy, one should wish the outcome to continue to be appreciated. But why should it matter that one's name be attached to it? After all one is not going to know anything about it. One runs no risk of suffering the humiliation of Max Beerbohm's Enoch Soames or the triumph that he would have felt if he had found a eulogistic record of his name in the British Museum's catalogue. All the same it does matter. I have the hope that some of my work will continue to be read after my death, perhaps even here and there in a hundred years' time. Yet I do not care at all for the idea that it will be attributed to one of my colleagues, however much I may like or admire him. Perhaps I should prefer that someone else should get the credit for my work, than that it should vanish without trace, but I cannot honestly say that this is a matter of indifference to me. If the work survives, I want my name also to survive as its author. Yet it is not a pleasure that I shall enjoy. I shall have no means of telling whether it has survived or not.

Nevertheless, my friends and my children and my grandchildren, if I have any, will know that it has survived; and the belief that they will take pride in the fact is a source of satisfaction to me. I think that this is true, though its importance may be overestimated. A childless curmudgeon may equally relish the thought of his posthumous fame. Moreover, it is a motive which does not reach far into the future. I care a great deal for my son, my stepdaughter and her three-year-old child, but the idea that persons in the twenty-fourth century will take any pleasure in my being their ancestor carries no weight with me. It is a matter of indifference to me, and I expect to most other people, if they think about it honestly, whether or not their family line continues for another three hundred years.

So far, I have been speaking about the satisfaction that people receive for the character and conduct of their personal lives. But for the most part when questions are raised about the meaning of life, they do not look for an answer at this level. The problem which is posed is much more general. Does the existence of the universe serve any purpose, and if it does serve a purpose, does the existence of human beings enter into it? There is a tendency to assume that an affirmative answer to the first question entails an affirmative answer to the second, but this need not be so. If any sense can be made of the statement that the universe has a purpose, then the purpose could be one in which the existence of human beings played no part. Admittedly, those who cleave to the superstition of determinism, are committed to holding that the original organization of the world causally necessitates the emergence of human beings, but even they are not obliged to attach value to this outcome. They could regard us as an excrescence on the scheme of things.

Nevertheless the vast majority of those who believe that the universe serves a purpose do so because they take this as conferring a meaning on life. How far down in the scale of organisms are they prepared to go is not always clear. The hymnodist Mrs Alexander boldly strikes out with 'All things bright and beautiful, All creatures great and small, All things wise and wonderful, the Lord God made them all.' The first and third lines seem to allow for a good many omissions, but perhaps the second line makes up for them. Everything after all must have some size.

We must not overlook the last line of the stanza. Not all theories that the world has a destiny are theistic. There are conceptions of the governance of all things, and of men in particular, by an impersonal fate. Nevertheless, the notion of human life as owing its meaning to its playing its part in a grand design is most commonly associated with the belief that the universe was created by a being of supernatural intelligence, and it is this belief that I now intend to discuss.

Let me begin by saying that I totally reject it. In my youth, when I published my first book, I argued with some force that the concept of a transcendent deity was literally nonsensical. Now I am prepared to be a little more conciliatory. I am, indeed, in doubt, whether the notion of an incorporeal subject of consciousness is logically coherent, but as a follower of Hume I am prepared to envisage a series of experiences which are not linked in the ordinary way with experiences of a physical body. The problem which he and the rest of us have failed to solve is to fashion an adequate criterion of identity for such a series. But let that pass. The hypothesis then would be that the course of nature, including the emergence of human beings and the vicissitudes of their individual lives, was planned by the owner of this disembodied consciousness. There are indeed, difficulties about time, since a series of experiences presumably occurs in time and therefore must be antecedent to whatever our cosmologists light upon as the first physical event, if any. The series of psychical events, if deified, presumably had no beginning, which is not an easy conclusion to accept. But the difficulties of embracing either side of Kant's antinomy that the world had or that it had not a beginning in time are notorious, and they are not lessened by assuming time to start off with the world's alleged creator.

Fortunately, we need not become entangled in them. The hypothesis of there being a creator, even if it is allowed to be intelligible, fails through its being vacuous. To have any content it would need to specify the end for which the world was designed and the way in which various features of it promote this end. But this it does not even attempt to do. The so-called argument from design owed its popularity to the occurrence of teleological processes within the world; the adaptation of animal and human organs, such as those of sight and hearing, to their functions, the pollination of flowers, the dependence of parasites upon their hosts, phenomena now explained, more or less adequately, by the theory of natural selection. What was overlooked, except by some philosophers such as Hume in his *Dialogues Concerning Natural Religion,* was that the analogy of a watch and a watchmaker, or a building and its architect, apart from its internal imperfections, since neither watchmakers nor architects are incorporeal, simply does not apply to the universe as a whole. From what we know of it, the universe bears no resemblance to a clock or any other artefact. It has some structure, since anything that we are capable of describing must have some structure or other, but not any structure that the hypothesis of a creator prescribes. Whatever happens, the believer in the creator is going to say that that was what was intended. And just for this reason his hypothesis is vacuous.

'It can't all just be a fluke,' a young philosopher said to me the other day. On the contrary a fluke is all that it can be. I do not know how much that goes on is capable of explanation. I suspect rather less than we are apt to assume. But let us be optimistic. Let us suppose that we command a physiological theory which accounts for all the phenomena of consciousness in terms of processes in the central nervous system, and let us suppose that this theory is derivable from some biochemical theory, and so along the line until we come to relativity theory and the subatomic theories of contemporary physics. And let us suppose that we realize Einstein's vision of integrating them. What have we then? A set of formulae that are at best contingently true. They happen to account for the phenomena, as they are so far known to us, and maybe they will continue to do so. Or maybe they will need to be modified, as their predecessors have been. It makes no difference which way it goes. In either case the phenomena are what they are and the theories are adapted to them. Both could logically have been otherwise.

Suppose now, what we have seen to be false, that sense could be made of ascribing these theories to the intentions of a supernatural being. That too would make no serious difference. We should still end up with a fluke. For the fact that the world was ordered in the way it is rather than some other, if not due to the limitation of his capacity, must simply be put down to his whim.

Though they commonly go together, religious belief and belief in an afterlife, not taking the form of reincarnation, are logically distinct. I know of two atheists, both of them Cambridge philosophers, one of whom, J. Ellis McTaggart, was quite certain that he would survive, since he held the strange metaphysical view that everything in the world was a disguised immortal soul, and the other, C. D. Broad, whose interest in psychical research led him to believe that there was about an even chance of his surviving.

What is curious about Broad is that he had no wish for this to happen. He thought poorly of this world and believed that the next world, if there was one, was quite likely to be even nastier.

I cannot claim to have gone deeply into the subject of psychical research, but such evidence as I have seen of what it has yielded has not seemed to be strong enough to overcome the main objections to the idea of one's surviving one's death; first the unsolved logical difficulty of defining personal identity in anything other than physical terms; and perhaps more importantly the abundant evidence which goes to show that all our conscious experiences are causally dependent upon our brains. I have already admitted that we do not have a set of well-established psychophysical hypotheses which correlate experiences one to one with states of the brain but the evidence for the overall, dependence of consciousness upon the brain is very strong.

Even if life had a meaning in the sense that we have just been discussing, it would not be known to the persons who had faith in it, nor would they have any inkling of the part that their own lives played in the overall plan. It might, therefore, seem surprising that the question was so important to them. Why should it matter to them that they followed a course which was not of their own choosing as a means to an end of which they were ignorant? Why should they derive any satisfaction from the belief that they were puppets in the hands of a superior agent?

I believe the answer is that most people are excited by the feeling that they are involved in a larger enterprise, even if they have no responsibility for its direction. This is a dangerous propensity since it makes them easier to manipulate, and so facilitates the growth of political and religious fanaticism. On the other hand, it can also serve the promotion of good causes, such as the agitation in favour of the victims of political injustice, or the organization of relief for the inhabitants of areas of famine. The case of war is an interesting example. I can speak, from experience, only of the second Great War, and only from an English point of view. I took part in it first as a soldier and then as a member of departments of intelligence. I suppose that I spent no more than half my time in England but it included the period of the blitz and that in which the V_1 rockets were replaced by the V_2s. The feature of this war, which concerns my argument, is that the civilian population was involved in it to a greater degree than in any previous war and certainly to a greater degree than they ever will be again, if our present strategy is maintained. As a result, it was apparent that they were living with a greater intensity, and also displaying in manner and action a greater amount of fellow feeling than they previously had or would have again. It may sound shocking, but I honestly believe that, with the exception of those who suffered personal injury or personal loss, especially in the form of death or maiming of those whom they loved, most English people enjoyed the war.

This is allied to the fact that if we take the intensity with which a life is lived as a criterion of its being meaningful we shall find no very close correlation between meaningful lives and those that we consider morally estimable. The same will be true if we attribute meaning to the lives of those who pass for having been great men or women, especially if their greatness consisted in their power. I do no know whether Lord Acton was justified in saying that great men are almost always bad, but it is certainly not the case that they have always been good. We need only think of Alexander the Great, Augustus Caesar, Jenghis Kahn, Cesare Borgia, Martin Luther, Peter the Great, Catherine the Great, Louis XIV, Florence Nightingale, John Pierpont Morgan, Lord Beaverbrook and David Lloyd George. I have avoided bringing the list up to date with Hitler and Stalin, in order to avoid the question whether we are going so to construe greatness that causing an inordinate amount of evil strips one of the title. There will still be no denying that they were major historical figures and I suspect that, on the whole, they were satisfied with their lives, Hitler at least until his last days and even then he seems to have seen the collapse of his fortunes more as the failure of the German people than his own; Stalin quite probably until the very end, since even if he was poisoned he was not aware of it.

In the realm of the arts, the disparity is not so flagrant, but still there is no positive correlation between being a great artist and an amiable man. Wagner is perhaps the most obvious counterexample. There is little correlation between goodness and happiness. If virtue is said to be its own reward it is because it so often acquires no other. As the Psalmist put it, it is the ungodly whom one sees 'flourishing like a green bay-tree.' In speaking of the ungodly I am not straying into deism. I am not even thinking of major criminals, who quite often come to grief, but of the multitude of minor villains who appear to have come to the fore in recent years, persons skilled in sharp practice on the stock exchange, hooligans, racists of one or other colour, persons whose principal aim is not merely to keep up with the Jones's but to outstrip them without being too scrupulous about the means.

The obvious disparity between virtue and prosperity in this world troubled the philosopher Immanuel Kant. He believed that there ought to be another world in which this balance would be redressed and thereby discovered a motive for believing in a God who would bring this about. I use the word 'motive' rather than 'reason' because, much as I dislike Kant's moral philosophy, I have too much respect for his intelligence to suppose that he regarded his pious hope as a serious argument. After all, it was Kant who first demolished the tricky ontological argument for the existence of God, the surprisingly durable pretence that the existence of a necessary being can be established by smuggling the factor of necessity into some grandiose concept, and went on to dispose with equal ease of the argument from design and the argument to a first cause.

My reasons for disliking Kant's moral philosophy are not only technical, inasmuch as he never succeeds in finding a way to bring his goodwill into action, but also moral. I do not care for the supremacy which he accords to the sense of duty over every human sympathy or principle of altruism. In his theory, indeed, it is only the sense of duty that counts. This is because he believed, mistakenly, that to act or fail to act in accordance with it lies in our power, in a way that the possession of the motives for other forms of action and our responses to them do not. In fact, actions done from a sense of duty are no less subject to causal conditioning than any others. Does the extent to which our actions are causally conditioned rob them of their moral value? I think not. I think that acts of cruelty or kindness are ugly or attractive in themselves, irrespective of their being correlated, in some measure, with states of our central nervous system, or explicable, however vaguely, in terms of our genetic endowment and the stimuli to which we have been subjected. This question is more difficult when it is directed towards the agent. Our ordinary moral judgments imply that he could not only have acted but in many cases chosen otherwise and it is not entirely clear to me what this means. I am inclined to think that the concept of desert which is included in our notion of moral responsibility is incoherent, but this is not a question into which I can enter here.

If I say that there are no such things as objective moral values, this is not to be taken as a profession of moral nihilism. I am not endorsing any moral principle that anybody happens to hold, still less alleging that all actions are morally neutral. On the contrary, I have strong moral sentiments and am anxious that other people should share them and act upon them. In saying that moral values are not objective, I am maintaining only that moral terms, while as it were, commenting on natural features of the world, do no themselves describe them. One consequence of this is that moral argument, in so far as it is not a dispute about some matter of fact, say, an agent's motive or the physical character of his action, is possible only on the basis of some common sentiment. For this reason, it is commonly *ad hominem*. One endeavours to convince one's opponent that his standpoint commits him to endorsing a course of action of which one is sure that he cannot honestly approve.

Evidently, there is no general answer to the question what constitutes a meaningful life. A life lived in one culture at a given social and economic level which satisfies one person might well fail to satisfy another who dwelt in a different or even in the same environment. Treating the question subjectively one can say, platitudinously, that it is a matter of the degree to which one achieves self-fulfilment. Treating it objectively, it is a matter of one's standing in one's society and the historical influence, if any, that one exerts. We have seen that the results of these different viewpoints need not coincide either with each other or with what we humane and liberal persons would regard as morally commendable.

I conclude with a question to which I do not know the answer. How far should our judgment of the worth of a person's life be affected by the fact that we take it to be based upon an illusion? Let us take the example of a nun, belonging to a strict order, leading a life of austerity, but serene in the performance of her devotions, confident that she is loved by her deity, and that she is destined for a blissful future in the world to come. If this example is considered to be too subjective, we can allot her a position of authority in the convent and locate her at a time and place when abbesses were historically important. It makes no difference to the problem. The question is whether it matters that the deity in whose love she rejoices does not exist and that there is no world to come.

I am inclined to say that it does matter, just as G. E. Moore in the last chapter of *Principia Ethica* goes so far as to say that 'a merely poetical contemplation of the Kingdom of Heaven *would* be superior to that of the religious believer, if it were the case (as he in fact thought it was) that the Kingdom of Heaven does not and will not really exist.'[3] I suppose that he was and I am yielding to what he called 'a strong respect for truth.' But what is our argument? It is not as if there were some end that the nun's life is failing to achieve. So far as one can survey the Universe *sub specie aeternitatis* one has to agree with Macbeth. It *is* 'a tale, told by an idiot, full of sound and fury, signifying nothing.' What is wrong with this quotation is its aura of disillusionment. It is not that we are sentenced to deprivation. It is open to us to make our lives as satisfying as our circumstances allow. But to return to the nun. It would indeed be terrible for her to discover that the point of her life was nonexistent. But *ex hypothesi* this is something that she will never know.

Notes

1. *The Problem of Knowledge*, p. 194.
2. *Tractatus Logico-Philosophicus*, 6.4311.
3. 2nd edn., p. 495.

PART TWO

Arguments for God's Existence: Is God's Existence Demonstrable to Reason?

In this section, classic arguments for the existence of God are presented. For centuries, believers in the West were convinced that the existence of God was virtually self-evident and that anyone who paid the matter any serious attention would come to realize that the issue was beyond rational dispute. Of course, the arguments eventually fell upon hard times philosophically, and reason's easy access to God is no longer taken for granted. Richard Taylor (1983) sets out a contemporary version of the cosmological argument, suggesting that the argument from causality can be philosophically defended. Next, William Paley (1802) offers his watch argument in favor of the argument from design and, finally, St. Anselm of Canterbury (1077–78), in his ontological argument, proposes the logical necessity of God's existence. Objections to and rebuttals of the three arguments are offered by David Hume (1779), Percy Bysshe Shelley (1814), and Jerome Shaffer (1962). In addition to introducing the arguments for the existence of God, the readings in this chapter also examine the degree to which reason can assist in establishing the foundation for religious faith.

5. The Cosmological Argument: A Defense

RICHARD TAYLOR

Suppose you were strolling in the woods and, in addition to the sticks, stones, and other accustomed litter of the forest floor, you one day came upon some quite unaccustomed object, something not quite like what you had ever seen before and would never expect to find in such a place. Suppose, for example, that it is a large ball, about

Source: Richard Taylor, "The Cosmological Argument: A Defense," in *Metaphysics,* 4th ed. (Englewood Cliffs, NJ: Prentice Hall, 1992), 99–108.

your own height, perfectly smooth and translucent. You would deem this puzzling and mysterious, certainly, but if one considers the matter, it is no more inherently mysterious that such a thing should exist than that anything else should exist. If you were quite accustomed to finding such objects of various sizes around you most of the time, but had never seen an ordinary rock, then upon finding a large rock in the woods one day you would be just as puzzled and mystified. This illustrates the fact that something that is mysterious ceases to seem so simply by its accustomed presence. It is strange indeed, for example, that a world such as ours should exist; yet few men are very often struck by this strangeness, but simply take it for granted.

Suppose, then, that you have found this translucent ball and are mystified by it. Now whatever else you might wonder about it, there is one thing you would hardly question; namely, that it did not appear there all by itself, that it owes its existence to something. You might not have the remotest idea whence and how it came to be there, but you would hardly doubt that there was an explanation. The idea that it might have come from nothing at all, that it might exist without there being any explanation of its existence, is one that few people would consider worthy of entertaining.

This illustrates a metaphysical belief that seems to be almost a part of reason itself, even though few men ever think upon it; the belief, namely, that there is some explanation for the existence of anything whatever, some reason why it should exist rather than not. The sheer nonexistence of anything, which is not to be confused with the passing out of existence of something, never requires a reason; but existence does. That there should never have been any such ball in the forest does not require any explanation or reason, but that there should ever be such a ball does. If one were to look upon a barren plain and ask why there is not and never has been any large translucent ball there, the natural response would be to ask why there should be; but if one finds such a ball, and wonders why it is there, it is not quite so natural to ask why it should *not* be, as though existence should simply be taken for granted. That anything should not exist, then, and that, for instance, no such ball should exist in the forest, or that there should be no forest for it to occupy, or no continent containing a forest, or no earth, nor any world at all, do not seem to be things for which there needs to be any explanation or reason; but that such things should be, does seem to require a reason.

The principle involved here has been called the principle of sufficient reason. Actually, it is a very general principle, and is best expressed by saying that, in the case of any positive truth, there is some sufficient reason for it, something which, in this sense, makes it true—in short, that there is some sort of explanation, known or unknown, for everything.

Now some truths depend on something else, and are accordingly called *contingent,* while others depend only upon themselves, that is, are true by their very natures and are accordingly called *necessary.* There is, for example, a reason why the stone on my window sill is warm; namely, that the sun is shining upon it. This happens to be true, but not by its very nature. Hence, it is contingent, and depends upon something other than itself. It is also true that all the points of a circle are equidistant from the center, but this truth depends upon nothing but itself. No matter what happens, nothing can make it false. Similarly, it is a truth, and a necessary one, that if the stone on my window sill is a body, as it is, then it has a form, because this fact depends upon nothing but itself for its confirmation. Untruths are also, of course, either contingent or necessary, it being contingently false, for example, that the stone on my window sill is cold, and necessarily false that it is both a body and formless, because this is by its very nature impossible.

The principle of sufficient reason can be illustrated in various ways, as we have done, and if one thinks about it, he is apt to find that he presupposes it in his thinking about reality, but it cannot be proved. It does not appear to be itself a necessary truth, and at the same time it would be most odd to say it is contingent. If one were to try proving it, he would sooner or later have to appeal to considerations that are less plausible than the principle itself. Indeed, it is hard to see how one could even make an argument for it, without already assuming it. For this reason it might properly be called a presupposition of reason itself. One can deny that it is true, without embarrassment or fear of refutation, but one is then apt to find that what he is denying is not really what the principle asserts. We shall, then, treat it here as a datum—not something that is provably true, but as something which all men, whether they ever reflect upon it or not, seem more or less to presuppose.

The Existence of a World

It happens to be true that something exists, that there is, for example, a world, and although no one ever seriously supposes that this might not be so, that there might exist nothing at all, there still seems to be nothing the least necessary in this, considering it just by itself. That no world should ever exist at all is perfectly comprehensible and seems to express not the slightest absurdity. Considering any particular item in the world it seems not at all necessary in itself that it should ever have existed, nor does it appear any more necessary that the totality of these things, or any totality of things, should ever exist.

From the principle of sufficient reason it follows, of course, that there must be a reason, not only for the existence of everything in the world but for the world itself, meaning by "the world" simply everything that ever does exist, except God, in case there is a god. This principle does not imply that there must be some purpose or goal for everything, or for the totality of all things; for explanations need not, and in fact seldom are, teleological or purposeful. All the principle requires is that there be some sort of reason for everything. And it would certainly be odd to maintain that everything in the world owes its existence to something, that nothing in the world is either purely accidental, or such that it just bestows its own being upon itself, and then to deny this of the world itself. One can indeed say that the world is in some sense a pure accident, that there simply is no reason at all why this or any world should exist, and one can equally say that the world exists by its very nature, or is an inherently necessary being. But it is at least very odd and arbitrary to deny of this existing world the need for any sufficient reason, whether independent of itself or not, while presupposing that there is a reason for every other thing that ever exists.

Consider again the strange ball that we imagine has been found in the forest. Now we can hardly doubt that there must be an explanation for the existence of such a thing, though we may have no notion what that explanation is. It is not, moreover, the fact of its having been found in the forest rather than elsewhere that renders an explanation necessary. It matters not in the least where it happens to be, for our question is not how it happens to be *there* but how it happens to exist at all. If we in our imagination annihilate the forest, leaving only this ball in an open field, our conviction that it is a contingent thing and owes its existence to something other than itself is not reduced in the least. If we now imagine the field to be annihilated, and in fact everything else as well to vanish into nothingness, leaving only this ball to constitute the entire physical universe, then we cannot for a moment suppose that its existence has thereby been explained, or the need of any explanation eliminated, or that its existence is suddenly rendered self-explanatory. If we now carry this thought one step further and suppose that no other reality ever has existed or ever will exist, that this ball forever constitutes the entire physical universe, then we must still insist on there being some reason independent of itself why it should exist rather than not. If there must be a reason for the existence of any particular thing, then the necessity of such a reason is not eliminated by the mere supposition that certain other things do *not* exist. And again, it matters not at all what the thing in question is, whether it be large and complex, such as the world we actually find ourselves in, or whether it be something small, simple and insignificant, such as a ball, a bacterium, or the merest grain of sand. We do not avoid the necessity of a reason for the existence of something merely by describing it in this way or that. And it would, in any event, seem quite plainly absurd to say that if the world were comprised entirely of a single ball about six feet in diameter, or of a single grain of sand, then it would be contingent and there would have to be some explanation other than itself why such a thing exists, but that, since the actual world is vastly more complex than this, there is no need for an explanation of its existence, independent of itself.

Beginningless Existence

It should now be noted that it is no answer to the question, why a thing exists, to state *how long* it has existed. A geologist does not suppose that he has explained why there should be rivers and mountains merely by pointing out that they are old. Similarly, if one were to ask, concerning the ball of which we have spoken, for some sufficient reason for its being, he would not receive any answer upon being told that it had been there since yesterday. Nor would it be any better answer to say that it had existed since before anyone could remember, or even that it had existed; for the question was not one concerning its age but its existence. If, to be sure, one were to ask where a given thing came from, or how it came into being, then upon learning that it had always existed he would learn that it never really *came* into being at all; but he could still reasonably wonder why it should exist at all. If, accordingly, the world—that is, the totality of all things excepting God, in case there is a god—had really no beginning at all, but has always existed in some form or other, then there is clearly no answer to the question, where it came from and when; it did not, on this supposition, *come* from anything at all, at any time. But still, it can be asked why there is a world, why indeed there is a beginningless world, why there should have perhaps always been something rather than nothing. And, if the principle of sufficient reason is a good principle, there must be an answer to that question, an answer that is by no means supplied by giving the world an age, or even an infinite age.

Creation

This brings out an important point with respect to the concept of creation that is often misunderstood, particularly by those whose thinking has been influenced by Christian ideas. People tend to think that creation—for example, the creation of the world by God—*means* creation *in time,* from which it of course logically follows that if the world had no beginning in time, then it cannot be the creation of God. This, however, is erroneous, for creation means essentially *dependence,* even in Christian theology. If one thing is the creation of another, then it depends for its existence on that other, and this is perfectly consistent with saying that both are eternal, that neither ever came into being, and hence, that neither was ever created at any point of time. Perhaps an analogy will help convey this point. Consider, then, a flame that is casting beams of light. Now there seems to be a clear sense in which the beams of light are dependent for their existence upon the flame, which is their source, while the flame, on the other hand, is not similarly dependent for its existence upon them. The beams of light arise from the flame, but the flame does not arise from them. In this sense, they are the creation of the flame; they derive their existence from it. And none of this has any reference to time; the relationship of dependence in such a case would not be altered in the slightest if we supposed that the flame, and with it the beams of light, had always existed, that neither had ever *come* into being.

Now if the world is the creation of God, its relationship to God should be thought of in this fashion; namely, that the world depends for its existence upon God, and could not exist independently of God. If God is eternal, as those who believe in God generally assume, then the world may (though it need not) be eternal too, without that altering in the least its dependence upon God for its existence, and hence without altering its being the creation of God. The supposition of God's eternality, on the other hand, does not by itself imply that the world is eternal too; for there is not the least reason why something of finite duration might not depend for its existence upon something of infinite duration—though the reverse is, of course, impossible.

God

If we think of God as "the creator of heaven and earth," and if we consider heaven and earth to include everything that exists except God, then we appear to have, in the foregoing considerations, fairly strong reasons for asserting that God, as so conceived, exists. Now of course most people have much more in mind than this when they think of

God, for religions have ascribed to God ever so many attributes that are not at all implied by describing him merely as the creator of the world; but that is not relevant here. Most religious persons do, in any case, think of God as being at least the creator, as that being upon which everything ultimately depends, no matter what else they may say about him in addition. It is, in fact, the first item in the creeds of Christianity that God is the "creator of heaven and earth." And, it seems, there are good metaphysical reasons, as distinguished from the persuasions of faith, for thinking that such a creative being exists.

If, as seems clearly implied by the principle of sufficient reason, there must be a reason for the existence of heaven and earth—i.e., for the world—then that reason must be found either in the world itself, or outside it, in something that is literally supranatural, or outside heaven and earth. Now if we suppose that the world—i.e., the totality of all things except God—contains within itself the reason for its existence, we are supposing that it exists by its very nature, that is, that it is a necessary being. In that case there would, of course, be no reason for saying that it must depend upon God or anything else for its existence; for if it exists by its very nature, then it depends upon nothing but itself, much as the sun depends upon nothing but itself for its heat. This, however, is implausible, for we find nothing about the world or anything in it to suggest that it exists by its own nature, and we do find, on the contrary, ever so many things to suggest that it does not. For in the first place, anything that exists by its very nature must necessarily be eternal and indestructible. It would be a self-contradiction to say of anything that it exists by its own nature, or is a necessarily existing thing, and at the same time to say that it comes into being or passes away, or that it ever could come into being or pass away. Nothing about the world seems at all like this, for concerning anything in the world, we can perfectly easily think of it as being annihilated, or as never having existed in the first place, without there being the slightest hint of any absurdity in such a supposition. Some of the things in the universe are, to be sure, very old; the moon, for example, or the stars and the planets. It is even possible to imagine that they have always existed. Yet it seems quite impossible to suppose that they owe their existence to nothing but themselves, that they bestow existence upon themselves by their very natures, or that they are in themselves things of such nature that it would be impossible for them not to exist. Even if we suppose that something, such as the sun, for instance, has existed forever, and will never cease, still we cannot conclude just from this that it exists by its own nature. If, as is of course very doubtful, the sun has existed forever and will never cease, then it is possible that its heat and light have also existed forever and will never cease; but that would not show that the heat and light of the sun exist by their own natures. They are obviously contingent and depend on the sun for their existence, whether they are beginningless and everlasting or not.

There seems to be nothing in the world, then, concerning which it is at all plausible to suppose that it exists by its own nature, or contains within itself the reason for its existence. In fact, everything in the world appears to be quite plainly the opposite, namely, something that not only need not exist, but at some time or other, past or future or both, does not in fact exist. Everything in the world seems to have a finite duration, whether long or short. Most things, such as ourselves, exist only for a short while; they come into being, then soon cease. Other things, like the heavenly bodies, last longer, but they are still corruptible, and from all that we can gather about them, they too seem destined eventually to perish. We arrive at the conclusion, then, that although the world may contain some things that have always existed and are destined never to perish, it is nevertheless doubtful that it contains any such thing and, in any case, everything in the world is capable of perishing, and nothing in it, however long it may already have existed and however long it may yet remain, exists by its own nature, but depends instead upon something else.

Although this might be true of everything in the world, is it necessarily true of the world itself? That is, if we grant, as we seem forced to, that nothing in the world exists by its own nature, that everything in the world is contingent and perishable, must we also say that the world itself, or the totality of all these perishable things, is also contingent and perishable? Logically, we are not forced to, for it is logically possible that the totality of all perishable things might itself be imperishable, and hence, that the world might exist by its own nature, even though it is comprised exclusively of things that are contingent. It is not logically necessary that a totality should share the defects of its members. For example, even though every man is mortal, it does not follow from this that the human race, or the totality of all men, is also mortal; for it is possible that there will always be human beings, even though there are no human beings who will always exist. Similarly, it is possible that the world is in itself a necessary thing, even though it is comprised entirely of things that are contingent.

This is logically possible, but it is not plausible. For we find nothing whatever about the world, any more than in its parts, to suggest that it exists by its own nature. Concerning anything in the world, we have not the slightest difficulty in supposing that it should perish, or even that it should never have existed in the first place. We have almost as little difficulty in supposing this of the world itself. It might be somewhat hard to think of everything as utterly perishing and leaving no trace whatever of its ever having been, but there seems to be not the slightest difficulty in imagining that the world should never have existed in the first place. We can, for instance, perfectly easily suppose that nothing in the world had ever existed except, let us suppose, a single grain of sand, and we can thus suppose that this grain of sand has forever constituted the whole universe. Now if we consider just this grain of sand, it is quite impossible for us to suppose that it exists by its very nature, and could never have failed to exist. It clearly depends for its existence upon something other than itself, if it depends on anything at all. The same will be true if we consider the world to consist, not of one grain of sand, but of two, or of a million, or, as we in fact find, of a vast number of stars and planets and all their minuter parts.

It would seem, then, that the world, in case it happens to exist at all—and this is quite beyond doubt—is contingent and thus dependent upon something other than itself for its existence, if it depends upon anything at all. And it must depend upon something, for otherwise there could be no reason why it exists in the first place. Now that upon which the world depends must be something that either exists by its own nature or does not. If it does not exist by its own nature, then it, in turn, depends for its existence upon something else, and so on. Now then, we can say either of two things: namely, (1) that the world depends for its existence upon something else, which in turn depends on still another thing, this depending upon still another, *ad infinitum;* or (2) that the world derives its existence from something that exists by its own nature and that is accordingly eternal and imperishable, and is the creator of heaven and earth. The first of these alternatives, however, is impossible, for it does not render a sufficient reason why anything should exist in the first place. Instead of supplying a reason why any world should exist, it repeatedly begs off giving a reason. It explains what is dependent and perishable in terms of what is itself dependent and perishable, leaving us still without a reason why perishable things should exist at all, which is what we are seeking. Ultimately, then, it would seem that the world, or the totality of contingent or perishable things, in case it exists at all, must depend upon something that is necessary and imperishable, and that accordingly exists, not in dependence upon something else, but by its own nature.

"Self-Caused"

What has been said thus far gives some intimation of what meaning should be attached to the concept of a self-caused being, a concept that is quite generally misunderstood, sometimes even by scholars. To say that something—God, for example—is self-caused, or is the cause of its own existence, does not mean that this being brings itself into existence, which is a perfectly absurd idea. Nothing can *bring* itself into existence. To say that something is self-caused (*causa sui*) means only that it exists, not contingently or in dependence upon something else, but by its own nature, which is only to say that it is a being which is such that it can neither come into being nor perish. Now whether such a being in fact exists or not, there is in any case no absurdity in the idea. We have found, in fact, that the principle of sufficient reason seems to point to the existence of such a being, as that upon which the world, with everything in it, must ultimately depend for its existence.

"Necessary Being"

A being that depends for its existence upon nothing but itself, and is in this sense self-caused, can equally be described as a necessary being; that is to say, a being that is not contingent, and hence not perishable. For in the case of anything that exists by its own nature and is dependent upon nothing else, it is impossible that it should not exist, which is equivalent to saying that it is necessary. Many persons have professed to find the gravest difficulties in this concept, too, but that is partly because it has been confused with other notions. If it makes sense to speak of anything as an *impossible* being, or something that by its very nature does not exist, then it is hard to see why the idea of a necessary being, or something that in its very nature exists, should not be just as comprehensible. And of course, we have not the slightest difficulty in speaking of something, such as a square circle or a formless body, as an impossible being. And if it makes sense to speak of something as being perishable, contingent, and dependent upon something other than itself for its existence, as it surely does, then there seems to be no difficulty in thinking of something as imperishable and dependent upon nothing other than itself for its existence.

"First Cause"

From these considerations we can see also what is properly meant by a first cause, an appellative that has often been applied to God by theologians, and that many persons have deemed an absurdity. It is a common criticism of this notion to say that there need not be any first cause, because the series of causes and effects that constitute the history of the universe might be infinite or beginningless and must, in fact, be infinite in case the universe itself had no beginning in time. This criticism, however, reflects a total misconception of what is meant by a first cause. *First* here does not mean first in time, and when God is spoken of as a first cause, he is not being described as a being which, at some time in the remote past, *started* everything. To describe God as a first cause is only to say that he is literally a *primary* rather than a secondary cause, an *ultimate* rather than a derived cause, or a being upon which all other things, heaven and earth, ultimately depend for their existence. It is, in short, only to say that God is the creator, in the sense of creation explained above. Now this, of course, is perfectly consistent with saying that the world is eternal or beginningless. As we have seen, one gives no reason for the existence of a world merely by giving it an age, even if it is supposed to have an infinite age. To use a helpful analogy, we can say that the sun is the first cause of daylight and, for that matter, of the moonlight of the night as well, which means only that daylight and moonlight ultimately depend upon the sun for their existence. The moon, on the other hand, is only a secondary or derivative cause of its light. This light would be no less dependent upon the sun if we affirmed that it had no beginning, for an ageless and beginningless light requires a source no less than an ephemeral one. If we supposed that the sun has always existed, and with it its light, then we would have to say that the sun has always been the first—i.e., the primary or ultimate—cause of its light. Such is precisely the manner in which God should be thought of, and is by theologians often thought of, as the first cause of heaven and earth.

6. The Watch and the Watchmaker

WILLIAM PALEY

Statement of the Argument

In crossing a heath, suppose I pitched my foot against a *stone,* and were asked how the stone came to be there, I might possibly answer, that, for anything I knew to the contrary, it had lain there for ever; nor would it, perhaps, be very easy to show the absurdity of this answer. But suppose I found a *watch* upon the ground, and it should be inquired how the watch happened to be in that place, I should hardly think of the answer which I had given—that, for anything I knew, the watch might have always been there. Yet why should not this answer serve for the watch as well as for the stone? why is it not as admissible in the second case as in the first? For this reason, and for no other; viz., that, when we come to inspect the watch, we perceive (what we could not discover in the stone) that its several parts are framed and put together for a purpose, e.g. that they are so formed and adjusted as to produce motion, and that motion so regulated as to point out the hour of the day; that, if the different parts had been differently shaped from what they are, if a different size from what they are, or placed after any other manner, or in any other order than that in which they are placed, either no motion at all would have been carried on in the machine, or none which would have answered the use that is now served by it. To reckon up a few of the plainest of these parts, and of their offices, all tending to one result:—We see a cylindrical box containing a coiled elastic spring, which, by its endeavor to relax itself, turns round the box. We next observe a flexible chain (artificially wrought for the sake of flexure) communicating the action of the spring from the box to the fusee. We then find a series of wheels, the teeth of which catch in, and apply to, each other, conducting the motion from the fusee to the balance, and from the balance to the pointer, and, at the same time, by the size and shape of those wheels, so regulating that motion as to terminate in causing an index, by an equable and measured progression, to pass over a given space in a given time. We take notice that the wheels are made of brass, in order to keep them from rust; the springs of steel, no other metal being so elastic; that over the face of the watch there is

Source: From William Paley, *Natural Theology, or Evidences of the Existence and Attributes of the Deity Collected from the Appearances of Nature* (1802).

placed a glass, a material employed in no other part of the work, but in the room of which, if there had been any other than a transparent substance, the hour could not be seen without opening the case. This mechanism being observed, (it requires indeed an examination of the instrument, and perhaps some previous knowledge of the subject, to perceive and understand it; but being once, as we have said, observed and understood,) the inference, we think, is inevitable, that the watch must have had a maker; that there must have existed, at some time, and at some place or other, an artificer or artificers who formed it for the purpose which we find it actually to answer; who comprehended its construction, and designed its use.

I. Nor would it, I apprehend, weaken the conclusion, that we had never seen a watch made; that we had never known an artist capable of making one; that we were altogether incapable of executing such a piece of workmanship ourselves, or of understanding in what manner it was performed; all this being no more than what is true of some exquisite remains of ancient art, of some lost arts, and, to the generality of mankind, of the more curious productions of modern manufacture. Does one man in a million know how oval frames are turned? Ignorance of this kind exalts our opinion of the unseen and unknown artist's skill, if he be unseen and unknown, but raises no doubt in our minds of the existence and agency of such an artist, at some former time, and in some place or other. Nor can I perceive that it varies at all the inference, whether the question arise concerning a human agent, or concerning an agent of a different species, or an agent possessing, in some respect, a different nature.

II. Neither, secondly, would it invalidate our conclusion, that the watch sometimes went wrong, or that it seldom went exactly right. The purpose of the machinery, the design, and the designer, might be evident, and, in the case supposed, would be evident, in whatever way we accounted for the irregularity of the movement, or whether we could account for it or not. It is not necessary that a machine be perfect, in order to show with what design it was made; still less necessary, where the only question is, whether it were made with any design at all.

III. Nor, thirdly, would it bring any uncertainty into the argument, if there were a few parts of the watch, concerning which we could not discover, or had not yet discovered, in what manner they conduced to the general effect; or even some parts, concerning which we could not ascertain whether they conduced to that effect in any manner whatever. For, as to the first branch of the case, if by the loss, or disorder, or decay of the parts in question, the movement of the watch were found in fact to be stopped, or disturbed, or retarded, no doubt would remain in our minds as to the utility or intention of these parts, although we should be unable to investigate the manner according to which, or the connection by which, the ultimate effect depended upon their action or assistance; and the more complex is the machine, the more likely is this obscurity to arise. Then, as to the second thing supposed, namely, that there were parts which might be spared without prejudice to the movement of the watch, and that he had proved this by experiment, these superfluous parts, even if we were completely assured that they were such, would not vacate the reasoning which we had instituted concerning other parts. The indication of contrivance remained, with respect to them, nearly as it was before.

IV. Nor, fourthly, would any man in his senses think the existence of the watch, with its various machinery, accounted for, by being told that it was one out of possible combinations of material forms; that whatever he had found in the place where he found the watch, must have contained some internal configuration or other; and that this configuration might be the structure now exhibited, viz., of the works of a watch, as well as a different structure.

V. Nor, fifthly, would it yield his inquiry more satisfaction, to be answered, that there existed in things a principle of order, which had disposed the parts of the watch into their present form and situation. He never knew a watch made by the principle of order; nor can he even form to himself an idea of what is meant by a principle of order, distinct from the intelligence of the watchmaker.

VI. Sixthly, he would be surprised to hear that the mechanism of the watch was no proof of contrivance, only a motive to induce the mind to think so:

VII. And not less surprised to be informed, that the watch in his hand was nothing more than the result of the laws of *metallic* nature. It is a perversion of language to assign any law as the efficient, operative cause of anything. A law presupposes an agent; for it is only the mode according to which an agent proceeds; it implies a power; for it is the order according to which that power acts. Without this agent, without this power, which are both distinct from itself, the *law* does nothing, is nothing. The expression, "the law of metallic nature," may sound strange and harsh to a philosophic ear; but it seems quite as justifiable as some others which are more familiar to him such as "the law of vegetable nature," "the law of animal nature," or, indeed, as "the law of nature" in general, when assigned as the cause of phenomena in exclusion of agency and power, or when it is substituted into the place of these.

VIII. Neither, lastly, would our observer be driven out of his conclusion, or from his confidence in its truth, by being told that he knew nothing at all about the matter. He knows enough for his argument: he knows the utility of the end: he knows the subserviency and adaptation of the means to the end. These points being known, his ignorance of other points, his doubts concerning other points, affect not the certainty of his reasoning. The consciousness of knowing little need not beget a distrust of that which he does know. . . .

Application of the Argument

Every indication of contrivance, every manifestation of design, which existed in the watch, exists in the works of nature; with the difference, on the side of nature, of being greater and more, and that in a degree which exceeds all computation. I mean that the contrivances of nature surpass the contrivances of art, in the complexity, subtilty, and curiosity of the mechanism; and still more, if possible, do they go beyond them in number and variety; yet in a multitude of cases, are not less evidently mechanical, not less evidently contrivances, not less evidently accommodated to their end, or suited to their office, than are the most perfect productions of human ingenuity. . . .

7. The Classical Ontological Argument

ST. ANSELM OF CANTERBURY

Truly there is a God, although the fool hath said in his heart, There is no God.

And so, Lord, do thou, who dost give understanding to faith, give me, so far as thou knowest it to be profitable, to understand that thou art as we believe; and that thou art that which we believe. And, indeed, we believe that thou art a being than which nothing greater can be conceived. Or is there no such nature, since the fool hath said in his heart, there is no God? (Psalms xiv. I). But, at any rate, this very fool, when he hears of this being of which I speak—a being than which nothing greater can be conceived—understands what he hears, and what he understands is in his understanding; although he does not understand it to exist.

For, it is one thing for an object to be in the understanding, and another to understand that the object exists. When a painter first conceives of what he will afterwards perform, he has it in his understanding, but he does not yet understand it to be, because he has not yet performed it. But after he has made the painting, he both has it in his understanding, and he understands that it exists, because he has made it.

Hence, even the fool is convinced that something exists in the understanding, at least, than which nothing greater can be conceived. For, when he hears of this, he understands it. And whatever is understood, exists in the understanding. And assuredly that, than which nothing greater can be conceived, cannot exist in the understanding alone. For, suppose it exists in the understanding alone: then it can be conceived to exist in reality; which is greater.

Therefore, if that, than which nothing greater can be conceived, exists in the understanding alone, the very being, than which nothing greater can be conceived, is one, than which a greater can be conceived. But obviously this is impossible. Hence, there is no doubt that there exists a being, than which nothing greater can be conceived, and it exists both in the understanding and in reality.

God cannot be conceived not to exist.—God is that, than which nothing greater can be conceived.—That which can be conceived not to exist is not God.

And it assuredly exists so truly, that it cannot be conceived not to exist. For, it is possible to conceive of a being which cannot be conceived not to exist; and this is

Source: St. Anselm, "The Ontological Argument," in *St. Anselm's Proslogion*, trans. M. J. Charlesworth (Notre Dame, IN: University of Notre Dame Press, 1979), 17, 19, 21.

greater than one which can be conceived not to exist. Hence, if that, than which nothing greater can be conceived, can be conceived not to exist, it is not that, than which nothing greater can be conceived. But this is an irreconcilable contradiction. There is, then, so truly a being than which nothing greater can be conceived to exist, that it cannot even be conceived not to exist; and this being thou art, O Lord, our God.

So truly, therefore, dost thou exist, O Lord, my God, that thou canst not be conceived not to exist; and rightly. For, if a mind could conceive of a being better than thee, the creature would rise above the Creator; and this is most absurd. And, indeed, whatever else there is, except thee alone, can be conceived not to exist. To thee alone, therefore, it belongs to exist more truly than all other beings, and hence in a higher degree than all others. For, whatever else exists does not exist so truly, and hence in a less degree it belongs to it to exist. Why, then, has the fool said in his heart, there is no God (Psalms xiv. I), since it is so evident, to a rational mind, that thou dost exist in the highest degree of all? Why, except that he is dull and a fool?

> How the fool has said in his heart what cannot be conceived.—A thing may be conceived in two ways: (1) when the word signifying it is conceived; (2) when the thing itself is understood As far as the word goes, God can be conceived not to exist; in reality he cannot.

But how has the fool said in his heart what he could not conceive; or how is it that he could not conceive what he said in his heart? since it is the same to say in the heart, and to conceive.

But, if really, nay, since really, he both conceived, because he said in his heart; and did not say in his heart, because he could not conceive; there is more than one way in which a thing is said in the heart or conceived. For, in one sense, an object is conceived, when the word signifying it is conceived; and in another, when the very entity, which the object is, is understood.

In the former sense, then, God can be conceived not to exist; but in the latter, not at all. For no one who understands what fire and water are can conceive fire to be water, in accordance with the nature of the facts themselves, although this is possible according to the words. So, then, no one who understands what God is can conceive that God does not exist; although he says these words in his heart, either without any, or with some foreign, signification. For, God is that than which a greater cannot be conceived. And he who thoroughly understands this, assuredly understands that this being so truly exists, that not even in concept can it be non-existent. Therefore, he who understands that God so exists, cannot conceive that he does not exist.

I thank thee, gracious Lord, I thank thee; because what I formerly believed by thy bounty, I now so understand by thine illumination, that if I were unwilling to believe that thou dost exist, I should not be able to understand this to be true.

8. The Cosmological Argument Dialogues: Part IX

DAVID HUME

BUT IF SO many difficulties attend the argument *a posteriori*, said DEMEA; had we not better adhere to that simple and sublime argument *a priori*, which, by offering to us infallible demonstration, cuts off at once all doubt and difficulty? By this argument, too, we may prove the INFINITY of the divine attributes, which, I am afraid, can never be ascertained with certainty from any other topic. For how can an effect, which either is finite, or, for aught we know, may be so; how can such an effect, I say, prove an infinite cause? The unity too of the divine nature, it is very difficult, if not absolutely impossible, to deduce merely from contemplating the works of nature; nor will the uniformity alone of the plan, even were it allowed, give us any assurance of that attribute. Whereas the argument *a priori*. . . .

You seem to reason, DEMEA, interposed CLEANTHES, as if those advantages and conveniences in the abstract argument were full proofs of its solidity. But it is first proper, in my opinion, to determine what argument of this nature you choose to insist on; and we shall afterwards, from itself, better than from its *useful* consequences, endeavour to determine what value we ought to put upon it.

The argument, replied DEMEA, which I would insist on is the common one. Whatever exists must have a cause or reason of its existence; it being absolutely impossible for any thing to produce itself, or be the cause of its own existence. In mounting up, therefore, from effects to causes, we must either go on in tracing an infinite succession, without any ultimate cause at all, or must at last have recourse to some ultimate cause, that is *necessarily* existent: Now that the first supposition is absurd may be thus proved. In the infinite chain or succession of causes and effects, each single effect is determined to exist by the power and efficacy of that cause which immediately preceded; but the whole eternal chain or succession, taken together, is not determined or caused by any thing: And yet it is evident that it requires a cause or reason, as much as any particular object, which begins to exist in time. The question is still reasonable, why this particular succession of causes existed from eternity, and not any other succession, or no succession at all. If there be no necessarily existent Being, any supposition, which can be

---

Source: David Hume, *Dialogues Concerning Natural Religion: Part IX* (1779).

formed, is equally possible; nor is there any more absurdity in nothing's having existed from eternity, than there is in that succession of causes, which constitutes the universe. What was it, then, which determined something to exist rather than nothing, and bestowed being on a particular possibility, exclusive of the rest? *External causes*, there are supposed to be none. *Chance* is a word without a meaning. Was it *nothing?* But that can never produce any thing. We must, therefore, have recourse to a necessarily existent Being, who carries the REASON of his existence in himself; and who cannot be supposed not to exist without an express contradiction. There is consequently such a Being, that is, there is a Deity.

I shall not leave it to PHILO, said CLEANTHES (thought I know that the starting objections is his chief delight), to point out the weakness of this metaphysical reasoning. It seems to me so obviously ill-grounded, and at the same time of so little consequence to the cause of true piety and religion, that I shall myself venture to show the fallacy of it.

(1)

I shall begin with observing, that there is an evident absurdity in pretending to demonstrate a matter of fact, or to prove it by any arguments *a priori*. Nothing is demonstrable, unless the contrary implies a contradiction. Nothing, that is distinctly conceivable, implies a contradiction. Whatever we conceive as existent, we can also conceive as non-existent. There is no Being, therefore, whose non-existence implies a contradiction. Consequently there is no Being, whose existence is demonstrable. I propose this argument as entirely decisive, and am willing to rest the whole controversy upon it.

(2)

It is pretended that the Deity is a necessarily existent Being; and this necessity of his existence is attempted to be explained by asserting, that, if we knew his whole essence or nature, we should perceive it to be as impossible for him not to exist as for twice two not to be four. But it is evident, that this can never happen, while our faculties remain the same as at present. It will still be possible for us, at any time, to conceive the non-existence of what we formerly conceived to exist; nor can the mind ever lie under a necessity of supposing any object to remain always in being; in the same manner as we lie under a necessity of always conceiving twice two to be four. The words, therefore, *necessary existence*, have no meaning; or, which is the same thing, none that is consistent.

(3)

But farther; why may not the material universe be the necessarily existent Being, according to this pretended explication of necessity? We dare not affirm that we know all the qualities of matter; and for aught we can determine, it may contain some qualities, which, were they known, would make its non-existence appear as great a contradiction as that twice two is five. I find only one argument employed to prove, that the material world is not the necessarily existent Being; and this argument is derived from the contingency both of the matter and the form of the world. "Any particle of matter," it is said, "may be *conceived* to be annihilated; and any form may be *conceived* to be altered. Such an annihilation or alteration, therefore, is not impossible." But it seems a great partiality not to perceive, that the same argument extends equally to the Deity, so far as we have any conception of him; and that the mind can at least imagine him to be non-existent, or his attributes to be altered. It must be some unknown, inconceivable qualities, which can make his non-existence appear impossible, or his attributes unalterable: And no reason can be assigned, why these qualities may not belong to matter. As they are altogether unknown and inconceivable, they can never be proved incompatible with it.

(4)

Add to this, that in tracing an eternal succession of objects, it seems absurd to inquire for a general cause or first Author. How can anything, that exists from eternity, have a cause, since that relation implies a priority in time and a beginning of existence?

   In such a chain too, or succession of objects, each part is caused by that which preceded it, and causes that which succeeds it. Where then is the difficulty? But the WHOLE, you say, wants a cause. I answer, that the uniting of these parts into a whole, like the uniting of several distinct counties into one kingdom, or several distinct members into one body, is performed merely by an arbitrary act of the mind, and has no influence on the nature of things. Did I show you the particular causes of each individual in a collection of twenty particles of matter, I should think it very unreasonable, should you afterwards ask me, what was the cause of the whole twenty. This is sufficiently explained in explaining the cause of the parts.

9. Against Revelation and Deism

PERCY BYSSHE SHELLEY

The Dialogue: A Refutation of Deism, 1814

PREFACE   The object of the following Dialogue is to prove that the system of Deism is untenable. It is attempted to shew that there is no alternative between Atheism and Christianity; that the evidences of the Being of a God are to be deduced from no other principles than those of Divine Revelation.

The Author endeavours to shew how much the cause of natural and revealed Religion has suffered from the mode of defence adopted by Theosophistical Christians. How far he will accomplish what he proposed to himself, in the composition of this Dialogue, the world will finally determine.

The mode of printing this little work may appear too expensive, either for its merits or its length. However inimical this practice confessedly is, to the general diffusion of knowledge, yet it was adopted in this instance with a view of excluding the multitude from the abuse of a mode of reasoning, liable to misconstruction on account of its novelty.

Eusebes and Theosophus

EUSEBES   Theosophus, I have long regretted and observed the strange infatuation which has blinded your understanding. It is not without acute uneasiness that I have beheld the progress of your audacious scepticism trample on the most venerable institutions of our forefathers, until it has rejected the salvation which the only begotten Son of God deigned to proffer in person to a guilty and unbelieving world. To this excess, then, has the pride of the human understanding at length arrived? To measure itself with Omniscience! To scan the intentions of Inscrutability!

Source: From Percy Bysshe Shelley, *A Refutation of Deism* (1814).

You can have reflected but superficially on this awful and important subject. The love of paradox, an affectation of singularity, or the pride of reason has seduced you to the barren and gloomy paths of infidelity. Surely you have hardened yourself against the truth with a spirit of coldness and cavil.

Have you been wholly inattentive to the accumulated evidence which the Deity has been pleased to attach to the revelation of his will? The antient books in which the advent of the Messiah was predicted, the miracles by which its truth has been so conspicuously confirmed, the martyrs who have undergone every variety of torment in attestation of its veracity? You seem to require mathematical demonstration in a case which admits of no more than strong moral probability. Surely the merit of that faith which we are required to repose in our Redeemer would be thus entirely done away. Where is the difficulty of according credit to that which is perfectly plain and evident? How is he entitled to a recompense who believes what he cannot disbelieve?

When there is satisfactory evidence that the witnesses of the Christian miracles passed their lives in labours, dangers, and sufferings, and consented severally to be racked, burned, and strangled, in testimony of the truth of their account, will it be asserted that they were actuated by a disinterested desire of deceiving others? That they were hypocrites for no end but to teach the purest doctrine that ever enlightened the world, and martyrs without any prospect of emolument or fame? The sophist, who gravely advances an opinion thus absurd, certainly sins with gratuitous and indefensible pertinacity.

The history of Christianity is itself the most indisputable proof of those miracles by which its origin was sanctioned to the world. It is itself one great miracle. A few humble men established it in the face of an opposing universe. In less than fifty years an astonishing multitude was converted, as Suetonius, Pliny, Tacitus, and Lucian attest; and shortly afterwards thousands who had boldly overturned the altars, slain the priests and burned the temples of Paganism, were loud in demanding the recompense of martyrdom from the hands of the infuriated heathens. Not until three centuries after the coming of the Messiah did his holy religion incorporate itself with the institutions of the Roman Empire, and derive support from the visible arm of fleshly strength. Thus long without any assistance but that of its Omnipotent author, Christianity prevailed in defiance of incredible persecutions, and drew fresh vigour from circumstances the most desperate and unpromising. By what process of sophistry can a rational being persuade himself to reject a religion, the original propagation of which is an event wholly unparalleled in the sphere of human experience?

The morality of the Christian religion is as original and sublime, as its miracles and mysteries are unlike all other portents. A patient acquiescence in injuries and violence; a passive submission to the will of sovereigns; a disregard of those ties by which the feelings of humanity have ever been bound to this unimportant world; humility and faith, are doctrines neither similar nor comparable to those of any other system. Friendship, patriotism, and magnanimity; the heart that is quick in sensibility, the hand that is inflexible in execution; genius, learning and courage, are qualities which have engaged the admiration of mankind, but which we are taught by Christianity to consider as splendid and delusive vices.

I know not why a Theist should feel himself more inclined to distrust the historians of Jesus Christ than those of Alexander the Great. What do the tidings of redemption contain which render them peculiarly obnoxious to discredit? It will not be disputed that a revelation of the Divine will is a benefit to mankind. It will not be asserted that even under the Christian revelation, we have too clear a solution of the vast enigma of the Universe, too satisfactory a justification of the attributes of God. When we call to mind the profound ignorance in which, with the exception of the Jews, the philosophers of antiquity were plunged; when we recollect that men, eminent for dazzling talents and fallacious virtues, Epicurus, Democritus, Pliny, Lucretius, Euripides, and innumerable others, dared publicly to avow their faith in Atheism with impunity, and that the Theists, Anaxagoras, Pythagoras and Plato, vainly endeavoured by that human reason, which is truly incommensurate to so vast a purpose, to establish among philosophers the belief in one Almighty God, the creator and preserver of the world; when we recollect that the multitude were grossly and ridiculously idolatrous, and that the magistrates, if not Atheists, regarded the being of a God in the light of an abstruse and uninteresting speculation; when we add to these considerations a remembrance of the wars and the oppressions, which about the time of the advent of the Messiah, desolated the human race, is it not more credible that the Deity actually interposed to check the rapid progress of human deterioration, than that he permitted a specious and pestilent imposture to seduce mankind into the labyrinth of a deadlier superstition? Surely the Deity has not created man immortal, and left him for ever in ignorance of his glorious destination. If the Christian Religion is false, I see not upon what foundation our belief in a moral governor of the universe, or our hopes of immortality can rest.

Thus then the plain reason of the case, and the suffrage of the civilized world, conspire with the more indisputable suggestions of faith, to render impregnable that system which has been so vainly and so wantonly assailed. Suppose, however, it were admitted that the conclusions of human reason and the lessons of worldly virtue should be found, in the detail, incongruous with Divine Revelation; by the dictates of which would it become us to abide? Not by that which errs whenever it is employed, but by that which is incapable of error: not by the ephemeral systems of vain philosophy, but by the word of God, which shall endure for ever.

Reflect, O Theosophus, that if the religion you reject be true, you are justly excluded from the benefits which result from a belief in its efficiency to salvation. Be not regardless, therefore, I entreat you, of the curses so emphatically heaped upon infidels by the inspired organs of the will of God: the fire which is never quenched, the worm that never dies. I dare not think that the God in whom I trust for salvation, would terrify his creatures with menaces of punishment which he does not intend to inflict. The ingratitude of incredulity is, perhaps, the only sin to which the Almighty cannot extend his mercy without compromising his justice. How can the human heart endure, without despair, the mere conception of so tremendous an alternative? Return, I entreat you, to that tower of strength which securely overlooks the chaos of the conflicting opinions of men. Return to that God who is your creator and preserver, by whom alone you are defended from the ceaseless wiles of your eternal enemy. Are human institutions so faultless that the principle upon which they are founded may strive with the voice of God? Know that faith is superior to reason, in as much as the creature is surpassed by the Creator; and that whensoever they are incompatible, the suggestions of the latter, not those of the former, are to be questioned.

Permit me to exhibit in their genuine deformity the errors which are seducing you to destruction. State to me with candour the train of sophisms by which the evil spirit has deluded your understanding. Confess the secret motives of your disbelief; suffer me to administer a remedy to your intellectual disease. I fear not the contagion of such revolting sentiments: I fear only lest patience should desert me before you have finished the detail of your presumptuous credulity.

Against Revelation

THEOSOPHUS   I am not only prepared to confess but to vindicate my sentiments. I cannot refrain, however, from premising, that in this controversy I labour under a disadvantage from which you are exempt. You believe that incredulity is immoral, and regard him as an object of suspicion and distrust whose creed is incongruous with your own. But truth is the perception of the agreement or disagreement of ideas. I can no more conceive that a man who perceives the disagreement of any ideas should be persuaded of their agreement, than that he should overcome a physical impossibility. The reasonableness or the folly of the articles of our creed is therefore no legitimate object of merit or demerit; our opinions depend not on the will, but on the understanding.

If I am in error (and the wisest of us may not presume to deem himself secure from all illusion) that error is the consequence of the prejudices by which I am prevented, of the ignorance by which I am incapacitated from forming a correct estimation of the subject. Remove those prejudices, dispel that ignorance, make truth apparent, and fear not the obstacles that remain to be encountered. But do not repeat to me those terrible and frequent curses, by whose intolerance and cruelty I have so often been disgusted in the perusal of your sacred books. Do not tell me that the All-Merciful will punish me for the conclusions of that reason by which he has thought fit to distinguish me from the beasts that perish. Above all, refrain from urging considerations drawn from reason, to degrade that which you are thereby compelled to acknowledge as the ultimate arbiter of the dispute. Answer my objections as I engage to answer your assertions, point by point, word by word.

You believe that the only and ever-present God begot a Son whom he sent to reform the world, and to propitiate its sins; you believe that a book, called the Bible, contains a true account of this event, together with an infinity of miracles and prophecies which preceded it from the creation of the world. Your opinion that these circumstances really happened appears to me, from some considerations which I will proceed to state, destitute of rational foundation.

To expose all the inconsistency, immorality and false pretensions which I perceive in the Bible, demands a minuteness of criticism at least as voluminous as itself. I shall confine myself, therefore, to the confronting of your tenets with those primitive and general principles which are the basis of all moral reasoning.

In creating the Universe, God certainly proposed to himself the happiness of his creatures. It is just, therefore, to conclude that he left no means unemployed, which did not involve an impossibility, to accomplish this design. In fixing a residence for this image of his own Majesty, he was doubtless careful that every occasion of detriment, every opportunity of evil, should be removed. He was aware of the extent of his powers, he foresaw the consequences of his conduct, and doubtless modelled his being consentaneously with the world of which he was to be the inhabitant, and the circumstances which were destined to surround him.

The account given by the Bible has but a faint concordance with the surmises of reason concerning this event.

According to this book, God created Satan, who, instigated by the impulses of his nature, contended with the Omnipotent for the throne of Heaven. After a contest for the empire, in which God was victorious, Satan was thrust into a pit of burning sulphur. On man's creation, God placed within his reach a tree whose fruit he forbade him to taste, on pain of death; permitting Satan, at the same time, to employ all his artifice to persuade this innocent and wondering creature to transgress the fatal prohibition.

The first man yielded to this temptation; and to satisfy Divine Justice the whole of his posterity must have been eternally burned in hell, if God had not sent his only Son on earth, to save those few whose salvation had been foreseen and determined before the creation of the world.

God is here represented as creating man with certain passions and powers, surrounding him with certain circumstances, and then condemning him to everlasting torments because he acted as omniscience had foreseen, and was such as omnipotence had made him. For to assert that the Creator is the author of all good, and the creature the author of all evil, is to assert that one man makes a straight line and a crooked one, and that another makes the incongruity.

Barbarous and uncivilized nations have uniformly adored, under various names, a God of which themselves were the model: revengeful, blood-thirsty, grovelling and capricious. The idol of a savage is a demon that delights in carnage. The steam of slaughter, the dissonance of groans, the flames of a desolated land, are the offerings which he deems acceptable, and his innumerable votaries throughout the world have made it a point of duty to worship him to his taste. The Phenicians, the Druids and the Mexicans have immolated hundreds at the shrines of their divinity, and the high and holy name of God has been in all ages the watchword of the most unsparing massacres, the sanction of the most atrocious perfidies.

But I appeal to your candor, O Eusebes, if there exists a record of such grovelling absurdities and enormities so atrocious, a picture of the Deity so characteristic of a demon as that which the sacred writings of the Jews contain. I demand of you, whether as a conscientious Theist you can reconcile the conduct which is attributed to the God of the Jews with your conceptions of the purity and benevolence of the divine nature.

The loathsome and minute obscenities to which the inspired writers perpetually descend, the filthy observances which God is described as personally instituting, the total disregard of truth and contempt of the first principles of morality, manifested on the most public occasions by the chosen favourites of Heaven, might corrupt, were they not so flagitious as to disgust.

When the chief of this obscure and brutal horde of assassins asserts that the God of the Universe was enclosed in a box of shittim wood, "two feet long and three feet wide," and brought home in a new cart, I smile at the impertinence of so shallow an imposture. But it is blasphemy of a more hideous and unexampled nature to maintain that the Almighty God expressly commanded Moses to invade an unoffending nation; and, on account of the difference of their worship, utterly to destroy every human being it contained, to murder every infant and unarmed man in cold blood, to massacre the captives, to rip up the matrons, and to retain the maidens alone for concubinage and violation. [See Exodus, 32:26; Numbers, 31: 7–18.] At the very time that philosophers of the most enterprising benevolence were founding in Greece those institutions which have rendered it the wonder and luminary of the world, am I required to believe that the weak and wicked king of an obscure and barbarous nation, a murderer, a traitor and a tyrant, was the man after God's own heart? A wretch, at the thought of whose unparalleled enormities the sternest soul must sicken in dismay! An unnatural monster, who sawed his fellow beings in sunder, harrowed them to fragments under harrows of iron, chopped them to pieces with axes, and burned them in brick-kilns, because they bowed before a different, and less bloody idol than his own. It is surely no perverse conclusion of an infatuated understanding that the God of the Jews is not the benevolent author of this beautiful world.

The conduct of the Deity in the promulgation of the Gospel, appears not to the eye of reason more compatible with his immutability and omnipotence than the history of his actions under the law accords with his benevolence.

You assert that the human race merited eternal reprobation because their common father had transgressed the divine command, and that the crucifixion of the Son of God was the only sacrifice of sufficient efficacy to satisfy eternal justice. But it is no less inconsistent with justice and subversive of morality that millions should be responsible for a crime which they had no share in committing, than that, if they had really committed it, the crucifixion of an innocent being could absolve them from moral turpitude. *Ferretne ulla civitas latorem istiusmodi legis, ut condemnaretur filius, aut nepos, si pater aut avus deliquisset?* Certainly this is a mode of legislation peculiar to a state of savageness and anarchy; this is the irrefragable logic of tyranny and imposture.

The supposition that God has ever supernaturally revealed his will to man at any other period than the original creation of the human race, necessarily involves a compromise of his benevolence. It assumes that he withheld from mankind a benefit which it was in his power to confer. That he suffered his creatures to remain in ignorance of truths essential to their happiness and salvation. That during the lapse of innumerable ages, every individual of the human race had perished without redemption, from an universal stain which the Deity at length descended in person to erase. That the good and wise of all ages, involved in one common fate with the ignorant and wicked, have been tainted by involuntary and inevitable error which torments infinite in duration may not avail to expiate.

In vain will you assure me with amiable inconsistency that the mercy of God will be extended to the virtuous, and that the vicious will alone be punished. The foundation of the Christian Religion is manifestly compromised by a concession of this nature. A subterfuge thus palpable plainly annihilates the necessity of the incarnation of God for the redemption of the human race, and represents the descent of the Messiah as a gratuitous display of Deity, solely adapted to perplex, to terrify and to embroil mankind.

It is sufficiently evident that an omniscient being never conceived the design of reforming the world by Christianity. Omniscience would surely have foreseen the inefficacy of that system, which experience demonstrates not only to have been utterly impotent in restraining, but to have been most active in exhaling the malevolent propensities of men. During the period which elapsed between the removal of the seat of empire to Constantinople in 328, and its capture by the Turks in 1453, what salutary influence did Christianity exercise upon that world which it was intended to enlighten? Never before was Europe the theatre of such ceaseless and sanguinary wars; never were the people so brutalized by ignorance and debased by slavery.

I will admit that one prediction of Jesus Christ has been indisputably fulfilled. *I come not to bring peace upon earth, but a sword.* Christianity indeed has equalled Judaism in the atrocities, and exceeded it in the extent of its desolation. Eleven millions of men, women, and children, have been killed in battle, butchered in their sleep, burned to death at public festivals of sacrifice, poisoned, tortured, assassinated, and pillaged in the spirit of the Religion of Peace, and for the glory of the most merciful God.

In vain will you tell me that these terrible effects flow not from Christianity, but from the abuse of it. No such excuse will avail to palliate the enormities of a religion pretended to be divine. A limited intelligence is only so far responsible for the effects of its agency as it foresaw, or might have foreseen them; but Omniscience is manifestly chargeable with all the consequences of its conduct. Christianity itself declares that the worth of the tree is to be determined by the quality of its fruit. The extermination of infidels; the mutual persecutions of hostile sects; the midnight massacres and slow burning of thousands, because their creed contained either more or less than the orthodox standard, of which Christianity has been the immediate occasion; and the invariable opposition which philosophy has ever encountered from the spirit of revealed religion, plainly show that a very slight portion of sagacity was sufficient to have estimated at its true value the advantages of that belief to which some Theists are unaccountably attached.

You lay great stress upon the originality of the Christian system of morals. If this claim be just, either your religion must be false, or the Deity has willed that opposite modes of conduct should be pursued by mankind at different times, under the same circumstances; which is absurd.

The doctrine of acquiescing in the most insolent despotism; of praying for and loving our enemies; of faith and humility, appears to fix the perfection of the human character in that abjectness and credulity which priests and tyrants of all ages have found sufficiently convenient for their purposes. It is evident that a whole nation of

Christians (could such an anomaly maintain itself a day) would become, like cattle, the property of the first occupier. It is evident that ten highwaymen would suffice to subjugate the world if it were composed of slaves who dared not to resist oppression.

The apathy to love and friendship, recommended by your creed, would, if attainable, not be less pernicious. This enthusiasm of antisocial misanthropy, if it were an actual rule of conduct, and not the speculation of a few interested persons, would speedily annihilate the human race. A total abstinence from sexual intercourse is not perhaps enjoined, but is strenuously recommended, and was actually practised to a frightful extent by the primitive Christians. [See I Cor. 7.]

The penalties inflicted by that monster Constantine, the first Christian Emperor, on the pleasures of unlicensed love, are so iniquitously severe, that no modern legislator could have affixed them to the most atrocious crimes. This cold-blooded and hypocritical ruffian cut his son's throat, strangled his wife, murdered his father-in-law and his brother-in-law, and maintained at his court a set of blood-thirsty and bigoted Christian Priests, one of whom was sufficient to excite the one half of the world to massacre the other.

I am willing to admit that some few axioms of morality, which Christianity has borrowed from the philosophers of Greece and India, dictate, in an unconnected state, rules of conduct worthy of regard; but the purest and most elevated lessons of morality must remain nugatory, the most probable inducements to virtue must fail of their effect, so long as the slightest weight is attached to that dogma which is the vital essence of revealed religion.

Belief is set up as the criterion of merit or demerit; a man is to be judged not by the purity of his intentions but by the orthodoxy of his creed; an assent to certain propositions, is to outweigh in the balance of Christianity the most generous and elevated virtue.

But the intensity of belief, like that of every other passion, is precisely proportioned to the degrees of excitement. A graduated scale, on which should be marked the capabilities of propositions to approach to the test of the senses, would be a just measure of the belief which ought to be attached to them: and but for the influence of prejudice or ignorance this invariably *is* the measure of belief. That is believed which is apprehended to be true, nor can the mind by any exertion avoid attaching credit to an opinion attended with overwhelming evidence. Belief is not an act of volition, nor can it be regulated by the mind: it is manifestly incapable therefore of either merit or criminality. The system which assumes a false criterion of moral virtue, must be as pernicious as it is absurd. Above all, it cannot be divine, as it is impossible that the Creator of the human mind should be ignorant of its primary powers.

The degree of evidence afforded by miracles and prophecies in favor of the Christian Religion is lastly to be considered.

Evidence of a more imposing and irresistible nature is required in proportion to the remoteness of any event from the sphere of our experience. Every case of miracles is a contest of opposite improbabilities, whether it is more contrary to experience that a miracle should be true, or that the story on which it is supported should be false:

whether the immutable laws of this harmonious world should have undergone violation, or that some obscure Greeks and Jews should have conspired to fabricate a tale of
wonder.

The actual appearance of a departed spirit would be a circumstance truly unusual
and portentous; but the accumulated testimony of twelve old women that a spirit had
appeared is neither unprecedented nor miraculous.

It seems less credible that the God whose immensity is uncircumscribed by space,
should have committed adultery with a carpenter's wife, than that some bold knaves or
insane dupes had deceived the credulous multitude. We have perpetual and mournful
experience of the latter: the former is yet under dispute. History affords us innumerable
examples of the possibility of the one: Philosophy has in all ages protested against the
probability of the other.

Every superstition can produce its dupes, its miracles, and its mysteries; each is
prepared to justify its peculiar tenets by an equal assemblage of portents, prophecies
and martyrdoms.

Prophecies, however circumstantial, are liable to the same objection as direct miracles: it is more agreeable to experience that the historical evidence of the prediction really having preceded the event pretended to be foretold should be false, or that a lucky
conjuncture of events should have justified the conjecture of the prophet, than that
God should communicate to a man the discernment of future events. I defy you to
produce more than one instance of prophecy in the Bible, wherein the inspired writer
speaks so as to be understood, wherein his prediction has not been so unintelligible and
obscure as to have been itself the subject of controversy among Christians.

That one prediction which I except is certainly most explicit and circumstantial.
It is the only one of this nature which the Bible contains. Jesus himself here predicts
his own arrival in the clouds to consummate a period of supernatural desolation, before the generation which he addressed should pass away. [See Matthew, 24.] Eighteen hundred years have past, and no such event is pretended to have happened. This
single plain prophecy, thus conspicuously false, may serve as a criterion of those
which are more vague and indirect, and which apply in an hundred senses to an hundred things.

Either the pretended predictions in the Bible were meant to be understood,
or they were not. If they were, why is there any dispute concerning them: if they were
not, wherefore were they written at all? But the God of Christianity spoke to
mankind in parables, that seeing they might not see, and hearing they might not
understand.

The Gospels contain internal evidence that they were not written by eye-witnesses
of the event which they pretend to record. The Gospel of St. Matthew was plainly not
written until some time after the taking of Jerusalem, that is, at least forty years after
the execution of Jesus Christ: for he makes Jesus say that *upon you may come all the
righteous blood shed upon the earth, from the blood of righteous Abel unto the blood of
Zacharias son of Barachias whom ye slew between the altar and the temple.* [See Matthew,
2.] Now Zacharias, son of Barachias, was assassinated between the altar and the temple
by a faction of zealots, during the siege of Jerusalem. [Josephus]

You assert that the design of the instances of supernatural interposition which the Gospel records was to convince mankind that Jesus Christ was truly the expected Redeemer. But it is as impossible that any human sophistry should frustrate the manifestation of Omnipotence, as that Omniscience should fail to select the most efficient means of accomplishing its design. Eighteen centuries have passed and the tenth part of the human race have a blind and mechanical belief in that Redeemer, without a complete reliance on the merits of whom, their lot is fixed in everlasting misery: surely if the Christian system be thus dreadfully important its Omnipotent author would have rendered it incapable of those abuses from which it has never been exempt, and to which it is subject in common with all human institutions, he would not have left it a matter of ceaseless cavil or complete indifference to the immense majority of mankind. Surely some more conspicuous evidences of its authenticity would have been afforded than driving out devils, drowning pigs, curing blind men, animating a dead body, and turning water into wine. Some theatre worthier of the transcendent event, than Judea, would have been chosen, some historians more adapted by their accomplishments and their genius to record the incarnation of the immutable God. The humane society restores drowned persons; every empiric can cure every disease; drowning pigs is no very difficult matter, and driving out devils was far from being an original or an unusual occupation in Judea. Do not recite these stale absurdities as proofs of the Divine origin of Christianity.

If the Almighty has spoken, would not the Universe have been convinced? If he had judged the knowledge of his will to have been more important than any other science to mankind, would he not have rendered it more evident and more clear?

Now, O Eusebes, have I enumerated the general grounds of my disbelief of the Christian Religion.—I could have collated its Sacred Writings with the Brahminical record of the early ages of the world, and identified its institutions with the antient worship of the Sun. I might have entered into an elaborate comparison of the innumerable discordances which exist between the inspired historians of the same event. Enough however has been said to vindicate me from the charge of groundless and infatuated scepticism. I trust therefore to your candour for the consideration, and to your logic for the refutation, of my arguments.

EUSEBES   I will not dissemble, O Theosophus, the difficulty of solving your general objections to Christianity, on the grounds of human reason. I did not assist at the councils of the Almighty when he determined to extend his mercy to mankind, nor can I venture to affirm that it exceeded the limits of his power to have afforded a more conspicuous or universal manifestation of his will.

But this is a difficulty which attends Christianity in common with the belief in the being and attributes of God. This whole scheme of things might have been, according to our partial conceptions, infinitely more admirable and perfect. Poisons, earthquakes, disease, war, famine and venomous serpents; slavery and persecution are the consequences of certain causes, which according to human judgment might well have been dispensed with in arranging the economy of the globe.

Is this the reasoning which the Theist will choose to employ? Will he impose limitations on that Deity whom he professes to regard with so profound a veneration? Will he place his God between the horns of a logical dilemma which shall restrict the fulness either of his power or his bounty?

Certainly he will prefer to resign his objections to Christianity, than pursue the reasoning upon which they are found, to the dreadful conclusions of cold and dreary Atheism.

I confess that Christianity appears not unattended with difficulty to the understanding which approaches it with a determination to judge its mysteries by reason. I will even confess that the discourse, which you have just delivered, ought to unsettle any candid mind engaged in a similar attempt. The children of this world are wiser in their generation than the children of light.

But if I succeed in convincing you that reason conducts to conclusions destructive of morality, happiness, and the hope of futurity, and inconsistent with the very existence of human society, I trust that you will no longer confide in a director so dangerous and faithless.

I require you to declare, O Theosophus, whether you would embrace Christianity or Atheism, if no other systems of belief shall be found to stand the touchstone of enquiry.

I do not hesitate to prefer the Christian system, or indeed any system of religion, however rude and gross, to Atheism. Here we truly sympathize; nor do I blame, however I may feel inclined to pity, the man who in his zeal to escape this gloomy faith, should plunge into the most abject superstition.

The Atheist is a monster among men. Inducements, which are omnipotent over the conduct of others, are impotent for him. His private judgment is his criterion of right and wrong. He dreads no judge but his own conscience, he fears no hell but the loss of his self-esteem. He is not to be restrained by punishments, for death is divested of its terror, and whatever enters into his heart to conceive, that will he not scruple to execute. *Iste non timet omnia providentem et cogitantem, et animadvertentem, et omnia ad se pertinere putantem, curiosum et plenum negotii Deum.*

This dark and terrible doctrine was surely the abortion of some blind speculator's brain; some strange and hideous perversion of intellect, some portentous distortion of reason. There can surely be no metaphysician sufficiently bigoted to his own system to look upon this harmonious world, and dispute the necessity of intelligence; to contemplate the design and deny the designer; to enjoy the spectacle of this beautiful Universe and not feel himself instinctively persuaded to gratitude and adoration. What arguments of the slightest plausibility can be adduced to support a doctrine rejected alike by the instinct of the savage and the reason of the sage?

I readily engage, with you, to reject reason as a faithless guide, if you can demonstrate that it conducts to Atheism. So little, however, do I mistrust the dictates of reason, concerning a supreme Being, that I promise, in the event of your success, to subscribe the wildest and most monstrous creed which you can devise. I will call credulity, faith; reason, impiety; the dictates of the understanding shall be the temptations of the Devil, and the wildest dreams of the imagination, the infallible inspirations of Grace.

EUSEBES   Let me request you then to state, concisely, the grounds of your belief in the being of a God. In my reply I shall endeavour to controvert your reasoning, and shall hold myself acquitted by my zeal for the Christian religion, of the blasphemies which I must utter in the progress of my discourse.

THEOSOPHUS   I will readily state the grounds of my belief in the being of a God. You can only have remained ignorant of the obvious proofs of this important truth, from a superstitious reliance upon the evidence afforded by a revealed religion. The reasoning lies within an extremely narrow compass; *quicquid enim nos vel meliores vel beatiores facturum est, aut in aperto, aut in proximo posuit natura.*

From every design we justly infer a designer. If we examine the structure of a watch, we shall readily confess the existence of a watchmaker. No work of man could possibly have existed from all eternity. From the contemplation of any product of human art, we conclude that there was an artificer who arranged its several parts. In like manner, from the marks of design and contrivance exhibited in the Universe, we are necessitated to infer a designer, a contriver. If the parts of the Universe have been designed, contrived, and adapted, the existence of a God is manifest.

But design is sufficiently apparent. The wonderful adaptation of substances which act to those which are acted upon; of the eye to light, and of light to the eye; of the ear to sound, and of sound to the ear; of every object of sensation to the sense which it impresses prove that neither blind chance, nor undistinguishing necessity has brought them into being. The adaptation of certain animals to certain climates, the relation borne to each other by animals and vegetables, and by different tribes of animals; the relation, lastly, between man and the circumstances of his external situation are so many demonstrations of Deity.

All is order, design, and harmony, so far as we can descry the tendency of things, and every new enlargement of our views, every new display of the material world, affords a new illustration of the power, the wisdom and the benevolence of God.

The existence of God has never been the topic of popular dispute. There is a tendency to devotion, a thirst for reliance on supernatural aid inherent in the human mind. Scarcely any people, however barbarous, have been discovered, who do not acknowledge with reverence and awe the supernatural causes of the natural effects which they experience. They worship, it is true, the vilest and most inanimate substances, but they firmly confide in the holiness and power of these symbols, and thus own their connexion with what they can neither see nor perceive.

If there is motion in the Universe, there is a God. The power of beginning motion is no less an attribute of mind than sensation or thought. Wherever motion exists it is evident that mind has operated. The phenomena of the Universe indicate the agency of powers which cannot belong to inert matter.

Every thing which begins to exist must have a cause: every combination, conspiring to an end, implies intelligence.

Against Deism

EUSEBES   Design must be proved before a designer can be inferred. The matter in controversy is the existence of design in the Universe, and it is not permitted to assume the contested premises and thence infer the matter in dispute. Insidiously to employ the words contrivance, design, and adaptation before these circumstances are made apparent in the Universe, thence justly inferring a contriver, is a popular sophism against which it behoves us to be watchful.

To assert that motion is an attribute of mind, that matter is inert, that every combination is the result of intelligence is also an assumption of the matter in dispute.

Why do we admit design in any machine of human contrivance? Simply because innumerable instances of machines having been contrived by human art are present to our mind, because we are acquainted with persons who could construct such machines; but if, having no previous knowledge of any artificial contrivance, we had accidentally found a watch upon the ground, we should have been justified in concluding that it was a thing of Nature, that it was a combination of matter with whose cause we were unacquainted, and that any attempt to account for the origin of its existence would be equally presumptuous and unsatisfactory.

The analogy which you attempt to establish between the contrivances of human art, and the various existences of the Universe, is inadmissible. We attribute these effects to human intelligence, because we know beforehand that human intelligence is capable of producing them. Take away this knowledge, and the grounds of our reasoning will be destroyed. Our entire ignorance, therefore, of the Divine Nature leaves this analogy defective in its most essential point of comparison.

What consideration remains to be urged in support of the creation of the Universe by a supreme Being? Its admirable fitness for the production of certain effects, that wonderful consent of all its parts, that universal harmony by whose changeless laws innumerable systems of worlds perform their stated revolutions, and the blood is driven through the veins of the minutest animalcule that sports in the corruption of an insect's lymph: on this account did the Universe require an intelligent Creator, because it exists producing invariable effects, and inasmuch as it is admirably organised for the production of these effects, so the more did it require a creative intelligence.

Thus have we arrived at the substance of your assertion, "That whatever exists, producing certain effects, stands in need of a Creator, and the more conspicuous is its fitness for the production of these effects, the more certain will be our conclusion that it would not have existed from eternity, but must have derived its origin from an intelligent creator."

In what respect then do these arguments apply to the Universe, and not apply to God? From the fitness of the Universe to its end you infer the necessity of an intelligent Creator. But if the fitness of the Universe, to produce certain effects, be thus conspicuous and evident, how much more exquisite fitness to his end must exist in the Author of this Universe? If we find great difficulty from its admirable arrangement in conceiving that the Universe has existed from all eternity, and to resolve this difficulty suppose a Creator, how much more clearly must we perceive the necessity of this very

Creator's creation whose perfections comprehend an arrangement far more accurate and just.

The belief of an infinity of creative and created Gods, each more eminently requiring an intelligent author of his being than the foregoing, is a direct consequence of the premises which you have stated. The assumption that the Universe is a design, leads to a conclusion that there are an infinity of creative and created Gods, which is absurd. It is impossible indeed to prescribe limits to learned error, when Philosophy relinquishes experience and feeling for speculation.

Until it is clearly proved that the Universe was created, we may reasonably suppose that it has endured from all eternity. In a case where two propositions are diametrically opposite, the mind believes that which is less incomprehensible: it is easier to suppose that the Universe has existed from all eternity, than to conceive an eternal being capable of creating it. If the mind sinks beneath the weight of one, is it an alleviation to increase the intolerability of the burthen?

A man knows, not only that he now is, but that there was a time when he did not exist; consequently there must have been a cause. But we can only infer, from effects, causes exactly adequate to those effects. There certainly is a generative power which is effected by particular instruments; we cannot prove that it is inherent in these instruments, nor is the contrary hypothesis capable of demonstration. We admit that the generative power is incomprehensible, but to suppose that the same effects are produced by an eternal Omnipotent and Omniscient Being, leaves the cause in the same obscurity, but renders it more incomprehensible.

We can only infer from effects causes exactly adequate to those effects. An infinite number of effects demand an infinite number of causes, nor is the philosopher justified in supposing a greater connexion or unity in the latter, than is perceptible in the former. The same energy cannot be at once the cause of the serpent and the sheep; of the blight by which the harvest is destroyed, and the sunshine by which it is matured; of the ferocious propensities by which man becomes a victim to himself, and of the accurate judgment by which his institutions are improved. The spirit of our accurate and exact philosophy is outraged by conclusions which contradict each other so glaringly.

The greatest, equally with the smallest motions of the Universe, are subjected to the rigid necessity of inevitable laws. These laws are the unknown causes of the known effects perceivable in the Universe. Their effects are the boundaries of our knowledge, their names the expressions of our ignorance. To suppose some existence beyond, or above them, is to invent a second and superfluous hypothesis to account for what has already been accounted for by the laws of motion and the properties of matter. I admit that the nature of these laws is incomprehensible, but the hypothesis of a Deity adds a gratuitous difficulty, which so far from alleviating those which it is adduced to explain, requires new hypotheses for the elucidation of its own inherent contradictions.

The laws of attraction and repulsion, desire and aversion, suffice to account for every phenomenon of the moral and physical world. A precise knowledge of the properties of any object, is alone requisite to determine its manner of action. Let the mathematician be acquainted with the weight and volume of a cannon ball, together with the degree of velocity and inclination with which it is impelled, and he will accurately delineate the course it must describe, and determine the force with which it will strike an object at a given distance. Let the influencing motive, present to the mind of any person be given, and the knowledge of his consequent conduct will result. Let the bulk and velocity of a comet be discovered, and the astronomer, by the accurate estimation of the equal and contrary actions of the centripetal and centrifugal forces, will justly predict the period of its return.

The anomalous motions of the heavenly bodies, their unequal velocities and frequent aberrations, are corrected by that gravitation by which they are caused. The illustrious Laplace has shewn that the approach of the Moon to the Earth, and the Earth to the Sun, is only a secular equation of a very long period, which has its maximum and minimum. The system of the Universe then is upheld solely by physical powers. The necessity of matter is the ruler of the world. It is vain philosophy which supposes more causes than are exactly adequate to explain the phenomena of things. *Hypotheses non fingo: quicquid enim ex phænomenis non deducitur, hypothesis vocanda est; et hypotheses vel metaphysicæ, vel physicae, vel qualitatum occultarum, seu mechanicae, in philosophiâ locum non habent.*

You assert that the construction of the animal machine, the fitness of certain animals to certain situations, the connexion between the organs of perception and that which is perceived; the relation between everything which exists, and that which tends to preserve it in its existence, imply design. It is manifest that if the eye could not see, nor the stomach digest, the human frame could not preserve its present mode of existence. It is equally certain, however, that the elements of its composition, if they did not exist in one form, must exist in another; and that the combinations which they would form, must so long as they endured, derive support for their peculiar mode of being from their fitness to the circumstances of their situation.

It by no means follows, that because a being exists, performing certain functions, he was fitted by another being to the performance of these functions. So rash a conclusion would conduct, as I have before shewn, to an absurdity; and it becomes infinitely more unwarrantable from the consideration that the known laws of matter and motion, suffice to unravel, even in the present imperfect state of moral and physical science, the majority of those difficulties which the hypothesis of a Deity was invented to explain.

Doubtless no disposition of inert matter, or matter deprived of qualities, could ever have composed an animal, a tree, or even a stone. But matter deprived of qualities, is an abstraction, concerning which it is impossible to form an idea. Matter, such as we behold it, is not inert. It is infinitely active and subtle. Light, electricity, and magnetism are fluids not surpassed by thought itself in tenuity and activity: like thought they are sometimes the cause and sometimes the effect of motion; and, distinct as they are from every other class of substances with which we are acquainted, seem to possess equal claims with thought to the unmeaning distinction of immateriality.

The laws of motion and the properties of matter suffice to account for every phenomenon, or combination of phenomena exhibited in the Universe. That certain animals exist in certain climates, results from the consentaneity of their frames to the circumstances of their situation: let these circumstances be altered to a sufficient degree, and the elements of their composition must exist in some new combination no less resulting than the former from those inevitable laws by which the Universe is governed.

It is the necessary consequence of the organization of man, that his stomach should digest his food: it inevitably results also from his gluttonous and unnatural appetite for the flesh of animals that his frame be diseased and his vigor impaired; but in neither of these cases is adaptation of means to end to be perceived. Unnatural diet, and the habits consequent upon its use are the means, and every complication of frightful disease is the end, but to assert that these means were adapted to this end by the Creator of the world, or that human caprice can avail to traverse the precautions of Omnipotence, is absurd. These are the consequences of the properties of organized matter; and it is a strange perversion of the understanding to argue that a certain sheep was created to be butchered and devoured by a certain individual of the human species, when the conformation of the latter, as is manifest to the most superficial student of comparative anatomy, classes him with those animals who feed on fruits and vegetables.

The means by which the existence of an animal is sustained requires a designer in no greater degree than the existence itself of the animal. If it exists, there must be means to support its existence. In a world where *omne mutatur nihil interit,* no organized being can exist without a continual separation of that substance which is incessantly exhausted, nor can this separation take place otherwise than by the invariable laws which result from the relations of matter. We are incapacitated only by our ignorance from referring every phenomenon, however unusual, minute or complex, to the laws of motion and the properties of matter; and it is an egregious offence against the first principles of reason to suppose an immaterial creator of the world, *in quo omnia moventur sed sine mutuâ passione:* which is equally a superfluous hypothesis in the mechanical philosophy of Newton, and a useless excrescence on the inductive logic of Bacon.

What then is this harmony, this order which you maintain to have required for its establishment, what it needs not for its maintenance, the agency of a supernatural intelligence? Inasmuch as the order visible in the Universe requires one cause, so does the disorder whose operation is not less clearly apparent, demand another. Order and disorder are no more than modifications of our own perceptions of the relations which subsist between ourselves and external objects, and if we are justified in inferring the operation of a benevolent power from the advantages attendant on the former, the evils of the latter bear equal testimony to the activity of a malignant principle, no less pertinacious in inducing evil out of good, than the other is unremitting in procuring good from evil.

If we permit our imagination to traverse the obscure regions of possibility, we may doubtless imagine, according to the complexion of our minds, that disorder may have a relative tendency to unmingled good, or order be relatively replete with exquisite and subtile evil. To neither of these conclusions, which are equally presumptuous and unfounded, will it become the philosopher to assent. Order and disorder are expressions denoting our perceptions of what is injurious or beneficial to ourselves, or to the beings in whose welfare we are compelled to sympathize by the similarity of their conformation to our own.

A beautiful antelope panting under the fangs of a tiger, a defenceless ox, groaning beneath the butcher's axe, is a spectacle which instantly awakens compassion in a virtuous and unvitiated breast. Many there are, however, sufficiently hardened to the rebukes of justice and the precepts of humanity, as to regard the deliberate butchery of thousands of their species, as a theme of exultation and a source of honour, and to consider any failure in these remorseless enterprises as a defect in the system of things. The criteria of order and disorder are as various as those beings from whose opinions and feelings they result.

Populous cities are destroyed by earthquakes, and desolated by pestilence. Ambition is everywhere devoting its millions to incalculable calamity. Superstition, in a thousand shapes, is employed in brutalizing and degrading the human species, and fitting it to endure without a murmur the oppression of its innumerable tyrants. All this is abstractedly neither good nor evil, because good and evil are words employed to designate that peculiar state of our own perceptions, resulting from the encounter of any object calculated to produce pleasure or pain. Exclude the idea of relation, and the words good and evil are deprived of import.

Earthquakes are injurious to the cities which they destroy, beneficial to those whose commerce was injured by their prosperity, and indifferent to others which are too remote to be affected by their influence. Famine is good to the corn-merchant, evil to the poor, and indifferent to those whose fortunes can at all times command a superfluity. Ambition is evil to the restless bosom it inhabits, to the innumerable victims who are dragged by its ruthless thirst for infamy to expire in every variety of anguish, to the inhabitants of the country it depopulates, and to the human race whose improvement it retards; it is indifferent with regard to the system of the Universe, and is good only to the vultures and the jackalls that track the conqueror's career, and to the worms who feast in security on the desolation of his progress. It is manifest that we cannot reason with respect to the universal system from that which only exists in relation to our own perceptions.

You allege some considerations in favor of a Deity from the universality of a belief in his existence.

The superstitions of the savage, and the religion of civilized Europe appear to you to conspire to prove a first cause. I maintain that it is from the evidence of revelation alone that this belief derives the slightest countenance.

That credulity should be gross in proportion to the ignorance of the mind which it enslaves, is in strict consistency with the principles of human nature. The idiot, the child, and the savage, agree in attributing their own passions and propensities to the inanimate substances by which they are either benefited or injured. The former become Gods and the latter Demons; hence prayers and sacrifices, by the means of which the rude Theologian imagines that he may confirm the benevolence of the one, or mitigate the malignity of the other. He has averted the wrath of a powerful enemy by supplications and submission; he has secured the assistance of his neighbour by offerings; he has felt his own anger subside before the entreaties of a vanquished foe, and has cherished gratitude for the kindness of another. Therefore does he believe that the elements will listen to his vows. He is capable of love and hatred towards his fellow beings, and is variously impelled by those principles to benefit or injure them. The source of his error is sufficiently obvious. When the winds, the waves and the atmosphere, act in such a manner as to thwart or forward his designs, he attributes to them the same propensities of whose existence within himself he is conscious when he is instigated by benefits to kindness, or by injuries to revenge. The bigot of the woods can form no conception of beings possessed of properties differing from his own: it requires, indeed, a mind considerably tinctured with science, and enlarged by cultivation to contemplate itself, not as the centre and model of the Universe, but as one of the infinitely various multitude of beings of which it is actually composed.

There is no attribute of God which is not either borrowed from the passions and powers of the human mind, or which is not a negation. Omniscience, Omnipotence, Omnipresence, Infinity, Immutability, Incomprehensibility, and Immateriality, are all words which designate properties and powers peculiar to organised beings, with the addition of negations, by which the idea of limitation is excluded.

That the frequency of a belief in God (for it is not universal) should be any argument in its favour, none to whom the innumerable mistakes of men are familiar, will assert. It is among men of genius and science that Atheism alone is found, but among these alone is cherished an hostility to those errors, with which the illiterate and vulgar are infected.

How small is the proportion of those who really believe in God, to the thousands who are prevented by their occupations from ever bestowing a serious thought upon the subject, and the millions who worship butterflies, bones, feathers, monkeys, calabashes and serpents. The word God, like other abstractions, signifies the agreement of certain propositions, rather than the presence of any idea. If we found our belief in the existence of God on the universal consent of mankind, we are duped by the most palpable of sophisms. The word God cannot mean at the same time an ape, a snake, a bone, a calabash, a Trinity, and a Unity. Nor can that belief be accounted universal against which men of powerful intellect and spotless virtue have in every age protested. *Non pudet igitur physicum, id est speculatorem venatoremque naturae, ex animis consuctudine imbutis petere testimonium veritatis?*

Hume has shewn, to the satisfaction of all philosophers, that the only idea which we can form of causation is derivable from the constant conjunction of objects, and the consequent inference of one from the other. We denominate that phenomenon the cause of another which we observe with the fewest exceptions to precede its occurrence. Hence it would be inadmissible to deduce the being of a God from the existence of the Universe; even if this mode of reasoning did not conduct to the monstrous conclusion of an infinity of creative and created Gods, each more eminently requiring a Creator than its predecessor.

If Power be an attribute of existing substance, substance could not have derived its origin from power. One thing cannot be at the same time the cause and the effect of another.—The word power expresses the capability of any thing to be or act. The human mind never hesitates to annex the idea of power to any object of its experience. To deny that power is the attribute of being, is to deny that being can be. If power be an attribute of substance, the hypothesis of a God is a superfluous and unwarrantable assumption.

Intelligence is that attribute of the Deity, which you hold to be most apparent in the Universe. Intelligence is only known to us as a mode of animal being. We cannot conceive intelligence distinct from sensation and perception, which are attributes to organized bodies. To assert that God is intelligent, is to assert that he has ideas; and Locke has proved that ideas result from sensation. Sensation can exist only in an organized body, an organised body is necessarily limited both in extent and operation. The God of the rational Theosophist is a vast and wise animal.

You have laid it down as a maxim that the power of beginning motion is an attribute of mind as much as thought and sensation.

Mind cannot create, it can only perceive. Mind is the recipient of impressions made on the organs of sense, and without the action of external objects we should not only be deprived of all knowledge of the existence of mind, but totally incapable of the knowledge of any thing. It is evident, therefore, that mind deserves to be considered as the effect, rather than the cause of motion. The ideas which suggest themselves too are prompted by the circumstances of our situation, these are the elements of thought, and from the various combinations of these our feelings, opinions, and volitions inevitably result.

That which is infinite necessarily includes that which is finite. The distinction therefore between the Universe, and that by which the Universe is upheld, is manifestly erroneous. To devise the word God, that you may express a certain portion of the universal system, can answer no good purpose in philosophy: In the language of reason, the words God and Universe are synonymous. *Omnia enim per Dei potentiam facta sunt, imo, quia naturae potentia nulla est nisi ipsa Dei potentia, artem est nos catemus Dei potentiam non intelligere quatenus causas naturales ignoramus; adeoque stultè ad eandam Dei potentiam recurritur quando rei alieujus, causam naturalem, sive est, ipsam Dei potentiam ignoramus.**

Thus from the principles of that reason to which you so rashly appealed as the ultimate arbiter of our dispute, have I shewn that the popular arguments in favour of the being of a God are totally destitute of colour. I have shewn the absurdity of attributing intelligence to the cause of those effects which we perceive in the Universe, and the fallacy which lurks in the argument from design. I have shewn that order is no more than a peculiar manner of contemplating the operation of necessary agents, that mind is the effect, not the cause of motion, that power is the attribute, not the origin of Being. I have proved that we can have no evidence of the existence of a God from the principles of reason.

You will have observed, from the zeal with which I have urged arguments so revolting to my genuine sentiments, and conducted to a conclusion in direct contradiction to that faith which every good man must eternally preserve, how little I am inclined to sympathise with those of my religion who have pretended to prove the existence of God by the unassisted light of reason. I confess that the necessity of a revelation has been compromised by treacherous friends to Christianity, who have maintained that the sublime mysteries of the being of a God and the immortality of the soul are discoverable from other sources than itself.

---

*Spinosa. *Tractus Theologico-Politicus*, chap. i.

I have proved that on the principles of that philosophy to which Epicurus, Lord Bacon, Newton, Locke and Hume were addicted, the existence of God is a chimera.

The Christian Religion then, alone, affords indisputable assurance that the world was created by the power, and is preserved by the Providence of an Almighty God, who, in justice has appointed a future life for the punishment of the vicious and the remuneration of the virtuous.

Now, O Theosophus, I call upon you to decide between Atheism and Christianity; to declare whether you will pursue your principles to the destruction of the bonds of civilized society, or wear the easy yoke of that religion which proclaims "peace upon earth, good-will to all men."

THEOSOPHUS   I am not prepared at present, I confess, to reply clearly to your unexpected arguments. I assure you that no considerations, however specious, should seduce me to deny the existence of my Creator.

I am willing to promise that if, after mature deliberation, the arguments which you have advanced in favour of Atheism should appear incontrovertible, I will endeavour to adopt so much of the Christian scheme as is consistent with my persuasion of the goodness, unity, and majesty of God.

---

10. Existence, Predication, and the Ontological Argument

JEROME SHAFFER

HUME said, "There is no being, . . . whose non-existence implies a contradiction,"[1] and Kant said, "The predicate of existence can . . . be rejected without contradiction."[2] In making these claims, Hume and Kant intended to bring out a peculiarity in assertions of existence, for they both would admit that assertions that something was (or was not), for example, round might turn out to be self-contradictory, whereas assertions that something exists (or does not exist) could never turn out to be self-contradictory.

Source: Jerome Shaffer, "Existence, Predication, and the Ontological Argument," *Mind* 71 (283): pp. 307–25 (July 1962). Reprinted by permission of Oxford University Press.

Now if this is a genuine peculiarity of assertions of existence, then it follows that any proof that something exists because its nonexistence implies a contradiction will be invalid.

A famous example of an argument which purports to prove the existence of something by showing that its nonexistence implies a contradiction is the Ontological Argument, which purports to show that it follows from a particular concept of God that such a being exists, and therefore that the assertion of the nonexistence of God is self-contradictory. Most philosophers have agreed with Hume and Kant that the Ontological Argument is invalid, although it has recently been defended.[3] My own view is that the argument is basically unsound, but I find the standard criticisms totally unconvincing. In this paper I shall show what I take to be the faults in the standard criticisms and then go on to show what I take to be the proper criticism of the argument.

The many versions of the Ontological Argument have in common the following feature: a definition of "God" is given from which, by the use of certain premises, the conclusion, "God exists," is deduced. The Ontological Argument has frequently been attacked by casting doubt upon the acceptability of these premises. I wish to avoid such controversies. I am interested in the move from a definition to an existential statement. Therefore I shall use an argument which brings attention to bear just on that move. This will be the specimen under discussion:

> Let the expression, "God," mean "an almighty being who exists and is eternal." Therefore "God is an almighty being who exists and is eternal" is true by definition, and that entails "God exists."

This argument purports to demonstrate that "God exists" is a tautology, true by definition. It is not necessary to show that the expression, "God," really does mean what it is here defined to mean, for the definition is purely stipulative. But given that meaning, it is argued, anyone who denies that God, in the sense laid down, exists has contradicted himself. Only the laws of logic are required to show that he has contradicted himself.

The following short objections to this argument will not do. (1) The question is begged from the start by using a proper name, "God." No, for "God" is not used here as a logically proper name. I have simply introduced an expression into discourse, an expression which is, grammatically, a proper noun. (2) Even if we grant the conclusion, "God exists," that does not imply that there is a God or that something is a God. Why not? In ordinary discourse the expressions are used interchangeably in most contexts. It must be shown, if it is true, that the implication does not hold here. (3) Tautologies only tell us about our use of language, about the meanings of our terms, not about what actually is the case. This objection begs the question. Proponents of the argument claim that here is a tautology which tells us about what actually is the case, namely that God exists. (4) But then with suitable definitions we could "prove" the existence of a number of things which we know perfectly well do not exist. No, for the things we know not to exist would necessarily be different from the things picked out by our definitions. (5) The argument involves a non-sequitur, for the premise is about a *word* but the conclusion is about something different, a thing. No, the definition of the word allows us to prove, by substitution, that the conclusion is a tautology.

The traditional attack on the Ontological Argument consists in trying to show that the definition is inadmissible because it is ill-formed. Kant argued that definitions can consist only of strings of predicates and since "exists" is not a predicate it cannot be a part of the definition. Others have argued that "exists" is a purely formal element, present in any definition of a thing, and therefore could not be used to show that some particular thing exists as opposed to anything else. I shall, in Part I, discuss these arguments in detail and show that none of them succeeds in establishing any impropriety in the definition of "God" I have proposed. In Part II, I shall show that the argument, although formally correct, does not do what the religious expect it to do. The agnostic will still be able to raise his doubt and the atheist will still be able to affirm his disbelief, no contradiction arising in either case, even if each accepts the specimen argument under consideration.

I

" 'Exists' Is Not a Predicate"

The Ontological Argument purports to show that God must exist because the condition that He exists is a part of the definition of the kind of thing He is. Kant argued that it could not be the case that existence was a defining feature of God or of anything else, because "exists" is not, as he put it (p. 504), a "real" or "determining" predicate (he admitted that, grammatically, "exists" is a predicate).

What is a "real" predicate? Kant defines it as something "which is added to the concept of the subject and enlarges it" (*ibid.*). This is a most unfortunate definition for Kant to use, however, since it leads to contradiction with another important doctrine of his, that *existential propositions are always synthetic* (*ibid.*). Synthetic judgments are those which "add to the concept of the subject a predicate which has not been in any wise thought in it" (p. 48), and if existential judgments are always synthetic then "exists" must be a predicate which adds to the concept of the subject, in short, a "real" predicate as defined above. But even without the difficulties this definition of "real" predicate raises within the Kantian system, it is not a very helpful definition, for it represents predicating something of a subject as *revising the concept* of the subject (by enlarging that concept), something only philosophers of a Reconstructionist bent do very often. But I shall say more of Kant's misrepresentation of predication below.

What argument does Kant give for holding that "exists" is not a "real" predicate, that is, not a predicate which adds something to the concept of the subject? He argues that if "exists" were a real predicate, then in asserting that something exists we would be altering our concept of that something, thereby ending up with a different concept from the one we started with. Since we now have a new and different concept, we will have failed to assert existence of the original subject. Thus if "exists" were a predicate, "we could not, therefore, say that the exact object of my concept exists" (p. 505). But since we obviously can say that, we cannot be adding anything to the concept of the subject when we say that the subject exists, and therefore "exists" cannot be a real predicate.

It is astonishing that this argument has stood up for so long and is still commended by philosophers, *e.g.* by Malcolm (*op. cit.* p. 44). For the argument, if sound, shows that nothing could be a real predicate. Suppose I wish to say that something is red, where "red" is intended as a real predicate. In asserting that the thing is red, I would be adding to my concept of the thing, and hence would be unable to say that the object as originally conceived is red, that "the exact object of my concept" is red. The argument which shows that "exists" is not a "real" predicate also show that nothing could be one.

The difficulty here lies in an incomplete picture of predication. Kant seems to think that when I say that so-and-so is such-and-such, I must be doing one of two things: either I am extracting the concept of such-and-such from the concept of so-and-so (an analytic judgment) or else I am revising my concept of so-and-so by adding to it the concept of such-and-such (a synthetic judgment). Now which of these two things am I doing when I say that so-and-so exits? Noticing that existential propositions are often justified by an appeal to experience (p. 506), Kant decides that they cannot be cases of extracting the concept of existence from the concept of the subject. So they must be cases of revising concepts; thus, "all existential propositions are synthetic." But this really will not do either, since to revise one's concept of the subject is simply to change the subject of the proposition. Hence in other places Kant concludes that "exists" is not a predicate at all. Kant's vacillation here comes from an overly narrow account of predication. To say that so-and-so is such-and-such is sometimes neither to analyse the concept of so-and-so nor to revise it, but, to put it roughly, to say something about the object conceived of. This use of language is obviously not peculiar to existential propositions. The sentence, "Crows are black," may be used to express a proposition not about the the concept of crows but about crows, and when so used would create as much difficulty for Kant, given his account of predication, as "Crows exist." There may well be important differences between ". . . are black" and ". . . exist," but Kant fails to bring them out by this line of argument.

Philosophers have tried to express what they took to be the truth in Kant's claim that "exists" is not a real predicate without appeal to that obscure notion of a real predicate. For example Malcolm restates Kant's argument in this way:

> Suppose that two royal councillors, A and B, were asked to draw up separately descriptions of the most perfect chancellor they could conceive, and that the descriptions they produced were identical except that A included existence in his list of attributes of a perfect chancellor and B did not. (I do not mean that B put nonexistence in his list.) One and the same person could satisfy both descriptions. More to the point, any person who satisfied A's description would *necessarily* satisfy B's description and *vice versa*. (p. 43–44)

While Malcom admits that this is not a "rigorous" argument, and "leave(s) the matter at the more or less intuitive level," he thinks it does show that "exists" is very different in character from the expressions which go to make up a description or list of attributes of something. But I cannot see how it goes to show that at all. For it seems to me false that any person who satisfies B's description necessarily satisfies A's. Could not a nonexistent person, say Merlin, satisfy B's description but not A's? It cannot be said that Merlin fails to satisfy B's description (B might have had Merlin in mind when he drew up the list), unless the notion of *satisfying a description* is such that only real things, existent beings, can be said to satisfy a description. But if one uses this rather technical notion, the argument loses its intuitive appeal.

Subject-Predicate Statements as Really Hypotheticals

Some philosophers have attempted to bring out the special feature of "exists" which debars it from appearing in a definition in the following way. If we take "Crows are black" as a typical affirmative subject-predicate statement and "Crows are not black" as a typical negative one, then they would claim that the affirmative statement is equivalent to the hypothetical, "If there exists anything which is a crow, then that thing is black," and the negative statement is equivalent to the hypothetical, "If there exists anything which is a crow, then that thing is not black." Now if we hold that existential statements are of the same form, then "Crows exist" would be equivalent to "If there exists anything which is a crow, then that thing exists," and "Crows do not exist" would be equivalent to "If there exists anything which is a crow, then that thing does not exist." But the former hypothetical is a tautology whereas "Crows exist" obviously is not a tautology, and the latter hypothetical is not readily intelligible whereas "Crows do not exist" is perfectly clear. Therefore it is most implausible to claim that existential statements are of the same form as the typical subject-predicate statements, that is, implausible to construe "exists" as a predicate.

I do not find this argument very compelling. It is a mistake to think that the hypothetical expresses the meaning of the typical subject-predicate statement. Notice that the hypothetical must be put in the form, "If *there exists* anything which is. . . ." If we allow the antecedent clause to range over nonexistent as well as existent things, then the hypothetical, "If anything is . . ., then it exists," is not tautological and the hypothetical, "If anything is . . ., then it does not exist," is perfectly clear. And therefore the main reason for saying they cannot be equivalent to categorical existential statements has disappeared. But if we take the antecedent in the strong existential sense, then the claim that such hypotheticals express the meaning of subject-predicate statements breaks down. Consider the following subject-predicate statement: "Unicorns are proper subject-matter for mythologists." It is not equivalent to "If there exists anything which is a unicorn, then that thing is proper subject-matter for mythologists," for the former is true but the latter is false. On the other hand, "Unicorns are proper subject-matter for zoologists" is false, but "If there exists anything which is a unicorn, then it is proper subject-matter for zoologists" is true. And these are not just odd cases. There are many other things which it would be true to say of unicorns, if they existed, *e.g.* that they would obey the laws of physics, be sought after by zoos, be mentioned in books which describe the species of animals, etc., but which are not true of them since they do not exist; and there would be many things which it would be false to say of them if they existed but which are not false since they do not exist. So the purported equivalence of subject-predicate statements to hypotheticals does not hold. The reason is evident enough. If a thing exists, then given the way the world is it will have certain features and lack others, so to say something about a thing is not the same as to say what the thing would be like if it existed. Of course a thing keeps its defining characteristics whether it exists or not, so analytic subject-predicate statements will entail analytic hypotheticals, but in general the equivalence does not hold. Nor does it hold if we understand the hypothetical as that of material implication, for "Unicorns do not have horns" is false but the parallel hypothetical, "If there exists anything which is a unicorn, then it does not have a horn," is true if taken materially, which shows that they cannot be equivalent.

Since it is a popular view that subject-predicate statements are equivalent to hypotheticals, it is important to see how someone might come to such a view. One way would be through the Kantian restriction of subject-predicate statements to statements about the *concept* of the subject. If this were correct, then the kind of counter-example I used, where the thing referred to by the concept turns out, given the nature of the world, to have some feature could not arise. All subject-predicate statements would be tautologous, either by analysis of the concept of the subject or by revision of the concept of the subject, and in this limited case the equivalence would hold.

But there is a line of argument more plausible to the modern mind which would yield the same result. Suppose one thought that for a series of words to express a meaningful subject-predicate statement, the grammatical subject must refer to some existent or set of existents. Then there would be no difference between attributing a property to a thing and attributing a property to the thing if it exists. Again my counter-examples could not arise. And philosophers have held such a view. Ryle once said:

> How can we make propositions about Mr. Pickwick or seaserpents, given that they do not exist? We cannot. For a proposition is only about something when something in fact answers to the designation in it. And nothing answers to the pseudo-designation "Mr. Pickwick" or "those sea-serpents."[4]

And Broad holds, "*Dragons do not exist* . . . cannot be about dragons; for there will be no such things as dragons for it to be about."[5] Since such propositions are not meaningless, they must be about something, however, and philosophers of this persuasion have offered various candidates for the subject of statements about nonexistents, urging that they are really about beliefs, books, paintings, propositional functions, properties, inscriptions, or story-tellers.

I do not see why statements cannot be made about non-existents. We can dream about them, think about them, and describe them, just as we can wait for them, hope to have them, and look for them. We can mention them, allude to or direct attention to them, and make reference to them. One thing we cannot do, of course, is to *point* to them, and someone who thinks of mentioning, alluding or referring as a substitute for pointing will be puzzled as to how we can point to what does not exist. But if we have not fallen prey to this overly narrow conception of what it is to mention something, then we will not be puzzled about how we can mention something nonexistent.

The most modest proposal along this line is that of Strawson, who abandoned his earlier position that the use of a referring expression in cases where the object referred to is nonexistent is "a spurious use"[6] in which we either "pretend to refer, in make-believe or in fiction, or mistakenly think we are referring when we are not referring to anything" (p. 40). His modified view is that the "primary" use of referring expressions occurs when the speaker believes the expression to refer to some existent, but that such expressions may be used to "refer in secondary ways, as in make-believe or in fiction."[7] But I take it that Strawson would still wish to say that unless we refer to an existent we do not succeed in expressing a subject-predicate "statement," that is, an assertion which admits of truth or falsity. And if he is right about this, then it becomes more plausible to claim that subject-predicate statements are equivalent to hypotheticals; (I do not wish to suggest that Strawson would claim they are equivalent).

But here again it seems perfectly obvious to me that statements which are true or false can be made about nonexistent things. After all, unicorns do have horns, giants are two-legged, and Mr. Pickwick is a most benevolent gentleman. Nor am I engaging in make-believe or story-telling when I assert these things. My grounds for such assertions are quite different from my grounds for claiming that my neighbour is a most benevolent gentleman, but that does not detract from the truth of such assertions.

To summarize, the claim that subject-predicate statements are equivalent to hypotheticals fails, although perhaps a case could be made for their equivalence with hypotheticals in those cases in which the grammatical subject refers to some existent or set of existents. If so, we might introduce a technical sense of "subject-predicate statement" for those statements which are translatable in the way that "Crows are black" is translatable into "If anything exists which is a crow, then that thing is black." For reasons which differ in each case, none of the following would be subject-predicate statements: "Crows are plentiful," "Crows scatter during storms," "Crows vary greatly," "Crows change over the centuries," and "Crows live in our barns." "Crows exist" would not be a subject-predicate statement either, since the requirement that the subject must refer to some existent would yield the result that if it were a subject-predicate statement it would have to be true.[8] No wonder it would only come to the trivial "If anything exists which is a crow, then it exists," if construed as a subject-predicate statement in the technical sense we have given that term. But none of the peculiarities of "exists" which are brought out by saying that it cannot be an element in a subject-predicate statement, in the sense specified, go to indicate any impropriety in framing a definition in which "exists" appears, such as the definition of "God" given above.

"Exists" as a Universal Predicate

When faced with the claim that if "exists" is taken as a predicate positive existential assertions become tautological and negative extential assertions not readily intelligible, most philosophers have decided that "exists" cannot be taken as a predicate. But some have boldly accepted the consequence that "exists" is a trivial predicate, predicable of everything conceivable. Hence the Ontological Argument becomes harmless, for "exists" is a necessary predicate not only of God but of everything conceivable. As recent supporters of this view have put it:

> Every conception involves the predicate "exists". Thus not only God's essence but every essence implies existence.[9]

And Hume suggested a doctrine very much like this when he said:

> To reflect on any thing simply, and to reflect on it as existent, are nothing different from each other. That idea, when conjoined with the idea of any object, makes no addition to it. Whatever we conceive, we conceive to be existent.[10]

Thus attributions of existence to anything I conceive become tautological, and denials of existence not readily intelligible.

Now whatever the intrinsic merits of this view, it is a most embarrassing one for Hume to hold. For he also wishes to maintain that "whatever we conceive as existent, we can also conceive as non-existent,"[11] and thus that "the non-existence of any being is as clear and distinct an idea as its existence,"[12] Since Hume uses "conceive to be existent" and "conceive as existent" interchangeably,[13] these two doctrines are flatly contradictory, for the first implies that whatever we conceive we *cannot* conceive as non-existent and the second states that whatever we conceive we *can* conceive as non-existent. Nor can we save Hume by interpreting the second to mean that whatever we can conceive we can believe to be non-existent, for if I cannot conceive of a thing except as existent, then surely I cannot believe in its non-existence.

Perhaps Hume was writing carelessly when he said that "what-ever we conceive, we conceive to be existent," and expressed his real thoughts more precisely when he said, "whatever the mind clearly conceives includes the idea of possible existence."[14] But if he did seriously hold the first view, there are many ways in which he might have come to it. The reason he does give,

> Since we never remember any idea or impression without attributing existence to it, the idea of existence . . . must be the very same with the idea of the perception or object.[15]

confuses the existence of the conception with the existence of what is conceived, the *realitas formalis* of the idea with its *realitas objectiva*. But he might have argued, in line with his notion of ideas as pictures, that we cannot form the picture of a thing as non-existent, and therefore cannot conceive such a thing. Also his attack on the abstract idea of existence as distinguishable and separable from the ideas of particular objects[16] and his connected claim that in making judgments that something exists we only entertain the idea of the thing in an especially lively and forceful way[17] lead him to say that the idea of existence cannot be something over and beyond the things we conceive, and therefore would incline him to say that whatever we conceive, we conceive to be existent.

Such a doctrine leaves most unclear what negative existential judgments could be, and yet it is obviously most important to be able to give such judgments sense. At one point, when Hume concerns himself with negative existential judgments, he abandons this doctrine, interpreting them as judgments in which the idea of the object is conjoined with the idea of non-existence,[18] although in another place he flatly rejects such an interpretation without giving what he takes to be the correct account.[19] So far as I can see, the contradiction here was one which Hume was never able to eliminate.[20] Nor, so far as I can see, is it possible to reconcile the two. If the definition of a substantive must include the notion that the thing exists (which is what I take Hume's doctrine to mean), then that the thing exists follows from the definition and is necessarily the case. To deny that the thing exists is to contradict oneself just as certainly as to deny that the thing possesses any other defining characteristic is to contradict oneself. And if all our conceptions of things include existence as necessary properties of the things, then no denials of existence will make sense.

Hume was mistaken in thinking that whatever we conceive of we must conceive to be existent. For suppose it is a necessary feature of a chimera that it be not only a she-monster of a particular sort but an imaginary she-monster. Then it would be a necessary statement that chimeras do not exist; anyone who held that chimeras exist would contradict himself. Could one conceive of a chimera? I do not see why not. But one would be conceiving of it as nonexistent.

I do not wish to suggest that philosophers were mistaken in thinking that "exists" is in many ways different from grammatically similar expressions, for it obviously is. To take Hume's point, for example, if I wish to picture an animal, it will make a difference whether I picture it as yellow or not; but one cannot make the same kind of sense out of speaking of picturing it as existent or non-existent. It does not follow from this that what-ever I picture I picture as existing, but Hume is certainly right in thinking that I cannot represent the existence or non-existence of the thing by adding to my picture in an exactly parallel way to the way in which I represent the yellowness or non-yellowness of the thing by adding to the picture. It requires some special convention to indicate that what is pictured is pictured as, say, imaginary. (Comic strip creators have special conventions for showing this, for example by encircling it and linking it by a stream of small circles to someone's head to show that he is just imagining it.) To make this point is to bring out a difference between "exists" and predicates like "is yellow." Further differences between "exists" and other predicates are brought out in the arguments for the slogan, " 'Exists' is not a predicate." What must be shown, however, is that these differences bear relevantly on the issue whether existential statements can be true by definition. I have been concerned to argue, in this section, that no differences have been noted which rule out existential statements which are true by definition.

II

Until further arguments are offered, it seems reasonable to hold that there is nothing logically improper in so defining the expression, "God," that "God exists" is a tautology and "God does not exist" self-contradictory. In fact it seems to me that the definition I have given expresses a concept of God (*i.e.,* as necessarily existing) which many people actually accept (just as it is a common conception of Satan that he merely happens to exist). I wish to show in this section that this concept of God can give no support to the religious. I shall argue that no matter what its content, this concept of God is still simply a concept. What must be shown, and what cannot be shown just by an analysis of the concept, is that there actually exists something which answers to the concept. Even if we have here the concept of an object which necessarily exists, a further question remains whether any existent meets the specifications of the concept. The difficulty lies in showing that this further question makes sense, for I have admitted that "God exists" is a necessary statement, analytically true, and therefore it looks as if there could be no further question. But that is an illusion. It must however be dispelled.

As a first step, I wish to point out that the concept of God is hardly unique in its capacity to generate a tautological existential statement. For one thing, we could invent new tautologies. Suppose we introduce the word, "particular," to mean "object which exists," and the word, "nonentity," to mean "object which does not exist." Then to bring out the difference between these two words we might properly say, tautologically, "Particulars exist and nonentities do not exist." Nor, for another thing, do we have to invent such words, for we already have many words with existential notions included in their meanings. The following sentences all have tautological uses: "Existents exists," "Fictitious objects do not exist," "Members of extinct species existed once but no longer exist," "Hallucinatory objects do not exist," "Historical persons have at some time existed." I do not suggest that these sentences can never be used in non-tautological ways, but I do suggest that they may be used tautologically in those circumstances in which we wish to emphasize that such concepts include as a necessary feature, as a defining element, notions of existence or non-existence.

As a preliminary to seeing what these tautological existential claims come to, let us examine the relation between expressions of the form, "A's exist," and of the form, "There are A's." Take the tautology, "Fictitious objects do not exist". One might think that "Fictitious objects do not exist" means the same as "There are no fictitious objects." But a moment's thought will show that this is incorrect, for although the former is true the latter is false. There are fictitious objects, many of them—Alice's looking glass, Jack's bean stalk, Wittgenstein's beetle, to mention only a few. So "Fictitious objects do not exist" does not mean the same as "There are no fictitious objects." Similarly "Particulars exist" does not mean the same as "There are particulars." In general, given a tautology of the form, "A's exist," we cannot deduce from it, "There are A's," nor from a tautology of the form, "A's do not exist," can we deduce "There are no A's." And specifically, given the tautology, "God exists," we cannot deduce from it, "There is a God." The statement, "God necessarily exists, but there is no God," is *not* self-contradictory.

As it stands, the situation is most paradoxical. For in many of its ordinary uses, "A's exist" is equivalent to "There are A's." If I raise a question about the existence of pearls as large as my fist, it usually does not matter whether you say, "Yes, such pearls exist," or "Yes, there are such pearls." So if there is a way of saying that certain things exist which does not mean that there are such things, then this must be explained.

Now I have misinterpreted the situation somewhat. I have spoken as if it were important whether we used the form "A's exist" rather than "There are A's." But this is not the case. "There are A's" is perhaps more resistant to being treated as a tautology but it is still possible to frame tautologies of the form, "There are A's." "There is what there is" and "There are what there are," are tautologies, and one could imagine situations in which one might say them in this tautological way. If I define "particulars" as "whatever entities there really are," then "There are particulars" is a tautology, namely, "There are whatever entities there really are." And if I define "a God" as "whatever divine being there is," then "There is a God" is tautological too. So there is nothing distinctive about the forms "A's exist" or "there are A's." They both function in very similar ways. But we do have both forms of expression, and that is most convenient. For it allows us to formulate a further existential question, using the alternative form, when we are presented with a tautological existential assertion. Thus if someone says, tautologically, "There are particulars [*i.e.,* there are whatever objects there are]," we can avoid the danger of formal contradiction in asking, "I grant that there are particulars, but do particulars *exist* ?"

What I am claiming is that if we are given a tautological existential assertion like "Particulars exist" or "God exists," the existential question is not settled. Just as the tautology, "Fictitious objects do not exist," leaves open the question whether there are fictitious objects, so the tautology, "God exists," leaves open the question whether there is a God. But what is this further question ? How paradoxical it seems to deny that "once one has grasped Anselm's proof of the necessary existence of a being a greater than which cannot be conceived, no question remains as to whether it exists or not."[21]

It is tempting to try to resolve the paradox in accordance with Aristotle's principle that "there are several senses in which a thing may be said to 'be.'" Then to say that fictitious objects do not exist would be to say that fictitious objects lacked, say, spatio-temporal existence, whereas to say that there are fictitious objects would be to say that they had some other kind of existence—hence no contradiction, since in a sense fictitious objects exist and in a sense they do not. But appeals to the systematic ambiguity of "exists" will not work in all cases, for we may deny that there are A's in precisely the same sense of "be" that we claim tautologically that A's exist. For example, it will be tautologically true that particulars exist in precisely the same sense of "exist," say, temporal existence, that it might be true that there are no particulars.

A more promising line of argument consists in showing that a tautological existential claim is quite different from a non-tautological existential claim. How are we to explain the difference ? Suppose we say that a tautological existential assertion consists in attributing to the subject a special property, the property of necessary existence. We could explain this property by saying, *à la* Malcolm, that a being which has this property is such that it is senseless to speak of its non-existence or of its coming into existence or going out of existence or of the existence of anything else as a condition of its existence (pp. 44–59). Now this account will not do. First, the attempt to explain the necessity of the statement by postulating a special property commits us to an infinite regress of properties, for presumably this special property might not be one which a being just happens to have but one which it necessarily has and which it is senseless to speak of its not having, and thus by similar reasoning we are led to necessary necessary-existence, etc. And it is most unclear what these properties could be or how we could distinguish them. But, secondly, it is not clear what this property of necessary existence is, if this is any more than a way of saying that the existential proposition is necessary. Am I making anything clearer when I say that squares, which are necessarily four-sided, have the special property of *necessary four-sidedness* ? A defining property is not a special kind of property. So the tautological character of the existential assertions I have been discussing cannot be explained by postulating a special predicate, necessary existence. Their tautological character arises from nothing but the definition we have stipulated for the subject term. But then we are still left with our puzzle: how is it possible to say that A's necessarily exist but there may be no A's?

I wish to consider one further attempt to remove the paradox, one suggested by some remarks by Carnap on a somewhat different issue:

> If someone wishes to speak in his language about a new kind of entities, he has to introduce a system of new ways of speaking, subject to new rules; we shall call this procedure the construction of a *framework* for the new entities in question. And now we must distinguish two kinds of questions of existence: first, question . . . *within* the *framework;* we call them *internal questions;* and second, question concerning the existence or reality *of the framework itself,* called *external question.*[22]

Carnap goes on to explain that "external questions" concern nothing but "whether or not to accept and use the forms of expression for the framework in question," a purely practical question to be answered in terms of expediency and fruitfulness (p. 23). To apply this distinction to our paradox, given the basic definitions and rules of a particular religious language it will be a necessary statement that God exists (although not, perhaps, a necessary statement that the Devil exists), but we may ask the further question, Is there a God? meaning, Is this language a useful one?

Now waiving objections we may have about the vagueness of talking of the "fruitfulness" of a set of expressions, it still remains the case that "Are there any A's" will not always be identical with asking if the language is fruitful, for it may be very fruitful to talk of perfect pendulums, frictionless pulleys, the ideal society, Euclidean points, and the economic man, even if it is perfectly clear that there do not exist such things. So the question whether there are such things cannot be identical with the question whether it is in some sense fruitful to use expressions which refer to them; a fiction or *façon de parler* may turn out to be useful and fruitful.

What lies at the heart of the puzzle about the Ontological Argument is the fact that our concepts have two quite different aspects, marked by the familiar philosophical distinction of intension and extension. A word like "horse" has a particular meaning and is logically connected with other words like "animal"; its corresponding concept, the concept of a horse, has a particular content and is connected with other concepts like the concept of an animal. It is this intensional feature of words and their corresponding concepts which makes certain assertions like "A horse is an animal" tautological. But words and concepts are also applicable to things. It turns out to be the case that there have existed, do now exist, and will exist entities such that it is true of each of them that it is a horse, true of each of them that the concept of a horse applies to it. And this fact we may express by saying that the word, "horse" or the concept of a horse has extension. In making assertions about the extension of a concept there are typical forms of expression which we use: ". . . exist," ". . . are non-existent," "There are. . . ," "There are no. . . ," ". . . are plentiful," ". . . are scarce," ". . . are extinct," ". . . are mythological," ". . . are found in Africa," etc. That such expressions are typically used in assertions about the extension (or lack thereof) of particular concepts is what is correctly brought out in the slogan, " 'Exists' is not a predicate." But the typical use is not the only use. Since any statement, with suitable definition, can be true by virtue of the meanings of the terms, sentences with existential expressions can be used to express tautological statements. The very same sentence which is typically used to make a claim about the extension of the concept may instead be used to make a claim about the intension of the concept. We cannot tell by the form of the expression how the expression is being used. "Particulars exist," when asserted tautologically, is used to make a claim about the *meaning* of the word, "particulars," and therefore cannot be used to make a claim about the extension of the term. Similarly, if someone uses the sentence, "God exists," tautologically, he tells us only that being an existent is a logical requirement for being God. If, on the other hand, someone asserts, "God exists," non-tautologically, then he claims that the term, "God," has extension, applies to some existent. In the case of the Ontological Argument the only valid conclusion is an intensional statement about the meaning of the concept of God. *A fortiori* the conclusion cannot be about whether anything exists to which the concept applies. The *prima facie* plausibility of the Argument comes from the use of a sentence intensionally when the typical use of that sentence is extensional. In this way it conceals the illicit move from an intensional to an extensional statement.

It looked as if the familiar distinction between intension and extension, stood in danger of breaking down in the case of existential tautologies. But we have seen that this is not the case. For even when we have an existential tautology like "Particulars exist" or "God exists," it still remains an open question whether the concept of particulars or the concept of God has application, applies to any existent. What is settled at one level is not settled at another level. It is important to see that we can go on to settle the question at the other level, too, for we can *make* it a priori true that the concept has application. For example, let the expression, "the concept of God," mean "a concept which has application and applies to a being such that . . . ." Then by definition the concept of God has application; the statement, "The concept of God has application," is now a tautology, given the definition. But nothing is gained by such a manoeuvre. We have given the expression, "the concept of God," a meaning; we have framed a concept, namely the concept of the concept of God, and this concept makes certain statements tautologically true. Yet we can still raise the extensional question, Does this concept refer to any existent? At this level the extensional question would be whether there actually is a concept of God such that this concept has extension, and there is such a concept only if there actually is a God. So making the condition of having application or extension a necessary condition for being a concept of God still leaves open the question, concerning *that* concept, whether it has extension. Nothing has been settled except the meaning of a certain expression.

Why is it that extensional assertions cannot be tautological? Because they do not merely tell us what the requirements are for being an *A* but, starting with these requirements, tell us whether anything meets these requirements. Even if it is a conceptual requirement that the thing exist in order to be an instance of the concept, that in no way settles whether the requirement is met. And if we *make* it a tautology that the requirement is met, by framing a concept of a concept, then we are left with the open question whether the newly framed concept has extension. That is what is true in the thesis that no "existential" proposition can be analytic. But we must remember that an "existential" proposition can turn out to be an intensional proposition, and therefore tautological.

Since much of what I have claimed depends upon the legitimacy of the intension-extension distinction, I wish to consider, finally, two threats to this distinction. The first concerns the so-called *intensional object.* When I conceive of an object, think about it, describe it, make a painting of it, long for it, look for it, and expect to find it, it may nevertheless be the case that the object does not exist, that the concept has no extension. But it is tempting to say that there must be something such that I conceive of it, think about it, describe it, etc., tempting to say that the object in some sense exists. And thus it is tempting to say that the mere fact that there is a concept of some object entails that the object in some sense exists. Well, even if one says that, it is obviously not the sense in which the religious usually wish to say that God exists nor the sense in which the atheist wishes to deny that God exists. They disagree about whether anything answers to that concept of an object, not about whether that concept is a concept of an object.

A second, and more troublesome, threat to the intension-extension distinction arises when we try to apply the distinction to certain concepts. We seem quite clear that the concept of a horse does have extension and that the concept of a unicorn does not have extension, and that these are contingent facts. But now suppose we ask whether the concept of a number has extension. If we hold that the concept ultimately has as its extension things in the world, then it still remains a contingent fact that the concept has extension. But suppose we are inclined to say that the concept has extension simply because, as we all know, there are (infinitely) many numbers. Surely it is not a contingent fact that there are (infinitely) many numbers. So if this fact leads us to say that the concept of a number has extension, then it will be a necessary proposition that the concept of a number has extension and, given the concept of a number, we can say a *priori* that the concept applies to (infinitely) many things.

What makes this case puzzling is that we have no idea what would count as establishing that the concept of a number has extension or that it does not have extension. We can investigate whether the concept of a number is a legitimate one, clear and self-consistent; we can note its logical connection with other mathematical concepts; and we can frame propositions which state these connections, even propositions like "There exists a number which is even and prime." But what would count as showing that the concept, over and above its intensional content, has extension as well? Where would one look for traces, signs, evidences, intimations, or testimonies of the existence of numbers? Would we not say of someone who did think such a search sensible that he had misconceived the nature of numbers ? Nothing would count as showing that the concept of numbers had extension over and above its intensional content, and this is to say that the notion of extension does not apply here. The most that could be said is that numbers are *in*tensional objects.

The same thing must be said for the existence of God. The most that the Ontological Argument establishes is the intensional object, God, even if this intensional object has the attribute of existence as an intensional feature. To establish that the concept of God has extension requires adducing some additional argument to show that over and above its intensional features, over and above the content of the concept (or the meaning of the word, "God"), the concept of God has extension as well. This additional argument will of necessity have to be an *a posteriori* argument to the effect that certain evidences make it reasonable to think that some actual existent answers to the concept. We are thus led to the result that the Ontological Argument of itself alone cannot show the existence of God, in the sense in which the concept is shown to have extension. And this is just as the religious wish it to be. They do not conceive of God as something whose being expresses itself entirely in the concepts and propositions of a language game. They conceive of Him as something which has effects on the world and can in some way be experienced. Here is a crucial respect in which His status is meant to be different from that of the numbers. The concept of God is a concept which *might* have extension. But some further argument is required to show whether it does or not.

Concepts are like nets. What they catch depends in part upon how we construct them and in part upon what is outside the net. Suppose I produce a net for catching fish one-millionth of an inch long. Of such a net we are entitled to say, "This net catches fish one-millionth of an inch long", and what shows that this statement is true is nothing but the construction of the net. Does the net catch anything? It catches fish one-millionth of an inch long. Still, a question remains. Shall we ever find such fish in our net? For those who hunger for such fish, the existence of the net does not in any way show that what they hunger for shall be given unto them.

Notes

1. *Dialogues Concerning Natural Religion,* Part IX.
2. *Critique of Pure Reason,* trans. Norman Kemp Smith, Macmillan, 1953, p. 504.
3. Norman Malcolm, "Anselm's Ontological Arguments," *Philosophical Review,* 69 (1960), 41–62.
4. G. Ryle, "Imaginary Objects," *Aristotelian Society,* Supplementary Volume XII, 1933, p. 27.
5. C. D. Broad, *Religion, Philosophy, and Psychical Research,* New York, 1953, p. 182.
6. P. F. Strawson, "On Referring," reprinted in *Essays in Conceptual Analysis,* ed. A. Flew, London, 1956, p. 35.
7. *Ibid.* footnote (added to original article), p. 40. See also Strawson's "A Reply to Mr. Sellars," *Philosophical Review,* 1954, p. 229.
8. *Cf.* P. F. Strawson, *Introduction to Logical Theory,* London, 1952, pp. 190–191.
9. G. Nakhnikian and W. Salmon, " 'Exists' as a Predicate," *Philosophical Review,* 1957, p. 541.
10. David Hume, *A Treatise of Human Nature,* ed. L. A. Selby-Bigge, Oxford, 1888, p. 66.
11. David Hume, *Dialogues Concerning Natural Religion,* Part IX.
12. David Hume, *Enquiries Concerning the Human Understanding,* ed. L. A. Selby-Bigge, Oxford, 1902, p. 164.

13. *Treatise, op. cit.* pp. 66–67.

14. *Ibid.* p. 32.

15. *Ibid.* p. 66.

16. *Ibid.* p. 623.

17. *Ibid.* p. 86 and *passim.*

18. *Ibid.* p. 15.

19. *Ibid.* p. 96, footnote.

20. J. A. Passmore, in his illuminating book, *Hume's Intentions* (Cambridge, 1952) diagnoses the difficulties which appear here as arising from Hume's attempt to produce "a logic in which the only links are psychological" (p. 27).

21. Malcolm, *op. cit.* p. 52.

22. R. Carnap, "Empiricism, Semantics, and Ontology," *Revue Internationale de Philosophie,* § 11, January 1950, pp. 21–22.

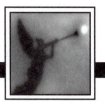

PART THREE

Models of Religious Faith

In Chapter 3, four models of religious faith are examined in critical detail. While any number of other approaches to faith could have been selected, including St. Augustine, Martin Luther, John Calvin, Paul Tillich, Karl Barth, and many others, the thinkers included represent distinctively different perspectives on the roles of reason, belief, will, knowledge, and language in the dynamic of faith, and offer a challenging cross section of explanatory models of the faith experience.

A. St. Thomas Aquinas: Faith, Belief, and Intellectual Assent

Aquinas (1265–1274), in the context of an extended conversation with the work of Aristotle, argues for a continuity between faith and reason. It is entirely within the domain of reason to come to the knowledge of God's existence, and even to be directed by historical evidence toward the supernatural truths of the Christian faith. While faith surpasses knowledge and clearly requires the assistance of divine grace, faith completes human reason and is never in conflict with it. Reason, properly employed, can prove the existence of God and propel the person of good will toward the church where the further mysteries of the Triune God can be appropriated in Christian faith. John Hick's essay (1957) assesses the consistency of Aquinas's position on faith, exposing what he takes to be difficulties in the argument, and Norwood Russell Hanson (1961) rejects Aquinas's confidence in reason to assert the existence of God. For Hanson, it is clear that reason not only cannot support believer's claims about God's existence but also negates them.

11. On Faith

St. Thomas Aquinas

Question I. Of Faith. (*In Ten Articles.*)

Having to treat now of the theological virtues, we shall begin with Faith, secondly we shall speak of Hope, and thirdly, of Charity.

The treatise on Faith will be fourfold: (1) Of faith itself: (2) Of the corresponding gifts, knowledge and understanding: (3) Of the opposite vices: (4) Of the precepts pertaining to this virtue.

About faith itself we shall consider: (1) its object: (2) its act: (3) the habit of faith.

Under the first head there are ten points of inquiry: (1) Whether the object of faith is the First Truth? (2) Whether the object of faith is something complex or incomplex, i.e. whether it is a thing or a proposition? (3) Whether anything false can come under faith? (4) Whether the object of faith can be anything seen? (5) Whether it can be anything known? (6) Whether the things to be believed should be divided into a certain number of articles? (7) Whether the same articles are of faith for all times? (8) Of the number of articles. (9) Of the manner of embodying the articles in a symbol (10) Who has the right to propose a symbol of faith?

First Article. Whether the Object of Faith Is the First Truth?

We proceed thus to the First Article:—

Objection 1. It seems that the object of faith is not the First Truth. For it seems that the object of faith is that which is proposed to us to be believed. Now not only things pertaining to the Godhead, i.e. the First Truth, are proposed to us to be believed, but also things concerning Christ's human nature, and the sacraments of the Church, and the condition of creatures. Therefore the object of faith is not only the First Truth.

Obj. 2. Further, Faith and unbelief have the same object since they are opposed to one another. Now unbelief can be about all things contained in Holy Writ, for whichever one of them a man denies, he is considered an unbeliever. Therefore faith also is about all things contained in Holy Writ. But there are many things therein, concerning man and other creatures. Therefore the object of faith is not only the First Truth, but also created truth.

Source: From St. Thomas Aquinas, *Summa Theologica,* Part II, Translated by the Fathers of the English Dominican Province, London: R. & T. Washbourne, Ltd., 1917.

Obj. 3. Further, Faith is condivided with charity, as stated above (I.-II., Q. LXII., A. 3). Now by charity we love not only God, who is the sovereign Good, but also our neighbour. Therefore the object of Faith is not only the First Truth.

On the contrary, Dionysius says (*Div. Nom.* vii.) that *faith is about the simple and everlasting truth.* Now this is the First Truth. Therefore the object of faith is the First Truth.

I answer that, The object of every cognitive habit includes two things: first, that which is known materially, and is the material object, so to speak, and, secondly, that whereby it is known, which is the formal aspect of the object. Thus in the science of geometry, the conclusions are what is known materially, while the formal aspect of the science is the mean of demonstration, through which the conclusions are known.

Accordingly if we consider, in faith, the formal aspect of the object, it is nothing else than the First Truth. For the faith of which we are speaking, does not assent to anything, except because it is revealed by God. Hence the mean on which faith is based is the Divine Truth. If, however, we consider materially the things to which faith assents, they include not only God, but also many other things, which, nevertheless, do not come under the assent of faith, except as bearing some relation to God, in as much as, to wit, through certain effects of the Divine operation, man is helped on his journey towards the enjoyment of God. Consequently from this point of view also the object of faith is, in a way, the First Truth, in as much as nothing comes under faith except in relation to God, even as the object of the medical art is health, for it considers nothing save in relation to health.

Reply Obj. 1. Things concerning Christ's human nature, and the sacraments of the Church, or any creatures whatever, come under faith, in so far as by them we are directed to God, and in as much as we assent to them on account of the Divine Truth.

The same answer applies to the Second Objection, as regards all things contained in Holy Writ.

Reply Obj. 3. Charity also loves our neighbour on account of God, so that its object, properly speaking, is God, as we shall show further on (Q. XXV., A. I).

Second Article. Whether the Object of Faith Is Something Complex, By Way of a Proposition?

We proceed thus to the Second Article:—

Objection 1. It seems that the object of faith is not something complex by way of a proposition. For the object of faith is the First Truth, as stated above (A. I). Now the First Truth is something simple. Therefore the object of faith is not something complex.

Obj. 2. Further, The exposition of faith is contained in the symbol. Now the symbol does not contain propositions, but things: for it is not stated therein that God is almighty, but: *I believe in God . . . almighty.* Therefore the object of faith is not a proposition but a thing.

Obj. 3. Further, Faith is succeeded by vision, according to I Cor. xiii. 12: *We see now through a glass in a dark manner: but then face to face. Now I know in part; but then*

I shall know even as I am known. But the object of the heavenly vision is something simple, for it is the Divine Essence. Therefore the faith of the wayfarer is also.

On the contrary, Faith is a mean between science and opinion. Now the mean is in the same genus as the extremes. Since, then, science and opinion are about propositions, it seems that faith is likewise about propositions; so that its object is something complex.

I answer that, The thing known is in the knower according to the mode of the knower. Now the mode proper to the human intellect is to know the truth by synthesis and analysis, as stated in the First Part (Q. LXXXV., A. 5). Hence things that are simple in themselves, are known by the intellect with a certain amount of complexity, just as on the other hand, the Divine intellect knows, without any complexity, things that are complex in themselves.

Accordingly the object of faith may be considered in two ways. First, as regards the thing itself which is believed, and thus the object of faith is something simple, namely the thing itself about which we have faith. Secondly, on the part of the believer, and in this respect the object of faith is something complex by way of a proposition.

Hence in the past both opinions have been held with a certain amount of truth.

Reply Obj. 1. This argument considers the object of faith on the part of the thing believed.

Reply Obj. 2. The symbol mentions the things about which faith is, in so far as the act of the believer is terminated in them, as is evident from the manner of speaking about them. Now the act of the believer does not terminate in a proposition, but in a thing. For as in science we do not form propositions, except in order to have knowledge about things through their means, so is it in faith.

Reply Obj. 3. The object of the heavenly vision will be the First Truth seen in itself, according to 1 John iii. 2: *We know that when He shall appear, we shall be like to Him: because we shall see Him as He is:* hence that vision will not be by way of a proposition but by way of simple understanding. On the other hand, by faith, we do not apprehend the First Truth as it is in itself. Hence the comparison fails. . . .

Fourth Article. Whether the Object of Faith Can Be Something Seen?

We proceed thus to the Fourth Article:—

Objection 1. It seems that the object of faith is something seen. For Our Lord said to Thomas (John xx. 29): *Because thou hast seen Me, Thomas, thou hast believed.* Therefore vision and faith regard the same object.

Obj. 2. Further, The Apostle, while speaking of the knowledge of faith, says (I Cor. xiii. 12): *We see now through a glass in a dark manner.* Therefore what is believed is seen.

Obj. 3. Further, Faith is a spiritual light. Now something is seen under every light. Therefore faith is of things seen.

Obj. 4. Further, *Every sense is a kind of sight,* as Augustine states (*De Verb. Domini, Serm.* xxxiii.). But faith is of things heard, according to Rom. x. 17: *Faith . . . cometh by hearing.* Therefore faith is of things seen.

On the contrary, The Apostle says (Heb. xi. I) that *faith is the evidence of things that appear not.*

I answer that, Faith implies assent of the intellect to that which is believed. Now the intellect assents to a thing in two ways. First, through being moved to assent by its very object, which is known either by itself (as in the case of first principles, which are held by the habit of understanding), or through something else already known (as in the case of conclusions which are held by the habit of science). Secondly the intellect assents to something, not through being sufficiently moved to this assent by its proper object, but through an act of choice, whereby it turns voluntarily to one side rather than to the other: and if this be accompanied by doubt and fear of the opposite side, there will be opinion, while, if there be certainty and no fear of the other side, there will be faith.

Now those things are said to be seen which, of themselves, move the intellect or the senses to knowledge of them. Wherefore it is evident that neither faith nor opinion can be of things seen either by the senses or by the intellect.

Reply Obj. 1. Thomas *saw one thing, and believed another.** he saw the Man, and believing Him to be God, he made profession of his faith, saying: *My Lord and my God.*

Reply Obj. 2. Those things which come under faith can be considered in two ways. First, in particular; and thus they cannot be seen and believed at the same time, as shown above. Secondly, in general, that is, under the common aspect of credibility; and in this way they are seen by the believer. For he would not believe unless, on the evidence of signs, or of something similar, he saw that they ought to be believed.

Reply Obj. 3. The light of faith makes us see what we believe. For just as, by the habits of the other virtues, man sees what is becoming to him in respect of that habit, so, by the habit of faith, the human mind is directed to assent to such things as are becoming to a right faith, and not to assent to others.

Reply Obj. 4. Hearing is of words signifying what is of faith, but not of the things themselves that are believed; hence it does not follow that these things are seen.

Fifth Article. Whether Those Things That Are of Faith Can Be an Object of Science?

We proceed thus to the Fifth Article:—

Objection 1. It seems that those things that are of faith can be an object of science. For where science is lacking there is ignorance, since ignorance is the opposite of science. Now we are not in ignorance of those things we have to believe, since ignorance of such things savours of unbelief, according to 1 Tim. i. 13: *I did it ignorantly in unbelief.* Therefore things that are of faith can be an object of science.

Obj. 2. Further, Science is acquired by reasons. Now sacred writers employ reasons to inculcate things that are of faith. Therefore such things can be an object of science.

S. Gregory: Hom. xxvi. in Evang.

Obj. 3. Further, Things which are demonstrated are an object of science, since a *demonstration is a syllogism that produces science.* Now certain matters of faith have been demonstrated by the philosophers, such as the Existence and Unity of God, and so forth. Therefore things that are of faith can be an object of science.

Obj. 4. Further, Opinion is further from science than faith is, since faith is said to stand between opinion and science. Now opinion and science can, in a way, be about the same object, as stated in *Poster.* i. Therefore faith and science can be about the same object also.

On the contrary, Gregory says (*Hom.* xxi. *in Ev.*) that *when a thing is manifest, it is the object, not of faith, but of perception.* Therefore things that are of faith are not the object of perception, whereas what is an object of science is the object of perception. Therefore there can be no faith about things which are an object of science.

I answer that, All science is derived from self-evident and therefore *seen* principles; wherefore all objects of science must needs be, in a fashion, seen.

Now as stated above (A. 4) it is impossible that one and the same thing should be believed and seen by the same person. Hence it is equally impossible for one and the same thing to be an object of science and of belief for the same person. It may happen, however, that a thing which is an object of vision or science for one, is believed by another: since we hope to see some day what we now believe about the Trinity, according to 1 Cor. xiii. 12: *We see now through a glass in a dark manner; but then face to face:* which vision the angels possess already; so that what we believe, they see. In like manner it may happen that what is an object of vision or scientific knowledge for one man, even in the state of a wayfarer, is, for another man, an object of faith, because he does not know it by demonstration.

Nevertheless that which is proposed to be believed equally by all, is equally unknown by all as an object of science: such are the things which are of faith simply. Consequently faith and science are not about the same things.

Reply Obj. 1. Unbelievers are in ignorance of things that are of faith, for neither do they see or know them in themselves, nor do they know them to be credible. The faithful, on the other hand, know them, not as by demonstration, but by the light of faith which makes them see that they ought to believe them, as stated above (A. 4, *ad* 2, 3).

Reply Obj. 2. The reasons employed by holy men to prove things that are of faith, are not demonstrations; they are either persuasive arguments showing that what is proposed to our faith is not impossible, or else they are proofs drawn from the principles of faith, i.e. from the authority of Holy Writ, as Dionysius declares (*Div. Nom.* ii.). Whatever is based on these principles is as well proved in the eyes of the faithful, as a conclusion drawn from self-evident principles is in the eyes of all. Hence again, theology is a science, as we stated at the outset of this work (P. I., Q. I., A. 2).

Reply Obj. 3. Things which can be proved by demonstration are reckoned among the articles of faith, not because they are believed simply by all, but because they are a necessary presuppositions to matters of faith, so that those who do not know them by demonstration must know them first of all by faith.

Reply Obj. 4. As the Philosopher says (*loc. cit.*), *science and opinion about the same object can certainly be in different men,* as we have stated above about science and faith; yet it is possible for one and the same man to have science and faith about the same thing relatively, i.e. in relation to the object, but not in the same respect. For it is possible for the same person, about one and the same object, to know one thing and to think another:

and, in like manner, one may know by demonstration the unity of the Godhead, and, by faith, the Trinity. On the other hand, in one and the same man, about the same object, and in the same respect, science is incompatible with either opinion or faith, yet for different reasons. Because science is incompatible with opinion about the same object simply, for the reason that science demands that its object should be deemed impossible to be otherwise, whereas it is essential to opinion, that its object should be deemed possible to be otherwise. Yet that which is the object of faith, on account of the certainty of faith, is also deemed impossible to be otherwise; and the reason why science and faith cannot be about the same object and in the same respect is because the object of science is something seen, whereas the object of faith is the unseen, as stated above. . . .

Tenth Article. Whether It Belongs to the Sovereign Pontiff to Draw up a Symbol of Faith?

We proceed thus to the Tenth Article:—

Objection 1. It seems that it does not belong to the Sovereign Pontiff to draw up a symbol of faith. For a new edition of the symbol becomes necessary in order to explain the articles of faith, as stated above (A. 9). Now, in the Old Testament, the articles of faith were more and more explained as time went on, by reason of the truth of faith becoming clearer through greater nearness to Christ, as stated above (A. 7). Since then this reason ceased with the advent of the New Law, there is no need for the articles of faith to be more and more explicit. Therefore it does not seem to belong to the authority of the Sovereign Pontiff to draw up a new edition of the symbol.

Obj. 2. Further, No man has the power to do what is forbidden under pain of anathema by the universal Church. Now it was forbidden under pain of anathema by the universal Church, to make a new edition of the symbol. For it is stated in the acts of the first council of Ephesus (P. ii., Act. 6) that *after the symbol of the Nicene council had been read through, the holy synod decreed that it was unlawful to utter, write or draw up any other creed, than that which was defined by the Fathers assembled at Nicaea together with the Holy Ghost,* and this under pain of anathema. The same was repeated in the acts of the council of Chalcedon (P. ii., Act. 5). Therefore it seems that the Sovereign Pontiff has no authority to publish a new edition of the symbol.

Obj. 3. Further, Athanasius was not the Sovereign Pontiff, but patriarch of Alexandria, and yet the published a symbol which is sung in the Church. Therefore it does not seem to belong to the Sovereign Pontiff any more than to other bishops, to publish a new edition of the symbol.

On the contrary, The symbol was drawn up by a general council. Now such a council cannot be convoked otherwise than by the authority of the Sovereign Pontiff, as stated in the Decretals (Dist. xvii., Cap. 4, 5). Therefore an edition of the symbol belongs to the authority of the Sovereign Pontiff.

I answer that, As stated above (*Obj.* 1), a new edition of the symbol becomes necessary in order to set aside the errors that may arise. Consequently to publish a new edition of the symbol belongs to that authority which is empowered to decide matters of faith finally, so that they may be held by all with unshaken faith. Now this belongs to the authority of the Sovereign Pontiff, to whom the more important and more difficult questions that arise in the Church are referred, as stated in the Decretals (Extra, *De Baptismo,* Cap. *Majores*). Hence Our Lord said to Peter whom he made Sovereign Pontiff (Luke xxii. 32): *I have prayed for thee,* Peter, *that thy faith fail not, and thou, being once converted, confirm thy brethren.* The reason of this is that there should be but one faith of the whole Church, according to 1 Cor. i. 10: *That you all speak the same thing, and that there be no schisms among you:* and this could not be secured unless any question of faith that may arise be decided by him who presides over the whole Church, so that the whole Church may hold firmly to his decision. Consequently it belongs to the sole authority of the Sovereign Pontiff to publish a new edition of the symbol, as do all other matters which concern the whole Church, such as to convoke a general council and so forth.

Reply Obj. 1. The truth of faith is sufficiently explicit in the teaching of Christ and the apostles. But since, according to 2 Pet. iii. 16, some men are so evil-minded as to pervert the apostolic teaching and other doctrines and Scriptures to their own destruction, it was necessary as time went on to express the faith more explicitly against the errors which arose.

Reply Obj. 2. This prohibition and sentence of the council was intended for private individuals, who have no business to decide matters of faith: for this decision of the general council did not take away from a subsequent council the power of drawing up a new edition of the symbol, containing not indeed a new faith, but the same faith with greater explicitness. For every council has taken into account that a subsequent council would expound matters more fully than the preceding council, if this became necessary through some heresy arising. Consequently this belongs to the Sovereign Pontiff, by whose authority the council is convoked, and its decision confirmed.

Reply Obj. 3. Athanasius drew up a declaration of faith, not under the form of a symbol, but rather by way of an exposition of doctrine, as appears from his way of speaking. But since it contained briefly the whole truth of faith, it was accepted by the authority of the Sovereign Pontiff, so as to be considered as a rule of faith.

Question II. Of The Act Of Faith. (*In Ten Articles.*)

We must now consider the act of faith, and (1) the internal act, (2) the external act.

Under the first head there are ten points of inquiry: (1) What is *to believe,* which is the internal act of faith? (2) In how many ways is it expressed? (3) Whether it is necessary for salvation to believe in anything above natural reason? (4) Whether it is necessary to believe those things that are attainable by natural reason? (5) Whether it is necessary for salvation to believe certain things explicitly? (6) Whether all are equally bound to explicit faith? (7) Whether explicit faith in Christ is always necessary for salvation? (8) Whether it is necessary for salvation to believe in the Trinity explicitly? (9) Whether the act of faith is meritorious? (10) Whether human reason diminishes the merit of faith?

First Article. Whether to Believe Is to Think with Assent?

We proceed thus to the First Article:—

Objection 1. It seems that to believe is not to think with assent. Because the Latin word *cogitatio* (*thought*) implies a research, for *cogitare* (*to think*) seems to be equivalent to *coagitare* i.e. *to discuss together.* Now Damascene says (*De Fide Orthod.* iv.) that faith is *an assent without research.* Therefore thinking has no place in the act of faith.

Obj. 2. Further, Faith resides in the reason, as we shall show further on (Q. IV., A. 2). Now to think is an act of the cogitative power, which belongs to the sensitive faculty, as stated in the First Part (Q. LXXVIII., A. 4). Therefore thought has nothing to do with faith.

Obj. 3. Further, To believe is an act of the intellect, since its object is truth. But assent seems to be an act not of the intellect, but of the will, even as consent is, as stated above (I.-II., Q. XV., A. 1, *ad* 3). Therefore to believe is not to think with assent.

On the contrary, This is how *to believe* is defined by Augustine (*De Praedest. Sanct.* ii.).

I answer that, To think can be taken in three ways. First, in a general way for any kind of actual consideration of the intellect, as Augustine observes (*De Trin.* xiv.): *By understanding I mean now the faculty whereby we understand when thinking.* Secondly, *to think* is more strictly taken for that consideration of the intellect, which is accompanied by some kind of inquiry, and which precedes the intellect's arrival at the stage of perfection that comes with the certitude of sight. In this sense Augustine says (*De Trin.* xv.) that *the Son of God is not called the Thought, but the Word of God. When our thought realizes what we know and takes form therefrom, it becomes our world. Hence the Word of God must be understood without any thinking on the part of God, for there is nothing there that can take form, or be unformed.* In this way thought is, properly speaking, the movement of the mind while yet deliberating, and not yet perfected by the clear sight of truth. Since, however, such a movement of the mind may be one of deliberation either about universal notions, which belongs to the intellectual faculty, or about particular matters, which belongs to the sensitive part, hence it is that *to think* is taken secondly for an act of the deliberating intellect, and thirdly for an act of the cogitative power.

Accordingly, if *to think* be understood broadly according to the first sense, then *to think with assent,* does not express completely what is meant by *to believe:* since, in this way, a man thinks with assent even when he considers what he knows by science, or understands. If, on the other hand, *to think* be understood in the second way, then this expresses completely the nature of the act of believing. For among the acts belonging to the intellect, some have a firm assent without any such kind of thinking, as when a man considers the things that he knows by science, or understands, for this consideration is already formed. But some acts of the intellect have unformed thought devoid of a firm assent, whether they incline to neither side, as in one who *doubts;* or incline to one side rather than the other, but on account of some slight motive, as in one who *suspects;* or incline to one side yet with fear of the other, as in one who *opines.* But this act *to believe,* cleaves firmly to one side, in which respect belief has something in common with science and understanding; yet its knowledge does not attain the perfection of clear sight, wherein it agrees with doubt, suspicion and opinion. Hence it is proper to the believer to think with assent: so that the act of believing is distinguished from all the other acts of the intellect, which are about the true or the false.

Reply Obj. 1. Faith has not that research of natural reason which demonstrates what is believed, but a research into those things whereby a man is induced to believe, for instance that such things have been uttered by God and confirmed by miracles.

Reply Obj. 2. *To think* is not taken here for the act of the cogitative power, but for an act of the intellect, as explained above.

Reply Obj. 3. The intellect of the believer is determined to one object, not by the reason, but by the will, wherefore assent is taken here for an act of the intellect as determined to one object by the will.

(Q.I., A. 1). One of these is the material object of faith, and in this way an act of faith is *to believe in a God;* because, as stated above (*ibid.*) nothing is proposed to our belief, except in as much as it is referred to God. The other is the formal aspect of the object, for it is the medium on account of which we assent to such and such a point of faith; and thus an act of faith is *to believe God,* since, as stated above (*ibid.*) the formal object of faith is the First Truth, to Which man gives his adhesion, so as to assent for Its sake to whatever he believes.

Thirdly, if the object of faith be considered in so far as the intellect is moved by the will, an act of faith is *to believe in God.* For the First Truth is referred to the will, through having the aspect of an end.

Reply Obj. 1. These three do not denote different acts of faith, but one and the same act having different relations to the object of faith.

This suffices for the *Reply* to the *Second Objection.*

Reply Obj. 3. Unbelievers cannot be said *to believe in a God* as we understand it in relation to the act of faith. For they do not believe that God exists under the conditions that faith determines; hence they do not truly believe in a God, since, as the Philosopher observes (*Met.* ix.) *to know simple things defectively is not to know them at all.*

Reply Obj. 4. As stated above (I.-II., Q. IX., A. 1) the will moves the intellect and the other powers of the soul to the end: and in this respect an act of faith is *to believe in God.*

Third Article. Whether It Is Necessary for Salvation to Believe Anything Above the Natural Reason?

We proceed thus to the Third Article:—

Objection 1. It seems unnecessary for salvation to believe anything above the natural reason. For the salvation and perfection of a thing seem to be sufficiently insured by its natural endowments. Now matters of faith, surpass man's natural reason, since they are things unseen as stated above (Q. I., A. 4). Therefore to believe seems unnecessary for salvation.

Obj. 2. Further, It is dangerous for man to assent to matters, wherein he cannot judge whether that which is proposed to him be true or false, according to Job xii. 11:

Doth not the ear discern words? Now a man cannot form a judgment of this kind in matters of faith, since he cannot trace them back to first principles, by which all our judgments are guided. Therefore it is dangerous to believe in such matters. Therefore to believe is not necessary for salvation.

Obj. 3. Further, Man's salvation rests on God, according to Ps. xxxvi. 39: *But the salvation of the just is from the Lord.* Now *the invisible things* of God *are clearly seen, being understood by the things that are made; His eternal power also and Divinity,* according to Rom. i. 20: and those things which are clearly seen by the understanding are not an object of belief. Therefore it is not necessary for man's salvation, that he should believe certain things.

On the contrary, It is written (Heb. xi. 6): *Without faith it is impossible to please God.*

I answer that, Wherever one nature is subordinate to another, we find that two things concur towards the perfection of the lower nature, one of which is in respect of that nature's proper movement, while the other is in respect of the movement of the higher nature. Thus water by its proper movement moves towards the centre (of the earth), while according to the movement of the moon, it moves round the centre by ebb and flow. In like manner the planets have their proper movements from west to east, while in accordance with the movement of the first heaven, they have a movement from east to west. Now the created rational nature alone is immediately subordinate to God, since other creatures do not attain to the universal, but only to something particular, while they partake of the Divine goodness either in *being* only, as inanimate things, or also in *living,* and in *knowing singulars,* as plants and animals; whereas the rational nature, in as much as it apprehends the universal notion of good and being, is immediately related to the universal principle of being.

Consequently the perfection of the rational creature consists not only in what belongs to it in respect of its nature, but also in that which it acquires through a supernatural participation of Divine goodness. Hence it was said above (I.-II., Q. III., A. 8) that man's ultimate happiness consists in a supernatural vision of God: to which vision man cannot attain unless he be taught by God, according to John vi. 45: *Every one that hath heard of the Father and hath learned cometh to Me.* Now man acquires a share of this learning, not indeed all at once, but by little and little, according to the mode of his nature: and every one who learns thus must needs believe, in order that he may acquire science in a perfect degree; thus also the Philosopher remarks (*Elench.* i.) that *it behoves a learner to believe.*

Hence, in order that a man arrive at the perfect vision of heavenly happiness, he must first of all believe God, as a disciple believes the master who is teaching him.

Reply Obj. 1. Since man's nature is dependent on a higher nature, natural knowledge does not suffice for its perfection, and some supernatural knowledge is necessary, as stated above.

Reply Obj. 2. Just as man assents to first principles, by the natural light of his intellect, so does a virtuous man, by the habit of virtue, judge aright of things concerning that virtue; and in this way, by the light of faith which God bestows on him, a man assents to matters of faith and not to those which are against faith. Consequently *there is no* danger or *condemnation to them that are in Christ Jesus,* and whom He has enlightened by faith.

Reply Obj. 3. In many respects faith perceives the invisible things of God in a higher way than natural reason does in proceeding to God from His creatures. Hence it is written (Ecclus. iii. 25): *Many things are shown to thee above the understanding of man.* . . .

Eighth Article. Whether It Is Necessary for Salvation To Believe Explicitly in the Trinity?

We proceed thus to the Eighth Article:—

Objection 1. It seems that it was not necessary for salvation to believe explicitly in the Trinity. For the Apostle says (Heb. xi. 6): *He that cometh to God must believe that He is, and is a rewarder to them that seek Him.* Now one can believe this without believing in the Trinity. Therefore it was not necessary to believe explicitly in the Trinity.

Obj. 2. Further, Our Lord said (John xvii. 5, 6): *Father,* . . . *I have manifested Thy name to men,* which words Augustine expounds (*Tract.* cvi.) as follows: *Not the name by which Thou art called God, but the name whereby Thou art called My Father,* and further on he adds: *In that He made this world, God is known to all nations; in that He is not to be worshipped together with false gods, 'God is known in Judea'; but, in that He is the Father of this Christ, through Whom He takes away the sin of the world, He now makes known to men this name of His, which hitherto they knew not.* Therefore before the coming of Christ it was not known that Paternity and Filiation were in the Godhead: and so the Trinity was not believed explicitly.

Obj. 3. Further, That which we are bound to believe explicitly of God is the object of heavenly happiness. Now the object of heavenly happiness is the sovereign good, which can be understood to be in God, without any distinction of Persons. Therefore it was not necessary to believe explicitly in the Trinity.

On the contrary, In the Old Testament the Trinity of Persons is expressed in many ways; thus at the very outset of Genesis it is written in manifestation of the Trinity: *Let Us make man to Our image and likeness* (Gen. i. 26). Therefore from the very beginning it was necessary for salvation to believe in the Trinity.

I answer that, It is impossible to believe explicitly in the mystery of Christ, without faith in the Trinity, since the mystery of Christ includes that the Son of God took flesh; that He renewed the world through the grace of the Holy Ghost; and again, that He was conceived by the Holy Ghost. Wherefore just as, before Christ, the mystery of Christ was believed explicitly by the learned, but implicitly and under a veil, so to speak, by the simple, so too was it with the mystery of the Trinity. And consequently, when once grace had been revealed, all were bound to explicit faith in the mystery of the Trinity: and all who are born again in Christ, have this bestowed on them by the invocation of the Trinity, according to Matth. xxviii. 19: *Going therefore teach ye all nations, baptizing them in the name of the Father, and of the Son, and of the Holy Ghost.*

Reply Obj. 1. Explicit faith in those two things was necessary at all times and for all people: but it was not sufficient at all times and for all people.

Reply Obj. 2. Before Christ's coming, faith in the Trinity lay hidden in the faith of the learned, but through Christ and the apostles it was shown to the world.

Reply Obj. 3. God's sovereign goodness as we understand it now through its effects, can be understood without the Trinity of Persons: but as understood in itself, and as seen by the Blessed, it cannot be understood without the Trinity of Persons. Moreover the mission of the Divine Persons brings us to heavenly happiness.

Ninth Article. Whether to Believe Is Meritorious?

We proceed thus to the Ninth Article:—

Objection 1. It seems that to believe is not meritorious. For the principle of all merit is charity, as stated above (I.-II., Q. CXIV., A. 4). Now faith, like nature, is a preamble to charity. Therefore, just as an act of nature is not meritorious, since we do not merit by our natural gifts, so neither is an act of faith.

Obj. 2. Further, Belief is a mean between opinion and scientific knowledge or the consideration of things scientifically known. Now the considerations of science are not meritorious, nor on the other hand is opinion. Therefore belief is not meritorious.

Obj. 3. Further, He who assents to a point of faith, either has a sufficient motive for believing, or he has not. If he has a sufficient motive for his belief, this does not seem to imply any merit on his part, since he is no longer free to believe or not to believe: whereas if he has not a sufficient motive for believing, this is a mark of levity, according to Ecclus. xix. 4: *He that is hasty to give credit, is light of heart,* so that, seemingly, he gains no merit thereby. Therefore to believe is by no means meritorious.

On the contrary, It is written (Heb. xi. 33) that the saints *by faith . . . obtained promises,* which would not be the case if they did not merit by believing. Therefore to believe is meritorious.

I answer that, As stated above (I.-II., Q. CXIV., AA. 3, 4), our actions are meritorious in so far as they proceed from the free-will moved with grace by God. Therefore every human act proceeding from the free-will, if it be referred to God, can be meritorious. Now the act of believing is an act of the intellect assenting to the Divine truth at the command of the will moved by the grace of God, so that it is subject to the free-will in relation to God; and consequently the act of faith can be meritorious.

Reply Obj. 1. Nature is compared to charity which is the principle of merit, as matter to form: whereas faith is compared to charity as the disposition which precedes the ultimate form. Now it is evident that the subject or the matter cannot act save by virtue of the form, nor can a preceding disposition, before the advent of the form: but after the advent of the form, both the subject and the preceding disposition act by virtue of the form, which is the chief principle of action, even as the heat of fire acts by virtue of the substantial form of fire. Accordingly neither nature nor faith can, without charity, produce a meritorious act; but, when accompanied by charity, the act of faith is made meritorious thereby, even as an act of nature, and a natural act of the free-will.

Reply Obj. 2. Two things may be considered in science; namely, the scientist's assent to a scientific fact, and his consideration of that fact. Now the assent of science is not subject to free-will, because the scientist is obliged to assent by the force of the demonstration, wherefore scientific assent is not meritorious. But the actual consideration of what a man knows scientifically is subject to his free-will for it is in his power to consider or not to consider. Hence scientific consideration may be meritorious if it be referred to the end of charity, i.e. to the honour of God or the good of our neighbour. On the other hand, in the case of faith, both these things are subject to the free-will, so that in both respects the act of faith can be meritorious: whereas in the case of opinion, there is no firm assent, since it is weak and infirm, as the Philosopher observes (*Poster.* i.), so that it does not seem to proceed from a perfect act of the will: and for this reason, as regards the assent, it does not appear to be very meritorious, though it can be as regards the actual consideration.

Reply Obj. 3. The believer has sufficient motive for believing, for he is moved by the authority of Divine teaching confirmed by miracles, and, what is more, by the inward instinct of the Divine invitation: hence he does not believe lightly. He has not, however, sufficient reason for scientific knowledge, hence he does not lose the merit. . . .

Third Article. Whether Charity Is the Form of Faith?

We proceed thus to the Third Article:—

Objection 1. It seems that charity is not the form of faith. For each thing derives its species from its form. When, therefore, two things are opposite members of a division, one cannot be the form of the other. Now faith and charity are stated to be opposite members of a division, as different species of virtue (I Cor. xiii. 13). Therefore charity is not the form of faith.

Obj. 2. Further, A form and the thing of which it is the form are in one subject, since together they form one simply. Now faith is in the intellect, while charity is in the will. Therefore charity is not the form of faith.

Obj. 3. Further, The form of a thing is a principle thereof. Now obedience, rather than charity, seems to be the principle of believing, on the part of the will, according to Rom. i. 5: *For obedience to the faith in all nations.* Therefore obedience rather than charity, is the form of faith.

On the contrary, Each thing works through its form. Now faith works through charity. Therefore the love of charity is the form of faith.

I answer that, As appears from what has been said above (I.-II., Q. I., A. 3: Q. XVIII., A. 6), voluntary acts take their species from their end which is the will's object. Now that which gives a thing its species, is after the manner of a form in natural things. Wherefore the form of any voluntary act is, in a manner, the end to which that act is directed, both because it takes its species therefrom, and because the mode of an action should correspond proportionately to the end. Now it is evident from what has been said (A. I), that the act of faith is directed to the object of the will, i.e. the good, as to its end: and this good which is the end of faith, viz. the Divine Good, is the proper object of charity. Therefore charity is called the form of faith, in so far as the act of faith is perfected and formed by charity.

Reply Obj. 1. Charity is called the form of faith because it quickens the act of faith. Now nothing hinders one act from being quickened by different habits, so as to be reduced to various species in a certain order, as stated above (I.-II., Q. XVIII., AA. 6, 7: Q. LXI., A. 2) when we were treating of human acts in general.

Reply Obj. 2. This objection is true of an intrinsic form. But it is not thus that charity is the form of faith, but in the sense that it *quickens the act of faith,* as explained above.

Reply Obj. 3. Even obedience, and hope likewise, and whatever other virtue might precede the act of faith, is quickened by charity, as we shall show further on (Q. XXIII., A. 8), and consequently charity is spoken of as the form of faith. . . .

Fifth Article. Whether Faith Is a Virtue?

We proceed thus to the Fifth Article:—

Objection 1. It seems that faith is not a virtue. For virtue is directed to the good, since *it is virtue that makes its subject good,* as the Philosopher states (*Ethic.* ii.). But faith is directed to the true. Therefore faith is not a virtue.

Obj. 2. Further, Infused virtue is more perfect than acquired virtue. Now faith, on account of its imperfection, is not placed among the acquired intellectual virtues, as the Philosopher states (*Ethic.* vi.). Much less, therefore, can it be considered an infused virtue.

Obj. 3. Further, Living and lifeless faith are of the same species, as stated above (A. 4). Now lifeless faith is not a virtue, since it is not connected with the other virtues. Therefore neither is living faith a virtue.

Obj. 4. Further, The gratuitous graces and the fruits are distinct from the virtues. But faith is numbered among the gratuitous graces (I Cor. xii. 9) and likewise among the fruits (Gal. v. 23). Therefore faith is not a virtue.

On the contrary, Man is justified by the virtues, since *justice is all virtue* as the Philosopher states (*Ethic.* v.). Now man is justified by faith according to Rom. v. I: *Being justified therefore by faith let us have peace,* etc. Therefore faith is a virtue.

I answer that, As shown above, it is by human virtue that human acts are rendered good; hence, any habit that is always the principle of a good act, may be called a human virtue. Such a habit is living faith. For since to believe is an act of the intellect assenting to the truth at the command of the will, two things are required that this act may be perfect: one of which is that the intellect should infallibly tend to its object, which is the true; while the other is that the will should be infallibly directed to the last end, on account of which it assents to the true: and both of these are to be found in the act of living faith. For it belongs to the very essence of faith that the intellect should ever tend to the true, since nothing false can be the object of faith, as proved above (Q. I., A. 3): while the effect of charity, which is the form of faith, is that the soul ever has its will directed to a good end. Therefore living faith is a virtue.

On the other hand, lifeless faith is not a virtue, because, though the act of lifeless faith is duly perfect on the part of the intellect, it has not its due perfection as regards the will: just as if temperance be in the concupiscible, without prudence being in the rational part, temperance is not a virtue, as stated above (I.-II., Q. LXV., A. 1), because the act of temperance requires both an act of reason, and an act of the concupiscible faculty, even as the act of faith requires an act of the will, and an act of the intellect.

Reply Obj. 1. The truth is itself the good of the intellect, since it is its perfection: and consequently faith has a relation to some good in so far as it directs the intellect to the true. Furthermore, it has a relation to the good considered as the object of the will, inasmuch as it is formed by charity.

Reply Obj. 2. The faith of which the Philosopher speaks is based on human reasoning in a conclusion which does not follow, of necessity, from its premises; and which is subject to be false: hence suchlike faith is not a virtue. On the other hand, the faith of which we are speaking is based on the Divine Truth, which is infallible, and consequently its object cannot be anything false; so that faith of this kind can be a virtue.

Reply Obj. 3. Living and lifeless faith do not differ specifically, as though they belonged to different species. But they differ as perfect and imperfect within the same species. Hence lifeless faith, being imperfect, does not satisfy the conditions of a perfect virtue, for virtue is a kind of perfection (*Phys.* vii.).

Reply Obj. 4. Some say that faith which is numbered among the gratuitous graces is lifeless faith. But this is said without reason, since the gratuitous graces, which are mentioned in that passage, are not common to all the members of the Church: wherefore the Apostle says: *There are diversities of graces,* and again: *To one is given* this grace and *to another* that. Now lifeless faith is common to all the members of the Church, because its lifelessness is not part of its substance, if we consider it as a gratuitous gift. We must, therefore, say that in that passage, faith denotes a certain excellency of faith, for instance, *constancy in faith,* according to a gloss, or the *word of faith.*

Faith is numbered among the fruits, in so far as it gives a certain pleasure in its act by reason of its certainty, wherefore the gloss on the fifth chapter to the Galatians, where the fruits are enumerated, explains faith as being *certainty about the unseen.* . . .

Second Article. Whether in the Demons There Is Faith?

We proceed thus to the Second Article:—

Objection 1. It seems that the demons have no faith. For Augustine says (*De Pradest. Sanct.* v.) that *faith depends on the believer's will:* and this is a good will, since by it man wishes to believe in God. Since then no deliberate will of the demons is good, as stated above (P. I., Q. LXIV., A. 2, *ad* 5), it seems that in the demons there is no faith.

Obj. 2. Further, Faith is a gift of Divine grace, according to Eph. ii. 8: *By grace you are saved through faith, . . . for it is the gift of God.* Now, according to a gloss on Osee iii. 1, *They look to strange gods, and love the husks of the grapes,* the demons lost their gifts of grace by sinning. Therefore faith did not remain in the demons after they sinned.

Obj. 3. Further, Unbelief would seem to be graver than other sins, as Augustine observes (*Tract.* lxxxix. *super Joan.*) on John xv. 22, *If I had not come and spoken to them, they would not have sin: but now they have no excuse for their sin.* Now the sin of unbelief is in some men. Consequently, if the demons have faith, some men would be guilty of a sin graver than that of the demons, which seems unreasonable. Therefore in the demons there is no faith.

On the contrary, It is written (James ii. 19): *The devils . . . believe and tremble.*

I answer that, As stated above (Q. I., A. 4: Q. II., A. 1), the believer's intellect assents to that which he believes, not because he sees it either in itself, or by resolving it to first self-evident principles, but because his will commands his intellect to assent. Now, that the will moves the intellect to assent, may be due to two causes. First, through the will being directed to the good, and in this way, to believe is a praiseworthy action. Secondly, because the intellect is convinced that it ought to believe what is said, though that conviction is not based on objective evidence. Thus if a prophet, while preaching the word of God, were to foretell something, and were to give a sign, by raising a dead person to life, the intellect of a witness would be convinced so as to recognize clearly that God, Who lieth not, was speaking, although the thing itself foretold would not be evident in itself, and consequently the essence of faith would not be removed.

Accordingly we must say that faith is commended in the first sense in the faithful of Christ: and in this way faith is not in the demons, but only in the second way, for they see many evident signs, whereby they recognize that the teaching of the Church is from God, although they do not see the things themselves that the Church teaches, for instance that there are three Persons in God, and so forth.

Reply Obj. 1. The demons are, in a way, compelled to believe, by the evidence of signs, and so their will deserves no praise for their belief.

Reply Obj. 2. Faith, which is a gift of grace, inclines man to believe, by giving him a certain affection for the good, even when that faith is lifeless. Consequently the faith which the demons have, is not a gift of grace. Rather are they compelled to believe through their natural intellectual acumen.

Reply Obj. 3. The very fact that the signs of faith are so evident, that the demons are compelled to believe, is displeasing to them, so that their malice is by no means diminished by their belief.

12. Of God and His Creatures

St. Thomas Aquinas

First Book: Chapter I

In What Consists the Office of a Wise Man

My mouth shall meditate truth, and my lips shall hate wickedness.—Prov. viii. 7.

The general use which, in the Philosopher's opinion, should be followed in naming things, has resulted in those men being called *wise* who direct things themselves and govern them well. Wherefore among other things which men conceive of the wise man, the Philosopher reckons that *it belongs to the wise man to direct things.* Now the rule of all things directed to the end of government and order must needs be taken from their end: for then is a thing best disposed when it is fittingly directed to its end, since the end of everything is its good. Wherefore in the arts we observe that the art which governs and rules another is the one to which the latter's end belongs: thus the medical art rules and directs the art of the druggist, because health which is the object of medicine is the end of all drugs which are made up by the druggist's art. The same may be observed in the art of sailing in relation to the art of ship-building, and in the military art in relation to the equestrian art and all warlike appliances. These arts which govern others are called *master-arts* (*architectonicæ*), that is *principal arts*, for which reason their craftsmen, who are called *master-craftsmen* (*architectores*), are awarded the name of wise men. Since, however, these same craftsmen, through being occupied with the ends of certain singular things, do not attain to the universal end of all things, they are called wise about this or that, in which sense it is said (1 Cor. iii. 10): *As a wise architect, I have laid the foundation;* whereas the name of being wise simply is reserved to him alone whose consideration is about the end of the universe, which end is also the beginning of the universe: wherefore, according to the Philosopher, it belongs to the wise man to consider the *highest causes.*

Source: From St. Thomas Aquinas, *Summa Contra Gentiles*, Translated (with some abridgements) by Joseph Rickaby, London: Burns & Oates, 1905. (Footnotes omitted.)

Now the last end of each thing is that which is intended by the first author or mover of that thing: and the first author and mover of the universe is an intellect, as we shall prove further on. Consequently the last end of the universe must be the good of the intellect: and this is truth. Therefore truth must be the last end of the whole universe; and the consideration thereof must be the chief occupation of wisdom. And for this reason divine Wisdom, clothed in flesh, declares that He came into the world to make known the truth, saying (Jo. xviii. 37): *For this was I born, and for this cause came I into the world, that I should give testimony to the truth.* Moreover the Philosopher defines the First Philosophy as being the *knowledge of truth,* not of any truth, but of that truth which is the source of all truth, of that, namely, which relates to the first principle of being of all things; wherefore its truth is the principle of all truth, since the disposition of things is the same in truth as in being.

Now it belongs to the same thing to pursue one contrary and to remove the other: thus medicine which effects health, removes sickness. Hence, just as it belongs to a wise man to meditate and disseminate truth, especially about the first principle, so does it belong to him to refute contrary falsehood.

Wherefore the twofold office of the wise man is fittingly declared from the mouth of Wisdom, in the words above quoted; namely, to meditate and publish the divine truth, which antonomastically is *the* truth, as signified by the words, *My mouth shall meditate truth;* and to refute the error contrary to truth, as signified by the words, *and my lips shall hate wickedness,* by which is denoted falsehood opposed to divine truth, which falsehood is contrary to religion that is also called *godliness,* wherefore the falsehood that is contrary thereto receives the name of *ungodliness.*

Chapter II

The Author's Intention in This Work

Now of all human pursuits, that of wisdom is the most perfect, the most sublime, the most profitable, the most delightful. It is the most perfect, since in proportion as a man devotes himself to the pursuit of wisdom, so much does he already share in true happiness: wherefore the wise man says (Ecclus. xiv. 22): *Blessed is the man that shall continue in wisdom.* It is the most sublime because thereby especially does man approach to a likeness to God, Who *made all things in wisdom:* wherefore since likeness is the cause of love, the pursuit of wisdom especially unites man to God by friendship: hence it is said (Wis. vii. 14) that *wisdom is an infinite treasure to men: which they that use, become the friends of God.* It is the most profitable, because by wisdom itself man is brought to the kingdom of immortality, for *the desire of wisdom bringeth to the everlasting kingdom* (Wis. vi. 21). And it is the most delightful because *her conversation hath no bitterness, nor her company any tediousness, but joy and gladness* (Wis. viii. 16).

Wherefore, taking heart from God's lovingkindness to assume the office of a wise man, although it surpasses our own powers, the purpose we have in view is, in our own weak way, to declare the truth which the Catholic faith professes, while weeding out contrary errors; for, in the words of Hilary, *I acknowledge that I owe my life's chief occupation to God, so that every word and every thought of mine may speak of Him.* But it is difficult to refute the errors of each individual, for two reasons. First, because the sacrilegious assertions of each erring individual are not so well known to us, that we are able from what they say to find arguments to refute their errors. For the Doctors of old used this method in order to confute the errors of the heathens, whose opinions they were able to know, since either they had been heathens themselves, or had lived among heathens and were conversant with their teachings. Secondly, because some of them, like the Mohammedans and pagans, do not agree with us as to the authority of any Scripture whereby they may be convinced, in the same way as we are able to dispute with the Jews by means of the Old Testament, and with heretics by means of the New: whereas the former accept neither. Wherefore it is necessary to have recourse to natural reason, to which all are compelled to assent. And yet this is deficient in the things of God.

And while we are occupied in the inquiry about a particular truth, we shall show what errors are excluded thereby, and how demonstrable truth is in agreement with the faith of the Christian religion.

Chapter III

In What Way It Is Possible to Make Known the Divine Truth

Since, however, not every truth is to be made known in the same way, *and it is the part of an educated man to seek for conviction in each subject, only so far as the nature of the subject allows,* as the Philosopher most rightly observes as quoted by Boethius, it is necessary to show first of all in what way it is possible to make known the aforesaid truth.

Now in those things which we hold about God there is truth in two ways. For certain things that are true about God wholly surpass the capability of human reason, for instance that God is three and one: while there are certain things to which even natural reason can attain, for instance that God is, that God is one, and others like these, which even the philosophers proved demonstratively of God, being guided by the light of natural reason.

That certain divine truths wholly surpass the capability of human reason, is most clearly evident. For since the principle of all the knowledge which the reason acquires about a thing, is the understanding of that thing's essence, because according to the Philosopher's teaching the principle of a demonstration is *what a thing is,* it follows that our knowledge about a thing will be in proportion to our understanding of its essence. Wherefore, if the human intellect comprehends the essence of a particular thing, for instance a stone or a triangle, no truth about that thing will surpass the capability of human reason. But this does not happen to us in relation to God, because the human intellect is incapable by its natural power of attaining to the comprehension of His essence: since our intellect's knowledge, according to the mode of the present life, originates from the senses: so that things which are not objects of sense cannot be comprehended by the human intellect, except in so far as knowledge of them is gathered from sensibles. Now sensibles cannot lead our intellect to see in them what God is, because they are effects unequal to the power of their cause. And yet our intellect is led by sensibles to the divine knowledge so as to know about God that He is, and other such truths, which need to be ascribed to the first principle. Accordingly some divine truths are attainable by human reason, while others altogether surpass the power of human reason.

Again. The same is easy to see from the degrees of intellects. For if one of two men perceives a thing with his intellect with greater subtlety, the one whose intellect is of a higher degree understands many things which the other is altogether unable to grasp; as instanced in a yokel who is utterly incapable of grasping the subtleties of philosophy. Now the angelic intellect surpasses the human intellect more than the intellect of the cleverest philosopher surpasses that of the most uncultured. For an angel knows God through a more excellent effect than does man, for as much as the angel's essence, through which he is led to know God by natural knowledge, is more excellent than sensible things, even than the soul itself, by which the human intellect mounts to the knowledge of God. And the divine intellect surpasses the angelic intellect much more than the angelic surpasses the human. For the divine intellect by its capacity equals the divine essence, wherefore God perfectly understands of Himself what He is, and He knows all things that can be understood about Him: whereas the angel knows not what God is by his natural knowledge, because the angel's essence, by which he is led to the knowledge of God, is an effect unequal to the power of its cause. Consequently an angel is unable by his natural knowledge to grasp all that God understands about Himself: nor again is human reason capable of grasping all that an angel understands by his natural power. Accordingly just as a man would show himself to be a most insane fool if he declared the assertions of a philosopher to be false because he was unable to understand them, so, and much more, a man would be exceedingly foolish, were he to suspect of falsehood the things revealed by God through the ministry of His angels, because they cannot be the object of reason's investigations.

Furthermore. The same is made abundantly clear by the deficiency which every day we experience in our knowledge of things. For we are ignorant of many of the properties of sensible things, and in many cases we are unable to discover the nature of those properties which we perceive by our senses. Much less therefore is human reason capable of investigating all the truths about that most sublime essence.

With this the saying of the Philosopher is in accord (2 *Metaph.*) where he says that *our intellect in relation to those primary things which are most evident in nature is like the eye of a bat in relation to the sun.*

To this truth Holy Writ also bears witness. For it is written (Job xi. 7): *Peradventure thou wilt comprehend the steps of God and wilt find out the Almighty perfectly?* and (xxxvi. 26): *Behold God is great, exceeding our knowledge,* and (1 Cor. xiii. 9): *We know in part.*

Therefore all that is said about God, though it cannot be investigated by reason, must not be forthwith rejected as false, as the Manicheans and many unbelievers have thought.

Chapter IV

That The Truth About Divine Things Which Is Attainable By Reason Is Fittingly Proposed To Man As An Object Of Belief

While then the truth of the intelligible things of God is twofold, one to which the inquiry of reason can attain, the other which surpasses the whole range of human reason, both are fittingly proposed by God to man as an object of belief. We must first show this with regard to that truth which is attainable by the inquiry of reason, lest it appears to some, that since it can be attained by reason, it was useless to make it an object of faith by supernatural inspiration. Now three disadvantages would result if this truth were left solely to the inquiry of reason. One is that few men would have knowledge of God: because very many are hindered from gathering the fruit of diligent inquiry, which is the discovery of truth, for three reasons. Some indeed on account of an indisposition of temperament, by reason of which many are naturally indisposed to knowledge: so that no efforts of theirs would enable them to reach to the attainment of the highest degree of human knowledge, which consists in knowing God. Some are hindered by the needs of household affairs. For there must needs be among men some that devote themselves to the conduct of temporal affairs, who would be unable to devote so much time to the leisure of contemplative research as to reach the summit of human inquiry, namely the knowledge of God. And some are hindered by laziness. For in order to acquire the knowledge of God in those things which reason is able to investigate, it is necessary to have a previous knowledge of many things: since almost the entire consideration of philosophy is directed to the knowledge of God: for which reason metaphysics, which is about divine things, is the last of the parts of philosophy to be studied. Wherefore it is not possible to arrive at the inquiry about the aforesaid truth except after a most laborious study: and few are willing to take upon themselves this labour for the love of a knowledge, the natural desire for which has nevertheless been instilled into the mind of man by God.

The second disadvantage is that those who would arrive at the discovery of the aforesaid truth would scarcely succeed in doing so after a long time. First, because this truth is so profound, that it is only after long practice that the human intellect is enabled to grasp it by means of reason. Secondly, because many things are required beforehand, as stated above. Thirdly, because at the time of youth, the mind, when tossed about by the various movements of the passions, is not fit for the knowledge of so sublime a truth, whereas *calm gives prudence and knowledge,* as stated in *7 Phys.* Hence mankind would remain in the deepest darkness of ignorance, if the path of reason were the only available way to the knowledge of God: because the knowledge of God which especially makes men perfect and good, would be acquired only by the few, and by these only after a long time.

The third disadvantage is that much falsehood is mingled with the investigations of human reason, on account of the weakness of our intellect in forming its judgments, and by reason of the admixture of phantasms. Consequently many would remain in doubt about those things even which are most truly demonstrated, through ignoring the force of the demonstration: especially when they perceive that different things are taught by the various men who are called wise. Moreover among the many demonstrated truths, there is sometimes a mixture of falsehood that is not demonstrated, but assumed for some probable or sophistical reason which at times is mistaken for a demonstration. Therefore it was necessary that definite certainty and pure truth about divine things should be offered to man by the way of faith.

Accordingly the divine clemency has made this salutary commandment, that even some things which reason is able to investigate must be held by faith: so that all may share in the knowledge of God easily, and without doubt or error.

Hence it is written (Eph. iv. 17, 18): That *henceforward you walk not as also the Gentiles walk in the vanity of their mind, having their understanding darkened:* and (Isa. liv. 13): *All thy children shall be taught of the Lord.*

Chapter V

That Those Things Which Cannot Be Investigated by Reason Are Fittingly Proposed to Man as an Object of Faith

It may appear to some that those things which cannot be investigated by reason ought not to be proposed to man as an object of faith: because divine wisdom provides for each thing according to the mode of its nature. We must therefore prove that it is necessary also for those things which surpass reason to be proposed by God to man as an object of faith.

For no man tends to do a thing by his desire and endeavour unless it be previously known to him. Wherefore since man is directed by divine providence to a higher good than human frailty can attain in the present life, as we shall show in the sequel, it was necessary for his mind to be bidden to something higher than those things to which our reason can reach in the present life, so that he might learn to aspire, and by his endeavours to tend to something surpassing the whole state of the present life. And this is especially competent to the Christian religion, which alone promises goods spiritual and eternal: for which reason it proposes many things surpassing the thought of man: whereas the old law which contained promises of temporal things, proposed few things that are above human inquiry. It was with this motive that the philosophers, in order to wean men from sensible pleasures to virtue, took care to show that there are other goods of greater account than those which appeal to the senses, the taste of which things affords much greater delight to those who devote themselves to active or contemplative virtues.

Again it is necessary for this truth to be proposed to man as an object of faith in order that he may have truer knowledge of God. For then alone do we know God truly, when we believe that He is far above all that man can possibly think of God, because the divine essence surpasses man's natural knowledge, as stated above. Hence by the fact that certain things about God are proposed to man, which surpass his reason, he is strengthened in his opinion that God is far above what he is able to think.

There results also another advantage from this, namely, the checking of presumption which is the mother of error. For some there are who presume so far on their wits that they think themselves capable of measuring the whole nature of things by their intellect, in that they esteem all things true which they see, and false which they see not.

Accordingly, in order that man's mind might be freed from this presumption, and seek the truth humbly, it was necessary that certain things far surpassing his intellect should be proposed to man by God.

Yet another advantage is made apparent by the words of the Philosopher (10 *Ethic.*). For when a certain Simonides maintained that man should neglect the knowledge of God, and apply his mind to human affairs, and declared that *a man ought to relish human things, and a mortal, mortal things:* the Philosopher contradicted him, saying that a *man ought to devote himself to immortal and divine things as much as he can.* Hence he says (11 *De Animal.*) that though it is but little that we perceive of higher substances, yet that little is more loved and desired than all the knowledge we have of lower substances. He says also (2 *De Cælo et Mundo*) that when questions about the heavenly bodies can be answered by a short and probable solution, it happens that the hearer is very much rejoiced. All this shows that however imperfect the knowledge of the highest things may be, it bestows very great perfection on the soul: and consequently, although human reason is unable to grasp fully things that are above reason, it nevertheless acquires much perfection, if at least it hold things, in any way whatever, by faith.

Wherefore it is written (Ecclus. iii. 25): *Many things are shown to thee above the understanding of men,* and (1 Cor. ii. 10, 11): *The things . . . that are of God no man knoweth, but the Spirit of God: but to us God hath revealed them by His Spirit.*

Chapter VI

That It Is Not a Mark of Levity to Assent to the Things That Are of Faith, Although They Are Above Reason

Now those who believe this truth, of *which reason affords a proof,* believe not lightly, as though *following foolish fables* (2 Pet. i. 16). For divine Wisdom Himself, Who knows all things most fully, deigned to reveal to man *the secrets of God's wisdom:* and by suitable arguments proves His presence, and the truth of His doctrine and inspiration, by performing works surpassing the capability of the whole of nature, namely, the wondrous healing of the sick, the raising of the dead to life, a marvellous control over the heavenly bodies, and what excites yet more wonder, the inspiration of human minds, so that unlettered and simple persons are filled with the Holy Ghost, and in one instant are endowed with the most sublime wisdom and eloquence. And after considering these arguments, convinced by the strength of the proof, and not by the force of arms, nor by the promise of delights, but—and this is the greatest marvel of all—amidst the tyranny of persecutions, a countless crowd of not only simple but also of the wisest men, embraced the Christian faith, which inculcates things surpassing all human understanding, curbs the pleasures of the flesh, and teaches contempt of all worldly things. That the minds of mortal beings should assent to such things, is both the greatest of miracles, and the evident work of divine inspiration, seeing that they despise visible things and desire only those that are invisible. And that this happened not suddenly nor by chance, but by the disposition of God, is shown by the fact that God foretold that He would do so by the manifold oracles of the prophets, whose books we hold in veneration as bearing witness to our faith. This particular kind of proof is alluded to in the words of Heb. ii. 3, 4: *Which*, namely the salvation of mankind, *having begun to be declared by the Lord, was confirmed with us by them that heard Him, God also bearing witness by signs and wonders, and divers . . . distributions of the Holy Ghost.*

Now such a wondrous conversion of the world to the Christian faith is a most indubitable proof that such signs did take place, so that there is no need to repeat them, seeing that there is evidence of them in their result. For it would be the most wondrous sign of all if without any wondrous signs the world were persuaded by simple and lowly men to believe things so arduous, to accomplish things so difficult, and to hope for things so sublime. Although God ceases not even in our time to work miracles through His saints in confirmation of the faith.

On the other hand those who introduced the errors of the sects proceeded in contrary fashion, as instanced by Mohammed, who enticed peoples with the promise of carnal pleasures, to the desire of which the concupiscence of the flesh instigates. He also delivered commandments in keeping with his promises, by giving the reins to carnal pleasure, wherein it is easy for carnal men to obey: and the lessons of truth which he inculcated were only such as can be easily known to any man of average wisdom by his natural powers: yea rather the truths which he taught were mingled by him with many fables and most false doctrines. Nor did he add any signs of supernatural agency, which alone are a fitting witness to divine inspiration, since a visible work that can be from God alone, proves the teacher of truth to be invisibly inspired: but he asserted that he was sent in the power of arms, a sign that is not lacking even to robbers and tyrants. Again, those who believed in him from the outset were not wise men practised in things divine and human, but beast-like men who dwelt in the wilds, utterly ignorant of all divine teaching; and it was by a multitude of such men and the force of arms that he compelled others to submit to his law.

Lastly, no divine oracles of prophets in a previous age bore witness to him; rather did he corrupt almost all the teaching of the Old and New Testaments by a narrative replete with fables, as one may see by a perusal of his law. Hence by a cunning device, he did not commit the reading of the Old and New Testament Books to his followers, lest he should thereby be convicted of falsehood. Thus it is evident that those who believe his words believe lightly.

Chapter VII

That the Truth of Reason Is Not in Opposition to the Truth of the Christian Faith

Now though the aforesaid truth of the Christian faith surpasses the ability of human reason, nevertheless those things which are naturally instilled in human reason cannot be opposed to this truth. For it is clear that those things which are implanted in reason by nature, are most true, so much so that it is impossible to think them to be false. Nor is it lawful to deem false that which is held by faith, since it is so evidently confirmed by God. Seeing then that the false alone is opposed to the true, as evidently appears if we examine their definitions, it is impossible for the aforesaid truth of faith to be contrary to those principles which reason knows naturally.

Again. The same thing which the disciple's mind receives from its teacher is contained in the knowledge of the teacher, unless he teach insincerely, which it were wicked to say of God. Now the knowledge of naturally known principles is instilled into us by God, since God Himself is the author of our nature. Therefore the divine Wisdom also contains these principles. Consequently whatever is contrary to these principles, is contrary to the divine Wisdom; wherefore it cannot be from God. Therefore those things which are received by faith from divine revelation cannot be contrary to our natural knowledge.

Moreover. Our intellect is stayed by contrary arguments, so that it cannot advance to the knowledge of truth. Wherefore if conflicting knowledges were instilled into us by God, our intellect would thereby be hindered from knowing the truth. And this cannot be ascribed to God.

Furthermore. Things that are natural are unchangeable so long as nature remains. Now contrary opinions cannot be together in the same subject. Therefore God does not instil into man any opinion or belief contrary to natural knowledge.

Hence the Apostle says (Rom. x. 8): *The word is nigh thee even in thy heart and in thy mouth. This is the word of faith which we preach.* Yet because it surpasses reason some look upon it as though it were contrary thereto; which is impossible.

This is confirmed also by the authority of Augustine who says (*Gen. ad lit.* ii): *That which truth shall make known can nowise be in opposition to the holy books whether of the Old or of the New Testament.*

From this we may evidently conclude that whatever arguments are alleged against the teachings of faith, they do not rightly proceed from the first self-evident principles instilled by nature. Wherefore they lack the force of demonstration, and are either probable or sophistical arguments, and consequently it is possible to solve them.

Chapter VIII

In What Relation Human Reason Stands to the Truth of Faith

It would also seem well to observe that sensible things from which human reason derives the source of its knowledge, retain a certain trace of likeness to God, but so imperfect that it proves altogether inadequate to manifest the substance itself of God. For effects resemble their causes according to their own mode, since like action proceeds from like agent; and yet the effect does not always reach to a perfect likeness to the agent. Accordingly human reason is adapted to the knowledge of the truth of faith, which can be known in the highest degree only by those who see the divine substance, in so far as it is able to put together certain probable arguments in support thereof, which nevertheless are insufficient to enable us to understand the aforesaid truth as though it were demonstrated to us or understood by us in itself. And yet however weak these arguments may be, it is useful for the human mind to be practised therein, so long as it does not pride itself on having comprehended or demonstrated: since although our view of the sublimest things is limited and weak, it is most pleasant to be able to catch but a glimpse of them, as appears from what has been said.

The authority of Hilary is in agreement with this statement: for he says (*De Trin.*) while speaking of this same truth: *Begin by believing these things, advance and persevere; and though I know thou will not arrive, I shall rejoice at thy advance. For he who devoutly follows in pursuit of the infinite, though he never come up with it, will always advance by setting forth. Yet pry not into that secret, and meddle not in the mystery of the birth of the infinite, nor presume to grasp that which is the summit of understanding: but understand that there are things thou canst not grasp.*

13. The Thomist-Catholic View of Faith

John Hick

According to the most widespread view of the matter today faith is unevidenced or inadequately evidenced belief. To quote a typical definition, "The general sense is belief, perhaps based on some evidence, but very firm, or at least more firm, or/and of more extensive content, than the evidence possessed by the believer rationally warrants."[1] Faith thus consists in believing strongly various propositions, of a theological nature, which the believer does not and cannot *know* to be true. To know here is taken to mean either to observe directly or to be able to prove by strict demonstration. Where this is possible, there is no room for faith. It is only that which lies beyond the scope of human knowledge that must be taken, if at all, on faith or trust. When in such a case we do adopt some belief, the lack of rational compulsion to assent is compensated by an act of will, a voluntary leap of trust, so that the man of faith comes to believe something which he cannot prove or see.

This general view of the nature of faith, so far as it goes, would probably be accepted today by many both Catholic and Protestant Christians, as well as by the agnostic and atheist critics of Christianity. For it represents the dominant Western tradition of thought on the subject from the time it was established by St. Thomas Aquinas in

Source: John Hick, *Faith and Knowledge* (Ithaca, NY: Cornell University Press, 1957), pages 11–31. Reprinted with the permission of the author.

the thirteenth century. It is, accordingly, to Aquinas that we must turn if we are to go to the roots of this tradition.

Aquinas discusses faith in all its aspects in his *Summa Theologica,* the second part of the second part, Questions 1–7.[2] His conclusions can be presented under three main headings.

1. First, faith is a propositional attitude: that is to say, it consists in assenting to propositions. This is unambiguously stated, and its implications unambiguously accepted, both by Aquinas and throughout the Catholic tradition that has followed him. Aquinas explains that since "the thing known is in the knower according to the mode of the knower" and "the mode proper to the human intellect is to know the truth by composition and division,"[3] man's knowledge of God takes the form of knowing propositions about him, though God himself is of course not a proposition but the supreme Being. There is thus a sense in which the ultimate object of faith is the living God—that is, the propositions which are believed by faith are propositions about him. But the immediate objects of faith are these propositions themselves, and our cognitive relation to God consists in our believing them. Faith, says Aquinas, occupies a position between knowledge (*scientia*) and opinion (*opinio*) and accordingly falls on a common scale with them; and since they are both concerned with propositions, so also is faith. The particular propositions which are the objects of Christian faith are the articles, or distinguishable segments, or Christian truth[4] which are authoritatively summarized in the Church's creeds.[5] Faith, then, for Aquinas, in practice means believing the articles of the creeds. It is necessary for salvation to believe explicitly such central articles as the Incarnation and the Trinity, but apart from these it is sufficient, especially in the case of the unlearned, to believe implicitly, that is, to be ready to believe the articles of the faith if and when they are explicitly presented to one's understanding.

At every point, then, faith is concerned with propositions. This is made clear once again in the definition promulgated by the First Vatican Council (1869–1870) as follows: faith "is a supernatural virtue by which we, with the aid and inspiration of the grace of God, believe that the things revealed by Him are true, not because the intrinsic truth of the revealed things has been perceived by the natural light of reason, but because of the authority of God Himself who reveals them, who can neither deceive nor be deceived."[6] And the object of faith is defined as "all those things . . . which are contained in the written word of God and in tradition, and those which are proposed by the Church, either in a solemn pronouncement or in her ordinary and universal teaching power, to be believed as divinely revealed."[7]

2. Second, the propositions which faith believes, or at any rate those that are of faith absolutely, i.e., that can be accepted only on faith, are of a special kind. They express "mysteries"; that is to say, they are propositions whose truth can never (in this life) be directly evident to us, and which therefore have to be accepted on authority. These Christian mysteries are such that the human mind could never discover them for itself, and such that the mind, having come to possess them, cannot fully penetrate and comprehend them. Chief examples of the Christian mysteries are the unity of deity and humanity in the person of Christ, and the nature of God as three in one and one in three.

It follows from this that faith is to be distinguished from knowledge or *scientia*. By *scientia* Aquinas means the direct and indubitable knowledge that we have when we

"see" self-evident truths or when we attain to further truths by strict logical demonstration. In *scientia* the truth compels assent either by self-evidence or by the force of the
demonstration that has led the mind to it: we cannot help—in so far as we are rational—believing that which is to us either self-evident or proved by strict logic. Faith,
however, differs from *scientia* in that the object of faith does not compel assent. For,
since the propositions that are believed by faith are mysteries, we cannot directly see or
prove their truth. Aquinas says, "Now the intellect assents to a thing in two ways. First,
through being moved to assent by its very object, which is known either by itself . . . or
through something else already known. [This is *scientia*.] . . . Secondly, the intellect assents to something, not through being sufficiently moved to this assent by its proper
object, but through an act of choice, whereby it turns voluntarily to one side rather
than to the other."[8] This is faith, which is thus characterized as "an act of the intellect
assenting to the truth at the command of the will."[9]

It is accordingly in the nature of the case impossible to have knowledge and faith
simultaneously in relation to the same object; knowledge is intellectual vision, whilst
faith is firm and undoubting belief concerning that which is not (at any rate in this life)
directly knowable. It is of course in some cases possible for two different people to have
knowledge and faith respectively in relation to the same object; for it may happen that
"what is an object of vision or scientific knowledge (*scitum*) for one man, even in the
state of a wayfarer, is, for another man, an object of faith, because he does not know it
by demonstration."[10] But "in one and the same man, about the same object, and in the
same respect, *scientia* is incompatible with either opinion or faith."[11]

As well as being distinguished from knowledge, faith is also to be distinguished
from opinion (*opinio*). Opinion, like faith, is an assent which is not compelled by its
object but produced by an act of choice; but it differs from faith in that if the choice
"be accompanied by doubt and fear of the opposite side, there will be opinion; while, if
there be certainty and no fear of the other side, there will be faith."[12] Faith thus involves an act of commitment which sets aside the uncertainty that would otherwise be
present in face of propositions which are not able by themselves to compel assent. Belief "cleaves firmly to one side,"[13] whereas in opinion there always remains a certain admixture of active or latent doubt.

Thus faith is distinguished from *scientia* by a difference between their objects: the
object of *scientia* is such as to compel the assent of the human mind, whilst the object
of faith is not.[14] And faith is distinguished from opinion by the subjective or psychological difference that opinion is and faith is not accompanied by an inner feeling of
doubt or uncertainty.

3. The third main aspect of Aquinas' doctrine of faith, its voluntary character, follows naturally; faith is belief which is not compellingly evoked by its object but which
requires an act of will on the believer's part. We must now ask the following questions:
What motivates this decision to believe? Is it an arbitrary and irrational "leap in the
dark"? Or are there reasons for it? According to the Thomist-Catholic tradition, there
are reasons. For faith, defined as belief in divinely authorized doctrines, presupposes the
previous knowledge both that there is a God and that he has authorized the doctrines
in question. This condition is acknowledged in Catholic theology, which provides "preambles to faith" designed to identify as divine the utterances which faith then

obediently accepts. The preambles begin with the scholastic proofs of God's existence, and then proceed along a well-defined path whose course is summarized by the Catholic theologian, M. C. D'Arcy as follows:

> It is easy to pass from these conclusions [of the existence and unity of God] to others, for instance that God might reveal further knowledge about Himself if He chose. The question, therefore, now is whether He has communicated such further knowledge to us. We find when we look at the history of the human race that man left to himself has made a bad muddle of religion, and that, nevertheless, he has always longed for some deeper and more intimate relation with and knowledge of God. This suggests that it is probable that God has come to the aid of mankind and taught the truth about His wishes for mankind and the way to realise them. We now turn to history, and in history we find that the founder of Christianity made the claim to be the messenger from God bringing a revelation of good news, and that the Catholic Church has unfailingly reiterated that claim. The next step is to examine that claim, since it is not impossible and is, indeed, even probable. An examination of it can end only in one conclusion, that it is made out. The historical evidence, the previous history of the Jewish people, the holiness and authority of Christ, which rule out the hypothesis that He could have been a dupe or deceiver, the miracles He worked, which are too closely bound up with the narrative of His teaching and character to be interpolations, the Resurrection, which has never successfully been gainsaid—all these facts can lead the reasonable inquirer to only one conclusion: Christ is the messenger of God or God. This once granted, the rest follows irresistibly.[15]

And so the conclusion is reached that the Roman hierarchy, culminating in the Pope, is the appointed guardian and teacher of the truths which God has imparted.

If we now ask more particularly whether these *preambula fidei* are held to be rationally compelling, so that anyone who examines them and who is not prejudiced against the truth must acknowledge them, or whether, on the contrary, some degree of faith enters into their acceptance, no satisfactorily unambiguous answer is forth-coming.

On the one hand it is held, in agreement with non-Catholic critics and commentators, that the preambles to faith must make out their case before the court of human reason. This was pointed out, for example, by the Protestant John Locke. He defines faith, in agreement with the scholastic tradition, as "the assent to any proposition, not . . . made out by the deductions of reason, but upon the credit of the proposer, as coming from God in some extraordinary way of communication."[16] He then points out that, within the terms of this definition, our reason must establish that a particular proposition has in fact come from God before our faith can have anything to exercise itself upon, and that therefore the certainty attaching to faith can never exceed that of the reasoning which preceded it: "though faith be founded on the testimony of God (who cannot lie) revealing any proposition to us, yet we cannot have an assurance of the truth of its being a divine revelation greater than our own rationally acquired knowledge; since the whole strength of the certainty depends upon our knowledge that God revealed it."[17] This idea is not resisted, but is on the contrary emphasized by many Catholic writers. For example Canon George D. Smith, writing on "Faith and Revealed Truth" in the composite work *The Teaching of the Catholic Church*, describes the evidence of miracles as "peremptory," and says:

> The human mind, then, is able to learn with certainty the existence of God; is able, by the proper investigation of the facts, to conclude that Christ is the bearer of a divine message, that he founded an infallible Church for the purpose of propagating that message; and fi-

nally, by the process indicated in apologetics, to conclude that the Catholic Church is that divinely appointed teacher of revelation. These things, I say, can be known and proved, and by those who have the requisite leisure, opportunity and ability, are actually known and proved with all the scientific certainty of which the subject is patient. The preambles of faith, therefore, rest upon the solid ground of human reason.[18]

Again, Aquinas, discussing the question whether the demons have faith (for "Even the demons believe—and shudder," James 2:19), says that they do, but that their faith is no credit to them since it is extorted by the evidence. "The demons are, in a way, compelled to believe by the evidence of signs, and so their will deserves no praise for their belief. . . . Rather are they compelled to believe by their natural intellectual acumen." Indeed, "The very fact that the signs of faith are so evident, that the demons are compelled to believe, is displeasing to them."[19] These statements seem to imply that there are coercive historical reasons for believing that the Church's message has the status of divine revelation.

On the other hand in his main discussion of the nature of faith Aquinas teaches that faith is a virtue precisely because it is *not* compelled. We have already noted his stress upon the part played by the will in the genesis of faith. Faith is belief which is not coercively evoked by intrinsic evidence but which is produced by a voluntary adhesion to divine revelation. The *preambula fidei* constitute reasons providing a motive for faith, but these reasons are not so compelling as to undermine the believer's freedom, and therefore merit, in believing. "The believer has sufficient motive for believing, for he is moved by the authority of divine teaching confirmed by miracles, and, what is more, by the inward instigation of the divine invitation; and so he does not believe lightly. He has not, however, sufficient reason for scientific knowledge [*ad sciendum*] and hence he does not lose the merit."[20] The act of belief is thus sufficiently evidenced to be rational and yet not so over-whelmingly evidenced as to cease to be a free and meritorious act. It is indeed required by the structure of Aquinas' theology as a whole, in which faith has its place as one of the three theological virtues, that faith be recognized as involving a responsible act of the human will. This recognition, however, is not easily reconciled with the claim that the demons are compelled by the visible evidences, even against their will, to acknowledge the Christian mysteries as divine revelations.

Aquinas' only suggestion for harmonizing these two divergent exigencies of his theology occurs in connection with the same problem of demonic faith. He here distinguishes two motives for faith. "Now, that the will moves the intellect to assent may be due to two causes. First, by the fact that the will is ordered towards the good; and in this way, to believe is a praiseworthy action. Secondly, because the intellect is convinced that it ought to believe what is said, though that conviction is not based on the evidence in the thing said [but on external evidences]. . . . Accordingly, we must say that faith is commended in the first sense in the faithful of Christ. And in this way faith is not in the demons, but only in the second way, for they see many evident signs, whereby they recognize that the teaching of the Church is from God."[21] The two motives then are the implicit direction of the will or the personality toward the Good or God, which occurs as a gift of divine grace, and the compulsion of the evidence of miracles, prophecy, and so forth. But this distinction does not remove the contradiction which Aquinas has built into his doctrine. On the one hand, in discussing human faith he teaches that the historical evidence for the revelatory status of the Church's teaching does not compel assent, and that faith motivated by assent accordingly remains free and meritorious; but, on the other hand, in discussing demonic faith he teaches that this same evidence does compel assent even in minds which are wickedly resistant to it. The contradiction remains in full force.

Aquinas' dilemma is caused by the necessity under which he labors to account for the epistemological condition of the demons as beings who believe God's revelation by faith rather than by sight, but whose faith is not meritorious since they are unqualifiedly evil and condemned creatures. The only effective solution would seem to be to jettison the demons, in the hope that they are mythological, and thus set aside the epicycle of theory that was developed to accommodate their faith. If this were done we could regard Aquinas' discussion of human belief as representing his central contribution to the epistemology of faith. His teaching is, then, that Christian faith is a voluntary acceptance of the Church's doctrine, not because this can be directly seen by our intellects to be true, but because the historical evidence of prophecy and miracles leads (without coercing) a mind disposed toward goodness and truth to accept that teaching as being of divine origin.

Many will account it a virtue that the Thomist-Catholic position makes its primary appeal to human reason, turning to ecclesiastical authority only after this authority has been accredited by reason. The Church's claim to be believed is based upon historical evidences which are to be assessed by the exercise of reason. But this virtue carries with it the danger that the court to which the Church thus appeals, the court of human reason, may not return a favorable verdict. Indeed, if the jury is mankind at large, the situation is that Catholics are convinced of the Roman Church's credentials, whilst the rest of humanity is not. Further, the appeal to reason must in practice be an appeal to the reason of individuals. As such, however, it is in grave danger, from the Catholic point of view, of being in effect an appeal to individual private judgment.

A common reply to this suggestion is that although private judgment is necessary to enable us to recognize a divine revelation, the revelation once accepted is found to be intrinsically authoritative and self-guaranteeing. In Cardinal Newman's simile, the lamp of private judgment may be required to enable us to find our way; but once we have reached home we no longer have need of it. Newman's analogy, however, is misleading. Once a traveler has safely reached his destination, it does not matter by what route he has arrived: he does not suddenly dissolve into thin air if it is discovered that he has come by an unauthorized path. The validity of a reasoned conclusion, however, is not correspondingly independent of the "route" by which it has been reached. If the arguments which have led to a conclusion are found to be invalid, it is left unsupported and must either collapse or be established afresh upon another basis. Again, rational argument has been likened to a ladder by which we climb up to a position of faith, but which can then be dispensed with. But to reach a conclusion by reason and then to renounce the authority of reason would be more like cutting off the branch on which one is sitting. The steps of an argument are not like the steps of a ladder: they are more akin to the links of a chain from which something is suspended. And a chain of reasoning can be no stronger than its weakest link; probable arguments never suffice to establish a certain conclusion. Thus we can never properly be more certain of the truth of a revealed proposition than of the soundness of our reasons for classifying it as revealed. We cannot claim that the revelation once accepted is self-guaranteeing, for (as John Locke pointed out) its guarantee is valid only if it is indeed a genuine revelation, and whether this is so must first be decided by reason.[22]

We now have the Thomist-Catholic analysis of faith before us. To introduce labels which will draw attention to the three main aspects of it which we have noted, we will say that it is intellectualist, in that it regards faith as a propositional attitude; fideistic, in that it regards faith and knowledge as mutually exclusive; and voluntaristic, in that it sees faith as the product of a conscious act of will. These three elements have remained linked together in Catholic thought down to the present day. In recent writings from the more liberal wing of Catholic thought an impulse is indeed evident toward a less rigidly intellectualist view. There is apparent a desire to escape from the older image of faith as merely the acceptance of theological propositions, and to draw into the doctrine of faith the "I-Thou" encounter between God and man which has been so much stressed in modern Protestant theology, partly under the influence of the Jewish thinker, Martin Buber. Thus Eugène Joly in the volume on faith in the *Twentieth-Century Encyclopedia of Catholicism* announces that his discussion is to be concerned "simply and solely with meeting the living God,"[23] and at one point he characterizes faith as "a personal encounter with the living God."[24] This sounds very different from the traditional view of faith as a believing of theological propositions on the authority of God who has revealed them. At the end of the book, however, Joly offers as normative the definition of faith promulgated by the First Vatican Council and quoted above on page 126, with its straight Thomist doctrine expressed in uncompromisingly intellectualist terms. In expounding it Joly himself falls back into the ways of thinking which it embodies and from which he fails to escape. "God," he says, "has revealed all that it was necessary for us to know about him and about his plans for the world. . . . The apostles, the hearers and witnesses of Christ, have handed on this revelation to the Church which has the mission of faithfully preserving and infallibly interpreting the revelation completed by Jesus Christ. . . . We admit [a doctrine] because Christ has declared it to us and because the Church has infallibly transmitted to us these words of Christ and their proper interpretation."[25] In this crucial discussion in Joly's book, to which the preceding discussions were "approaches,"[26] there is no reference to the divine-human encounter or to meeting the living God; faith has reverted to its traditional character as belief in the dogmas of the Church. Again, even so impressively bold and independent a Catholic as the late Father Gustave Weigel, S.J., said in his last book, "To a Catholic, the word 'faith' conveys the notion of an intellectual assent to the content of revelation as true because of the witnessing authority of God the Revealer. . . . Faith is the Catholic's response to an intellectual message communicated by God."[27]

We will now note briefly the wider context of theological thought within which this intellectualist understanding of faith has its place. Faith and revelation are correlative terms, faith being the cognitive aspect of man's response to divine revelation, so that a conception of the nature of faith develops in partnership with a corresponding conception of revelation. The Thomist-Catholic notion of faith is accompanied by a view of revelation as the divine communication to man of the truths, belief in which comprises faith. In the words of *The Catholic Encyclopedia*, "Revelation may be defined as the communication of some truth by God to a rational creature through means which are beyond the ordinary course of nature."[28] God has communicated the knowledge that is necessary to man's salvation, first through the prophets of Israel and then in a fuller and final way through Christ, and this knowledge has ever since been preserved and propagated by the Church. The Bible finds its place within this scheme of thought as the book in which the saving truths are written down and made available, under the Church's guardianship, to all mankind. This view requires of course a theory of the Bible's ultimate divine authorship and hence its verbal inerrancy, such as was laid down in the pronouncement of the First Vatican Council concerning the books of the Bible that "having been written by the inspiration of the Holy Spirit, they have God as their author."[29] (Whether God's revelation is wholly contained within the Bible, or whether there is essential supplementary knowledge in the oral traditions of the Church seems, in the light of the Second Vatican Council, to be at present an open question for Catholics.)

These various principles also determine the Thomist-Catholic account of the relation between faith and reason. According to this account there are two sets of theological truths: those that are accessible to human reason and that can be established by philosophical demonstration (such as that God exists and that he is one), and those exceeding the scope of reason (such as that God is triune). The former constitute the corpus of natural theology and the latter of revealed theology; and the former are grasped by reason, the latter by faith. The truths of natural theology, however, as well as being rationally available, are also presented for acceptance by faith. For otherwise many would fail to attain them, being too unlearned, too busy or too indolent to pursue the abstruse metaphysical reasonings required for a philosophical knowledge of God. Again, those few who did come to know God by the way of rational reflection would arrive at that knowledge only late in life, since metaphysical reasoning presupposes considerable previous training and study. And finally, the conclusions of human reasoning are subject to a certain suspicion in the minds of nonphilosophers because of the possibility of errors in reasoning, and therefore the truths of natural theology are always treated by many with a certain reserve. For all these reasons "it was necessary that the unshakeable certitude and pure truth concerning divine things should be presented to men by way of faith."[30]

The Thomist-Catholic understanding of faith as the believing of revealed truths likewise determines a view of the nature of theological thinking. The theologian's task is not to create doctrines as a philosopher may create metaphysical theories. The Christian truths are already known, having been given in revelation, and the theologian's task is to systematize them, expound them, and guard them from erroneous and misleading modes of exposition.

The central thread which holds these conceptions together is the intellectualist assumption which restricts the entire discussion to propositional truths: revelation is God's communicating of such truths to man, faith is man's obedient believing of them; and they are written down in the Bible and systematized by the theologians. This intellectualist assumption is to be found not only throughout the greater part of Christian thought, past and present, but also in most of the criticism of Christianity, which has not unnaturally been a reaction against the dominant Christian view. For example, Julian Huxley in his *Religion without Revelation* speaks of "the hypothesis of revelation," which is "that the truth has been revealed in a set of god-given commandments, or a holy book, or divinely-inspired ordinances."[31] Again, Walter Kaufmann, in his hard-hitting *Critique of Religion and Philosophy*, reveals his understanding of the Christian concept of revelation when he says, "Even if we grant, for the sake of the present argument, that God exists and sometimes reveals propositions to mankind. . . ."[32] And again, Richard Robinson, in *An Atheist's Values*, a book often of singular beauty, defines faith as "assuming a certain belief without reference to its probability," and as "belief reckless of evidence and probability." He therefore urges the virtue of undermining faith: "We ought to do what we can towards eradicating the evil habit of believing without regard to evidence."[33]

Is there any alternative account of religious faith which does not proceed from this widespread intellectualist assumption? An alternative has always been implicit in the piety of ordinary religious men and women within both Judaism and Christianity, and has now been made explicit in the main streams of twentieth-century Protestant theology. According to this alternative view revelation consists, not in the divine communication of religious truths, but in the self-revealing actions of God within human history. God has acted above all in that special stream of history which Christianity sees as *Heilsgeschichte*, holy history: beginning with the calling out of the Hebrews as a people in covenant with their God; continuing through their stormy career, during which God was seeking through events and circumstances, as interpreted to them by the prophets, to lead his people into a fuller knowledge of himself; and culminating in the Christ event, in which God's love for mankind was seen directly at work on earth in the actions of Jesus. Revelation, considered as completed communication, consists in the conjunction of God's activity within our human experience, with the human recognition that the events in question *are* God's actions. As William Temple wrote, "there is event and appreciation; and in the coincidence of these the revelation consists."[34] The events are always in themselves ambiguous, capable of being seen either simply as natural happenings or as happenings through which God is acting towards us. For example, in the prophetic interpretation of history embodied in the Old Testament records, events which would be described by a secular historian as the outcome of political, economic, sociological and geographical factors are seen as incidents in a dialogue which continues through the centuries between God and his people. Again, the central figure of the New Testament could be regarded in purely human terms, as a political agitator or as a dangerous critic of the religious establishment, but could also be seen and worshiped as the one in whom the world encounters the divine Son made man. Thus, when the revelatory events are seen and responded to as divine actions, man exists in a conscious relation to, and with knowledge of, God: and this total occurrence is revelation. Faith is an element within this totality in that it is the human recognition of ambiguous events as revelatory, and hence the experiencing of them as mediating the presence and activity of God.

So understood, revelation is not a divine promulgation of propositions, nor is faith a believing of such propositions. The theological propositions formulated on the basis of revelation have a secondary status. They do not constitute the content of God's self-revelation but are human and therefore fallible verbalizations, constructed to aid both the integration of our religious experience into our own minds and the communication of religious experience to others. The formulation and approval of doctrine is thus a work not of faith but of reason—reason operating upon the data of revelation. The function of faith in this sphere is to establish the premises, not the conclusions, of theological reasoning.

According to this view the two objects of "natural" and "revealed" theology, God's existence and God's revelation, merge into one. The divine Being and the divine self-communication are known in a single apprehension which is the awareness of God as acting self-revealingly toward us. The believer does not make two separate acts of faith, nor an act of reason and an act of faith, directed respectively to divine existence and to divine revelation. He claims to know "that God exists" because he knows God as existing and having to do with him in the events of the world and of his own life.

It would be an oversimplification to say that this non-propositional, *heilsgeschichtliche* conception of the revelation-faith complex represents the Reformed in distinction from the Catholic point of view. In the early days of the Reformation, as part of the great upsurge of direct, personal religious experience and piety which in the sixteenth century burst the limits of a decadent and legalistic scholasticism, the foundations were laid for a nonpropositional doctrine of faith. For Luther, faith was not primarily acceptance of the Church's dogmas but a wholehearted response of trust and gratitude toward the divine grace revealed in Jesus Christ. Indirectly it included acceptance of all the fundamental Christian beliefs; but Luther's primary emphasis was upon faith as a total reliance upon the omnipotent goodness of God. In a distinction that Luther himself drew, faith is not belief *that* but belief *in*.[35] But Protestant theology suffered a rapid decline after Luther's insight. Calvin, the great systematizer of Reformed theology, represents an intermediate position, with his definition of faith as "a firm and certain knowledge of God's benevolence towards us, founded upon the truth of the freely given promise in Christ, both revealed to our minds [in the Bible] and sealed upon our hearts through the Holy Spirit."[36] But after Calvin there was a decisive relapse into a Protestant scholasticism as narrowly intellectualist as that of the Thomist-Catholic tradition. In the Westminster Confession of Faith of 1647, for instance, it is said of "saving faith" that "By this faith, a Christian believeth to be true whatsoever is revealed in the word, for the authority of God himself speaking therein";[37] and more than two hundred years later a Calvinist theologian was writing as though he were strict Thomist: "And we define faith. . . to be the assent of the mind to truth, upon the testimony of God, conveying knowledge to us through supernatural channels. . . . Reason establishes the fact that God speaks, but when we know what he says, we believe it because he says it."[38]

In more recent times the notion of divinely revealed propositions has virtually disappeared from Protestant theology, being replaced by the idea of revelation through history.[39] But among philosophers discussing the problems of religion, the basic intellectualist assumption that faith means primarily and centrally the holding of unevidenced beliefs has continued to operate and has produced some of the theories of faith. . . .

Notes

1. C. J. Ducasse, *A Philosophical Scrutiny of Religion* (New York, 1953), pp. 73–74. This type of formulation goes back to Kant, with his account of faith (*Glaube*) as belief on grounds that are subjectively sufficient but objectively insufficient (*Critique of Pure Reason*, 2d ed., p. 850; trans. by Norman Kemp Smith [London, 1933], p. 646).

2. For an attractive contemporary restatement of the Thomist position, see Josef Pieper, *Belief and Faith,* trans. by R. Winston and C. Winston (New York, 1963, and London, 1964).

3. *Summa Theologica,* pt. II, II, Q. 1, Art. 2. English Dominican translation, revised by Anton C. Pegis, *Basic Writings of Saint Thomas Aquinas* (New York, 1945).

4. *Ibid.,* Q. 1, Art. 6.

5. *Ibid.,* Q. 1, Art. 9.

6. Dogmatic Constitution, ch. 3, in Denzinger, *Enchiridion Symbolorum,* no. 1789.

7. *Ibid.,* no. 1792.

8. *Summa Theologica,* pt. II, II, Q. 1, Art. 4.

9. *Ibid.,* Q. 4, Art. 5.

10. *Ibid.,* Q. 1, Art. 5.

11. *Ibid.,* Q. 1, Art. 5.

12. *Ibid.,* Q. 1, Art. 4.

13. *Ibid.,* Q. 2, Art. 1.

14. In this respect faith is less certain than *scientia.* In another sense however it is more certain than *scientia:* for its object, which is a divine truth, is in itself more certain than are the mundane objects of human *scientia* (*ibid., Q.* 4, Art. 8).

15. M. C. D'Arcy, *The Nature of Belief* (London, 1945), pp. 224–225.

16. *Essay concerning the Human Understanding,* bk. IV, ch. 18, sec. 2.

17. *Ibid.,* sec. 5.

18. New York, 1927, I, 13.

19. *Summa Theologica,* pt. II, II, Q. 5, Art. 2.

20. *Ibid., Q.* 2, Art. 9.

21. *Ibid.,* Q. 5, Art. 2.

22. On the question of the rational coerciveness or otherwise of the *premabula fidei,* and their relation to the act of faith, there have been several writings by English Catholic theologians who are fully aware of the difficulty noticed above, e.g., Dom Mark Pontifex, *Religious Assent* (London, 1927); M. C. D'Arcy, *The Nature of Belief* (London, 1945); Dom Illtyd Trethowan, *Certainty* (London, 1948).

23. *Qu'est-ce que croire?* (Paris, 1956), trans. by Dom Illtyd Trethowan as *What is Faith?* (New York, 1958), p. 7.

24. *Ibid.,* p. 86.

25. *Ibid.,* pp. 131–132.

26. *Ibid.,* p. 130.

27. *Faith and Understanding in America* (New York, 1959), p. 1. Note however Weigel's description of faith as "an intellectual act which is simultaneously an orientation of man towards the revealing Lord," in his contribution to the New York University Institute of Philosophy in 1960, *Religious Experience and Truth,* edited by Sidney Hook (New York, 1961), p. 104.

28. New York, 1912, XIII, 1.

29. *Dogmatic Constitution,* ch. 2. Denzinger, *Enchiridion Symbolorum,* no. 1789.

30. *Summa contra Gentiles,* bk. I, ch. 4, par. 5.

31. Revised ed.; London, 1957, p. 207.

32. New York, 1958, p. 89.

33. Oxford, 1964, pp. 120, 121.

34. *Nature, Man and God* (London, 1934), p. 314.

35. *Werke* (Weimar ed.), VII, 215.

36. *Institutes,* bk. III, ch. 2, par. 7.

37. Ch. 14, par. 2.

38. A. A. Hodge, *Outlines of Theology* (London, 1863), pp. 49–50.

39. On this development see John Baillie, *The Idea of Revelation in Recent Thought* (New York, 1956).

14. The Agnostic's Dilemma

NORWOOD RUSSELL HANSON

An agnostic maintains himself in a state of perfect doubt concerning God's existence, a position I regard as unsound. The agnostic achieves his equipoise of dubiety only by shifting his ground where logic requires him to stand fast.

Is religious belief reasonable? This question pivots on reactions to the claim 'God exists.' This claim could be false. Its denial is consistent, hence the claim is synthetic. Otherwise it would be as uninformative to be told that God exists as it is to hear that bachelors are male.

Distinguishing theists from atheists, and these from agnostics, depends on there being alternative answers to the question "Does God exist?" The theist answers "Yes." The atheist answers "No." The agnostic doesn't know, or cannot decide.

There is a fund of subtle literature concerning this existence claim. Sometimes it is construed as synthetic but necessarily true. But this would make atheism impossible, which it is not. This point also cuts against 'God exists' being analytic. Again, some think the claim to be factual, yet established beyond all reasonable doubt. This makes atheism unreasonable, which it is not.

Many theologians hold the claim 'God exists' not to be central to the core of religious belief at all. In different ways, Niebuhr, Tillich, and Braithwaite have argued that the role of belief within human life remains fundamental whatever our decisions about the logical or factual status of the claim 'God exists.' Apparently it matters little to the reasonableness of one's religious beliefs whether or not he believes in God: indeed, it might remain reasonable for one to persist as a believer even after further thought has led him to deny God's existence.

Source: Reprinted from *The American Rationalist,* July–August 1961, Courtesy of the Center for Inquiry, Inc.

This apologia has gained in popularity what it has lost in rationality. Clearly, a rational man will not continue to believe in what he has grounds for supposing does not exist. Nor will he maintain belief in that chain of claims which hang on a proposition he no longer thinks is true.

Hence, in this paper, 'God exists' is a synthetic claim; it could be false. Moreover, the claim could be contingently confirmed, as some theists say it already is. What have theists, atheists, and agnostics been arguing about, if not whether this existence claim is, or can be, factually established? Logically, the claim belongs in the center of our discussion. Historically, that is where it always has been. Despite the hocus-pocus of theologians, the claim is also central within the lives of genuinely religious people. Surely most streetlevel believers would be affected in their religion by the disclosure that the New Testament was a forgery, or by a demonstration that God could not exist—assuming such a disclosure or demonstration to be possible.

Many theists will not be moved by these considerations. They will insist that 'God exists' is not the sort of claim that could be amenable to scientific observation, or even to logical scrutiny. Both reason and the senses fail when issues which turn on faith arise. This, of course, is a flight from reason. If neither logic nor experience can be allowed to affect our attitudes towards God's existence, then no argument and no ordinary experience can affect the theist's belief. However, it then becomes a university's function to stress that religious belief, so construed, is not reasonable. Nor is it connected with ordinary experience—since, if the latter cannot count against such belief, then neither can it count for it. A university must help young adults to distinguish positions for which there are good grounds from other positions for which the grounds are not so good. When the theist lets his appeal collapse into faith alone, he concedes that his position rests on no rational grounds at all.

The agnostic, however, cannot adopt any such theistic device. He must grant, without qualification, that 'God exists' is contingent. He feels, nonetheless, that there are no compelling factual grounds for deciding the issue one way or the other. After the atheist has exposed as inadequate all known arguments for God's existence, someone will ask, "But can you prove God does not exist?". Instead of realizing he has already done this, the atheist often hedges. This the agnostic mistakenly makes the basis for his universal dubiety.

If the argument between theists and atheists could have been settled by reflection, this would long since have been done. The theist's appeal to faith cannot settle any argument. So the agnostic adopts the only alternative, viz., that the argument concerns a matter of fact—whether or not God does in fact exist. But he remains in an equipoise of noncommitment by proclaiming that neither theist nor atheist has factual grounds for supposing the other's position to be refuted. How in detail does the agnostic argue this point?

Consider some logical preliminaries: entertain the claim 'All A's are B's.' If this ranges over a potential infinitude, then it can never be completely established by any finite number of observations of A's being B's. 'All bats are viviparous' receives each day a higher probability—but it is always less than 1, since the claim ranges over all past, present, and future bats, anywhere and everywhere.

This claim is easily disconfirmed, however. Discovering one oviparous bat would do it. Consider now the different claim: 'There exists an A which is a B.' This can never be disconfirmed. Being told that some bat is oviparous cannot be disconfirmed by appealing to everything now known about bats, as well as to all extant bats. The 'any-where-everywhere' and 'past-present-future' conditions operate here too. However, we can confirm this claim by discovering one oviparous bat.

So, 'All A's are B's' can be disconfirmed, but never completely established. 'There exists an A which is B' can be established, but never disestablished.

'There is a God' has never been factually established. Any account of phenomena which at first seems to require God's existence is always explicable via some alternative account requiring no supernatural reference. Since appealing to God constitutes an end to further inquiry, the alternative accounts have been the more attractive; indeed, the history of science is a history of finding accounts of phenomena alternative to just appealing to God's existence.

Thus there is not one clearcut natural happening, nor any constellation of such happenings, which establishes God's existence—not as witnessing a bat laying an egg would establish 'There is an oviparous bat.'

In principle, God's existence could be established with the same clarity and directness one would expect in a verification of the claim 'some bats are oviparous.' Suppose that tomorrow morning, after breakfast, all of us are knocked to our knees by an ear-shattering thunderclap. Trees drop their leaves. The earth heaves. The sky blazes with light, and the clouds pull apart, revealing an immense and radiant Zeus-like figure. He frowns. He points at me and exclaims, for all to hear.

"Enough of your logic-chopping and word-watching matters of theology. Be assured henceforth that I most assuredly exist." Nor is this a private transaction between the heavens and myself. Everyone in the world experienced this, and heard what was said to me.

Do not dismiss this example as a playful contrivance. The conceptual point is that were this to happen, I should be entirely convinced that God exists. The subtleties with which the learned devout discuss this existence claim would seem, after such an experience, like a discussion of color in a home for the blind. That God exists would have been confirmed for me, and everyone else, in a manner as direct as that involved in any noncontroversial factual claim. Only, there is no good reason for supposing anything remotely like this ever to have happened, biblical mythology notwithstanding.

In short, not only is 'God exists' a factual claim—one can even specify what it would be like to confirm it. If the hypothetical description offered above is not rich or subtle enough, the reader can make the appropriate adjustments. But if no description, however rich and subtle, could be relevant to confirming the claim, then it could never be reasonable to believe in God's existence. Nor would it then be reasonable to base one's life on such a claim.

What about disconfirming 'God exists'? Here the agnostic should face the logical music—but he doesn't. What he does do, and as an agnostic must do, is as follows:

The agnostic treats 'God exists' as he should, as a factual claim the supporting evidence for which is insufficient for verification. However, he treats the denial of that claim quite differently. Now the agnostic chooses the logical point we sharpened above. No finite set of experiences which fail to support claims like 'Oviparous bats exist' and 'God exists' can by itself conclusively disconfirm such claims. Perhaps we have not been looking in the right places, or at the right things. We do not even know what it would be like to disconfirm such claims, since we cannot have all the possibly relevant experiences. But we do know what it would be like to establish that 'God exists.' Variations of the alarming encounter with the thundering God described above would confirm this claim.

The logical criterion invoked when the agnostic argues that 'there is a God' cannot be falsified applies to all existence claims. Hence, he has no grounds for denying that there is a Loch Ness Monster, or a five-headed Welshman, or a unicorn in New College garden. But there are excellent grounds for denying such claims. They consist in there being no reason whatever for supposing that these claims are true. And there being no reason for thinking a claim true is itself good reason for thinking it false. We know what it would be like to fish up the Loch Ness monster, or to encounter a five-headed Welshman, or to trap the New College unicorn. It just happens that there are no such things. We have the best factual grounds for saying this. Believers will feel that 'God exists' is better off than these other claims. They might even think it confirmed. But if they think this they must also grant that the evidence could go in the opposite direction. For if certain evidence can confirm a claim, other possible evidence must be such that, had it obtained, it would have disconfirmed that claim.

Precisely here the agnostic slips. While he grants that some possible evidence could confirm that God exists, but that it hasn't yet, he insists that no possible evidence could disconfirm this claim. The agnostic shifts logical ground when he supposes that evidence against the 'God exists' claim never could be good enough. Yet he must do this to remain agnostic. Otherwise, he could never achieve his 'perfect indecision' concerning whether God exists. For usually, when evidence is not good enough for us to conclude that X exists, we infer directly that X does not exist. Thus, the evidence fails to convince us that there is a Loch Ness monster, or a five-headed Welshman, or a New College unicorn; and since this is so, we conclude directly that such beings do not exist. These are the grounds usually offered for saying of something that it does not exist, namely, the evidence does not establish that it does.

The agnostic dons the mantle of rationality in the theist vs. atheist dispute. He seeks to appear as one whose reasonableness lifts him above the battle. But he can maintain this attitude only by being unreasonable, i.e., by shifting ground in his argument. If the agnostic insists that we could never disconfirm God's existence, then he must grant that we could never confirm the claim either. But if he feels we could confirm the claim, then he must grant that we could disconfirm it, too. To play the logician's game when saying that 'there are no oviparous bats' cannot be established, one must play the same game with 'there is an oviparous bat.' Even were a bat to lay an egg before such a person's very eyes, he would have to grant that, in strict logic, 'there exists an oviparous bat' was no more confirmed than its denial. But this is absurd. To see such a thing is to have been made able to claim that there is an oviparous bat. By this same criterion we assert today that 'there are no oviparous bats.' We take this to be confirmed in just that sense appropriate within any factual context.

The agnostic's position is therefore impossible. He begins by assessing 'God exists' as a fact-gatherer. He ends by appraising the claim's denial not as a fact-gatherer but as a logician. But consistency demands he either be a fact-gatherer on both counts or play logician on both counts. If the former, he must grant that there is ample factual reason for denying that God exists, namely, that the evidence in favor of his existence is just not good enough. If the latter, however—if he could make logical mileage out of "it is not the case that God exists" by arguing that it can never be established—then he must treat 'God exists' the same way. He must say not only that the present evidence is not good enough, but that it never could be good enough.

In either case, the conclusion goes against the claim that God exists. The moment the agnostic chooses consistency he becomes an atheist. For, as either fact-gatherer or logician, he will discover that there are no good grounds for claiming that God exists. The alternative is for him to give up trying to be consistent and reasonable, and assert that God exists in faith. But then he will have to doff the mantle of rationality which so attracted him when he adopted his original position.

The drift of this argument is not new: it is not reasonable to believe in the existence of God. Reflective people may have other grounds for believing in God's existence, but these hinge not on any conception of 'having good reasons' familiar in science, logic, or philosophy. The point is that the agnostic, despite his pretensions, is not more reasonable than the atheist or the theist. The next step for him is easy: if he chooses to use his head, he will become an atheist. If he chooses to react to his glands, he will become a theist. Either he will grant that there is no good reason for believing in the existence of God, or he will choose to believe in the existence of God on the basis of no good reason.

B. Blaise Pascal and William James: Faith, Will, and Prudential Options

For both Pascal and James, reason plays a critical part in establishing the framework of one's conviction, but offers less certitude than suggested by Aquinas. Even at its best, reason cannot lead us with any assurance directly to a First Cause or Principle; instead, it can take us only to a state of objective uncertainty, with nowhere to turn for additional evidenciary support. Nonetheless, this lesser degree of certainty is sufficient justification for both thinkers to defend a willful movement toward faith. For Pascal (1660), one who acknowledges that the matter of God's existence cannot be decided by objective means is then faced with a prudential wager, weighing the prospective temporal and eternal benefits and losses accruing from possible belief and nonbelief. As Pascal explains it, for reasons of enlightened self-interest, one ought to put aside skeptical thoughts and place oneself in the position most likely to generate religious faith, namely, in the church. Having thus willed oneself into the community of faith one will, over time, come to genuine faith presumably through the workings of grace, and look back with regret at the self-interested wagerer he used to be. Although James (1897) is highly critical of Pascal, their pathways to faith are not as dissimilar as James suggests. Both argue for the reasonableness of faith on prudential or pragmatic grounds, rather than on evidenciary ones. As an empiricist, James argues that one can never know anything with absolute certainty, since experience may bring us new evidence to overturn our most deeply held and cherished convictions. The most we can say about the God question, or the religious hypothesis ("Perfection is Eternal") as James calls it, is that many regard it as objectively uncertain. If this is an option that one can regard as objectively uncertain, or a live option, James believes that it is also an option that is obviously forced (unavoidable) and momentous, or potentially life-changing. When an option is living, forced, and momentous it constitutes a genuine option for James, and one can rationally permit oneself to believe it in order to discern its practical value. In short, for James a trusting will can lead one to a confirmatory experience of faith as a pragmatically satisfying conviction. Faith is always open to doubt, for subsequent experience may confirm or disconfirm one's belief. James Cargile ((1966) and Thomas V. Morris (1986) debate the coherence of Pascal's wager, whereas James's essay itself is a classic response to the more restricted version of rational decision making offered by William Clifford (1879). D. M. Yeager corrects misconceptions of James's argument and offers a contemporary clarification and defense of his position.

15. The Wager

Blaise Pascal

Infinite, nothing.—The soul of man is cast into the body, in which it finds number, time, dimension; it reasons thereon, and calls this nature or necessity, and cannot believe aught else.

Unity joined to infinity increases it not, any more than a foot measure added to infinite space. The finite is annihilated in presence of the infinite and becomes simply nought. Thus our intellect before God, thus our justice before the divine justice. There is not so great a disproportion between our justice and that of God, as between unity and infinity.

The justice of God must be as vast as his mercy, but justice towards the reprobate is less vast, and should be less amazing than mercy towards the elect.

Source: From Blaise Pascal, *Thoughts,* Translated from the text of August Molinier by C. Kegan Paul, London: Kegan Paul, Trench & Oates, 1888.

We know that there is an infinite, but are ignorant of its nature. As we know it to be false that numbers are finite, it must therefore be true that there is an infinity in number, but what this is we know not. It can neither be odd nor even, for the addition of an unit can make no change in the nature of number; yet it is a number, and every number is either odd or even, at least this is understood of every finite number.

Thus we may well know that there is a God, without knowing what he is.

We know then the existence and the nature of the finite, because we also are finite and have dimension.

We know the existence of the infinite, and are ignorant of its nature, because it has dimension like us, but not limits like us. But we know neither the existence nor the nature of God, because he has neither dimension nor limits.

But by faith we know his existence, by glory we shall know his nature. Now I have already shown that we can know well the existence of a thing without knowing its nature.

Let us now speak according to the light of nature.

If there be a God, he is infinitely incomprehensible, since having neither parts nor limits he has no relation to us. We are then incapable of knowing either what he is or if he is. This being so, who will dare to undertake the solution of the question? Not we, who have no relation to him.

Who then will blame Christians for not being able to give a reason for their faith; those who profess a religion for which they cannot give a reason? They declare in putting it forth to the world that it is a foolishness, *stultitiam,* and then you complain that they do not prove it. Were they to prove it they would not keep their word, it is in lacking proof that they are not lacking in sense.—Yes, but although this excuses those who offer it as such, and takes away from them the blame of putting it forth without reason, it does not excuse those who receive it.—Let us then examine this point, and say "God is, or he is not." But to which side shall we incline? Reason can determine nothing about it. There is an infinite gulf fixed between us. A game is playing at the extremity of this infinite distance in which heads or tails may turn up. What will you wager? There is no reason for backing either one or the other, you cannot reasonably argue in favour of either.

Do not then accuse of error those who have already chosen, for you know nothing about it.—No, but I blame them for having made, not this choice, but a choice, for again both the man who calls 'heads' and his adversary are equally to blame, they are both in the wrong; the true course is not to wager at all.—

Yes, but you must wager; this depends not on your will, you are embarked in the affair. Which will you choose? Let us see. Since you must choose, let us see which least interests you. You have two things to lose, truth and good, and two things to stake, your reason and your will, your knowledge and your happiness; and your nature has two things to avoid, error and misery. Since you must needs choose, your reason is no more wounded in choosing one than the other. Here is one point cleared up, but what of your happiness? Let us weigh the gain and the loss in choosing heads that God is. Let us weigh the two cases: if you gain, you gain all; if you lose, you lose nothing. Wager then unhesitatingly that he is.—You are right. Yes, I must wager, but I may stake too much.—Let us see. Since there is an equal chance of gain and loss, if you had only to gain two lives for one, you might still wager. But were there three of them to gain, you would have to play, since needs must that you play, and you would be imprudent, since you must play, not to chance your life to gain three at a game where the chances of loss or gain are even. But there is an eternity of life and happiness. And that being so, were there an infinity of chances of which one only would be for you, you would still be right to stake one to win two, and you would act foolishly, being obliged to play, did you refuse to stake one life against three at a game in which out of an infinity of chances there be one for you, if there were an infinity of an infinitely happy life to win. But there is here an infinity of an infinitely happy life to win, a chance of gain against a finite number of chances of loss, and what you stake is finite; that is decided. Wherever the infinite exists and there is not an infinity of chances of loss against that of gain, there is no room for hesitation, you must risk the whole. Thus when a man is forced to play he must renounce reason to keep life, rather than hazard it for infinite gain, which is as likely to happen as the loss of nothingness.

For it is of no avail to say it is uncertain that we gain, and certain that we risk, and that the infinite distance between the certainty of that which is staked and the uncertainty of what we shall gain, equals the finite good which is certainly staked against an uncertain infinite. This is not so. Every gambler stakes a certainty to gain an uncertainty, and yet he stakes a finite certainty against a finite uncertainty without acting unreasonably. It is false to say there is infinite distance between the certain stake and the uncertain gain. There is in truth an infinity between the certainty of gain and the certainty of loss. But the uncertainty of gain is proportioned to the certainty of the stake, according to the proportion of chances of gain and loss, and if therefore there are as many chances on one side as on the other, the game is even. And thus the certainty of the venture is equal to the uncertainty of the winnings, so far is it from the truth that there is infinite distance between them. So that our argument is of infinite force, if we stake the finite in a game where there are equal chances of gain and loss, and the infinite is the winnings. This is demonstrable, and if men are capable of any truths, this is one.

I confess and admit it. Yet is there no means of seeing the hands at the game?— Yes, the Scripture and the rest, etc.

—Well, but my hands are tied and my mouth is gagged: I am forced to wager and am not free, none can release me, but I am so made that I cannot believe. What then would you have me do?

True. But understand at least your incapacity to believe, since your reason leads you to belief and yet you cannot believe. Labour then to convince yourself, not by increase of the proofs of God, but by the diminution of your passions. You would fain arrive at faith, but know not the way; you would heal yourself of unbelief, and you ask remedies for it. Learn of those who have been bound as you are, but who now stake all that they possess; these are they who know the way you would follow, who are cured of a disease of which you would be cured. Follow the way by which they began, by making believe that they believed, taking the holy water, having masses said, etc. Thus you will naturally be brought to believe, and will lose your acuteness.—But that is just what I fear.—Why? what have you to lose?

But to show you that this is the right way, this it is that will lessen the passions, which are your great obstacles, etc.—

What you say comforts and delights me, etc.—If my words please you, and seem to you cogent, know that they are those of one who has thrown himself on his knees before and after to pray that Being, infinite, and without parts, to whom he submits all his own being, that you also would submit to him all yours, for your own good and for his glory, and that this strength may be in accord with this weakness.

The end of this argument.—Now what evil will happen to you in taking this side? You will be trustworthy, honourable, humble, grateful, generous, friendly, sincere, and true. In truth you will no longer have those poisoned pleasures, glory and luxury, but you will have other pleasures. I tell you that you will gain in this life, at each step you make in this path you will see so much certainty of gain, so much nothingness in what you stake, that you will know at last that you have wagered on a certainty, an infinity, for which you have risked nothing.

Objection.—Those who hope for salvation are so far happy, but they have as a counterpoise the fear of hell.

Answer.—Who has most reason to fear hell, the man who is in ignorance if there be a hell, and who is certain of damnation if there be; or he who is certainly convinced that there is a hell, and has a hope of being saved if there be?

"I would soon have given up pleasure," say they, "had I but faith." But I say to you, "you would soon have faith did you leave off your pleasures. Now it is for you to begin. If I could, I would give you faith. I cannot do this, nor discover therefore if what you say is true. But you can easily give up pleasure, and discover if what I say is true."

Probabilities.—We must live differently in the world, according to these different suppositions:

---

16. Pascal's Wager

JAMES CARGILE

A. Pascal's statement of his wager argument[1,2] is couched in terms of the theory of probability and the theory of games, and the exposition is unclear and unnecessarily complicated. The following is a "creative" reformulation of the argument designed to avoid *some* of the objections which have been or might be raised against the original.

Source: Reprinted from *Philosophy* 41 (1966), by permission of Cambridge University Press. Notes edited.

B. *Premises:*

1. "If there is a God, we are incapable of knowing either what he is, or whether he exists" (Pascal). And further, we have no way of knowing that God does not exist.
2. If you perform religious rites with enthusiasm, and never question the claims of some religion, you will come to be devoutly religious. "Go then and take holy water, and have masses said; belief will come and stupefy your scruples" (William James' version[3] of a remark by Pascal).
3. If you are devoutly religious—Christian, Jew, Moslem, Hindu, polytheist, etc.—and there is a God, then he will send you to heaven when you die.

Conclusion: Solely on grounds of rational self-interest, you should participate in religious rites, refrain from skeptical thoughts, etc.

Proof: Consider the following case. A very rich man who is fond of jazz promises that in two years, he is going to toss an unbiased coin. If it lands heads, he will give each devoted jazz fan a million dollars. If it lands tails, he won't do anything. Every Sunday for the next two years, a one-hour jazz concert is scheduled. It is known to be highly likely that if you attend these concerts religiously, and avoid listening to classical music, you will become a devoted jazz fan.

This case is clearly analogous to the situation of the man who is reflecting as to whether or not he should take up religious observances. And in either case the answer is obvious: you had better start listening uncritically to a lot of jazz. You may return to classical music as a millionaire, and you may get to heaven and not have to listen to sermons any more.

It may be objected that the person who "wagers" by attending concerts loses, if he loses, only two years of classical music, while the person who "wagers" by participating in religious rites and avoiding skeptical thoughts loses, if he loses, the only chance for thinking he will ever have. But after all, what is thinking? You have only to pass up philosophical quibbling which everyone knows is silly anyway. You can keep your mind exercised on mathematics or formal logic or approved scientific topics. Concession to religion needn't be much, even when you strive for real faith. Look what subtle reasoners even fanatics can be!

It may be objected that God may save atheists and agnostics as well as religious people. And the rich man *might* give a million dollars to a lover of classical music—but why depend on *kindness* when you can get a *contract* (or rather, a covenant)?

Someone might plan to delay attending the concerts until the second year so as to get in as much classical music as possible. Similarly, someone might plan to follow the advice of Pascal's argument in forty years, after enjoying his skepticism as long as he can. But if the rich man announces that he *may* exclude people who are not jazz fans from his offer if they delay attending the concerts, it would obviously be foolish to delay. And if you plan to delay religious observance, you may not live that long. It is foolish to be even a little careless with an opportunity for infinite gain.

C. This argument is designed to convince an open-minded agnostic acting out of rational self-interest that he ought to take up religious practices in the hope of becoming religious. Pascal has other arguments which will then be brought forward to bring the newly won religious sympathizer into Pascal's own particular church, but the Wager argument is not one of these. William James (loc. cit.) criticizes Pascal's argument on the grounds that it would not convert a Moslem to Catholicism. But it wasn't intended to. James has probably been misled by Pascal's comment about holy water and masses. But this needn't occur in the presentation of the Wager argument; the point which the reference to holy water and masses is designed to illustrate could be made just as well with respect to Moslem rituals. The argument is aimed at convincing skeptics, whose coolness about their prospects for immortality horrifies Pascal, that they should become *involved* on the side of those committed to belief in immortality.

James also criticizes Pascal's argument as immoral, and says indignantly, "We feel that a faith in masses and holy water adopted wilfully after such a mechanical calculation would lack the inner soul of faith's reality: and if we were ourselves in the place of the Deity, we should probably take particular pleasure in cutting off believers of this pattern from their infinite reward." It seems that James is over-looking the fact that "*believers* of this pattern" are going to be just the same as other believers. Their belief isn't *sustained* by the argument, nor is it acquired by simply deciding to believe—James rightly regards the idea of "believing by our volition" as "simply silly"—rather, their faith is acquired as a result of actions which they were persuaded by the argument to perform. Once belief comes, the believer may genuinely despise his old skeptical self and shudder to think that such considerations as self-interest ever moved him. He may sincerely perform acts of faith, with no thought of his ultimate reward. A cynic may decide that the most convenient arrangement is a deathbed conversion; but if he is really converted, no one will despise this cynicism more than he.

Since James says that he is presenting Pascal's words "translated freely," it seems fair to protest against his representing Pascal as saying that "any finite loss is reasonable, even a certain one is reasonable, if there is but the possibility of infinite gain." Pascal's exposition is unclear, but he doesn't make such a mistake as this. James also presents the choice as one between belief and unbelief, which is probably one reason why he considers the argument immoral. But Pascal doesn't put it as a choice between belief and unbelief. He speaks obscurely of "risking your life," where he seems to be asking, not that you believe, but that you observe religious rites and abstain from criticism in the hope of being led to belief.

James also presents Pascal's argument as starting with the claim that human reason can't tell us what to do and ending with the claim that a certain course is obviously the reasonable one. This is especially reprehensible when presented as a translation. Jean Mesnard makes the same mistake in paraphrasing Pascal's argument,[4] apparently with approval, as starting with the claim that "reason cannot determine our choice" and ending with "Our reason therefore commands us to bet on the existence of God!" Pascal actually starts by saying that reason cannot settle the question as to whether or not there *is* a God, and concludes by saying that reason does clearly advise us to "*bet*" that there is a God—which for Pascal means being religious or sincerely trying to become so.

D. Various presentations of the Wager argument defend it against the charge that it is an immoral argument. But no presentation I know of notices that the argument, which is presented as an appeal to a self-interested, rational skeptic who is completely uncommitted,[5] is simply invalid, because no such person could accept the premises.

Premise (1) might not be acceptable to an agnostic because it considers only the possibility of a transcendent God. The agnostic might think that investigation of occult phenomena *could* answer the God question, though of course only an affirmative answer would be so obtainable. Still, the skeptic would certainly admit that the God question is pretty much up in the air. So with "could not know" changed to "do not know," premise (1) would be acceptable to a skeptic.

The skeptic might doubt that he is the sort of person of whom the factual claim of premise (2) is true. But he would probably admit that there are measures sufficient to bring him into a religious frame of mind, even if the measures required were somewhat more severe than are needed by the average man. So he might accept premise (2) while still preserving his title as a skeptic or agnostic.

However, no self-respecting skeptic could accept premise (3). For one thing, if he accepts premise (1) as stated, that is, accepts that if there is a God, then "we are incapable of knowing what he is," then he cannot consistently agree with premise (3) that one thing we can be sure of about the possible owner-operator of the universe is that he is the sort of being who will send religious people to heaven. And premise (1) apart, why should not the neutral skeptic think it just as likely that God will save atheists and agnostics as that he will save believers? He might hope that it is more likely, either purely for his own sake, or on moral grounds.

The fact that, say, Christianity or Mohammedanism *promise* their adherents an infinite reward, while, say, dialectical materialism does not, cannot be produced as a good reason for a neutral adopting one of the former positions rather than the latter. The argument, "If you become devoutly religious, and religion is right about there being a God, then you will get an infinite reward," is just invalid. It would be all right to argue, "If you become devoutly religious, and religion is right about there being a God and religion is right about one claim it makes about his character, then you will get an infinite reward." But with these premises, there are no longer just the two possibilities, "Religion is right about there being a God or it isn't right about there being a God." There are three possibilities: religion is right about there being a God and right about his character; or religion is right about there being a God and wrong about his character; or religion is wrong about there being a God.

E. However, an attempt might be made to reinstate the Wager argument in spite of the observations in (D), as follows:

Either (a) there is a god who will send only religious people to heaven or (b) there is not. To be religious is to wager for (a). To fail to be religious is to wager for (b). We can't settle the question whether (a) or (b) is the case, at least not at present. But (a) is clearly vastly better than (b). With (a), infinite bliss is *guaranteed,* while with (b) we are still in the miserable human condition of facing death with no assurance as to what lies beyond. So (a) is clearly the best wager.

This arrangement does indeed appeal to a self-interested, *uncommitted* skeptic—it does not *presuppose* anything about the nature of god—the assumption about the nature of god is explicit in the argument. A skeptic might accept this argument and still deserve the title of "skeptic," but he would not deserve the title of "clear thinker."

The argument just presented is formally similar to the following:

Either (a) there is a god who will send you to heaven only if you commit a painful ritual suicide within an hour of first reading this, or (b) there is not. We cannot settle the question whether (a) or (b) is the case; or it is at least not settled yet. But (a) is vastly preferable to (b), since in situation (a) infinite bliss is *guaranteed,* while in (b) we are left in the usual miserable human condition. So we should wager for (a) by performing the suicidal ritual.

It might be objected that we can be sure that there is not a god who will send us to heaven only if we commit suicide but we can't be sure that there is not a god who will send us to heaven only if we are religious. However, a skeptic would demand proof for this.

Both the foregoing arguments might gain plausibility through confusing possibility with probability. Certainly Pascal's application of probability theory could be severely criticized. However, my purpose has not been to criticize this aspect of the argument, but only to point out that the argument cannot stand as an appeal to someone who subscribes to no religious presuppositions.

F. Though my criticism of Pascal's argument has not been based on attacking his use of probability theory, it may be worth noting that if his use of probability theory were right, probability theory would be in a bad way.

Pascal uses a certain method from probability theory for calculating whether a given bet is a good one, to support his argument. The method is as follows: given a bet on whether or not an event E will happen, you multiply the probability of E by the odds offered (with the largest number in the odds, if there is one, in the numerator). If this product exceeds one, and you are getting the high end of the odds, then the bet is a good one for you no matter how low the probability of E may be.

The limitations of this method are well-known, and Pascal's application of it creates a situation somewhat like the Petersburg Paradox.[6] But I think we need not go as far as the Petersburg Paradox to criticize Pascal's application of this method. It is enough to observe that in applying the method, Pascal takes for granted that the hypothesis that there is a God has some nonzero probability.

The only support Pascal could have for this is the so-called "Principle of Indifference," the fallaciousness of which is well-known,[7] Pascal assumes that if a proposition is logically possible and not known to be false, then it has some nonzero probability. But the propositional function, "There exists a God who prefers contemplating the real number x more than any other activity," provides us with a set of mutually incompatible propositions, each of which is logically and epistemically possible, such that there could not be a nonzero probability for each member of the set. Even if this "propositional function" is rejected as nonsense, such a function as "There are *n* rabbits in the universe" would provide a set of mutually incompatible propositions, infinitely many of which would be both logically and epistemically possible. They could all be assigned probability numbers, e.g., from the series ½, ¼, ⅛, . . . , but such an assignment would be absurd.

G. Of course, there remains the argument that if you become devoutly religious (and not a Calvinist!) you will *think* that you are going to get an infinite reward, and this is pleasanter than not thinking so. Whether Pascal would have stooped to this is a question outside the scope of the present essay.

H. It must be emphasized that my criticisms have not been intended to suggest that religious belief is unreasonable. It is one thing to hold that reason directs us to be religious, quite another to hold that it is (perfectly) reasonable to be religious.

Even in this connection, it is not the belief in an infinite gain which makes it reasonable to be religious. I may get the idea into my head that setting fire to the bus station will get me into heaven, but this belief does not make it *reasonable* for me to perform this religious act. *How I got the belief* would be crucial in determining whether the religious act of setting fire to the bus station is reasonable.

For example, if someone were dressed as an angel in a very convincing way, and lowered by an invisible wire to hang in front of me as I was climbing a cliff where I had every reason to think no one else was present, and this "angel" told me to burn the bus station, and I did, and the judge found out about the prank, and found out how diabolically convincing it had been, he might well dismiss my case, calling my action reasonable. Or again, if a heavenly host actually appeared to me and to all mankind, and promised us all eternal bliss if I burn down the bus station, my fellow men might consider me irrational to refuse.

On the other hand, if I were talked into burning the bus station by some sleazy prophet, my religious observance might well be called irrational.

I. There remains one way of reconstruing the Wager argument so as to make the preceding criticisms inapplicable. It might be observed that many professed skeptics have lingering tendencies to believe in some religion, and that proposing a wager is an effective way to exploit these tendencies to bring them back into the fold.

Thus a lapsed Christian might feel that there is a 1/100 chance that Christianity is right, while assigning no likelihood at all to the claims of other religions. Furthermore, he may be sure that if Christianity is right, then however ordinary sinners and believers in other religions may fare, hard-boiled atheists will fare very badly indeed. For such a person as this, the wager might be thought to exert a powerful attraction to return to active Christianity.

However, this doesn't seem to be true in actual practice, and there are good reasons why this should be so. For one thing, if someone is a hard-boiled atheist, he won't assign any positive probability to Christian claims about God. And if he isn't a hard-boiled atheist and does assign a positive probability to Christian claims, he is likely to imagine the Christian God as too nice to be stingy with rewards for people in his category, so the Wager won't lead him to change his schedule.

Furthermore, lingering religiosity is not in itself enough to make the Wager appetizing. It has to be lingering religiosity which the agent will express in a positive probability estimate, or otherwise the Wager won't get started. And many people who have superstitious tendencies would still not attach any positive probability to these superstitions.

And finally, even when someone does attach a positive probability to some religion's god-claims (and to no other's), the Wager argument is not sure to bind him. Let us very roughly distinguish between objective and subjective theories of probability by noting that on an objective theory, it is not necessary that someone's judgment of a probability have any connection with his wagering behavior; while on a subjective view, given the person's value scheme, his wagering behavior is essential to determining his probability judgments. Then on the objective view, even given a positive probability estimate for some religion and a definite preference for heaven, being willing to make the wager doesn't follow and it is even a vexed question (at least) to show that wager-reluctance in such circumstances would even be less than reasonable. And on the subjective view, the probability estimate won't be of much use in persuading the agent to wager, considering that willingness to wager was an essential feature in determining the probability estimate.

Notes

1. *Pascal's Pensees,* bilingual ed., trans. H. F. Stewart (New York: Modern Library, 1947).

2. Georges Brunet, in *Le Pari de Pascal,* pp. 62–63, points out that Pascal was not the originator of the Wager argument. Other writings on the background of Pascal's argument are A. Ducas, *Le Pari de Pascal,* and M. J. Orcibal, "Le Fragment Infini-Rien et ses Sources," in *Blaise Pascal, L'Homme et L'Oeuvre,* (Paris, 1956), Sec. V.

3. William James, *The Will to Believe* (New York, 1897), pp. 5–6.

4. Jean Mesnard, *Pascal, His Life and Works,* trans. G. S. Fraser (London: Harvill Press, 1952), pp. 156–57.

5. M. L. Goldmann ("Le Pari, est-il Ecrit 'Pour le Libertin'?" in *Blaise Pascal: L'Homme et L'Oeuvre,* Sec. IV) argues that the argument is not for the skeptic who is *satisfied* with this world, but is rather for the man who is conscious of the miserable human condition. It is certainly consistent for a self-interested, rational skeptic to feel unhappy with man's lot. But even if he has the appropriate human longings, the rational skeptic must find Pascal's argument invalid.

6. See, for example, Harald Cramer, *The Elements of Probability Theory* (New York: Wiley, 1955), p. 95; or William Feller, *Introduction to Probability Theory and its Applications* (New York: Wiley, 1957), pp. 199–201.

7. See William Kneale, *Probability and Induction* (Oxford, Engl.: Clarendon Press, 1949), pp. 184–85.

17. Pascalian Wagering

Thomas V. Morris

> Either God is or he is not. But to which view shall we be inclined? Reason cannot decide this question. Infinite chaos separates us. At the far end of this infinite distance, a coin is being spun which will come down heads or tails. How will you wager? Reason cannot make you choose either, reason cannot prove either wrong.

In this vivid and memorable passage, Blaise Pascal began to develop the famous argument which has come to be known as "Pascal's Wager."[1] The Wager is widely regarded as an argument for the rationality of belief in God which completely circumvents all considerations of proof or evidence that there is a God. Viewed as such, it has both excited and aggravated philosophers for years. Some have applauded it as a simple, down-to-earth, practical, and decisive line of reasoning which avoids altogether the esoteric, mind-boggling intricacies and apparently inevitable indecisiveness of the traditional theistic arguments that year after year continue to be revised and reevaluated. They seem to share the view of Pascal himself who once wrote that

> The metaphysical proofs for the existence of God are so remote from human reasoning and so involved that they make little impact, and, even if they did help some people, it would only be for the moment during which they watched the demonstration, because an hour later they would be afraid they had made a mistake.[2]

Others have been exceedingly offended by the very idea of wagering on God in hopes of obtaining infinite gain, and shocked by the suggestion that rational belief can be established by wholly nonevidential, or nonepistemic means. Such philosophers have succeeded in raising an impressive number of objections to Pascal's case, objections which in the eyes of many render the argument of the Wager a failure. In this essay, I propose to examine this common view of the Wager as intended to secure the rationality of religious belief without any regard to purely epistemic matters. I want to suggest that such a view involves a misunderstanding of the Wager based on a neglect to take seriously an important feature of its original context, manifested by those initial remarks which Pascal used to launch his argument and from which this paper began. A proper understanding of the epistemic context within which the Wager was intended to be used can provide us with a way of answering a number of the most standard and imposing objections to this interesting argument.

Source: Thomas Morris, "Pascalian Wagering," *Canadian Journal of Philosophy* 16 no. 3 (1986): 437–54.

I

In attempting to show on prudential grounds that everyone ought to be a theist, Wager enthusiasts often seek to maximize the rhetorical force of their argument by conceding almost everything to the epistemically reasonable atheist and then producing from his own premises their desired conclusion. The rhetoric of their presentation often develops like this. First, it is pointed out that rational gamblers seeking to maximize their gains over the long run bet in accordance with the highest mathematical expectation, where expectation is established with the formula

$$\text{(E) (Probability} \times \text{Payoff)} - \text{Cost} = \text{Expectation}$$

and is ranked for all possible bets in the contest or game situation. Then the confident Pascalian announces that in this life we are all in a forced betting situation in which the possible wagers are that there is a God and that there is no God. The situation is said to be forced in the sense that not acting as if there is a God—not praying, not seeking God's will for one's life, not being thankful to God—is considered to be the equivalent to acting as if there is no God, practically speaking.[3] So one either acts as if there is a God, thereby betting on God, or one does not so act, thereby betting there is no God. Which bet should a rational person make? To answer this question, we must make assignments to the expectation formula and compare outcomes for the bets of theism and atheism. And this is where the rhetorical flourishes come into play whose assumptions result in disaster for the argument.

Let atheism be assigned an extremely high probability, and theism accordingly a very low one, the modern-day Pascalian suggests. It will not matter, so long as neither value is 0 or 1. And so long as theism is even a possibility, it is claimed, its probability is greater than 0, however small, and atheism's is less than 1. Now consider the question of cost. What does it cost to be an atheist? The Pascalian is typically ready to concede that it costs nothing. For, remember, in betting situations the cost is figured under the presumption that the outcome is unknown. So atheism cannot be said here to cost the loss of eternal bliss. And further, any values of the religious life whose descriptions do not entail the existence of God, such as the aesthetic pleasures of liturgy, and the social fulfillment of religious community, are in principle available to atheists as well as theists, if they are sufficiently shrewd. Even the comfort of believing in an afterlife need not be the exclusive possession of theists. So even in this life atheism can be conceded to bear no cost. But religious belief, on the contrary, can be acknowledged to exact quite a cost from the believer. An adherent to typical theistic religions finds himself under all sorts of prohibitions and rules not recognized by the nonbeliever. So, the Pascalian is often quick to agree, the cost of betting on God is great.

Unlike standard betting situations, we have not to this point had determinate, precise assignments of probability and cost, but rather have contented ourselves with very general, comparative indications. According to the view of the Wager under consideration, this does not matter, however, since the values we must assign to the payoff variable will work in the formula for expectation in such a way as to render any precision with respect to the other variables irrelevant. Theism promises infinite, eternal reward. Atheism at best carries with it a promise of finite rewards—whatever pleasures in this life would have been prohibited to the theist. So the Pascalian claims.

Respective expectations of atheism and theism are then figured and ranked as follows. In the case of atheism, multiplying a very high probability by a great finite payoff, and subtracting no cost at all will yield at best a very large finite value. For theism, on the other hand, the product of an infinite payoff and any positive finite probability, however small, will yield an infinite expectation, regardless of how great a finite cost is subtracted. So theism has an infinitely higher expectation than atheism. Thus, the rational person seeking to maximize his gains in this betting situation ought to bet on God.

II

Many objections have been raised against Pascal's Wager. I want to focus for a moment on those which I think to be particularly problematic for the sort of presentation of the Wager just elucidated. Let us refer to that development of the argument as the epistemically unconcerned version of the Wager, a version in which it does not matter what the precise epistemic status of theism or of atheism is, as long as neither is certainly true. Such a version is vulnerable to a number of objections.

First of all, many people who accept (E) as a formula appropriate for use in normal betting situations may hesitate or refuse to use it in this situation. For the conditions under which it is appropriately used may not obtain with respect to this quite unusual bet. In normal situations, for which the formula was constructed, possible payoffs are always finite in value. The insertion of an infinite value here so overrides considerations of probability and cost as to render them nearly irrelevant. Can (E) be expected to serve its ordinary function with such an extraordinary assignment to one of its variables?

Likewise, in normal betting situations there is usually a controlled range of divergence between probability values when the cost of some bet is high. And, again, it is in such situations that (E) has its appropriate application. Often, this feature of a betting situation is not perceived as being so important. And it need not be, so long as there is, as there usually is, a direct correlation and otherwise proper sort of relation between magnitude of cost and magnitude of probability. But in this version of the Wager, there is an inverse correlation between these factors. Under such conditions, degree of divergence between probabilities becomes a concern. The epistemically unconcerned version of the Wager purports to work regardless of the disparity between the probabilities of theism and atheism, even if, for example. there is only a one in a trillion chance, or less, of theism's being true. It can be rational to distrust the formula's application under such conditions. Further, there is some serious question about the use of probability assignments at all by this version of the Wager. It seems clear that the only interpretation of probability relevant and useable here is the subjective one; yet, how are even subjective probability assignments supposed to arise out of the mere insistence that theism is not demonstrably impossible? Its mere possibility need not be taken to endow it with any positive probability at all.

Third, (E) clearly functions to aid a rational gambler in maximizing his gains over the long run. And this it does, since long-run success is compatible with the losing of many individual bets along the way. Now, despite the fact that one often hears Pascalians insist on the formula's appropriateness in this case since "there is no longer run than eternity," it is clear that in the bet concerning God we do not have a situation of repetitive wagering, in which ultimate maximization of gain is compatible with numerous losses along the way. And so again it could be argued that conditions do not obtain in which the rational bettor is best guided by (E). But of course, if (E) is not used, this popular form of the Wager does not work.

A fourth objection to the Wager we must consider, one raised and developed by numerous critics in recent years, is the Many Claimants Objection, one which is often characterized as resulting from a partitioning problem. The Wager, it is said, partitions the variously possible bets on the issue of God inadequately, presenting us with only two options, theism and atheism, when in reality there are many, perhaps innumerably many. And this is much more than an easily correctable oversight. First of all, there are numerous different versions of theism extant, all vying for credence. For any which promises eternal bliss, and many do, (E) will yield an infinite expectation, as long as there is the slightest positive probability that it is true. And if mere possibility yields some positive probability, as the epistemically unconcerned version of the Wager alleges, matters are even worse. For if it is even logically possible that there exists a being who promises infinite eternal reward to all and only those who deny the existence of all other claimants to worship, including the Christian God, (E) yields a dilemma equivalent to a practical contradiction: a rational person both ought and ought not bet on, say, the Christian God. Further, as if this were not enough, not even will it be the case that some theism or other will be preferable to all forms of atheism. For consider the apparent logical possibility that there is no God and that by some weird law of nature there will be an infinite, eternally blissful afterlife for all and only those who in this life live as convinced atheists. On the basic assumptions of the epistemically unconcerned version of the Wager, the expectation associated with this form of atheism will also be infinite. Clearly, we have here a serious problem.[4]

Most recent commentators have seen one or more of these objections as decisive against the Wager, sufficient to show it to have no rational force. And this is, I think, a correct judgment with respect to the epistemically unconcerned version of the Wager. But it is neither the only version of a Wager-style argument nor, I believe, the sort of version we should attribute to Pascal. When the formula (E) is allowed to work on very low probability values, even those so low as to be approaching 0, and the positive probability of a bet is thought to be provided by the mere logical possibility of its outcome, a context is created in which the production of absurd results is unavoidable. But this is not the context of the original Wager.

It is almost anyone's guess as to what Pascal's planned defense of the Christian faith would have looked like in detail had he lived to complete it. One thing that is clear, though, is that it was not an epistemically unconcerned project. In fact, even a fairly casual reading of the *Pensées* will show that Pascal felt it important to try to defeat prima facie evidential considerations which could be held to count seriously against the truth of Christian beliefs, considerations such as, for example, the hidden-ness of God, and the rejection by most of his Jewish contemporaries of the Christian claim that Jesus was the long-awaited Messiah sent from God. Furthermore, although he engages in no natural theology at all, Pascal does marshal together quite a few considerations in favor of the reliability of the Bible and the trustworthiness of Christian claims. We have no reason to think that he intended his Wager argument to operate in complete isolation from any purely epistemic. considerations. In fact quite the contrary is indicated even by the remarks with which he launched the argument. Recall the claim that "Reason cannot decide this question." If epistemic conditions were such that Christian theism could properly receive a very low assignment of subjective probability by any well-informed rational person, and its denial a correspondingly high value, it would not be the case that "reason cannot decide this question." I think we have here sufficient textual indication that the Wager argument was intended to work only for people who judge the theism Pascal had in mind and its denial to be in rough epistemic parity.

If reason cannot decide whether the Christian God exists or not, there cannot be a clear preponderance of purely epistemic considerations either way. Thus there cannot be a great disparity between the assigned probability values of theism and atheism. If it can be rational for a person to judge these positions to be in rough epistemic parity, it can be rational to dismiss altogether one objection to the Wager we considered, the one in which hesitation is expressed concerning the application of (E) to situations with greatly disparate probability values. The objection in this context becomes irrelevant.

Likewise, the hesitation to employ (E) with an infinite value for one of its variables is groundless unless there is reason to believe that allowing such a value assignment will have obviously absurd or unacceptable consequences. And a moment's consideration will show that the only problematic and absurd consequences of applying (E) with an infinite payoff value are displayed in the famous Many Claimants problem, a problem which as we have seen results only from the additional assumptions as well that (1) apparent logical possibility should be translated into some positive nonzero probability value, and (2) the Wager formula can and should be employed regardless of the probability disparity between possible bets. But if both these assumptions are rejected, the Many Claimants problem does not arise, and the importation of an infinite value into (E) has no clearly problematic results.

So holding the Wager to be appropriate only under conditions of rough epistemic parity between Christian theism and its denial avoids altogether three otherwise interesting and worrisome objections. What about the fourth we considered? We do not have here a repetitive wagering situation in which short-term loss is compatible with long-term gain. There is only one bet; it is either won or lost. But if (E) is thought not to be relevant, how is a decision between theism and atheism to be made? If theism and atheism are in rough epistemic parity, no decision between them can be made on purely epistemic grounds. Some form of agnosticism would be the appropriate doxastic stance if no considerations other than purely epistemic ones could or should enter into such decisions. But, according to Pascal, this is betting against God. One's doxastic stance is a form of, and a function of, behavior which amounts, in the context, to the placing of a bet. And surely there are values other than purely epistemic values which are relevant in the placing of a bet. What sort of values? Just the ones which function in (E). So even though the wager concerning God is not only one episode in a repetitive wagering situation, there seems to be no good alternative to (E) to employ here when choosing one's bet. So given our restriction of the Wager argument to conditions of rough epistemic parity, this objection is neutralized as well.

This view of the wager is an improvement over the epistemically unconcerned version, then, in two respects. It seems to be more in line with Pascal's original intentions, and it is immune to certain difficult objections which plague the more contemporary version. But this version of the wager can have use for a rational person only if it can be reasonable to judge Christian theism and its denial to be in rough epistemic parity. Pascal seems to have thought this was possible. But others have offered reasons to think otherwise. So this is an issue which will merit some consideration.

III

There are two possible ways in which theism and atheism can be in rough epistemic parity for a person. It seems possible for a person rationally to think that there is no positive evidence or any other epistemic ground for thinking that there is a God, nor any good evidence or other epistemic ground for thinking that there is not. Such a person might be aware of traditional arguments for both positions but find all of them flawed to such an extent that he reasonably judges none of them to endow either conclusion with any positive epistemic status. And he might lack any other purely epistemic consideration either way. For example, he could also lack any natural inclination to believe either way, and so find himself with neither a properly basic theistic belief nor a properly basic atheistic belief. Let us say that with respect to the issue of theism versus atheism, such a person would find himself in epistemically null conditions. The other way in which theism and atheism can be in rough epistemic parity for a person obtains when each is judged to have some positive epistemic status, but neither is more evident than, or clearly outweighs, the other. Let us say that a person who reasonably makes such a judgment is in epistemically ambiguous conditions regarding theism and atheism. Initially, it would seem that if either epistemically null, or epistemically ambiguous conditions can reasonably be thought sometimes to obtain, we have reason to believe that a version of the Wager requiring rough epistemic parity can be formulated as a potentially useful decision making device.

Both N. R. Hanson and Michael Scriven, however, have argued that it is impossible to be in epistemically null conditions with respect to any positive existence claim. In the posthumously published "What I Don't Believe," Hanson wrote: "When there is no good reason for thinking a claim to be true, *that* in itself is good reason for thinking the claim to be false"[5] and, accordingly, "a 'proof' of x's non-existence usually derives from the fact that there is no good reason for supposing that x *does* exist."[6] In the line with this, Scriven wrote in *Primary Philosophy* that: "The proper alternative, when there is no evidence, is not mere suspension of belief; it is disbelief."[7] Applying this to the question of theism, Scriven went on to say that, "Atheism is obligatory in the absence of any evidence for God's existence."[8] If epistemically null conditions could obtain for any proposition *p* and its denial − *p,* then according to Hanson and Scriven, it seems, we would be forced to disbelieve *p,* thereby believing − *p,* and to disbelieve − *p,* thereby believing *p.* But this is absurd, so epistemically null conditions cannot obtain both for a proposition and its denial. The absence of a positive epistemic consideration in favor of *p* will just be a positive epistemic consideration in favor of − *p,* and vice versa.

On close inspection of their arguments, however, it becomes clear that Hanson and Scriven are not concerned to make a completely general claim about the epistemic dynamics of just any sort of proposition whatsoever, but rather that they want to lay down a rule for the evaluation only of positive existence claims, propositions which assert that some sort of object exists. One feature of such propositions Hanson points out is this: it is possible in principle to gather conclusive evidence concerning any positive existential generalization; whereas, it is not possible in principle to gather such evidence for the denial of an unrestricted, positive existential, a proposition of the form of an unrestricted universal generalization. Hanson sees this asymmetry as setting the logical backdrop for what we can call the Hanson-Scriven Thesis:

> HST For any rational subject S and any positive existence claim P, if S is in possession of no good evidence or any other positive epistemic ground for thinking that P is true, then S ought to adopt the cognitive relation to P of denial.

Now of course, the evidential asymmetry between unrestricted positive and negative existentials does not entail or in any other way dictate the HST. But the intuitive force the HST has had for many philosophers need not be impugned in the least by this fact. For it just seems that in many ordinary situations we do govern our assent by something like it.

Suppose I am seated in my office, which is neither excessively large nor unusually cluttered. The proposition suddenly occurs to me that there is a large boa constrictor in the room. I make a quick but cautious, thorough inspection of the place. Suppose I find absolutely no trace of such an animal anywhere in the office. What is the most rational stance for me to take concerning the suddenly entertained proposition? Affirmation? Certainly not. Agnosticism? Surely this would be just as inappropriate. The only rational stance to take in absence of any evidence or any other positive epistemic consideration at all will be one of denial. And that judgment seems to accord perfectly with the HST. Any number of such examples from everyday life could be produced as well which seem to show that Hanson and Scriven have indeed captured in their thesis one of our ordinary principles for rational judgment. And if we are committed to such a principle, we are committed to refusing to allow the claim that epistemically null conditions concerning both theism and atheism can obtain for any rational subject. The absence of any evidence or any other positive epistemic consideration for theism will just count as providing a good, decisive consideration for atheism.

An ingenious rejoinder to Hanson and Scriven has been devised by Alvin Plantinga.[9] Plantinga asks us to consider the proposition

1. There is at least one human being that was not created by God.

Since it is, he suggests, a necessary truth about God (at least about the God of orthodox Christian theology) that

2. If God exists, then God has created all the human beings there are,

any set of epistemic considerations in favor of the truth of (1)—evidences, arguments, etc.—will have to contain an argument that there is no God. But suppose that

A. There is no good argument against God's existence.

Then we shall have in consequence no good argument for (1) and so, according to Hanson and Scriven, we must believe its denial:

1'. All human beings are created by God.

Now suppose also, Plantinga suggests, that

B. There is no good argument for God's existence,

a supposition which surely would be dear to the hearts of both Hanson and Scriven. Then when considering

3. There is a God

we find that we are obliged to believe its denial

3'. There is no God.

But then, Plantinga continues, assuming that

C. There are no good arguments for or against the existence of God,

the Hanson-Scriven view forces us to believe

4. There is no God and all human beings are created by him,

which is awkward and embarassing enough for anyone, but which also, along with the obvious truths that

5. Some human beings exist

and that

6. No human being was created by God unless God exists

entails a contradiction. And certainly, no principle which produces this sort of absurdity is worthy of rational acceptance.

But, of course, we can well imagine that Hanson and Scriven would reply that this attempted refutation of their principle just begs the question against them. For on their principle, assumption (C) could never be true. The absence of any good argument *for* the existence of God would just itself provide us with a good argument *against* the existence of God. The epistemically null situation portrayed by (C) could not obtain. So this argument against the principle espoused by Hanson and Scriven cannot after all show it to be unacceptable.

Is there anything wrong with their principle? It has stood for years in the literature, unrefuted, and apparently endorsed by many philosophers. Further, it has the apparent backing of common intuitions about the proper governance of our assent, as illustrated by the story of the boa constrictor. However, it is easy to show that such backing is apparent only for the specific HST formulation we are considering and which is necessary for blocking the possibility of epistemically null conditions obtaining for both theism and atheism.

Circumstances in which the lack of any positive epistemic considerations (evidence, etc.) for some positive existence claim P rationally oblige a subject S to deny P rather than to withhold on it are those in which S reasonably believes he is in *good epistemic position* with respect to P, where being in good epistemic position relative to a proposition is understood in such a way that any subject S is in good epistemic position relative to P if and only if (1) P is such that if it were true, there would exist positive epistemic considerations indicating or manifesting its truth, and (2) S is such that if there existed such considerations, he would, or most likely would, possess them. When I have completed my search for the boa, I am in good epistemic position to assess the claim that such a thing exists in my office. *In that position,* and only in that position, lack of any positive epistemic consideration for the claim amounts to as decisive a consideration against the claim as one could want. It is only when a person reasonably believes himself to be in good epistemic position for assessing an existence claim that an absence of any evidence or other positive epistemic consideration for it can warrant and require his denial of the claim.

So the HST should be revised to read something like

HST' For any rational subject S and any positive existence claim P, if S rationally believes himself to be in good epistemic position relative to P, and S is in possession of no good evidence or any other positive epistemic ground for thinking that P is true, then S ought to adopt the cognitive relation to P of denial.

Suppose that someone believes there to be no positive epistemic support for theism. Can he also believe there to be no such support for atheism? Can he rationally judge himself to be in epistemically null conditions regarding both claims? According to the HST', he can so long as he is rationally unsure whether he is in a good epistemic position relative to theism, or rationally believes himself not to be in such a position.

A rational person lacking any positive epistemic considerations can certainly be agnostic about his epistemic position on theism. For suppose he thinks there to be no good evidence or any other positive epistemic consideration either way. Either the Christian God exists or he does not. If the Christian God exists, any failure to have positive considerations of this (any lack of evidence, or of a natural inclination to believe, etc.) may be due to the noetic effects of sin. And on the other hand, if there is no such being, a failure to see that there is not may be due to low-grade effects of a deep psychological need not to know. In either case, one who lacks evidence or other positive considerations would not be in good epistemic position, having his cognitive abilities clouded in one way or another. Realizing these possibilities can rationally warrant agnosticism with respect to one's epistemic position on this issue.[10] And that condition is sufficient for one's rationally judging the situation to be epistemically null, and on purely epistemic grounds withholding on both theism and atheism. HST' does not require otherwise.

Any perceived condition of epistemic parity between a proposition and its denial can be expressed in a subjective probability assignment of ½ to each option. And for anyone in a condition of epistemic nullity with respect to Christian theism and its denial who is willing to register this with a probability estimation (a function of expectations) of "50/50," Pascal's wager can be formulated to suggest prudential reasons for venturing in behavior beyond the agnosticism which only epistemic considerations alone would require.

But of course, as I have indicated earlier, Pascal did not believe that any well-informed inquirer would find himself in epistemically null conditions concerning Christian theism and its denial. So on this count it might seem unimportant to have argued the possibility of such conditions obtaining with respect to these alternatives. Furthermore, anyone willing to assign a subjective probability assignment to these two alternatives of each, despite being bereft of any positive epistemic consideration for either, seems clearly to be adopting the procedure of assigning positive probability values on the ground of logical possibility alone, a policy which I have suggested is unwise, and has been partly responsible for actually weakening the reasoning of the Wager. So on its own, it is not so important to have established, against the contentions of Hanson and Scriven, the possibility of epistemically null conditions obtaining here. What is important is seeing how an HST-style principle requiring denial under conditions of no positive grounds for an existence claim must be qualified. For such a principle could be reformulated quite naturally and easily for circumstances in which the epistemic considerations relevant to such a proposition (distinct from any arising from the application of such a principle itself) were ambiguous, or counterbalanced in such a way that there existed no sufficient consideration for the purely epistemic endorsement of the proposition. Such an extension of the original HST might be thought to be in full accord with the basic intent of its proponents. And such a principle could be taken to rule out the possibility that any rational, well-informed inquirer be in epistemically ambiguous conditions with respect to any positive existence claim and its denial. But this is precisely what Pascal envisioned to be possible in the case of Christian theism and its denial. Once we have seen how the original HST must be qualified in such a way that it allows epistemically null conditions to obtain here, it surely will require no separate argument to see how a properly qualified version will allow the possibility of conditions of epistemic ambiguity. And surely, many people confess to finding themselves in just such conditions on the issue of Pascal's concern, seeing some reason to think Christian theism to be true, some reason to think it false. This perspective is very naturally reflected by such subjective probability assessments as "roughly 50/50." In any situation of rough epistemic parity the famous and much maligned Principle of Indifference can even be produced to yield a probability assignment of exactly ½ for each of the two competitors.[11] If it is rational for anyone to make such an assignment as a reflection of his subjective doxastic state, it is reasonable, so far, to think that Pascal's Wager has a context of rational application.

IV

It seems to have been Pascal's conviction that a person's epistemic condition with respect to theism and atheism is a function of his attitudes, desires, and other commitments, and that in turn these are a function of the sorts of patterns of behavior he liked to call "habit." It is a dangerous illusion to think of our epistemic capacities as existing and operating independently of the other features of our lives. The person who loves God, according to Pascal, is able to see that everything is created by him (781). The person with contrary passions is bereft of this perspicacity. It was Pascal's view that there exists evidence for the truth of Christian theism which exceeds, or at least equals, evidence to the contrary (835). But he was convinced that it is a person's passional state which will determine how he sees the evidence, and what he does on the basis of it.

The enjoinder to wager on God is the recommendation, on prudential grounds, to adopt a Christian form of life to the extent that one is able. Pascal thought that an entry into that sort of life pattern would have a long-term and cumulative effect on a person's attitudes, desires, and epistemic state. As contrary passions were bridled and finally put aside, he was convinced that anyone who formerly was incapable of seeing or knowing God would attain this capacity, and only with the onset of such a capacity could true faith come.

It is not an assumption of the Wager that God will reward a person for a deliberate, calculated charade of belief undertaken and maintained on grounds of the grossest self-interest. So the famous objection of William James, who was offended by such an assumption, misses the point. There is no doubt that the argument as constructed by Pascal appeals to self-interest. But its intent and goal is to induce a wager whose outcome will yield true faith, an attitudinal state in which self-interest takes its rightful and subordinate place as a behavior motivation. Furthermore, the Wager need not be formulated as an appeal to self-interest at all. It can be presented as an appeal to altruism. One then bets on God so that one will be in a proper position nonhypocritically to urge others to do so, thereby potentially providing them with the greatest amount of good one possibly could.

Likewise, other moral objections to the Wager are easily defeated. James found it morally offensive that God would reward those who want reward. Terence Penelhum apparently has found it repugnant that God would punish anyone who did not otherwise believe for failing to following such a course of attempted aggrandizement.[12] Both James and Penelhum impose a conception of the eternal economy on the argument which it in no way requires and then object to their own creations. In particular, they have what we may call an inappropriately externalist conception of afterlife. One reads Pascal's original

Wager passage in vain for the language of rewards and punishment. He does not there portray God at all as either granting or withholding benefits in accordance with how people bet. It seems on the contrary that a more internalist conception of eternal beatitude can both accord with Pascal's own Wager presentation and serve to neutralize the James and Penelhum type of objection. One's state after bodily death is then viewed as being in proper moral and spiritual continuity with one's earthly existence. Those who have hungered and thirsted after righteousness are satisfied. Those who have not, are not. Now, it might appear odd to characterize all those who align themselves with the Christian God as those who hunger and thirst after righteousness. In particular this may seem an inappropriate description of those who are, on Pascalian grounds, wagering on God. However, as indicated already, this is the sort of mind-set meant to eventuate from the particular wagering behavior recommended. Further, the infinite "payoff" as characterized in the Christian tradition, if delineated carefully enough, just may not appeal to a person with no taste for moral and spiritual good. For the heaven of Pascal is not the heaven of, say, popular Islam. It is not an infinite expansion of sensual delights. In fact, it is the sort of infinite bliss which will be attractive only to those with at least a latent capacity to exemplify the attitude characterized biblically as a hunger and thirst for righteousness. And only such as these are, in the theology of Christian theism, able to commune with God at all.

It is not my intent here to defend Pascal's Wager against all extant criticism, although I think it eminently more defensible than most recent commentators have allowed. My primary aim has been merely to suggest that when we attend carefully to some important clues in Pascal's text, we can see that the sort of argument he intended is immune to numerous potent objections which have been raised against contemporary versions of the argument differing in important respects from his own. When these objections have been cleared away, it becomes possible to consider more seriously other philosophical and religious questions raised by the whole idea of Pascalian Wagering.

Notes

1. Blaise Pascal, *Pensées,* trans. A. J. Krailsheimer (Harmondsworth, Middlesex [Engl.]: Penguin Books, 1966), p. 150

2. Pascal, p. 86, pensée 190; hereafter citations from the *Pensées* will all be from the edition cited above, and will be given by the pensée numbering therein adopted.

3. Such a claim has been made or implied by many theists in different contexts. Recently, for example, Peter Geach has written: "Now for those who believe in an Almightly God, a man's every act is an act either of obeying or of ignoring or of defying that God . . ." ("The Moral Law and the Law of God," in *Divine Commands and Morality,* ed. Paul Helm [Oxford, Engl.: Oxford University Press, 1980], p. 173). It is easy to see how ignoring and defying God could be categorized together as acting as if there is no God.

4. One of the best recent explications of this sort of problem is Michael Martin's essay "Pascal's Wager as an Argument for Not Believing in God," *Religious Studies* 19 (1983): 57–64.

5. From N. R. Hanson, *What I Do Not Believe and Other Essays,* ed. Stephen Toulmin and Harry Woolf (Dordrecht, Neth.: D. Reidel, 1972), p. 323. I have explored the views of Hanson and Scriven in "Agnosticism," *Analysis* 45 (1985): 219–24, from which the present section derives some of its points.

6. Hanson, p. 310. (Eds.: For another statement of the thesis presented by Hanson and Scriven, see the Antony Flew article, "The Presumption of Atheism," reprinted in Part I of this volume, pp. 19–32.)

7. Michael Scriven, *Primary Philosophy* (New York: McGraw-Hill, 1966), p. 103.

8. Scriven, p. 103.

9. The argument is presented in his major paper, "Reason and Belief in God," in *Faith and Rationality*, ed. A. Plantinga and N. Wolterstorff (Notre Dame, IN: The University of Notre Dame Press, 1983), pp. 27–29.

10. I lay out a different ground for rational doubt here than in "Agnosticism."

11. The Principle of Indifference has recently received impressive defense at the hands of George N. Schlesinger. See his book *The Intelligibility of Nature* (Aberdeen: Aberdeen University Press, 1985).

12. Terence Penelhum, *Religion and Rationality* (New York: Random House, 1971), pp. 211–19.

---

18. The Ethics of Belief

W. K. CLIFFORD

A shipowner was about to send to sea an emigrant ship. He knew that she was old, and not over-well built at the first; that she had seen many seas and climes, and often had needed repairs. Doubts had been suggested to him that possibly she was not seaworthy. These doubts preyed upon his mind and made him unhappy; he thought that perhaps he ought to have her thoroughly overhauled and refitted, even though this should put him to great expense. Before the ship sailed, however, he succeeded in overcoming these melancholy reflections. He said to himself that she had gone safely through so many voyages and weathered so many storms that it was idle to suppose she would not come safely home from this trip also. He would put his trust in Providence, which could hardly fail to protect all these unhappy families that were leaving their fatherland to seek for better times elsewhere. He would dismiss from his mind all ungenerous suspicions about the honesty of builders and contractors. In such ways he acquired a sincere and comfortable conviction that his vessel was thoroughly safe and seaworthy; he watched her departure with a light heart, and benevolent wishes for the success of the exiles in their strange new home that was to be; and he got his insurance money when she went down in midocean and told no tales.

What shall we say of him? Surely this, that he was verily guilty of the death of those men. It is admitted that he did sincerely believe in the soundness of his ship; but the sincerity of his conviction can in no wise to help him, because he had no right to believe on

---

Source: Reprinted from W. K. Clifford, *Lectures and Essays* (London: Macmillan, 1879).

such evidence as was before him. He had acquired his belief not by honestly earning it in patient investigation, but by stifling his doubts. And although in the end he may have felt so sure about it that he could not think otherwise, yet inasmuch as he had knowingly and willingly worked himself into that frame of mind, he must be held responsible for it.

Let us alter the case a little, and suppose that the ship was not unsound after all; that she made her voyage safely, and many others after it. Will that diminish the guilt of her owner? Not one jot. When an action is once done, it is right or wrong forever; no accidental failure of its good or evil fruits can possibly alter that. The man would not have been innocent, he would only have been not found out. The question of right or wrong has to do with the origin of his belief, not the matter of it; not what it was, but how he got it; not whether it turned out to be true or false, but whether he had a right to believe on such evidence as was before him.

There was once an island in which some of the inhabitants professed a religion teaching neither the doctrine of original sin nor that of eternal punishment. A suspicion got abroad that the professors of this religion had made use of unfair means to get their doctrines taught to children. They were accused of wresting the laws of their country in such a way as to remove children from the care of their natural and legal guardians; and even of stealing them away and keeping them concealed from their friends and relations. A certain number of men formed themselves into a society for the purpose of agitating the public about this matter. They published grave accusations against individual citizens of the highest position and character, and did all in their power to injure those citizens in the exercise of their professions. So great was the noise they made, that a Commission was appointed to investigate the facts; but after the Commission had carefully inquired into all the evidence that could be got, it appeared that the accused were innocent. Not only had they been accused on insufficient evidence, but the evidence of their innocence was such as the agitators might easily have obtained, if they had attempted a fair inquiry. After these disclosures the inhabitants of that country looked upon the members of the agitating society, not only as persons whose judgment was to be distrusted, but also as no longer to be counted honorable men. For although they had sincerely and conscientiously believed in the charges they had made, yet they had no right to believe on such evidence as was before them. Their sincere convictions, instead of being honestly earned by patient inquiring, were stolen by listening to the voice of prejudice and passion.

Let us vary this case also, and suppose, other things remaining as before, that a still more accurate investigation proved the accused to have been really guilty. Would this make any difference in the guilt of the accusers? Clearly not; the question is not whether their belief was true or false, but whether they entertained it on wrong grounds. They would no doubt say, "Now you see that we were right after all; next time perhaps you will believe us." And they might be believed, but they would not thereby become honorable men. They would not be innocent, they would only be not found out. Every one of them, if he chose to examine himself *in foro conscientiae,* would know that he had acquired and nourished a belief, when he had no right to believe on such evidence as was before him; and therein he would know that he had done a wrong thing.

It may be said, however, that in both of these supposed cases it is not the belief which is judged to be wrong, but the action following upon it. The shipowner might say, "I am perfectly certain that my ship is sound, but still I feel it my duty to have her examined, before trusting the lives of so many people to her." And it might be said to the agitator, "However convinced you were of the justice of your cause and the truth of your convictions, you ought not to have made a public attack upon any man's character until you had examined the evidence on both sides with the utmost patience and care."

In the first place, let us admit that, so far as it goes, this view of the case is right and necessary; right, because even when a man's belief is so fixed that he cannot think otherwise, he still has a choice in regard to the action suggested by it, and so cannot escape the duty of investigating on the ground of the strength of his convictions; and necessary, because those who are not yet capable of controlling their feelings and thoughts must have a plain rule dealing with overt acts.

But this being premised as necessary, it becomes clear that it is not sufficient, and that our previous judgment is required to supplement it. For it is not possible so to sever the belief from the action it suggests as to condemn the one without condemning the other. No man holding a strong belief on one side of a question, or even wishing to hold a belief on one side, can investigate it with such fairness and completeness as if he were really in doubt and unbiased; so that the existence of a belief not founded on fair inquiry unfits a man for the performance of this necessary duty.

Nor is that truly a belief at all which has not some influence upon the actions of him who holds it. He who truly believes that which prompts him to an action has looked upon the action to lust after it, he has committed it already in his heart. If a belief is not realized immediately in open deeds, it is stored up for the guidance of the future. It goes to make a part of that aggregate of beliefs which is the link between sensation and action at every moment of all our lives, and which is so organized and compacted together that no part of it can be isolated from the rest, but every new addition modifies the structure of the whole. No real belief, however trifling and fragmentary it may seem, is ever truly insignificant; it prepares us to receive more of its like, confirms those which resembled it before, and weakens others; and so gradually it lays a stealthy train in our inmost thoughts, which may some day explode into overt action, and leave its stamp upon our character forever.

And no one man's belief is in any case a private matter which concerns himself alone. Our lives are guided by that general conception of the course of things which has been created by society for social purposes. Our words, our phrases, our forms and processes and modes of thought are common property, fashioned and perfected from age to age; an heirloom which every succeeding generation inherits as a precious deposit and a sacred trust to be handed on to the next one, not unchanged but enlarged and purified, with some clear marks of its proper handiwork. Into this, for good or ill, is woven every belief of every man who has speech of his fellows. An awful privilege, and an awful responsibility, that we should help to create the world in which posterity will live.

In the two supposed cases which have been considered, it has been judged wrong to believe on insufficient evidence, or to nourish belief by suppressing doubts and avoiding investigation. The reason of this judgment is not far to seek: it is that in both these cases the belief held by one man was of great importance to other men. But for as much as no belief held by one man, however seemingly trivial the belief, and however obscure the believer, is ever actually insignificant or without its effect on the fate of mankind, we have no choice but to extend our judgment to all cases of belief whatever. Belief, that sacred faculty which prompts the decisions of our will, and knits into harmonious working all the compacted energies of our being, is ours not for ourselves, but for humanity. It is rightly used on truths which have been established by long experience and waiting toil, and which have stood in the fierce light of free and fearless questioning. Then it helps to bind men together, and to strengthen and direct their common action. It is desecrated when given to unproved and unquestioned statements, for the solace and private pleasure of the believer; to add a tinsel splendor to the plain straight road of our life and display a bright mirage beyond it; or even to drown the common sorrows of our kind by a self-deception which allows them not only to cast down, but also to degrade us. Whoso would deserve well of his fellows in this matter will guard the purity of his belief with a very fanaticism of jealous care, lest at any time it should rest on an unworthy object, and catch a stain which can never be wiped away.

It is not only the leader of men, statesman, philosopher or poet, that owes this bounden duty to mankind. Every rustic who delivers in the village alehouse his slow, infrequent sentences, may help to kill or keep alive the fatal superstitions which clog his race. Every hard-worked wife of an artisan may transmit to her children beliefs which shall knit society together, or rend it in pieces. No simplicity of mind, no obscurity of station, can escape the universal duty of questioning all that we believe.

It is true that this duty is a hard one, and the doubt which comes out of it is often a very bitter thing. It leaves us bare and powerless where we thought that we were safe and strong. To know all about anything is to know how to deal with it under all circumstances. We feel much happier and more secure when we think we know precisely what to do, no matter what happens, than when we have lost our way and do not know where to turn. And if we have supposed ourselves to know all about anything, and to be capable of doing what is fit in regard to it, we naturally do not like to find that we are really ignorant and powerless, that we have to begin again at the beginning, and try to learn what the thing is and how it is to be dealt with—if indeed anything can be learned about it. It is the sense of power attached to a sense of knowledge that makes men desirous of believing, and afraid of doubting.

This sense of power is the highest and best of pleasures when the belief on which it is founded is a true belief, and has been fairly earned by investigation. For then we may justly feel that it is common property, and holds good for others as well as for ourselves. Then we may be glad, not that I have learned secrets by which I am safer and stronger, but that we men have got mastery over more of the world; and we shall be strong, not for ourselves, but in the name of Man and in his strength. But if the belief has been accepted on insufficient evidence, the pleasure is a stolen one. Not only does it deceive ourselves by giving us a sense of power which we do not really possess, but it is sinful, because it is stolen in defiance of our duty to mankind. That duty is to guard ourselves from such beliefs as from a pestilence, which may shortly master our own body and then spread to the rest of the town. What would be thought of one who, for the sake of a sweet fruit, should deliberately run the risk of bringing a plague upon his family and his neighbors?

And, as in other such cases, it is not the risk only which has to be considered; for a bad action is always bad at the time when it is done, no matter what happens afterwards. Every time we let ourselves believe for unworthy reasons, we weaken our powers of self-control, of doubting, of judicially and fairly weighing evidence. We all suffer severely enough from the maintenance and support of false beliefs and the fatally wrong actions which they lead to, and the evil born when one such belief is entertained is great and wide. But a greater and wider evil arises when the credulous character is maintained and supported, when a habit of believing for unworthy reasons is fostered and made permanent. If I steal money from any person, there may be no harm done by the mere transfer of possession; he may not feel the loss, or it may prevent him from using the money badly. But I cannot help doing this great wrong towards Man, that I make myself dishonest. What hurts society is not that it should lose its property, but that it should become a den of thieves; for then it must cease to be society. This is why we ought not to do evil that good may come; for at any rate this great evil has come, that we have done evil and are made wicked thereby. In like manner, if I let myself believe anything on insufficient evidence, there may be no great harm done by the mere belief; it may be true after all, or I may never have occasion to exhibit it in outward acts. But I cannot help doing this great wrong toward Man, that I make myself credulous. The danger to society is not merely that it should believe wrong things, though that is great enough; but that it should become credulous, and lose the habit of testing things and inquiring into them; for then it must sink back into savagery.

The harm which is done by credulity in a man is not confined to the fostering of a credulous character in others, and consequent support of false beliefs. Habitual want of care about what I believe leads to habitual want of care in others about the truth of what is told to me. Men speak the truth to one another when each reveres the truth in his own mind and in the other's mind; but how shall my friend revere the truth in my mind when I myself am careless about it, when I believe things because I want to believe them, and because they are comforting and pleasant? Will he not learn to cry, "Peace," to me, when there is no peace? By such a course I shall surround myself with a thick atmosphere of falsehood and fraud, and in that must live. It may matter little to me, in my closed castle of sweet illusions and darling lies; but it matters much to Man that I have made my neighbors ready to deceive. The credulous man is father to the liar and the cheat; he lives in the bosom of this his family, and it is no marvel if he should become even as they are. So closely are our duties knit together, that whoso shall keep the whole law, and yet offend in one point, he is guilty of all.

To sum up: it is wrong always, everywhere and for anyone, to believe anything upon insufficient evidence.

If a man, holding a belief which he was taught in childhood or persuaded of afterwards, keeps down and pushes away any doubts which arise about it in his mind, purposely avoids the reading of books and the company of men that call in question or discuss it, and regards as impious those questions which cannot easily be asked without disturbing it—the life of that man is one long sin against mankind.

If this judgment seems harsh when applied to those simple souls who have never known better, who have been brought up from the cradle with a horror of doubt, and taught that their eternal welfare depends on what they believe, then it leads to the very serious question, Who hath made Israel to sin? . . .

Inquiry into the evidence of a doctrine is not to be made once for all, and then taken as finally settled. it is never lawful to stifle a doubt; for either it can be honestly answered by means of the inquiry already made, or else it proves that the inquiry was not complete.

"But," says one, "I am a busy man; I have no time for the long course of study which would be necessary to make me in any degree a competent judge of certain questions, or even able to understand the nature of the arguments." Then he should have no time to believe. . . .

---

19. The Will to Believe

WILLIAM JAMES

In the recently published Life by Leslie Stephen of his brother, Fitz-James, there is an account of a school to which the latter went when he was a boy. The teacher, a certain Mr. Guest, used to converse with his pupils in this wise: "Gurney, what is the difference between justification and sanctification?—Stephen, prove the omnipotence of God!" etc. In the midst of our Harvard freethinking and indifference we are prone to imagine that here at your good old orthodox College conversation continues to be somewhat upon this order; and to show you that we at Harvard have not lost all interest in these vital subjects, I have brought with me to-night something like a sermon on justification by faith to read to you,—I mean an essay in justification *of* faith, a defence of our right to adopt a believing attitude in religious matters, in spite of the fact that our merely logical intellect may not have been coerced. 'The Will to Believe,' accordingly, is the title of my paper.

I have long defended to my own students the lawfulness of voluntarily adopted faith; but as soon as they have got well imbued with the logical spirit, they have as a rule refused to admit my contention to be lawful philosophically, even though in point of fact they were personally all the time chock-full of some faith or other themselves. I am all the while, however, so profoundly convinced that my own position is correct, that your invitation has seemed to me a good occasion to make my statements more clear. Perhaps your minds will be more open that those with which I have hitherto had to deal. I will be as little technical as I can, though I must begin by setting up some technical distinctions that will help us in the end.

Source: An Address to the Philosophical Clubs of Yale and Brown Universities. Published in the New World, June, 1896.

I.

Let us give the name of *hypothesis* to anything that may be proposed to our belief; and just as the electricians speak of live and dead wires, let us speak of any hypothesis as either *live* or *dead*. A live hypothesis is one which appeals as a real possibility to him to whom it is proposed. If I ask you to believe in the Mahdi, the notion makes no electric connection with your nature,—it refuses to scintillate with any credibility at all. As an hypothesis it is completely dead. To an Arab, however (even if he be not one of the Mahdi's followers), the hypothesis is among the mind's possibilities: it is alive. This shows that deadness and liveness in an hypothesis are not intrinsic properties, but relations to the individual thinker. They are measured by his willingness to act. The maximum of liveness in an hypothesis means willingness to act irrevocably. Practically, that means belief; but there is some believing tendency wherever there is willingness to act at all.

Next, let us call the decision between two hypotheses an *option*. Options may be of several kinds. They may be—1, *living* or *dead;* 2, *forced* or *avoidable;* 3, *momentous* or *trivial;* and for our purposes we may call an option a *genuine* option when it is of the forced, living, and momentous kind.

1. A living option is one in which both hypotheses are live ones. If I say to you: "Be a theosophist or be a Mohammedan," it is probably a dead option, because for you neither hypothesis is likely to be alive. But if I say: "Be an agnostic or be a Christian," it is otherwise: trained as you are, each hypothesis makes some appeal, however small, to your belief.

2. Next, if I say to you: "Choose between going out with your umbrella or without it," I do not offer you a genuine option, for it is not forced. You can easily avoid it by not going out at all. Similarly, if I say, "Either love me or hate me," "Either call my theory true or call it false," your option is avoidable. You may remain indifferent to me, neither loving nor hating, and you may decline to offer any judgment as to my theory. But if I say, "Either accept this truth or go without it," I put on you a forced option, for there is no standing place outside of the alternative. Every dilemma based on a complete logical disjunction, with no possibility of not choosing, is an option of this forced kind.

3. Finally, if I were Dr. Nansen and proposed to you to join my North Pole expedition, your option would be momentous; for this would probably be your only similar opportunity, and your choice now would either exclude you from the North Pole sort of immortality altogether or put at least the chance of it into your hands. He who refuses to embrace a unique opportunity loses the prize as surely as if he tried and failed. *Per contra,* the option is trivial when the opportunity is not unique, when the stake is insignificant, or when the decision is reversible if it later prove unwise. Such trivial options abound in the scientific life. A chemist finds an hypothesis live enough to spend a year in its verification: he believes in it to that extent. But if his experiments prove inconclusive either way, he is quit for his loss of time, no vital harm being done.

It will facilitate our discussion if we keep all these distinctions well in mind.

II.

The next matter to consider is the actual psychology of human opinion. When we look at certain facts, it seems as if our passional and volitional nature lay at the root of all our convictions. When we look at others, it seems as if they could do nothing when the intellect had once said its say. Let us take the latter facts up first.

Does it not seem preposterous on the very face of it to talk of our opinions being modifiable at will? Can our will either help or hinder our intellect in its perceptions of truth? Can we, by just willing it, believe that Abraham Lincoln's existence is a myth, and that the portraits of him in McClure's Magazine are all of some one else? Can we, by any effort of our will, or by any strength of wish that it were true, believe ourselves well and about when we are roaring with rheumatism in bed, or feel certain that the sum of the two one-dollar bills in our pocket must be a hundred dollars? We can *say* any of these things, but we are absolutely impotent to believe them; and of just such things is the whole fabric of the truths that we do believe in made up,—matters of fact, immediate or remote, as Hume said, and relations between ideas, which are either there or not there for us if we see them so, and which if not there cannot be put there by any action of our own.

In Pascal's Thoughts there is a celebrated passage known in literature as Pascal's wager. In it he tries to force us into Christianity by reasoning as if our concern with truth resembled our concern with the stakes in a game of chance. Translated freely his words are these: You must either believe or not believe that God is—which will you do? Your human reason cannot say. A game is going on between you and the nature of things which at the day of judgment will bring out either heads or tails. Weigh what your gains and your losses would be if you should stake all you have on heads, or God's existence: if you win in such case, you gain eternal beatitude; if you lose, you lose nothing at all. If there were an infinity of chances, and only one for God in this wager, still you ought to stake your all on God; for though you surely risk a finite loss by this procedure, any finite loss is reasonable, even a certain one is reasonable, if there is but the possibility of infinite gain. Go, then, and take holy water, and have masses said; belief will come and stupefy your scruples,—*Cela vous fera croire et vous abêtira.* Why should you not? At bottom, what have you to lose?

You probably feel that when religious faith expresses itself thus, in the language of the gaming-table, it is put to its last trumps. Surely Pascal's own personal belief in masses and holy water had far other springs; and this celebrated page of his is but an argument for others, a last desperate snatch at a weapon against the hardness of the unbelieving heart. We feel that a faith in masses and holy water adopted wilfully after such a mechanical calculation would lack the inner soul of faith's reality; and if we were ourselves in the place of the Deity, we should probably take particular pleasure in cutting off believers of this pattern from their infinite reward. It is evident that unless there be some pre-existing tendency to believe in masses and holy water, the option offered to the will by Pascal is not a living option. Certainly no Turk ever took to masses and holy water on its account; and even to us Protestants these means of salvation seem such foregone impossibilities that Pascal's logic, invoked for them specifically, leaves us unmoved. As well might the Mahdi write to us, saying, "I am the Expected One whom God has created in his effulgence. You shall be infinitely happy if you confess me; otherwise you shall be cut off from the light of the sun. Weigh, then, your infinite gain if I am genuine against your finite sacrifice if I am not!" His logic would be that of Pascal; but he would vainly use it on us, for the hypothesis he offers us is dead. No tendency to act on it exists in us to any degree.

The talk of believing by our volition seems, then, from one point of view, simply silly. From another point of view it is worse than silly, it is vile. When one turns to the magnificent edifice of the physical sciences, and sees how it was reared; what thousands of disinterested moral lives of men lie buried in its mere foundations; what patience and postponement, what choking down of preference, what submission to the icy laws of outer fact are wrought into its very stones and mortar; how absolutely impersonal it stands in its vast augustness,—then how besotted and contemptible seems every little sen-timentalist who comes blowing his voluntary smoke-wreaths, and pretending to decide things from out of his private dream! Can we wonder if those bred in the rugged and manly school of science should feel like spewing such subjectivism out of their mouths? The whole system of loyalties which grow up in the schools of science go dead against its toleration; so that it is only natural that those who have caught the scientific fever should pass over to the opposite extreme, and write sometimes as if the incorruptibly truthful in-tellect ought positively to prefer bitterness and unacceptableness to the heart in its cup.

> It fortifies my soul to know
> That, though I perish, Truth is so—

sings Clough, while Huxley exclaims: "My only consolation lies in the reflection that, however bad our posterity may become, so far as they hold by the plain rule of not pre-tending to believe what they have no reason to believe, because it may be to their ad-vantage so to pretend [the word 'pretend' is surely here redundant], they will not have reached the lowest depth of immorality." And that delicious *enfant terrible* Clifford writes: "Belief is desecrated when given to unproved and unquestioned statements for the solace and private pleasure of the believer. . . . Whoso would deserve well of his fel-lows in this matter will guard the purity of his belief with a very fanaticism of jealous care, lest at any time it should rest on an unworthy object, and catch a stain which can never be wiped away. . . . If [a] belief has been accepted on insufficient evidence [even though the belief be true, as Clifford on the same page explains] the pleasure is a stolen one. . . . It is sinful because it is stolen in defiance of our duty to mankind. That duty is to guard ourselves from such beliefs as from a pestilence which may shortly master our own body and then spread to the rest of the town. . . . It is wrong always, everywhere, and for every one, to believe anything upon insufficient evidence."

III.

All this strikes one as healthy, even when expressed, as by Clifford, with somewhat too much of robustious pathos in the voice. Free-will and simple wishing do seem, in the matter of our credences, to be only fifth wheels to the coach. Yet if any one should thereupon assume that intellectual insight is what remains after wish and will and sentimental preference have taken wing, or that pure reason is what then settles our opinions, he would fly quite as directly in the teeth of the facts.

It is only our already dead hypotheses that our willing nature is unable to bring to life again But what has made them dead for us is for the most part a previous action of our willing nature of an antagonistic kind. When I say 'willing nature,' I do not mean only such deliberate volitions as may have set up habits of belief that we cannot now escape from,—I mean all such factors of belief as fear and hope, prejudice and passion, imitation and partisanship, the circumpressure of our caste and set. As a matter of fact we find ourselves believing, we hardly know how or why. Mr. Balfour gives the name of 'authority' to all those influences, born of the intellectual climate, that make hypotheses possible or impossible for us, alive or dead. Here in this room, we all of us believe in molecules and the conservation of energy, in democracy and necessary progress, in Protestant Christianity and the duty of fighting for 'the doctrine of the immortal Monroe,' all for no reasons worthy of the name. We see into these matters with no more inner clearness, and probably with much less, than any disbeliever in them might possess. His unconventionality would probably have some grounds to show for its conclusions; but for us, not insight, but the *prestige* of the opinions, is what makes the spark shoot from them and light up our sleeping magazines of faith. Our reason is quite satisfied, in nine hundred and ninety-nine cases out of every thousand of us, if it can find a few arguments that will do to recite in case our credulity is criticised by some one else. Our faith is faith in some one else's faith, and in the greatest matters this is most the case. Our belief in truth itself, for instance, that there is a truth, and that our minds and it are made for each other,—what is it but a passionate affirmation of desire, in which our social system backs us up? We want to have a truth; we want to believe that our experiments and studies and discussions must put us in a continually better and better position towards it; and on this line we agree to fight out our thinking lives. But if a pyrrhonistic sceptic asks us *how we know* all this, can our logic find a reply? No! certainly it cannot. It is just one volition against another,—we willing to go in for life upon a trust or assumption which he, for his part, does not care to make.[1]

As a rule we disbelieve all facts and theories for which we have no use. Clifford's cosmic emotions find no use for Christian feelings. Huxley belabors the bishops because there is no use for sacerdotalism in his scheme of life. Newman, on the contrary, goes over to Romanism, and finds all sorts of reasons good for staying there, because a priestly system is for him an organic need and delight. Why do so few 'scientists' even look at the evidence for telepathy, so called? Because they think, as a leading biologist, now dead, once said to me, that even if such a thing were true, scientists ought to band together to keep it suppressed and concealed. It would undo the uniformity of Nature and all sorts of other things without which scientists cannot carry on their pursuits. But if this very man had been shown something which as a scientist he might *do* with telepathy, he might not only have examined the evidence, but even have found it good enough. This very law which the logicians would impose upon us—if I may give the name of logicians to those who would rule out our willing nature here—is based on nothing but their own natural wish to exclude all elements for which they, in their professional quality of logicians, can find no use.

Evidently, then, our non-intellectual nature does influence our convictions. There are passional tendencies and volitions which run before and others which come after belief, and it is only the latter that are too late for the fair; and they are not too late when the previous passional work has been already in their own direction. Pascal's argument, instead of being powerless, then seems a regular clincher, and is the last stroke needed to make our faith in masses and holy water complete. The state of things is evidently far from simple; and pure insight and logic, whatever they might do ideally, are not the only things that really do produce our creeds.

IV.

Our next duty, having recognized this mixed-up state of affairs, is to ask whether it be simply reprehensible and pathological, or whether, on the contrary, we must treat it as a normal element in making up our minds. The thesis I defend is, briefly stated, this: *Our passional nature not only lawfully may, but must, decide an option between propositions, whenever it is a genuine option that cannot by its nature be decided on intellectual grounds; for to say, under such circumstances, "Do not decide, but leave the question open," is itself a passional decision,—just like deciding yes or no,—and is attended with the same risk of losing the truth.* The thesis thus abstractly expressed will, I trust, soon become quite clear. But I must first indulge in a bit more of preliminary work.

V.

It will be observed that for the purposes of this discussion we are on 'dogmatic' ground,—ground, I mean, which leaves systematic philosophical scepticism altogether out of account. The postulate that there is truth, and that it is the destiny of our minds to attain it, we are deliberately resolving to make, though the sceptic will not make it. We part company with him, therefore, absolutely, at this point. But the faith that truth exists, and that our minds can find it, may be held in two ways. We may talk of the *empiricist* way and of the *absolutist* way of believing in truth. The absolutists in this matter say that we not only can attain to knowing truth, but we can *know when* we have attained to knowing it; while the empiricists think that although we may attain it, we cannot infallibly know when. To *know* is one thing, and to know for certain *that* we know is another. One may hold to the first being possible without the second; hence the empiricists and the absolutists, although neither of them is a sceptic in the usual philosophic sense of the term, show very different degrees of dogmatism in their lives.

If we look at the history of opinions, we see that the empiricist tendency has largely prevailed in science, while in philosophy the absolutist tendency has had everything its own way. The characteristic sort of happiness, indeed, which philosophies yield has mainly consisted in the conviction felt by each successive school or system that by it bottom-certitude had been attained. "Other philosophies are collections of opinions, mostly false; *my* philosophy gives standing-ground forever."—who does not recognize in this the key-note of every system worthy of the name? A system, to be a system at all, must come as a *closed* system, reversible in this or that detail, perchance, but in its essential features never!

Scholastic orthodoxy, to which one must always go when one wishes to find perfectly clear statement, has beautifully elaborated this absolutist conviction in a doctrine which it calls that of 'objective evidence.' If, for example, I am unable to doubt that I now exist before you, that two is less than three, or that if all men are mortal then I am mortal too, it is because these things illumine my intellect irresistibly. The final ground of this objective evidence possessed by certain propositions is the *adæquatio intellectûs nostri cum rê.* The certitude it brings involves an *aptitudinem ad extorquendum certum assensum* on the part of the truth envisaged, and on the side of the subject a *quietem in cognitione,* when once the object is mentally received, that leaves no possibility of doubt behind; and in the whole transaction nothing operates but the *entitas ipsa* of the object and the *entitas ipsa* of the mind. We slouchy modern thinkers dislike to talk in Latin,— indeed, we dislike to talk in set terms at all; but at bottom our own state of mind is very much like this whenever we uncritically abandon ourselves: You believe in objective evidence, and I do. Of some things we feel that we are certain: we know, and we know that we do know. There is something that gives a click inside of us, a bell that strikes twelve, when the hands of our mental clock have swept the dial and meet over the meridian hour. The greatest empiricists among us are only empiricists on reflection: when left to their instincts, they dogmatize like infallible popes. When the Cliffords tell us how sinful it is to be Christians on such 'insufficient evidence,' insufficiency is really the last thing they have in mind. For them the evidence is absolutely sufficient, only it makes the other way. They believe so completely in an anti-christian order of the universe that there is no living option: Christianity is a dead hypothesis from the start.

VI.

But now, since we are all such absolutists by instinct, what in our quality of students of philosophy ought we to do about the fact? Shall we espouse and indorse it? Or shall we treat it as a weakness of our nature from which we must free ourselves, if we can?

I sincerely believe that the latter course is the only one we can follow as reflective men. Objective evidence and certitude are doubtless very fine ideals to play with, but where on this moonlit and dream-visited planet are they found? I am, therefore, myself a complete empiricist so far as my theory of human knowledge goes. I live, to be sure, by the practical faith that we must go on experiencing and thinking over our experience, for only thus can our opinions grow more true; but to hold any one of them—I absolutely do not care which—as if it never could be reinterpretable or corrigible, I believe to be a tremendously mistaken attitude, and I think that the whole history of philosophy will bear me out. There is but one indefectibly certain truth, and that is the truth that pyrrhonistic scepticism itself leaves standing,—the truth that the present phenomenon of consciousness exists. That, however, is the bare starting-point of knowledge, the mere admission of a stuff to be philosophized about. The various philosophies are but so many attempts at expressing what this stuff really is. And if we repair to our libraries what disagreement do we discover! Where is a certainly true answer found? Apart from abstract propositions of comparison (such as two and two are the same as four), propositions which tell us nothing by themselves about concrete reality, we find no proposition ever regarded by any one as evidently certain that has not either been called a falsehood, or at least had its truth sincerely questioned by some one else. The transcending of the axioms of geometry, not in play but in earnest, by certain of our contemporaries (as Zöllner and Charles H. Hinton), and the rejection of the whole Aristotelian logic by the Hegelians, are striking instances in point.

No concrete test of what is really true has ever been agreed upon. Some make the criterion external to the moment of perception, putting it either in revelation, the *consensus gentium,* the instincts of the heart, or the systematized experience of the race. Others make the perceptive moment its own test,—Descartes, for instance, with his clear and distinct ideas guaranteed by the veracity of God; Reid with his 'common-sense'; and Kant with his forms of synthetic judgment *a priori.* The inconceivability of the opposite; the capacity to be verified by sense; the possession of complete organic unity or self-relation, realized when a thing is its own other,—are standards which, in turn, have been used. The much lauded objective evidence is never triumphantly there; it is a mere aspiration or *Grenzbegriff,* marking the infinitely remote ideal of our thinking life. To claim that certain truths now possess it, is simply to say that when you think them true and they *are* true, then their evidence is objective, otherwise it is not. But practically one's conviction that the evidence one goes by is of the real objective brand, is only one more subjective opinion added to the lot. For what a contradictory array of opinions have objective evidence and absolute certitude been claimed! The world is rational through and through,—its existence is an ultimate brute fact; there is a personal God,—a personal God is inconceivable; there is an extra-mental physical world immediately known,—the mind can only know its own ideas; a moral imperative exists,—obligation is only the resultant of desires; a permanent spiritual principle is in every one,—there are only shifting states of mind; there is an endless chain of causes,—there is an absolute first cause; an eternal necessity,—a freedom; a purpose,—no purpose; a primal One,—a primal Many; a universal continuity,—an essential discontinuity in things; an infinity,—no infinity. There is this,—there is that; there is indeed nothing which some one has not thought absolutely true, while his neighbor deemed it absolutely false; and not an absolutist among them seems ever to have considered that the trouble may all the time be essential, and that the intellect, even with truth directly in its grasp, may have no infallible signal for knowing whether it be truth or no. When, indeed, one remembers that the most striking practical application to life of the doctrine of objective certitude has been the conscientious labors of the Holy Office of the Inquisition, one feels less tempted than ever to lend the doctrine a respectful ear.

But please observe, now, that when as empiricists we give up the doctrine of objective certitude, we do not thereby give up the quest or hope of truth itself. We still pin our faith on its existence, and still believe that we gain an ever better position towards it by systematically continuing to roll up experiences and think. Our great difference from the scholastic lies in the way we face. The strength of his system lies in the principles, the origin, the *terminus a quo* of his thought; for us the strength is in the outcome, the upshot, the *terminus ad quem.* Not where it comes from but what it leads to is to decide. It matters not to an empiricist from what quarter an hypothesis may come to him: he may have acquired it by fair means or by foul; passion may have whispered or accident suggested it; but if the total drift of thinking continues to confirm it, that is what he means by its being true.

VII.

One more point, small but important, and our preliminaries are done. There are two ways of looking at our duty in the matter of opinion,—ways entirely different, and yet ways about whose difference the theory of knowledge seems hitherto to have shown very little concern. *We must know the truth;* and *we must avoid error,*—these are our first and great commandments as would-be knowers; but they are not two ways of stating an identical commandment, they are two separable laws. Although it may indeed happen that when we believe the truth *A,* we escape as an incidental consequence from believing the falsehood *B,* it hardly ever happens that by merely disbelieving *B* we necessarily believe *A.* We may in escaping *B* fall into believing other falsehoods, *C* or *D,* just as bad as *B;* or we may escape *B* by not believing anything at all, not even *A.*

Believe truth! Shun error!—these, we see, are two materially different laws; and by choosing between them we may end by coloring differently our whole intellectual life. We may regard the chase for truth as paramount, and the avoidance of error as secondary; or we may, on the other hand, treat the avoidance of error as more imperative, and let truth take its chance. Clifford, in the instructive passage which I have quoted, exhorts us to the latter course. Believe nothing, he tells us, keep your mind in suspense forever, rather than by closing it on insufficient evidence incur the awful risk of believing lies. You, on the other hand, may think that the risk of being in error is a very small matter when compared with the blessings of real knowledge, and be ready to be duped many times in your investigation rather than postpone indefinitely the chance of guessing true. I myself find it impossible to go with Clifford. We must remember that these feelings of our duty about either truth or error are in any case only expressions of our passional life. Biologically considered, our minds are as ready to grind out falsehood as veracity, and he who says, "Better go without belief forever than believe a lie!" merely shows his own preponderant private horror of becoming a dupe. He may be critical of many of his desires and fears, but this fear he slavishly obeys. He cannot imagine any one questioning its binding force. For my own part, I have also a horror of being duped; but I can believe that worse things than being duped may happen to a man in this world: so Clifford's exhortation has to my ears a thoroughly fantastic sound. It is like a general informing his soldiers that it is better to keep out of battle forever than to risk a single wound. Not so are victories either over enemies or over nature gained. Our errors are surely not such awfully solemn things. In a world where we are so certain to incur them in spite of all our caution, a certain lightness of heart seems healthier than this excessive nervousness on their behalf. At any rate, it seems the fittest thing for the empiricist philosopher.

VIII.

And now, after all this introduction, let us go straight at our question. I have said, and now repeat it, that not only as a matter of fact do we find our passional nature influencing us in our opinions, but that there are some options between opinions in which this influence must be regarded both as an inevitable and as a lawful determinant of our choice.

I fear here that some of you my hearers will begin to scent danger, and lend an inhospitable ear. Two first steps of passion you have indeed had to admit as necessary,— we must think so as to avoid dupery, and we must think so as to gain truth; but the surest path to those ideal consummations, you will probably consider, is from now onwards to take no further passional step.

Well, of course, I agree as far as the facts will allow. Wherever the option between losing truth and gaining it is not momentous, we can throw the chance of *gaining truth* away, and at any rate save ourselves from any chance of *believing falsehood,* by not making up our minds at all till objective evidence has come. In scientific questions, this is almost always the case; and even in human affairs in general, the need of acting is seldom so urgent that a false belief to act on is better than no belief at all. Law courts, indeed, have to decide on the best evidence attainable for the moment, because a judge's duty is to make law as well as to ascertain it, and (as a learned judge once said to me) few cases are worth spending much time over: the great thing is to have them decided on *any* acceptable principle, and got out of the way. But in our dealings with objective nature we obviously are recorders, not makers, of the truth; and decisions for the mere sake of deciding promptly and getting on to the next business would be wholly out of place. Throughout the breadth of physical nature facts are what they are quite independently of us, and seldom is there any such hurry about them that the risks of being duped by believing a premature theory need be faced. The questions here are always trivial options, the hypotheses are hardly living (at any rate not living for us spectators), the choice between believing truth or falsehood is seldom forced. The attitude of sceptical balance is therefore the absolutely wise one if we would escape mistakes. What difference, indeed, does it make to most of us whether we have or have not a theory of the Röntgen rays, whether we believe or not in mind-stuff, or have a conviction about the causality of conscious states? It makes no difference. Such options are not forced on us. On every account it is better not to make them, but still keep weighing reasons *pro et contra* with an indifferent hand.

I speak, of course, here of the purely judging mind. For purposes of discovery such indifference is to be less highly recommended, and science would be far less advanced than she is if the passionate desires of individuals to get their own faiths confirmed had been kept out of the game. See for example the sagacity which Spencer and Weismann now display. On the other hand, if you want an absolute duffer in an investigation, you must, after all, take the man who has no interest whatever in its results: he is the warranted incapable, the positive fool. The most useful investigator, because the most sensitive observer, is always he whose eager interest in one side of the question is balanced by an equally keen nervousness lest he become deceived.[2] Science has organized this nervousness into a regular *technique,* her so-called method of verification; and she has fallen so deeply in love with the method that one may even say she has ceased to care for truth by itself at all. It is only truth as technically verified that interests her. The truth of truths might come in merely affirmative form, and she would decline to touch it. Such truth as that, she might repeat with Clifford, would be stolen in defiance of her duty to mankind. Human passions, however, are stronger than technical rules. "Le cœur a ses raisons," as Pascal says, "que la raison ne connaît pas"; and however indifferent to all but the bare rules of the game the umpire, the abstract intellect, may be, the concrete players who furnish him the materials to judge of are usually, each one of them, in love with some pet 'live hypothesis' of his own. Let us agree, however, that wherever there is no forced option, the dispassionately judicial intellect with no pet hypothesis, saving us, as it does, from dupery at any rate, ought to be our ideal.

The question next arises: Are there not somewhere forced options in our speculative questions, and can we (as men who may be interested at least as much in positively gaining truth as in merely escaping dupery) always wait with impunity till the coercive evidence shall have arrived? It seems *a priori* improbable that the truth should be so nicely adjusted to our needs and powers as that. In the great boarding-house of nature, the cakes and the butter and the syrup seldom come out so even and leave the plates so clean. Indeed, we should view them with scientific suspicion if they did.

IX.

Moral questions immediately present themselves as questions whose solution cannot wait for sensible proof. A moral question is a question not of what sensibly exists, but of what is good, or would be good if it did exist. Science can tell us what exists; but to compare the *worths,* both of what exists and of what does not exist, we must consult not science, but what Pascal calls our heart. Science herself consults her heart when she lays it down that the infinite ascertainment of fact and correction of false belief are the supreme goods for man. Challenge the statement, and science can only repeat it oracularly, or else prove it by showing that such ascertainment and correction bring man all sorts of other goods which man's heart in turn declares. The question of having moral beliefs at all or not having them is decided by our will. Are our moral preferences true or false, or are they only odd biological phenomena, making things good or bad for *us,* but in themselves indifferent? How can your pure intellect decide? If your heart does not *want* a world of moral reality, your head will assuredly never make you believe in one. Mephistophelian scepticism, indeed, will satisfy the head's play-instincts much better than any rigorous idealism can. Some men (even at the student age) are so naturally cool-hearted that the moralistic hypothesis never has for them any pungent life, and in their supercilious presence the hot young moralist always feels strangely ill at ease. The appearance of knowingness is on their side, of *naïveté* and gullibility on his. Yet, in the inarticulate heart of him, he clings to it that he is not a dupe, and that there is a realm in which (as Emerson says) all their wit and intellectual superiority is no better than the cunning of a fox. Moral scepticism can no more be refuted or proved by logic than intellectual scepticism can. When we stick to it that there *is* truth (be it of either kind), we do so with our whole nature, and resolve to stand or fall by the results. The sceptic with his whole nature adopts the doubting attitude; but which of us is the wiser, Omniscience only knows.

Turn now from these wide questions of good to a certain class of questions of fact, questions concerning personal relations, states of mind between one man and another. *Do you like me or not?*—for example. Whether you do or not depends, in countless instances, on whether I meet you half-way, am willing to assume that you must like me, and show you trust and expectation. The previous faith on my part in your liking's existence is in such cases what makes your liking come. But if I stand aloof, and refuse to budge an inch until I have objective evidence, until you shall have done something apt, as the absolutists say, *ad extorquendum assensum meum,* ten to one your liking never comes. How many women's hearts are vanquished by the mere sanguine insistence of some man that they *must* love him! he will not consent to the hypothesis that they cannot. The desire for a certain kind of truth here brings about that special truth's existence; and so it is in innumerable cases of other sorts. Who gains promotions, boons, appointments, but the man in whose life they are seen to play the part of live hypotheses, who discounts them, sacrifices other things for their sake before they have come, and takes risks for them in advance? His faith acts on the powers above him as a claim, and creates its own verification.

A social organism of any sort whatever, large or small, is what it is because each member proceeds to his own duty with a trust that the other members will simultaneously do theirs. Wherever a desired result is achieved by the co-operation of many independent persons, its existence as a fact is a pure consequence of the precursive faith in one another of those immediately concerned. A government, an army, a commercial system, a ship, a college, an athletic team, all exist on this condition, without which not only is nothing achieved, but nothing is even attempted. A whole train of passengers (individually brave enough) will be looted by a few highwaymen, simply because the latter can count on one another, while each passenger fears that if he makes a movement of resistance, he will be shot before any one else backs him up. If we believed that the whole car-full would rise at once with us, we should each severally rise, and train-robbing would never even be attempted. There are, then, cases where a fact cannot come at all unless a preliminary faith exists in its coming. *And where faith in a fact can help create the fact,* that would be an insane logic which should say that faith running ahead of scientific evidence is the 'lowest kind of immorality' into which a thinking being can fall. Yet such is the logic by which our scientific absolutists pretend to regulate our lives!

X.

In truths dependent on our personal action, then, faith based on desire is certainly a lawful and possibly an indispensable thing.

But now, it will be said, these are all childish human cases, and have nothing to do with great cosmical matters, like the question of religious faith. Let us then pass on to that. Religions differ so much in their accidents that in discussing the religious question we must make it very generic and broad. What then do we now mean by the religious hypothesis? Science says things are; morality says some things are better than other things; and religion says essentially two things.

First, she says that the best things are the more eternal things, the overlapping things, the things in the universe that throw the last stone, so to speak, and say the final word. "Perfection is eternal,"—this phrase of Charles Secrétan seems a good way of putting this first affirmation of religion, an affirmation which obviously cannot yet be verified scientifically at all.

The second affirmation of religion is that we are better off even now if we believe her first affirmation to be true.

Now, let us consider what the logical elements of this situation are *in case the religious hypothesis in both its branches be really true.* (Of course, we must admit that possibility at the outset. If we are to discuss the question at all, it must involve a living option. If for any of you religion be a hypothesis that cannot, by any living possibility be true, then you need go no farther. I speak to the 'saving remnant' alone.) So proceeding, we see, first, that religion offers itself as a *momentous* option. We are supposed to gain, even now, by our belief, and to lose by our non-belief, a certain vital good. Secondly, religion is a *forced* option, so far as that good goes. We cannot escape the issue by remaining sceptical and waiting for more light, because, although we do avoid error in that way *if religion be untrue,* we lose the good, *if it be true,* just as certainly as if we positively chose to disbelieve. It is as if a man should hesitate indefinitely to ask a certain woman to marry him because he was not perfectly sure that she would prove an angel after he brought her home. Would he not cut himself off from that particular angel-possibility as decisively as if he went and married some one else? Scepticism, then, is not avoidance of option; it is option of a certain particular kind of risk. *Better risk loss of truth than chance of error,*—that is your faith-vetoer's exact position. He is actively playing his stake as much as the believer is; he is backing the field against the religious hypothesis, just as the believer is backing the religious hypothesis against the field. To preach scepticism to us as a duty until 'sufficient evidence' for religion be found, is tantamount therefore to telling us, when in presence of the religious hypothesis, that to yield to our fear of its being error is wiser and better than to yield to our hope that it may be true. It is not intellect against all passions, then; it is only intellect with one passion laying down its law. And by what, forsooth, is the supreme wisdom of this passion warranted? Dupery for dupery, what proof is there that dupery through hope is so much worse than dupery through fear? I, for one, can see no proof; and I simply refuse obedience to the scientist's command to imitate his kind of option, in a case where my own stake is important enough to give me the right to choose my own form of risk. If religion be true and the evidence for it be still insufficient, I do not wish, by putting your extinguisher upon my nature (which feels to me as if it had after all some business in this matter), to forfeit my sole chance in life of getting upon the winning side,—that chance depending, of course, on my willingness to run the risk of acting as if my passional need of taking the world religiously might be prophetic and right.

All this is on the supposition that it really may be prophetic and right, and that, even to us who are discussing the matter, religion is a live hypothesis which may be true. Now, to most of us religion comes in a still further way that makes a veto on our active faith even more illogical. The more perfect and more eternal aspect of the universe is represented in our religions as having personal form. The universe is no longer a mere *It* to us, but a *Thou,* if we are religious; and any relation that may be possible from person to person might be possible here. For instance, although in one sense we are passive portions of the universe, in another we show a curious autonomy, as if we were small active centres on our own account. We feel, too, as if the appeal of religion to us were made to our own active good-will, as if evidence might be forever withheld from us unless we met the hypothesis half-way. To take a trivial illustration: just as a man who in a company of gentlemen made no advances, asked a warrant for every concession, and believed no one's word without proof, would cut himself off by such churlishness from all the social rewards that a more trusting spirit would earn,—so here, one who should shut himself up in snarling logicality and try to make the gods extort his recognition willy-nilly, or not get it at all, might cut himself off forever from his only opportunity of making the gods' acquaintance. This feeling, forced on us we know not whence, that by obstinately believing that there are gods (although not to do so would be so easy both for our logic and our life) we are doing the universe the deepest service we can, seems part of the living essence of the religious hypothesis. If the hypothesis *were* true in all its parts, including this one, then pure intellectualism, with its veto on our making willing advances, would be an absurdity; and some participation of our sympathetic nature would be logically required. I, therefore, for one, cannot see my way to accepting the agnostic rules for truth-seeking, or wilfully agree to keep my willing nature out of the game. I cannot do so for this plain reason, that *a rule of thinking which would absolutely prevent me from acknowledging certain kinds of truth if those kinds of truth were really there, would be an irrational rule.* That for me is the long and short of the formal logic of the situation, no matter what the kinds of truth might materially be.

I confess I do not see how this logic can be escaped. But sad experience makes me fear that some of you may still shrink from radically saying with me, *in abstracto,* that we have the right to believe at our own risk any hypothesis that is live enough to tempt our will. I suspect, however, that if this is so, it is because you have got away from the abstract logical point of view altogether, and are thinking (perhaps without realizing it) of some particular religious hypothesis which for you is dead. The freedom to 'believe what we will' you apply to the case of some patent superstition; and the faith you think of is the faith defined by the schoolboy when he said, "Faith is when you believe something that you know ain't true." I can only repeat that this is misapprehension. *In concreto,* the freedom to believe can only cover living options which the intellect of the individual cannot by itself resolve; and living options never seem absurdities to him who has them to consider. When I look at the religious question as it really puts itself to concrete men, and when I think of all the possibilities which both practically and theoretically it involves, then this command that we shall put a stopper on our heart, instincts, and courage, and *wait*—acting of course meanwhile more or less as if religion were *not* true[3]—till doomsday, or till such time as our intellect and senses working together may have raked in evidence enough,—this command, I say, seems to me the queerest idol ever manufactured in the philosophic cave. Were we scholastic absolutists, there might be more excuse. If we had an infallible intellect with its objective certitudes, we might feel ourselves disloyal to such a perfect organ of knowledge in not trusting to it exclusively, in not waiting for its releasing word. But if we are empiricists, if we believe that no bell in us tolls to let us know for certain when truth is in our grasp, then it seems a piece of idle fantasticality to preach so solemnly our duty of waiting for the bell. Indeed we *may* wait if we will,—I hope you do not think that I am denying that,—but if we do so, we do so at our peril as much as if we believed. In either case we *act,* taking our life in our hands. No one of us ought to issue vetoes to the other, nor should we bandy words of abuse. We ought, on the contrary, delicately and profoundly to respect one another's mental freedom: then only shall we bring about the intellectual republic; then only shall we have that spirit of inner tolerance without which all our outer tolerance is soulless, and which is empiricism's glory; then only shall we live and let live, in speculative as well as in practical things.

I began by a reference to Fitz James Stephen; let me end by a quotation from him. "What do you think of yourself? What do you think of the world? . . . These are questions with which all must deal as it seems good to them. They are riddles of the Sphinx, and in some way or other we must deal with them. . . . In all important transactions of life we have to take a leap in the dark. . . . If we decide to leave the riddles unanswered, that is a choice; if we waver in our answer, that, too, is a choice: but whatever choice we make, we make it at our peril. If a man chooses to turn his back altogether on God and the future, no one can prevent him; no one can show beyond reasonable doubt that he is mistaken. If a man thinks otherwise and acts as he thinks, I do not see that any one can prove that *he* is mistaken. Each must act as he thinks best; and if he is wrong, so much the worse for him. We stand on a mountain pass in the midst of whirling snow and blinding mist, through which we get glimpses now and then of paths which may be deceptive. If we stand still we shall be frozen to death. If we take the wrong road we shall be dashed to pieces. We do not certainly know whether there is any right one. What must we do? 'Be strong and of a good courage.' Act for the best, hope for the best, and take what comes. . . . If death ends all, we cannot meet death better."[4]

Notes

1. Compare the admirable page 310 in S. H. Hodgson's "Time and Space," London, 1865.

2. Compare Wilfrid Ward's Essay, "The Wish to Believe," in his *Witnesses to the Unseen,* Macmillan & Co., 1893.

3. Since belief is measured by action, he who forbids us to believe religion to be true, necessarily also forbids us to act as we should if we did believe it to be true. The whole defence of religious faith hinges upon action. If the action required or inspired by the religious hypothesis is in no way different from that dictated by the naturalistic hypothesis, then religious faith is a pure superfluity, better pruned away, and controversy about its legitimacy is a piece of idle trifling, unworthy of serious minds. I myself believe, of course, that the religious hypothesis gives to the world an expression which specifically determines our reactions, and makes them in a large part unlike what they might be on a purely naturalistic scheme of belief.

4. Liberty, Equality, Fraternity, p. 353, 2d edition. London, 1874.

20. Passion and Suspicion: Religious Affections in "The Will to Believe"

D. M. YEAGER

> We first need to look at the phenomenon of "longing" in general;
> for longing itself is a peculiar and rarely examined state of mind.
> [BERNARD YACK, *The Longing for Total Revolution*]

In his treatment of "The Will to Believe" in *Protestant Thought in the Nineteenth Century*, Claude Welch links William James with Pascal, Kierkegaard, and Coleridge (as opposed to Schleiermacher, Ritschl, or Herrmann) on the grounds that James "stood with those for whom faith is essentially a matter of willing and choosing, rather than a feeling or a knowing, even the knowing of a practical reason."[1] He attributes to James the view that "believing in something, deciding that it shall be true for us, can itself be a means of making it true."[2] He identifies James with the party that holds that "faith is capable of generating data for its verification."[3] Widely read in this way, James's argument has come to be dismissed as dangerous and unreliable. While I concur that the intellectual position that people have come to describe under the rubric of "the will to believe" is indeed dangerous and unreliable, my purpose in this essay is to show that James is falsely accused and to construct his vindication. To approach the essay in the conventional way, that is, as an investigation of the grounds and warrants for belief, would only contribute further to the problem. To understand James rightly is to recognize that the issue of giving grounds and finding warrants for belief is, in his view, an irrelevant issue—a consideration for which there is no logical space.

The "will to believe" is a passion, a feature of the passional or willing nature. This willing nature has *sources* that can, in part, be traced, but it is finally simply "given," like the body. It does not have grounds and warrants. It is not chosen or constructed. It

Source: D. M. Yeager, "Passion and Suspicion: Religious Affection in 'The Will to Believe,'" *The Journal of Religion,* 69, no. 4 (October 1989), pages 467–83. Reprinted with the permission of the University of Chicago and the author.

cannot be invaded and assessed. And it cannot by any specific conscious decision be changed. It does not follow that the trustworthiness of such passions is beyond examination. Neither does it follow that we inevitably do or must act on these passions. As a matter of fact, James holds that the passions are subject to considerable suspicion—and if we want to talk about grounds and warrants at all, we should talk about the grounds and warrants of our *suspicions* regarding our passional longings. It is when we *obstruct* the play of passion that we require justification because these passions are synonymous with the power of action.

The defense that I propose to offer here is not without precedent. My reading is consonant with the work of scholars who have studied James in depth, and the misinterpretation against which I write was clearly identified (and denounced) by John Smith twenty-five years ago: noting that "there is no idea in James, or in any other American philosopher for that matter, which is more widely known and more universally misinterpreted than the will to believe," Smith complained that the essay has been erroneously interpreted to advance the view that "you not only can, but that you should, believe anything you care to believe and that, with regard to anything you desire to be true, you can force yourself to believe it to be true against all evidence if only your will is strong enough."[4] It was Smith's intention to set matters right. He did not, apparently, succeed. The phrase "the will to believe" is everywhere used to signify belief by fiat, an irrational and subjective decision to believe in the absence of motive or reason, a naked act of arbitrary self-determination; and this misconstruction perdures in spite of the work of careful students of James and in face of explicit attempts at correction.[5] The durability of error is always worrisome, but it is particularly troublesome here because the considerable creative resources of James's thought are thus restricted to the small circle of those who have immersed themselves in his work. It is nonetheless intriguing. Might readers *need* to believe that James said something other than he did? Do contemporary presuppositions and preoccupations bias us toward misconstrual? Perhaps the attempts at correction share so many of the assumptions of the misinterpretation that they cannot function effectively as correctives.

Smith rightly locates the source of the interpretive difficulty in the notion of will because "the term 'will' . . . often connotes arbitrariness; it implies belief by fiat or by sheer power unconnected with reasons or grounds."[6] Thereupon Smith joins the army of interpreters who argue that all would have been well if James had just substituted "right" for "will" in the title—a substitution which, as they are quick to point out, James himself later saw that he might have made and thought perhaps that he should have made. This conventional defense does not invite, much less require, us to reconsider our operant notion of "will." In fact, Smith interprets "will" in the same way that James's adversaries interpret it; thus his defense of James rests entirely in showing that James has defined the sphere of operation of "will" more narrowly than is generally appreciated. Though will does involve belief by fiat, belief by fiat is epistemologically justifiable in certain narrowly defined circumstances; thus, in such circumstances, we do have a right to believe. In point of fact, however, the title James chose is, if properly understood, precisely the correct title; to suggest that "The Right to Believe" is as good or better is systematically misleading because it obscures James's analysis of the factors that come into play when an individual must respond to the challenge presented by *"a genuine option that cannot by its nature be decided on intellectual grounds."*[7] While it is true and helpful to say that James has defended our right to adopt a posture of belief in a certain set of narrowly defined cases, the genius of the essay only becomes clear once we move beyond issues of epistemic necessity to examine (1) James's understanding of the positive role of the passions in the activity of living and (2) his conviction that among the longings of the willing nature are certain dispositions to believe specific things about the nature of reality. It behooves us, then, to examine with greater care the notion of "will."

I

In *The Illusion of Technique,* William Barrett sets one understanding of the slippery word "will" against another. On the one hand, "will" is used to name self-assertion and the struggle for dominance; in this characteristically modern usage, the word connotes the will to power. On the other hand, it can also be used in a more traditional sense to name "deliberative desire," that is, "that place in our psychic landscape where reason and appetite meet; where our wishes and emotions submit to reason, and reason in turn is activated by desire";[8] in this usage, the word "will" is short-hand for "the moral will." Barrett's own avowed project is "to try to restore the moral will to a central and primary role in the human personality."[9] Any such restoration, he insists, requires the repudiation of the self-assertive willing that our culture normally celebrates and cultivates. In championing the moral will, Barrett recognizes in James a general ally;[10] however, Barrett is disappointed by "The Will to Believe" and treats the essay as an uncharacteristic and inconsistent lapse in an otherwise sound body of work. Indeed, Barrett takes on the author of "The Will to Believe" as his adversary, arguing that the essay represents a classic instance of the now-entrenched habit of interpreting will as raw and primitive self-assertion. Accordingly, Barrett argues that James attributes to the will a power to accomplish what does not actually lie within the powers of the will: the creation of conviction in the midst of doubt. The essay, he writes, "smacks a little too much of a muscular YMCA kind of Christianity. James is exhorting us to make an effort, which is normally admirable counsel; but in this case the goal of the effort is not something we can arrive at by sheer force of will."[11] According to Barrett, James urges the reader "to produce out of oneself something that is not there to begin with" and proposes that we summon the will to believe at just those moments when, according to Barrett, "we may not be able to summon up a will for anything."[12] Barrett then lodges this objection: "We stand on one side of an abyss that has to be crossed, and on the other side is belief and everything positive that follows from it. On the one side, belief; on the other side, our will, naked of all belief. We are to tense all our muscles and leap. But where is the will to fetch its strength for that leap? Is a will naked of belief capable of willing at all?"[13] Barrett's questions are important and revealing questions, but he is putting them to the wrong author. The notion of "naked will" that disposes of itself gratuitously, arbitrarily, in some sort of unwarranted and ungrounded leap that produces belief where antecedently there was no belief is the furthest possible conception from the conception actually operating in the essay. James's argument treats belief as antecedent to, not consequent to, the acceptance of risk; the impulse toward belief is precisely the impelling power that Barrett cannot find in the essay.

In her last book, *Willing*, Hannah Arendt also asserts that in our culture there are operative "two altogether different ways of understanding the faculty [of will]";[14] interestingly, however, the two usages she describes differ from those described by Barrett. According to Arendt, will is, on the one hand, understood "as a faculty of *choice* between objects or goals, the *liberum arbitrium*, which acts as arbiter between given ends and deliberates freely about means to reach them; and, on the other hand, [it is understood] as our 'faculty for beginning spontaneously a series in time' (Kant) or Augustine's '*initium ut esset homo creatus est*,' man's capacity for beginning because he himself is a beginning."[15] These are, she notes, typically modern readings of "will," and in both cases "will" is so construed as to be capable of securing the locus of human freedom. Arendt also acknowledges the lingering shadow of a third understanding or usage, one that is less typical and certainly less modern. On this third model, "will" is construed to mean "inclination, desire, longing, liking, or pleasure." In this usage, according to Arendt, "will" is properly construed as the locus of bondage.

In trying to understand James's essay, we do best if we begin with this last, presumably archaic, concept of the will—though I will return at the very end of this essay to a consideration of felicities obtaining between James's argument and Barrett's attempt to resurrect "deliberative desire." The will to believe is not a resolute voluntary act; the will to believe is a prevoluntary passion. The nature of James's quarrel with W. K. Clifford and the definition he offers of "our willing nature" (a definition that is pivotal to the meaning of his thesis) make it quite clear that when he writes of the will to believe, James is thinking not in terms of some arbitrary mental act of self-commitment carried out in some sort of affective vacuum, but is thinking instead of our deep powers of longing and attachment, wondering to what degree they may be trusted as, like an undertow, they pull us into the depths of commitment. The will is, then, in the view of James, a constellation of prerational passions and predispositions that constitute the indelible affective core of the individual personality.[16] Among these affections or sentiments is a will to believe that has no warrant and needs none—indeed, that leaves no logical or affective space for the intrusion of the very considerations that the language of grounds and warrants entails and reflects.

For this reason, James's essay is most reliably read against the background of Jonathan Edwards's *Religious Affections* rather than being read against the background of Jean-Paul Sartre's theory of value creation in the exercise of free decision. The problem with most of the interpreters of James is that they have spent more time in Argos than in the City on the Hill.

Edwards's thesis is that "true religion, in great part, consists of holy affections."[17] This is to say that it belongs to the domain of will, where will-as-desire is experienced with uncommon intensity. Edwards holds that "God has endued the soul with two faculties," the speculative understanding that perceives and considers things and the faculty of inclination that approves/accepts or opposes/rejects that which the soul in its other faculty merely views and considers.[18] Inclination governs the direction of understanding, and it necessarily governs all action. In its connection with action, it is called will. The affections constitute a narrow class of instances of inclination or will; only where the inclination is intense and vigorous in its capacity to inspire action can we legitimately speak of affection. Since the relationship of the person to God is not reducible to detached, impartial, speculative reflection and since religiousness must show itself in action and since religion, to be serious, must be intense and vigorous, "true religion consists, in great measure, in vigorous and lively actings of the inclination and will of the soul"—that is, in affections.[19] However, Edwards does not assume that any and all affections are trustworthy; on the contrary, he devotes the rest of the treatise to the problem of discriminating between true and false affections and between holy and unholy ones. "The right way, is not to reject all affections, nor to approve all; but to distinguish between affections, approving some, and rejecting others; separating between the wheat and the chaff, the gold and the dross, the precious and the vile."[20]

James, like Edwards, is acutely aware of the way in which consciousness is structured by prephilosophical and indeed prerational inclinations that color our thinking as well as our actions. This is precisely what he describes by means of his interchangeable terms "our passional nature" and "our willing nature." Though always impressively attentive to actualities, James never confuses what *is* the case with what *ought* to be the case. That these inclinations do in fact color our thinking and action does not mean that they necessarily should. W. K. Clifford is the primary adversary in the essay because he has explicitly, articulately, and unambiguously argued that, under no circumstances, ought these affections/inclinations ever to be allowed to influence action or reflection. Making of suspicion a matter of principle, Clifford holds that all affections are, from the point of view of human moral obligation, unholy and destructive. Will, in this sense, should play no role in our arguments, our decisions, or our actions. The essay "The Will to Believe" is an extraordinarily subtle and intricate consideration of this question of the legitimacy of permitting the impetuous affections a pivotal place in our intellectual, moral, and religious life. To interpret the essay as one that proposes that we commit ourselves to belief in the absence of any cause for belief is to declare Clifford the winner by refusing to concede any importance to the heartfelt longing to embrace the religious hypothesis, the longing James names "the will to believe." What James actually argues is that, in the absence of any specific experiential impugning of the religious longings, reliance on such passional needs offends neither intellect nor duty. The very affective tangle of desires, hopes, and fears, which is denounced by Clifford on the grounds that it corrupts the morally obligatory dispassionate search for truth, is celebrated by James as the only available means by which the truth of things may be found out when we confront a live, momentous, forced option not resolvable by rational or empirical investigation.

The pattern is incomplete, however, unless we understand that the longings themselves must be subjected to assessment; if they can be shown to be untrustworthy foundations for action, we may not legitimately rely on these longings even in these most difficult cases. This dimension of the essay, evident primarily in the development of the distinction between absolutism and empiricism, has not been adequately appreciated. In the typical epistemologically focused reading of the essay as a defense of the right to believe, the extended critique of absolutism is treated as an aside. Only when we study the essay as an investigation of the legitimacy of giving rein to our natural passion for believing do we begin to appreciate the pivotal character of the discussion of absolutism as an exercise in discriminating between true and false affections. The passion for certainty—the urge or inclination to believe we have laid hold once and for all of the absolute truth—can be shown by appeal to communal experience to be fundamentally untrustworthy; it therefore constitutes a form of longing that may *never* legitimately guide our actions and choices.

II

In the secondary literature, the complaint that James has argued for the self-validating character of all beliefs is closely bound up with the habit of modeling will on the concept of deliberation and self-disposition. The logic of the connection is this: if human commitment is a matter of arbitrary decision in an experiential vacuum, then the act of deciding to think that something is true establishes a framework for interpretation that is beyond any challenge from the experiential realm; indeed, the invented structure of interpretation that constitutes the belief will so bias the assessment of experience that all experience will seem to validate and reinforce the initial arbitrary assumptions. It is helpful to see that James does not advance the notion of belief by fiat, but that, in itself, does not suffice to dispatch the deeper complaint that he is careless of truth and encourages us in the dubious practice of adopting beliefs that can be expected to be self-legitimating. The unwarranted and self-serving beliefs against which Clifford railed were not exercises of untrammeled naked will but were instances of the blinding (and Arendt would say binding) power of unrestrained desire hell-bent in its own interests. If James is to be rescued from subjectivism, it will take more than the substitution of prerational desire in place of arbitrary decision.

To better appreciate the intricacy of the essay, we can best begin by examining a structural oddity. Though James asserts that he has written the essay to defend the adoption of "a believing attitude in religious matters,"[21] the logic of his argument in no way forecloses the possibility of adopting the contrary of the religious hypothesis when one confronts the religious option (i.e., the option of believing either that it is true that "the best things are the more eternal things" and that our lives will be better if we believe that or that it is true that our lives will not be improved by believing such non-sense).[22] Because this is a genuine option, we cannot decline to take a position; to imagine that one is withholding judgment is to choose to believe the second hypothesis. It is plain that we can neither settle the question by factual investigation nor delay decision until conclusive evidence is obtained. How then shall we decide? Well, we not only *may* consult our passional longings, but we *must* consult our passional longings; there is nothing else to do. Since each must act according to the inclinations of the willing nature, the person who inclines toward hypothesis B rather than hypothesis A will properly adopt the belief that talk of eternal things is nonsense and will live accordingly. If we have a right to religious belief, we also have a right to disbelief. And, of course, if religious belief "is capable of generating data for its verification," so is humanistic naturalism or Manichaean cynicism.

Now, to be sure, James does not discuss this atheistic option in the essay; his failure to recognize or remark on this possibility is instructive. When James turns to the passional nature, he does not believe he is turning to some whimsical and arbitrary faculty; he believes himself to be turning to a settled and stable set of deeply rooted longings, convictions, and affections that constitute the very fabric of the particular personality in question. James defines the willing nature unambiguously: "When I say 'willing nature,' . . . I mean all such factors of belief as fear and hope, prejudice and passion, imitation and partisanship, the circumpressure of our caste and set."[23] It never occurs to him that in consulting one's passional nature one might discover there some deep passionate hope that our lives might be pointless and our suffering blank and our sorrows without hope. Thus he operates under the assumption, rooted in his own experience as well as in his observation of the attitudes and behavior of others, that if the appeal to the willing nature is unobstructed, the person who confronts the religious option will *naturally* choose the religious hypothesis rather than its contrary.

This preference arising out of the willing nature authorizes no metaphysical claims. In this essay, James neither assumes nor argues that our passional longings necessarily signal something to us about the nature of reality. On the contrary, his discussion of absolutism makes it plain that our longings may entirely mislead us. Having differentiated himself from true subjectivists—or, as he names them, skeptics—by confessing that he "deliberately" postulates "that there is truth, and that it is the destiny of our minds to attain it," James distinguishes among truth-seekers on the basis of their beliefs about the certainty with which knowledge claims can be advanced.[24] The absolutists enjoy a self-certifying subjective sense of infallibility in their confidence that they have laid hold of eternal truth; they develop closed systems and generate concrete truth criteria that are thought to provide "objective evidence" or inerrant demonstration. The empiricists understand the intellectual life in terms of risk and adventure; their criterion of truth is future fruitfulness. What arrests attention here is his assertion that "the greatest empiricists among us are only empiricists on reflection."[25] That is to say, we *feel* we are certain. We *long* to be right. Moved by our willing nature, we "dogmatize like infallible popes."[26] There is hardly any feature of our passional nature that is stronger than our fear of being wrong. This leads James to a critical question: "Since we are all such absolutists by instinct, what in our quality of students of philosophy ought we to do about the fact? Shall we espouse and indorse it? Or shall we treat it as a weakness of our nature from which we must free ourselves, if we can?"[27] The answer is immediate and decisive: "I sincerely believe that the latter course is the only one we can follow as reflective men."[28] Here, then, is a will, a longing, a passion that is clearly ruled illegitimate. It is ruled illegitimate on the basis of the history of the intellectual projects it has motivated—all of which have been, in the end, disastrous. This is a passion, a commitment, an inclination or affection that clearly is not self-validating and does not "generate data for its verification." There are longings, then, that James believes to be illegitimate. Thus, clearly, even when the option is genuine and cannot be decided on any intellectual grounds, we are still not permitted to give free rein to the headstrong passional nature. The problem with Clifford is not simply that he is an intellectual hypocrite whose project of forbidding reliance on passional longings is motivated by the unrecognized play of passional longings in his own life. If self-delusion were the only problem, he and James would be operationally on equal footing in the search for truth, though they would be testing vastly different hypotheses. The deeper problem is that Clifford has given himself up to an untrustworthy will, to a feature of our willing nature that we should recognize by now to be a weakness—or, we might say, an unholy affection. It is a false faith, and over time, the data generated by action on this hypothesis plainly disconfirms the hypothesis.

The longing for infallible certainty battles in the soul with the longing for truth; this is the point of James's disquisition on the difference between the intellectual commandment to avoid error and the intellectual commandment to seek truth. Let us stop then, for a moment, to examine the theory of truth that is put forward in the essay. While James dismisses as a species of chimera the popular notion that human beings are capable of dispassionate, neutral, perfectly impersonal and objective formulations of apprehended Truth, he rejects equally the position of the Pyrrhonistic skeptic. It is his view—or faith—"that truth exists, and that our minds can find it."[29] He adroitly avoids the view that some people have laid hold of truth while others lack it altogether; rather, he suggests that truth-seeking is an open project in an open universe. The proper question is not, "Have I got the truth?" but, "Am I making any progress?" Thus James writes, "We must go on experiencing and thinking over our experience, for only thus can our opinions grow more true."[30] We do not so much lay hold of truth as we "gain an ever better position towards it by systematically continuing to roll up experiences and think."[31] This leads James to ask what is going on when William James says of any view or proposition that it is a *true* view or proposition, and he concludes with an interesting piece of linguistic analysis. When a person says that something is true, the person makes a more modest claim than is conventionally thought: "If the total drift of thinking continues to confirm it, that is what he means by its being true."[32] That is all that anybody can possibly mean. We may passionately desire to be able to say more for our claims, but that is all that we can actually say—and when you think of it, it is quite a lot. It is, interestingly, science that provides James with his dominant image of what it means to concern oneself with truth, to search after truth in this processive way, and to finally feel reasonably confident in claiming that one's views are true. But the scientific model James employs as a paradigm is quite different from the scientific model Clifford employs. For James, the paradigm case is the scientist who has committed himself to the testing of a hypothesis and who goes into the laboratory—or out into the field—to gather experience by means of which the hypothesis will either be confirmed or challenged. If experience confirms the hypothesis, the scientist is justified in claiming that the hypothesis is true; if experience does not confirm it, the scientist is obliged to give it up—or modify it in some significant way. The religious hypothesis is no different. Whether one elects to commit oneself to the religious hypothesis or to its contrary, one has at least something to test. If one refuses the option—or never advances to it (as is the case with Clifford) because prior choices have rendered the option dead—then one has no means by which one's view might be made more nearly true. This is what James has in mind in the last section when he accuses Clifford of foreclosing the search for truth in religious matters.[33] Since we cannot know in advance which hypothesis is true and since we must have something to test if we are to have any hope of discovering truth, we may and, in fact, must, rely on our passional nature to settle the initial quandary so that we may get on with the business of accumulating the experience that will enable us to discriminate the true from the false. There are, of course, difficulties. The "evidence" of "experience" is much more ambiguous in the testing of the religious hypothesis than in the testing of some specific hypothesis about the operations of material entities and physical forces. It is also vastly more difficult to figure out what counts decisively and what does not.

Another difficulty arises because James posits an essential asymmetry between the inquiries of science and the inquiries of the moral and religious realm. One reason the misreading of the essay persists is that the subtle points James makes at this point in his argument lend themselves to misinterpretation. There are a number of claims in section 9 that appear to assert that, in the moral and religious realm, beliefs become self-validating such that if we begin with a heart-felt longing or hope that the religious tradition embodies some important truth, we will surely end up having lived our lives in such a way that our very belief produces the verifying experiences that ensure that we may feel justified in our initial hopes. Speaking of friendship and love, James remarks, "The desire for a certain kind of truth here brings about the special truth's existence; and so it is in innumerable cases of other sorts."[34] Speaking of the way in which a person's dedication to a cause often results in the rewards the person sought, James observes, "His faith acts on the powers above him as a claim, and creates its own verification."[35] Toward the end of the section, we find in italics the apparently damaging assertion: "*Faith in a fact can help create the fact.*"[36] It would seem, then, that James has argued for the self-validating character of beliefs and in so doing has dispensed with the question of the truth of beliefs altogether.

Yet James has made it so insistently obvious that he does "stick to it that there *is* truth" that it would be, at the least, very odd if he were, here at the end, to exempt whole areas of human reflection—and, by his own account, the most important areas of human reflection—from the domain of truth.[37]

To grasp James's actual intent, we must distinguish between self-validating beliefs and reality-transforming commitments. The phrase "self-validating beliefs" is part of a cluster of essentially subjectivistic concepts, and it posits as given the closed character of systems of belief where the belief imposes a framework of interpretation that systematically reinforces the beliefs to the exclusion of all other interpretive possibilities. The notion of reality-transforming commitments is part of a completely different cluster of concepts. It does not concern truth and knowing; rather, it concerns action and the contingent character of certain human realities. The two one-dollar bills in our pocket are there in our pocket whether we believe them to be there or not; if we forget that they are there, they do not disappear; they simply get wrinkled in the wash. The continuing existence of the building we call the White House is not in any sense immediately contingent on the beliefs of people that it is there at 1600 Pennsylvania Avenue. While it is possible that Abraham Lincoln will be altogether forgotten if American education continues on its dread course, such universal forgetfulness would not alter the fact that there once was a sixteenth president of the United States and that that man

was Abraham Lincoln and that all future events will bear the indelible trace of his having lived, at least insofar as we have this present when we might have had some other
present. There are, however, human realities that lack this remarkable durability.
Friendship is one such reality; a just society would be another; a vital religious community or church would be a third. What James wishes to say is that if people fail to commit themselves to the possibility of creating a just society, a just society cannot come to
exist. It is the nature of such realities that they do not happen accidentally in the absence of "precursive faith." Sometimes people commit themselves to such a dream and
are unable to bring it about. The does not mean that they were deluded, but it does
mean that belief in a just society is not a self-validating belief. The one thing that is certain is that a just society is a reality that is entirely dependent on human belief in its
possibility; if a just society is ever achieved, it will be because a sufficient number of
people believed it to be possible and worked to bring it about. There can be no working
to bring it about without precursive believing in it as a realizable possibility. This is
what James has in mind when he argues that "faith . . . created its own verification" or
"*faith in a fact can help create the fact.*"[38] This is something quite different, of course,
from saying that believing that a given social order is just will, in fact, make it just—or
even make it appear to be just in the eyes of the believer. The difference between the
notion of self-validating belief and the notion of reality-transforming commitment is
that, in the first case, we posit belief as the efficacious agency in the creation of a perceived state of affairs; in the second case, we posit activity arising from belief as the efficacious agency in the creation of a contingent actual state of affairs, recognizing that
neither the precursive belief nor the activity guarantees a successful outcome.

    The last section of "The Will to Believe" is not as clear as one might like, but the
motifs of passion and suspicion are conjoined there in an explicit way, and the entire
section builds on the idea of "truths dependent on our personal action" that was established in the preceding section.[39] We face an option between the religious hypothesis
and the naturalistic hypothesis. We have, James asserts, a "passional need of taking the
world religiously."[40] There is no means by which we can determine dispassionately and
in advance which of these hypotheses is the more true hypothesis. This is partly because
these are hypotheses, like the hypothesis "that there is truth, and that it is the destiny of
our minds to attain it,"[41] which are not subject to conclusive verification on empirical
or intellectual grounds. But it is also because the religious hypothesis is a hypothesis
not about what is the case independent of human action but a hypothesis about dimensions of human experience that are dependent on human action of a particular sort;
thus, even if the religious hypothesis concerns a true *possibility*, if no one believes in or
makes a commitment to the realization of this possibility, the naturalistic hypothesis
becomes, by default, the more reliable hypothesis about the way things are. By a curious twist of logic, then, it is belief in the truth of the naturalistic hypothesis that proves
to be a potentially delusive self-validating belief—a belief that forecloses the discovery
of error and that necessarily renders itself apparently true to the person who holds it. In
the language of James, it turns the religious hypothesis into a dead hypothesis.

    So, as James brings us to face this genuine option at the end of his essay, he en-
courages us in the direction of religious faith for two reasons: (1) we are in the grip of a

"will to believe" that is quite powerful and that has not been shown to be untrustworthy and (2) dedication to the truth seems to compel us in the direction of assenting to the religious hypothesis since only insofar as we assent and act on this belief do we have any means of assessing beliefs of this sort. We commit ourselves not because commitment will render moot the question of the rectitude of our passional longings, but rather in order that we may discover whether "my passional need of taking the world religiously might be prophetic and right."[42]

Yet, as we have seen, James is suspicious of the maneuvers of the will, and James is appreciative of the fact that this assenting to a passional need is a dangerous thing. It is wholly unacceptable if we know in advance that this passional need is pernicious—as is the case in our passional need for certainty. He can only counsel "the right to choose my own form of risk" because the present state of reflection on the matter permits "the supposition that it [my passional need of taking the world religiously] really may be prophetic and right."[43] Clifford is the primary adversary because he has universalized the suspicion of the willing nature that James recognizes to be sometimes justified. However, after careful examination, James is finally able to dismiss as "absurd" Clifford's unqualified advances.[44] This dismissal rests on three discoveries about Clifford's project: (1) Clifford's witnessing presence is at odds with his theoretical claims; he himself has not been successful in keeping his intellectual life free of all taint of will. (2) Though Clifford is motivated at a deep level by a passion for truth, which we are still entitled to trust and act on, his love of truth languishes under the sovereignty of a still stronger power rising up out of the willing nature: fear—specifically fear of error. This fear is the dramatic underside of the will to noetic closure. Thus, Clifford's whole project is shaped by passions that are shown by human experience to be untrustworthy motivations. (3) Despite all Clifford's fulminations, he has given no sound reason for distrusting, much less vetoing, our longing—that is, our will—to believe that the religious hypothesis rather than its contrary is true. The reasons that he gives, if deconstructed, can be shown to conceal a covert attack of quite another sort. What he actually opposes is the human condition; he therefore begins his consideration with no tolerance at all for intellectual risk and thus is a useless guide when it comes to a consideration of the truth or falsity of hypotheses concerning the reality-transforming character of certain commitments and patterns of action.

III

By way of conclusion, I would like to return to the argument advanced by William Barrett in *The Illusion of Technique*. Barrett finds fault with James on two counts: (1) Failing to understand the affective content folded into James's conception of "will," he criticizes James for falling prey to our culture's infatuation with arbitrary self-assertion. (2) He believes that James, through a failure to appreciate the mystical side of religion (the concern with Being itself) and through the philosopher's typical fault of writing about religion rather than writing from within the circle of religious faith, has misunderstood the essential character of religious faith. Barrett himself describes this essential character as the invocation of Being—an invocation that Barrett calls prayer. He therefore complains that James made true apprehension of the dynamics of the religious life inaccessible by "putting the question of the credibility of beliefs at the center of religion."[45]

Barrett is correct to present the religious life in terms of practice rather than thought—and he is correct to see that one of the most durable and appealing features of the corpus of James's writings is his "grasp of feeling as the central fact for any human life."[46] Barrett, like Welch, goes awry in failing to appreciate the way in which feeling, as the central fact of life, is foundational to the argument of "The Will to Believe." In this matter, as in the usage of the term, "will," "The Will to Believe" reinforces rather than departs from the "tone" and insights of James's other arguments. James has built the affective dimension of invocation, prayer, worship, and apprehension of mystery into his consideration through his construct of the passional or willing nature that is the origin of the "will to believe" that presses us quite vigorously toward the posture of faith. If James joins the sorry ranks of those who posit *"an agent who is in fact a spectator at his own life,"*[47] it is not because he is unfamiliar with the emotional depths of the religious sensibility but because he and others like him have been brought to face a genuine option that is wholly alien to the experience of the simple folk that Barrett invokes toward the end of his discussion.[48] Under pressure from Clifford, James has advanced to a peculiar stage of self-consciousness in which it is not enough to have "simple faith" or a desire for simple faith because the question is not whether one might have that but whether, having it, one dares to trust it, to give oneself up to it, to embrace it in the confidence that it at least might be "prophetic and right" rather than delusive and self-betraying. It would seem that, rather than expressing such disappointment in the essay, Barrett ought to have hailed it as precisely the sort of endeavor that he advocates—the careful operation of the moral will as deliberative desire: "the place in our psychic landscape where reason and appetite meet; where our wishes and emotions submit to reason, and reason in turn is activated by desire."[49]

Notes

1. Claude Welch, *Protestant Thought in the Nineteenth Century*, vol. 2: *1870–1914* (New Haven, Conn.: Yale University Press, 1985), p. 60.

2. *Ibid.*, p. 61.

3. *Ibid.*, p. 67.

4. John E. Smith, *The Spirit of American Philosophy*, rev. ed. (1963; reprint, Albany: State University of New York Press, 1983), p. 69.

5. I particularly recommend Robert J. Vanden Burgt, *The Religious Philosophy of William James* (Chicago: Nelson-Hall, 1981): and H. S. Thayer, "The Right to Believe," *Kenyon Review*, no. 5 (Winter 1983).

6. Smith, p. 69.

7. William James, *The Will to Believe and Other Essays in Popular Philosophy* (1897: reprint, Cambridge, Mass.: Harvard University Press, 1979), p. 20.

8. William Barrett, *The Illusion of Technique* (Garden City, N. Y.: Anchor/Doubleday, 1978), p. 252.

9. *Ibid.*, p. 254.

10. *Ibid.*, p. 291.

11. *Ibid.,* p. 308.

12. *Ibid.,* p. 309.

13. *Ibid.*

14. Hannah Arendt, *Willing,* vol. 2 of *The Life of the Mind* (New York: Harcourt Brace Jovanovich, 1978), p. 158.

15. *Ibid.,* p. 158.

16. It has been objected to me that this interpretation of the content of "will" is not consistent with the treatment of "will" in William James, *The Principles of Psychology* (originally published 1890), 3 vols., in *The Works of William James,* ed. F. H. Burkhardt, F. Bowers, and I. K. Skrupskelis (Cambridge, Mass.: Harvard University Press, 1981). Readers focus on the material in the subsection "Action after Deliberation" in the chapter "Will"; in that section James discusses the linkage of will with those stubborn and difficult cases in which "we are said to *decide,* or to *utter our voluntary fiat* in favor of one of the other course" (2:1136). My first response is that, if we are looking for antecedents of "The Will to Believe" in *The Principles of Psychology,* we should probably look not at the explicit treatment of "Will" in vol. 2 (a chapter largely devoted to the technical physiological question of how what goes on in the mind is translated into bodily motion) but at the chapters concerning "The Consciousness of Self" (particularly the spiritual self) and "Attention" in vol. 1. The notion of "the inner nucleus of my spiritual self, that collection of obscurely felt 'adjustments,' *plus* perhaps that still more obscurely perceived subjectivity as such" (1:303) is a better analogue of "the willing [or passional] nature" than anything we find in the chapter "Will." In the chapter "Attention" we find such revealing observations as these: "When we reflect that the turnings of our attention form the nucleus of our inner self; when we see (as in the chapter on the Will we shall see) that volition is nothing but attention . . ." (1:423–24) and "When we come to the chapter on the Will, we shall see that the whole drama of the voluntary life hinges on the amount of attention . . . which rival motor ideas may receive" (1:429). Furthermore, in examining the chapter titled "Will," the reader must keep the structure of the entire consideration clearly in mind. What we might best call the deliberative will is a special case of the operations of will, not the paradigm case of the operations of will. The material, social, and spiritual self is awash in desires. Some of these desires are immediately recognized as unattainable and therefore father no activity, remaining mere wishes. The others function as motives of action— and this constitutes will. In other words, will is in its root nothing other than desire precipitating action ("volition is nothing but attention"). James is exceptionally careful to specify that normal action does *not* require over and above a mental impulse/desire some "*additional mental antecedent, in the shape of a fiat, decision, consent, volitional mandate, or other synonymous phenomenon of consciousness*" (2:1130). Such normal functioning is not, of course, very interesting to the psychologist; cases of conflict, particularly paralyzing conflict, are much more absorbing. Here James treats of two different sorts of cases, both arising when normal action upon desire is *inhibited* by some obstructive factor. (1) Reflecting on immobility that arises when the cozy sleeper, just waking, desires to get up but cannot mobilize himself to leap out of his warm bed into his freezing bedroom, James suggests, not that we finally by force of will overcome the conflict by resolving to ignore the cold and rise, but rather that "we more often than not get up without any struggle or decision at all" (2:1132). The quandary is circumvented as we fall to reflecting on the things that we have to do in the coming hours, and we simply find that the desire to get on with X or Y has taken shape in our leaving the bed. "It was our acute consciousness of both the warmth and the cold during the period of struggle, which paralyzed our activity then and kept our idea of rising in the condition of *wish* and not of *will.* The moment these inhibitory ideas ceased, the original idea

exerted its effects" (2:1133). In other words, it is not the case that paralysis is overcome by willful fiat; will takes hold when the equilibrium of one desire with its inhibiting fear is superseded by a stronger desire activating action in the event of will. (2) There are, however, cases of more obdurate conflict in which no more shift of attention serves to get round the difficulty. These are the cases in which the strictly deliberative will plays a pivotal role because "the express fiat, or act of mental consent to the movement, comes in when the neutralization of the antagonistic and inhibitory idea is required" (2:1134). It is not my purpose to argue that James denied that there is any such thing as "will force" or that will sometimes operates by "fiat"; it is only my purpose to insist that James regards will-as-determination as a special case operating in rare and problematic instances, and that the argument of the essay "The Will to Believe" is impoverished if "will" is understood in this reduced way. It is also very important to notice that, when he examines deliberative will, he presents its operation as the "neutralization" of that which inhibits action, a formulation which (1) presumes that there is some sort of primitive vector toward action (passion, inclination, will) in place, simply waiting to be freed or released, and (2) is remote indeed from any voluntaristic conception of creating an entity where no entity previously exists.

17. Jonathan Edwards, *Religious Affections,* ed. John E. Smith (New Haven, Conn.: Yale University Press, 1959), p. 95.

18. *Ibid.,* p. 96.

19. *Ibid.,* p. 99.

20. *Ibid.,* p. 121.

21. James, *Will to Believe* (n. 7 above), p. 13.

22. *Ibid.,* p. 29.

23. *Ibid.,* p. 18.

24. *Ibid.,* p. 20.

25. *Ibid.,* p. 21.

26. *Ibid.*

27. *Ibid.,* p. 22.

28. *Ibid.*

29. *Ibid.,* p. 20.

30. *Ibid.,* p. 22.

31. *Ibid.,* p. 24.

32. *Ibid.*

33. *Ibid.,* pp. 31–32.

34. *Ibid.,* p. 28.

35. *Ibid.,* pp. 28–29.

36. *Ibid.,* p. 29.

37. *Ibid.,* p. 28.

38. *Ibid.,* pp. 28–29.

39. *Ibid.,* p. 29.

40. *Ibid.,* p. 31.

41. *Ibid.,* p. 20.

42. *Ibid.,* p. 31.

43. *Ibid.*

44. *Ibid.*
45. Barrett (n. 8 above), p. 307.
46. *Ibid.*, p. 279.
47. *Ibid.*, p. 286.
48. See *ibid.*, p. 303.
49. *Ibid.*, p. 252.

C. Søren Kierkegaard: Faith, Subjectivity, and Religious Possibility

Søren Kierkegaard (1844) argues that faith and reason are far less compatible. Christian faith does not complete reason, as in Aquinas, nor is the paradox of the incarnation objectively uncertain in the sense intended by Pascal and James. According to Kierkegaard, the absolute otherness of God transcends the categories of human understanding. In addition, the distinctively Christian claim that God became man is an affront to reason and borders on nonsense; moreover, it represents an absurdity that, when considered objectively, is almost assuredly not true. Faith, then, for Kierkegaard represents a leap well beyond reason, and perhaps contrary to reason, into the appropriation of a religious possibility that offers eternal consolation to the believer but no objective security. Faith is marked by its subjective passion, not by its objective or prudential grounding. C. Stephen Evans (1998) and Mark C. Taylor (1975) both offer analysis and interpretation of Kierkegaard, along with incisive objections to the logic and implications of his approach.

21.　Truth Is Subjectivity

SØREN KIERKEGAARD

To objective reflection, truth becomes something objective, an object, and the point is to disregard the subject. To subjective reflection, truth becomes appropriation, inwardness, subjectivity, and the point is to immerse oneself, existing, in subjectivity.

Source: Søren Kierkegaard, *Concluding Unscientific Postscript,* © 1992, Princeton University Press. Reprinted by permission of Princeton University Press.

But what then? Are we to remain in this disjunction, or does mediation offer its kind assistance here, so that truth becomes subject-object? Why not? But can mediation then help the existing person so that he himself, as long as he is existing, becomes mediation, which is, after all, *sub specie aeterni,* whereas the poor existing one is existing? It certainly does not help to make a fool of a person, to entice him with the subject-object when he himself is prevented from entering into the state in which he can relate himself to it, prevented because he himself, by virtue of existing, is in the process of becoming. Of what help is it to explain how the eternal truth is to be understood eternally when the one to use the explanation is prevented from understanding it in this way because he is existing and is merely a fantast if he fancies himself to be *sub specie aeterni,* consequently when he must avail himself precisely of the explanation of how the eternal truth is to be understood in the category of time by someone who by existing is himself in time, something the honored professor himself admits, if not always, then every three months when he draws his salary. . . .

We return, then, to the two ways of reflection and have not forgotten that it is an existing spirit who is asking, simply an individual human being, and are not able to forget, either, that his existing is precisely what will prevent him from going both ways at once, and his concerned questions will prevent him from light-mindedly and fantastically becoming a subject-object. Now, then, which of the ways is the way of truth for the existing spirit? Only the fantastical *I-I* is simultaneously finished with both ways or advances methodically along both ways simultaneously, which for an existing human being is such an inhuman way of walking that I dare not recommend it.

Since the questioner specifically emphasizes that he is an existing person, the way to be commended is naturally the one that especially accentuates what it means to exist.

The way of objective reflection turns the subjective individual into something accidental and thereby turns existence into an indifferent, vanishing something. The way to the objective truth goes away from the subject, and while the subject and subjectivity become indifferent [*ligegyldig*], the truth also becomes indifferent, and that is precisely its objective validity [*Gyldighed*], because the interest, just like the decision, is subjectivity. The way of objective reflection now leads to abstract thinking, to mathematics, to historical knowledge of various kinds, and always leads away from the subjective individual, whose existence or nonexistence becomes, from an objective point of view, altogether properly, infinitely indifferent, altogether properly, because, as Hamlet says, existence and nonexistence have only subjective significance.[1] At its maximum, this way will lead to a contradiction, and to the extent that the subject does not become totally indifferent to himself, this is merely an indication that his objective striving is not objective enough. At its maximum, it will lead to the contradiction that only objectivity has come about, whereas subjectivity has gone out, that is, the existing subjectivity that has made an attempt to become what in the abstract sense is called subjectivity, the abstract form of an abstract objectivity. And yet, viewed subjectively, the objectivity that has come about is at its maximum either a hypothesis or an approximation, because all eternal decision is rooted specifically in subjectivity.

But the objective way is of the opinion that it has a security that the subjective way does not have (of course, existence, what it means to exist, and objective security cannot be thought together). It is of the opinion that it avoids a danger that lies in wait for the subjective way, and at its maximum this danger is madness. In a solely subjective definition of truth, lunacy and truth are ultimately indistinguishable, because they may both have inwardness.* But one does not become lunatic by becoming objective. At this point I might perhaps add a little comment that does not seem superfluous in an objective age. Is the absence of inwardness also lunacy? The objective truth as such does not at all decide that the one stating it is sensible; on the contrary, it can even betray that the man is lunatic, although what he says is entirely true and especially objectively true.

I shall here allow myself to relate an incident that, without any modification whatever by me, comes directly from a madhouse. A patient in such an institution wants to run away and actually carries out his plan by jumping through a window. He now finds himself in the garden of the institution and wishes to take to the road of freedom. Then it occurs to him (shall I say that he was sagacious enough or lunatic enough to have this whimsical idea?): When you arrive in the city, you will be recognized and will very likely be taken back right away. What you need to do, then, is to convince everyone completely, by the objective truth of what you say, that all is well as far as your sanity is concerned. As he is walking along and pondering this, he sees a skittle ball lying on the ground. He picks it up and puts it in the tail of his coat. At every step he takes, this ball bumps him, if you please, on his r——, and every time it bumps him he says, "Boom! The earth is round." He arrives in the capital city and immediately visits one of his friends. He wants to convince him that he is not lunatic and therefore paces up and down the floor and continually says, "Boom! The earth is round!" But is the earth not round? Does the madhouse demand yet another sacrifice on account of this assumption, as in those days when everyone assumed it to be as flat as a pancake? Or is he lunatic, the man who hopes to prove that he is not lunatic by stating a truth universally accepted and universally regarded as objective? And yet, precisely by this it became clear to the physician that the patient was not yet cured, although the cure certainly could not revolve around getting him to assume that the earth is flat. But not everyone is a physician, and the demand of the times has considerable influence on the question of lunacy. Now and then, one would indeed almost be tempted to assume that the modern age, which has modernized Christianity, has also modernized Pilate's question,[2] and that the need of the age to find something in which to repose declares itself in the question: What is lunacy? When an assistant professor, every time his coattail reminds him to say something, says *de omnibus dubitandum est* [everything must be doubted][3] and briskly writes away on a system in which there is sufficient internal evidence in every other sentence that the man has never doubted anything—he is not considered lunatic. . . .

Subjective reflection turns inward toward subjectivity and in this inward deepening will be of the truth, and in such a way that, just as in the preceding, when

---

*Even this is not true, however, because madness never has the inwardness of infinity. Its fixed idea is a kind of objective something, and the contradiction of madness lies in wanting to embrace it with passion. The decisive factor in madness is thus not the subjective, but the little finitude that becomes fixed, something the infinite can never become.

objectivity was advanced, subjectivity vanished, here subjectivity as such becomes the final factor and objectivity the vanishing. Here it is not forgotten, even for a single moment, that the subject is existing, and that existing is a becoming, and that truth as the identity of thought and being is therefore a chimera of abstraction and truly only a longing of creation,[4] not because truth is not an identity, but because the knower is an existing person, and thus truth cannot be an identity for him as long as he exists. If this is not held fast, then with the aid of speculative thought we promptly enter into the fantastical *I-I* that recent speculative thought certainly has used but without explaining how a particular individual relates himself to it, and, good Lord, of course no human being is more than a particular individual.

If the existing person could actually be outside himself, the truth would be something concluded for him. But where is this point? The *I-I* is a mathematical point that does not exist at all; accordingly anyone can readily take up this standpoint—no one stands in the way of anyone else. Only momentarily can a particular individual, existing, be in a unity of the infinite and the finite that transcends existing. This instant is the moment of passion. Modern speculative thought has mustered everything to enable the individual to transcend himself objectively, but this just cannot be done. Existence exercises its constraint, and if philosophers nowadays had not become pencil-pushers serving the trifling busyness of fantastical thinking, it would have discerned that suicide is the only somewhat practical interpretation of its attempt. But pencil-pushing modern speculative thought takes a dim view of passion, and yet, for the existing person, passion is existence at its very highest—and we are, after all, existing persons. In passion, the existing subject is infinitized in the eternity of imagination and yet is also most definitely himself. The fantastical *I-I* is not infinitude and finitude in identity, since neither the one nor the other is actual; it is a fantastical union with a cloud,[5] an unfruitful embrace, and the relation of the individual *I* to this mirage is never stated.[6]

All essential knowing pertains to existence, or only the knowing whose relation to existence is essential is essential knowing. Essentially viewed, the knowing that does not inwardly in the reflection of inwardness pertain to existence is accidental knowing, and its degree and scope, essentially viewed, are a matter of indifference. . . .

[7]*When the question about truth is asked objectively, truth is reflected upon objectively as an object to which the knower relates himself. What is reflected upon is not the relation but that what he relates himself to is the truth, the true. If only that to which he relates himself is the truth, the true, then the subject is in the truth. When the question about truth is asked subjectively, the individual's relation is reflected upon subjectively. If only the how of this relation is in truth, the individual is in truth, even if he in this way were to relate himself to untruth.* *

Let us take the knowledge of God as an example. Objectively, what is reflected upon is that this is the true God; subjectively, that the individual relates himself to a something *in such a way* that his relation is in truth a God-relation. Now, on which side is the truth? Alas, must we not at this point resort to mediation and say: It is on neither side; it is in the mediation? Superbly stated, if only someone could say how an existing

---

*The reader will note that what is being discussed here is essential truth, or the truth that is related essentially to existence, and that it is specifically in order to clarify it as inwardness or as subjectivity that the contrast is pointed out.

person goes about being in mediation, because to be in mediation is to be finished; to exist is to become. An existing person cannot be in two places at the same time, cannot be subject-object. When he is closest to being in two places at the same time, he is in passion; but passion is only momentary, and passion is the highest pitch of subjectivity.

The existing person who chooses the objective way now enters upon all approximating deliberation intended to bring forth God objectively, which is not achieved in all eternity, because God is a subject and hence only for subjectivity in inwardness. The existing person who chooses the subjective way instantly comprehends the whole dialectical difficulty because he must use some time, perhaps a long time, to find God objectively. He comprehends this dialectical difficulty in all its pain, because he must resort to God at that very moment, because every moment in which he does not have God is wasted.* At that very moment he has God, not by virtue of any objective deliberation but by virtue of the infinite passion of inwardness. The objective person is not bothered by dialectical difficulties such as what it means to put a whole research period into finding God, since it is indeed possible that the researcher would die tomorrow, and if he goes on living, he cannot very well regard God as something to be taken along at his convenience, since God is something one takes along *à tout prix* [at any price], which, in passion's understanding, is the true relationship of inwardness with God.

It is at this point, dialectically so very difficult, that the road swings off for the person who knows what it means to think dialectically and, existing, to think dialectically, which is quite different from sitting as a fantastical being at a desk and writing about something one has never done oneself, quite different from writing *de omnibus dubitandum* and then as an existing person being just as credulous as the most sensate human being. It is here that the road swings off, and the change is this: whereas objective knowledge goes along leisurely on the long road of approximation, itself not actuated by passion, to subjective knowledge every delay is a deadly peril and the decision so infinitely important that it is immediately urgent, as if the opportunity had already passed by unused.

Now, if the problem is to calculate where there is more truth (and, as stated, simultaneously to be on both sides equally is not granted to an existing person but is only a beatifying delusion for a deluded *I-I*), whether on the side of the person who only objectively seeks the true God and the approximating truth of the God-idea or on the side of the person who is infinitely concerned that he in truth relate himself to God with the infinite passion of need—then there can be no doubt about the answer for anyone who is not totally botched by scholarship and science. If someone who lives in the midst of Christianity enters, with knowledge of the true idea of God, the house of God, the house of the true God, and prays, but prays in untruth, and if someone lives in an idolatrous land but prays with all the passion of infinity, although his eyes are resting upon the image of an idol—where, then, is there more truth? The one prays in

---

*[8]In this way God is indeed a postulate, but not in the loose sense in which it is ordinarily taken. Instead, it becomes clear that this is the only way an existing person enters into a relationship with God: when the dialectical contradiction brings passion to despair and assists him in grasping God with "the category of despair" (faith), [9]so that the postulate, far from being the arbitrary, is in fact *necessary* defense [*N ø d værge*], self-defense; in this way God is not a postulate, but the existing person's postulating of God is—a necessity [*Nødvendighed*].

truth to God although he is worshiping an idol; the other prays in untruth to the true God and is therefore in truth worshiping an idol.

If someone objectively inquires into immortality, and someone else stakes the passion of the infinite on the uncertainty—where, then, is there more truth, and who has more certainty? The one has once and for all entered upon an approximation that never ends, because the certainty of immortality is rooted in subjectivity; the other is immortal and therefore struggles by contending with the uncertainty.

Let us consider Socrates. These days everyone is dabbling in a few proofs or demonstrations—one has many, another fewer. But Socrates! He poses the question objectively, problematically: if there is an immortality.[10] So, compared with one of the modern thinkers with the three demonstrations, was he a doubter? Not at all. He stakes his whole life on this "if"; he dares to die, and with the passion of the infinite he has so ordered his whole life that it might be acceptable—*if* there is an immortality. Is there any better demonstration for the immortality of the soul? But those who have the three demonstrations do not order their lives accordingly. If there is an immortality, it must be nauseated by their way of living—is there any better counterdemonstration to the three demonstrations? The "fragment" of uncertainty helped Socrates, because he himself helped with the passion of infinity. The three demonstrations are of no benefit whatever to those others, because they are and remain slugs and, failing to demonstrate anything else, have demonstrated it by their three demonstrations.

In the same way a girl has perhaps possessed all the sweetness of being in love through a weak hope of being loved by the beloved, because she herself staked everything on this weak hope; [11]on the other hand, many a wedded matron, who more than once has submitted to the strongest expression of erotic love, has certainly had demonstrations and yet, strangely enough, has not possessed *quod erat demonstrandum* [that which was to be demonstrated]. The Socratic ignorance was thus the expression, firmly maintained with all the passion of inwardness, of the relation of the eternal truth to an existing person, and therefore it must remain for him a paradox as long as he exists. Yet it is possible that in the Socratic ignorance there was more truth in Socrates than in the objective truth of the entire system that flirts with the demands of the times and adapts itself to assistant professors.

[12]*Objectively the emphasis is on* **what** *is said; subjectively the emphasis is on* **how** *it is said.* This distinction applies even esthetically and is specifically expressed when we say that in the mouth of this or that person something that is truth can become untruth. Particular attention should be paid to this distinction in our day, for if one were to express in a single sentence the difference between ancient times and our time, one would no doubt have to say: In ancient times there were only a few individuals who knew the truth; now everyone knows it, but inwardness has an inverse relation to it.* Viewed esthetically, the contradiction that emerges when truth becomes untruth in this and that person's mouth is best interpreted comically. Ethically-religiously, the emphasis is again on: *how*. But this is not to be understood as manner, modulation of voice, oral delivery, etc., but it is to be understood as the relation of the existing person, in his very exis-

*See *Stages on Life's Way*, p. 366 fn.[13]

tence, to what is said. Objectively, the question is only about categories of thought; subjectively, about inwardness. At its maximum, this "how" is the passion of the infinite, and the passion of the infinite is the very truth. But the passion of the infinite is precisely subjectivity, and thus subjectivity is truth. From the objective point of view, there is no infinite decision, and thus it is objectively correct that the distinction between good and evil is canceled, along with the principle of contradiction, and thereby also the infinite distinction between truth and falsehood. Only in subjectivity is there decision, whereas wanting to become objective is untruth. The passion of the infinite, not its content, is the deciding factor, for its content is precisely itself. In this way the subjective "how" and subjectivity are the truth.

[14]But precisely because the subject is existing, the "how" that is subjectively emphasized is dialectical also with regard to time. In the moment of the decision of passion, where the road swings off from objective knowledge, it looks as if the infinite decision were thereby finished. But at the same moment, the existing person is in the temporal realm, and the subjective "how" is transformed into a striving that is motivated and repeatedly refreshed by the decisive passion of the infinite, but it is nevertheless a striving.

When subjectivity is truth, the definition of truth must also contain in itself an expression of the antithesis to objectivity, a memento of that fork in the road, and this expression will at the same time indicate the resilience of the inwardness. Here is such a definition of truth: *An objective uncertainty, held fast through appropriation with the most passionate inwardness, is the truth*, the highest truth there is for an *existing* person. At the point where the road swings off (and where that is cannot be stated objectively, since it is precisely subjectivity), objective knowledge is suspended. Objectively he then has only uncertainty, but this is precisely what intensifies the infinite passion of inwardness, and truth is precisely the daring venture of choosing the objective uncertainty with the passion of the infinite. I observe nature in order to find God, and I do indeed see omnipotence and wisdom, but I also see much that troubles and disturbs. The *summa summarum* [sum total] of this is an objective uncertainty, but the inwardness is so very great, precisely because it grasps this objective uncertainty with all the passion of the infinite. In a mathematical proposition, for example, the objectivity is given, but therefore its truth is also an indifferent truth.

But the definition of truth stated above is a paraphrasing of faith. [15]Without risk, no faith. Faith is the contradiction between the infinite passion of inwardness and the objective uncertainty. If I am able to apprehend God objectively, I do not have faith; but because I cannot do this, I must have faith. If I want to keep myself in faith, I must continually see to it that I hold fast the objective uncertainty, see to it that in the objective uncertainty I am "out on 70,000 fathoms of water" and still have faith.

[16]The thesis that subjectivity, inwardness, is truth contains the Socratic wisdom, the undying merit of which is to have paid attention to the essential meaning of existing, of the knower's being an existing person. That is why, in his ignorance, Socrates was in the truth in the highest sense within paganism. To comprehend this, that the misfortune of speculative thought is simply that it forgets again and again that the knower is an existing person, can already be rather difficult in our objective age. "But

to go beyond Socrates when one has not even comprehended the Socratic—that, at least, is not Socratic."

Notes

1. See Shakespeare, *Hamlet*, III, 1, 56; Foersom and Wulff, 1, p. 97; Ortlepp, I, p. 289; Schlegel and Tieck, VI, p. 63; Kittredge, p. 1167: "To be, or not to be—that is the question. . . ."
2. John 18:38, "What is truth?"
3. An allusion to Descartes, *A Discourse on Method*, II, IV; *Renati DesCartes opera philosophica* (Amsterdam: 1685; *ASKB* 473 [1678]), pp. 7, 20; *A Discourse on Method and Selected Writings*, tr. John Veitch (New York: Dutton, 1951), pp. 9, 27:

   > I was then in Germany, attracted thither by the wars in that country, which have not yet been brought to a termination; and as I was returning to the army from the coronation of the emperor, the setting in of winter arrested me in a locality where, as I found no society to interest me, and was besides fortunately undisturbed by any cares or passions, I remained the whole day in seclusion[1] with full opportunity to occupy my attention with my own thoughts. . . . I had long before remarked that, in relation to practice, it is sometimes necessary to adopt, as if above doubt, opinions which we discern to be highly uncertain, as has been already said; but as I then desired to give my attention solely to search after truth, I thought that a procedure exactly the opposite was called for, and that I ought to reject as absolutely false all opinions in regard to which I could suppose the least ground for doubt, in order to ascertain whether after that there remained aught in my belief that was wholly indubitable.
   >
   > [1]Literally, in a room heated by means of a stove.—Tr.

   See, for example, *Johannes Climacus*, pp. 133–59, *KW* VII (*Pap.* IV B 1, pp. 116–41); *Fear and Trembling*, pp. 5–6, *KW* VI (*SV* III 57–58).
4. Cf. Romans 8:19.
5. 269. In Greek mythology, Zeus punished Ixion for making love to Hera (Roman Juno) by sending him a cloud resembling Hera. From this union came the centaurs. See Paul Friedrich A. Nitsch, *neues mythologisches Wörterbuch*, I–II, rev. Friedrich Gotthilf Klopfer (Leipzig, Sorau: 1821; *ASKB* 1944–45), II, pp. 122–23. See also Faust's attempted union with Helena, *Faust*, II, 3, 9939–54, *Werke*, XLI, pp. 244–45; Taylor, p. 183.
6. For continuation of the sentence and paragraph, see Supplement, pp. 2.45–46 (*Pap.* VI B 40:22).
7. With reference to the following paragraph, see Supplement, p. 2.46 (*Pap.* VI B 19.7,8).
8. With reference to the following note, see Supplement, p. 2.46 (*Pap.* VI B 40:23).
9. See, for example, *Sickness unto Death*, pp. 67, 116 fn., *KW* XIX (*SV* XI 178, 226).
10. See, for example, Plato, *Apology*, 40 c–41 a; *Opera*, VIII, pp. 154–55; *Dialogues*, p. 25; *Phaedo*, 91 b; *Opera*, 1, pp. 554–55; Heise, I, pp. 69–70; *Dialogues*, p. 73:

    > Death is one of two things. Either it is annihilation, and the dead have no consciousness of anything, or, as we are told, it is really a change—a migration of the soul from this place to another. Now if there is no consciousness but only a dreamless sleep, death must be a marvelous gain. I suppose that if anyone were told to pick out the night on which he slept so soundly as not even to dream, and then to compare it with all the other nights and days of his life, and then were told to say, after due consideration, how many better and happier days and nights than this he had spent in the course of his life—well, I think that the Great King himself, to say nothing of any private person, would find these days and nights easy to

count in comparison with the rest. If death is like this, then, I call it gain, because the whole of time, if you look at it in this way, can be regarded as no more than one single night. If on the other hand death is a removal from here to some other place, and if what we are told is true, that all the dead are there, what greater blessing could there be than this, gentlemen? If on arrival in the other world, beyond the reach of our so-called justice, one will find there the true judges who are said to preside in those courts, Minos and Rhadamanthus and Aeacus and Triptolemus and all those other half-divinities who were upright in their earthly life, would that be an unrewarding journey? Put it in this way. How much would one of you give to meet Orpheus and Musaeus, Hesiod and Homer? I am willing to die ten times over if this account is true.

If my theory is really true, it is right to believe it, while, even if death is extinction, at any rate during this time before my death I shall be less likely to distress my companions by giving way to self-pity, and this folly of mine will not live on with me—which would be a calamity—but will shortly come to an end.

11. With reference to the remainder of the paragraph, see Supplement, p. 2.47 (*Pap.* VI B 40:24).
12. With reference to the following sentence, see Supplement, p. 2.11 (*Pap.* VI B 17).
13. *Stages*, pp. 471–72, *KW* XI (*SV* VI 438).
14. With reference to the following three paragraphs, see Supplement, p. 2.47 (*Pap.* VI B 18).
15. With reference to the remainder of the paragraph, see Supplement, pp. 2.47–48 (*Pap.* VI B 18, 19:3,10).
16. With reference to the following fourteen pages, see Supplement, pp. 2.48–51 (*Pap.* VI B 40:26).

22. Eulogy on Abraham[1]

SØREN KIERKEGAARD

If a human being did not have an eternal consciousness,[2] if underlying everything there were only a wild, fermenting power that writhing in dark passions produced everything, be it significant or insignificant, if a vast, never appeased emptiness hid beneath everything, what would life be then but despair? If such were the situation, if there were no sacred bond that knit humankind together, if one generation emerged after another like forest foliage,[3] if one generation succeeded another like the singing of birds in the forest, if a generation passed through the world as a ship through the sea, as wind through

Source: Søren Kierkegaard, *Fear and Trembling,* © 1973, Princeton University Press. Reprinted by permission of Princeton University Press.

the desert, an unthinking and unproductive performance, if an eternal oblivion, perpetually hungry, lurked for its prey and there were no power strong enough to wrench that away from it—how empty and devoid of consolation life would be! But precisely for that reason it is not so, and just as God created man and woman, so he created the hero and the poet or orator. The poet or orator can do nothing that the hero does; he can only admire, love, and delight in him. Yet he, too, is happy—no less than that one is, for the hero is, so to speak, his better nature, with which he is enamored—yet happy that the other is not himself, that his love can be admiration. He is recollection's genius. He can do nothing but bring to mind what has been done, can do nothing but admire what has been done; he takes nothing of his own but is zealous for what has been entrusted. He follows his heart's desire, but when he has found the object of his search, he roams about to every man's door with his song and speech so that all may admire the hero as he does, may be proud of the hero as he is. This is his occupation, his humble task; this is his faithful service in the house of the hero. If he remains true to his love in this way, if he contends night and day against the craftiness of oblivion, which wants to trick him out of his hero, then he has fulfilled his task, then he is gathered together with the hero, who has loved him just as faithfully, for the poet is, so to speak, the hero's better nature, powerless, to be sure, just as a memory is, but also transfigured just as a memory is. Therefore, no one who was great will be forgotten, and even though it takes time, even though a cloud[4] of misunderstanding takes away the hero, his lover will nevertheless come, and the longer the passage of time, the more faithfully he adheres to him.

No! No one who was great in the world will be forgotten, but everyone was great in his own way, and everyone in proportion to the greatness of that which *he loved*. He who loved himself became great by virtue of himself, and he who loved other men became great by his devotedness, but he who loved God became the greatest of all. Everyone shall be remembered, but everyone became great in proportion to his *expectancy*. One became great by expecting the possible, another by expecting the eternal; but he who expected the impossible became the greatest of all. Everyone shall be remembered, but everyone was great wholly in proportion to the magnitude of that with which he *struggled*. For he who struggled with the world became great by conquering the world, and he who struggled with himself became great by conquering himself, but he who struggled with God became the greatest of all. Thus did they struggle in the world, man against man, one against thousands, but he who struggled with God was the greatest of all. Thus did they struggle on earth: there was one who conquered everything by his power, and there was one who conquered God by his powerlessness. There was one who relied upon himself and gained everything; there was one who in the security of his own strength sacrificed everything; but the one who believed God was the greatest of all. There was one who was great by virtue of his power, and one who was great by virtue of his wisdom, and one who was great by virtue of his hope, and one who was great by virtue of his love, but Abraham was the greatest of all, great by that power whose strength is powerlessness, great by that wisdom whose secret is foolishness, great by that hope whose form is madness, great by the love that is hatred to oneself.

By faith Abraham emigrated from the land of his fathers and became an alien in the promised land.[5] He left one thing behind, took one thing along: he left behind his worldly understanding, and he took along his faith. Otherwise he certainly would not have emigrated but surely would have considered it unreasonable [*urimeligt*]. By faith he was an alien in the promised land, and there was nothing that reminded him of what he cherished, but everything by its newness tempted his soul to sorrowful longing. And yet he was God's chosen one in whom the Lord was well pleased! As a matter of fact, if he had been an exile, banished from God's grace, he could have better understood it—but now it was as if he and his faith were being mocked. There was also in the world one who lived in exile from the native land he loved.[6] He is not forgotten, nor are his dirges of lamentation when he sorrowfully sought and found what was lost. There is no dirge by Abraham. It is human to lament, human to weep with one who weeps, but it is greater to have faith, more blessed to contemplate the man of faith.

By faith Abraham received the promise that in his seed all the generations of the earth would be blessed.[7] Time passed, the possibility was there, Abraham had faith; time passed, it became unreasonable, Abraham had faith. There was one in the world who also had an expectancy.[8] Time passed, evening drew near; he was not so contemptible as to forget his expectancy, and therefore he will not be forgotten, either. Then he sorrowed, and his sorrow did not disappoint him as life had done, it did everything it could for him; in the sweetness of his sorrow he possessed his disappointed expectancy. It is human to sorrow, human to sorrow with the sorrowing, but it is greater to have faith, more blessed to contemplate the man of faith. We have no dirge of sorrow by Abraham. As time passed, he did not gloomily count the days; he did not look suspiciously at Sarah, wondering if she was not getting old; he did not stop the course of the sun so she would not become old and along with her his expectancy; he did not soothingly sing his mournful lay for Sarah. Abraham became old, Sarah the object of mockery in the land, and yet he was God's chosen one and heir to the promise that in his seed all the generations of the earth would be blessed. Would it not have been better, after all, if he were not God's chosen? What does it mean to be God's chosen? Is it to be denied in youth one's youthful desire in order to have it fulfilled with great difficulty in one's old age? But Abraham believed and held to the promise. If Abraham had wavered, he would have given it up. He would have said to God, "So maybe it is not your will that this should be; then I will give up my wish. It was my one and only wish, it was my blessedness. My soul is open and sincere; I am hiding no secret resentment because you denied me this." He would not have been forgotten, he would have saved many by his example, but he still would not have become the father of faith, for it is great to give up one's desire, but it is greater to hold fast to it after having given it up; it is great to lay hold of the eternal, but it is greater to hold fast to the temporal after having given it up.

Then came the fullness of time. If Abraham had not had faith, then Sarah would surely have died of sorrow, and Abraham, dulled by grief, would not have understood the fulfillment but would have smiled at it as at a youthful dream. But Abraham had faith, and therefore he was young, for he who always hopes for the best grows old and is deceived by life, and he who is always prepared for the worst grows old prematurely, but he who has faith—he preserves an eternal youth. So let us praise and honor that story! For Sarah, although well advanced in years, was young enough to desire the pleasure of motherhood, and Abraham with his gray hairs was young enough to wish to be a father. Outwardly, the wonder of it is that it happened according to their expectancy; in the more profound sense, the wonder of faith is that Abraham and Sarah were young enough to desire and that faith had preserved their desire and thereby their youth. He accepted the fulfillment of the promise, he accepted it in faith, and it happened according to the promise and according to his faith. Moses struck the rock with his staff, but he did not have faith.[9]

So there was joy in Abraham's house when Sarah stood as bride on their golden wedding day.

But it was not to remain that way; once again Abraham was to be tried [forsøges].[10] He had fought with that crafty power that devises all things, with that vigilant enemy who never dozes, with that old man who outlives everything—he had fought with time and kept his faith. Now all the frightfulness of the struggle was concentrated in one moment. "And God tempted [fristede][11] Abraham and said to him, take Isaac, your only son, whom you love, and go to the land of Moriah and offer him as a burnt offering on a mountain that I shall show you."

So everything was lost, even more appallingly than if it had never happened! So the Lord was only mocking Abraham! He wondrously made the preposterous come true; now he wanted to see it annihilated. This was indeed a piece of folly, but Abraham did not laugh at it as Sarah did when the promise was announced.[12] All was lost! Seventy years[13] of trusting expectancy, the brief joy over the fulfillment of faith. Who is this who seizes the staff from the old man, who is this who demands that he himself shall break it! Who is this who makes a man's gray hairs disconsolate, who is this who demands that he himself shall do it! Is there no sympathy for this venerable old man, none for the innocent child? And yet Abraham was God's chosen one, and it was the Lord who imposed the ordeal [Prøvelse].[14] Now everything would be lost! All the glorious remembrance of his posterity, the promise in Abraham's seed—it was nothing but a whim, a fleeting thought that the Lord had had and that Abraham was now supposed to obliterate. That glorious treasure,[15] which was just as old as the faith in Abraham's heart and many, many years older than Isaac, the fruit of Abraham's life, sanctified by prayer, matured in battle, the blessing on Abraham's lips—this fruit was now to be torn off prematurely and rendered meaningless, for what meaning would it have if Isaac should be sacrificed! That sad but nevertheless blessed hour when Abraham was to take leave of everything he held dear, when he once more would raise his venerable head, when his face would shine as the Lord's, when he would concentrate all his soul upon a blessing that would be so powerful it would bless Isaac all his days—this hour was not to come! For Abraham would indeed take leave of Isaac, but in such a way that he himself would remain behind; death would separate them, but in such a way that Isaac would become its booty. The old man would not, rejoicing in death, lay his hand in blessing on Isaac, but, weary of life, he would lay a violent hand upon Isaac. And it was God who tested him! Woe to the messenger who brought such news to Abraham! Who would have dared to be the emissary of this sorrow? But it was God who tested [prøvede][16] Abraham.

Yet Abraham had faith, and had faith for this life. In fact, if his faith had been only for a life to come, he certainly would have more readily discarded everything in order to rush out of a world to which he did not belong. But Abraham's faith was not of this sort, if there is such a faith at all, for actually it is not faith but the most remote possibility of faith that faintly sees its object on the most distant horizon but is separated from it by a chasmal abyss in which doubt plays its tricks. But Abraham had faith specifically for this life—faith that he would grow old in this country, be honored among the people, blessed by posterity, and unforgettable in Isaac, the most precious thing in his life, whom he embraced with a love that is inadequately described by saying he faithfully fulfilled the father's duty to love the son, which is indeed stated in the command:[17] the son, whom you love. Jacob had twelve sons, one of whom he loved;[18] Abraham had but one, whom he loved.

But Abraham had faith and did not doubt; he believed the preposterous. If Abraham had doubted, then he would have done something else, something great and glorious, for how could Abraham do anything else but what is great and glorious! He would have gone to Mount Moriah, he would have split the firewood, lit the fire, drawn the knife. He would have cried out to God, "Reject not this sacrifice; it is not the best that I have, that I know very well, for what is an old man compared with the child of promise, but it is the best I can give you. Let Isaac never find this out so that he may take comfort in his youth." He would have thrust the knife into his own breast.[19] He would have been admired in the world, and his name would never be forgotten; but it is one thing to be admired and another to become a guiding star that saves the anguished.

But Abraham had faith. He did not pray for himself, trying to influence the Lord; it was only when righteous punishment fell upon Sodom and Gomorrah that Abraham came forward with his prayers.[20]

We read in sacred scripture:[21] "And God tempted [*fristede*] Abraham and said: Abraham, Abraham, where are you? But Abraham answered: Here am I." You to whom these words are addressed, was this the case with you? When in the far distance you saw overwhelming vicissitudes approaching, did you not say to the mountains, "Hide me," and to the hills, "Fall on me"?[22] Or, if you were stronger, did your feet nevertheless not drag along the way, did they not long, so to speak, for the old trails? And when your name was called, did you answer, perhaps answer softly, in a whisper? Not so with Abraham. Cheerfully, freely, confidently, loudly he answered: Here am I. We read on: "And Abraham arose early in the morning." He hurried as if to a celebration, and early in the morning he was at the appointed place on Mount Moriah. He said nothing to Sarah, nothing to Eliezer[23]—who, after all, could understand him, for did not the nature of the temptation [*Fristelsen*] extract from him the pledge of silence? "He split the firewood, he bound Isaac, he lit the fire, he drew the knife."[24] My listener! Many a father has thought himself deprived of every hope for the future when he lost his child, the dearest thing in the world to him; nevertheless, no one was the child of promise in the sense in which Isaac was that to Abraham. Many a father has lost his child, but then it was God, the unchangeable, inscrutable will of the Almighty, it was his hand that took it. Not so with Abraham! A harder test [*Prøve*] was reserved for him, and Isaac's fate was placed, along with the knife, in Abraham's hand. And there he stood, the old man with his solitary hope. But he did not doubt, he did not look in anguish to the left and to the right, he did not challenge heaven with his prayers. He knew it was God the Almighty who was testing [*prøvede*] him; he knew it was the hardest sacrifice that could be demanded of him; but he knew also that no sacrifice is too severe when God demands it—and he drew the knife.

Who strengthened Abraham's arm, who braced up his right arm so that it did not sink down powerless! Anyone who looks upon this scene is paralyzed. Who strengthened Abraham's soul lest everything go black for him and he see neither Isaac nor the ram! Anyone who looks upon this scene is blinded. And yet it perhaps rarely happens that anyone is paralyzed or blinded, and still more rarely does anyone tell what happened as it deserves to be told. We know it all—it was only an ordeal [*Prøvelse*].

If Abraham had doubted as he stood there on Mount Moriah, if irresolute he had looked around, if he had happened to spot the ram before drawing the knife, if God had allowed him to sacrifice it instead of Isaac—then he would have gone home, everything would have been the same, he would have had Sarah, he would have kept Isaac, and yet how changed! For his return would have been a flight, his deliverance an accident, his reward disgrace, his future perhaps perdition. Then he would have witnessed neither to his faith nor to God's grace but would have witnessed to how appalling it is to go to Mount Moriah. Then Abraham would not be forgotten, nor would Mount Moriah. Then it would not be mentioned in the way Ararat,[25] where the ark landed, is mentioned, but it would be called a place of terror, for it was here that Abraham doubted.

Venerable Father Abraham! When you went home from Mount Moriah, you did not need a eulogy to comfort you for what was lost, for you gained everything and kept Isaac—was it not so? The Lord did not take him away from you again, but you sat happily together at the dinner table in your tent, as you do in the next world for all eternity. Venerable Father Abraham! Centuries have passed since those days, but you have no need of a late lover to snatch your memory from the power of oblivion, for every language calls you to mind—and yet you reward your lover more gloriously than anyone else. In the life to come you make him eternally happy in your bosom; here in this life you captivate his eyes and his heart with the wonder of your act. Venerable Father Abraham! Second Father of the race! You who were the first to feel and to bear witness to that prodigious passion that disdains the terrifying battle with the raging elements and the forces of creation in order to contend with God, you who were the first to know that supreme passion, the holy, pure, and humble expression for the divine madness[26] that was admired by the pagans—forgive the one who aspired to speak your praise if he has not done it properly. He spoke humbly, as his heart demanded; he spoke briefly, as is seemly. But he will never forget that you needed 100 years to get the son of your old age against all expectancy, that you had to draw the knife before you kept Isaac; he will never forget that in 130 years[27] you got no further than faith.[28]

Notes

1. See Supplement, pp. 248–49 (*Pap.* IV B 72).
2. Here for the first time in the pseudonymous writings the expression "eternal consciousness" and variants are used. See, for example, *Philosophical Fragments, KW* VII (*SV* IV 173, 224, 271); *The Concept of Anxiety*, p. 153, *KW* VIII (*SV* IV 418); *Stages on Life's Way, KW* XI (*SV* VI 91); *Postscript, KW* XII (*SV* VII 6, 122, 483, 500); *Upbuilding Discourses in Various Spir-*

its, KW XV (*SV* VIII 226); *The Sickness unto Death*, pp. 70–71, 79, 113, *KW* XIX (*SV* XI 182, 191, 223). In brief, it signifies consciousness of selfhood, particularly in the context of recollection (as in Plato) and ultimately before God.

3. See Homer, *Iliad*, VI, 146–48.

4. See ibid., III, 381, where Paris is carried away in a cloud.

5. See Hebrews 11:8–19.

6. Presumably the Roman poet Ovid (43 B.C.–A.D. 17?), who in A.D. 8 was banished by Caesar Augustus to Tomi on the Black Sea. See his *Tristia* and *Ex Ponto*, *P. Ovidii Nasonis opera quae extant*, ed. A. Richter (Leipzig: 1828; *ASKB* 1265); *Tristia [and] Ex Ponto*, tr. A. L. Wheeler (Loeb Classics, New York: Putnam, 1924).

7. See p. 12 and note 12.

8. See note 6.

9. See Numbers 20:11.

10. See p. 9 and note 2.

11. See p. 9 and note 2.

12. See Genesis 18:12. See also Genesis 17:17; Supplement, p. 255 (*Pap.* IV B 69).

13. See note 27.

14. See p. 9 and note 2.

15. See Genesis 12:2.

16. See p. 9 and note 2.

17. See Genesis 22:2.

18. Joseph. See Genesis 35:22–23, 37:3.

19. See Supplement, pp. 248–49 (*Pap.* IV B 72).

20. See Genesis 18:23.

21. Genesis 22:1–3. See Supplement, pp. 239–40 (*Pap.* III C 4). See p. 9 and note 2.

22. See Luke 23:30; Supplement, pp. 248–49 (*Pap.* IV B 72).

23. See p. 14, note 16.

24. A free rendition of Genesis 22:3, 9–10.

25. See Genesis 8:4. Ararat: a high or holy place.

26. Plato, *Phaedrus*, 244–45 c, 265 b; *Platonis quae exstant opera*, I–XI, ed. Fridericus Astius (Leipzig: 1819–32; *ASKB* 1144–54), 1, pp. 164–67, 216–17: *The Collected Dialogues of Plato*, ed. Edith Hamilton and Huntington Cairns (Princeton: Princeton University Press, 1963), pp. 491–92, 511.

27. Since Abraham was 100 years old at the time of Isaac's birth, Isaac's age is placed here at 30. Kierkegaard was 30 years old at the time *Fear and Trembling* was written.

28. See Supplement, p. 249 (*Pap.* IV B 87:2).

Epilogue[1]

O nce when the price of spices in Holland fell, the merchants had a few cargoes sunk in the sea in order to jack up the price. This was an excusable, perhaps even necessary, deception. Do we need something similar in the world of the spirit? Are we so sure that we have achieved the highest, so that there is nothing left for us to do except piously to delude ourselves into thinking that we have not come that far, simply in order to have something to occupy our time? Is this the kind of self-deception the present generation needs? Should it be trained in a virtuosity along that line, or is it not, instead, adequately perfected in the art of deceiving itself? Or, rather, does it not need an honest earnestness that fearlessly and incorruptibly points to the tasks, an honest earnestness that lovingly maintains the tasks, that does not disquiet people into wanting to attain the highest too hastily but keeps the tasks young and beautiful and lovely to look at, inviting to all and yet also difficult and inspiring to the noble-minded (for the noble nature is inspired only by the difficult)? Whatever one generation learns from another, no generation learns the essentially human from a previous one. In this respect, each generation begins primitively, has no task other than what each previous generation had, nor does it advance further, insofar as the previous generations did not betray the task and deceive themselves. The essentially human is passion, in which one generation perfectly understands another and understands itself. For example, no generation has learned to love from another, no generation is able to begin at any other point than at the beginning, no later generation has a more abridged task than the previous one, and if someone desires to go further and not stop with loving as the previous generation did, this is foolish and idle talk.

But the highest passion in a person is faith, and here no generation begins at any other point than where the previous one did. Each generation begins all over again; the next generation advances no further than the previous one, that is, if that one was faithful to the task and did not leave it high and dry. That it should be fatiguing is, of course, something that one generation cannot say, for the generation does indeed have the task and has nothing to do with the fact that the previous generation had the same task, unless this particular generation, or the individuals in it, presumptuously assumes the place that belongs to the spirit who rules the world and who has the patience not to become weary. If the generation does that, it is wrong, and no wonder, then, that all existence seems wrong to it, for there surely is no one who found existence more wrong than the tailor who, according to the fairy story,[2] came to heaven while alive and contemplated the world from that vantage point. As long as the generation is concerned only about its task, which is the highest, it cannot become weary, for the task is always adequate for a person's lifetime.[3] When children on vacation have already played all the games before twelve o'clock and impatiently ask: Can't somebody think up a new game—does this show that these children are more developed and more advanced than the children in the contemporary or previous generation who make the well-known games last all day long? Or does it show instead that the first children lack what I would call the endearing earnestness belonging to play?

Faith is the highest passion in a person. There perhaps are many in every generation who do not come to faith, but no one goes further. Whether there also are many in our day who do not find it, I do not decide. I dare to refer only to myself, without concealing that he has a long way to go, without therefore wishing to deceive himself or what is great by making a trifle of it, a childhood disease one may wish to get over as soon as possible. But life has tasks enough also for the person who does not come to faith, and if he loves these honestly, his life will not be wasted, even if it is never comparable to the lives of those who perceived and grasped the highest. But the person who has come to faith (whether he is extraordinarily gifted or plain and simple does not matter) does not come to a standstill in faith. Indeed, he would be indignant if anyone said this to him, just as the lover would resent it if someone said that he came to a standstill in love; for, he would answer, I am by no means standing still. I have my whole life in it. Yet he does not go further, does not go on to something else, for when he finds this, then he has another explanation.

[4]"One must go further, one must go further." This urge to go further is an old story in the world. Heraclitus the obscure, who deposited his thoughts in his books and his books in Diana's temple[5] (for his thoughts had been his armor in life, and therefore he hung it in the temple of the goddess), Heraclitus the obscure said: One cannot walk through the same river twice.*[6] Heraclitus the obscure had a disciple who did not remain standing there but went further—and added: One cannot do it even once.† Poor Heraclitus, to have a disciple like that! By this improvement, the Heraclitean thesis was amended into an Eleatic thesis that denies motion, and yet that disciple wished only to be a disciple of Heraclitus who went further, not back to what Heraclitus had abandoned.

Notes

1. For sketches of pp. 121–23, see Supplement, pp. 256–57 (*Pap.* IV B 92, 94, 76).
2. "*Der Schneider im Himmel,*" no. 35, *Kinder- und Haus-Märchen gesammelt durch die Brüder Grimm,* I–III (2 ed., Berlin: 1819–22; *ASKB* 1425–27), I, pp. 177–79; *The Complete Grimm's Fairy Tales,* tr. Padraic Colum (New York: Pantheon, 1972), pp. 175–77.
3. With reference to the following sentence, see Supplement, p. 256 (*Pap.* IV B 94).
4. For a draft of the following two sentences, see Supplement, p. 257 (*Pap.* IV B 95:3).
5. See *JP* II 2285 (*Pap.* IV A 58).
6. For a draft of the following sentence, see Supplement, p. 257 (*Pap.* IV B 95:4).
7. *Collected Dialogues,* p. 439.

*Καὶ ποταμοῦ ῥοῇ ἀπεικάζων τά ὂυτα λέγει ὡς δίς ἐς τὸν αὐτὸν ποταμὸν οὐκ ὀμβαίης [He compares being to the stream of a river and says that you cannot go into the same river twice]. [7]See Plato, *Cratylus,* 402. Ast., III, p. 158.

†Cf. Tennemann, *Gesch. d. Philos.,* I, p. 220.

23. The Strategy of the Authorship

MARK C. TAYLOR

A. Religious Truth as Subjectivity

Kierkegaard's use of the pseudonymous method depends upon his conception of the nature of religious truth. Therefore if we are to understand his pseudonymous authorship and his purpose in these writings, we must begin by examining the way in which he views religious truth.

For Kierkegaard religious truth is subjectivity. Although this dictum is well-known, it is frequently misinterpreted. In holding that religious truth is subjectivity, Kierkegaard certainly is not arguing that religious truth is solipsistic or that it is the function of the capricious desire or interest of the individual. We can begin to understand what he means by comparing subjectivity with its opposite, objectivity.

Kierkegaard argues that one can be concerned with the problem of truth either from an objective or a subjective point of view. "*The objective accent falls on* WHAT [*hvad*] *is said, the subjective accent on* HOW [*hvorledes*] *it is said.*"[1] When one seeks truth objectively, he adopts the standpoint of objective apprehension. His attention is turned away from himself and toward a certain object (the "what"), which he attempts to understand. "*When the question of truth is raised in an objective manner, reflection is directed objectively to the truth, as an object to which the knower relates himself.*"[2] The person involved in this pursuit of truth is fundamentally an observer to whom objects become manifest.[3] The ideal toward which such knowledge is directed is the correspondence between one's idea and the object of that idea. Truth is regarded as the identity of thought and being. In cognition one endeavors accurately to re-present the object with which he is concerned. To attain the desired unity of thought and being, the inquirer must remove as far as possible his own subjectivity and become fully receptive to the object:

"The way of objective reflection makes the subject accidental, and thereby transforms existence into something indifferent, something vanishing. Away from the subject the objective way of reflection leads to the objective truth, and while the subject

Source: Mark C. Taylor, *Kierkegaard's Pseudonymous Authorship,* ©1973, Princeton University Press. Reprinted by permission of Princeton University Press.

and his subjectivity become indifferent, the truth also becomes indifferent, and this indifference is precisely its objective validity; for all interest [*Interessen*], like all decisiveness, is rooted in subjectivity. The way of objective reflection leads to abstract thought, to mathematics, to historical knowledge of different kinds; and always it leads away from the subject, whose existence or non-existence, and from the objective point of view quite rightly, becomes infinitely indifferent [*uendelig ligegyldig*]."[4]

Thus when truth is pursued objectively, attention is directed to the "what," or to the object of inquiry. The aim is to attain a knowledge, i.e., a correspondence of thought (idea) and being (object), which is valid independent of the particular knower conducting the investigation. This intention is only hindered by subjectivity and its interests.

Kierkegaard criticizes such an approach to truth. In the first place, there is a contradiction directly built into the ideal of objective truth. Because an objective approach to truth requires that subjectivity be excluded as far as is possible, the ideal would seem to be the complete elimination of subjectivity so that the object can be accurately known. But this would mean the elimination of the thinker himself, and therefore the end of the process of cognition. "As its maximum this way will lead to the contradiction that only the objective has come into being, while the subjective has gone out; that is to say, the existing subjectivity has vanished . . . ."[5]

In the second place, and more importantly, Kierkegaard holds that although it is correct to view truth as the conformity of thought and being, it is necessary to define the sort of being with which one is concerned.[6] The being that objective contemplation deals with is *conceptual being*. Although objective contemplation may be directed to empirical reality, it can never arrive at that empirical reality. One reason for this is that while empirical reality is irreducibly particular, thought is fundamentally general. Thought always deals with concepts that abstract from the particularities of empirical existence, and not immediately with that existence itself. Thus the object with which such objective contemplation comes into relation is, in the final analysis, a conceptual object; the being with which it deals is conceptual being. Kierkegaard surely does not deny that such being, in a certain sense, "is." "That the content of my thought *is* in the conceptual sense needs no proof, or needs no argument to prove it, since it is proved by my thinking it."[7] However, since the being with which such objective contemplation is concerned is conceptual being, the truth at which at arrives (truth, it will be recalled, is the conformity of thought and being) is completely tautologous. Such thought constantly relates itself to concepts that abstract from concrete reality, and does not treat that reality itself. These concepts certainly "are," and insofar as the thinker's thoughts correspond to these concepts, there is a conformity of thought and being. But this conformity is between thought and *conceptual* being. This is only another way of saying that there is a conformity of thought with itself.[8]

The fact that empirical reality is particular and thought is general is not, however, the only reason that objective reflection cannot break away from itself and become related to concrete existence. We have seen that for Kierkegaard, one who argues that truth is the conformity of thought and being must always be aware of the nature of the being with which he is concerned. If the being involved is not conceptual being, but is empirical being, a conformity of thought and being is possible only as an ideal toward which one strives. The reason for this lies in the very nature of empirical being: "If being . . . is understood as empirical being [*empiriske Væren*], truth is at once transformed into a desideratum, and everything must be understood in terms of becoming; for the empirical object is unfinished and the existing cognitive spirit is itself in the process of becoming. Thus the truth becomes an approximation [*Approximeren*] whose beginning cannot be posited absolutely, precisely because the conclusion is lacking, the effect of which is retroactive."[9]

Because the nature of empirical reality is to be in the process of becoming, it never is, but always becomes. Truth, as the conformity of thought and *being*, could, therefore, be attained only when the process of becoming had stopped. But this would mean that truth could be achieved only after empirical being had ceased to be what it fundamentally is. Kierkegaard thinks that such an alteration of empirical reality takes place in objective reflection. When this procedure is followed, there is an abstraction from the process of becoming that is indigenous to empirical reality. Again, it is apparent that such reflection deals with a constructed conception (a mental object) and not with the empirical object: ". . . for the correspondence between thought and being is, from the abstract point of view, always finished. Only with the concrete does becoming enter in, and it is from the concrete that abstract thought abstracts."[10] Such an abstraction from the process of becoming negates concrete reality. However, if the process of cognition so changes that which it cognizes that it ceases to be what it is, one can hardly say that he attains the truth of what he had been examining. Therefore, Kierkegaard thinks that objective reflection is unable to grasp the truth of empirical reality.

The implications, for his understanding of religious truth, of Kierkegaard's contention that empirical being is a process of becoming become more evident when the exact form that becoming takes in the life of the self is examined. While the general character of all becoming is, for Kierkegaard, a process of moving from potentiality to actuality, the peculiar feature of human becoming is that here this process is self-directed. In order for such a self-directed actualization of possibility to occur, two things are necessary: first, one must be able to imagine possibilities, and, second, one must be able to realize what has been imagined. Let us consider each of these conditions of human becoming. For the self, imaginative thought is the means by which possibilities are apprehended. "Knowledge places everything in possibility, and to the extent that it is in possibility, it is outside the actuality of existence."[11] Kierkegaard elaborates this important issue in somewhat more complex terms when he says: "Abstract thought considers both possibility and actuality, but its understanding of actuality is a false reflection, since the medium within which the concept is thought is not actuality but possibility. Abstract thought can get hold of actuality only by nullifying [*ophæve*] it, but to nullify actuality is to transform it into possibility."[12]

To clarify the point that Kierkegaard is making in this obscure passage, let us take an example from interpersonal relationships. Suppose one person, *A,* says to another person, *B,* "Would you please do *X* for me?" *B* must first hear *A* and comprehend what *A* has requested. In this process, *B* translates the request of *A* into a possibility for himself. Whether explicitly or implicitly, *B* says to himself, "It is possible for me either to do what *A* has asked or to refuse to do it." The grasping of possibility through the thought process is not, however, the actualization of possibility. It is quite evident that, in this instance, thought and being do not conform to each other. To *think* a possibility is not to *be* the one who has accomplished that possibility by translating it into actuality. Therefore Kierkegaard argues, "Man thinks and exists, and existence separates thought and being, holding them apart from one another in succession."[13] If this were not the case, then to think of doing *X* would be the same as doing *X*. This Kierkegaard certainly does not allow.

If we turn from the first to the second condition of human becoming, it is apparent that while thought is the means by which possibilities are apprehended, imagined possibilities are actualized through the will. Between conceiving a possibility (thought) and the actualization of that possibility (being) lies the will. In brief, possibilities are actualized by the assertion of the individual's will. Returning to our previous example, after *B* has recognized the possibilities posed to him by *A*'s request, he must decide which of the possibilities he will realize. On the basis of this insight, Kierkegaard claims that "reality is an *inter-esse* between the moments of that hypothetical unity of thought and being that abstract thought presupposes."[14] By this Kierkegaard means that reality—here human existence—is a "being between," or is a being that moves between potentiality and actuality. In other words, concrete existence is a process of becoming. It is also important to note in this context that there is another nuance to "*inter-esse*" with which Kierkegaard plays. For Kierkegaard it is "interest" that motivates the will, and hence commences the process of becoming. When one is moved to actualize potentialities, it is the result of one's own subjective interest. Therefore, the "being between" actuality and potentiality is the exertion of the will, moved by interest, to realize possibilities.[15] This, Kierkegaard argues, is reality.

For the existing individual, thought and being can never fully coincide. As long as one exists, one is in a process of becoming in which one seeks to enact that about which one has thought, thereby striving to effect a unity of one's thought and being. The conclusion of Kierkegaard's argument is that *the unity of thought and being is a task that is posed to the existing individual and is not an accomplished fact.*

We are now in a position to understand what Kierkegaard means when he says that "religious truth is subjectivity." He defines religious truth as follows: "Here is such a definition of truth: *An objective uncertainty held fast in an appropriation-process [Tilegnelse] of the most passionate inwardness is truth,* the highest truth attainable for an *existing* individual."[16] The important phrase in this definition for our present purpose is "an appropriation-process." Because the existing individual is in a state of becoming, his life is a constant approximation of the ideals that he conceives. "Subjectivity" indicates the process by which an individual appropriates what he thinks, or constitutes his actuality by realizing his possibilities.[17]

Kierkegaard proceeds to identify subjectivity (the process of appropriating what one has conceived) with truth for the existing individual: ". . . the truth consists in nothing else than the self-activity of personal appropriation. . . ."[18] Kierkegaard's argument at this juncture is not intended to deny the general notion of truth as the conformity of thought and being. However, due to the fact that the existing individual is in a process of becoming, Kierkegaard holds that such a conformity is never reached as long as existence continues, but remains an ideal that is asymptotically approximated: "Not for a single moment is it forgotten that the subject is an existing individual, and that existence is a process of becoming, and that therefore the notion of truth as identity of thought and being is a chimera of abstraction, in its truth only an expectation of the creature; not because truth is not such an identity, but because the knower is an existing individual for whom the truth cannot be such an identity as long as he lives in time."[19]

Therefore, after defining religious truth as subjectivity, Kierkegaard elaborates his meaning in terms of the process by which an individual appropriates what he thinks. We have considered two aspects of this process. While thought grasps the possibilities with which actuality confronts the individual (i.e., thought moves from *esse* to *posse*), the will actualizes these possibilities (i.e., moves from *posse* to *esse*).[20]

As will become increasingly apparent as the argument progresses, the process by which possibilities are actualized results in an alteration of the self's actuality. Upon the basis of such insights, Kierkegaard proceeds to extend the implications of his argument one step further by holding that to say "truth is subjectivity" is to say that "truth is the subject's transformation in himself."[21] The following passage is one of Kierkegaard's clearest statements about the subjectivity of truth:

"Truth in its very being is not the simple duplication of being in terms of thought, which yields only the thought of being, merely ensures that the act of thinking shall not be a cobweb of the brain without relation to reality, guaranteeing the validity of thought, that the thing thought actually is, i.e., has validity. No, truth in its very being is the duplication [*Fordoblelse*] in me, in thee, in him, so that my, that thy, that his life, approximately in the striving to attain it, is the very being of truth, is a *life*, as the truth was in Christ, for he was the truth. And hence, Christianly understood, the truth consists not in knowing the truth but in being the truth."[22]

As this quotation makes clear, truth, when considered subjectively, is not identified with the accuracy of certain propositions, but is the quality of an individual's *life*. The English phrases "he is true to . . ." or "he is faithful to . . ." express the way in which Kierkegaard understands religious truth.

Kierkegaard frequently points to the identification of truth with the life of the individual. The following is a concise example: ". . . only then do I truly know the truth when it becomes a life in me. Therefore Christ compares truth with food, and the appropriation of it with eating; for just as food, corporally by being appropriated [*Tilegnes*] (assimilated) becomes the sustenance of life, so also is truth, spiritually, both the giver of life and its sustenance; it is life."[23] The logic of the identification of truth with the life of an individual is implicit in what has gone before, and forms a convenient summary of our argument about the nature of religious truth.

1. Human reality is a "being between" possibility and actuality, or is a process in which one constitutes his actuality by realizing that which he has conceived.
2. Subjectivity is "the process by which an individual appropriates what he thinks."
3. Therefore, subjectivity is the reality of the self (a reality that the self defines by the realization of possibility through decision).

Because Kierkegaard identifies religious truth with subjectivity, religious truth refers to the processive or dynamic life of the individual.[24] A person reaches truth when he is true to the ideal to which he pledges his loyalty. Kierkegaard stresses that in religious matters, truth does not concern intellectual assent to propositions, but entails volitional commitment to ideals. Religious truth must always be embodied in the life of the individual, and this can be accomplished only by the consistent and disciplined assertion of the will. Kierkegaard does not, however, intend to set the intellect and the will in opposition. Rather, they are closely related. Through the intellectual capacity to use language and reason, the individual is enabled to articulate goals and to specify possibilities. Once these ideals have been established, they pose a task for the individual. Here thought and being do not coincide; i.e., to think about an ideal is not to have realized what one has thought. Through the will, the imagined possibilities can be actualized. In this instance, truth is not the duplication of being in thought, but the duplication of thought in being (in the individual's personal being). To put this in other terms, in the actualization of possibility, the existing individual defines the truth of his own self.

Two important consequences of the view that religious truth is subjectivity must be noted here. In the first place, one's attention is turned toward the subject and the subject's striving to realize his potentialities: "For a subjective reflection the truth becomes a matter of appropriation, of inwardness, of subjectivity, and thought must probe more and more deeply into the subject and his subjectivity."[25] This movement is exactly opposite that of objective reflection, which, as we saw, directs itself away from the subject. Secondly, by contending that the locus of truth is the individual's life, Kierkegaard gives more importance to the quality of the relationship to one's goal, or his possibility, than to the nature of that goal or possibility. This raises a rather startling possibility that Kierkegaard is fully prepared to acknowledge: "If one who lives in the midst of Christendom goes up to the house of God, the house of the true God, with the true conception of God in his knowledge, and prays, but prays in a false spirit; and one who lives in an idolatrous community prays with the entire passion of the infinite, although his eyes rest upon the image of an idol: where is there most truth? The one prays in truth to God though he worships an idol; the other prays falsely to the true God, and hence worships in fact an idol."[26]

On the basis of this passage, some critics argue that by his view that religious truth is subjectivity Kierkegaard, in effect, denies the objective (i.e., extra-subjective) existence of God.[27] Although there are a few points at which Kierkegaard seems to suggest such a view, most notably in the Journals,[28] this certainly is not his intention. He never doubts that God exists apart from the subjectivity of the believer.[29] To contend that Kierkegaard's proposal that truth is subjectivity restricts the being of God to the believer's belief in God is to misapprehend the import of his argument. What he intends to stress is that religious faith is not to be identified with the cognitive assent to propositions, but must be related to the assertion of the individual's will, or to the transformation of one's life.

This is the appropriate place to clarify another of Kierkegaard's terms that bears on the subjectivity of truth: reduplication. At times it seems as if he unnecessarily complicates this category. For example, he offers the following comment on the nature of reduplication: "However, coming into existence may present a reduplication, i.e., the possibility of a second coming into existence within the first coming into existence. Here we have the historical in the stricter sense, subject to a dialectic with respect to time. The coming into existence that in this sphere is identical with the coming into existence of nature is a possibility, a possibility that for nature is its whole reality. But this historical coming into existence in the stricter sense is a coming into existence within a coming into existence."[30]

Here reduplication is defined as "a coming into existence within a coming into existence." Furthermore, it seems to have a special relationship to time. Kierkegaard's point is that reduplication is the actualization of possibilities. The first coming into existence is the conceptualization of possibility. Possibility, as will become evident in chapter three, is fundamentally related to the *future* as that toward which the individual moves. The second coming into existence is the realization of possibilities. This takes place, as we have seen, through one's *present* decisions, which thereby come to constitute his *past*. Kierkegaard's most concise definition of "reduplication" is: ". . . to reduplicate [*at redupplicere*] is to 'exist' in what one understands."[31] Reduplication is, therefore, another way of indicating the process by which an individual strives to embody in his life that which he has understood. It is another way of pointing to the fact that, for an existing individual, religious truth is subjectivity.

By holding that religious truth is subjectivity, Kierkegaard feels that he is fully in line with what he regards as the two most authoritative sources of the Christian tradition: the Bible and Luther.[32] *The Letter of James* is Kierkegaard's favorite book of the Bible, and from this source he draws the biblical justification for his stance with respect to religious truth.[33] The particular text, to which Kierkegaard frequently refers in this connection, is James I:22–25: "But be doers of the word, and not hearers only, deceiving yourselves. For if any one is a hearer of the word and not a doer, he is like a man who observes his natural face in a mirror; for he observes himself and goes away and at once forgets what he was like. But he who looks into the perfect law, the law of liberty, and perseveres, being no hearer that forgets but a doer that acts, he shall be blessed in his doing."[34]

Kierkegaard finds the issue of personal appropriation raised in Luther's writings, especially in the theme of *pro me* or *pro nobis*. Kierkegaard writes: "Take away from the Christian determinations the factor of personal appropriation, and what becomes of Luther's merit? But open to any page of his writings, and note in every line the strong pulse-beat of personal appropriation. Note it in the entire trembling propulsive movement of his style, which is as if it were driven from behind by the terrible thunderstorm that killed Alexius and created Luther. Did not the papacy have objectivity enough, objective determinations to the point of superfluity? What then did it lack? It lacked appropriation, inwardness."[35]

Kierkegaard argues, therefore, that his thesis that religious truth is subjectivity grows out of the biblical and the Lutheran tradition. It refers to the process by which an individual appropriates what he has conceived as a possibility. In so doing, the individual himself becomes true and "truth exists for the particular individual only as he himself produces it in action."[36]

B. Socratic Midwifery: Method and Intention of the Authorship

Our purpose in taking up the foregoing discussion of Kierkegaard's notion of religious truth was to arrive at an understanding of his use of the pseudonymous method. We must now turn our attention to the relationship between the view of truth just examined and the method of the authorship.

Notes

1. *Postscript,* p. 181; S.V., VIII, 196.
2. *Ibid.,* p. 178; S.V., VII, 166.
3. In the introduction to his translation to *Crisis in the Life of an Actress and Other Essays on Drama* (New York: Harper Torchbooks, 1967), pp. 20–26, Stephen Crites points out that this use of "objectivity" by Kierkegaard is very similar to Kant's view of the "theoretical" employment of reason.
4. *Postscript,* p. 173; S.V., VII, 161.
5. *Ibid.,* p. 173; S.V., VII, 161.
6. *Ibid.,* p. 169; S.V., VII, 157.
7. *Ibid.,* p. 172; S.V., VII, 161.
8. This is one of the bases upon which Kierkegaard forms his criticism of speculative philosophy of Hegel's sort. He contends that such thought deals only with thought itself, and not with existing reality.
9. *Postscript,* p. 169; S.V., VII, 157.
10. *Ibid.,* p. 170; S.V., VII, 158.
11. *Works of Love,* p. 218; S.V., IX, 221.
12. *Postscript,* p. 279; S.V., VII, 270. Compare p. 280: "All knowledge about actuality is possibility." S.V., VII, 287.
13. *Ibid.,* p. 296; S.V., VII, 271.
14. *Ibid.,* p. 279; S.V., VII, 270.
15. It will be recalled that it is precisely "subjective interest" that objective contemplation excludes.
16. *Postscript,* p. 182; S.V., VII, 170.
17. Compare Louis Mackey, "Kierkegaard and the Problem of Existential Philosophy, II," *The Review of Metaphysics,* vol. 9, 1956, p. 572.
18. *Postscript,* p. 217; S.V., VII, 203.
19. *Ibid.,* p. 176; S.V., VII, 279.
20. *Ibid.,* p. 288; S.V., VII, 279.
21. *Ibid.,* p. 38; S.V., VII, 27. Compare Carnell's comment: "The Subjective is character change." *The Burden of Søren Kierkegaard, op. cit.,* p. III; and Thomte's point when he says that for Kierkegaard, "truth was consigned to the realm of personality." *Kierkegaard's Philosophy of Religion, op.cit.,* p. 205.

22. *Training in Christianity,* p. 201; S.V., XII, 189.

23. *Ibid.,* p. 202; S.V., XII, 190. It is interesting to note in this context that the Danish *"at ti-legne"* can also be translated "to dedicate."

24. For this reason, Kierkegaard calls subjective truth "edifying" [*opbygge*]. Literally translated, *"opbygge"* means to build (*bygge*) up (*op*). This is precisely what is accomplished in the subjective pursuit of truth. The personality of the individual is built up insofar as he appropriates the truth with which he is concerned, or as he strives to achieve his ideals. See *Works of Love,* pp. 199–212; S.V., IX, 201–215.

25. *Postscript,* p. 171; S.V., VII, 159–160.

26. *Ibid.,* pp. 179–180; S.V., VII, 168.

27. Karl Löwith offers the most striking instance of this line of argument. He presents his views in the context of pointing out certain similarities between Feuerbach's analysis of Christianity in terms of subjective feeling and Kierkegaard's principle of subjectivity. Löwith, however, overstates the similarities between the two thinkers. See *From Hegel to Nietzsche* (New York: Doubleday and Co., 1967), pp. 357ff. Compare his argument in "On The Historical Understanding of Kierkegaard," *Review of Religion,* 1943, pp. 234ff., esp. p. 241.

28. See *Journals,* ed. Dru, *op.cit.,* no. 605; *Papirer,* VII A 139.

29. For support of this interpretation, see Paul Holmer, "Kierkegaard and Theology," *Union Seminary Quarterly Review,* vol. XII, 1957, pp. 21–31; Valter Lindström, "The Problem of Objectivity and Subjectivity in Kierkegaard," *A Kierkegaard Critique,* edited by Howard A. Johnson and Niels Thulstrup (Chicago: Henry Regnery Co., 1961), pp. 228–243; David F. Swenson, *Something About Kierkegaard,* ed. Lillian M. Swenson (Minneapolis: Augsburg Publishing Co., 1956), pp. 126ff.; James Brown, *Kierkegaard, Heidegger, Buber,* and *Barth: Subject and Object in Modern Theology* (New York: Collier Books, 1962), p. 90.

30. *Philosophical Fragments,* p. 94; S.V., IV, 240.

31. *Training in Christianity,* p. 133; S.V., XII, 125.

32. There are certain anticipations of Kierkegaard's view of religious truth in Hegel's work. See Crites, *In the Twilight of Christendom, op.cit.,* part I; Karl Löwith, "On the Historical Understanding of Kierkegaard," *op. cit.,* p. 243; and Jean Wahl, *Études Kierkegaardiennes* (Paris: Fernard Aubier, n.d.). J. Heywood Thomas notes anticipations in Von Braeder, Schelling, Hamann, and Lessing. *Subjectivity and Paradox* (New York: Macmillan Co., 1957), pp. 44–59. Finally, there are evident parallels between Kierkegaard's "subjectivity" and Kant's "practical reason." See Crites, *In the Twilight of Christendom, op. cit.,* part I; "Introduction," *Crisis in the Life of an Actress,* pp. 19–28; Jerry H. Gill, "Kant, Kierkegaard, and Religious Knowledge," *Essays on Kierkegaard,* ed. J. H. Gill, (Minneapolis: Burgess Publishing Co., 1969), pp. 58–73; Louis Mackey, "Kierkegaard and the Problem of Existential Philosophy, II," *op. cit.,* pp. 575, 608; H. Richard Niebuhr, *The Responsible Self* (New York: Harper and Row, 1963), p. 92; Günter Rohrmoser, "Kierkegaard und das Problem der Subjectivität," *Neue Zeitschrift für Systematische Theologie und Religionsphilosophie,* vol. 8, no. 3, pp. 289–310, esp. p. 292.

33. Kierkegaard could never quite forgive Luther for his dismissal of *The Letter of James.* He tried to explain it by holding that Luther's historical situation demanded that grace and not works be stressed. See *Journals,* ed. Dru, *op. cit.,* nos. 88 and 1008; *Papirer,* I A 328 X^2 A 244.

34. See *Edifying Discourses,* vol. II, pp. 84–85.

35. *Postscript,* pp. 327–328; S.V., VII, 317. Compare his remark in his Journal: "Formally the category of 'for thee' (Subjectivity, Inwardness) with which *Either-Or* ended (only the truth that edifies is the truth for thee) is exactly Luther's." *Papirer,* VII A 465.

36. *The Concept of Dread,* p. 123; S.V., IV, 405. It should be noted that many writers give special emphasis to the way in which the theme of *imitatio Christi* develops in Kierkegaard's later works. But, as Lindström correctly observes ("The Problem of Objectivity and Subjectivity in Kierkegaard," *op.cit.,* p. 240), this is only another form of the view that truth is subjectivity.

■

---

24. Faith against Reason: Kierkegaard

C. STEPHEN EVANS

Why does Kierkegaard so frequently assert that faith is not merely *above* but *against* reason? Faith is said to believe what is 'impossible' and 'absurd.'[1] Faith revels in the improbability of what is believed; a 'proof' of the content of what is to be believed, so far from being an aid to faith, would make faith impossible.[2] Can this be responsible fideism?

As we have noted, Kierkegaard is often understood to be asserting that faith involves a rejection of rationality altogether. If this were indeed Kierkegaard's view, I would urge that it be rejected, since I argued in Chapter 2 that such a rejection of reason cannot be rationally defended, and ultimately comes at a steep price for the fideist. Fortunately, I do not think that this irrationalism is a fair characterisation of Kierkegaard. As I also noted in Chapter 2, the term 'reason' is ambiguous. The concept is partly normative; it connotes those patterns of thinking that ought to be emulated because they are most likely to lead to truth. A purely normative concept is, however, abstract and empty. In reality every human society holds up particular concrete patterns and modes of thinking as constitutive of reason because they are thought to realise those normative ideals.

This descriptive content of reason is not beyond challenge, however. There is constant debate among philosophers concerning human perception, induction, testimony, self-evident principles, memory, and other cognitive practices. There are arguments about whether these practices need some kind of validation or backing to be rational, arguments about which are most 'basic' and reliable, arguments about the criteria within each practice

Source: C. Stephen Evans, *Faith Beyond Reason: A Kierkegaardian Account,* © 1998, C. Stephen Evans, published by Wm. B. Eerdmans Publishing Company, Grand Rapids, MI. Used by permission.

for detecting reliable perceptions, memories, testimonies, etc. So the question as to what practices actually constitute 'reason' is a real one that is the subject of ongoing debate.

Most sociologists argue, with a good degree of plausibility, that by and large what counts as 'reasonable' is what is accepted as reasonable in a society by those with the power and authority to shape the process of socialisation. We accept as reasonable what we are taught as reasonable, and those who control society also control what is transmitted through teaching.[3] The important French thinker Michel Foucault devoted almost his entire career to exploring the ways in which claims about reason, knowledge and truth reflect social power exerted by some over others.[4] Concrete judgments about what is rational are thus not dropped from Olympus, and it is thus quite conceivable that some individual might come to question whether the accepted judgments about what counts as 'reason' are those that in fact best realise the normative goals of reason. A critique of 'reason' is not *per se* a rejection of rationality, if rationality is a commitment to practices that are aimed at truth.

Suppose that a set of religious beliefs were true, but that the intellectual practices designated as 'reasonable' in a society (or in all human societies) were such as to make it impossible to recognise those truths. In that case, there would be a tension between the normative and descriptive aspects of reason. One might say that what is accepted as 'reason' concretely would be a barrier to achieving the goals of reason in an ideal normative sense. We might call these two different senses of reason the *concrete* and the *ideal* senses. I want to argue that a rejection of concrete reason is not necessarily a rejection of ideal reason, but may in fact be motivated by a commitment to ideal reason. My proposal is that some people who are called fideists, including Kierkegaard, are actually engaging in such a critique of concrete reason, though it is not always clear whether or not the fideists themselves clearly see the difference between the two forms of reason.

Of course such a proposal raises many questions. The person who rejects concrete reason must see it as suffering from some radical defects. If that were the case, one might wonder how human beings could ever come to recognise these defects. Must we not suppose that concrete reason is generally reliable if we are to detect particular instances where it is not reliable and in need of correction?

This is a pressing problem for critics of concrete reason and there are other problems as well. Nevertheless, I believe that this is precisely how Kierkegaard thinks about human reason and the truth of Christianity. He thinks that concrete human reason has a tendency to judge Christian faith irrational. Since the Enlightenment, though not only during that period, religious faith in general and Christian faith in particular have been under attack. Some theologians have thought it necessary to modify and reshape Christian faith so as to make it acceptable to reason, as Schleiermacher attempted to do when he defended religion against its 'cultured despisers.'[5] This strategy of reshaping religious beliefs to make them acceptable to modern culture is in fact the essence of what is often called 'modernism' or 'liberalism' in theology. For example, a common proposal has been to abandon any claims that miracles have occurred, or to abandon claims about the full deity of Jesus so as to make Christianity more acceptable to 'modern minds.'

Kierkegaard thinks that the appropriate Christian response to the intellectual attacks of modernity is to go on the offensive, rather than to attempt to shore up the battlements apologetically or to concede ground in the hope that some territory can still be preserved. The concrete human reason that wishes to indict faith is itself charged by him with being radically defective. Terminologically, he makes his point by conceding, or rather exuberantly asserting, that judged by the concrete standards of 'reason' faith is necessarily unreasonable. He then goes on to claim that the reason that makes this charge is itself 'a blockhead and a dunce.'[6]

One might wish that Kierkegaard had not been so quick to give the term 'reason' to the opponents of faith, by identifying 'reason' with what we have termed 'concrete reason.' His terminology here invites the misunderstanding that the person of faith simply does not care about truth, since reason in its normative sense is defined in terms of a search for truth. In attacking concrete reason under the label of 'reason,' Kierkegaard might seem to be rejecting reason in the normative sense as well. However, Kierkegaard makes it clear that from his point of view, faith does aim at truth. In fact, he charges that a major reason people do not have faith is that they do not want truth; they prefer to believe what makes them happy. People prefer to live in illusions, even though the illusion masks the truth that their condition is one of despair, and they regard anyone who wishes to give them the truth about their condition as their enemy:

> It is far from being the case that men regard the relationship to truth, relating themselves to the truth, as the highest good, and it is very far from being the case that they Socratically regard being in error in this manner as the worst misfortune—the sensuous aspect in them usually far outweighs their intellectuality. For example, if a man is presumably happy, imagines himself to be happy, although considered in the light of truth he is unhappy, he is usually far from wanting to be wrenched out of his error . . . Why? Because he is completely dominated by the sensuous and the sensuous-psychical. . . .[7]

Thus Kierkegaard reverses the common charge that religious belief is a form of wish-fulfilment, by claiming that this is true of religious *unbelief*. (However, he agrees with Freud that wish-fulfilment is characteristic of many inauthentic forms of religious faith as well.)

How Sin Damages Human Reason

We saw in the previous chapter that Kierkegaard agrees with Aquinas and Kant that faith is above human reason, because of the finitude and temporality of that human reason. The claim that faith is not only above but against human reason is rooted, not merely in the recognition of human finitude, but in the charge that human reason is radically defective. For Kierkegaard the damage is due to human sin.

How exactly is sin supposed to affect concrete human reason negatively? I believe that for Kierkegaard there are two primary ways that concrete reason is damaged by sin. I shall explain each in turn and then try to show that the two are in fact closely connected. Both kinds of damage presuppose that reason is a characteristic of actual persons, and that the reasoning of such persons is shaped by their character. The first kind of damage is that which is caused by reason's *pride* or what might be termed its imperialistic, domineering character. The second kind of problem is grounded in the *selfish* or egoistic character of reason. I shall first examine the damaging effects of pride.

Kierkegaard shares with Aquinas and Kant the conviction that God transcends the powers of the human mind, and he thinks that this limitation of human reason is particularly present when it comes to understanding God's incarnation in human form. By itself this seems to imply only that God as the object of faith is mysterious, something that is above reason. However, Kierkegaard combines this view of God as mysterious with some particular claims about the character of concrete human thinking.

Kierkegaard believes that reason has what we might term a restless, domineering quality, in that it is always striving to master or appropriate whatever it encounters. He claims that it is the supreme passion of all human thinking to 'want to discover something that thought itself cannot think.'[8] He claims that 'this passion is fundamentally present everywhere in thought.'[9] The attitude of reason is the attitude that wishes to explain, to make intelligible. When the scientist discovers some strange phenomenon, when something occurs that is unexpected and inexplicable in terms of current scientific theory, the scientist may indeed feel a sense of wonder and awe. That sense, however, is not the end but the beginning of scientific inquiry. The scientist is motivated to try to explain this new phenomenon, to make what is mysterious explicable. This recalcitrant reality must be mastered, forced to yield its secrets. When reason behaves in this way, Kierkegaard interprets it as seeking its own limits, testing each 'unknown' it encounters to see if it is truly resistant to reason's mastery.

Insofar as reason is confident that it will always be victorious in its continued quest, it will necessarily reject any claim that there is an *ultimate* mystery, anything that is in principle resistant to reason's domination and control. Kierkegaard thinks that this is precisely what might be termed the 'natural attitude' of human reason. Such an attitude of reason is really a claim of omniscience—not a claim of actual omniscience, but a claim that human reason as an infinite process of discovery is essentially omniscient. Two things become clear when reason is seen in this light.

1. We can easily see why faith is not merely above but is in some sense against reason. Faith is indeed above reason, but a reason that recognises its own limitations will not necessarily reject the possibility of faith. However, to the degree that reason insists that there is nothing that lies outside its power, it finds itself in tension with a faith that insists that its object exceeds reason's grasp.

2. We can also see why this natural tension between reason and faith is linked by Kierkegaard to sin. The classical Christian understanding of sin is to view sin as an expression of pride. Pride here is not the virtue of properly appreciating one's achievements; it is rather the vice of overestimating one's place in the universe. The Christian understanding of sin is that it involves a human being's confusion of himself or herself with God. In the Genesis account of the first temptation, the serpent offers the alluring line, 'You shall be as gods.' The sinful human being then sees himself or herself as the centre of the universe. The person sees himself or herself as completely self-sufficient, and therefore as possessing the final criterion of truth. The attitude is 'What (in principle) I cannot understand must be nonsense.' The understanding 'cannot get the paradox into its head,' and thinks that this is an objection, even though in reality this claim is simply an echo of what the paradox says about itself and its relation to reason.[10] If there is a reality that is essentially mysterious to human reason, then such a prideful attitude is

indeed damaging, because it blocks us from a recognition of this truth and from whatever kind of encounter and relation might be possible with such a mysterious reality.

The second feature of human sinfulness that Kierkegaard sees as damaging lies in what we could term the egoistic or selfish character of human reason. Of course human reason will not be flattered by this description of it as selfish, and it may well find it jarring. Reason in fact prides itself on its disinterestedness and objectivity.

Kierkegaard does not deny that a kind of disinterestedness on the part of reason is possible. Such objectivity, he says, is the glory of the scholar; it can be seen in the devoted historian, the scientist, the mathematician.[11] Strictly speaking, even this attitude is not purely disinterested; human reason cannot be absolutely pure, for human thinking is always the thinking of a concrete, existing human being. Even the objective scholar is motivated by interests of various kinds, and what Kierkegaard calls *pure thought* is a mirage that does not exist:

> Pure thinking is—what shall I say—piously or thoughtlessly unaware of the relation that abstraction still continually has to that from which it abstracts. Here in this pure thinking there is rest for every doubt; here is the eternal positive truth and whatever else one cares to say. This means that pure thinking is a phantom. And if Hegelian philosophy is free from all postulates, it has attained this with one insane postulate: the beginning of pure thinking.[12]

Abstract thought is possible. The objective scholar can have an interest in distancing himself from the subject, attempting to think about issues in ways that do not take into account his or her personal relation to the issues.

However, to the degree that this happens, the thinking of the scholar is divorced from existence. The scholar 'abstracts' from life, though he can never do so completely or purely. Insofar as a person is actually thinking about life and how life should be lived, such disinterestedness is not possible at all, according to Kierkegaard, because human actions and choices are moved by what he terms the passions. 'Existing, if this is not to be understood as just any sort of existing, cannot be done without passion.'[13] Merely thinking about a possibility is never sufficient to move an individual to act; one must care about the possibility, value it in some way. 'Am I the good because I think it, or am I good because I think the good? Not at all.'[14] Existential thinking, or thinking about life and what is related to life, is thus necessarily 'interested' thinking. 'For an existing person, existing is for him his highest interest, and his interestedness in existing is his actuality.'[15] Ethical and religious questions are pre-eminently questions about life and how it should be lived, and thus Kierkegaard argues that it is not possible to think in a purely neutral way about such questions.

Human beings think as whole persons. It is human beings who reflect, not brains or minds detached from concrete human persons. Their thinking therefore necessarily reflects the shape of their human interests and habits. One of the dominant characteristics of the thinking of sinful human beings is precisely its self-centred character. Even the disinterested scholar looks first to the index of a new book to see how many times he or she may be cited. A large proportion of human thinking is what might be termed 'cost-benefit analysis'—calculative thinking—and when we do our calculations, the cost and benefit to ourselves seems to weigh heavily, however much ethicists may prescribe a strict objectivity. Kant, whose ethic stressed the necessity of impartiality as much as anyone, nevertheless notes how pervasively we show our concern for what he terms 'the dear self.'[16]

For Kierkegaard human understanding is 'the stockbroker of the finite,' that power we have to calculate the relative value of goods and the costs associated with them.[17] What we might call the self-interested character of human reasoning for Kierkegaard comes through clearly in a satirical passage in which he pokes fun at the 'sensible individual' who allows faith to be supported by (and controlled by) rational arguments:

> See, the wader feels his way with his foot, lest he go out so far that he cannot touch bottom. In the same way, with his understanding, the sensible person feels his way in probability and finds God where probability suffices, and thanks him on the great festival days of probability when he has obtained a really good job and there is the probability of quick advancement to boot. And he thanks him when for a wife he finds a girl both beautiful and congenial, and even Councillor of War Marcussen says that it will be a happy marriage, that the girl has the kind of beauty that in all probability will last a good time, and that she is built in such a way that in all probability she will bear healthy and strong children. To believe against the understanding is something else, and to believe with the understanding cannot be done at all, because the person who believes with the understanding talks only about job and wife and field and oxen and the like, which are in no way the object of faith.[18]

Kierkegaard here seems to be saying that human thinking not only deals with what is finite, but considers that finitude in a self-interested way.

The implication of this is that the story of the incarnation is doubly impervious to human reason. For the story of the God-man is not merely the story of what is infinite. It is a story of love—pure self-giving love. The God who gives himself for humans is a God who does not need human beings at all. His motivation for becoming human to redeem us can only be a love that differs from every human love.[19] For all human love, even the purest love of parent for child, or the grandest romantic passion, aims at least partly at self-satisfaction. We love, but our love does not aim simply at the benefit of the other, but also at our own happiness. The kind of love that God's incarnation represents is therefore a love of which we have no experience at all apart from the incarnation itself.

Kierkegaard accepts the ancient maxim that 'like can only be known by like.' Because we ourselves have never loved in the manner that God loves, it is a love we cannot understand. The person who is selfish naturally sees the actions of others as motivated by the same desires. Our natural response is suspicion; there must be an angle, we think. 'What's in it for God, anyway?' we cynically wonder. We find ourselves sceptical even when confronted with apparently altruistic human behaviour, but the reckless lack of concern for his own privilege that God displays in becoming human totally goes beyond our understanding:

> Divine compassion, however, the unlimited *recklessness* in concerning oneself only with the suffering, not in the least with oneself, and of unconditionally recklessly concerning oneself with *each* sufferer—people can interpret this only as a kind of madness over which we are not sure whether we should laugh or cry.[20]

Because of our sinful self-centredness, we cannot do anything but find this story the 'strangest possible thing,'[21] the 'most improbable thing' we can imagine.[22]

The incarnation cannot be understood because it is a story of how the absolutely different (God), moved by unfathomable love, has become absolutely human. But what is the difference between the divine and the human that makes such an understanding so difficult? Kierkegaard says unequivocally that the difference lies in human sinfulness.[23] The problem is not fundamentally the speculative problem of seeing how a being with properties like omnipotence and omniscience could become human, even though Kierkegaard has no doubt that this theoretical task is one that human reason cannot accomplish. That theoretical failure, however, only means that faith is above reason. It is sin that makes faith appear to be against reason. The problem is that God's nature is love and we are so self-centred that we cannot understand God's love, even when, especially when, it is expressed in human form.

There is of course a link between the two ways sin operates to damage our rational capacities. It is our self-centredness that makes us prideful and self-sufficient. It is because we are so fundamentally concerned with self that we want to make ourselves the centre of the universe and become as gods. Or, looking at things from the other direction, it is our prideful self-sufficiency that makes it impossible for us to love, that blocks us from truly seeing and caring about the other for the other's sake.

Can Reason Recognise Its Own Limits?

In the series of movies that made him famous, Clint Eastwood played a character who often informed a villain (before dispatching him to the next life) 'A man's gotta know his limitations.' Indeed, it is beneficial for all of us to know our limits. However, if human reason is as limited as Kierkegaard maintains, can this be recognised? If reason is so damaged, then it appears that it will be unable to recognise that it has been damaged.

Kierkegaard maintains that one of the effects of sin is typically to blind reason to the damaging effects of sin. Self-deception or what Marxists call 'false consciousness' is indeed the common condition of human thinking. However, Kierkegaard does not think that a recognition of the limits of reason is impossible for reason. It is true that he says that the 'natural' response of reason to the God-man as the object of faith is to be offended. However, it is very important to see that this 'natural' response is not inevitable; it is not the only possible response. Nor is it in any objective sense more 'rational' than the other option, which is to respond in faith.

The two possible relations between reason and the incarnation, that paradox which is the object of faith, are illustrated by Kierkegaard through an analogy with romantic love. It is true, he says, that reason has 'strong objections' to the paradox, since 'the understanding certainly cannot think it, cannot hit upon it on its own, and if it is proclaimed, the understanding cannot understand it.'[24] Yet, there is also something about the paradox that attracts reason, since reason is steadily seeking 'that which thought cannot think.' Reason is in fact trying to discover its own ultimate limit, 'seeking its own downfall.'[25] To see the two possible relations between reason and the paradox, we must look at romantic love:

> Self-love lies at the basis of love, but at its peak its paradoxical passion wills its own down-fall. Erotic love also wills this, and therefore these two forces are in mutual understanding in the moment of passion, and this passion is precisely love . . . So also with the paradox's rela-tion to the understanding, except that this passion has another name, or rather, we must simply try to find a name for it.[26]

The name he ultimately decides to give this passion is, unsurprisingly, faith.

I believe that the thought that underlies this somewhat obscure passage is some-thing like this. Self-love and genuine love appear to be at odds; it looks as if egoism and altruism are opposing orientations. However, romantic love, when it becomes genuine love, overcomes this opposition. It is true that love begins as self-love; the lover initially wants to be with the loved one out of a desire for the lover's own happiness. However, as love grows, and the lover really begins to care for the other person, happiness comes from seeking the happiness of that other. In this relation self-love 'founders but is not annihilated.'[27] Self-love fulfils its goal of personal happiness by in a sense relinquishing it, ceasing to make egoistic satisfaction its primary end.

Of course not everyone is capable of such love, and Kierkegaard says that the per-son who, out of selfishness, shrinks from love, cannot really understand love and is in-capable of grasping it.[28] The idea seems to be that one's ability to conceive of love depends on whether one has been gripped by the passion itself. The selfish person be-comes embittered by love, perhaps sensing unconsciously that in rejecting love, the per-son is in fact rejecting what he or she truly wants.

Returning to the relation between reason and the paradox, faith and offence are clearly supposed to be analogous to love and the embittered selfishness that shrinks from love. If offence is more 'natural' than faith, the ground for this clearly lies in the character of human nature as it concretely is. When reason is willing to recognise its own limits, as Kant and Aquinas urge it to do, then Kierkegaard says it can find fulfilment. When rea-son shrinks from such a recognition, obstinately and imperialistically insisting on its own completeness and autonomy, then it becomes bitter and angry at what it refuses, much as the selfish egoist becomes bitter and angry at love. The crucial point is that faith and of-fence are opposite *passions*. It is not cool rationality that determines the response of reason to the object of faith, but the nature of the passion that grips the reasoner.

Kierkegaard's claim then is that human reason is not inevitably offended by the Christian revelation, even if offence is in some sense 'natural.' Reason can itself recog-nise its limits. As Kierkegaard puts it, faith is the happy passion in which 'reason limits itself, the paradox bestows itself.'[29] The prevalence of offence and the widespread ten-sion between reason and the paradox, a tension that makes it necessary for faith to be defined as something that goes against reason, are both due to the imperialistic and egoistic character of human reasoners. To come to faith reason must recognise both its finitude and its own 'damaged' character; it must see that its tendency to reject the ob-ject of faith is due to a prideful, egoistic character that is in fact an impediment to truth. To acquire the ability to believe the paradox and avoid offence, people must acquire a new passion that will reshape their characters from the ground up.

How Can a Damaged Reason Recognise Its Problems?

A serious problem emerges at this point for any view of faith and reason that is like Kierkegaard's. Perhaps it is possible that reason is indeed defective in the ways Kierkegaard alleges. However, if this is so, then it may appear that reason will be powerless to discover this truth, for if reason is fundamentally damaged, then it would seem impossible for it to recognise the damage. It is precisely this point that underlies the criticisms made in Chapter 2 against fideists such as Van Til, who appear to endorse such a view of the total helplessness of reason. Is Kierkegaard subject to the same type of criticism?

Kierkegaard himself considers the competency of reason by looking at the figure of Socrates, considered as a paradigm of rational thought. For Kierkegaard, the ability of human reason to discover Truth is symbolised in the Platonic doctrine of recollection, here attributed to Socrates.[30] Recollection affirms that Truth is within human beings; at least the essential capacity to grasp Truth is, and it is the capacity or ability that is crucial.[31] If Recollection were valid, then humans would be autonomous and would have no need of any special revelation from God. From this Socratic viewpoint, a human being can teach another human being, but when such teaching occurs, the teacher should understand his or her essential equality with the learner. Socrates understood this, and saw himself simply as a 'midwife' who helped others to grasp the Truth that was present within them already.[32] The Socratic teacher sees himself only as an 'occasion' for the other to acquire what belongs to humans as humans. 'Viewed Socratically, any point of departure in time is *eo ipso* something accidental, a vanishing point, an occasion. Nor is the teacher anything more. . . .'[33]

When put into this language, the Christian critique of 'reason' is a claim that Recollection is not possible for humans; we have within us neither the Truth nor the capacity to discover the Truth.[34] Instead we need a Teacher who can bring us the Truth, and even more important, transform us into the kind of beings who can grasp the Truth. For Kierkegaard this means the Teacher must be God himself, for only God can transform a person in such a fundamental way that the person is essentially re-created. Thus the Christian narrative of the incarnation requires a rejection of the assumption of Recollection.

However, within the Christian picture, is there any room for anything resembling Recollection, any remnant of autonomy? For Kierkegaard there is one point of analogy between the Socratic picture of Truth and the Christian picture. The Christian view is that human beings do not possess the Truth but are in fact in a state of Untruth.[35] The first thing the God who is to be my teacher must impart to me is the truth about my condition of being in Untruth. It is only if I learn that I am in Untruth that Christianity begins to makes sense to me. But if the learner can make this discovery, then there is a possibility that he or she will gain a kind of understanding of Christianity, or at least an understanding of why Christianity cannot be understood by autonomous reason.

With regard to the discovery of my Untruth, Kierkegaard says that 'the Socratic principle applies: the teacher is only an occasion, whoever he may be, even if he is a god, because I can only discover my own untruth by myself, because only when *I* discover it is it discovered, not before, even though the whole world knew it.'[36] Within the Christian account of things, 'this becomes the one and only analogy to the Socratic.'[37]

On this crucial question, then, Kierkegaard recognises that even a 'damaged' reason must not be so damaged that it is impossible for it to recognise the truth about its condition. Does this mean that the defective character of reason is not taken seriously or that reason is not really so damaged as initially appears? I do not think that it does. Even to recognise its sinful 'untruthful' character reason may need assistance. The Kierkegaardian account does not imply that reason can discover its problematic character all by itself; if that were the case, then it would seem that reason would be in pretty good shape after all. The discovery of my Untruth is precipitated by a revelation in which I meet God and in light of that meeting come to understand myself in a new way. So Kierkegaard has not really reverted to a faith in the soundness of autonomous reason.

Nevertheless, if we take seriously the historical character of reason, reason should be open to the possibility of such a 'transformative encounter.' If reason is a capacity that is developed in time, both individually and socially, then we must recognise that people do at times acquire insights that what they previously took to be 'rational' is not in fact 'truth-conducive.' The child learns that a particular pattern of reasoning is in fact fallacious. The scientist discovers that apparently 'self-evident' assumptions about the character of space and time are not really self-evident after all. How are such discoveries made? Typically, they are made when the ideas of the person we might call 'the learner' are challenged by someone else who thinks differently. Such changes require an encounter with an 'Other,' an encounter in which the learner is changed.

The contemporary Jewish philosopher Emmanuel Levinas has much to say about the encounter with 'the Other.'[38] Levinas has argued that much of modern Western philosophy has been turned inward into self-consciousness. The focus has been on epistemology, with the search for truth rooted in the certainty of self-consciousness. Levinas argues for 'ethics' instead of epistemology as 'first philosophy,' but by 'ethics' he does not mean simply systematic thinking about ethical theories, but a kind of philosophical thinking that takes as its starting point 'the gaze of the Other.' It is when I look into the face of the Other that I come to understand my own character.

Kierkegaard would I think be sympathetic to Levinas's claim that to know the truth people must not simply burrow into their own consciousness, but open themselves up to the transforming look of the Other. His worry, however, concerns our ability to see the Other in the right way. All around the world the sorry tale of ethnic strife and racism shows that the persistent human response to the Other is to fail to see the Other as my neighbour. Kierkegaard thinks that in order properly to see the Other who is my human neighbour as a neighbour, I must first allow myself to be transformed by the gaze of the Other who allowed himself to be crucified for my sake.

It does seem possible therefore for Kierkegaard to hold both that reason suffers from some major defects, but also that reason might be able to recognise those defects under certain conditions. The conditions in question include some kind of transformative encounter which enables reason to understand something about its condition.

Of course it by no means follows that because reason can recognise its condition that it has the ability to change that condition.[39] Just as I might, for example, recognise that my eyesight is bad without being able to remedy the problem, so also I might come to see that my 'natural' reasoning is corrupted by pride and egoism without being able to transform myself so as to become humble and loving. The recognition of the problem, while it may be a precondition to a solution, is not the solution itself.

We could imagine such a transformative encounter as simply producing a new perspective in the learner automatically; in such a case we might say the learner has simply been 'overpowered' by the experience. This would be analogous to the assertion by Van Til that the only remedy for human sinfulness is for God to 'force an entry.' However, Kierkegaard does not envision the encounter along these lines, because God chose to reveal himself in the form of a humble human being. God could of course have used his omnipotence to ensure that the learner is transformed, but by doing so the learner would have been 'crushed.'[40] God's love is such that he desires the learner to respond to him freely and out of love. In revealing himself in the paradoxical form of the humble servant, God makes it possible for the learner to come to see God's true character (pure love), and, in contrast, the learner's own selfishness. However, God also makes it possible for the learner to refuse the insight offered. After all, the one who claims to be divine cannot be immediately recognised as God, since to all outward appearances he is an ordinary human being.

In the final analysis, therefore, Kierkegaard offers us a form of responsible fideism which is not like the irrational fideisms criticised in Chapter 2. It is true that Kierkegaard argues that the Christian view of faith is that it requires autonomous reason to 'surrender' or 'yield itself' to God's revelation.[41] However, he also insists that it is possible for reason itself to recognise the need for this. In one sense the autonomy of reason is respected; reason is not set aside in an authoritarian manner, but *sets itself aside*.[42] When the individual is gripped by the passion of faith, then reason and God's paradoxical revelation 'are on good terms.'[43] Since the encounter with God does not force the new insight on reason, it is also possible for reason to recoil from the revelation, in that passionate clinging to autonomy that Kierkegaard calls offence. However, Kierkegaard stresses that though offence is in one sense natural (and thus faith must be understood as 'against' reason as it functions apart from the transforming encounter), offended reason is no more 'rational' than reason that has been transformed by faith. Faith and offence are 'opposite passions.' Both stem from the passionate response of the person who has encountered God's revelation in Jesus.[44]

Does Kierkegaard Leave Room for Objective Reasoning?

My discussion has focused on what seems to me to be the central and deepest element in Kierkegaard's critique of reason. However, there are many other fideistic elements in his thought. His arguments often contain valuable insights, but in some cases these insights are mingled with claims that I do not think are defensible.

Perhaps the strongest critique of Kierkegaard's fideistic arguments is found in Robert Adams' article, 'Kierkegaard's Arguments Against Objective Reasoning in Religion.' Adams discusses and criticises three arguments he finds in Kierkegaard against objective reasoning in religion: the approximation argument, the postponement argument and the passion argument. Adams finds the first argument to be mistaken; the other two have some plausibility but depend on a conception of religious faith that he does not wish to accept. In all three cases Adams rightly focuses on Kierkegaard's view that Christian faith contains historical beliefs, and thus raises the question of the relation of such faith to historical inquiry and evidence.

The approximation argument hinges on the claim that historical evidence, on Kierkegaard's view, can never be completely certain, but can only lead to a belief that has a certain level of probability. However, as Adams reads Kierkegaard, religious faith involves an 'infinite interest' in the truth of at least some of its beliefs, and there is an incommensurability between such an infinite interest and even the smallest chance of error.[45] Or, as Kierkegaard says, 'in relation to an eternal happiness, and an impassioned, infinite interest in this (the former can be only in the latter), an iota is of importance, of infinite importance. . . .'[46]

Adams rightly points out that this argument does not really show that reasoning is not of value to the religious believer. It does show, he thinks, that for a person with such an 'infinite interest' in the truth of a belief, even the smallest possibility of error would be of concern.[47] However, Adams argues that the believer may still *reason* that he or she is justified in disregarding the chance of error, because the chances of not satisfying the infinite interest will be much greater if this is not done. For example, suppose that I have a passionate desire for eternal life, and believe that there is a 99 per cent probability that I will receive it if I believe in the truth of a particular doctrine. It is true that I may rightly worry about the chance of error, since the stakes are so high, but it is also true that my chance of achieving my goal will be much greater if I follow the probabilities here and ignore the uncertainty. In some sense this is the rational thing for me to do.

I think Adams is quite right about this, but I am not sure that the point is really a criticism of Kierkegaard. When Kierkegaard argues that faith should not be based on objective reasoning he has in mind what I would term evidential scholarship, inquiry that focuses solely on the objective probability of the truth of the belief, with no consideration given to the subjective desires of the individual. Kierkegaard does not wish to reject thinking or reflection altogether. In fact, a substantial portion of *Concluding Unscientific Postscript* is an exploration of what he calls 'subjective thinking,' which is thinking that is, we might say, situated by taking account of the needs and desires of the thinker.[48] The argument that Adams presents, however, is manifestly one that does take into account the situation of the potential believer. It does not focus solely on the probability of the belief but rather says that belief makes sense because it is the best way for the believer to realise his or her desires.

So it seems correct that Adams has demonstrated that Kierkegaard's argument does not show that what Adams calls 'objective thinking' is not valuable for faith, but it is not clear that Kierkegaard means to reject this kind of thinking. I think that Adams has in fact missed the heart of Kierkegaard's concern, which does not lie in the approximative character of historical evidence, but in the incommensurability between such evidence and the passionate commitment which faith demands.

Something like this problem of incommensurability underlies the second argument Adams finds in Kierkegaard, what Adams calls the 'postponement argument.' The idea here is that historical inquiry is never completed, and thus historical beliefs based on such inquiry must always be tentative. It is always possible, at least theoretically, that new evidence will emerge that will overturn any historical conviction. Thus, if religious beliefs were based on such evidence, they would have to be of this tentative character. Kierkegaard thinks, however, that religious beliefs should have a kind of finality that differs from this kind of scholarly judgment. Even if Kierkegaard is wrong to say that such evidence has no bearing on religious belief, it seems right to claim that religious beliefs with the right kind of decisiveness will not stem solely from such 'objective' evidential concerns, but will be motivated by subjective needs and desires.

In fact, Kierkegaard's concern here is very similar to that of William James, in the argument for 'the will to believe' that was discussed in Chapter 3.[49] I interpreted James's argument there as a form of anti-evidentialism. Specifically, following George Mavrodes, I argued that James wishes to reject what could be called proportionality evidentialism, which holds that belief must be proportioned to evidence. Even if belief requires some evidence (a threshold requirement), it does not follow that the character of a belief is determined solely by evidence. What Mavrodes calls the 'meatloaf factor,' an asymmetry between the value of the consequences of believing and disbelieving, helps determine the amount of evidence we require and also may give the belief a qualitative character that does not come only from evidence.

Kierkegaard's argument can also be understood as a rejection of evidentialism; perhaps he can be understood as rejecting both proportionality and threshold evidentialism. Like James (and Pascal) he wants to argue that if you want something like an eternal happiness more than anything else, then it may be reasonable to commit yourself wholeheartedly to something that promises to help you obtain it, even if the chances of obtaining what you seek are not high because the objective probability that eternal happiness is truly to be gained in this way is not high either. Perhaps Kierkegaard wishes to argue that if your desire for this good is great enough (infinitely high, whatever that might mean), then even a very low probability would be sufficient to motivate belief, so that a passionate believer simply ceases to worry about evidence at all. We might say that for such a believer any amount of evidence at all will be sufficient.

Of course one way that this might occur will be if the beliefs in question are *basic* in character, as Plantinga has argued.[50] If a belief is not based on evidence at all, then it will not be affected by the quality or quantity of the evidence, and the kind of incommensurability that Kierkegaard sees between scholarly inquiry and religious faith will not be a problem. Of course even basic beliefs for Plantinga require a ground of some kind, a situation in which a true belief is elicited through some process or mechanism that is designed to produce such a belief. One way to think about Kierkegaard's claims about subjectivity is to see them as claims about the character of the ground of religious beliefs.[51] The specifically Christian beliefs he is discussing, for example, can be understood as beliefs that require a particular set of emotions (or 'passions' in Kierkegaard's language). A person cannot come to believe in Christ without a strong sense of sinfulness and a desperate desire for God's forgiveness. Those are the factors that produce the beliefs. When they are present, the evidence is always sufficient; when they are lacking, no amount of evidence is enough.[52]

This interpretation of Kierkegaard as arguing that religious beliefs should be understood as basic in character, and grounded partly in subjective factors, also helps us understand the third argument that Adams attributes to Kierkegaard. The final argument that Adams considers is what he terms the 'passion argument.' The claim here is not that there is never enough objective evidence to produce the certainty that faith demands. Rather, the claim is that faith does not even want objective certainty; it thrives on uncertainty:

> The almost probable, the probable, the to-a-high-degree and exceedingly probable—that he can almost know, or as good as know, to a higher degree and exceedingly almost *know*—but *believe* it, that cannot be done, for the absurd is precisely the object of faith and only that can be believed.[53]

The true religious believer is like a lover who does not need probable arguments that the beloved is worth loving. A need for such an argument would be a sign that love is in fact fading. The genuine lover actually welcomes a chance to show the genuineness of the love by running risks and paying a price:

> it never occurs to a girl truly in love that she has purchased her happiness at too high a price, but rather that she has not purchased it at a price high enough . . . so it is also the case with the highest that you get what you pay for.[54]

Adams objects that this passion argument does not take into account the dispositional character of faith. It may be true that faith requires a willingness to undergo risks if necessary, but a willingness to run such risks does not mean that one must actually run them. There is a parallel here with the love relationship; perhaps a genuine lover shows love by continuing to love even when there is reason to doubt. However, a willingness to do that does not mean love requires the doubt to be actual.

I think that Adams is correct to argue that even if faith involves a willingness to believe in the face of difficulties, this does not mean that one must actually have the difficulties in order to have genuine faith. I have faith in my wife if I am willing to believe in her even when I have evidence that she has wronged me; however, I do not have to be in the situation where it appears she has wronged me to have this faith in her.

However, it is true that love may grow and develop in ways that it would not otherwise when it is tested. And it may also be the case that faith may similarly grow and develop in ways that it would not otherwise when it is tested by uncertainty. So even if faith does not require uncertainty, it may welcome it, and perhaps this is all Kierkegaard really needs to maintain. For it appears that our world offers opportunities enough for uncertainty, both for those who possess religious faith and those who are committed to some secular faith.

Defeaters and the Value of Evidence

In the end, however, I believe that Kierkegaard does go too far in dismissing the value of evidence. He may be right in claiming that faith is properly basic and not based on evidence. He may also be right in claiming that faith has qualities that stem from its grounds in what he terms 'subjectivity.' Objective evidence may be neither necessary nor sufficient for faith. However, it does not follow from this that objective evidence is simply irrelevant for faith, or that the believer will have no concern for evidence.

Even a belief that is properly basic is subject to being 'defeated' or overturned by evidence. As Plantinga develops the notion, properly basic beliefs are not infallible, and Kierkegaard, with his stress on human finitude and sinfulness, would certainly agree that a human being must admit to the possibility of being mistaken. So I believe, right now, in a basic manner, that I had pancakes for breakfast this morning. However, if I return to the house and discover that I left bowls of half-eaten cereal in the kitchen sink, and see no evidence of pancake preparation, I am prepared to admit that my belief is false. So a claim that a belief is basic does not imply that it is immune to falsification.

Of course if the original ground for my belief is strong enough, I may simply cling to the belief and reject the defeater. Perhaps someone sneaked into my house, cleaned up the pancake makings, and then left the appearances of a cereal breakfast in order to deceive me. It is not always clear when it is reasonable to think a belief has been defeated, and when to continue to hold it in the face of new evidence that cuts against it.

In the case of a religious belief that has historical content, such as Kierkegaard thinks is the case for Christianity, it seems wrong to say that the believer would always be right to ignore evidence that falsified the belief. Suppose, for example, that we found overwhelmingly powerful evidence that Jesus never existed, and that the whole of Christianity, along with its early history, had been invented in the fifth century. If the evidence were really powerful, would it still be possible to continue to believe that an historical figure from first-century Palestine, Jesus of Nazareth, was divine?[55]

So even if religious beliefs are basic in character, I doubt that evidence can be simply ignored or dismissed as irrelevant. However, the heart of Kierkegaard's position can I think still be maintained. What he wants to assert is that faith, with all its passion and decisiveness, does not stem from evidence. That may be true, even if it is important to the believer that there is no decisive evidence that would disprove his or her belief. The intellectual inquiry and amount of evidence that might be necessary in order to 'defeat the defeater' is quite different than what would be required if the belief itself were based simply in objective evidence. It may be important for the believer that there is no overwhelmingly powerful evidence that the story of Jesus was invented in the fifth century; it may not be important that the historical truth of the story cannot be proved to secular historians.[56]

As we shall see in the next chapter, when I examine the project of looking for evidence for God's existence, it is not always clear that evidence precludes the need for faith, or that faith considers evidence unimportant. There may be evidence that can only be seen as evidence by the eyes of faith, but such evidence might still be important for those who have those eyes of faith. Perhaps Kierkegaard draws too sharp a distinction between 'objective' and 'subjective' ways of thinking about religious truths. Pure objectivity may be a myth, as he himself argues. But pure subjectivity may be mythical as well, particularly if religious questions are ones that have real answers, answers that may be true or false. For one of our deepest subjective concerns is truth.

But this objection to Kierkegaard, even if it is sound, does not touch what I take to be his deepest concerns, which are I think twofold: an emphasis on the ways that sinfulness and finitude limit human thinking, and on the ways that certain emotions and passions are necessary in order to get at religious truth. If Kierkegaard is right, then a good deal of the intellectual practices and attitudes that are taken as 'reasonable' by sinful human beings do not in fact help us get on track with truth. To make contact with truth we need to be reshaped from the ground up, and for Kierkegaard that requires a reorientation of our deepest desires.

Notes

1. Actually, these terms are usually found in Kierkegaard's pseudonymous writings and there is some debate about whether or not this language is characteristic of Kierkegaard's own position. See Chapter 6, n. 1 for more about the problem of pseudonymity.

2. Søren Kierkegaard, *Concluding Unscientific Postscript,* trans. by Howard V. and Edna H. Hong (Princeton:. Princeton University Press, 1992) pp. 211, 233.

3. A very strong version of this claim is found in the so-called 'strong program' in the sociology of knowledge, which tries to explain all beliefs as accepted for social reasons, reasons that cannot be linked to objective truth or transcendent rationality. For an example, see Barry Barnes and David Bloor, 'Relativism, Rationalism, and the Sociology of Knowledge,' in *Rationality and Relativism,* ed. Martin Hollis and Steven Lukes (Cambridge, Massachusetts: MIT Press, 1984) pp. 21–47. One does not have to accept this strong claim and its accompanying relativism to accept the weaker thesis that a great deal of what is accepted as 'reason' is due to sociological factors.

4. For a good brief account of Foucault's thinking, see his 'Afterword' that appears at the end of Hubert L. Dreyfus and Paul Rabinow, *Michel Foucault: Beyond Structuralism and Hermeneutics* (Chicago: University of Chicago Press, 1983). For longer statements of Foucault's views, see Gordon Colin, ed., *Power/Knowledge: Selected Interviews and Other Writings, 1971–77* (New York: Pantheon, 1980) and Paul Rabinow, ed., *The Foucault Reader* (New York: Pantheon, 1985).

5. See Friedrich Schleiermacher, *On Religion: Speeches to Its Cultured Despisers,* trans. John Oman (New York: Harper, 1958).

6. Søren Kierkegaard, *Philosophical Fragments,* trans. Howard V. and Edna H. Hong (Princeton: Princeton University Press, 1985) p. 53 (translation modified).

7. Søren Kierkegaard, *The Sickness Unto Death,* trans. by Howard V. and Edna H. Hong (Princeton: Princeton University Press, 1980) pp. 42–3 (translation modified).

8. *Philosophical Fragments,* p. 37.

9. Ibid.

10. *Philosophical Fragments,* p. 53.

11. See, for example, Kierkegaard's praise of the critical Biblical scholar who tries to establish the Biblical text accurately and understand its origin historically. He says that this kind of scholarship deserves our admiration except, as is so often the case, when it implies that this scholarly work has some implications for faith. See *Concluding Unscientific Postscript,* pp. 24–6. In another passage (*Postscript,* p. 193) he says the indifference of the scholar is the basis of the objective validity of the work of the mathematician or historian.

12. *Concluding Unscientific Postscript,* p. 314.

13. *Concluding Unscientific Postscript,* p. 311.

14. *Concluding Unscientific Postscript,* p. 330.

15. *Concluding Unscientific Postscript,* p. 314.

16. Immanuel Kant, *Grounding for the Metaphysics of Morals,* 3rd edn trans. James W. Ellington (Indianapolis, Indiana: Hackett Publishing Co., 1993) p. 20.

17. Søren Kierkegaard, *Fear and Trembling,* trans. Howard V. and Edna H. Hong (Princeton: Princeton University Press, 1983) p. 36.

18. *Concluding Unscientific Postscript,* p. 233.

19. See *Philosophical Fragments,* Chp. 2.

20. Søren Kierkegaard, *Practice in Christianity,* trans. Howard V. Hong and Edna H. Hong (Princeton: Princeton University Press, 1991) p. 58.

21. *Philosophical Fragments,* p. 101.

22. *Philosophical Fragments,* p. 52.

23. See *Philosophical Fragments,* p. 47.

24. *Ibid.*

25. *Philosophical Fragments,* p. 37.

26. *Philosophical Fragments,* p. 48.

27. *Ibid.*

28. *Ibid.*

29. See *Philosophical Fragments,* pp. 54 and 59, for two different versions of this formula for faith. The translation used here is my own.

30. *Philosophical Fragments,* p. 9.

31. See *Philosophical Fragments,* p. 15 for a discussion of 'the condition.'

32. *Philosophical Fragments,* p. 10.

33. *Philosophical Fragments,* p. 11.

34. Kierkegaard means by 'the Truth' here not just any propositional truth, but the grasping of the Truth that transforms a person; in other words, having Truth in this sense is equivalent to the religious concept of salvation. See Chp. 1 of *Philosophical Fragments.*

35. In Kierkegaard's Danish, all nouns are capitalised. Thus, it is difficult to decide when a noun such as 'Truth' is being used as a proper noun designating a particular kind of truth. In my view, the concepts of Truth and Untruth in *Philosophical Fragments* should be capitalised.

36. *Philosophical Fragments,* p. 14.

37. *Ibid.*

38. See Emmanuel Levinas, *Totality and Infinity,* trans. Alphonso Lingis (Pittsburgh: Duquesne University Press, 1969), particularly pp. 187–219.

39. Kierkegaard argues this in a lengthy footnote on pp. 16 and 17 in *Philosophical Fragments.*

40. See *Philosophical Fragments,* pp. 27–32.

41. *Philosophical Fragments,* p. 54.

42. *Philosophical Fragments,* 59.

43. *Philosophical Fragments,* p. 54.

44. Robert Adams, 'Kierkegaard's Arguments Against Objective Reasoning in Religion,' in *The Virtue of Faith and Other Essays in Philosophical Theology* (Oxford: Oxford University Press, 1987) pp. 25–41. Originally published in *The Monist* 60 (1976).

45. Adams, pp. 25–27.

46. *Concluding Unscientific Postscript,* p. 26. (Adams himself, writing before the new Hong translation appeared, cites the old Lowrie-Swenson translation; I here follow the new translation.)

47. Adams, p. 28.

48. Many sections of *Concluding Unscientific Postscript* deal with the nature of the subjective thinker, but one of the central descriptions is found on pp. 349–60, where we have an account of the 'subjective thinker: his task, his form, his style.'

49. See Chp. 3, pp. 47–52.

50. See Chp. 3, pp. 41–7.

51. See my article, 'Kierkegaard and Plantinga on Belief in God: Subjectivity as the Ground of Properly Basic Beliefs,' *Faith and Philosophy* (v, 1), 1988.

52. This is exactly what Kierkegaard argues, both in *Philosophical Fragments* and *Concluding Unscientific Postscript*. In both books, he performs thought experiments in which he imagines first that the religious apologist has all the evidence he or she could possibly want, and then that the sceptic has all the negative evidence he or she could want. In both cases Kierkegaard suggests that the results have no decisive importance for faith. See *Fragments*, pp. 58–61, and *Postscript*, pp. 28–31.

53. *Concluding Unscientific Postscript*, p. 211.

54. *Concluding Unscientific Postscript*, p. 231.

55. For a fuller development of this point, as well as a fuller discussion of what is defensible and what is not in Kierkegaard's view of the relation of faith to historical evidence, see Chp. 9 of my *Passionate Reason: Making Sense of Kierkegaard's* Philosophical Fragments (Bloomington, Indiana: Indiana University Press, 1992).

56. For a full account of how historical religious beliefs could be properly basic and yet still vulnerable to defeat by evidence, see my *The Historical Christ and the Jesus of Faith: The Incarnational Narrative as History* (Oxford: Oxford University Press, 1996), especially Chps. 10–12.

D. John Hick: Faith, Language, and Experience of God

John Hick argues that the believer's faith experience of reality is not incompatible with the way persons experience the world in general. As he explains, we experience the world as having significance for us through the application of language. To experience an object as a particular kind of object requires that one possess a sense of the physical structure of a thing along with its function in relation to human interests. For example, in order to experience a pen "as" a pen one requires a familiarity with the tools of written communication. Without such an understanding one could not experience a long, thin object as a pen, and would have no awareness of its function. In the same manner, without moral concepts or a sense of the moral order, one lacks the capacity to experience a situation as having moral significance. At the moral level, one cannot literally perceive the presence or absence of moral responsibility, but one's ability to discern significance in events through the prism of moral language helps create distinctive moral experiences. In an analogous way, the presence of religious concepts, despite the

absence of empirical evidence for the divine, makes possible the believer's experi-
ence of the transcendent. Hick is not arguing for the truth or falsity of religious
faith or its claims; rather, he is suggesting that the believer's experience is justified
as corresponding with the ways in which all of us, believer or nonbeliever, come
to experience the world. James Heaney (1979) argues that Hick's attempt to draw
an analogy between religious faith and perceptual experience is seriously flawed,
and J. Wesley Robbins (1974) critiques Hick's suggestion that the unbeliever can-
not object to the believer's experience of God without, at the same time, calling
into question his own perceptual awareness of the physical world.

25. The Nature of Faith

JOHN HICK

We come now to our main problem. What manner of cognition is the religious man's awareness of God, and how is it related to his other cognitions?

We become conscious of the existence of other objects in the universe, whether things or persons, either by experiencing them for ourselves or by inferring their existence from evidences within our experience. The awareness of God reported by the ordinary religious believer is of the former kind. He professes, not to have inferred that there is a God, but that God as a living being has entered into his own experience. He claims to enjoy something which he describes as an experience of God. The ordinary believer does not, however, report an awareness of God as existing in isolation from all other objects of experience. His consciousness of the divine does not involve a cessation of his consciousness of a material and social environment. It is not a vision of God in solitary glory, filling the believer's entire mind and blotting out his normal field of perception. Whether such phrases correctly describe the mystic's goal, the ultimate Beatific Vision which figures in Christian doctrine, is a question for a later chapter. But at any rate the ordinary person's religious awareness here on earth is not of that kind. He claims instead an apprehension of God meeting him in and through his material and social environments. He finds that in his dealings with the world of men and things he is somehow having to do with God, and God with him. The moments of ordinary life possess, or may possess, for him in varying degrees a religious significance. As has been well said, religious experience is "the whole experience of religious persons."[1] The believer meets God not only in moments of worship, but also when through the urgings of conscience he feels the pressure of the

Source: John Hick, *Faith and Knowledge* (Ithaca, N.Y.: Cornell University Press, 1957), pages 95–119. Reprinted with the permission of the author.

divine demand upon his life; when through the gracious actions of his friends he appre-hends the divine grace; when through the marvels and beauties of nature he traces the hand of the Creator; and he has increasing knowledge of the divine purpose as he re-sponds to its behests in his own life. In short, it is not apart from the course of mundane life, but in it and through it, that the ordinary religious believer claims to experience, however imperfectly and fragmentarily, the divine presence and activity.

This at any rate, among the variety of claims to religious awareness which have been and might be made, is the claim whose epistemological credentials we are to examine. Can God be known through his dealings with us in the world which he has made? The question concerns human experience, and the possibility of an awareness of the divine being mediated through awareness of the world, the supernatural through the natural.

In answer to this query I shall try to show, in various fields, that "mediated" knowl-edge, such as is postulated by this religious claim, is already a common and accepted fea-ture of our cognitive experience. To this end we must study a basic characteristic of human experience, which I shall call "significance," together with the correlative mental activity by which it is apprehended, which I shall call "interpretation." We shall find that interpretation takes place in relation to each of the three main types of existence, or or-ders of significance, recognized by human thought—the natural, the human, and the di-vine; and that in order to relate ourselves appropriately to each, a primary and unevidenceable act of interpretation is required which, when directed toward God, has traditionally been termed "faith." Thus I shall try to show that while the object of reli-gious knowledge is unique, its basic epistemological pattern is that of all our knowing.

This is not to say that the logic of theistic belief has no peculiarities. It does indeed display certain unique features; and these (I shall try to show) are such as follow from the unique nature of its object, and are precisely the peculiarities which we should ex-pect if that object is real. In the present chapter, then, we shall take note of the com-mon epistemological pattern in which religious knowledge partakes, and in the following chapter we shall examine some special peculiarities of religious knowing, and especially its noncompulsory character.

"Significance" seems to be the least misleading word available to name the fundamen-tal characteristic of experience which I wish to discuss. Other possible terms are "form" and "meaning." But "form," as the word is used in the traditional matter-form distinction, would require careful editing and commentary to purge it of unwanted Aristotelian associ-ations. "Meaning," on the other hand, has been so overworked and misused in the past, not only by plain men and poets, but also by theologians and philosophers,[2] as to be al-most useless today, except in its restricted technical use as referring to the equivalence of symbols. We may perhaps hope that after a period of exile the wider concept of "meaning" will be readmitted into the philosophical comity of notions. Indeed Brand Blanshard has long braved the post–Ogden and Richards ban by his use of the phrase "perceptual mean-ing."[3] I propose here, however, to use the less prejudged term "significance."

By significance I mean that fundamental and all-pervasive characteristic of our con-scious experience which *de facto* constitutes it for us the experience of a "world" and not of a mere empty void or churning chaos. We find ourselves in a relatively stable and or-dered environment in which we have come to feel, so to say, "at home." The world has become intelligible to us, in the sense that it is a familiar place in which we have learned to act and react in appropriate ways. Our experience is not just an unpredictable kaleidoscope of which we are bewildered spectators, but reveals to us a familiar, settled cosmos in which we live and act, a world in which we can adopt purposes and adapt means to ends. It is in virtue of this homely, familiar, intelligible character of experience—its possession of significance—that we are able to inhabit and cope with our environment.

If this use of "significance" be allowed it will, I think, readily be granted that our consciousness is essentially consciousness of significance. Mind could neither emerge nor persist in an environment which was totally nonsignificant to it. For this reason it is not possible to define "significance" ostensively by pointing to contrasting examples of significant and nonsignificant experience. In its most general form at least, we must accept the Kantian thesis that we can be aware only of that which enters into a certain framework of basic relations which is correlated with the structure of our own consciousness. These basic relations represent the minimal conditions of significance for the human mind. The totally nonsignificant is thus debarred from entering into our experience. A completely undifferentiated field, or a sheer "buzzing, booming confusion," would be incapable of sustaining consciousness. For our consciousness is (to repeat) essentially consciousness of significance. Except perhaps in very early infancy or in states of radical breakdown, the human mind is always aware of its environment as having this quality of fundamental familiarity or intelligibility. Significance, then, is simply the most general characteristic of our experience.

Significance, so defined, has an essential reference to action. Consciousness of a particular kind of environmental significance involves a judgment, implicit or explicit, as to the appropriateness of a particular kind, or range of kinds, of action in relation to that environment. The distinction between types of significance is a distinction between the reactions, occurrent and dispositional, which they render appropriate. For the human psychophysical organism has evolved under the pressure of a continual struggle to survive, and our system of significance-attributions has as a result an essentially pragmatic orientation. Our outlook is instinctively empirical and practical. Physiologically we are so constituted as to be sensitive only to a minute selection of the vast quantity and complexity of the events taking place around us—that precise selection which is practically relevant to us. Our ears, for example, are attuned to a fragment only of the full range of sound waves, and our eyes to but a fraction of the multitudinous variations of light. Our sense organs automatically select from nature those aspects in relation to which we must act. We apprehend the world only at the macroscopic level at which we have practical dealings with it. As Norman Kemp Smith has said, "The function of sense-perception, as of instinct, is not knowledge but power, not insight but adaptation."[4] For an animal to apprehend more of its environment than is practically relevant to it would prove a fatal complication; it would be bemused and bewildered, and unable to react selectively to the stimuli indicating danger, food, and so on. And it is equally true at the human level that the significance of a given object or situation for a given individual consists in the practical *difference* which the existence of that object makes to that individual. It is indeed one of the marks of our status as dependent beings that we live by continual adaptation to our environment; and from this follows the essentially practical bearing of that which constitutes significance for us.

Although the locus of significance is primarily our environment as a whole, we can in thought divide this into smaller units of significance. We may accordingly draw a provisional distinction between two species of significance, object-significance and situational significance, and note the characteristics of significance first in terms of the former.

Every general name, such as "hat," "book," "fire," "house," names a type of object-significance. For these are isolable aspects of our experience which (in suitable contexts) render appropriate distinctive patterns of behavior. The word "hat," for example, does not name a rigidly delimited class of objects but a particular use to which things can be put, namely, as a covering for the head. Objects are specially manufactured for this use; but if necessary many other items can be made to fulfill the function of a hat. This particular way of treating things, as headgear, is the behavioral correlate of the type of object-significance which we call "being a hat." Indeed the boundaries of each distinguishable class of objects are defined by the two *foci* of (1) physical structure and (2) function in relation to human interests. Our names are always in part names for functions or uses or kinds of significance as apprehended from the standpoint of the agent.

Significance, then, is a relational concept. A universe devoid of consciousness would be neither significant nor non-significant. An object or a sense-field is significant *for* or *to* a mind. We are only concerned here with significance for the human mind, but it is well to remember that the lower animals also are aware of their environment as being significant, this awareness being expressed not in words or concepts but in actions and readinesses for action.

There is, I hope, no suggestion of anything occult about this fundamental feature of our experience which I am calling "significance." The difficulty in discussing it is not novelty but, on the contrary, overfamiliarity. It is so completely obvious that we can easily overlook its importance, or even its existence. There is also the related difficulty that we do not apprehend significance as such, but only each distinguishable aspect of our experience as having its own particular type of significance. For significance is a genus which exists only in its species. Just as we perceive the various colors, but never color in general, so we perceive this and that kind of significance, but never significance *simpliciter*.

After this preliminary characterization of the nature of significance, we may take note of the mental activity of interpretation which is its subjective correlate. The word "interpretation" suggests the possibility of differing judgments; we tend to call a conclusion an interpretation when we recognize that there may be other and variant accounts of the same subject matter. It is precisely because of this suggestion of ambiguity in the given, and of alternative modes of construing data, that "interpretation" is a suitable correlate term for "significance."

Two uses of "interpretation" are to be distinguished. In one of its senses, an interpretation is a (true or false) *explanation,* answering the question, Why? We speak, for example, of a metaphysician's interpretation of the universe. In its other sense, an interpretation is a (correct or incorrect) *recognition,*[5] or attribution of significance, answering the question, What? ("What is that, a dog or a fox?") These two meanings are closely connected. For all explanation operates ultimately in terms of recognition. We explain a puzzling phenomenon by disclosing its context, revealing it as part of a wider whole which does not, for us, stand in need of explanation. We render the unfamiliar intellectually acceptable by relating it to the already recognizable, indicating a connection or continuity between the old and the new. But in the unique case of the universe as a whole the distinction between explanation and recognition fails to arise. For the universe has no wider context in terms of which it might be explained; an explanation of it can therefore only consist in a perception of its significance. In this case, therefore, interpretation is both recognition and explanation. Hence the theistic recognition, or significance-attribution, is also a metaphysical explanation or theory. However, although the explanatory and the recognition aspects of theistic faith are inseparable, they may usefully be distinguished for purposes of exposition. In the present chapter we shall be examining interpretation, including the religious interpretation, as a recognition, or perception of significance.

An act of recognition, or of significance-attribution, is a complex occurrence dealing with two different types of ambiguity in the given. There are, on the one hand, interpretations which are mutually exclusive (e.g., "That is a fox" and "That is a dog," referring to the same object), and on the other hand interpretations which are mutually compatible (e.g., "That is an animal" and "That is a dog"; or "He died by asphyxiation" and "He was murdered"). Of two logically alternative interpretations only one (at most) can be the correct interpretation. But two compatible interpretations may both be correct. We shall be concerned henceforth with this latter kind of difference, in which several levels or layers or orders of significance are found in the same field of data.

The following are some simple examples of different levels or orders of object-significance.

(a) I see a rectangular red object on the floor in the corner. So far I have interpreted it as a "thing" (or "substance"), as something occupying space and time. On looking more closely, however, I see that it is a red-covered book. I have now made a new interpretation which includes my previous one, but goes beyond it.

(b) There is a piece of paper covered with writing. An illiterate savage can perhaps interpret it as something made by man. A literate person, who does not know the particular language in which it is written, can interpret it as being a document. But someone who understands the language can find in it the expression of specific thoughts. Each is answering the question, "What is it?" correctly, but answering it at different levels. And each more adequate attribution of significance presupposes the less adequate ones.

This relationship between types of significance, one type being superimposed upon and interpenetrating another, is a pattern which we shall find again in larger and more important spheres.

We have already noted that significance is essentially related to action. The significance of an object to an individual consists in the practical difference which that object makes to him, the ways in which it affects either his immediate reactions or his more long-term plans and policies. There is also a reciprocal influence of action upon our interpretations. For it is only when we have begun to act upon our interpretations, and have thereby verified that our environment is capable of being successfully inhabited in terms of them, that they become fully "real" modes of experience. Interpretations which take the dispositional form of readinesses for action, instead of immediate overt activity, borrow this feeling of "reality" from cognate interpretations which are being or have already been confirmed in action. (For example, when I see an apple on the sideboard, but do not immediately eat it, I nevertheless perceive it as entirely "real" because I have in the past verified similar interpretations of similar apple-like appearances.) It is by acting upon our interpretations that we build up an apprehension of the world around us; and in this process interpretations, once confirmed, suggest and support further interpretations. The necessity of acting-in-terms-of to "clinch" or confirm an interpretation has its importance, as we shall note later, in relation to the specifically religious recognition which we call theistic faith.

We have been speaking so far only of object-significance. But, as already indicated, object-significance as contrasted with situational significance is an expository fiction. An object absolutely per se and devoid of context would have no significance for us. It can be intelligible only as part of our familiar world. What significance would remain, for example, to a book without the physical circumstance of sight, the conventions of language and writing, the acquired art of reading, and even the literature of which the book is a part and the civilization within which it occurs? An object owes its signifi-cance as much to its context as to itself; it is what it is largely because of its place in a wider scheme of things. We are indeed hardly ever conscious of anything in complete isolation. Our normal consciousness is of groups of objects standing in recognizable patterns of relations to one another. And it is the resulting situation taken as a whole that carries significance for us, rendering some ranges of action and reaction appropri-ate and others inappropriate. We live and plan and act all the time in terms of the situa-tional significance of our environment; although of course our interest may focus at any given moment upon a particular component object within the current situation.

We do not, it is true, as plain men generally think of the familiar situations which constitute our experience from moment to moment as having "significance" and of our actions as being guided thereby. But in the fundamental sense in which we are using the term, our ordinary consciousness of the world is undoubtedly a continuous consciousness of significance. It is normally consciousness of a routine or humdrum significance which is so familiar that we take it entirely for granted. The significance for me, for example, of my situation at the present moment is such that I go on quietly working; this is the re-sponse rendered appropriate by my interpretation of my contemporary experience. No fresh response is required, for my routine reactions are already adjusted to the prevailing context of significance. But this significance is none the less real for being undramatic.

The component elements of situational significance are not only physical ob-jects—tables, mountains, stars, houses, hats, and so on—but also such nonmaterial en-tities as sounds and lights and odors and, no less important, such psychological events and circumstances as other peoples' thoughts, emotions, and attitudes. Thus the kinds of situational significance in terms of which we act and react are enormously complex. Indeed the philosopher who would trace the morphology of situational significance must be a dramatist and poet as well as analyst. Attempts at significance-mapping have been undertaken by some of the existentialist writers: what they refer to as the existen-tial character of experience is the fact that we are ourselves by definition *within* any re-lational system which constitutes a situation for us. However, these writers have usually been concerned to bring out the more strained and hectic aspects of human experience, presenting it often as a vivid nightmare of metaphysical anxieties and perils. They are undoubtedly painting from real life, particularly in this anguished age, but I venture to think that they are depicting it in a partial and one-sided manner.

A "situation" may be defined, then, as a state of affairs which, when selected for at-tention by an act of interpretation, carries its own distinctive practical significance for us. We may be involved in many different situations at the same time and may move by swift or slow transitions of interpretation from one to another. There may thus occur an indefinitely complex interpenetration of situations. For example I am, let us say, sitting in a room playing a game of chess with a friend. The game, isolated by the brackets of imagination, is a situation in itself in which I have a part to play as one of the two competing intelligences presiding over the chess board. Here is an artificial situation with its conventional boundaries, structure, and rules of procedure. But from time to time my attention moves from the board to the friend with whom I am playing, and I exchange some conversation with him. Now I am living in another situation which contains the game of chess as a sub-situation. Then suddenly a fire breaks out in the building, and the attention of both of us shifts at once to our wider physical situation; and so on. There are the wider and wider spatial situations of the street, the city, the state, continent, globe, Milky Way, and finally, as the massive permanent background situation inclusive of all else, the physical universe. And there are also the widening circles of family, class, nation, civilization, and all the other groupings within the inclusive group of the human species as a whole. The complex web of interplays within and between these two expanding series gives rise to the infinite variety of situations of which our human life is composed.

Finally, enfolding and interpenetrating this interlocking mass of finite situations there is also, according to the insistent witness of theistic religion, the all-encompassing situation of being in the presence of God and within the sphere of an on-going divine purpose. Our main concern, after these prolonged but unavoidable preliminaries, is to be with this alleged ultimate and inclusive significance and its relation to the more limited and temporary significances through which it is mediated.

Our inventory, then, shows three main orders of situational significance, corresponding to the threefold division of the universe, long entertained by human thought, into nature, man, and God. The significance for us of the physical world, nature, is that of an objective environment whose character and "laws" we must learn, and toward which we have continually to relate ourselves aright if we are to survive. The significance for us of the human world, man, is that of a realm of relationships in which we are responsible agents, subject to moral obligation. This world of moral significance is, so to speak, superimposed upon the natural world, so that relating ourselves to the moral world is not distinct from the business of relating ourselves to the natural world but is rather a particular manner of so doing. And likewise the more ultimately fateful and momentous matter of relating ourselves to the divine, to God, is not distinct from the task of directing ourselves within the natural and ethical spheres; on the contrary, it entails (without being reducible to) a way of so directing ourselves.

In the case of each of these three realms, the natural, the human, and the divine, a basic act of interpretation is required which discloses to us the existence of the sphere in question, thus providing the ground for our multifarious detailed interpretations within that sphere.

Consider first the level of natural significance. This is the significance which our environment has for us as animal organisms seeking survival and pleasure and shunning pain and death. In building houses, cooking food, avoiding dangerous precipices, whirlpools, and volcanoes, and generally conducting ourselves prudently in relation to the material world, we are all the time taking account of what I am calling (for want of a better name) the *natural* significance of our environment.

We have already noted some instances of natural significance when discussing the recognition of objects and situations. It is a familiar philosophical tenet, and one which may perhaps today be taken as granted, that all conscious experience of the physical world contains an element of interpretation. There are combined in each moment of experience a presented field of data and an interpretative activity of the subject. The perceiving mind is thus always in some degree a selecting, relating and synthesizing agent, and experiencing our environment involves a continuous activity of interpretation. "Interpretation" here is of course an unconscious and habitual process, the process by which a sense-field is perceived, for example, as a three-dimensional room, or a particular configuration of colored patches within that field as a book lying upon a table. Interpretation in this sense is generally recognized as a factor in the genesis of sense perception. We have now to note, however, the further and more basic act of interpretation which reveals to us the very existence of a material world, a world which we explore and inhabit as our given environment. In attending to this primary interpretative act we are noting the judgment which carries us beyond the solipsist predicament into an objective world of enduring, causally interacting objects, which we share with other people. Given the initial rejection of solipsism (or rather given the interpretative bias of human nature, which has prevented all but the most enthusiastic of philosophers from falling into solipsism) we can, I think, find corroborations of an analogical kind to support our belief in the unobserved continuance of physical objects and the reality of other minds. But the all-important first step, or assumption, is unevidenced and unevidenceable—except for permissive evidence, in that one's phenomenal experience is "there" to be interpreted either solipsistically or otherwise. But there is no event within our phenomenal experience the occurrence or nonoccurrence of which is relevant to the truth or falsity of the solipsist hypothesis. That hypothesis represents one possible interpretation of our experience as a whole, and the contrary belief in a plurality of minds existing in a common world represents an alternative and rival interpretation.

It may perhaps be objected that it does not make any practical difference whether solipsism be true or not, and that these are not therefore two *different* interpretations of our experience. For if our experience, phenomenally considered, would be identical on either hypothesis, then the alternative (it will be said) is a purely verbal one; the choice is merely a choice of synonyms. I do not think, however, that this is the case. Phenomenally, there is no difference between a dream in which we know that we are dreaming and one in which we do not. But, nevertheless, there is a total difference between the two experiences—total not in the sense that every, or indeed any, isolable aspects of them differ, but in the sense that the two experiences taken as wholes are of different kinds. We are aware of precisely the same course of events, but in the one case this occurs within mental brackets, labeled as a dream, while in the other case we are ourselves immersed within the events and live through them as participants. The phenomena are apprehended in the one case as dream constituents and in the other case as "real." And the difference caused by a genuine assent to solipsism would be akin to the sudden realization during an absorbing dream that it *is* only a dream. If the solipsist interpretation were to be seriously adopted and wholeheartedly believed, experience would take on an unreal character in contrast with one's former nonsolipsist mode of experience. Our personal relationships in particular, our loves and friendships, our hates and enmities, rivalries and co-operations, would have to be treated not as transsubjective meetings with other personalities, but as dialogues and dramas with oneself. There would be only one person in existence, and other "people," instead of being apprehended as independent centers of intelligence and purpose, would be but human-like appearances. They could not be the objects of affection or enmity, nor could their actions be subjected to moral judgment in our normal nonsolipsist sense. In short, although it must be very difficult, if not impossible, for the sanely functioning mind seriously to assent to solipsism and to apperceive in terms of it, yet this does represent at least a logically possible interpretation of experience, and constitutes a *different* interpretation from our ordinary belief in an independently existing world of things and persons. It follows that our normal mode of experience is itself properly described as an interpretation, an interpretation which we are unable to justify by argument but which we have nevertheless no inclination or reason to doubt. Indeed as Hume noted, nature has not left this to our choice, "and has doubtless esteem'd it an affair of too great importance to be trusted to our uncertain reasonings and speculations. We may well ask, What causes induce us to believe in the existence of body [i.e., matter]? but 'tis vain to ask, Whether there be body or not? That is a point, which we must take for granted in all our reasonings."[6]

But the ordering of our lives in relation to an objective material environment thus revealed to us by a basic act of interpretation is not the most distinctively human level of experience. It is characteristic of mankind to live not only in terms of the natural significance of his world but also in the dimension of personality and responsibility. And so we find that presupposing consciousness of the physical world, and supervening upon it, is the kind of situational significance which we call "being responsible" or "being under obligation." The sense of moral obligation, or of "oughtness," is the basic datum of ethics. It is manifested whenever someone, in circumstances requiring practical decision, feels "obligated" to act, or to refrain from acting, in some particular way. When this occurs, the natural significance of his environment is interpenetrated by another, ethical significance. A traveler on an unfrequented road, for example, comes upon a stranger who has met with an accident and who is lying injured and in need of help. At the level of natural significance this is just an empirical state of affairs, a particular configuration of stone and earth and flesh. But an act or reflex of interpretation at the moral level reveals to the traveler a situation in which he is under obligation to render aid. He feels a categorical imperative laid upon him, demanding that he help the injured man. The situation takes on for him a peremptory ethical significance, and he finds himself in a situation of inescapable personal responsibility.

As has often been remarked, it is characteristic of situations exhibiting moral significance that they involve, directly or indirectly, more than one person. The other or others may stand either in an immediate personal relationship to the moral agent or, as in large-scale social issues, in a more remote causal relationship. (The sphere of politics has been defined as that of the *im*personal relationships between persons.) Ethical significance, as the distinctive significance of situations in which persons are components, includes both of these realms. To feel moral obligation is to perceive (or misperceive) the practical significance for oneself of a situation in which one stands in a responsible relationship to another person or to other people. That the perception of significance in personal situations sets up (in Kant's terms) a categorical imperative, while natural situations give rise only to hypothetical imperatives, conditional upon our own desires, is a defining characteristic of the personal world.

Clearly, moral significance presupposes natural significance. For in order that we may be conscious of moral obligations, and exercise moral intelligence, we must first be aware of a stable environment in which actions have foreseeable results, and in which we can learn the likely consequences of our deeds. It is thus a precondition of ethical situations that there should be a stable medium, the world, with its own causal laws, in which people meet and in terms of which they act. The two spheres of significance, the moral and the physical, interpenetrate in the sense that all occasions of obligation have reference, either immediately or ultimately, to overt action. Relating oneself to the ethical sphere is thus a particular manner of relating oneself to the natural sphere: ethical significance is mediated to us in and through the natural world.

As in the case of natural situational significance, we can enter the sphere of ethical significance only by our own act of interpretation. But at this level the interpretation is a more truly voluntary one. That is to say, it is not forced upon us from outside, but depends upon an inner capacity and tendency to interpret in this way, a tendency which we are free to oppose and even to overrule. If a man chooses to be a moral solipsist, or absolute egoist, recognizing no responsibility toward other people, no one can prove to him that he has any such responsibilities. The man who, when confronted with some standard situation having ethical significance, such as a bully wantonly injuring a child, fails to see it as morally significant, could only be classified as suffering from a defect of his nature analogous to physical blindness. He can of course be compelled by threats of punishment to conform to a stated code of behavior; but he cannot be compelled to feel moral obligation. He must see and accept for himself his own situation as a responsible being and its corollary of ethical accountability.

Has this epistemological paradigm—of one order of significance superimposed upon and mediated through another—any further application? The contention of this chapter is that it has. As ethical significance interpenetrates natural significance, so religious significance interpenetrates both ethical and natural. The divine is the highest and ultimate order of significance, mediating neither of the others and yet being mediated through both of them.

But what do we man by religious significance? What is it that, for the ethical monotheist, possesses this significance, and in what does the significance consist?

The primary locus of religious significance is the believer's experience as a whole. The basic act of interpretation which reveals to him the religious significance of life is a uniquely "total interpretation," whose logic will be studied in Part III. But we must at this point indicate what is intended by the phrase "total interpretation," and offer some preliminary characterization of its specifically theistic form.

Consider the following imagined situation. I enter a room in a strange building and find that a militant secret society appears to be meeting there. Most of the members are armed, and as they take me for a fellow member I judge it expedient to acquiesce in the role. Subtle and blood-thirsty plans are discussed for a violent overthrow of the constitution. The whole situation is alarming in the extreme. Then I suddenly notice behind me a gallery in which there are batteries of arc lights and silently whirring cameras, and I realize that I have walked by accident onto the set of a film. This realization consists in a change of interpretation of my immediate environment. Until now I had automatically interpreted it as being "real life," as a dangerous situation demanding considerable circumspection on my part. Now I interpret it as having practical significance of a quite different kind. But there is no corresponding change in the observable course of events. The meeting of the "secret society" proceeds as before, although now I believe the state of affairs to be quite other than I had previously supposed it to be. The same phenomena are interpreted as constituting an entirely different practical situation. And yet not quite the same phenomena, for I have noticed important new items, namely, the cameras and arc lights. But let us now in imagination expand the room into the world, and indeed expand it to include the entire physical universe. This is the strange room into which we walk at birth. There is no space left for a photographers' gallery, no direction in which we can turn in search of new clues which might reveal the significance of our situation. Our interpretation must be a *total* interpretation, in which we assert that the world as a whole (as experienced by ourselves) is of this or that kind, that is to say, affects our plans and our policies in such and such ways.

The monotheist's faith-apprehension of God as the unseen Person dealing with him in and through his experience of the world is from the point of view of epistemology an interpretation of this kind, an interpretation of the world as a whole as mediating a divine presence and purpose. He sees in his situation as a human being a significance to which the appropriate response is a religious trust and obedience. His interpretative leap carries him into a world which exists through the will of a holy, righteous, and loving Being who is the creator and sustainer of all that is. Behind the world—to use an almost inevitable spatial metaphor—there is apprehended to be an omnipotent, personal Will whose purpose toward mankind guarantees men's highest good and blessedness. The believer finds that he is at all times in the presence of this holy Will. Again and again he realizes, either at the time or in retrospect, that in his dealings with the circumstances of his own life he is also having to do with a transcendent Creator who is the determiner of his destiny and the source of all good.

Thus the primary religious perception, or basic act of religious interpretation, is not to be described as either a reasoned conclusion or an unreasoned hunch that there is a God. It is, putatively, an apprehension of the divine presence within the believer's human experience. It is not an inference to a general truth, but a "divine-human encounter," a mediated meeting with the living God.

As ethical significance presupposes natural, so religious significance presupposes both ethical and natural. Entering into conscious relation with God consists in large part in adopting a particular style and manner of acting towards our natural and social environments. For God summons men to serve him *in* the world, and in terms of the life of the world. Religion is not only a way of cognizing but also, and no less vitally, a way of living. To see the world as being ruled by a divine love which sets infinite value upon each individual and includes all men in its scope, and yet to live as though the world were a realm of chance in which each must fight for his own interests against the rest, argues a very dim and wavering vision of God's rule. So far as that vision is clear it issues naturally in a trust in the divine purpose and obedience to the divine will. We shall be able to say more about this practical and dispositional response, in which the apprehension of the religious significance of life so largely consists, when we come in Part IV to examine a particular form of theistic faith. At present we are concerned only with the general nature of the awareness of God.

Rudolf Otto has a somewhat obscure doctrine of the schematization of the Holy in terms of ethics.[7] Without being committed to Otto's use of the Kantian notion, or to his general philosophy of religion, we have been led to a parallel conception of the religious significance of life as schematized in, mediated through, or expressed in terms of, its natural and moral significance. As John Oman says of the Hebrew prophets,

> What determines their faith is not a theory of the Supernatural, but an attitude towards the Natural, as a sphere in which a victory of deeper meaning than the visible and of more abiding purpose than the fleeting can be won. . . . The revelation of the Supernatural was by reconciliation to the Natural: and this was made possible by realising in the Natural the meaning and purpose of the Supernatural.[8]

In one respect this theistic interpretation is more akin to the natural than to the ethical interpretation. For while only *some* situations have moral significance, *all* situations have for embodied beings a continuous natural significance. In like manner the sphere of the basic religious interpretation is not merely this or that isolable situation, but the uniquely total situation constituted by our experience as a whole and in all its aspects, up to the present moment.

But on the other hand the theistic interpretation is more akin to the ethical than to the natural significance-attribution in that it is clearly focused in some situations and imperceptible in others. Not all the moments of life mediate equally the presence of God to the ordinary believer. He is not continuously conscious of God's presence (although possibly the saint is), but conscious rather of the divine Will as a reality in the background of his life, a reality which may at any time emerge to confront him in absolute and inescapable demand. We have already observed how one situation may interpenetrate another, and how some sudden pressure or intrusion can cause a shift of interpretation and attention so that the mind moves from one interlocking context to another. Often a more important kind of significance will summon us from a relatively trivial kind. A woman may be playing a game of cards when she hears her child crying in pain in another room; and at once her consciousness moves from the artificial world of the game to the real world in which she is the mother of the child. Or an officer in the army reserve may be living heedless of the international situation until sudden mobilization recalls him to his military responsibility. The interrupting call of duty may summon us from trivial or relatively unimportant occupations to take part in momentous events. Greater and more ultimate purposes may without warning supervene upon lesser ones and direct our lives into a new channel. But the final significance, which takes precedence over all others as supremely important and overriding, is (according to theism) that of our situation as being in the presence of God. At any time a man may be confronted by some momentous decision, some far-reaching moral choice either of means or of ends, in which his responsibility as a servant of God intrudes upon and conflicts with the requirements of his earthly "station and its duties," so that the latter pales into unimportance and he acts in relation to a more ultimate environment whose significance magisterially overrules his customary way of life. When the call of God is clearly heard other calls become inaudible, and the prophet or saint, martyr or missionary, the man of conscience or of illumined mind may ignore all considerations of worldly prudence in responding to a claim with which nothing else whatever may be put in the balance.

To recapitulate and conclude this stage of the discussion, the epistemological point which I have sought to make is this. There is in cognition of every kind an unresolved mystery. The knower-known relationship is in the last analysis *sui generis:* the mystery of cognition persists at the end of every inquiry—though its persistence does not prevent us from cognizing. We cannot explain, for example, how we are conscious of sensory phenomena as constituting an objective physical environment; we just find ourselves interpreting the data of our experience in this way. We are aware that we live in a real world, though we cannot prove by any logical formula that it *is* a real world. Likewise we cannot explain how we know ourselves to be responsible beings subject to moral obligations; we just find ourselves interpreting our social experience in this way. We find ourselves inhabiting an ethically significant universe, though we cannot prove that it *is* ethically significant by any process of logic. In each case we discover and live in terms of a particular aspect of our environment through an appropriate act of interpretation; and having come to live in terms of it we neither require nor can conceive any further validation of its reality. The same is true of the apprehension of God. The theistic believer cannot explain *how* he knows the divine presence to be mediated through his human experience. He just finds himself interpreting his experience in this way. He lives in the presence of God, though he is unable to prove by any dialectical process that God exists.

To say this is not of course to demonstrate that God *does* exist. The outcome of the discussion thus far is rather to bring out the similarity of epistemological structure and status between men's basic convictions in relation to the world, moral responsibility, and divine existence. The aim of the present chapter has thus been to show how, if there be a God, he is known to mankind, and how such knowledge is related to other kinds of human knowing. I hope that at least the outline of a possible answer to these questions has now been offered.

Notes

1. William Temple, *Nature, Man and God* (London, 1934), p. 334.

2. Cf. Ogden and Richards, *The Meaning of Meaning* (7th ed.; London, 1945), ch. 8.

3. *The Nature of Thought* (London, 1939), I, chs. 4–6.

4. *Prolegomena to an Idealist Theory of Knowledge* (London, 1924), pp. 32–33.

5. This is a slightly off-dictionary sense of "recognition," equating it, not with the identification of the appearances of an object at different times as appearances of the same object, but with the apprehension of what has been discussed above as the "significance" of objects.

6. *Treatise*, bk. I, pt. IV, sec. 2 (Selby-Bigge's ed., pp. 187–188).

7. *The Idea of the Holy*, trans. by J. W. Harvey (London, 1923), ch. 7.

8. *The Natural and the Supernatural* (Cambridge, 1931), p. 448.

26. Faith and the Logic of Seeing-As

JAMES HEANEY

1. Faith and Experience

In *Philosophical Investigations* IIxi, Wittgenstein concentrated on a visual phenomenon he dubbed "seeing-as." Briefly, it is the same phenomenon familiar to us all in trick visual figures which can be seen in more than one way: the drawing of a staircase which looks at one moment as if it leads upward and at another as if downward; the line drawing of a free-standing cube which tends at one moment toward the upper portion of our visual field and at the next moment the lower; the "Christ in the snow" print where a face can be discerned in an otherwise uninteresting assortment of light and dark patches. Wittgenstein included several examples of these in this section of the *Investigations,* not the least striking of which is the Jastrow figure of the "duck-rabbit."[1]

Although it might not at first appear that visual oddities like seeing-as could provide new and fertile ground for Christian apologetics, nonetheless it is precisely upon such grounds, and for some time, that John Hick has attempted to construct an accurate and defensible account of religious faith. Hick's claim, spelled out most clearly in the paper "Religious Faith as Experiencing-As" and implicit in a great deal of his other writing, is that religious faith is so similar as to be almost identical with the sort of perceptual experiences exemplified by seeing-as. In using it as a paradigm he hopes to bring faith and perception closer together and thereby to solve a problem endemic to Christian theology, belief in God as an absent theological entity rather than a present personal reality. He wants, he says, to establish faith as a mode of "cognition in presence" rather than "cognition in absence"[2] and is concerned that his account will produce a description of faith that both believers and skeptics can agree to, even if they cannot agree to the truth of religion. There are, I think, four theses which serve as the philosophical mainsprings of his argument:

a. All seeing is seeing-as.
b. All experiencing is experiencing-as.

Source: James Heaney, "Faith and the Logic of Seeing-As," *International Journal for Philosophy of Religion* 10 (1979), 189–98.

   c. "Recognizing" something, e.g., a fork, is "experiencing-as in terms of a concept."

   d. In instances of seeing-as, the object is seen as either one of two mutually exclusive things at different times, or it is seen as more than one "level" of thing at one and the same time.[3]

These theses are connected somewhat as follows: (A) brings to our attention that not all perceptual experiences are as simple and straightforward as we might think them to be. That is, there is an ineradicable element of interpretation in some of them which implies that we bring as much to our experiences as the objects involved bring, if not more.[4] The fullness of this doctrine is embodied in (B), under which Hick intends to include not only seeing, but, and minimally, the activities of all the other senses as well. (B) says, in short, that there is *no* experiencing that is without its interpretive element. Faith, which Hick has long believed to be fundamentally interpretive,[5] must therefore be a form of experiencing-as, not only because of its interpretive character, but also because it is a mode of experiencing the world and must thereby fall under the jurisdiction of (B). Thesis (C) is vital to the development of the argument, because it enables Hick to bridge the gap between seeing-as in visual instances and such more problematic instances as seeing an event as the action of God. The "recognitions" of (C) include some cases of seeing-as which Wittgenstein may not have wished to place under this heading, but they enable Hick to introduce two notions of some importance. The first is that recognition can be learned, i.e., that one does not need prior acquaintance with an object in order to learn to identify it as what it is. One need not, thus, have prior acquaintance with acts of God in order to learn to recognize some event as one. The second is that religious language is closely tied to religious experience: when one knows how to speak religiously, he applies the proper concepts and in so doing expresses that he sees events as they really are, as acts of God. Thesis (D) aims at covering instances which, unlike the difference between the believer seeing the world as the arena of God's action and the unbeliever seeing it as the domain of chance, demand that we be able to see the same event as a physical occurrence, moral imperative, and result of divine purpose all at once. Hick's contention is that faith is just such a seeing-as, and he goes on to illustrate from both the Old and New Testaments that such a view is not out of harmony with Christianity. He even suggests that the sacramental beliefs of the Christian churches may be construed along such lines:

> In themselves, apart from the sacramental context of worshipping faith, the bread and wine or the water are ordinary material things; they have no magical properties. What happens in the sacramental event is that they are experienced as channels of divine grace.[6]

Quite aside from the difficulties with suggest themselves immediately with regard to the four theses, there are problems here. One general problem is that Hick has promised us an account of faith which would assimilate it as closely as possible to perceptual experience, to "cognition in presence" rather than to "cognition in absence." Much to one's surprise, however, his sequence of theses far more modestly claims to establish only an "analogy" between faith, which he assumes to be a form of knowledge by acquaintance, and sense perception. Another is that there is surely some confusion in claiming that a faith assumed to be a form of knowledge by acquaintance will be assimilated to sense perception by way of analogy: sense perception *is* knowledge by acquaintance. What we have here is no more than a tacitly assumed tautology that makes Hick's expansion of his case by further analogy merely a mistake.[7]

More specifically, the most unsettling thing about Hick's argument is his consistent willingness for analogies to supply the missing links between dissimilar situations, between the seeing-as and experiencing-as of (A) and (B), for instance, and his simultaneous unwillingness to recognize disanalogies where they would be damaging to his case. When one recognizes something, a bird, to use Hick's own example to be referred to below in more detail, this is allegedly both a perceptual event and the application of a concept. The unity of perception and concept-application in this one act of recognition is, therefore, supposed to prove the continuity between theses (A), (B), and (C). This cannot be, however, due to a very clear dissimilarity between knowledge by acquaintance and the application of a concept, or, put as a logical difficulty, by a difference in category between sentences which would instantiate these.

Experiences are of particulars: one sees individuals, but "sees" categories or concepts only by greatly stretching the primary sense of "sees." "Bird," of course, is a general term or concept, but to claim that one can see "in terms of" a general term or concept seems illegitimate when one is also claiming to remain steadfastly within the realm of real experiences.

Even if we pass over the differences between seeing a bird and "seeing" a "bird," it is plain that recognizing something to be a bird as Hick construes it depends upon much more than knowledge by acquaintance:

> Here, too, to recognize is to apply a concept; and this is always to cognise the thing as being much more than is currently perceptible. For example, to identify a moving object in the sky as a bird is not only to make implicit claims about its present shape, size, and structure beyond what we immediately observe but also about its past (for instance, that it came out of an egg, not a factory) about its future (for instance, that it will one day die), and about its behavior in various hypothetical circumstances (for instance, that it will tend to be frightened by loud noises).[8]

Of this it seems only necessary to ask whether acquaintance need be involved here at all: surely we knew, most of us of city origins at any rate, that birds came from eggs long before we ever saw a robin's nest, and the eventual death of any bird we might see was not a matter of knowledge by acquaintance. The conventions surrounding the use of the word "bird" incorporate knowledge gained by means quite different from acquaintance and perhaps even altogether unconnected with it. This disanalogy makes it seem impossible to move uninterruptedly from thesis (A) to thesis (C) on the grounds that both are really knowledge by acquaintance.

Another troubling disanalogy arises in regard to the levels mentioned in thesis (D). That there are differences of a sort that might be called levels in cases of seeing-as is not a difficult notion. One can see the duck-rabbit as a duck, as a rabbit, or, presumably, as a figure of either, something we express by referring to it as a "picture-duck" or a "picture-rabbit." Hick develops this thesis as follows:

As an example, first, of mutually exclusive experiencing-as, one cannot see the tuft of grass simultaneously as a tuft of grass and as a rabbit; or the person whose face we are watching as both furiously angry and profoundly delighted. On the other hand, as an example of supplementary experiencing-as, we may see what is moving above us in the sky as a bird; we may further see it as a hawk; and we may further see it as a hawk engaged in searching for prey; and if we are extremely expert bird watchers we may even see it as a hawk about to swoop down on something on the far side of that low hump of ground. These are successively higher-level recognitions in the sense that each later member of the list presupposes and goes beyond the previous one.[9]

Hick thinks this illustrates the continuity between recognitions of a simpler sort, those concerned with rabbits for instance, and the far more elevated recognitions of religious awareness. What we must ask first, however, is whether this example works as it stands. Is it, in fact, a 'higher level" of awareness to recognize that a moving object is a bird? Does the class of all birds "include," i.e., is it more general than the class of all moving objects? Obviously not, since many moving objects are not birds, and birds do sit still. Is it a "higher level" recognition to know that a particular bird is a hawk, when the class of hawks is likewise smaller than the class of birds in general? True, it is a more specific piece of information, but as in our argument above we may not have learned it by acquaintance but by some other means, and knowledge by acquaintance *is* supposed to be the criterion and *point d'appui* of Hick's argument. Finally, knowing enough about the bird in question to be able to predict its impending behavior is more specific still, and may in fact have been learned by acquaintance, but it still lacks the necessary connection that one would hope a "higher level" recognition would have. This is simply to say that not all that swoops is a hawk. Hick, therefore, is right when he says that each of these details about the moving object that turns out to be hawk "goes beyond" the previous one, but he is wrong in saying that each later member of the list "presupposes" the previous one, certainly in any binding way. Most problematic of all, however, is that this example illustrates a progressively narrower and more specific knowledge about the object in question, whereas the religious awareness it is hopefully analogous to must of necessity be broader and less specific. The progression of religious awareness is not a spelling-out of the subclasses of our perceptions, but of our perceptions as subclasses of something far greater, as "physical situation" leads to "moral situation" and, finally, to "religious situation" in regard to a specific event. As was the case with the first three theses, it is hard to see that anything has been accomplished by the use of Hick's chosen example, and its failure to establish the hoped-for analogy is very damaging to his case.

2. The Varieties of Seeing-As

As we now see, Hick's claim for the coextensiveness of faith and perception rests on the conviction that all of one's experience, including the faith experience, is concerned to interpret material reality, not merely to acknowledge its presence. When this line of attack becomes too difficult to stick with, however, when it becomes apparent that identifying faith and perceptual experience too closely with each other leads, besides the objections voiced above, to positivistic objections about the absence of a perceptual object for these faith experiences, Hick reduces his claim to an analogical one. But, while his analogies are undoubtedly interesting, they add to that tenuousness endemic to analogical argument a decided lack of force at exactly those points where the analogies need to be strongest. I think the source of these problems is that Hick's notion of seeing-as is far too vague to work with. My contention is that once we have more amply described seeing-as, we may find that some instances of seeing-as do have some important common features with religious faith, although nowhere suggesting identity with it.

Consider the following five examples:

1. seeing a fork as a fork,
2. seeing a dot on the horizon as Don Quixote,
3. seeing the duck-rabbit of *Investigations* IIxi as a duck,
4. seeing a toy chest as a house,
5. seeing a geometric figure as a concave or a convex step.[10]

In (1) when someone comes to the table and sees a fork, he sees it correctly as a fork, and can be said to do so appropriately because, due perhaps to some visual problem created by the lighting or by a lack of perceptual acuity on his part, he *might* wrongly see it as something else, a spoon, an insect, or whatever. If seeing incorrectly, runs the arguments, includes seeing-as, so also must seeing correctly. Besides, who could ever see something and say he didn't see it as anything at all? In (2), I see a dot moving on the horizon, see it a bit later and closer as an animate figure, see it still later as a man on horseback, and finally see it to be Don Quixote on Rosinante his faithful steed. Here it is alleged that seeing a dot as an animate figure is first a potential instance of (1) and then a real instance of it. In the case of the duck-rabbit, (3), a more plainly legitimate instance, the figure is seen alternately as a picture of a duck or as a picture of a rabbit. The interesting difference between this example and the previous ones is that alternating descriptions of the figure are each correct, while in (1) we cannot switch back and forth between a fork seen as a fork and as an insect. Similarly, getting Quixote back to being a dot requires having him ride off into the distance again. Further, while forks are indeed forks and Quixote remains adamantly himself, whether in disguise or in the distance, the duck-rabbit is neither just a figure, nor a duck, nor a rabbit, but rather a picture of a duck or rabbit. Wittgenstein noted this oddity by saying that such a figure refers to something, but "indirectly."[11] Imagining a chest to be a house, (4), as children do in games, is also a species of seeing-as: the child sees the chest as a house, his companions as its residents, its top as a roof, and so on. While this may not obviously be a case of genuine visual seeing-as, we should not overlook the many behavioral indications that what the child sees there he sees as a house. Our final instance, (5), the concave-convex step figure, has some things in common with the earlier instances, but adds some interesting elements. With the duck-rabbit one cannot see the figure just as a figure, but in the house-chest one can, and in fact only ever does, see a chest, without the possibility of mutually exclusive alternate aspects. The step figure, on the other hand, can be seen as concave, convex, *or* as two-dimensional, i.e., without any interpretive third dimension added at all. Equally importantly, in (5) these alternate possibilities retain mutual exclusiveness.

Where, in these examples, can there be an adequate analogy for faith? (1), besides being, as Wittgenstein noted, an uninformative tautology,[12] demands that what we are seeing give clear evidence for what it is. The world, however, is not this clearly the arena of God's action, the full scope of which, for Hick, we can understand only in the life to come.[13] (2) suffers from the same problem, although it does show how one can learn to see something, a progressive element faith hopes lifelong to nurture. (3) introduces a feature quite important to faith, namely, that one's feelings of faith wax and wane throughout life, but it remains nonetheless firmly coupled to the purely representative character of what is seen. Faith wants more than simply a *picture* of how the world might or might not be. It wants, and paradoxically so, *both* is picture *and* the reality of the world as it is. (4), although it includes some of the benefits of (3), remains unalterably committed to the notion that what things are seen as is purely imaginary or fictive. (5), oddly enough, seems to present the best case for an analogy, in that it provides views of an object that may be either three-dimensional in one of two possible ways or simply two-dimensional. One may alternate these views without holding more than one at once, and one may start out seeing only one of them and learn to see the other two.

3. The Analogy of Faith

The case for an analogy between (5) and religious faith would have to be based on the following similarities. First, and foreseen perhaps by John Wisdom thirty years ago in his essay "Gods,"[14] in both faith as it sees the world and in the perception of the step figure there is something not unlike a decision to exclude certain possibilities: the figure is one of three possible and mutually exclusive views, and the world is either providentially governed or not. "Decision," of course, is not meant to refer to a judgment of a specific kind, but simply to this process of exclusion. Different individuals, believing and unbelieving, see the same world and, as Kant knew, can say equally justified but very different things about it at the same time. In (5), justification of the report of what is seen proceeds from the experience of the perceiver, who has learned at some time what steps look like, when things are convex or concave, and in which directions three-dimensional objects point. If I happen to be either temporarily or permanently "aspect blind"[15] about one of the ways the figure can be seen, I nevertheless can understand someone else's claim to seeing it that way. That is, his claim need not be unintelligible to me but merely frustrating. Again, although I might be "aspect blind" at the moment, it can clear to me that if there is another aspect and the necessary changes in my point of view occur, I too could see that aspect. Equally evident is that my ability to know when I am seeing something under a new aspect does not depend on my having seen that aspect before, while with (3) I must know what ducks and rabbits are to begin with.

Also important to this analogy is the accidental characteristic that the step figure is, so to speak, differently describable than the duck-rabbit. Describing the figure as convex or concave is as much a description of one's experience of it as it is a claim about the nature of the object: "I see it opening *this* way." That the figure is of a duck is a more publicly ascertainable fact than that the step figure is convex or concave as *I* see it; that God acts in the world is surely less ascertainable than that my neighbor does.

Can we really claim an analogy between (5) and religious faith? If by an analogy we mean something like a covert identity, of course not. The relation between God and man that is faith is a relation of which we can know only one of the terms for sure. We cannot know for certain, therefore, that faith is at all like anything else in our experience. If, however, by an analogy I mean a comparison which, although limited, can enhance my understanding of faith by some striking similarities to believing as I know it, then perhaps there is one. And, indeed, there is something like a decision or selectivity of views in each, there is a process by which experiences justify assertions which describe these views, particularly in regard to Christian beliefs in providence; there is tolerance for other views; there are criteria for recognition which do not necessarily require prior experience; and there is a certain privacy to the justifying of descriptive assertions which, though not something religion has always been comfortable with, seems unavoidable. None of this, plainly, will serve to establish that faith is a mode of "cognition in presence," nor will it make faith a kind of "experiencing-as." What it can tell us, and this hopefully is helpful, is that faith is not completely unlike the rest of our cognitive activties.

Notes

1. Ludwig Wittgenstein, *Philosophical Investigations,* trans. G. E. M. Anscombe (New York: Macmillan, 1953), p. 194. Hereafter referred to as *PI* (1953), with either page or section numbers.
2. "Religious Faith as Experiencing-As," in *Talk of God,* Royal Institute of Philosophy Lectures. II (1967–68), (London: Macmillan, 1969), pp. 20–35. Cf. Hick, *Faith and Knowledge* (Ithaca: Cornell University Press, 1957), pp. 109–196; *Philosophy of Religion,* Foundations of Philosophy Series (Englewood Cliffs: Prentice-Hall, 1963), pp. 70–77; *Christianity at the Center* (London: SCM Press, 1968), pp. 50–57. For a different approach to Hick's problem, see J. Wesley Robbins, "John Hick on Religious Experience and Perception," *International Journal for the Philosophy of Religion* (1974): 108–18.
3. Hick, "Religious Faith," pp. 25–28.
4. In all fairness, I must admit that Hick never explicitly asserts (A). On the other hand, the discussion of "Religious Faith," pp. 22–23 demands it, as does (B), not to mention its apparent use as a paradigm case.
5. See "The Nature of Faith," Chapter Five of Hick, *Faith and Knowledge,* pp. 95–119.
6. Hick, "Religious Faith," p. 35.
7. *Ibid.,* pp. 21–22.
8. *Ibid.,* p. 25.
9. *Ibid.,* p. 28. The putative consequences are discussed on pp. 28–31.
10. Cf. *PI* (1953), pp. 195, 197, 206, 203.
11. *Ibid.,* pp. 193–94.
12. *Ibid.,* p. 195.
13. Cf. the notion of "eschatological verification," discussed in *Faith and Knowledge,* pp. 169–199.
14. In *Logic and Language,* ed. Anthony Flew (Garden City: Doubleday, 1965), pp. 194–214.
15. *PI* (1953), pp. 213–14.

27. John Hick on Religious Experience and Perception

J. WESLEY ROBBINS

In several of his writings Professor John Hick has sought to point out certain parallels between religious experience and perception in order to make it more difficult to justify treating religious experience and perceptual experience differentially so far as their being sources of knowledge is concerned.

In his latest work,[1] Hick has again taken up this theme. He asks us to consider the case of a theistic believer who has certain distinctively religious experiences (which a non-religious person does not have) and who, because of these experiences, considers himself to be experientially aware of God (to know God). This case, he argues, is paralleled in certain important ways by the case of a percipient who has certain perceptual experiences and who, because of these experiences, considers himself to be perceptually aware of the physical world. Against those critics who would argue that religious experience cannot reasonably be considered to provide an experiential awareness of God, the main thrust of Hick's argument is that, given the parallels between the two cases, if one were to deny the legitimacy of the theistic believer's considering himself to be experientially aware of God, then one would also have to deny the legitimacy of any ordinary percipient's considering himself to be perceptually aware of the physical world.

In what follows I want to show that Hick has failed to provide any good reason for believing that the alleged parallels between the two cases, upon which his argument depends, in fact exist.

Both the experiential awareness of God and the perceptual awareness of physical objects can profitably be thought of as involving three elements:

1. certain states of the person—religious experiential states in the one case, perceptual states in the other;
2. the object or reality in question—the Judaeo-Christian God in the one case, physical objects in the other;

Source: J. Wesley Robbins, "John Hick on Religious Experience and Perception," *International Journal for Philosophy and Religion* (1974), 108–18. A portion of the research for this paper was subsidized through an Indiana University Faculty Summer Fellowship.

3. an appropriate relation between the states of the person and the object—e.g., that the latter causes the former in a certain manner.

In order for there to be instances, respectively, of persons' being experientially aware of God or of persons' perceiving physical objects certain states of the person are a necessary condition. Theories of religious experience and of perception, respectively, are especially devoted to specifying exactly what states of the person are necessary (e.g., is being presented with sense data a necessary condition of a person's perceiving physical objects?) and what the nature of these states is (e.g., do a person's perceptual states consist in certain behavioral dispositions?). Additionally they are concerned with determining to what extent, if any, the specified states provide knowledge of the object in question.

With the case of perception as an example, a distinction can now be made between a general and a specific sceptical question concerning the occurrence of instances of a person's perceiving physical objects:

  a. given that it is logically possible that the very perceptual states (1) (whatever they may be) which are a necessary condition of a person's perceiving physical objects should occur in the absence of the additional elements (2) and (3), how could a person who knows that he is in the appropriate perceptual states ever know that he is in fact perceiving some physical object(s)?
  b. given that the perceptual states which are a necessary condition of a person's perceiving physical objects are of a specific sort (e.g., that they include the person's having sense data), how could a person who knows that he is in the appropriate perceptual state (who knows, e.g., that he is having sense data of a certain sort) ever determine from that specific basis that he is in fact perceiving some physical object(s)?

The former question (a) would apply to any account of perception regardless of how it viewed the nature of the perceptual states (1). But Hick's arguments are not directed against those who would raise this general question.

Hick is concerned with those critics who would raise the specific question (b) against religious experience but not against perceptual experience. Such individuals may be taken as holding that, given the nature of religious experiential states (1), any claims to be experientially aware of God are unwarranted and gratuitous, whereas such is not the case with perceptual states and the claim to be perceptually aware of physical objects.

In response to this sort of contention, Hick's thesis may be stated as follows:

> since the states of a person (1) which are a necessary condition of his being experientially aware of God are of the same sort as those which are a necessary condition of his being perceptually aware of physical objects, the presence of specific states of this sort is not peculiar to the case of religious experience, and thus does not provide good reason for holding that although persons can on occasion justifiably consider themselves to be perceptually aware of physical objects, they could never justifiably consider themselves to be experientially aware of God.

In support of this line of argument Hick contends that a necessary condition of both a person's being experientially aware of God and a person's being perceptually aware of physical objects is an awareness of a medium epistemologically prior to the awareness of the ultimate object (God in the one case, physical objects in the other) and an interpretation, or taking, of this medium, in the absence of logically sufficient evidence, as being the medium of the reality of the ultimate object in question.[2] The presence of this sort of interpretation of one thing as being a medium of the reality of something else does not, then, by itself provide a good reason for denying that there are instances of a person's being experientially aware of God unless one is also prepared to cite it as a good reason for denying that there are instances of a person's being perceptually aware of physical objects.

Let us suppose, for the sake of the argument, that the principal reason for someone's denying that there are any instances of a person's being experientially aware of God is the fact that states of the person such as those described by Hick would be necessary components. The sceptical question would be of the specific sort (b): given that such a state consists in the person's taking something (which in and of itself has nothing, logically or evidentially, to do with God) as being the medium of God's reality, how can a person who knows that he is in the appropriate religious experiential state ever justifiably consider himself, on that basis, to be experientially aware of God? We might put the sceptical question in this way: how can a person's simply taking it for granted that something is so (e.g., that there is a God) ever provide a basis for his justifiably considering himself to be aware that something is so (e.g., that there is a God)? And since, in effect, this is what a person's religious experiential states consist in, how can anyone ever determine from that specific basis that he is in fact experientially aware of God? For would not that simply amount to reasserting what had already been taken for granted in the first place? Would not this be a case of what Hick himself calls "a subjective response which gratuitously projects meanings into the world"[3] rather than the awareness of some objective reality?

Before we look at the alleged parallel with the case of perception, we need to examine in more detail Hick's account of religious experience. Hick adopts the standard criticisms of the usual arguments for the existence of God. He holds that there is nothing about the physical world, or about morality, which provides premises for an argument that conclusively demonstrates that there is a God, or for one that makes such a conclusion even probable. It is further his belief that, for reasons having to do both with the nature of God and the preservation of human personality, God would not be available as a direct (immediate) object of experiential awareness.

On Hick's view it is a necessary condition of a person's being experientially aware of God that he take what in and of itself offers no logically acceptable evidence for the reality of God—the physical world, events in human history, moral experience—as being the medium of God's reality. Of course this interpretative state of the person does not itself suffice as being an instance of a person's being experientially aware of God. If there be a God, he is not created as part of the interpretative state of the human believer. But such an interpretative state of the person is necessary because if there is a God at all, his way with humans must be indirect so as to preserve their freedom and integrity as persons in the face of his being. Apart from such an interpretative state persons would, so to speak, have their minds on nothing that is God. In such a case even if there were a God such persons would overlook him. For these reasons Hick argues that there would be no such thing as a person's being experientially aware of God apart from the person's being in the interpretative state of taking something that in and of itself is evidentially insufficient and ambiguous as far as the reality of God is concerned as being the medium of God's reality.

It is precisely this interpretative state of the person which Hick describes as the theistic "sense of the presence of God." The question, then, is one of the reliability of this state. Since this state is, according to Hick, a necessary condition for a person's being experientially aware of God, there are two alternatives. One can consider it to be unreliable, i.e., its occurrence is no indication of the fulfillment of the other required conditions, and hold that there are no instances of a person's being experientially aware of God. Or, if one is going to hold that there are such instances, one must consider these states to be reliable in at least some cases since it is only through them that a person can be aware of the object in question.

We have, then, the following confrontation. On the one hand a sceptic asks how a person could ever be experientially aware of God given that what he would have to do— because of the lack of logically acceptable evidence—is to "jump to the conclusion" that there is a God. But, on the other hand, Hick argues that just such an arrangement is what is to be expected, given that the experiential awareness would involve God on the one hand and human individuals on the other. This demands the very indirectness and ambiguity which the sceptic sees as making awareness of God impossible.

It is in connection with this account of religious experience that Hick makes the claim that exactly the same sort of interpretative state of the person is a necessary condition for the occurrence of any instances of a person's perceiving physical objects, and that in that case such a state is not considered to make perceptual awareness of physical objects impossible. Quite the contrary, the occurrence of just this sort of interpretative state is normally taken as an indication of the fulfillment of the other conditions of a person's perceiving physical objects. In this case, the claim that there are instances of persons perceiving physical objects is justified, and the accompanying belief in the reality of the physical world is reasonable, at least for those persons who find themselves in the appropriate perceptual state. Consistency therefore demands that the same assessment be made in the case of those persons who find themselves in the analogous religious experiential state.

To hold that the cases in question are parallel, Hick must argue that a necessary condition of a person's perceiving physical objects is the person's being in the interpretative state of taking something in and of itself evidentially insufficient and ambiguous as far as the reality of the physical world is concerned, as being the medium of the physical world's reality nonetheless. And this is exactly what he does hold. He speaks in *Faith and Knowledge* (p. 109) of one's phenomenal experience which in and of itself is just "there" to be interpreted—itself offering no sufficient evidence of the reality of a world of physical objects. The first step—interpreting this phenomenal data as being the medium of the physical world's reality—is, in Hick's words, "unevidenced and unevidenceable." And apart from this interpretative step, the physical world (if there is one) would remain hidden and unrevealed. As in the case of God, apart from such a state persons would have their minds on nothing that is a world of physical objects. They would have their minds only on their own private phenomenal experience. Even if there were a world of physical objects, such persons would overlook it.

There is, then, little question that Hick believes both religious experience and perceptual experience to involve states of the person that are exactly similar in that they consist in the person's taking something that is in and of itself evidentially insufficient and ambiguous as being the medium of the reality of something else. In both cases it is argued that, apart from the person's being in this interpretative state, the object in question, if there is such, would remain unrevealed and unknown. In both cases the alternatives are the same. If, for some reason, one considers such a state to be unreliable, then one must conclude that there are no instances of a person's being experientially aware (of God or of the physical world). Whereas, if one believes that there are such instances, one must consider such an interpretative state to be reliable, serving as an adequate indication to the person that the other conditions of his being experientially aware (of God or of physical objects) are also fulfilled.

Now in the case of religious experience Hick does have certain fairly definite reasons (whatever one may think of their soundness) for holding that the interpretative state in question is indeed a necessary condition of a person's being experientially aware of God. However, the matter is not so clear in the case of perception. If it is held, as Hick does, that the latter is also a form of mediated awareness, it would have to be for different reasons. For presumably there is no reason to suppose that confrontation with physical objects *per se* would be destructive of human freedom or of personal identity.

The question is: what reasons are there for holding that a necessary condition of a person's perceiving physical objects is the person's having before his mind something itself evidentially insufficient and ambiguous so far as the reality of the physical world is concerned and yet interpreting this to be the medium of the reality of the physical world? So far as I can determine, Hick has one reason to offer, namely that solipsism is a theoretical possibility which cannot decisively be refuted by any sort of philosophical reasoning. Thus in his essay "Sceptics and Believers" he says:

> . . . in neither case can we prove demonstratively, or even show to be probable, that the object of our cognition exists independently of those states of mind in which we suppose ourselves to be cognizing it. If anyone were seriously inclined to interpret his sense experience solipsistically we could not expect to argue him out of this.[4]

And in *Arguments for the Existence for God:*

> In each instance a realm of putatively cognitive experience is taken to be veridical and is acted upon as such, even though its veridical character cannot be logically demonstrated. (p. 110)
> . . . In each case there is a solipsist alternative in which one can affirm *solus ipse* to the exclusion of the transcendent . . .
> . . . It should be noted that this analogy . . . is grounded in our awareness of an objective external world as such and turns upon the contrast between this and a theoretically possible solipsist interpretation of the same stream of conscious experience. (p. 112–13)

If I am correct, Hick's response, if challenged concerning the necessity of a person's being in an interpretative state of the short in question as part of his perceiving physical objects, would be an argument along the following lines:

1. Given a person's perceptual states on any given occasion, it is logically possible for the person to consider these to be either unrelated to a public physical

environment, or to be related to a public physical environment in such a way as to be an instance of his perceiving physical objects;

2. It is a necessary condition for a person to perceive physical objects that he "have physical objects in mind" (as opposed to "having in mind" only something that is essentially private, e.g., sense data);

3. Therefore, a necessary condition of a person's perceiving physical objects is his being in the interpretative state of taking something (phenomenal experience) that in and of itself is evidentially insufficient and ambiguous so far as the reality of the physical world is concerned as being the medium of the physical world's reality.

This response is clearly unsatisfactory. It involves a confusion of what I referred to earlier as the general sceptical question (a) with the specific sceptical question (b). It holds that since it is logically possible for a person's perceptual states (whatever they may be specifically) to occur in the absence of the additional conditions which together constitute his perceiving physical objects (a), the person's perceptual states must therefore be of a certain specific sort (b)—they must include the interpretative state previously described.

Even if we grant premise (1), which is an admission of the point made in the general sceptical question (a), and even if we grant premise (2), which says that a person cannot correctly be described as perceiving physical objects unless he *in some way* "has his mind on" physical objects; it by no means follows that the only way in which this can be done is by means of the sort of interpretative state that Hick contends is necessary.

The following is an alternative account of perception (essentially that developed by George Pitcher,[5] which admits these points without including Hick's interpretative state as one of the necessary perceptual states. According to this account the basic perceptual states of a person are belief-states of a certain specified sort, which are beliefs about physical objects in the first place. Thus, for example, the expression "Person Q sees an x that is at place u" is analyzed in the following manner:

i. There is an x at place u;

ii. Person Q is caused to receive by means of the use of his eyes in the standard visual way the belief that there is a y at place w, where at least some components of this belief are true of the x at u;

iii. The x at place u is involved in the generation of the perceptual state (ii) in a manner specified by examples, e.g., as when I look at my hand in good light my hand is causally responsible for its looking to me as though there is a hand before me.

(Different letters are used in (ii) to allow for cases in which the thing that is seen—the x, for example, a leaf—looks to the person like something else—y, for example, a bird.)

This account agrees with premise (2) above that in order for a person to be correctly described as perceiving physical objects he must "have his mind on" physical objects. But it holds that this necessary condition is accomplished by the person's being in one or another of the states of believing, being inclined to believe, or having the suppressed inclination to believe, for example, that there is some physical object x at place u. It expressly denies that this perceptual state consists in the person's interpreting something evidentially ambiguous (sense data) as being a medium of the physical world's reality.

At the same time it admits that it is logically possible for a person to be in the belief-states which are said to constitute the perceptual states of the person necessary for a person's perceiving physical objects even though these belief-states are not produced by the physical objects thought to be perceived, but by some other means. In such a case what occurs would not be an instance of a person's perceiving some physical object(s). The point of the general sceptical question (a) is admitted, namely that it is impossible to demonstrate, solely from the occurrence of those perceptual states of the person deemed necessary for a person's perceiving some physical objects, that the other, additional conditions are also fulfilled, i.e. that there are instances of a person's perceiving physical objects. The general sceptical question (a) is met by arguing that the supposition that the other, additional conditions are in fact met offers a more plausible, simple explanation in most cases of the occurrence of the specified perceptual states of the person than do other available explanations. One reason for preferring this alternative account to an account of perception such as Hick's, which holds that perception is a mediated form of awareness, is precisely that the former is not open to the specific sort of sceptical question (b) concerning those interpretative states of the person which are crucial to Hick's account.

The point is this. Hick's defense of the claim that there are instances of a person's being experientially aware of God rests upon his contending that the occurrence of a perceptual state exactly similar in character to an interpretative state which he holds to be a necessary condition of a person's being experientially aware of God does not in the former case stop us from holding that there are instances of persons' perceiving physical objects. Consistency therefore demands that the occurrence of just such an interpretative state in the latter case not be a reason for holding that there are not instances of a persons' being experientially aware of God. There is, on this particular point, nothing to be said against persons who take the alternative of considering the religious interpretative state to be reliable, thus holding that there are instances of persons being experientially aware of God.

But, as we have seen, Hick offers no good reason for supposing that a perceptual interpretative state of the sort in question is indeed a necessary condition of a person's perceiving physical objects. The alternative account which has been outlined admits the points which he makes, but yet accommodates these in a theory of perception which does not include the sort of interpretative state which Hick describes. From the point of view of this alternative account of perception one can quite consistently hold that there are instances of a person's perceiving physical objects (as outlined above) and yet remain sceptical as to the occurrence of instances of persons' being experientially aware of God—on the ground that the latter *would* involve as a necessary condition a person's being in the very sort of interpretative state described by Hick.

Finally, it would be useless for Hick to shift his thesis and argue that since exactly the same sceptical question (a) applies in both the cases of perception and religious experience, there is no justification for holding that a person can know in the one case that he is perceiving physical objects, but not know in the other case that he is experientially aware of God. For then we have solely the point raised in the general sceptical question (a). But this point cannot be discussed in any deatil until some account is offered as to the specific perceptual and/or religious experiential states thought to be necessary components of the two sorts of cases. As we have seen, Hick has specific religious, theological reasons for holding that a religious interpretative state of the sort described is indeed a necessary condition of a person's being experientially aware of God. But once this specific point about the conditions for a person's being experientially aware of God is made, the sceptical question of the specific sort (b), about this particular religious experiential state of the person, arises. At this point it will do no good to shift back to the general sceptical question (a) and point out that it can still be raised about perceptual states as well as about religious experiential states. For, unless the same sort of specific sceptical question (b) which is raised about religious experiential states can now also be raised about perceptual states, the general question will be beside the point, given the specific religious interpretative state described by Hick.

It is my conclusion that Hick has failed to make good his case for the claim that a person who finds himself in the religious experiential state which he calls "the sense of the presence of God" has as good reason to consider himself to be experientially aware of God as the person who finds himself in the appropriate perceptual states has for considering himself to be perceptually aware of physical objects. The principal reason for this failure would seem to be the preferability of an account of perception which has no place for, and no need for, the sort of interpretative state of the person which is crucial to Hick's argument.

Notes

1. John Hick, *Arguments for the Existence of God* (New York: Herder and Herder, 1971). chap. 7.
2. John Hick, *Faith and Knowledge,* 2nd ed., (Ithaca, New York: Cornell University Press, 1966), chap. 5.
3. John Hick, "Religious Faith as Experiencing-As," in *Royal Instirute of Philosophy Lectures,* Vol. II (New York: St. Martin's Press, 1969), p. 26.
4. John Hick, "Sceptics and Believers," in *Faith and the Philosophers* (New York: St. Martin's Press, 1964), p. 244.
5. George Pitcher, *A Theory of Perception* (Princeton, New Jersey: Princeton University Press, 1971).

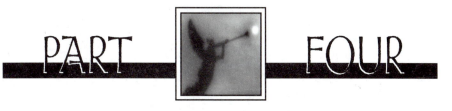

PART FOUR

The Rationality of Religious Faith

In this section, we return to the question of whether religious faith can be said to be rational or irrational. Ludwig Wittgenstein (1938) asks whether believers and unbelievers are even capable of understanding one another, since the structure of believers' thought and experience seems incommensurate with the rational standards adhered to by others. The discrepancy between believing forms of life and their language games and unbelieving forms appears to create a logical and experiential impasse that challenges the notion that there is a single standard for rationality. Other essayists in this section take seriously the notion that the framework principles of rationality itself are shaped by cultural-linguistic and communal systems and examine the implications that this way of thinking has for assessing the meaning, truth, and justification of religious faith claims. Norman Malcolm (1977), expressing support for the direction of Wittgenstein's inquiry, indicates that the making of claims, along with their verification and justification, occurs within such cultural-linguistic systems. Alvin Plantinga (1981), Jay Van Hook (1981), and Nicholas Wolsterstorff (1981) offer different perspectives on how religious faith may justifiably shape the convictions of the believer in ways that are foreign to the understanding of the outsider. Michael Martin (1990) raises objections to Plantinga's Reformed epistemology in particular, but his criticisms flag deeper concerns about the claim that rationality itself is tied to cultural-linguistic forms of life.

28. Lectures
on Religious Belief

LUDWIG WITTGENSTEIN

I

An Austrian general said to someone: "I shall think of you after my death, if that should be possible." We can imagine one group who would find this ludicrous, another who wouldn't.

(During the war, Wittgenstein saw consecrated bread being carried in chromium steel. This struck him as ludicrous.)

Suppose that someone believed in the Last Judgement, and I don't, does this mean that I believe the opposite to him, just that there won't be such a thing? I would say: "not at all, or not always."

Suppose I say that the body will rot, and another says "No. Particles will rejoin in a thousand years, and there will be a Resurrection of you."

If some said: "Wittgenstein, do you believe in this?" I'd say: "No." "Do you contradict the man?" I'd say: "No."

If you say this, the contradiction already lies in this.

Would you say: "I believe the opposite," or "There is no reason to suppose such a thing"? I'd say neither.

Suppose someone were a believer and said: "I believe in a Last Judgement," and I said: "Well, I'm not so sure. Possibly." You would say that there is an enormous gulf between us. If he said "There is a German aeroplane overhead," and I said "Possibly I'm not so sure," you'd say we were fairly near.

It isn't a question of my being anywhere near him, but on an entirely different plane, which you could express by saying: "You mean something altogether different, Wittgenstein."

The difference might not show up at all in any explanation of the meaning.

Why is it that in this case I seem to be missing the entire point?

Source: Ludwig Wittgenstein, *Lectures and Conversations on Aesthetics, Psychology, and Religious Belief,* translated/edited by Cyril Barrett (Berkeley, CA.: University of California Press, 1996), pp. 53–66.

Suppose somebody made this guidance for this life: believing in the Last Judgment. Whenever he does anything, this is before his mind. In a way, how are we to know whether to say he believes this will happen or not?

Asking him is not enough. He will probably say he has proof.

But he has what you might call an unshakeable belief. It will show, not by reasoning or by appeal to ordinary grounds for belief, but rather by regulating for in all his life.

This is a very much stronger fact—foregoing pleasures, always appealing to this picture. This is one sense must be called the firmest of all beliefs, because the man risks things on account of it which he would not do on things which are by far better established for him. Although he distinguishes between things well-established and not well-established.

Lewy: Surely, he would say it is extremely well-established.

First, he may use "well-established" or not use it at all. He will treat this belief as extremely well-established, and in another way as not well-established at all.

If we have a belief, in certain cases we appeal again and again to certain grounds, and at the same time we risk pretty little—if it came to risking our lives on the ground of this belief.

There are instances where you have a faith—where you say "I believe"—and on the other hand this belief does not rest on the fact on which our ordinary everyday beliefs normally do rest.

How should we compare beliefs with each other? What would it mean to compare them?

You might say: 'We compare the states of mind.'

How do we compare states of mind? This obviously won't do for all occasions. First, what you say won't be taken as the measure for the firmness of a belief? But, for instance, what risks you would take?

The strength of a belief is not comparable with the intensity of a pain.

An entirely different way of comparing beliefs is seeing what sorts of grounds he will give.

A belief isn't like a momentary state of mind. "At 5 o'clock he had very bad toothache."

Suppose you had two people, and one of them, when he had to decide which course to take, thought of retribution, and the other did not. One person might, for instance, be inclined to take everything that happened to him as a reward or punishment, and another person doesn't think of this at all.

If he is ill, he may think: "What have I done to deserve this?" This is one way of thinking of retribution. Another way is, he thinks in a general way whenever he is ashamed of himself: "This will be punished."

Take two people, one of whom talks of his behaviour and of what happens to him in terms of retribution, the other one does not. These people think entirely differently. Yet, so far, you can't say they believe different things.

Suppose someone is ill and he says: "This is a punishment," and I say: "If I'm ill, I don't think of punishment at all." If you say: "Do you believe the opposite?"—you can call it believing the opposite, but it is entirely different from what we would normally call believing the opposite.

I think differently, in a different way. I say different things to myself. I have different pictures.

It is this way: if someone said: "Wittgenstein, you don't take illness as punishment, so what do you believe?"—I'd say: "I don't have any thoughts of punishment."

There are, for instance, these entirely different ways of thinking first of all—which needn't be expressed by one person saying one thing, another person another thing.

What we call believing in a Judgement Day or not believing in a Judgement Day— The expression of belief may play an absolutely minor role.

If you ask me whether or not I believe in a Judgement Day, in the sense in which religious people have belief in it, I wouldn't say: "No. I don't believe there will be such a thing." It would seem to me utterly crazy to say this.

And then I give an explanation: "I don't believe in . . . ," but then the religious person never believes what I describe.

I can't say. I can't contradict that person.

In one sense, I understand all he says—the English words "God," "separate," etc. I understand. I could say: "I don't believe in this," and this would be true, meaning I haven't got these thoughts or anything that hangs together with them. But not that I could contradict the thing.

You might say: "Well, if you can't contradict him, that means you don't understand him. If you did understand him, then you might." That again is Greek to me. My normal technique of language leaves me. I don't know whether to say they understand one another or not.

These controversies look quite different from any normal controversies. Reasons look entirely different from normal reasons.

They are, in a way, quite inconclusive.

The point is that if there were evidence, this would in fact destroy the whole business.

Anything that I normally call evidence wouldn't in the slightest influence me.

Suppose, for instance, we knew people who foresaw the future; make forecasts for years and years ahead; and they described some sort of a Judgement Day. Queerly enough, even if there were such a thing, and even if it were more convincing than I have described but, belief in this happening wouldn't be at all a religious belief.

Suppose that I would have to forego all pleasures because of such a forecast. If I do so and so, someone will put me in fires in a thousand years, etc. I wouldn't budge. The best scientific evidence is just nothing.

A religious belief might in fact fly in the face of such a forecast, and say "No. There it will break down."

As it were, the belief as formulated on the evidence can only be the last result—in which a number of ways of thinking and acting crystallize and come together.

A man would fight for his life not to be dragged into the fire. No induction. Terror. That is, as it were, part of the substance of the belief.

That is partly why you don't get in religious controversies, the form of controversy where one person is *sure* of the thing, and the other says: 'Well, possibly.'

You might be surprised that there hasn't been opposed to those who believe in Resurrection those who say "Well, possibly."

Here believing obviously plays much more this role: suppose we said that a certain picture might play the role of constantly admonishing me, or I always think of it. Here, an enormous difference would be between those people for whom the picture is constantly in the foreground, and the others who just didn't use it at all.

Those who said: "Well, possibly it may happen and possibly not" would be on an entirely different plane.

This is partly why one would be reluctant to say: "These people rigorously hold the opinion (or view) that there is a Last Judgement." "Opinion" sounds queer.

It is for this reason that different words are used: 'dogma,' 'faith.'

We don't talk about hypothesis, or about high probability. Nor about knowing.

In a religious discourse we use such expressions as: "I believe that so and so will happen," and use them differently to the way in which we use them in science.

Although, there is a great temptation to think we do. Because we do talk of evidence, and do talk of evidence by experience.

We could even talk of historic events.

It has been said that Christianity rests on an historic basis.

It has been said a thousand times by intelligent people that indubitability is not enough in this case. Even if there is as much evidence as for Napoleon. Because the indubitability wouldn't be enough to make me change my whole life.

It doesn't rest on an historic basis in the sense that the ordinary belief in historic facts could serve as a foundation.

Here we have a belief in historic facts different from a belief in ordinary historic facts. Even, they are not treated as historical, empirical, propositions.

Those people who had faith didn't apply the doubt which would ordinarily apply to *any* historical propositions. Especially propositions of a time long past, etc.

What is the criterion of reliability, dependability? Suppose you give a general description as to when you say a proposition has a reasonable weight of probability. When you call it reasonable, is this *only* to say that for it you have such and such evidence, and for others you haven't?

For instance, we don't trust the account given of an event by a drunk man.

Father O'Hara[1] is one of those people who make it a question of science.

Here we have people who treat this evidence in a different way. They base things on evidence which taken in one way would seem exceedingly flimsy. They base enormous things on this evidence. Am I to say they are unreasonable? I wouldn't call them unreasonable.

I would say, they are certainly not *reasonable*, that's obvious.

'Unreasonable' implies, with everyone, rebuke.

I want to say: they don't treat this as a matter of reasonability.

Anyone who reads the Epistles will find it said: not only that it is not reasonable, but that it is folly.

Not only is it not reasonable, but it doesn't pretend to be.

What seems to me ludicrous about O'Hara is his making it appear to be *reasonable*.

Why shouldn't one form of life culminate in an utterance of belief in a Last Judgement? But I couldn't either say "Yes" or "No" to the statement that there will be such a thing. Nor "Perhaps," nor "I'm not sure."

It is a statement which may not allow of any such answer.

If Mr. Lewy is religious and says he believes in a Judgement Day, I won't even know whether to say I understand him or not. I've read the same things as he's read. In a most important sense, I know what he means.

If an atheist says: "There won't be a Judgment Day, and another person says there will," do they mean the same?—Not clear what criterion of meaning the same is. They might describe the same things. You might say, this already shows that they mean the same.

We come to an island and we find beliefs there, and certain beliefs we are inclined to call religious. What I'm driving at is, that religious beliefs will not . . . They have sentences, and there are also religious statements.

These statements would not just differ in respect to what they are about. Entirely different connections would make them into religious beliefs, and there can easily be imagined transitions where we wouldn't know for our life whether to call them religious beliefs or scientific beliefs.

You may say they reason wrongly.

In certain cases you would say they reason wrongly, meaning they contradict us. In other cases you would say they don't reason at all, or "It is an entirely different kind of reasoning." The first, you would say in the case in which they reason in a similar way to us, and make something corresponding to our blunders.

Whether a thing is a blunder or not—it is a blunder in a particular system. Just as something is a blunder in a particular game and not in another.

You could also say that where we are reasonable, they are not reasonable—meaning they don't use *reason* here.

If they do something very like one of our blunders, I would say, I don't know. It depends on further surroundings of it.

It is difficult to see, in cases in which it has all the appearances of trying to be reasonable.

I would definitely call O'Hara unreasonable. I would say, if this is religious belief, then it's all superstition.

But I would ridicule it, not by saying it is based on insufficient evidence. I would say: here is a man who is cheating himself. You can say: this man is ridiculous because he believes, and bases it on weak reasons.

II

The word 'God' is amongst the earliest learnt—pictures and catechisms, etc. But not the same consequences as with pictures of aunts. I wasn't shown [that which the picture pictured].

The word is used like a word representing a person. God sees, rewards, etc.

"Being shown all these things, did you understand what this word meant?" I'd say: "Yes and no. I did learn what it didn't mean. I made myself understand. I could answer questions, understand questions when they were put in different ways—and in that sense could be said to understand."

If the question arises as to the existence of a god or God, it plays an entirely differ-ent role to that of the existence of any person or object I ever heard of. One said, had to say, that one *believed* in the existence, and if one did not believe, this was regarded as something bad. Normally if I did not believe in the existence of something no one would think there was anything wrong in this.

Also, there is this extraordinary use of the word 'believe.' One talks of believing and at the same time one doesn't use 'believe' as one does ordinarily. You might say (in the normal use): "You only believe—oh well. . . ." Here it is used entirely differently; on the other hand it is not used as we generally use the word 'know'.

If I even vaguely remember what I was taught about God, I might say: "Whatever believing in God may be, it can't be believing in something we can test, or find means of testing." You might say: "This is nonsense, because people say they believe on *evidence* or say they believe on religious experiences." I would say: "The mere fact that someone says they believe on evidence doesn't tell me enough for me to be able to say now whether I can say of a sentence 'God exists' that your evidence is unsatisfactory or insufficient."

Suppose I know someone, Smith. I've heard that he has been killed in a battle in this war. One day you come to me and say: "Smith is in Cambridge." I inquire, and find you stood at Guild-hall and saw at the other end a man and said: "That was Smith." I'd say: "Listen. This isn't sufficient evidence." If we had a fair amount of evi-dence he was killed I would try to make you say that you're being credulous. Suppose he was never heard of again. Needless to say, it is quite impossible to make inquiries: "Who at 12.05 passed Market Place into Rose Crescent?" Suppose you say: "He was there." I would be extremely puzzled.

Suppose there is a feast on Mid-Summer Common. A lot of people stand in a ring. Suppose this is done every year and then everyone says he has seen one of his dead rela-tives on the other side of the ring. In this case, we could ask everyone in the ring. "Who did you hold by the hand?" Nevertheless, we'd all say that on that day we see our dead relatives. You could in this case say: "I had an extraordinary experience. I had the expe-rience I can express by saying: 'I saw my dead cousin.'" Would we say you are saying this on insufficient evidence? Under certain circumstances I would say this, under other circumstances I wouldn't. Where what is said sounds a bit absurd I would say: "Yes, in this case insufficient evidence." If altogether absurd, then I wouldn't.

Suppose I went to somewhere like Lourdes in France. Suppose I went with a very credulous person. There we see blood coming out of something. He says: "There you are, Wittgenstein, how can you doubt?" I'd say: "Can it only be explained one way? Can't it be this or that?" I'd try to convince him that he'd seen nothing of any conse-quence. I wonder whether I would do that under all circumstances. I certainly know that I would under normal circumstances.

"Oughtn't one after all to consider this?" I'd say: "Come on. Come on." I would treat the phenomenon in this case just as I would treat an experiment in a laboratory which I thought badly executed.

"The balance moves when I will it to move." I point out it is not covered up, a draught can move it, etc.

I could imagine that someone showed an extremely passionate belief in such a phenomenon, and I couldn't approach his belief at all by saying: "This could just as well have been brought about by so and so" because he could think this blasphemy on my side. Or he might say: "It is possible that these priests cheat, but nevertheless in a different sense a miraculous phenomenon takes place there."

I have a statue which bleeds on such and such a day in the year. I have red ink, etc. "You are a cheat, but nevertheless the Deity uses you. Red ink in a sense, but not red ink in a sense."

Cf. Flowers at seance with label. People said: "Yes, flowers are materialized with label." What kind of circumstances must there be to make this kind of story not ridiculous?

I have a moderate education, as all of you have, and therefore know what is meant by insufficient evidence for a forecast. Suppose someone dreamt of the Last Judgement, and said he now knew what it would be like. Suppose someone said: "This is poor evidence." I would say: "If you want to compare it with the evidence for it's raining to-morrow it is no evidence at all." He may make it sound as if by stretching the point you may call it evidence. But it may be more than ridiculous as evidence. But now, would I be prepared to say: "You are basing your belief on extremely slender evidence, to put it mildly." Why should I regard this dream as evidence—measuring its validity as though I were measuring the validity of the evidence for meteorological events?

If you compare it with anything in Science which we call evidence, you can't credit that anyone could soberly argue: "Well, I had this dream . . . therefore . . . Last Judgement." You might say: "For a blunder, that's too big." If you suddenly wrote numbers down on the blackboard, and then said: "Now, I'm going to add," and then said: "2 and 21 is 13," etc. I'd say: "This is no blunder."

There are cases where I'd say he's mad, or he's making fun. Then there might be cases where I look for an entirely different interpretation altogether. In order to see what the explanation is I should have to see the sum, to see in what way it is done, what he makes follow from it, what are the different circumstances under which he does it, etc.

I mean, if a man said to me after a dream that he believed in the Last Judgement, I'd try to find what sort of impression it gave him. One attitude: "It will be in about 2,000 years. It will be bad for so and so and so, etc." Or it may be one of terror. In the case where there is hope, terror, etc., would I say there is insufficient evidence if he says: "I believe . . ."? I can't treat these words as I normally treat 'I believe so and so.' It would be entirely beside the point, and also if he said his friend so and so and his grandfather had had the dream and believed, it would be entirely beside the point.

I would not say: "If a man said he dreamt it would happen to-morrow," would he take his coat? etc.

Case where Lewy has visions of his dead friend. Cases where you don't try to locate him. And case where you try to locate him in a business-like way. Another case where I'd say: "We can pre-suppose we have a broad basis on which we agree."

In general, if you say: "He is dead" and I say: "He is not dead" no-one would say: "Do they mean the same thing by 'dead'?" In the case where a man has visions I wouldn't offhand say: "He means something different."

Cf. A person having persecution mania.

What is the criterion for meaning something different? Not only what he takes as evidence for it, but also how he reacts, that he is in terror, etc.

How am I to find out whether this proposition is to be regarded as an empirical proposition—'You'll see your dead friend again?' Would I say: "He is a bit superstitious?" Not a bit.

He might have been apologetic. (The man who stated it categorically was more intelligent than the man who was apologetic about it).

'Seeing a dead friend,' again means nothing much to me at all. I don't think in these terms. I don't say to myself: "I shall see so and so again" ever.

He always says it, but he doesn't make any search. He puts on a queer smile. "His story had that dreamlike quality." My answer would be in this case "Yes," and a particular explanation.

Take "God created man.' Pictures of Michelangelo showing the creation of the world. In general, there is nothing which explains the meanings of words as well as a picture, and I take it that Michelangelo was as good as anyone can be and did his best, and here is the picture of the Deity creating Adam.

If we ever saw this, we certainly wouldn't think this the Deity. The picture has to be used in an entirely different way if we are to call the man in that queer blanket 'God,' and so on. You could imagine that religion was taught by means of these pictures. "Of course, we can only express ourselves by means of picture." This is rather queer . . . I could show Moore the pictures of a tropical plant. There is a technique of comparison between picture and plant. If I showed him the picture of Michelangelo and said: "Of course, I can't show you the real thing, only the picture". . . . The absurdity is, I've never taught him the technique of using this picture.

It is quite clear that the role of pictures of Biblical subjects and rôle of the picture of God creating Adam are totally different ones. You might ask this question: "Did Michelangelo think that Noah in the ark looked like this, and that God creating Adam looked like this?" He wouldn't have said that God or Adam looked as they look in this picture.

It might seem as though, if we asked such a question as: "Does Lewy *really* mean what so and so means when he says so and so is alive?"—it might seem as though there were two sharply divided cases, one in which he would say he didn't mean it literally. I want to say this is not so. There will be cases where we will differ, and where it won't be a question at all of more or less knowledge, so that we can come together. Sometimes it will be a question of experience, so you can say: "Wait another 10 years." And I would say: "I would disencourage this kind of reasoning" and Moore would say: "I wouldn't disencourage it." That is, one would *do* something. We would take sides, and that goes so far that there would really be great differences between us, which might come out in Mr. Lewy saying: "Wittgenstein is trying to undermine reason," and this wouldn't be false. This is actually where such questions rise.

III

Today I saw a poster saying: " 'Dead' Undergraduate speaks."

The inverted commas mean: "He isn't really dead." "He isn't what people call dead. They call it 'dead' not quite correctly."

We don't speak of "door" in quotes.

It suddenly struck me: "If someone said 'He isn't really dead, although by the ordinary criteria he is dead'—couldn't I say "He is not only dead by the ordinary criteria; he is what we all call 'dead.'"

If you now call him 'alive,' you're using language in a queer way, because you're almost deliberately preparing misunderstandings. Why don't you use some other word, and let "dead" have the meaning it already has?

Suppose someone said: "It didn't always have this meaning. He's not dead according to the old meaning" or "He's not dead according to the old idea."

What is it, to have different ideas of death? Suppose you say: "I have the idea of myself being a chair after death" or "I have the idea of myself being a chair in half-an-hour"—you all know under what circumstances we say of something that it has become a chair.

C.f. (1) "This shadow will cease to exist."

(2) "This chair will cease to exist." You say that you know what this chair ceasing to exist is like. But you have to think. You may find that there isn't a use for this sentence. You think of the use.

I imagine myself on the death-bed. I imagine you all looking at the air above me. You say "You have an idea."

Are you clear when you'd say you had ceased to exist?

You have six different ideas [of 'ceasing to exist'] at different times.

If you say: "I can imagine myself being a disembodied spirit. Wittgenstein, can you imagine yourself as a disembodied spirit?"—I'd say: "I'm sorry. I[so far] connect nothing with these words."

I connect all sorts of complicated things with these words. I think of what people have said of sufferings after death, etc.

"I have two different ideas, one of ceasing to exist after death, the other of being a disembodied spirit."

What's it like to have two different ideas? What is the criterion for one man having one idea, another man having another idea?

You gave me two phrases, "ceasing to exist," "being a disembodied spirit." "When I say this, I think of myself having a certain set of experiences." What is it like to think of this?

If you think of your brother in America, how do you know that what you think is, that the thought inside you is, of your brother being in America? Is this an experiential business?

Cf. How do you know that what you want is an apple? [Russell].

How do you know that you believe that your brother is in America?

A pear might be what satisfied you. But you wouldn't say: "What I wanted was an apple."

Suppose we say that the thought is some sort of process in his mind, or his saying something, etc.—then I could say: "All right, you call this a thought of your brother in America, well, what is the connection between this and your brother in America?"

Lewy: You might say that this is a question of convention.

Why is it that you don't doubt that it is a thought of your brother in America?

One process [the thought] seems to be a shadow or a picture of something else.

How do I know that a picture is a picture of Lewy?—Normally by its likeness to Lewy, or, under certain circumstances, a picture of Lewy may not be like him, but like Smith. If I give up the business of being like [as a criterion], I get into an awful mess, because anything may be his portrait, given a certain method of projection.

If you said that the thought was in some way a picture of his brother in America— Yes, but by what method of projection is it a picture of this? How queer it is that there should be no doubt what its a picture of.

If you're asked: "How do you know it is a thought of such and such?" the thought that immediately comes to your mind is one of a shadow, a picture. You don't think of a causal relation. The kind of relation you think of is best expressed by "picture," "shadow," etc.

The word "picture" is even quite all right—in many cases it is even in the most ordinary sense, a picture. You might translate my very words into a picture.

But the point is this, suppose you drew this, how do I know it is my brother in America? Who says it is him—unless it is here ordinary similarity?

What is the connection between these words, or anything substitutable for them, with my brother in America?

The first idea [you have] is that you are looking at your own thought, and are absolutely sure that it is a thought that so and so. You are looking at some mental phenomenon, and you say to yourself "obviously this is a thought of my brother being in America." It seems to be a super-picture. It seems, with thought, that there is no doubt whatever. With a picture, it still depends on the method of projection, whereas here it seems that you get rid of the projecting relation, and are absolutely certain that this is thought of that.

Smythies's muddle is based on the idea of a super—picture.

We once talked about how the idea of certain superlatives came about in Logic. The idea of a super-necessity, etc.

"How do I know that this is the thought of my brother in America?"—that *what* is the thought?

Suppose my thought consists of my *saying* "My brother is in America"—how do I know that I *say* my brother is in America?

How is the connection made?—We imagine at first a connection like strings.

Lewy: The connection is a convention. The word designates.

You must explain "designates" by examples. We have learnt a rule, a practice, etc.

Is thinking of something like painting or shooting at something?

It seems like a projection connection, which seems to make it indubitable, although there is not a projection relation at all.

If I said "My brother is in America"—I could imagine there being rays projecting from my words to my brother in America. But what if my brother isn't in America?— then the rays don't hit anything.

[If you say that the words refer to my brother by expressing the proposition that my brother is in America—the proposition being a middle link between the words and what they refer to]—What has the proposition, the mediate link, got to do with America?

The most important point is this—if you talk of painting, etc. your idea is that the connection exists *now*, so that it seem as though as long as I do this thinking, this connection exists.

Whereas, if we said it is a connection of convention, there would be no point in saying it exists while we think. There is a connection by convention—What do we mean?—This connection refers to events happening at various times. Most of all, it refers to a technique.

["Is thinking something going on at a particular time, or is it spread over the words?" "It comes in a flash." "Always?—it sometimes does come in a flash, although this may be all sorts of different things."]

If it does refer to a technique, then it can't be enough, in certain cases, to explain what you mean in a few words; because there is something which might be thought to be in conflict with the idea going on from 7 to 7.5, namely the practice of using it [the phrase].

When we talked of: "So and so is an automaton," the strong hold of that view was [due to the idea] that you could say: "Well, I know what I mean" . . ., as though you were looking at something happening while you said the thing, entirely independent of what came before and after, the application [of the phrase]. It looked as though you could talk of understanding a word, without any reference to the technique of its usage. It looked as though Smythies said he could understand the sentence, and that we then had nothing to say.

What was it like to have different ideas of death?—What I meant was—Is having an idea of death something like having a certain picture, so that you can say "I have an idea of death from 5 to 5.1 etc."? "In whatever way anyone will use this word, I have now a certain idea"—if you call this "having an idea," then it is not what is commonly called "having an idea," because what is commonly called "having an idea," has a reference to the technique of the word, etc.

We are all here using the word "death," which is a public instrument, which has a whole technique [of usage]. Then someone says he has an idea of death. Something queer; because you might say "You are using the word 'death', which is an instrument functioning in a certain way."

If you treat this [your idea] as something private, with what right are you calling it an idea of death?—I say this, because we, also, have a right to say what is an idea of death.

He might say "I have my own private idea of death"—why call this an 'idea of death' unless it is something you connect with death. Although this [your 'idea'] might not interest us at all. [In this case,] it does not belong on the game played with 'death,' which we all know and understand.

If what he calls his "idea of death" is to become relevant, it must become part of our game.

'My idea of death is the separation of the soul from the body'—if we know what to do with these words. He can also say: "I connect with the word 'death' a certain picture—a woman lying in her bed"—that may or may not be of some interest.

If he connects

with death, and this was his idea, this might be interesting psychologically.

"The separation of soul from body" [only had a public interest]. This may act like black curtains or it may not act like black curtains. I'd have to find out what the consequences [of your saying it] are. I am not, at least, at present at all clear. [You say this]— "So what?"—I know these words, I have certain pictures. All sorts of things go along with these words.

If he says this, I won't know yet what consequences he will draw. I don't know what he opposes this to.

Lewy: "You oppose it to being extinguished."

If you say to me—"Do you cease to exist?"—I should be bewildered, and would not know what exactly this is to mean. "If you dont cease to exist, you will suffer after death," there I begin to attach ideas, perhaps ethical ideas of responsibility. The point is, that although these are well-known words, and although I can go from one sentence to another sentence, or to pictures [I don't know what consequences you draw from this statement].

Suppose someone said: "What do you believe, Wittgenstein? Are you a sceptic? Do you know whether you will survive death?" I would really, this is a fact, say "I can't say. I don't know," because I haven't any clear idea what I'm saying when I'm saying "I don't cease to exist," etc.

Spiritualists make one kind of connection.

A Spiritualist says "Apparition" etc. Although he gives me a picture I don't like, I do get a clear idea. I know that much, that some people connect this phrase with a particular kind of verification. I know that some people don't—religious people e.g.—they don't refer to a verification, but have entirely different ideas.

A great writer said that, when he was a boy, his father set him a task, and he suddenly felt that nothing, not even death, could take away the responsibility [in doing this task]; this was his duty to do, and that even death couldn't stop it being his duty. He said that this was, in a way, a proof of the immortality of the soul—because if this lives on [the responsibility won't die]. The idea is given by what we call the proof. Well, if this is the idea, [all right].

If a Spiritualist wishes to give *me* an idea of what he means or doesn't mean by 'survival,' he can say all sorts of things—

[If I ask what idea he has, I may be given what the Spiritualists say or I may be given what the man I quoted said, etc., etc.]

I would at least [in the case of the Spiritualist] have an idea of what this sentence is connected up with, and get more and more of an idea as I see what he does with it.

As it is, I hardly connect anything with it at all.

Suppose someone, before going to China, when he might never see me again, said to me: "We might see one another after death"—would I necessarily say that I don't understand him? I might say [want to say] simply, "Yes. I *understand* him entirely."

Lewy "In this case, you might only mean that he expressed a certain attitude."

I would say "No, it isn't the same as saying 'I'm very fond of you'"—and it may not be the same as saying anything else. It says what it says. Why should you be able to substitute anything else?

Suppose I say: "The man used a picture."

"Perhaps now he sees he was wrong." What sort of remark is this?

"God's eye sees everything"—I want to say of this that it uses a picture.

I don't want to belittle him [the person who says it.]

Suppose I said to him "You've been using a picture," and he said "No, this is not all"—mightn't he have misunderstood me? What do I want to do [by saying this]? What would be the real sign of disagreement? What might be the real criterion of his disagreeing with me?

Lewy: "If he said: 'I've been making preparations [for death].'"

Yes, this might be a disagreement—if he himself were to use the word in a way in which I did not expect, or were to draw conclusions I did not expect him to draw. I wanted only to draw attention to a particular technique of usage. We should disagree, if he was using a technique I didn't expect.

We associate a particular use with a picture.

Smythies: 'This isn't all he does—associate a use with a picture.'

Wittgenstein: Rubbish. I meant: what conclusions are you going to draw? etc. Are eyebrows going to be talked of, in connection with the Eye of God?

"He could just as well have said so and so"—this [remark] is foreshadowed by the word "attitude." He couldn't just as well have said something else.

If I say he used a picture, I don't want to say anything he himself wouldn't say. I want to say that he draws these conclusions.

Isn't it as important as anything else, what picture he does use?

Of certain pictures we say that they might just as well be replaced by another—e.g. we could, under certain circumstances, have one projection of an ellipse drawn instead of another.

[He *may* say]: "I would have been prepared to use another picture, it would have had the same effect. . . ."

The whole *weight* may be in the picture.

We can say in chess that the exact shape of the chess-men plays no rôle. Suppose that the main pleasure was, to see people ride; then, playing it in writing wouldn't be playing the same game. Someone might say: "All he's done is change the shape of the head"—what more could he do?

When I say he's using a picture I'm merely making a *grammatical* remark: [What I say] can only be verified by the consequences he does or does not draw.

If Smythies disagrees, I don't take notice of this disagreement.

All I wished to characterize was the conventions he wished to draw. If I wished to say anything more I was merely being philosophically arrogant.

Normally, if you say "He is an automaton" you draw consequences, if you stab him, [he'll feel pain]. On the other hand, you may not wish to draw any such consequences, and this is all there is to it—except further muddles.

Note

1. Contribution to a Symposium on *Science and Religion* (London: Gerald Howe, 1931, pp. 107–116).

29. The Groundlessness of Belief

NORMAN MALCOLM

I

In his final notebooks Wittgenstein wrote that it is difficult "to realize the groundlessness of our believing."[1] He was thinking of how much mere acceptance, on the basis of no evidence, shapes our lives. This is obvious in the case of small children. They are told the names of things. They accept what they are told. They do not ask for grounds. A child does not demand a proof that the person who feeds him is called "Mama." Or are we to suppose that the child reasons to himself as follows: "The others present seem to know this person who is feeding me, and since they call her 'Mama' that probably is her name"? It is obvious on reflection that a child cannot consider evidence or even doubt anything until he has already learned much. As Wittgenstein puts it: "The child learns by believing the adult. Doubt comes *after* belief" (*OC*, 160).

Source: Reprinted from Norman Malcolm, "The Groundlessness of Belief," in *Reason and Religion*, ed. Stuart Brown, © 1977 Royal Institute of Philosophy. Used by permission of the publisher, Cornell University Press.

What is more difficult to perceive is that the lives of educated, sophisticated adults are also formed by groundless beliefs. I do not mean eccentric beliefs that are out on the fringes of their lives, but fundamental beliefs. Take the belief that familiar material things (watches, shoes, chairs) do not cease to exist without some physical explanation. They don't "vanish in thin air." It is interesting that we do use that very expression: "I *know* I put the keys right here on this table. They must have vanished in thin air!" But this exclamation is hyperbole: we are not speaking in literal seriousness. I do not know of any adult who would consider, in all gravity, that the keys might have inexplicably ceased to exist.

Yet it is possible to imagine a society in which it was accepted that sometimes material things do go out of existence without having been crushed, melted, eroded, broken into pieces, burned up, eaten, or destroyed in some other way. The difference between those people and ourselves would not consist in their *saying* something that we don't say ("It vanished in thin air"), since we say it too. I conceive of those people as acting and thinking differently from ourselves in such ways as the following: if one of them could not find his wallet, he would give up the search sooner than you or I would; also he would be less inclined to suppose that it was stolen. In general what we would regard as convincing circumstantial evidence of theft those people would find less convincing. They would take fewer precautions than we would to protect their possessions against loss or theft. They would have less inclination to save money, since it too can just disappear. They would not tend to form strong attachments to material things. They would stand in a looser relation to the world than we do. The disappearance of a desired object, which would provoke us to a frantic search, they would be more inclined to accept with a shrug. Of course their scientific theories would be different; but also their attitude toward experiment, and inference from experimental results, would be more tentative. If the repetition of a familiar chemical experiment did not yield the expected result, this *could* be because one of the chemical substances had vanished.

The outlook I have sketched might be thought to be radically incoherent. I do not see that this is so. Although those people consider it to be possible that a wallet might have inexplicably ceased to exist, it is also true that they regard that as unlikely. For things that are lost usually do turn up later; or if not, their fate can often be accounted for. Those people use pretty much the same criteria of identity that we do; their reasoning would resemble ours quite a lot. Their thinking would not be incoherent. But it would be different, since they would leave room for possibilities that we exclude.

If we compare their view that material things do sometimes go out of existence inexplicably with our own rejection of that view, it does not appear to me that one position is supported by *better evidence* than is the other. Each position is compatible with ordinary experience. On the one hand it is true that familiar objects (watches, wallets, lawn chairs) occasionally disappear without any adequate explanation. On the other hand it happens, perhaps more frequently, that a satisfying explanation of the disappearance is discovered.

Our attitude in this matter is striking. We would not be willing to consider it even as *improbable* that a missing lawn chair had "just ceased to exist." We would not entertain such a suggestion. If anyone proposed it we would be sure he was joking. It is no exaggeration to say that this attitude is part of the foundations of our thinking. I do not want to say that this attitude is *un*reasonable; but rather that it is something that we do not *try* to support with grounds. It could be said to belong to "the framework" of our thinking about material things.

Wittgenstein asks: "Does anyone ever test whether this table remains in existence when no one is paying attention to it?" (*OC*, 163). The answer is: Of course not. Is this because we would not call it "a table" if that were to happen? But we do call it "a table" and none of us makes the test. Doesn't this show that we do not regard that occurrence as a possibility? People who did so regard it would seem ludicrous to us. One could imagine that they made ingenious experiments to decide the question; but this research would make us smile. Is this because experiments were conducted by our ancestors that settled the matter once and for all? I don't believe it. The principle that material things do not cease to exist without physical cause is an unreflective part of the framework within which physical investigations are made and physical explanations arrived at.

Wittgenstein suggests that the same is true of what might be called "the principle of the continuity of nature":

> Think of chemical investigations. Lavoisier makes experiments with substances in his laboratory and now concludes that this and that takes place when there is burning. He does not say that it might happen otherwise another time. He has got hold of a world-picture—not of course one that he invented: he learned it as a child. I say world-picture and not hypothesis, because it is the matter-of-course (*selbstver-ständliche*) foundation for his research and as such also goes unmentioned (*OC*, 167).

> But now, what part is played by the presupposition that a substance A always reacts to a substance B in the same way, given the same circumstances? Or is that part of the definition of a substance? (*OC*, 168).

Framework principles, such as the continuity of nature or the assumption that material things do not cease to exist without physical cause, belong to what Wittgenstein calls a "system." He makes the following observation, which seems to me to be true: "All testing, all confirmation and disconfirmation of a hypothesis takes place already within a system. And this system is not a more or less arbitrary and doubtful point of departure for all our arguments; no, it belongs to the nature of what we call an argument. The system is not so much the point of departure, as the element in which arguments have their life" (*OC*, 105).

A "system" provides the boundaries within which we ask questions, carry out investigations, and make judgments. Hypotheses are put forth, and challenged, *within* a system. Verification, justification, the search for evidence, occur *within* a system. The framework propositions of the system are not put to the test, not backed up by evidence. This is what Wittgenstein means when he says: "Of course there is justification; but justification comes to an end" (*OC*, 192); and when he asks: "Doesn't testing come to an end?" (*OC*, 164); and when he remarks that "whenever we test anything we are already presupposing something that is not tested" (*OC*, 163).

That this is so is not to be attributed to human weakness. It is a conceptual requirement that our inquiries and proofs stay within boundaries. Think, for example, of the activity of calculating a number. Some steps in a calculation we will check for correctness, but others we won't: for example, that 4 + 4 = 8. More accurately, some beginners might check it, but grown-ups won't. Similarly, some grown-ups would want to determine by calculation whether 25 × 25 = 625, whereas others would regard that as laughable. Thus the boundaries of the system within which *you* calculate may not be exactly the same as my boundaries. But we do calculate; and, as Wittgenstein remarks, "In certain circumstances . . . we regard a calculation as sufficiently checked. What gives us a right to do so? . . . Somewhere we must be finished with justification, and then there remains the proposition that *this* is how we calculate" (*OC*, 212). If someone did not accept any boundaries for calculating, this would mean that he had not learned *that* language-game: "If someone supposed that *all* our calculations were uncertain and that we could rely on none of them (justifying himself by saying that mistakes are always possible) perhaps we would say he was crazy. But can we say he is in error? Does he not just react differently? We rely on calculations, he doesn't; we are sure, he isn't" (*OC*, 217). We are taught, or we absorb, the systems within which we raise doubts, make inquiries, draw conclusions. We grow into a framework. We don't question it. We accept it trustingly. But this acceptance is not a consequence of reflection. We do not *decide* to accept framework propositions. We do not decide that we live on the earth, any more than we decide to learn our native tongue. We do come to adhere to a framework proposition, in the sense that it shapes the way we think. The framework propositions that we accept, grow into, are not idiosyncrasies but common ways of speaking and thinking that are pressed on us by our human community. For our acceptances to have been withheld would have meant that we had not learned how to count, to measure, to use names, to play games, or even *to talk*. Wittgenstein remarks that "a language-game is only possible if one trusts something." Not *can*, but *does* trust something (*OC*, 509). I think he means by this trust or acceptance what he calls belief "in the sense of religious belief" (*OC*, 459). What does he mean by belief "in the sense of religious belief"? He explicitly distinguishes it from *conjecture* (*Vermutung*: ibid). I think this means that there is nothing tentative about it; it is not adopted as an hypothesis that might later be withdrawn in the light of new evidence. This also makes explicit an important feature of Wittgenstein's understanding of belief, in the sense of "religious belief," namely, that it does not rise or fall on the basis of evidence or grounds: it is "groundless."

II

In our Western academic philosophy, religious belief is commonly regarded as unreasonable and is viewed with condescension or even contempt. It is said that religion is a refuge for those who, because of weakness of intellect or character, are unable to confront the stern realities of the world. The objective, mature, *strong* attitude is to hold beliefs solely on the basis of *evidence*.

It appears to me that philosophical thinking is greatly influenced by this veneration of evidence. We have an aversion to statements, reports, declarations, beliefs, that are not based on grounds. There are many illustrations of this philosophical bent.

For example, in regard to a person's report that he has an image of the Eiffel Tower we have an inclination to think that the image must *resemble* the Eiffel Tower. How else could the person declare so confidently what his image is *of*? How could he know?

Another example: a memory-report or memory-belief must be based, we think, on some mental *datum* that is equipped with various features to match the corresponding features of the memory-belief. This datum will include an image that provides the *content* of the belief, and a peculiar feeling that makes one refer the image to a *past* happening, and another feeling that makes one believe that the image is an *accurate* portrayal of the past happening, and still another feeling that informs one that it was *oneself* who witnessed the past happening. The presence of these various features makes memory-beliefs thoroughly reasonable.

Another illustration: if interrupted in speaking one can usually give a confident account, later on, of what one had been *about* to say. How is this possible? Must not one remember *a feeling of tendency to say just those words*? This is one's basis for knowing what one had been about to say. It justifies one's subsequent account.

Still another example: after dining at a friend's house you announce your intention to go home. How do you know your intention? One theory proposes that you are presently aware of a particular mental state or bodily feeling which, as you recall from your past experience, has been highly correlated with the behavior of going home; so you infer that *that* is what you are going to do now. A second theory holds that you must be aware of some definite mental state or event which reveals itself, not by experience but *intrinsically*, as the intention to go home. Your awareness of that mental item *informs* you of what action you will take.

Yet another illustration: this is the instructive case of the man who, since birth, has been immune to sensations of bodily pain. On his thirtieth birthday he is kicked on the shins, and for the first time he responds by crying out, hopping around on one foot, holding his leg, and exclaiming "The pain is terrible!" We have an over-whelming inclination to wonder, "How could he tell, *this first time*, that what he felt was *pain?*" Of course the implication is that *after* the first time there would be *no* problem. Why not? Because his first experience of pain would provide him with a sample that would be preserved in memory; thereafter he would be equipped to determine whether any sensation he feels is or isn't pain; he would just compare it with the memory-sample to see whether the two match! Thus he will have a *justification* for believing that what he feels is pain. But the *first time* he will not have this justification. This is why the case is so puzzling. Could it be that this first time he *infers* that he is in pain from his own behavior?

A final illustration: consider the fact that after a comparatively few examples and bits of instruction a person can go on to carry out a task, apply a word correctly in the future, continue a numerical series from an initial segment, distinguish grammatical from ungrammatical constructions, solve arithmetical problems, and so on. These correct performances will be dealing with new and different examples, situations, combinations. The performance output will be far more varied than the instruction input. How is this possible? What carries the person from the meager instruction to his rich performance? The explanation has to be that an effect of his training was that he abstracted the Idea, perceived the Common Nature, "internalized" the Rule, grasped the Structure. What else could bridge the gap between the poverty of instruction and the wealth of performance? Thus we postulate an intervening mental act or state which removes the inequality and restores the balance.

My illustrations belong to what could be called the *pathology* of philosophy. Wittgenstein speaks of a "general disease of thinking" which attempts to explain occurrences of discernment, recognition, or understanding, by postulating mental states or processes from which those occurrences flow "as from a reservoir" (*BB*, p. 143). These mental intermediaries are assumed to contribute to the causation of the various cognitive performances. More significantly for my present purpose, they are supposed to *justify* them; they provide our *grounds* for saying or doing this rather than that; they *explain how we know*. The Image, or Cognitive State, or Feeling, or Idea, or Sample, or Rule, or Structure, *tells* us. It is like a road map or a signpost. It guides our course.

What is "pathological" about these explanatory constructions and pseudo-scientific inferences? Two things at least. First, the movement of thought that demands these intermediaries is circular and empty, unless it provides criteria for determining their presence and nature *other than* the occurrence of the phenomena they are postulated to explain—and of course no such criteria are forthcoming. Second, there is the great criticism by Wittgenstein of this movement of philosophical thought: namely, his point that no matter what kind of state, process, paradigm, sample, structure, or rule is conceived of as giving us the necessary guidance, *it* could be taken, or understood, as indicating a *different* direction from the one in which we actually did go. The assumed intermediary Idea, Structure, or Rule does not and cannot reveal that because of it we went in the only direction it was reasonable to go. Thus the internalized intermediary we are tempted to invoke to bridge the gap between training and performance, as being that which shows us what we must do or say if we are to be rational, cannot do the job it was invented to do. It cannot fill the epistemological gap. It cannot provide the bridge of justification. It cannot put to rest the How-do-we-know? question. Why not? Because it cannot tell us how *it itself* is to be taken, understood, applied. Wittgenstein puts the point briefly and powerfully: "Don't always think that you read off your words from facts; that you portray these in words according to rules. For even so you would have to apply the rule in the particular case without guidance" (*PI*, 292). Without guidance! Like Wittgenstein's signpost arrow that cannot tell us whether to go in the direction of the arrow tip or in the opposite direction, so too the Images, Ideas, Cognitive Structures, or Rules that we philosophers imagine as devices for guidance cannot interpret themselves to us. The signpost does not tell the traveler how to read it. A second signpost might tell him how to read the first one; we can imagine such a case. But this can't go on. If the traveler is to continue his journey he will have to do something on his own, without guidance.

The parable of the traveler speaks for *all* of the language-games we learn and practice, even those in which there is the most disciplined instruction and the most rigorous standards of conformity. Suppose that a pupil has been given thorough training in some procedure, whether it is drawing patterns, building fences, or proving theorems. But then he has to carry on by himself in new situations. How does he know what to do? Wittgenstein presents the following dialogue: " 'However you instruct him in the continuation of a pattern—how can he *know* how he is to continue by himself?'—Well, how do *I* know?—If that means 'Have I grounds?', the answer is: the grounds will soon give out. And then I shall act, without grounds" (*PI*, 211). Grounds come to an end. Answers to How-do-we-know? questions come to an end. Evidence comes to an end. We must speak, act, live, without evidence. This is so not just on the fringes of life and language, but at the center of our most regularized activities. We do learn rules and learn to follow them. But our training was in the past! We had to leave it behind and proceed on our own.

It is an immensely important fact of nature that as people carry on an activity in which they have received a common training, they do largely *agree* with one another, accepting the same examples and analogies, taking the same steps. We agree in what to say, in how to apply language. We agree in our responses to particular cases.

As Wittgenstein says, "That is not agreement in opinions but in form of life" (*PI*, 241). We cannot explain this agreement by saying that we are just doing what the rules tell us—for our agreement in applying rules, formulae and signposts is what gives them their *meaning*.

One of the primary pathologies of philosophy is the feeling that we must *justify* our language-games. We want to establish them as well grounded. But we should consider here Wittgenstein's remark that a language-game "is not based on grounds. It is there—like our life" (*OC*, 559).

Within a language-game there is justification and lack of justification, evidence and proof, mistakes and groundless opinions, good and bad reasoning, correct measurements and incorrect ones. One cannot properly apply these terms to a language-game itself. It may, however, be said to be "groundless," not in the sense of a groundless opinion, but in the sense that we accept it, we live it. We can say, "This is what we do. This is how we are."

In this sense religion is groundless; and so is chemistry. Within each of these two systems of thought and action there is controversy and argument. Within each there are advances and recessions of insight into the secrets of nature or the spiritual condition of humankind and the demands of the Creator, Savior, Judge, Source. Within the framework of each system there is criticism, explanation, justification. But we should not expect that there might be some sort of rational justification of the framework itself.

A chemist will sometimes employ induction. Does he have evidence for a Law of Induction? Wittgenstein observes that it would strike him as nonsense to say, "I know that the Law of Induction is true." ("Imagine such a statement made in a law court.") It would be more correct to say, "I believe in the Law of Induction" (*OC*, 500). This way of putting it is better because it shows that the attitude toward induction is belief in the sense of "religious" belief—that is to say, an acceptance which is not conjecture or surmise and for which there is no reason—it is a groundless acceptance.

It is intellectually troubling for us to conceive that a whole system of thought might be groundless, might have no rational justification. We realize easily enough, however, that grounds soon give out—that we cannot go on giving reasons for our reasons. There arises from this realization the conception of a reason that is *self-justifying*—something whose credentials as a reason cannot be questioned.

This metaphysical conception makes its presence felt at many points—for example, as an explanation of how a person can tell what his mental image is *of*. We feel that the following remarks, imagined by Wittgenstein, are exactly right: " 'The image must be more similar to its object than any picture. For however similar I make the picture to what it is supposed to represent, it can always be the picture of something else. But it is essential to the image that it is the image of *this* and of nothing else'" (*PI*, 389). A pen and ink drawing represents the Eiffel Tower; but it could represent a mine shaft or a new type of automobile jack. Nothing prevents this drawing from being taken as a representation of something other than the Eiffel Tower. But my mental image of the Eiffel Tower is *necessarily* an image of the Eiffel Tower. Therefore it must be a "remarkable" kind of picture. As Wittgenstein observes: "Thus one might come to regard the image as a super-picture" (ibid.). Yet we have no intelligible conception of how a super-picture would differ from an ordinary picture. It would seem that it has to be a *super-likeness*—but what does this mean?

There is a familiar linguistic practice in which one person *tells* another what his image is of (or what he intends to do, or what he was about to say) and no question is raised of how the first one *knows* that what he says is true. This question is imposed from outside, artificially, by the philosophical craving for justification. We can see here the significance of these remarks: "It isn't a question of explaining a language-game by means of our experiences, but of noting a language-game" (*PI*, 665). "Look on the language-game as the *primary* thing" (*PI*, 656). Within a system of thinking and acting there occurs, *up to a point*, investigation and criticism of the reasons and justifications that are employed in that system. This inquiry into whether a reason is good or adequate cannot, as said, go on endlessly. We stop it. We bring it to an end. We come upon something that *satisfies* us. It is *as if* we made a decision or issued an edict: "*This* is an adequate reason!" (or explanation, or justification). Thereby we fix a boundary of our language-game.

There is nothing wrong with this. How else could we have disciplines, systems, games? But our fear of groundlessness makes us conceive that we are under some logical compulsion to terminate at *those particular* stopping points. We imagine that we have confronted the self-evident reason, the self-justifying explanation, the picture or symbol whose meaning cannot be questioned. This obscures from us the *human* aspect of our concepts—the fact that what we call "a reason," "evidence," "explanation," "justification," is what appeals to and satisfies *us*.

III

The desire to provide a rational foundation for a form of life is especially prominent in the philosophy of religion, where there is an intense preoccupation with purported proofs of the existence of God. In American universities there must be hundreds of courses in which these proofs are the main topic. We can be sure that nearly always the critical verdict is that the proofs are invalid and consequently that, up to the present time at least, religious belief has received no rational justification.

Well, of course not! The obsessive concern with the proofs reveals the assumption that in order for religious belief to be intellectually respectable it *ought* to have a rational justification. *That* is the misunderstanding. It is like the idea that we are not justified in relying on memory until memory has been proved reliable.

Roger Trigg makes the following remark: "To say that someone acts in a certain way because of his belief in God does seem to be more than a redescription of his action. . . . It is to give a reason for it. The belief is distinct from the commitment which may follow it, and is the justification for it."[2] It is evident from other remarks that by "belief in God" Trigg means "belief in the existence of God" or "belief that God exists." Presumably, by the *acts* and *commitments* of a religious person Trigg refers to such things as prayer, worship, confession, thanksgiving, partaking of sacraments, and participation in the life of a religious group.

For myself I have great difficulty with the notion of belief in *the existence* of God, whereas the idea of belief *in* God is to me intelligible. If a man did not ever pray for help or forgiveness, or have any inclination toward it; nor ever felt that it is "a good and joyful thing" to thank God for the blessings of this life; nor was ever concerned about his failure to comply with divine commandments—then, it seems clear to me, he could not be said to believe in God. Belief in God is not an all or none thing; it can be more or less; it can wax and wane. But belief in God in any degree does require, as I understand the words, some religious action, some commitment, or if not, at least a bad conscience.

According to Trigg, if I take him correctly, a man who was entirely devoid of any inclination to religious action or conscience might believe in *the existence* of God. What would be the marks of this? Would it be that the man knows some theology, can recite the Creeds, is well-read in Scripture? Or is his belief in the existence of God something different from this? If so, what? What would be the difference between a man who knows some articles of faith, heresies, Scriptural writings, and in addition believes in the existence of God, and one who knows these things but does not believe in the existence of God? I assume that both of them are indifferent to the acts and commitments of religious life.

I do not comprehend this notion of belief in *the existence* of God which is thought to be distinct from belief *in* God. It seems to me to be an artificial construction of philosophy, another illustration of the craving for justification.

Religion is a form of life; it is language embedded in action—what Wittgenstein calls a "language-game." Science is another. Neither stands in need of justification, the one no more than the other.

Present-day academic philosophers are far more prone to challenge the credentials of religion than of science. This is probably due to a number of things. One may be the illusion that science can justify its own framework. Another is the fact that science is a vastly greater force in our culture. Still another reason may be the fact that by and large religion is to university people an alien form of life. They do not participate in it and do not understand what it is all about. This nonunderstanding is of an interesting nature. It derives, at least in part, from the inclination of academics to suppose that their employment as scholars demands of them the most severe objectivity and dispassionateness. For an academic philosopher to become a religious believer would be a stain on his professional competence! Here I will quote from Nietzsche, who was commenting on the relation of the German scholar of his day to religious belief; yet his remarks continue to have a nice appropriateness for the American and British scholars of our own day:

> Pious or even merely church-going people seldom realize *how much* good will, one might even say willfulness, it requires nowadays for a German scholar to take the problem of religion seriously; his whole trade . . . disposes him to a superior, almost good-natured merriment in regard to religion, sometimes mixed with a mild contempt directed at the "uncleanliness" of spirit which he presupposes wherever one still belongs to the church. It is only with the aid of

history (thus *not* from his personal experience) that the scholar succeeds in summoning up a reverent seriousness and a certain shy respect towards religion; but if he intensifies his feelings towards it even to the point of feeling grateful to it, he has still in his own person not got so much as a single step closer to that which still exists as church or piety; perhaps the reverse. The practical indifference to religious things in which he was born and raised is as a rule sublimated in him into a caution and cleanliness which avoids contact with religious people and things; . . . Every age has its own divine kind of naïvety for the invention of which other ages may envy it—and how much naïvety, venerable, childlike and boundlessly stupid naïvety there is in the scholar's belief in his superiority, in the good conscience of his tolerance, in the simple unsuspecting certainty with which his instinct treats the religious man as an inferior and lower type which he himself has grown beyond and *above.*[3]

Notes

1. Ludwig Wittgenstein, *On Certainty*, ed. G. E. M. Anscombe and G. H. von Wright; trans. D. Paul and G.E.M. Anscombe (Oxford, Engl.: Basil Blackwell, 1969), paragraph 166. Henceforth I include references to this work in the text, employing the abbreviation "*OC*" followed by paragraph number. References to Wittgenstein's *The Blue and Brown Books* (Oxford, Engl.: Basil Blackwell, 1958) are indicated in the text by "*BB*" followed by page number. References to his *Philosophical Investigations*, ed. G.E.M. Anscombe and R. Rhees; trans. G.E.M. Anscombe (Oxford, Engl.: Basil Blackwell, 1967) are indicated by "*PI*" followed by paragraph number. In *OC* and *PI* I have mainly used the translations of Paul and Elizabeth Anscombe, but with some departures.

2. Roger Trigg, *Reason and Commitment* (Cambridge, Engl.: Cambridge University Press, 1973), p. 75.

3. Friedrich Nietzsche, *Beyond Good and Evil*, trans. R. J. Hollingdale (Harmondsworth, Middlesex [Engl.]: Penguin, 1972), para. 58.

30. Knowledge, Belief, and Reformed Epistemology

JAY M. VAN HOOK

Philosophers have long been perplexed by the problem of which, and under what conditions, human beliefs may properly lay claim to being not merely beliefs, but also "knowledge." Christian thinkers, too, have labored over this issue, and not only in general, but also with reference to religious beliefs. May any of our beliefs about God, for example, ever properly be considered *knowledge?* If so, which and when? If not, why not?

The claim to know is ordinarily construed by philosophers and laymen alike as stronger than the claim to believe. Beliefs may turn out to be mistaken. We find nothing unusual about a friend's confession that one of his beliefs has turned out to be false. But we would consider it peculiar if someone admitted that some of her knowledge had proven to be false. Knowledge, unlike belief, is supposed to be immune to falsity. And in a case where a knowledge claim does turn out to be false, the conclusion to be drawn is that the person did not know what he thought he knew rather than that his knowledge itself is false.

The dominant theories of knowledge in Western philosophy have been one or another version of what is often termed "foundationalism." According to this view, a statement of belief may be taken as knowledge if and only if it is either a "foundational" (or "basic") proposition or one which is derived from foundational propositions in some appropriate way. Foundational propositions are alleged to be self-evident and incorrigible; they are grasped immediately and with certitude. While there is little agreement as to which propositions are properly foundational, Descartes's well-known "I think, therefore I am" and the reports of immediate sensations such as "I am in pain" are frequently advanced as candidates. Both deduction and induction (or probabilism) have been advocated as appropriate methods for building additional knowledge upon the foundational certitudes. Thus for some foundationalists, propositions which can be deduced from foundational propositions meet the requirement for inclusion in the house of knowledge, while for others propositions justified probabilistically in terms of basic propositions will so qualify.

Of late, considerable discussion has taken place among Reformed philosophers about the relation of religious beliefs to the foundation of knowledge. This discussion

Source: Jay Van Hook, "Knowledge, Belief, and Reformed Epistemology," *The Reformed Journal* (July 1981), published by Wm. B. Eerdmans Publishing Company, Grand Rapids, MI. Used by permission.

has been occasioned, I think, by at least two factors: first, the foundationalist theory just outlined has itself fallen upon hard times; and second, Reformed Christians have felt a continuing need to address a persistent legacy of logical positivism according to which statements of religious belief are at best emotive utterances which fall completely outside the scope of knowledge.

In what follows, I want to take up the issue of religious belief and knowledge as it has been dealt with by philosophers Nicholas Wolterstorff, whose critique of foundationalism is familiar to many professionals both within and beyond the Reformed community, and Alvin Plantinga, whose work in the philosophy of religion has received international attention (and earned him the designation from *Time* magazine as "orthodox Christianity's leading philosopher of God"). I shall be especially concerned here with what Plantinga has recently called "Reformed epistemology." Along the way, I shall detour in order to consider Princeton University philosopher Richard Rorty's notion of knowledge as "what our peers will let us get away with saying." My aim is more to raise some questions in the hope of provoking further discussion than it is to try to defend or refute some particular theory of knowledge.

The basic question I shall pose is this: What precisely is "knowledge" on a post-foundationalist or Reformed model and how, if at all, does it differ from mere "belief," or even from "rational" belief?

First, a further look at foundationalism and Wolterstorff's criticism of it.

As noted above, foundationalism attempts to set down the conditions upon which beliefs may properly be taken as knowledge. Its aim is to separate the prejudice and conjecture associated with opinion from objectively certain knowledge. To achieve this aim, it attempts to construct the super-structure of knowledge on a firm foundation of certitude using the method either of deduction or of induction. Wolterstorff contends, however, that both of these methods face insurmountable difficulties.

The appeal of deduction, of course, is not hard to discern. Every elementary logic student learns the simple deductive syllogism: "All men are mortal; Socrates is a man; therefore, Socrates is mortal." The advantage of deduction is that if the premises are true and the argument form valid, the conclusion follows with inexorable necessity. So propositions deduced from indubitable foundational propositions would seem also to have the prized characteristic of indubitability. But the problem for the deductive approach lies in the fact that little of what we know proves deducible from foundational certitudes. Thus Wolterstorff observes that while deduction promises certainty, "most universal propositions about physical objects would not be warranted."[1] "All swans have wings," for example, cannot be deduced from my knowledge (even if that knowledge were certain) that the specific swans I have encountered (however great the number) all have wings. But neither is "All swans have wings" a foundational proposition. There is nothing immediately self-evident about it.

Since deductivism has not worked very well, many foundationalists have turned instead to an inductive or probabilistic approach to adding propositions to the stock of foundational certitudes. The inductive method proceeds from the foundational certitudes to propositions which are seen as having more or less probability with respect to that foundation. But Wolterstorff correctly notes that the shift to probabilism already involves "a radical lowering of standards" as to what constitutes knowledge, one which would be rejected by deductivists who "would have refused to regard conjectures—no matter how probable—as knowledge at all."[2] Thus, even if successful, the probabilistic route involves weakening the original goal of certainty and incorrigibility. And beyond all this, Wolterstorff argues that theorists have so far failed to provide a convincing justification for induction itself.

Another way of looking at the same matter is this: the foundationalist is confronted with the difficulty of finding an adequate supply of foundational propositions to support the superstructure of knowledge; for these must be both true and "known noninferentially and with certitude to be true."[3] It turns out that basic propositions are not easy to come by. If one wishes to take the reports of immediate perception as basic, one must then face the problem that our reports of these perceptions are by no means infallible. I may be wrong about what I think I see, though perhaps I can't be wrong that I *seem* to see what I think I see. Thus even such an elementary report of sense perception as "I see a cat on the roof" seems to dissolve, after a hard-nosed search for the incorrigible, into the much more cautious claim that "I am appeared to cat-on-roofishly." Statements attempting to discuss real objects turn out to be statements about our own states of consciousness. And as Wolterstorff puts it, "It seems unlikely that from our introspective knowledge of propositions about our own states of consciousness we could erect the whole structure of objective science."[4] We apparently do not have enough basic propositions on which to build the house of knowledge.

These considerations provide the background for Wolterstorff's verdict that foundationalism is mortally ill and must be given up. He is careful to stress, however, that his rejection of foundationalism involves neither skepticism (the view that nothing can be known) nor epistemological permissiveness ("anything goes"). It is not entirely clear, though, just how skepticism is to be avoided. Given the demise of foundationalism, it seems to me that essentially two routes are open. One may either adhere to the foundationalist criterion and simply concede that we do not have any knowledge (or at least not much), or adopt a weaker criterion which makes knowledge possible (just as, by analogy, one can always give a passing grade to all of one's students if the standards are lowered sufficiently). It is not clear to me, moreover, that either of these approaches is intrinsically superior to the other. Wolterstorff, I believe, opts for a weakened criterion, though he has not yet published a formulation of such a criterion. If this indeed is what he wishes to do, then we need to recognize that the standards for what counts as knowledge have in fact been lowered.

My point, quite simply, is this. The basic aim of the whole enterprise of epistemology from Plato to our own day has been to provide what can be called a "common ground" on the basis of which knowledge claims can be made, criticized, justified, and settled. Now it may well be the case, as many philosophers and others have begun to suspect, that no such common ground exists or can be identified. But to say that we can have knowledge anyway, without a common ground, is surely to propose a radical alteration in the very idea of knowledge. Even so, there may be nothing amiss; perhaps the idea of knowledge needs to be altered. But one may legitimately ask, I think, what the criterion for knowledge is now going to be. But to this question Wolterstorff has not as yet provided an answer. Perhaps the new "Reformed epistemology" will furnish the needed criterion.

Before taking up Reformed epistemology, however, I wish to focus my concern by considering Richard Rorty's suggestion that knowledge is basically "what our peers will let us get away with saying." I do so not because I expect Reformed thinkers to find this suggestion congenial, but because it is not clear to me that even a Reformed epistemology can get very far beyond such a view.

Like Wolterstorff, Rorty believes that foundationalism is untenable. He also thinks that we need not trouble ourselves about trying to replace current theories of knowledge with a new and better epistemology. He suggests instead that we learn to do without epistemology altogether, and that we substitute "edifying conversation" for the scholastic argumentation (that is, abstruse logical arguments comprehensible only to other logicians) which constitutes the bulk of contemporary philosophizing. These are refreshing recommendations, the more so because they come from a recent president of the American Philosophical Association. But they cannot be pursued here. I shall consider, however, Rorty's admittedly pragmatic view of knowledge.

At first glance, to be sure, the notion of knowledge as "what our peers let us get away with saying" seems a rather slim and disappointing result of 2500 years of earnest philosophical reflection. But there is some plausibility about the idea, and it may well contain more truth than most of us would happily admit to. Consider the following examples (which are not Rorty's). . . .

Among the things I claim to know is that George Washington was the first president of the United States. Now on what basis can I be so audacious as to claim to know this? I never saw Washington at all, and certainly not functioning presidentially. My teachers told me? But surely my teachers are not infallible. I read it in books? But I can't rely on everything I read. Government documents? Perhaps a part of government myth-making. And on we could go. Is it all that farfetched to say that a claim to know holds in this case precisely because no one challenges the claim? In those cases where I believe just what everyone else also believes, I am very likely to be able to "get away with saying" that I *know.*

A person's claims to know will also ordinarily go unchallenged in cases where he is thought to have privileged access (for example, his own pains or mental states), where he is regarded as an expert, or where the claim simply doesn't arouse enough interest to make it worth challenging. I say "ordinarily" because there may be exceptional cases where even a person's knowledge of his own pain would be challenged (consider the skeptical reaction to Roberto Duran's alleged stomach cramps during his fight with Sugar Ray Leonard . . .) and in all of these cases one's status in the opinion of his peers will have much to do with whether or not the claim to know is challenged. Some people have the good fortune to have their every pronouncement taken as almost oracular (such people, I believe, are likely to feel little inclination to skepticism); but others try in vain to have their words taken seriously.

The claims to know in the examples above are rather trivial. But now suppose that I claim to know that God exists and created the world. This is a controversial claim, and not all of my peers will let it pass. My fellow church members and Christian colleagues may well accept the claim; a typical gathering of American philosophers probably would not. So it appears that I can properly be said to know things about God in some groups of peers, but not in others. Thus Rorty's view seems to have the unsatisfying result that one both knows and does not know the truth of certain controversial propositions, or at least the consequence that the more narrowly one construes her peers the more she will be able to know (a consequence which explains, as sociologists of religion have long understood, why many religious groups discourage contact with the outside world). Knowledge is peer-group relative.

As unhappy as we may be with such a relativistic theory of knowledge, we need to recognize that it stems from the failure to locate a common ground which could serve as a neutral basis for human knowledge. Although Rorty does not construe the idea of a common ground in a specifically theological way, his claim that there appears to be no common ground seems not all that far removed from what some Reformed theologians (notably followers of Cornelius Van Til) have also claimed. My purpose here, however, is not to engage in a critique of Rorty but to ask whether "Reformed epistemology" will serve us better. For this we turn to Alvin Plantinga.

Plantinga, too, concurs in the judgment that the usual versions of foundationalism (what he calls "strong" or "classical" foundationalism) are untenable and even incoherent. But Plantinga is inclined to accept what he calls "weak" foundationalism. Indeed, he argues that belief in God may be placed in the foundation of knowledge; or, to put it another way, belief in God is "properly basic." What this means is that Plantinga will not attempt to deduce God's existence from some other self-evident propositions (as does a traditional deductivist like Descartes), nor will he try to reach God's existence inductively from some indubitable givens of sensation (like, say, Aquinas). Instead he begins by boldly placing God's existence in the foundation of knowledge. As attractive as this move will surely appear to many Reformed Christians, the question I suppose is whether it will wash outside of Grand Rapids (or some similar place).

Now as I understand Plantinga's work in the philosophy of religion, its main thrust is to refute the charge that belief in God is irrational. Through powerful and often complicated arguments, Plantinga has repeatedly demolished the claims of anti-theists that belief in God is unjustified, irrational, and perhaps even immoral. One of his tactics has been to show that belief in God is in the same boat, epistemically, with beliefs which the anti-theists (and virtually everyone else) *do* hold, but which can no more easily be demonstrated than can the existence of God. Such beliefs include the belief in the existence of other minds and in the existence of a physical world which has existed for more than five minutes. But if it is not irrational to believe in the existence of minds other than our own (even though such existence can't be proved), Plantinga asks, why is it irrational to believe in God? The anti-theist has not demonstrated that such belief *is* irrational. Hence the theist violates no epistemological principles by believing in God.

Plantinga's work in this area has been a major achievement. Its primary beneficiaries, I think, are those theists who feel rather defensive and even apologetic about holding beliefs which "rational" people consider irrational. Armed with Plantinga, the theist need not allow herself to be bamboozled by the slurs of secularists.

I have no objection to Plantinga's contention that belief in God is rational even if, for some people, it is basic. It is not clear, however, why we can move from this to the claim of *knowledge*. Further, some of the theist's peers will undoubtedly protest that if belief in God can be properly basic, then just any belief can be claimed to be basic. But Plantinga anticipates and replies to this objection:

> If belief in God is properly basic, why can't *just any* belief be properly basic? Couldn't we say the same for any bizarre aberration we can think of? What about voodoo or astrology? What about the belief that the Great Pumpkin returns every Halloween? . . . If we say that belief in God is properly basic, won't we be committed to holding that just anything, or nearly anything, can properly be taken as basic, thus throwing wide the gates to irrationalism and superstition?
>
> Certainly not. What might lead one to think the Reformed epistemologist is in this kind of trouble? The fact that he rejects the criteria for proper basicality purveyed by classical foundationalism? But why should *that* be thought to commit him to such tolerance of irrationality?[5]

Now it seems to me that Plantinga takes this objection too lightly. Surely, as he says, the Reformed epistemologist is not *herself* committed to taking belief in the Great Pumpkin as properly basic! But that isn't the point. The question is whether the Reformed epistemologist could show a serious Great Pumpkin advocate (let's call him a "Pumpkinite") that *his* belief is *not* properly basic. And if she cannot show this, aren't we back to Rorty's relativistic peer groups? Couldn't a disinterested observer judge that the main difference between the theist and the Pumpkinite claims to proper basicality is that one has a much larger supporting community than the other? But how is that relevant? Even if we concede Plantinga's point that not anything goes and agree to throw out seemingly absurd candidates for basicality, it is difficult to see why, at the very lest, the adherents of the world's major religions and anti-religions could not claim that their beliefs are properly placed in the foundation of knowledge.

One of the problems here, I think is that the standard of "rationality" is too permissive and relativistic to serve as a criterion for knowledge. As Plantinga construes rationality, whether or not a person is rational has to do with the relations among her various beliefs, or with what he calls a person's "noetic structure." A person whose beliefs are mutually consistent or who has good reasons for some particular beliefs, for example, may be considered rational even though many of his beliefs are false. If all of the weather reports call for a major snow storm, a person's belief that it will snow and that he should take his boots to work would be considered rational. But the storm may pass over. One can hold a belief rationally which turns out to be false. Rationality is not truth-guaranteeing.

Consider one of Plantinga's examples:

> What about a fourteen-year-old theist brought up to believe in God in a community where everyone believes? This fourteen-year-old theist, we may suppose, doesn't believe on the basis of evidence. . . . Instead, he simply believes what he is taught. Is he violating an all-things-considered intellectual duty? Surely not.[6]

The fourteen-year-old theist, I take it, may be considered "rational" in this case. He violates no epistemological principles. But, of course, the very same thing can be said for *any* fourteen year old who believes what he is taught (perhaps even a fourteen-year-old Pumpkinite raised in an isolated rural Pumpkinite community). So rationality will not help us make the transition from belief to knowledge; or so it seems to me. And this is made quite clear, I think, in Plantinga's reply to one of his questioners at the Wheaton Conference:

> I think it's not appropriate to take as basic the proposition that God doesn't exist. But it doesn't follow from that that I either do or ought to think that I could prove to somebody who thinks it is appropriate to take that proposition as basic that he's wrong. Maybe I can't. Maybe when he and I sit down together to work out our criteria for proper basicality, maybe we don't start from enough of the same examples, maybe we just won't arrive at the same criteria. So I can't prove it to him. But nonetheless, I've got my views and he's got his. He thinks I'm starting in the wrong place. I think he's starting in the wrong place.

Can either of the parties in the unresolvable dispute above claim to know? I rather doubt it. Both parties may be rational in the sense that they think consistently relative to what they take to be properly basic. But rationality, as we have seen, does not guarantee truth; so rational belief, while surely preferable to irrational belief, does not seem to add up to knowledge.

I do not dispute Plantinga's claim that belief in God is rational as he construes the term "rationality." But the question remains: Can we *know* anything about God? Can we advance beyond the choice between skepticism and peer-group relativism? At one point Plantinga seems close to opting for peer-group relativism. He says:

> . . . perhaps a religious belief (as opposed to a memory belief, or a sense belief) is properly basic only if it is *shared by a community;* perhaps a merely private religion is irrational.[7]

But here again he is talking about rationality, not about knowledge. And even if the rationality of religious belief depends on community sharing, the questions of truth and knowledge are still unanswered. Contradictory sets of beliefs can be rational relative to their adherents.

While further developments in Reformed epistemology may serve to clarify some of the issues I have raised, it appears so far to have failed to supply a criterion for knowledge to replace that of the classical foundationalism which it rejects. Lacking a criterion for what may legitimately count as knowledge (and specifically for what sorts of propositions may be taken as foundational or basic), one may wonder whether Reformed epistemology can avoid a relativism like that of Rorty. Or perhaps knowledge as a sort of universal currency negotiable among all peoples is simply not available to mortals. But then one may also wonder whether the choice between Reformed epistemology and a fideistic skepticism (one, say, which believes in God but doesn't claim to know) involves much more than mere linguistic preference about how to use the admittedly useful word "knowledge." For as the noted historian of skepticism Richard Popkin has observed, skepticism about the merits of knowledge claims is by no means necessarily incompatible with religious belief. One can heartily believe in "God the father, almighty, maker of heaven and earth, and in Jesus Christ his only son, our Lord" without claiming to *know* these things. Does a claim to know here *add* anything to the heartfelt belief, and inner certainty? Does it mean *more* than that the belief is without doubt, unshakeable, and at the very core of one's being? If so, what more?

Notes

1. Nicholas Wolterstorff, *Reason within the Bounds of Religion* (Grand Rapids: Eerdmans, 1976), p. 33.
2. Wolterstorff, *Reason,* p. 34.
3. Wolterstorff, *Reason,* p. 42.
4. Wolterstorff, *Reason,* p. 50.
5. Plantinga, "Reformed Objection." Also, Lecture III presented at Wheaton Annual Philosophy Conference, 1980.
6. Plantinga, Wheaton Lecture, 1.
7. Plantinga, "Reformed Objection."

---

31. Is Reason Enough?

NICHOLAS WOLTERSTORFF

One of the characteristic differences between the Reformed and the Anglo-American Evangelical traditions of Christendom is their difference in attitude toward the project of giving arguments for the Christian faith. Reformed people characteristically have a deep intuitive revulsion against this project. They are convinced that it is useless, or worse, pernicious and idolatrous, to give preeminence to Reason rather than to Christ. Yet they have not been reluctant to meet head-on the arguments of the objectors to the faith. Neither have they been reluctant to give theoretical articulation to the Christian faith. Nor have they been reluctant to engage in the academic disciplines in the light of the Christian faith. In short, though Reformed people are profoundly convinced of the importance of theoretical activity in the life of the Christian community and in the life of humanity generally, of the giving of arguments for the faith they want no part.

Evangelicals are typically just the opposite. Often they have been suspicious of the worth of academic theology. Only episodically have they been persuaded of the worth—or even the *sense*—of engaging in the academic disciplines in the light of the Christian faith. What leaps to their attention when they read the history of culture is the dangerous and seductive character of theorizing. They perceive that over and over the theoretician has served the false god of Reason. And yet the project of giving evidences for the Christian faith exercises an irresistible lure for them.

Reformed persons have no taste at all for undergirding the Christian faith with evidences. Yet they are deeply committed to expressing their faith by way of theorizing.

Source: Nicholas Wolterstorff, "Is Reason Enough?" *The Reformed Journal* (April 1981), published by Wm. B. Eerdmans Publishing Company, Grand Rapids, MI. Used by permission.

Evangelicals have little taste for expressing the faith by way of theorizing. Yet they are profoundly committed to assembling evidences to undergird the faith. What strange and surprising oppositions!

I

What brings these reflections to mind is my recent reading of a new book by an articulate theologian from the Evangelical tradition, Clark H. Pinnock. The book is entitled *Reason Enough: A Case for the Christian Faith.*[1] I should say at once, however, that Pinnock is not at all a typical member of the Evangelical tradition—at least if I have represented that tradition correctly above. He is not suspicious of theorizing; he sees its importance as one of the ways in which the Christian community gives expression to its faith. He is characteristic, though, in his insistence that giving evidence for the faith is both legitimate and important.

I want here to engage him in discussion on what he says. And I do mean *engage him in discussion.* I do not propose to trot out all the old positions and arguments and do battle. The times for that are over, if ever they were present. I want to put my questions to Pinnock in the expectation that there is something here for each to learn from the other.

For whom is Pinnock's book meant? To whom does he wish to present his evidences for the truth of the Christian faith? To the person considering whether or not to accept the Christian faith. The person Pinnock has in mind is not the person ignorant of Christianity, nor the person who already has faith and is confident therein; rather, his concern is the person who pretty much knows the content of the faith and is wondering whether to accept it or not (or to continue accepting it):

> My purpose in writing this book is to communicate with people who are interested in investigating the truth claims made on behalf of the Christian message. Is Christianity, in fact, true? . . . I am writing, then, for those who do not believe and for those who experience difficulties in their believing.[2]

However, not every person considering whether to accept the faith is Pinnock's intended audience here. The person he has in mind is the one who, before she accepts the faith, wants to be sure that it would be rational for her to do so. The person Pinnock is addressing is the person who is willing to consider accepting the faith but not at the cost of sacrificing her intellect. And what Pinnock proposes to do is meet her demand. Pinnock proposes to show her that it would be rational to accept the faith. For Pinnock regards this demand as appropriate. "I do not believe," he says, "that we need to commit ourselves without reasonable grounds."[3] Pinnock urges that his apologetic efforts be placed "in the proper context, which is to test belief in God from the point of view of its rationality."[4]

Thus Pinnock sees himself as a fair-minded lawyer before what he hopes will be an equally fair-minded jury:

> I see my task as that of Christian persuasion. I am in the role of a fair-minded lawyer seeking to convince you the jury of the truth of the Christian message through the presentation of the evidences at my disposal. . . . I am . . . aiming at . . . a testing of faith in the light of knowledge which will enable you to take that step of commitment without sacrificing your intellect.[5]

"I am committed," says Pinnock,

> to appealing to reason to try to persuade those yet unconvinced to make a decision for Jesus
> Christ. Faith according to the Bible does not involve a rash decision made without reflec-
> tion or a blind submission in the face of an authoritarian claim.[6]

But do not expect too much of the evidential arguments that he will offer, says
Pinnock. He is not, in the fashion of Thomistic natural theology, going to offer
demonstrations—deductive arguments from premises which are self-evident to the attentive mind or evident to the senses. Rather, he is going to argue that Christianity is
the best available explanation of various phenomena. And this gives us something
weaker than demonstrations.

> I am not aiming at rational proof. . . . We will be dealing here with reasonable probabilities.
> No world view offers more than that, and Christianity offers nothing less. There will come a
> day I believe when God will reveal his glory in an unmistakable way and there will no
> longer be any room for doubt and hesitation. But that day is not yet, and in the meantime
> we work with reasonable probabilities which, while they do not create or compel belief, do
> establish the credible atmosphere in which faith can be born and can grow.[7]

What does Pinnock hope for as the outcome of his efforts at persuasion? A more
or less tentative acceptance of Christianity as the best explanation of various phenomena? Not at all. What he asks of his jury is that, once he has met their demand to show
them that it would be rational to accept the Christian faith, they *commit* themselves to
Jesus Christ. God's "way is to provide us with good and sufficient evidence of reasonable, persuasive force, and then to invite us to enter into the trustful certitude of
faith."[8] Such faith "is the act of wholehearted trust in the goodness and promises of the
God who confronts us with his reality and gives us ample reason to believe that he is
there."[9] And so, says Pinnock, "open yourself up to God, confess your failure to live a
just and holy life, and determine to follow the Lord Jesus. Act upon the evidence that
stands before you and accept the saving offer that is being extended."[10] Pinnock never
explicates the relation between believing with some tentativity that Christianity is the
best explanation of various phenomena and adopting the trustful certitude of faith. But
clearly he does not blur the difference between the two.

Pinnock's project then is to show to the person who wonders whether Christianity
is rational that it is indeed that. And he proposes to accomplish this by giving evidence
for the truth of Christianity.

What does he propose to allow as evidence? A proposition that is evident with respect to one body of propositions may not be such with respect to another. Or to put it
the other way round: one set of propositions may be good evidence for a certain proposition while another set is not. So when someone proposes to give evidence for Christianity, we must ask what he proposes to take as evidence. Where does he start? Well,
since the project is to persuade the unbeliever, we have to start with something that the
unbeliever accepts, and is justified in accepting. What Pinnock proposes to start with is
our perceptual knowledge. This will provide us the evidence. And from this we are to
make what anyone recognizes as reasonable inferences to Christianity:

I do not want to make any special demands in the area of knowledge. I have no hidden assumptions, no special philosophy. My contention is that the truth claims of the Christian gospel can be checked out in the ordinary ways we verify the things we know.[11]

The full picture then is this: Pinnock is addressing himself to that person wondering whether to accept the Christian faith who has stipulated that before he accepts it he be shown that it is rational to do so. Pinnock then undertakes to meet this demand. He does so by, as he sees it, trying to show that Christianity is more probable than not with respect to our perceptual knowledge. In particular, he tries to show that Christianity is the best explanation of various phenomena. And then, having met the demand to show that it is rational to accept the faith, he urges the person to commit himself to Christ.

II

I do not here wish to scrutinize Pinnock's actual arguments. I wish rather to reflect on the project he has set to himself. Before I do so, however, let me say that among my acquaintances is one for whom the decisive step in his conversion to Christianity some years back was his consideration of the evidence for the truth of Christianity. So let the Reformed person not leap into the fray here insisting that arguments presented to unbelievers for the truth of Christianity are always useless, or even pernicious. They are not. One can appropriately ask what exactly they do, under what circumstances they do it, etc., but what is not in question is that sometimes they work beneficially.

The person Pinnock has in mind is the person who is considering whether or not to accept Christianity and who has resolved to do so only if he or she is assured that it is rational to do so. Now evidently Pinnock believes that the characteristic difficulty for such a person—that which hinders him from accepting the faith—is that the evidence for the truth of Christianity is not available to him or has not been presented vividly enough to him. He hasn't perceived the evidential hookup between his perceptual knowledge and Christian teaching. For what Pinnock addresses to this person is a discourse in which he presents to him evidence for the truth of Christianity.

The first question I want to pose is whether Pinnock's analysis of the typical situation is correct. Characteristic of the Reformed tradition is quite a different analysis. What the Reformed person would suspect as operative in this and other cases of unbelief is not so much insufficient awareness of the evidence, as it is *resistance* to the available evidence. Calvin's thought, for example—which he bases in part on Romans 1—is that God has planted in every human being a disposition to believe in the existence of a divine Creator, and that this disposition is triggered, or activated, by our awareness of the richly complex design of the cosmos and of ourselves. It was not Calvin's thought that we *inferred* the existence of a divine Creator from perceptual knowledge of the existence of design. It was rather his thought that the awareness of the design immediately causes the belief—just as having certain sensations immediately convinces us that we are in the presence of another human person. It is possible, though, said Calvin, to resist the workings of this disposition. And one of the characteristic effects of sin is that we do resist it. The sinner prefers *not* to acknowledge the existence of a divine Creator.

Thus Calvin's picture of the unbeliever is of one who characteristically resists acknowledging what he really knows, not of course because he has any evidence for its falsehood, rather because he does not *like* to believe it.

Of course it's perfectly compatible with what Calvin says to acknowledge that a given person may feel very little or none of this resistance anymore. It may now be only a dim memory with him; he may feel little or no impulse anymore to believe that God exists.

Now of course one treats differently the person one views as resisting God than the person one views as having insufficient evidence of God. And one of the reasons the Reformed tradition has been so skeptical of the benefit of giving evidence is that it sees resistance as the key factor. For what, after all, does one do to overcome resistance to this truth? Well, for one thing, one attacks whatever defenses have been built up; thus it is that the Reformed tradition has characteristically gone on the attack against objections to Christianity. For the rest, one tries to bring to light the roots of the resistance, in the hope that God through his Spirit will work in the heart of the unbeliever so as to move him or her from resistance to love.

Let me give an analogy. Marx and Freud have taught us that often what shapes our beliefs is more or less hidden desires to protect our economic position or overcome our sense of insecurity. We construct ideologies, or rationalizations. Given its sources, the way to relieve someone of an ideology or rationalization is not to lay in front of him or her evidence for its falsehood. Usually that won't work. One must get at those hidden dynamics and bring them to light. Critique or therapy, rather than presenting evidence, is what is required.

Who is right here? Well, is it not in fact characteristic of converts to the Christian faith to confess that they had been resisting? And is this not the biblical picture of our human situation as well? But perhaps we must distinguish here, as Calvin himself did. Perhaps the person who refuses to be a theist knows better, and is resisting. But perhaps sometimes the person who is a theist but not a Christian has never had the reasons for accepting the gospel of Jesus Christ forcefully laid before him. Perhaps he has never been presented with the authenticity of the apostolic teaching, and its testimony to the resurrection of Jesus Christ. It is true that there are those who, when presented with this, resist. But probably there are also those who, having imbibed the anti-religious spirit of the modern Western world, have never seriously faced up to the grounds for accepting the Christian faith. To such a person, then, one presents as forcefully as one can the evidence for the truth of Christianity.

My guess, then, is that sometimes Pinnock's strategy is relevant. I judge, though, that it is relevant to fewer people than he seems to suppose. And in any case, Pinnock seriously neglects that fundamental factor of resistance.

III

Pinnock, to say it once again, has his eye on those who are considering whether or not to accept the Christian faith and want to be assured that it would be rational for them to do so. And since Pinnock agrees that God asks us to believe only what is rational for us to believe, he tries to meet the challenge. But is the assumption correct? Does God in fact ask us to believe only what is rational to believe?

The Christian, in my judgment, is not entitled to deal with this question by dismissing the issue of rationality out of hand. Rationality is one of the things God asks of us. To say that it is rational for me to believe something is to say that I am *justified* in believing it. And to say that I am justified in believing it is to say that I am *permitted* to believe it. Further, to say that I am permitted to believe it is to say that believing it is *not in violation of the norms* that pertain to my believings—that my believing it does not represent any failure on my part to have governed my believings as I ought to have done.

Now surely the Christian agrees that we do have obligations with respect to our believings. It is not true that anything goes in our treatment of other human beings; neither is it true that anything goes in our believings. And as with moral obligations, so with intellectual obligations: ultimately these are grounded in our responsibility to God. The reason the Christian cannot dismiss the claims of rationality, then, is that these are God's claims on him. It is as shallow to suppose that God asks us in general to choose between Christ and rationality as it would be shallow to suppose that God asks us in general to choose between Christ and morality.

Nonetheless, I do not think we can conclude that God will never ask us to believe what would not be rational for us to believe. For intellectual obligations are only one among various types of obligations; and in specific cases they may well be overridden by obligations of other types. This is clear in simple cases. Sometimes I have to choose between taking my daughter boating and calculating my bank account with sufficient care for me to be fully justified in my belief as to the size of the balance; and in some such cases, I ought to choose the former. May it not be so in the matter of Christian belief as well? Suppose that a relatively unsophisticated believer listens to a powerful attack on Christianity and finds herself incapable of finding any flaw in the attack. Suppose that she talks to others, and that they too can find no flaw. May it not be then that she is no longer intellectually justified in accepting the faith—that she does so in violation of the evidence available to her? Nonetheless, I do not believe that she should give up the faith, and neither, I suspect, does Pinnock.

Such a situation can best be understood, I think, as a situation in which God has permitted the person to enter into a trial. The biblical witness makes clear that faith may be tried. Usually the trial is that of suffering. But may the trial not sometimes take the form of an intellectual trial in which we are asked to endure in the faith in spite of the fact that we find ourselves with adequate reason to give it up?

IV

Many in the Reformed tradition would object to Pinnock's undertaking because, they would argue, there is in fact no point of contact, no common ground, between believer and unbeliever, and thus Pinnock's project cannot possibly succeed. Either he will surreptitiously grant something to the unbeliever that he should not grant, or the unbeliever will unwittingly grant something to Pinnock that he or she as an unbeliever should not grant.

I do not share this objection. When the believer tries to offer evidence to the unbeliever for the truth of Christianity, he tries to find beliefs that both of them believe and are justified in believing, and with respect to which Christianity is evident. I see no reason to suppose that this is in principle impossible. Believers and unbelievers do in fact share justified beliefs—many of them. And I see no reason to suppose that Christianity is never evident with respect to such shared beliefs.

Actually, whether or not there are *shared* justified beliefs is not actually relevant. What counts is simply whether the unbeliever has justified beliefs with respect to which Christianity is evident. Whether those justified beliefs are shared is not to the point. And if Christianity *is* evident with respect to the justified beliefs of some unbeliever, what could possibly be wrong with pointing this out to him or her?

Nonetheless, there are questions to be raised about Pinnock's procedure—or his understanding of it. The way in which the traditional dispute over common ground was conducted seems to me to have seriously misconceived the situation. One party assumed that there was no common ground between believer and unbeliever. The other party assumed that there *was* common ground. The truth is that, for any pair of believer and unbeliever, there will be shared justified beliefs; but the particular beliefs shared will differ from pair to pair. The common ground between a Barthian Christian and a positivist is very different from that between a liberal Christian and a Muslim.

What this means is that apologetics must always be person-specific. It must always be contextual. An apologetic satisfactory for all comers is impossible. Granted, as Pinnock observes, the New Testament writers gave reasons for the faith that was in them. But the reasons Peter gave on Pentecost were peculiarly relevant to Jews, and the reasons Paul gave in Athens were peculiarly relevant to Greeks—and neither of these sets of reasons is directly relevant to contemporary positivists.

Pinnock proposes to start solely from some items of perceptual knowledge. Presumably his reason for doing so is that he thinks these items are common to all—that everyone is justified in believing them. That is more than dubious. But in any case, even a hasty glance at his arguments will make clear that they are far indeed from all starting out solely from perceptual knowledge. In fact, what Pinnock does is construct an apologetic relevant to typical Western twentieth-century university students.

V

I raise one last point. "We must," says Pinnock, "exercise critical judgment in the context of our beliefs, so that the faith we hold is reasonable." And presumably he is speaking to everyone here, not just to inquirers. Now if an unbeliever comes along and asks to be shown that it would be reasonable for him to accept the faith, and if one thinks it best to meet this request head-on rather than treating it "therapeutically," then one thing one might try doing is present evidence for the truth of Christianity, starting from things that it is already reasonable for him to believe. But where does that leave you and me, who are already believers? We also are enjoined to be reasonable in our beliefs, other things being equal. Must we also have evidential arguments? Starting from what? From sensory experience? And what about the simple believer in Uganda? Must she also, if she is to be justified in her belief, have evidential arguments of the Pinnockian sort?

It is crucial here to distinguish two situations, all too often confused. It is one thing, given a person's set of beliefs, to distinguish those that are rational from those that are not, and then to raise the question: What accounts for the rationality of those that are rational? It is quite another thing, when a person does not yet believe a certain thing, to answer his question whether it *would be* rational for him to believe it, by presenting him with evidence for its truth.

Deeply embedded in the Reformed tradition is the conviction that a person's belief that God exists may be a justified belief even though that person has not inferred that belief from others of his beliefs which provide good evidence for it. After all, not all the things we are justified in believing have been inferred from other beliefs. We have to start somewhere! And the Reformed tradition has insisted that the belief that God exists, that God is Creator, etc., may justifiably be found there in the foundation of our system of beliefs. In that sense, the Reformed tradition has been fideist, not evidentialist, in its impulse. It seems to me that that impulse is correct. It is not in general true that to be justified in believing in God one has to believe this on the basis of evidence provided by one's other beliefs. We are entitled to reason *from* our belief in God without first having reasoned *to* it.

But if fideism is true, then perhaps there is available another and quite different way of answering the inquirer than the way Pinnock pursues. Pinnock tries to show the inquirer that it would be rational for him to accept the faith by showing him that the faith is probable with respect to his justified beliefs. Perhaps it would be just as well or better to point out to some inquirers that justifiably believing in God does not always require holding that belief on the basis of arguments.

Notes

1. Clark H. Pinnock, *Reason Enough: A Case for the Christian Faith* (Downers Grove, IL: Inter-Varsity Press, 1980).
2. Pinnock, *Reason Enough,* pp. 9–10.
3. Pinnock, *Reason Enough,* p. 10.
4. Pinnock, *Reason Enough,* p. 69.
5. Pinnock, *Reason Enough,* pp. 17–18.
6. Pinnock, *Reason Enough,* p. 13.
7. Pinnock, *Reason Enough,* p. 18.
8. Pinnock, *Reason Enough,* p. 121.
9. Pinnock, *Reason Enough,* p. 13.
10. Pinnock, *Reason Enough,* pp. 121–22.
11. Pinnock, *Reason Enough,* p. 17.

32. Is Belief in God Properly Basic?

ALVIN PLANTINGA

Many philosophers have urged the *evidentialist* objection to theistic belief; they have argued that belief in God is irrational or unreasonable or not rationally acceptable or intellectually irresponsible or noetically substandard, because, as they say, there is insufficient evidence for it.[1] Many other philosophers and theologians—in particular, those in the great tradition of natural theology—have claimed that belief in God is intellectually acceptable, but only because the fact is there is sufficient evidence for it. These two groups unite in holding that theistic belief is rationally acceptable only if there is sufficient evidence for it. More exactly, they hold that a person is rational or reasonable in accepting theistic belief only if she has sufficient evidence for it—only if, that is, she knows or rationally believes some *other* propositions which support the one in question, and believes the latter on the basis of the former. In "Is Belief in God Rational?," I argued that the evidentialist objection is rooted in *classical foundationalism*,[2] an enormously popular picture or total way of looking at faith, knowledge, justified belief, rationality, and allied topics. This picture has been widely accepted ever since the days of Plato and Aristotle; its near relatives, perhaps, remain the dominant ways of thinking about these topics. We may think of the classical foundationalist as beginning with the observation that some of one's beliefs may be *based upon* others; it may be that there are a pair of propositions A and B such that I believe A *on the basis of B*. Although this relation isn't easy to characterize in a revealing and nontrivial fashion, it is nonetheless familiar. I believe that the word "umbrageous" is spelled u-m-b-r-a-g-e-o-u-s; this belief is based on another belief of mine: the belief that that's how the dictionary says it's spelled. I believe that $72 \times 71 = 5112$. This belief is based upon several other beliefs I hold: that $1 \times 72 = 72$; $7 \times 2 = 14$; $7 \times 7 = 49$; $49 + 1 = 50$; and others. Some of my beliefs, however, I accept but don't accept on the basis of any other beliefs. Call these beliefs *basic*. I believe that $2 + 1 = 3$, for example, and don't believe it on the basis of other propositions. I also believe that I am seated at my desk, and that there is a mild pain in my right knee. These too are basic to me; I don't believe them on the basis of any other propositions. According to the classical foundationalist, some propositions are *properly* or *rightly* basic for a person and some are not. Those that are not, are rationally accepted only on the basis of *evidence*, where the evidence must trace back, ultimately, to what is properly basic. The existence of God, furthermore, is not among the propositions that are properly basic; hence a person is rational in accepting theistic belief only if he has evidence for it.

Source: Alvin Plantinga, "Is Belief in God Properly Basic?" *Nous* 15 1(1981), 41–51.

Now many Reformed thinkers and theologians[3] have rejected *natural theology* (thought of as the attempt to provide proofs or arguments for the existence of God). They have held not merely that the proffered arguments are unsuccessful, but that the whole enterprise is in some way radically misguided. In "The Reformed Objection to Natural Theology," I argue that the reformed rejection of natural theology is best construed as an inchoate and unfocused rejection of classical foundationalism.[4] What these Reformed thinkers really mean to hold, I think, is that belief in God need not be based on argument or evidence from other propositions at all. They mean to hold that the believer is entirely within his intellectual rights in believing as he does even if he doesn't know of any good theistic argument (deductive or inductive), even if he doesn't believe that there is any such argument, and even if in fact no such argument exists. They hold that it is perfectly rational to accept belief in God without accepting it on the basis of any other beliefs or propositions at all. In a word, they hold that *belief in God is properly basic*. In this paper I shall try to develop and defend this position.

But first we must achieve a deeper understanding of the evidentialist objection. It is important to see that this contention is a *normative* contention. The evidentialist objector holds that one who accepts theistic belief is in some way irrational or noetically substandard. Here 'rational' and 'irrational' are to be taken as normative or evaluative terms; according to the objector, the theist fails to measure up to a standard he ought to conform to. There is a right way and a wrong way with respect to belief as with respect to actions; we have duties, responsibilities, obligations with respect to the former just as with respect to the latter. So Professor Blanshard:

> . . . everywhere and always belief has an ethical aspect. There is such a thing as a general ethics of the intellect. The main principle of that ethic I hold to be the same inside and outside religion. This principle is simple and sweeping: Equate your assent to the evidence.[5]

This "ethics of the intellect" can be construed variously; many fascinating issues—issues we must here forebear to enter—arise when we try to state more exactly the various options the evidentialist may mean to adopt. Initially it looks as if he holds that there is a duty or obligation of some sort not to accept without evidence such propositions as that God exists—a duty flouted by the theist who has no evidence. If he has no evidence, then it is his duty to cease believing. But there is an oft-remarked difficulty: one's beliefs, for the most part, are not directly under one's control. Most of those who believe in God could not divest themselves of that belief just by trying to do so, just as they could not in that way rid themselves of the belief that the world has existed for a very long time. So perhaps the relevant obligation is not that of divesting myself of theistic belief if I have no evidence (that is beyond my power), but to try to cultivate the sorts of intellectual habits that will tend (we hope) to issue in my accepting as basic only propositions that are properly basic.

Perhaps this obligation is to be thought of *teleologically*: it is a moral obligation arising out of a connection between certain intrinsic goods and evils and the way in which our beliefs are formed and held. (This seems to be W. K. Clifford's way of construing the matter.) Perhaps it is to be thought of *aretetically*: there are valuable noetic or intellectual states (whether intrinsically or extrinsically valuable); there are also corresponding intellectual virtues, habits of acting so as to promote and enhance those valuable states. Among one's obligations, then, is the duty to try to foster and cultivate these virtues in oneself or others. Or perhaps it is to be thought of *deontologically:* this obligation attaches to us just by virtue of our having the sort of noetic equipment human beings do in fact display; it does not arise out of a connection with valuable states of affairs. Such an obligation, furthermore, could be a special sort of moral obligation; on the other hand, perhaps it is a sui generis non-moral obligation.

Still further, perhaps the evidentialist need not speak of duty or obligation here at all. Consider someone who believes that Venus is smaller than Mercury, not because he has evidence of any sort, but because he finds it amusing to hold a belief no one else does—or consider someone who holds this belief on the basis of some outrageously bad argument. Perhaps there isn't any obligation he has failed to meet. Nevertheless his intellectual condition is deficient in some way; or perhaps alternatively there is a commonly achieved excellence he fails to display. And the evidentialist objection to theistic belief, then, might be understood as the claim, not that the theist without evidence has failed to meet an obligation, but that he suffers from a certain sort of intellectual deficiency (so that the proper attitude toward him would be sympathy rather than censure).

These are some of the ways, then, in which the evidentialist objection could be developed; and of course there are still other possibilities. For ease of exposition, let us take the claim deontologically; what I shall say will apply mutatis mutandis if we take it one of the other ways. The evidentialist objection, therefore, presupposes some view as to what sorts of propositions are correctly, or rightly, or justifiably taken as basic; it presupposes a view as to what is *properly* basic. And the minimally relevant claim for the evidentialist objector is that belief in God is *not* properly basic. Typically this objection has been rooted in some form of *classical foundationalism*, according to which a proposition *p* is properly basic for a person *S* if and only if *p* is either self-evident or incorrigible for *S* (modern foundationalism) or either self-evident or 'evident to the senses' for *S* (ancient and medival foundationalism). In "Is Belief in God Rational?" I argued that both forms of foundationalism are self-referentially incoherent and must therefore be rejected.[6]

Insofar as the evidentialist objection is rooted in classical foundationalism, it is poorly rooted indeed: and so far as I know, no one has developed and articulated any other reason for supposing that belief in God is not properly basic. Of course it doesn't follow that it *is* properly basic; perhaps the class of properly basic propositions is broader than classical foundationalists think, but still not broad enough to admit belief in God. But why think so? What might be the objections to the Reformed view that belief in God is properly basic?

I've heard it argued that if I have no evidence for the existence of God, then if I accept that proposition, my belief will be groundless, or gratuitous, or arbitrary. I think this is an error; let me explain.

Suppose we consider perceptual beliefs, memory beliefs, and beliefs which ascribe mental states to other persons: such beliefs as

1. I see a tree,
2. I had breakfast this morning,

and

3. That person is angry.

Although beliefs of this sort are typically and properly taken as basic, it would be a mistake to describe them as *groundless*. Upon having experience of a certain sort, I believe that I am perceiving a tree. In the typical case I do not hold this belief on the basis of other beliefs; it is nonetheless not groundless. My having that characteristic sort of experience—to use Professor Chisholm's language, my being appeared treely to—plays a crucial role in the formation and justification of that belief. We might say this experience, together, perhaps, with other circumstances, is what *justifies* me in holding it; this is the *ground* of my justification, and, by extension, the ground of the belief itself.

If I see someone displaying typical pain behavior, I take it that he or she is in pain. Again, I don't take the displayed behavior as *evidence* for that belief; I don't infer that belief from others I hold; I don't accept it on the basis of other beliefs. Still, my perceiving the pain behavior plays a unique role in the formation and justification of that belief; as in the previous case, it forms the ground of my justification for the belief in question. The same holds for memory beliefs. I seem to remember having breakfast this morning; that is, I have an inclination to believe the proposition that I had breakfast, along with a certain past-tinged experience that is familiar to all but hard to describe. Perhaps we should say that I am appeared to pastly; but perhaps this insufficiently distinguishes the experience in question from that accompanying beliefs about the past not grounded in my own memory. The phenomonology of memory is a rich and unexplored realm; here I have no time to explore it. In this case as in the others, however, there is a justifying circumstance present, a condition that forms the ground of my justification for accepting the memory belief in question.

In each of these cases, a belief is taken as basic, and in each case properly taken as basic. In each case there is some circumstance or condition that confers justification; there is a circumstance that serves as the *ground* of justification. So in each case there will be some true proposition of the sort

4. In condition C, S is justified in taking p as basic.

Of course C will vary with p. For a perceptual judgment such as

5. I see a rose-colored wall before me,

C will include my being appeared to in a certain fashion. No doubt C will include more. If I'm appeared to in the familiar fashion but know that I'm wearing rose-colored glasses, or that I am suffering from a disease that causes me to be thus appeared to, no matter what the color of the nearby objects, then I'm not justified in taking (5) as basic. Similarly for memory. Suppose I know that my memory is unreliable; it often plays me tricks. In particular, when I seem to remember having breakfast, then, more often than not, I *haven't* had breakfast. Under these conditions I am not justified in taking it as basic that I had breakfast, even though I seem to remember that I did.

So being appropriately appeared to, in the perceptual case, is not sufficient for justification; some further condition—a condition hard to state in detail—is clearly necessary. The central point, here, however, is that a belief is properly basic only in certain conditions; these conditions are, we might say, the ground of its justification and, by extension, the ground of the belief itself. In this sense, basic beliefs are not, or are not necessarily, *groundless* beliefs.

Now similar things may be said about belief in God. When the Reformers claim that this belief is properly basic, they do not mean to say, of course, that there are no justifying circumstances for it, or that it is in that sense groundless or gratuitious. Quite the contrary. Calvin holds that God "reveals and daily discloses himself to the whole workmanship of the universe," and the divine art "reveals itself in the innumerable and yet distinct and well-ordered variety of the heavenly host." God has so created us that we have a tendency or disposition to see his hand in the world about us. More precisely, there is in us a disposition to believe propositions of the sort *this flower was created by God* or *this vast and intricate universe was created by God* when we contemplate the flower or behold the starry heavens or think about the vast reaches of the universe.

Calvin recognizes, at least implicitly, that other sorts of conditions may trigger this disposition. Upon reading the Bible, one may be impressed with a deep sense that God is speaking to him. Upon having done what I know is cheap, or wrong, or wicked I may feel guilty in God's sight and form the belief *God disapproves of what I've done.* Upon confession and repentence, I may feel forgiven, forming the belief *God forgives me for what I've done.* A person in grave danger may turn to God, asking for his protection and help; and of course he or she then forms the belief that God is indeed able to hear and help if he sees fit. When life is sweet and satisfying, a spontaneous sense of gratitude may well up within the soul; someone in this condition may thank and praise the Lord for his goodness, and will of course form the accompanying belief that indeed the Lord is to be thanked and praised.

There are therefore many conditions and circumstances that call forth belief in God: guilt, gratitude, danger, a sense of God's presence, a sense that he speaks, perception of various parts of the universe. A complete job would explore the phenomenology of all these conditions and of more besides. This is a large and important topic; but here I can only point to the existence of these conditions.

Of course none of the beliefs I mentioned a moment ago is the simple belief that God exists. What we have instead are such beliefs as

6. God is speaking to me,
7. God has created all this,
8. God disapproves of what I have done,
9. God forgives me,

and

10. God is to be thanked and praised.

These propositions are properly basic in the right circumstances. But it is quite consistent with this to suppose that the proposition *there is such a person as God* is neither properly basic nor taken as basic by those who believe in God. Perhaps what they take as basic are such propositions as (6)–(10), believing in the existence of God on the basis of propositions such as those. From this point of view, it isn't exactly right to say that it is belief in God that is properly basic; more exactly, what are properly basic are such propositions as (6)–(10), each of which self-evidently entails that God exists. It isn't the relatively high level and general proposition *God exists* that is properly basic, but instead propositions detailing some of his attributes or actions.

Suppose we return to the analogy between belief in God and belief in the existence of perceptual objects, other persons, and the past. Here too it is relatively specific and concrete propositions rather than their more general and abstract colleagues that are properly basic. Perhaps such items as

11. There are trees,
12. There are other persons,

and

13. The world has existed for more than five minutes,

are not in fact properly basic; it is instead such propositions as

14. I see a tree,
15. That person is pleased,

and

16. I had breakfast more than an hour ago,

that deserve that accolade. Of course propositions of the latter sort immediately and self-evidently entail propositions of the former sort; and perhaps there is thus no harm in speaking of the former as properly basic, even though so to speak is to speak a bit loosely.

The same must be said about belief in God. We may say, speaking loosely, that belief in God is properly basic; strictly speaking, however, it is probably not that proposition but such propositions as (6)–(10) that enjoy that status. But the main point, here, is that belief in God, or (6)–(10), are properly basic; to say so, however, is not to deny that there are justifying conditions for these beliefs, or conditions that confer justification on one who accepts them as basic. They are therefore not groundless or gratuitous.

A second objection I've often heard: if belief in God is properly basic, why can't *just any* belief be properly basic? Couldn't we say the same for any bizarre abberation we can think of? What about voodoo or astrology? What about the belief that the Great Pumpkin returns every Halloween? Could I properly take *that* as basic? And if I can't, why can I properly take belief in God as basic? Suppose I believe that if I flap my arms with sufficient vigor, I can take off and fly about the room; could I defend myself against the charge of irrationality by claiming this belief is basic? If we say that belief in God is properly basic, won't we be committed to holding that just anything, or nearly anything, can properly be taken as basic, thus throwing wide the gates to irrationalism and superstition?

Certainly not. What might lead one to think the Reformed epistemologist is in this kind of trouble? The fact that he rejects the criteria for proper basicality purveyed by classical foundationalism? But why should *that* be thought to commit him to such tolerance of irrationality? Consider an analogy. In the palmy days of positivism, the positivists went about confidently wielding their verifiability criterion and declaring meaningless much that was obviously meaningful. Now suppose someone rejected a formulation of that criterion—the one to be found in the second edition of A. J. Ayer's *Language, Truth and Logic*, for example. Would that mean she was committed to holding that

17. Twas brillig; and the slithy toves did gyre and gymble in the wabe,

contrary to appearances, makes good sense? Of course not. But then the same goes for the Reformed epistemologist; the fact that he rejects the classical foundationalist's criterion of proper basicality does not mean that he is committed to supposing just anything is properly basic.

But what then is the problem? Is it that the Reformed epistemologist not only rejects those criteria for proper basicality, but seems in no hurry to produce what he takes to be a better substitute? If he has no such criterion, how can he fairly reject belief in the Great Pumpkin as properly basic?

This objection betrays an important misconception. How do we rightly arrive at or develop criteria for meaningfulness, or justified belief, or proper basicality? Where do they come from? Must one have such a criterion before one can sensibly make any judgments—positive or negative—about proper basicality? Surely not. Suppose I don't know of a satisfactory substitute for the criteria proposed by classical foundationalism; I am nevertheless entirely within my rights in holding that certain propositions are not properly basic in certain conditions. Some propositions seem self-evident when in fact they are not; that is the lesson of some of the Russell paradoxes. Nevertheless it would be irrational to take as basic the denial of a proposition that seems self-evident to you. Similarly, suppose it seems to you that you see a tree; you would then be irrational in taking as basic the proposition that you don't see a tree, or that there aren't any trees. In the same way, even if I don't know of some illuminating criterion of meaning, I can quite properly declare (17) meaningless.

And this raises an important question—one Roderick Chisholm has taught us to ask. What is the status of criteria for knowledge, or proper basicality, or justified belief? Typically, these are universal statements. The modern foundationalist's criterion for proper basicality, for example, is doubly universal:

18. For any proposition A and person S, A is properly basic for S if and only if A is incorrigible for S or self-evident to S.

But how could one know a thing like that? What are its credentials? Clearly enough, (18) isn't self-evident or just obviously true. But if it isn't, how does one arrive at it? What sorts of arguments would be appropriate? Of course a foundationalist might find (18) so appealing, he simply takes it to be true, neither offering argument for it nor accepting it on the basis of other things he believes. If he does so, however, his noetic structure will be self-referentially incoherent. (18) itself is neither self-evident nor incorrigible; hence in accepting (18) as basic, the modern foundationalist violates the condition of proper basicality he himself lays down in accepting it. On the other hand, perhaps the foundationalist will try to produce some argument for it from premises that are self-evident or incorrigible: it is exceedingly hard to see, however, what such an argument might be like. And until he has produced such arguments, what shall the rest of us do—we who do not find (18) at all obvious or compelling? How could he use (18) to show us that belief in God, for example, is not properly basic? Why should we believe (18), or pay it any attention?

The fact is, I think, that neither (18) nor any other revealing necessary and sufficient condition for proper basicality follows from clearly self-evident premises by clearly acceptable arguments. And hence the proper way to arrive at such a criterion is, broadly speaking, *inductive*. We must assemble examples of beliefs and conditions such that the former are obviously properly basic in the latter, and examples of beliefs and conditions such that the former are obviously *not* properly basic in the latter. We must then frame hypotheses as to the necessary and sufficient conditions of proper basicality and test these hypothesis by reference to those examples. Under the right conditions, for example, it is clearly rational to believe that you see a human person before you: a being who has thoughts and feelings, who knows and believes things, who makes decisions and acts. It is clear, furthermore, that you are under no obligation to reason to this belief from others you hold; under those conditions that belief is properly basic for you. But then (18) must be mistaken; the belief in question, under those circumstances, is properly basic, though neither self-evident nor incorrigible for you. Similarly, you may seem to remember that you had breakfast this morning, and perhaps you know of no reason to suppose your memory is playing you tricks. If so, you are entirely justified in taking that belief as basic. Of course it isn't properly basic on the criteria offered by classical foundationalists; but that fact counts not against you but against those criteria.

Accordingly, criteria for proper basicality must be reached from below rather than above; they should not be presented as ex cathedra, but argued to and tested by a relevant set of examples. But there is no reason to assume, in advance, that everyone will agree on the examples. The Christian will of course suppose that belief in God is entirely proper and rational; if he doesn't accept this belief on the basis of other propositions, he will conclude that it is basic for him, and quite properly so. Followers of Bertrand Russell and Madelyn Murray O'Hare may disagree, but how is that relevant? Must my criteria, or those of the Christian community, conform to their examples? Surely not. The Christian community is responsible to *its* set of examples, not to theirs.

Accordingly, the Reformed epistemologist can properly hold that belief in the Great Pumpkin is not properly basic, even though he holds that belief in God is properly basic and even if he has no full-fledged criterion of proper basicality. Of course he is committed to supposing that there is a relevant *difference* between belief in God and belief in the Great Pumpkin, if he holds that the former but not the latter is properly basic. But this should prove no great embarrassment; there are plenty of candidates. These candidates are to be found in the neighborhood of the conditions I mentioned in the last section that justify and ground belief in God. Thus, for example, the

Reformed epistemologist may concur with Calvin in holding that God has implanted in us a natural tendency to see his hand in the world around us; the same cannot be said for the Great Pumpkin, there being no Great Pumpkin and no natural tendency to accept beliefs about the Great Pumpkin.

By way of conclusion then: being self-evident, or incorrigible, or evident to the senses is not a necessary condition of proper basicality. Furthermore, one who holds that belief in God *is* properly basic is not thereby committed to the idea that belief in God is groundless or gratuitous or without justifying circumstances. And even if he lacks a general criterion of proper basicality, he is not obliged to suppose that just any or nearly any belief—belief in the Great Pumpkin, for example—is properly basic. Like everyone should, he begins with examples; and he may take belief in the Great Pumpkin as a paradigm of irrational basic belief.

Notes

1. See, for example, Brand Blanshard, *Reason and Belief* (London: Allen & Unwin, 1974), pp. 400ff.; W. K. Clifford, "The Ethics of Belief," in his *Lectures and Essays* (London: Macmillan, 1879), p. 345ff.; A.G.N. Flew, *The Presumption of Atheism* (London: Pemberton Publishing Co., 1976), p. 22 (see the paper by Flew in Part I of this volume, pp. 19–32); Bertrand Russell, "Why I Am Not a Christian," in his *Why I Am Not a Christian* (New York: Simon & Schuster, 1957), p. 3ff.; and Michael Scriven, *Primary Philosophy* (New York: McGraw-Hill, 1966), p. 87ff.

2. Alvin Plantinga, "Is Belief in God Rational?" in *Rationality and Religious Belief*, ed. C.F. Delaney (Notre Dame, IN: University of Notre Dame Press, 1979), pp. 7–27.

3. A Reformed thinker or theologian is one whose intellectual sympathies lie with the Protestant tradition going back to John Calvin (not someone who was formerly a theologian and has since seen the light).

4. Alvin Plantinga, "The Reformed Objection to Natural Theology," *Proceedings of the American Catholic Philosophical Association* 15 (1980), 49–63.

5. Blanshard, *Reason and Belief*, p. 401.

6. Plantinga, "Is Belief in God Rational?"

33. A Critique of Plantinga's Religious Epistemology

MICHAEL MARTIN

One recent attempt to justify religious beliefs argues that some religious beliefs—for example, the belief that God exists—should be considered as basic beliefs that form the foundations of all other beliefs. The best-known advocate of this position is Alvin Plantinga, whose theory is based on a critique of classical foundationalism.

Foundationalism

Foundationalism was once a widely accepted view in epistemology; and although it has undergone modifications, it still has many advocates. The motivation for the view seems compelling. If we try to justify all our beliefs in terms of other beliefs, the justification generates an infinite regress or vicious circularity. Therefore, there must be some beliefs that do not need to be justified by other beliefs. Because they form the foundation of all knowledge, these are called basic beliefs, and the statements expressing them are called basic statements.

Foundationalism is usually considered a normative theory. It sets standards of what are properly basic beliefs and standards of how nonbasic beliefs are to be related to basic ones. Not every belief could be basic, and not every relation could link nonbasic beliefs to basic ones. According to the classical normative account of foundationalism, if one believes that a self-evident statement P is true because of the statement's self-evidence, then P is a properly basic one. According to this view, if a statement is self-evident, no conscious inference or calculation is required to determine its truth; one can merely look at it and know immediately that it is true. For example, certain simple and true statements of mathematics ($2 + 2 = 4$) and logic (Either p or ~p) are self-evidently true to almost everyone, while some more complex statements of mathematics and logic are self-evidently true only to some. Consequently, statements such as $2 + 2 = 4$ are considered basic statements for almost everyone while the more complex statements are basic only to some.

Source: From "Religious Beliefs and Basic Beliefs" as it appears in *Atheism: A Philosophical Justification,* by Michael Martin. Reprinted by permission of Temple University Press, © 1990 by Temple University. All rights reserved.

In addition to self-evident statements, classical foundationalists held that beliefs based on direct perception are properly basic and the statements expressing such beliefs—sometimes called statements that are evident to the senses—were considered basic statements. Some foundationalists included, in the class of statements that are evident to the senses, ones about observed physical objects (There is a blue bird in the tree). However, in modern times it has been more common for foundationalists to restrict statements that are evident to the senses to ones about immediate sense impressions (I seem to see a blue bird in the tree, or I am being appeared to bluely, or perhaps, Here now blue sense datum). According to the classical foundationalist account, statements that are evident to the senses are incorrigible; that is, one can decide not to believe such statements and be mistaken.

Denying that any statement is incorrigible, many contemporary epistemologists, although sympathetic with the foundationalist program, have maintained that statements that are evident to the senses are either initially credible or self-warranted. Moreover, some contemporary foundationalists have argued that memory statements, such as "I remember having breakfast ten minutes ago" should be included in the class of properly basic statements. Classical foundationalism also maintained that nonbasic beliefs had to be justified in terms of basic beliefs. Thus in order for a person P's nonbasic statement NS_1 (Other people have minds) to be justified, it would either have to follow logically from P's set of basic statements BS_1 & BS_2 & . . . BS_n or be probable relative to that set of statements. However, those contemporary foundationalists who maintain that properly basic statements are only initially credible allow that it is possible that a person P's basic statements BS_1 could be shown to be false if it conflicted with many of the well-supported nonbasic statements NS_1 & NS_2 & . . . NS_n of P. In addition, some have argued that deductive and inductive principles of inference must be supplemented with other principles of derivation. Consequently, a person P's nonbasic statement NS_1 is justified only if it follows from P's set of basic statements or is probable relative to this set or is justified relative to this set by means of certain special epistemic principles.

Plantinga's Critique of Foundationalism

Plantinga characterizes foundationalism as follows:

> Ancient and medieval foundationalism tended to hold that a proposition is properly basic for a person only if it is either self-evident or evident to the senses; modern foundationalism—Descartes, Locke, and Leibniz, and the like—tended to hold that a proposition is properly basic for S only if either self-evident or incorrigible for S. . . . Let us now say that a *classical foundationalist* is anyone who is either an ancient and medieval or a modern foundationalist.

He defines properly basic statements in terms of this understanding of foundationalism. Consider:

(1) A proposition p is properly basic for a person S if and only if p is self-evident to S, or incorrigible, or evident to the senses.

Plantinga gives two basic arguments against foundationalism so understood. (a) He maintains that many of the statements we know to be true cannot be justified in foundationalist terms. These statements are not properly basic according to the definition given above, nor can they be justified by either deductive or inductive inference from properly basic statements. As examples of such statements Plantinga cites "Other people have minds" and "The world existed five minutes ago." To be sure, he says, such statements are basic for most people in a descriptive sense. According to classical foundationalists, however, they should not be, since they are not self-evident, not incorrigible, and not evident to the senses. According to Plantinga, examples such as these show that there is something very wrong with classical foundationalism.

(b) Plantinga argues also that foundationalists are unable to justify (1) in their own terms; that is, they have not shown that (1) follows from properly basic statements or is probable relative to these. Moreover, (1) is not itself self-evident or incorrigible or evident to the senses. Consequently, he argues, a foundationalist who accepts (1) is being "self-referentially inconsistent"; such a person accepts a statement that does not meet the person's own conditions for being properly basic. Thus he concludes that classical foundationalism is "bankrupt."

Belief in God as Properly Basic

Following a long line of reformed thinkers—that is, thinkers influenced by the doctrines of John Calvin, Plantinga contends that traditional arguments for the existence of God are not needed for rational belief. He cites with approval Calvin's claim that God created humans in such a way that they have a strong tendency to believe in God. According to Plantinga, Calvin maintained:

> Were it not for the existence of sin in the world human beings would believe in God to the same degree and with the same natural spontaneity that we believe in the existence of other persons, an external world, or the past. This is a natural human condition; it is because of our presently unnatural sinful condition that many of us find belief in God difficult or absurd. The fact is, Calvin thinks, one who does not believe in God is in an epistemically substandard position—rather like a man who does not believe that his wife exists, or thinks that she is like a cleverly constructed robot and has no thoughts, feelings, or consciousness.

Although this natural tendency to believe in God may be partially suppressed, Plantinga argues, it is triggered by "a widely realizable condition." For example, it may be triggered "in beholding the starry heavens, or the splendid majesty of the mountains, or the intricate, articulate beauty of a tiny flower." This natural tendency to accept God in these circumstances is perfectly rational. No argument for God is needed. Plantinga maintains that the best interpretation of Calvin's views, as well as those of the other reformed thinkers he cites, is that they rejected classical foundationalism and maintained that belief in God can itself be a properly basic belief.

Surprisingly, Plantinga insists that although belief in God and belief about God's attributes and actions are properly basic, for reformed epistemologists this does not mean that there are no justifying circumstances or that they are without grounds. The circumstances that trigger the natural tendency to believe in God and to believe certain things about God provide the justifying circumstances for belief. So although beliefs about God are properly basic, they are not groundless.

How can we understand this? Plantinga draws an analogy between basic state-ments of religion and basic statements of perceptual belief and memory. A perceptual belief, he says, is taken as properly basic only under certain circumstances. For exam-ple, if I know that I am wearing rose-tinted glasses, then I am not justified in saying that the statement "I see a rose-colored wall before me" is properly basic; and if I know that my memory is unreliable, I am not justified in saying that the statement "I remember that I had breakfast" is properly basic. Although Plantinga admits that these conditions may be hard to specify, he maintains that their presence is necessary in order to claim that a perceptual or memory statement is basic. Similarly, he main-tains that not every statement about God that is not based on argument or evidence should be considered properly basic. A statement is properly basic only in the right circumstances. What circumstances are right? Plantinga gives no general account, but in addition to the triggering conditions mentioned above, the right conditions in-clude reading the Bible, having done something wrong, and being in grave danger. Thus if one is reading the Bible and believes that God is speaking to one, then the belief is properly basic.

Furthermore, Plantinga insists that although reformed epistemologists allow belief in God as a properly basic belief, this does not mean they must allow that anything at all can be a basic belief. To be sure, he admits that he and other reformed epistemolo-gists have not supplied us with any criterion of what is properly basic. He argues, how-ever, that this is not necessary. One can know that some beliefs in some circumstances are not properly basic without having an explicitly formulated criterion of basicness. Thus Plantinga says that reformed epistemologists can correctly maintain that belief in voodoo or astrology or the Great Pumpkin is not a basic belief.

How is one to arrive at a criterion for being properly basic? According to Plantinga the route is "broadly speaking, *inductive*." He adds, "We must assemble examples of be-liefs and conditions such that the former are obviously properly basic in the latter. . . . We must frame hypotheses as to the necessary and sufficient conditions of proper basi-cality and test these hypotheses by reference to these examples."

He argues that, using this procedure,

the Christian will of course suppose that belief in God is entirely proper and rational; if he does not accept this belief on the basis of other propositions, he will conclude that it is basic for him and quite properly so. Followers of Russell and Madelyn Murray O'Hare [*sic*] may disagree; but how is that relevant? Must my criteria, or those of the Christian community, conform to their examples? Surely not. The Christian community is responsible to *its* set of examples, not to theirs.

Evaluation of Plantinga's Critique of Foundationalism

Recall that Plantinga argues that classical foundationalists are being self-referentially inconsistent. But as James Tomberlin has pointed out, since what is self-evident is relative to persons, a classical foundationalist (CF) could argue that (1) is self-evident and that if Plantinga were sufficiently attentive, the truth of (1) would become clear to him. Tomberlin argues that this response is similar to Calvin's view that in beholding the starry heavens, the properly attuned theist senses the existence of God. As Tomberlin puts it: "If the theist may be so attuned, why can't the classical foundationalist enjoy a similar relation to (1)? No, I do not think that Plantinga has precluded CF's rejoinder; and consequently he has not proved that (1) fails to be self-evident to the classical foundationalist."

However, even if Plantinga can show that (1) is not self-evident for classical foundationalists, he has not shown that (1) could not be deductively or inductively inferred from statements that are self-evident or incorrigible or evident to the senses. As Philip Quinn has argued, the classical foundationalist can use the broadly inductive procedures suggested by Plantinga to arrive at (1). Since the community of classical foundationalists is responsible for its own set of examples of properly basic beliefs and the conditions that justify them, it would not be surprising that the hypothesis they came up with in order to account for their examples would be (1).

Furthermore, even if Plantinga has refuted classical foundationalism, this would hardly dispose of foundationalism. Contemporary foundationalism has seriously modified the classical theory, and it is not at all clear that in the light of these modifications, Plantinga's critique could be sustained. Recall that one of his criticisms was that a statement such as "The world existed five minutes ago" could not be justified on classical foundationalist grounds. Since contemporary foundationalists include memory statements in the class of basic statements, there would not seem to be any particular problem in justifying such a statement, for "I remember having my breakfast ten minutes ago" can be a properly basic statement. Furthermore, if basic statements only have to be initially credible and not self-evident or incorrigible or evident to the senses, the criticism of self-referential inconsistency is much easier to meet. It is not at all implausible to suppose that a criterion of basicality in term of initial credibility is itself either initially credible or based on statements that are.

Plantinga is aware that there is more to foundationalism than the classical formulation of it. He says:

> Of course the evidentialist objection *need* not presuppose classical foundationalism; someone who accepted a different version of foundationalism could no doubt urge this objection. But in order to evaluate it, we should have to see what criterion of properly basic was being invoked. In the absence of such specification the objection remains at best a promissory note. So far as the present discussion goes, then, the next move is up to the evidential objector.

Many contemporary foundationalist theories have been constructed on nonclassical lines. Indeed, it may be safe to say that few contemporary foundationalists accept the classical view or even take it seriously. Moreover, these contemporary versions are hardly promissory notes, as Plantinga must be aware. Indeed, his refutation of classical foundationalism has just about as much relevance for contemporary foundationalism as a refutation of the emotive theory in ethics has for contemporary ethical noncognitivism. The next move, therefore, does not seem to be up to contemporary foundationalists. Plantinga must go on to show that his critique has relevance to the contemporary foundationalist program and that, given the best contemporary formulations of foundationalism, beliefs about God can be basic statements. This he has yet to do.

The Trouble with Reformed Foundationalism

What can one say about Plantinga's ingenious attempt to save theism from the charge of irrationality by making beliefs about God basic?

(1) Plantinga's claim that his proposal would not allow just any belief to become a basic belief is misleading. It is true that it would not allow just any belief to become a basic belief *from the point of view of Reformed epistemologists*. However it would seem to allow any belief at all to become basic from the point of view of *some* community. Although reformed epistemologists would not have to accept voodoo beliefs as rational, voodoo followers would be able to claim that insofar as they are basic in the voodoo community they are rational and, moreover, that reformed thought was irrational in this community. Indeed, Plantinga's proposal would generate many different communities that could *legitimately* claim that their basic beliefs are rational and that these beliefs conflict with basic beliefs of other communities. Among the communities generated might be devil worshipers, flat earthers, and believers in fairies just so long as belief in the devil, the flatness of the earth, and fairies was basic in the respective communities.

(2) On this view the rationality of any belief is absurdly easy to obtain. The cherished belief that is held without reason by *any* group could be considered properly basic by the group's members. There would be no way to make a critical evaluation of any beliefs so considered. The community's most cherished beliefs and the conditions that, according to the community, correctly trigger such beliefs would be accepted uncritically by the members of the community as just so many more examples of basic beliefs and justifying conditions. The more philosophical members of the community could go on to propose hypotheses as to the necessary and sufficient conditions for inclusion in this set. Perhaps, using this inductive procedure, a criterion could be formulated. However, what examples the hypotheses must account for would be decided by the community. As Plantinga says, each community would be responsible only to its own set of examples in formulating a criterion, and each would decide what is to be included in this set.

(3) Plantinga seems to suppose that there is a consensus in the Christian community about what beliefs are basic and what conditions justify these beliefs. But this is not so. Some Christians believe in God on the basis of the traditional arguments or on the basis of religious experiences; their belief in God is not basic. There would, then, certainly be no agreement in the Christian community over whether belief in God is basic or nonbasic. More important, there would be no agreement on whether doctrinal beliefs

concerning the authority of the pope, the make-up of the Trinity, the nature of Christ, the means of salvation, and so on were true, let alone basic. Some Christian sects would hold certain doctrinal beliefs to be basic and rational; others would hold the same beliefs to be irrational and, indeed, the gravest of heresies. Moreover, there would be no agreement over the conditions for basic belief. Some Christians might believe that a belief is properly basic when it is triggered by listening to the pope. Others would violently disagree. Even where there was agreement over the right conditions, these would seem to justify conflicting basic beliefs and, consequently, conflicting religious sects founded on them. For example, a woman named Jones, the founder of sect S_1, might read the Bible and be impressed that God is speaking to her and telling her that p. A man named Smith, the founder of sect S_2, might read the Bible and be impressed that God is speaking to him and telling him that ~p. So Jones's belief that p and Smith's belief that ~p would both be properly basic. One might wonder how this differs from the doctrinal disputes that have gone on for centuries among Christian sects and persist to this day. The difference is that on Plantinga's proposal each sect could *justifiably* claim that its belief, for which there might be no evidence or argument, was completely rational.

(4) So long as belief that there is no God was basic for them, atheists could also justify the claim that belief in God is irrational relative to their basic beliefs and the conditions that trigger them without critically evaluating any of the usual reasons for believing in God. Just as theistic belief might be triggered by viewing the starry heavens above and reading the Bible, so atheistic beliefs might be triggered by viewing the massacre of innocent children below and reading the writings of Robert Ingersoll. Theists may disagree, but is that relevant? To paraphrase Plantinga: Must atheists' criteria conform to the Christian communities' criteria? Surely not. The atheistic community is responsible to *its* set of examples, not to theirs.

(5) There may not at present be any clear criterion for what can be a basic belief, but belief in God seems peculiarly inappropriate for inclusion in the class since there are clear disanalogies between it and the basic beliefs allowable by classical foundationalism. For example, in his critique of classical foundationalism, Plantinga has suggested that belief in other minds and the external world should be considered basic. There are many plausible alternatives to belief in an all-good, all-powerful, all-knowing God, but there are few, if any, plausible alternatives to belief in other minds and the external world. Moreover, even if one disagrees with these arguments that seem to provide evidence against the existence of God, surely one must attempt to meet them. Although there are many skeptical arguments against belief in other minds and the external world, there are in contrast no seriously accepted arguments purporting to show that there are no other minds or no external world. In this world, atheism and agnosticism are live options for many intelligent people; solipsism is an option only for the mentally ill.

(6) As we have seen, Plantinga, following Calvin, says that some conditions that trigger belief in God or particular beliefs about God also justify these beliefs and that, although these beliefs concerning God are basic; they are not groundless. Although Plantinga gave no general account of what these justifying conditions are, he presented some examples of what he meant and likened these justifying conditions to those of properly basic perceptual and memory statements. The problem here is the weakness of the

analogy. As Plantinga points out, before we take a perceptual or memory belief as properly basic we must have evidence that our perception or memory is not faulty. Part of the justification for believing that our perception or memory is not faulty is that in general it agrees with the perception or memory of our epistemological peers—that is, our equals in intelligence, perspicacity, honesty, thoroughness, and other relevant epistemic virtues, as well as with our other experiences. For example, unless my perceptions generally agreed with other perceivers with normal eyesight in normal circumstances and with my nonvisual experience—for example, that I feel something solid when I reach out—there would be no justification for supposing that my belief that I see a rose-colored wall in front of me is properly basic. Plantinga admits that if I know my memory is unreliable, my belief that I had breakfast should not be taken as properly basic. However, one knows that one's memory is reliable by determining whether it coheres with the memory reports of other people whose memory is normal and with one's other experiences.

As we have already seen, lack of agreement is commonplace in religious contexts. Different beliefs are triggered in different people when they behold the starry heavens or when they read the Bible. Beholding the starry heavens can trigger a pantheistic belief or a purely aesthetic response without any religious component. Sometimes no particular response or belief at all is triggered. From what we know about the variations of religious belief, it is likely that people would not have theistic beliefs when they beheld the starry heavens if they had been raised in nontheistic environments. Similarly, a variety of beliefs and responses are triggered when the Bible is read. Some people are puzzled and confused by the contradictions, others become skeptical of the biblical stories, others believe that God is speaking to them and has appointed them as his spokesperson, others believe God is speaking to them but has appointed no one as His spokesperson. In short, there is no consensus in the Christian community, let alone among Bible readers generally. So unlike perception and memory, there are no grounds for claiming that a belief in God is properly basic since the conditions that trigger it yield widespread disagreement among epistemological peers.

(7) Part of the trouble with Plantinga's account of basic belief is the assumption he makes concerning what it means to say that a person accepts one proposition on the basis of accepting another. According to Michael Levine, Plantinga understands the relation in this way:

(A) For any person S, and distinct propositions p and q, S believes q on the basis of p only if S entertains p, S accepts p, S infers q from p, and S accepts q.

Contemporary foundationalists do not accept (A) as a correct account of the relation of accepting one proposition on the basis of another. The following seems more in accord with contemporary understanding:

(B) For any person S and distinct propositions p and q, if S believes q, and S would cite p if queried under optional conditions about his reasons for believing in q, then S believes q on the basis of p.

On (B) it seems unlikely that any nonepistemologically deficient person—for example, a normal adult—would be unable to cite any reason for believing in God if this person did believe in God. Consequently, Plantinga's claim that "the mature theist does not typically accept belief in God . . . as a conclusion from other things that he believes" is irrelevant if his claim is understood in terms of (A) and probably false if understood in terms of (B).

(8) Finally, to consider belief in God as a basic belief seems completely out of keeping with the spirit and intention of foundationalism. Whatever else it was and whatever its problems, foundationalism was an attempt to provide critical tools for objectively appraising knowledge claims and provide a nonrelativistic basis for knowledge. Plantinga's foundationalism is radically relativistic and puts any belief beyond rational appraisal once it is declared basic.

The Trouble with Foundationalism

So far in my critique of Plantinga's attempt to incorporate beliefs in or about God into the set of properly basic beliefs that form the foundation of knowledge, I have uncritically accepted the idea that the structure of knowledge must have a foundation in terms of basic beliefs. But, as Laurence BonJour has recently shown, there is a serious problem with any foundationalist account of knowledge.

According to all foundationalist accounts, basic statements are justified noninferentially. For example, contemporary foundationalists who hold a moderate position maintain that properly basic statements, although not incorrigible or self-evident, are highly justified without inductive or deductive support. But, it may be asked, where does this justification come from? As BonJour argues, a basic constraint on any standards of justification for empirical knowledge is that there is a good reason for thinking that those standards lead to truth. So if basic beliefs are to provide a foundation for knowledge for the moderate foundationalist, then whatever the criterion for being properly basic, it must provide a good reason for supposing that basic beliefs are true. Further, such a criterion must provide grounds for the person who holds a basic belief to suppose that it is true. Thus moderate foundationalism must hold that for any person P, basic belief B, and criterion of being properly basic ϕ, in order for P to be justified in holding properly basic belief B, P must be justified in believing the premises of the following justifying argument:

(1) B has feature ϕ.
(2) Beliefs having feature ϕ are likely to be true.

_____

(3) Therefore, B is highly likely to be true.

Although, as BonJour argues, it might be possible that one of the two premises in the above argument could be known to be true on an *a priori* basis, it does not seem possible that both premises could be known *a priori*. Once this is granted, it follows that B is not basic after all, since B's justification would depend on some other empirical belief. But if B is properly basic, its justification cannot depend on any other empirical belief. BonJour goes on to meet objections to his argument, showing that a coherent account of the structure of empirical knowledge can be developed to overcome this problem of foundationalism and that the objections usually raised against the coherence theory can be answered. Surely any defender of foundationalism must meet BonJour's challenge.

As we have seen, when Plantinga proposes that belief about God can be considered properly basic, he admits that he did not have any criterion for being properly basic. But BonJour's argument tends to show that whatever criterion Plantinga might offer, there will be a problem for reformed foundationalism. If BonJour is correct, whatever this criterion is, it will have to provide a good reason for supposing that properly basic beliefs are true, and this will involve knowledge of further empirical beliefs. In order to defend his position, Plantinga must refute BonJour's argument.

Conclusion

In Chapter 1 it was argued that there was a strong presumption that belief in God should be based on epistemic reasons. Some theists disagree, maintaining that religious belief is basic or should be based on faith. The conclusion here is that this argument fails. Although not all theories of faith have been examined here, the ones that were are representative enough to give us confidence that all such arguments will fail.

In a way Aquinas seems to agree with our position. He maintains that belief in the existence of God should be based on epistemic reasons; and, as we shall see in Chapter 14, he believed the arguments he produced provided such reasons. However, he believed that certain Christian dogmas were not provable by means of argument and must be based on faith. But even here he thought that one could have good epistemic reason to believe that these dogmas were revealed by God. He was wrong, however, to suppose that they were. Kierkegaard's view that faith in God should be based on absurdities and improbabilities was rejected, since the arguments he used to support this view were unsound and, in any case, his view led to fanaticism. Wittgensteinian fideism was also rejected, since it led to absurdities and presupposed an indefensible view of meaning and language.

Plantinga's reformed foundationalism has some interesting similarities to the doctrine that belief in God should be based on faith, but should not be identified with it. To be sure, his view is similar to that of Aquinas, who maintains that particular Christian doctrines, although not themselves based on reason, are rational. The basic difference between the Aquinas and Plantinga positions is that Aquinas attempts to provide epistemic reasons that would persuade all rational beings to accept certain propositions as revealed truths. Plantinga provides no such reasons other than the argument that belief in God is basic and some such beliefs, including belief in God, are completely rational. Thus Plantinga's views differ markedly from those of Kierkegaard, who forsook any appeal to rationality in justifying religious belief. Plantinga's views also differ in important respects from Wittgensteinian fideism. While Wittgensteinian fideism appeals to ordinary religious practice and language to justify belief in God, Plantinga appeals to theoretical considerations from epistemology. Nevertheless, Plantinga's reformed foundationalism should be rejected since his arguments against classical foundationalism are weak, the logic of his position leads to a radical and absurd relativism, and foundationalism in general has serious problems.

PART  FIVE

Religious Faith and the Issue of Pluralism

Hick's discussion of religious faith as "experiencing-as" leads naturally to a consideration of how one is to assess the phenomenon of religious pluralism. Hick's own pluralistic response (1973) underscores his thesis that experience is constructed by language and that different religious traditions may have developed from distinctive cultural-linguistic responses to revelation. From Hick's perspective, one is unable to adjudicate between the conflicting truth claims of the major traditions, since to do so is akin to determining the truthfulness of languages or cultures, a feat that could only be accomplished from a vantage point outside of, and superior to, all existing cultures. Each tradition is equally true and equally false in the same sense that languages themselves express reality in quite different forms. If an Eternal One and a life beyond death exist, each tradition represents an equally valid pathway to salvation. Sumner Twiss (1990) presents Hick's position and the objections it has generated, and provides a sense of the unfolding conversation. Karl Rahner's essay on anonymous Christianity (1976) offers a version of the late-twentieth-century position of the Roman Catholic Church, namely, that all expressions of religious faith are made possible by, and are related to, the salvific work of Jesus Christ. In short, Rahner wishes to be more inclusive than the Roman Catholic Church had been in the past, but he continues to insist that the theological assertions of other traditions are categorically erroneous. It is only their intrinsic desire for truth, an implicit desire for Christ, that opens their adherents to the possibility of salvation. Wilfred Cantwell Smith's essay (1987) is a classic on the truthfulness of all major religious traditions and the value of their unfolding dialogue.

34. Religious Pluralism and Ultimate Reality

JOHN HICK

Let me begin by proposing a working definition of religion as an understanding of the universe, together with an appropriate way of living within it, which involves reference beyond the natural world to God or gods or to the Absolute or to a transcendent order or process. Such a definition includes such theistic faiths as Judaism, Christianity, Islam, Sikhism; the theistic Hinduism of the Bhagavad Gītā; the semi-theistic faith of Mahayana Buddhism and the non-theistic faiths of Theravada Buddhism and non-theistic Hinduism. It does not however include purely naturalistic systems of belief, such as communism and humanism, immensely important though these are today as alternatives to religious life.

When we look back into the past we find that religion has been a virtually universal dimension of human life—so much so that man has been defined as the religious animal. For he has displayed an innate tendency to experience his environment as being religiously as well as naturally significant, and to feel required to live in it as such. To quote the anthropologist, Raymond Firth, "religion is universal in human societies."[1] "In every human community on earth today," says Wilfred Cantwell Smith, "there exists something that we, as sophisticated observers, may term religion, or a religion. And we are able to see it in each case as the latest development in a continuous tradition that goes back, we can now affirm, for at least one hundred thousand years."[2] In the life of primitive man this religious tendency is expressed in a belief in sacred objects endowed with *mana*, and in a multitude of natural and ancestral spirits needing to be carefully propitiated. The divine was here crudely apprehended as a plurality of quasianimal forces which could to some extent be controlled by ritualistic and magical procedures. This represents the simplest beginning of man's awareness of the transcendent in the infancy of the human race—an infancy which is also to some extent still available for study in the life of primitive tribes today.

The development of religion and religions begins to emerge into the light of recorded history as the third millennium B.C. moves towards the period around 2000 B.C. There are two main regions of the earth in which civilisation seems first to have arisen and in which religions first took a shape that is at least dimly discernible to us as we peer back through the mists of time—these being Mesopotamia in the Near East and the Indus valley of northern India. In Mesopotamia men lived in nomadic shepherd tribes, each worshipping its own god. Then the tribes gradually coalesced into

Source: God and the Universe of Faiths, © John Hick, 1883. Reproduced by permission of Oneworld Publicatio

nation states, the former tribal gods becoming ranked in hierarchies (some however being lost by amalgamation in the process) dominated by great national deities such as Marduk of Babylon, the Sumerian Ishtar, Amon of Thebes, Jahweh of Israel, the Greek Zeus, and so on. Further east in the Indus valley there was likewise a wealth of gods and goddesses, though apparently not so much tribal or national in character as expressive of the basic forces of nature, above all fertility. The many deities of the Near East and of India expressed man's awareness of the divine at the dawn of documentary history, some four thousand years ago. It is perhaps worth stressing that the picture was by no means a wholly pleasant one. The tribal and national gods were often martial and cruel, sometimes requiring human sacrifices. And although rather little is known about the very early, pre-Aryan Indian deities, it is certain that later Indian deities have vividly symbolised the cruel and destructive as well as the beneficent aspects of nature.

These early developments in the two cradles of civilisation, Mesopotamia and the Indus valley, can be described as the growth of natural religion, prior to any special intrusions of divine revelation or illumination. Primitive spirit-worship expressed man's fears of unknown forces; his reverence for nature deities expressed his sense of dependence upon realities greater than himself; and his tribal gods expressed the unity and continuity of his group over against other groups. One can in fact discern all sorts of causal connections between the forms which early religion took and the material circumstances of man's life, indicating the large part played by the human element within the history of religion. For example, Trevor Ling points out that life in ancient India (apart from the Punjab immediately prior to the Aryan invasions) was agricultural and was organised in small village units; and suggests that "among agricultural peoples, aware of the fertile earth which brings forth from itself and nourishes its progeny upon its broad bosom, it is the mother-principle which seems important."[3] Accordingly God the Mother, and a variety of more specialised female deities, have always held a prominent place in Indian religious thought and mythology. This contrasts with the characteristically male expression of deity in the Semitic religions, which had their origins among nomadic, pastoral, herd-keeping peoples in the Near East. The divine was known to the desert-dwelling herdsmen who founded the Israelite tradition as God the King and Father; and this conception has continued both in later Judaism and in Christianity, and was renewed out of the desert experience of Mohammed in the Islamic religion. Such regional variations in our human ways of conceiving the divine have persisted through time into the developed world faiths that we know today. The typical western conception of God is still predominantly in terms of the male principle of power and authority; and in the typical Indian conceptions of deity the female principle still plays a distinctly larger part than in the west.

Here then was the natural condition of man's religious life: religion without revelation. But sometime around 800 B.C. there began what has been called the golden age of religious creativity. This consisted in a remarkable series of revelatory experiences occurring during the next five hundred or so years in different parts of the world, experiences which deepened and purified men's conception of the ultimate, and which religious faith can only attribute to the pressure of the divine Spirit upon the human spirit. First came the early Jewish prophets, Amos, Hosea and first Isaiah, declaring that they had heard the Word of the Lord claiming their obedience and demanding a new level of righteousness and justice in the life of Israel. Then in Persia the great prophet Zoroaster appeared; China produced Lao-tzu and then Confucius; in India the Upanishads were written, and Gotama the Buddha lived, and Mahavira, the founder of the Jain religion and, probably about the end of this period, the writing of the Bhagavad Gītā,[4] and Greece produced Pythagoras and then, ending this golden age, Socrates and Plato. Then after the gap of some three hundred years came Jesus of Nazareth and the emergence of Christianity; and after another gap the prophet Mohammed and the rise of Islam.

The suggestion that we must consider is that these were all moments of divine revelation. But let us ask, in order to test this thought, whether we should not expect God to make his revelation in a single mighty act, rather than to produce a number of different, and therefore presumably partial, revelations at different times and places? I think that in seeing the answer to this question we receive an important clue to the place of the religions of the world in the divine purpose. For when we remember the facts of history and geography we realise that in the period we are speaking of, between two and three thousand years ago, it was not possible for God to reveal himself through any human mediation to all mankind. A world-wide revelation might be possible today, thanks to the inventions of printing, and even more of radio, TV and communication satellites. But in the technology of the ancient world this was not possible. Although on a time scale of centuries and millennia there has been a slow diffusion and interaction of cultures, particularly within the vast Euro-Asian land mass, yet the more striking fact for our present purpose is the fragmented character of the ancient world. Communications between the different groups of humanity was then so limited and slow that for all practical purposes men inhabited different worlds. For the most part people in Europe, in India, in Arabia, in Africa, in China were unaware of the others' existence. And as the world was fragmented, so was its religious life. If there was to be a revelation of the divine reality to mankind it had to be a pluriform revelation, a series of revealing experiences occurring independently within the different streams of human history. And since religion and culture were one, the great creative moments of revelation and illumination have influenced the development of the various cultures, giving them the coherence and impetus to expand into larger units, thus creating the vast, many-sided historical entities which we call the world religions.

Each of these religio-cultural complexes has expanded until it touched the boundaries of another such complex spreading out from another centre. Thus each major occasion of divine revelation has slowly transformed the primitive and national religions within the sphere of its influence into what we now know as the world faiths. The early Dravidian and Aryan polytheisms of India were drawn through the religious experience and thought of the Brahmins into what the west calls Hinduism. The national and mystery cults of the Mediterranean world and then of northern Europe were drawn by influences stemming from the life and teaching of Christ into what has become Christianity. The early polytheism of the Arab peoples has been transformed under the influence of Mohammed and his message into Islam. Great areas of Southeast Asia, of China, Tibet and Japan were drawn into the spreading Buddhist movement. None of these expansions from different centres of revelation has of course been simple and uncontested, and a number of alternatives which proved less durable have perished or been absorbed in the process—for example, Mithraism has disappeared altogether; and Zoroastrianism, whilst it greatly influenced the development of the Judaic-Christian tradition, and has to that extent been absorbed, only survives directly today on a small scale in Parseeism.

Seen in this historical context these movements of faith—the Judaic-Christian, the Buddhist, the Hindu, the Muslim—are not essentially rivals. They began at different times and in different places, and each expanded outwards into the surrounding world of primitive natural religion until most of the world was drawn up into one or other of the great revealed faiths. And once this global pattern had become established it has ever since remained fairly stable. It is true that the process of establishment involved conflict in the case of Islam's entry into India and the virtual expulsion of Buddhism from India in the medieval period, and in the case of Islam's advance into Europe and then its retreat at the end of the medieval period. But since the frontiers of the different world faiths became more or less fixed there has been little penetration of one faith into societies moulded by another. The most successful missionary efforts of the great faiths continue to this day to be "downwards" into the remaining world of relatively primitive religions rather than "sideways" into territories dominated by another world faith. For example, as between Christianity and Islam there has been little more than rather rare individual conversions; but both faiths have successful missions in Africa. Again, the Christian population of the Indian subcontinent, after more than two centuries of missionary effort, is only about 2.7 per cent; but on the other hand the Christian missions in the South Pacific are fairly successful. Thus the general picture, so far as the great world religions is concerned, is that each has gone through an early period of geographical expansion, converting a region of the world from its more primitive religious state, and has thereafter continued in a comparatively settled condition within more of less stable boundaries.

Now it is of course possible to see this entire development from the primitive forms of religion up to and including the great world faiths as the history of man's most persistent illusion, growing from crude fantasies into sophisticated metaphysical speculations. But from the standpoint of religious faith the only reasonable hypothesis is that this historical picture represents a movement of divine self-revelation to mankind. This hypothesis offers a general answer to the question of the relation between the different world religions and of the truths which they embody. It suggests to us that the same divine reality has always been self-revealingly active towards mankind, and that the differences of human response are related to different human circumstances. These circumstances—ethnic, geographical, climatic, economic, sociological, historical—have produced the existing differentiations of human culture, and within each main cultural region the response to the divine has taken its own characteristic forms. In each case the post-primitive response has been initiated by some spiritually outstanding individual or succession of individuals, developing in the course of time into one of the great religio-cultural phenomena which we call the world religions. Thus Islam embodies the main response of the Arabic peoples to the divine reality; Hinduism, the main (though not the only) response of the peoples of India; Buddhism, the main response of the peoples of South-east Asia and parts of northern Asia; Christianity, the main response of the European peoples, both within Europe itself and in their emigrations to the Americas and Australasia.

Thus it is, I think, intelligible historically why the revelation of the divine reality to man, and the disclosure of the divine will for human life, had to occur separately within the different streams of human life. We can see how these revelations took different forms related to the different mentalities of the peoples to whom they came and developed within these different cultures into the vast and many-sided historical phenomena of the world religions.

But let us now ask whether this is intelligible theologically. What about the conflicting truth claims of the different faiths? Is the divine nature personal or non-personal; does deity become incarnate in the world; are human beings born again and again on earth; is the Bible, or the Koran, or the Bhagavad Gītā the Word of God? If what Christianity says in answer to these questions is true, must not what Hinduism says be to a large extent false? If what Buddhism says is true, must not what Islam says be largely false?

Let us begin with the recognition, which is made in all the main religious traditions, that the ultimate divine reality is infinite and as such transcends the grasp of the human mind. God, to use our Christian term, is infinite. He is not a thing, a part of the universe, existing alongside other things; nor is he a being falling under a certain kind. And therefore he cannot be defined or encompassed by human thought. We cannot draw boundaries around his nature and say that he is this and no more. If we could fully define God, describing his inner being and his outer limits, this would not be God. The God whom our minds can penetrate and whom our thoughts can circumnavigate is merely a finite and partial image of God.

From this it follows that the different encounters with the transcendent within the different religious traditions may all be encounters with the one infinite reality; though with partially different and overlapping aspects of that reality. This is a very familiar thought in Indian religious literature. We read, for example, in the ancient Rig-Vedas, dating back to perhaps as much as a thousand years before Christ:

> They call it Indra, Mitra, Varuna, and Agni
> And also heavenly, beautiful Garutman:
> The real is one, though sages name it variously.[5]

We might translate this thought into the terms of the faiths represented today in Britain:

> They call it Jahweh, Allah, Krishna, Param Atma,
> And also holy, blessed Trinity:
> The real is one, though sages name it differently.

And in the Bhagavad Gītā the Lord Krishna, the personal God of love, says, "However men approach me, even so do I accept them: for, on all sides, whatever path they may choose is mine."[6]

Again, there is the parable of the blind men and the elephant, said to have been told by the Buddha. An elephant was brought to a group of blind men who had never encountered such an animal before. One felt a leg and reported that an elephant is a great living pillar. Another felt the trunk and reported that an elephant is a great snake. Another felt the tusk and reported than an elephant is like a sharp ploughshare. And so on. And then they all quarrelled together, each claiming that his own account was the truth and therefore all the others false. In fact of course they were all true, but each referring only to one aspect of the total reality and all expressed in very imperfect analogies.

Now the possibility, indeed the probability, that we have seriously to consider is that many different accounts of the divine reality may be true, though all expressed in imperfect human analogies, but that none is "the truth, the whole truth, and nothing but the truth." May it not be that the different concepts of God, as Jahweh, Allah, Krishna, Param Atma, Holy Trinity, and so on: and likewise the different concepts of the hidden structure of reality, as the eternal emanation of Brahman or as an immense cosmic process culminating in Nirvana, are all images of the divine, each expressing some aspect or range of aspects and yet none by itself fully and exhaustively corresponding to the infinite nature of the ultimate reality?

Two immediate qualifications however to this hypothesis. First, the idea that we are considering is not that any and every conception of God or of the transcendent is valid, still less all equally valid; but that every conception of the divine which has come out of a great revelatory religious experience and has been tested though a long tradition of worship, and has sustained human faith over centuries of time and in millions of lives, is likely to represent a genuine encounter with the divine reality. And second, the parable of the blind men and the elephant is of course only a parable and like most parables it is designed to make one point and must not be pressed as an analogy at other points. The suggestion is not that the different encounters with the divine which lie at the basis of the great religious traditions are responses to different *parts* of the divine. They are rather encounters from different historical and cultural standpoints with the same infinite divine reality and as such they lead to differently focused awareness of the reality. The indications of this are most evident in worship and prayer. What is said about God in the theological treatises of the different faiths is indeed often widely different. But it is in prayer that a belief in God comes alive and does its main work. And when we turn from abstract theology to the living stuff of worship we meet again and again the overlap and confluence of faiths.

Here, for example, is a Muslim prayer at the feast of Ramadan:

> Praise be to God, Lord of creation, Source of all livelihood, who orders the morning, Lord of majesty and honour, of grace and beneficence. He who is so far that he may not be seen and so near that he witnesses the secret things. Blessed be he and for ever exalted.[7]

And here is a Sikh creed used at the morning prayer:

> There is but one God. He is all that is.
> He is the Creator of all things and He is all pervasive.
> He is without fear and without enmity.
> He is timeless, unborn and self-existent. He is the Enlightener
> And can be realised by grace of Himself alone. He was in the
> beginning; He was in all ages.
> The True One is, was, O Nanak, and shall for ever be.[8]

And here again is a verse from the Koran:

> To God belongs the praise. Lord of the heavens and Lord of the earth, the Lord of all being. His is the dominion in the heavens and in the earth: he is the Almighty, the All-wise.[9]

Turning now to the Hindu idea of the many incarnations of God, here is a verse from the Rāmāyaṇa:

Seers and sages, saints and hermits, fix on Him their reverent gaze,
And in faint and trembling accents, holy scripture hymns His praise.
He the omnipresent spirit, lord of heaven and earth and hell,
To redeem His people, freely has vouchsafed with men to dwell.[10]

And from the rich literature of devotional song here is a Bhakti hymn of the Vaishnavite branch of Hinduism:

Now all my days with joy I'll fill, full to the brim
With all my heart to Vitthal cling, and only Him.
He will sweep utterly away all dole and care;
And all in sunder shall I rend illusion's snare.
O altogether dear is He, and He alone,
For all my burden He will take to be His own.
Lo, all the sorrow of the world will straight way cease,
And all unending now shall be the reign ofpeace.[11]

And a Muslim mystical verse:

Love came a guest
Within my breast,
My soul was spread,
Love banqueted.[12]

And finally another Hindu (Vaishnavite) devotional hymn:

O save me, save me, Mightiest, Save me and set me free.
O let the love that fills my breast Cling to thee lovingly.
Grant me to taste how sweet thou art; Grant me but this, I pray.
And never shall my love depart Or turn from thee away.
Then I thy name shall magnify And tell thy praise abroad,
For very love and gladness I Shall dance before my God.[13]

Such prayers and hymns as these must express, surely, diverse encounters with the same divine reality. These encounters have taken place within different human cultures by people of different ways of thought and feeling, with different histories and different frameworks of philosophical thought, and have developed into different systems of theology embodied in different religious structures and organisations. These resulting large-scale religio-cultural phenomena are what we call the religions of the world. But must there not lie behind them the same infinite divine reality, and may not our divisions into Christian, Hindu, Muslim, Jew, and soon, and all that goes with them, accordingly represent secondary, human, historical developments?

There is a further problem, however, which now arises. I have been speaking so far of the ultimate reality in a variety of terms—the Father, Son and Spirit of Christianity, the Jahweh of Judaism, the Allah of Islam, and so on—but always thus far in theistic terms, as a personal God under one name or another. But what of the non-theistic religions? What of the non-theistic Hinduism according to which the ultimate reality, Brahman, is not He but It; and what about Buddhism, which in one form is agnostic concerning the existence of God even though in another form it has come to worship the Buddha himself? Can these non-theistic faiths be seen as encounters with the same divine reality that is encountered in theistic religion?

Speaking very tentatively, I think it is possible that the sense of the divine as non-personal may indeed reflect an aspect of the same infinite reality that is encountered as personal in theistic religious experience. The question can be pursued both as a matter of pure theology and in relation to religious experience. Theologically, the Hindu distinction between Nirguna Brahman and Saguna Brahman is important and should be adopted into western religious thought. Detaching the distinction, then from its Hindu context we may say that Nirguna God is the eternal self-existent divine reality, beyond the scope of all human categories, including personality; and Saguna God is God in relation to his creation and with the attributes which express this relationship, such as personality, omnipotence, goodness, love and omniscience. Thus the one ultimate reality is both Nirguna and non-personal, and Saguna and personal, in a duality which is in principle acceptable to human understanding. When we turn to men's religious awareness of God we are speaking of Saguna God, God in relation to man. And here the larger traditions of both east and west report a dual experience of the divine as personal and as other than personal. It will be a sufficient reminder of the strand of personal relationship with the divine in Hinduism to mention Iswaru, the personal God who represents the Absolute as known and worshipped by finite persons. It should also be remembered that the characterisation of Brahman as *satcitananda*, absolute being, consciousness and bliss, is not far from the conception of infinitely transcendent personal life. Thus there is both the thought and the experience of the personal divine within Hinduism. But there is likewise the thought and the experience of God as other than personal within Christianity. Rudolph Otto describes this strand in the mysticism of Meister Eckhart. He says:

> The divine, which on the one hand is conceived in symbols taken from the social sphere, as Lord, King, Father, Judge—a person in relation to persons—is on the other hand denoted in dynamic symbols as the power of life, as light and life, as spirit ebbing and flowing, as truth, knowledge, essential justice and holiness, a glowing fire that penetrates and pervades. It is characterized as the principle of a renewed, supernatural Life, mediating and giving itself, breaking forth in the living man as his nova vita, as the content of his life and being. What is here insisted upon is not so much an immanent God, as an "experienced" God, known as an inward principle of the power of new being and life. Eckhart knows this *deuteros theos* besides the personal God . . .[14]

Let me now try to draw the threads together and to project them into the future. I have been suggesting that Christianity is a way of salvation which, beginning some two thousand years ago, has become the principal way of salvation in three continents. The other great faiths are likewise of salvation, providing the principal path to the divine reality for other large sections of humanity. I have also suggested that the idea that Jesus proclaimed himself as God incarnate, and as the sole point of saving contact between God and man, is without adequate historical foundation and represents a doctrine developed by the church. We should therefore not infer, from the christian experience of redemption through Christ, that salvation cannot be experienced in any other way. The alternative possibility is that the ultimate divine reality—in our christian terms, God—has always been pressing in upon the human spirit, but in ways which leave men free to open or close themselves to the divine presence. Human life has developed along characteristically different lines in the main areas of civilisation, and these differences have naturally entered into the ways in which men have apprehended and responded to God. For the great religious figures through whose experience divine revelation has come have each been conditioned by a particular history and culture. One can hardly imagine Gotama the Buddha except in the setting of the India of his time, or Jesus the Christ except against the background of Old Testament Judaism, or Mohammed except in the setting of Arabia. And human history and culture have likewise shaped the development of the webs of religious creeds, practices and organisations which we know as the great world faiths.

It is thus possible to consider the hypothesis that they are all, at their experiential roots, in contact with the same ultimate reality, but that their differing experiences of that reality, interacting over the centuries with the different thought-forms of different cultures, have led to increasing differentiation and contrasting elaboration—so that Hinduism, for example, is a very different phenomenon from Christianity, and very different ways of conceiving and experiencing the divine occur within them.

However, now that the religious traditions are consciously interacting with each other in the "one world" of today, in mutual observation and dialogue, it is possible that their future developments may be on gradually converging courses. For during the next few centuries they will no doubt continue to change, and it may be that they will grow closer together, and even that one day such names as "Christianity," "Buddhism," "Islam," "Hinduism," will no longer describe the then current configurations of men's religious experience and belief. I am not here thinking of the extinction of human religiousness in a universal wave of secularisation. This is of course a possible future; and indeed many think it the most likely future to come about. But if man is an indelibly religious animal he will always, even in his secular cultures, experience a sense of the transcendent by which he will be both troubled and uplifted. The future I am thinking of is accordingly one in which what we now call the different religions will constitute the past history of different emphases and variations within a global religious life. I do not mean that all men everywhere will be overtly religious, any more than they are today. I mean rather that the discoveries now taking place by men of different faiths of central common ground, hitherto largely concealed by the variety of cultural forms in which it was expressed, may eventually render obsolete the sense of belonging to rival ideological communities. Not that all religious men will think alike, or worship in the same way or experience the divine identically. On the contrary, so long as there is a rich variety of human cultures—and let us hope there will always be this—we should expect there to be correspondingly different forms of religious cult, ritual and organisation, conceptualised in different theological doctrines. And so long as there is a wide spectrum of human psychological types—and again let us hope that there will always be this—we should expect there to be correspondingly different emphases between, for example, the sense of the divine as just and as merciful, between *karma* and *bhakti*; or between worship as formal and communal and worship as free and personal. Thus we may expect the different world faiths to continue as religio-cultural phenomena, though phenomena which are increasingly influencing one another's development. The relation between them will then perhaps be somewhat like that now obtaining between the different denominations of Christianity in Europe or the United States. That is to say, there will in most countries be a dominant religious tradition, with other traditions present in varying strengths, but with considerable awareness on all hands of what they have in common; with some degree of osmosis of membership through their institutional walls; with a large degree of practical cooperation; and even conceivably with some interchange of ministry.

Beyond this the ultimate unity of faiths will be an eschatological unity in which each is both fulfilled and transcended—fulfilled in so far as it is true, transcended in so far as it is less than the whole truth. And indeed even such fulfilling must be a transcending; for the function of a religion is to bring us to a right relationship with the ultimate divine reality, to awareness of our true nature and our place in the Whole, into the presence of God. In the eternal life there is no longer any place for religions; the pilgrim has no need of a way after he has finally arrived. In St. John's vision of the heavenly city at the end of our christian scriptures it is said that there is no temple—no christian church or chapel, no jewish synagogue, no hindu or buddhist temple, no muslim mosque, no sikh gurdwara. . . . For all these exist in time, as ways through time to eternity.

Notes

1. *Elements of Social Organization*, 3rd ed. (London: Tavistock Publications, 1969) p. 216.
2. *The Meaning and End of Religion* (New York: Mentor Books, 1963) p. 22.
3. *A History of Religion East and West* (London: Macmillan and New York: St. Martin's Press, 1968) p. 27.
4. The dating of the Bhagavad Gītā has been a matter of much debate; but R. C. Zaehner in his recent monumental critical edition says that "One would probably not be going far wrong if one dated it as some time between the fifth and second centuries B.C." *The Bhagavad* Gītā (Oxford: Clarendon Press, 1969) p. 7.
5. I 164.
6. IV II.
7. Kenneth Cragg, *Alive to God: Muslim and Christian Prayer* (London and New York: Oxford University Press, 1970) p. 65.
8. Harbans Singh, *Guru Nanak and Origins of the Sikh Faith* (Bombay, London and New York: Asia Publishing House, 1969), pp. 96–7.
9. *Alive to God*, p. 61 (Surah of the Kneeling, v. 35).
10. *Sacred Books of the World*, edited by A. C. Bouquet (London: Pelican Books, 1954) p. 226 (The Rāmāyana of Tulsi Das, Canto 1, Chandha 2, translated by F. S. Growse).
11. Ibid., p. 245 (A Hymn of Namdev, translated by Nicol MacNicol).
12. *Alive to God*, p. 79 (From Ibn Hazm, "The Ring of the Dove").
13. *Sacred Books of the World*, p. 246 (A Hymn of Tukaram).
14. Rudolph Otto, *Mysticism East and West*, trans. Bertha L. Bracey and Richenda C. Payne (New York: Meridian Books, 1957), p. 131.

35. The Philosophy of Religious Pluralism: A Critical Appraisal of Hick and His Critics*

SUMNER B. TWISS

For well over a decade now, John Hick has been publishing important, illuminating, and provocative articles about the nature of religion and the meaning of religious diversity.[1] His main thesis is that there is an underlying unity to this diversity that is explicated as a set of differential responses to a transcendent reality conceived and perceived in alternative ways by different cultural and religious traditions. In effect, this is a thesis about the higher transcendental unity of all religions. This is an important thesis for a philosopher to propound at this time because there are signs that the philosophy of religion is becoming an increasingly comparative and cross-cultural discipline, with a concomitant need to make sense of the diversity of religions. Hick's thesis, the core of his emerging philosophy of religious pluralism, is one coherent response to this need.

Needless to say, Hick's work on the philosophy of religious pluralism has generated considerable critical response in the journal literature. Indeed, there are even alternative—some might say divergent or incompatible—critical readings of the conceptual and epistemological nature and significance of Hick's project. Griffiths and Lewis and Byrne, for example, see Hick as advancing a noncognitive, neo-Wittgensteinian position on the diversity of religious belief, while Netland and Corliss, respectively, see him as developing a cognitive metatheory and a nonevidentialist pragmatic position on religious belief.[2] And each of these readings argues—on different grounds, of course—that Hick's theory founders on issues of hermeneutical adequacy, internal conceptual coherence, and epistemic convincingness.

Such divergent readings of one theory, of course, raise the critical problem of its precise nature and import, as well as posing the question of whether the tensions and weakness identified, in fact, undercut the theory's validity and coherence. In order to

*I want to express my gratitude to colleagues who read and commented on drafts of this essay: Wendell S. Dietrich (Brown University), Mark J. Franklin (Reed College), John P. Kenny (Reed College), and most especially John P. Reeder, Jr. (Brown University).

Source: From Sumner B. Twiss, "The Philosophy of Religious Pluralism: A Critical Appraisal of Hick and His Critics," *The Journal of Religion* 70 (1990): 533–68. Copyright © 1990 by The University of Chicago Press. Reprinted with the permission of the author and The University of Chicago Press.

answer these questions, I propose first to offer my own reading of what Hick is saying. Then I will go on to analyze and discuss in some detail four areas of tension and weakness identified by Hick's critics, offering my own views of their nature, significance, and possible resolution. As will become clear, unlike most of his critics, I have a rather favorable view of Hick's theory and its prospects; this is in large part due to my belief that Hick's theory constitutes a rich organic web of more than one theoretical strand, giving it considerable resilience and subtlety in dealing with difficult philosophical challenges. The overarching issue, of course, is whether this organic web is finally coherent and satisfies criteria of economy, explanatory power, and the like. I believe it does. Let me now provide my reading of Hick's theory.

Hick's theory of religious pluralism advances and defends the hypothesis of a noumenal transcendent divine reality (in itself infinite and unknowable) underlying and serving as the ultimate referent of the diverse phenomenal religions (viewed as culturally shaped and differentiated conceptualizations of and responses to the divine noumenon). The development of the theory falls into four interconnected phases: philosophical presuppositions, methodological first steps, rational ontological postulate, and epistemological consequences. Let us sketch each of these phases in turn, keeping in mind that they constitute a web of mutually supportive and interactive beliefs and arguments.

Philosophical Presuppositions

Hick adopts a Wittgensteinian perspective on the nature of religions, conceiving of them as cultural-linguistic systems (language games) making possible corresponding forms of life, experience, and expression.[3] According to Hick, these systems are structured around the practical soteriological aim of encouraging and regulating transformation of the self in relation to differing conceptions of the ultimately real and valuable. Consonant with this perspective, Hick confers a degree of priority on religious practice (religious forms of life) as contrasted with doctrine and theory. Nonetheless, quite unlike other neo-Wittgensteinian philosophers of religion, he explicitly maintains that the practical language of worship and prayer presupposes the sincere user's belief in the independent reality of the divine ultimate reality. (At times he also characterizes this language as metaphoric and mythic but nonetheless referential in intention.)

There is, then, in the very "basement" of Hick's theory a striking tension. On the one hand, his theory adheres to a Wittgensteinian view of religious language and belief, which is usually understood to conceive of divine reality as internally related to practices and to construe religious discourse as grammatical rather than referential.[4] On the other hand, it also adheres to the view that religious language and belief are properly understood as presupposing an independent and ontologically real ultimate divine. One of Hick's problems, of course, is precisely how to put these two presuppositions (or theoretical strands) together into one coherent view that does justice to each and to the fact of the diversity of religions. We will need to return to this seeming tension or incompatibility; for now, however, let us just note these two presuppositions since together they explain much of the apparent structural duality in the subsequent phases of

Hick's theory as well as offer one possible explanation of such different critical readings of the epistemology of Hick's project.

Methodological First Steps

Hick initiates the formal development of his theory by explicitly proposing a "revisionist" conception of, and approach to, religious diversity—involving the notion that the same soteriological process of human transformation takes place within the contexts of the different religious and cultural traditions—and then adopting as a methodological assumption the basic religious conviction that religious experience and thought mediate real contact with a higher reality (in-principled veridicality of religious experience and thought).[5] Defending the reasonability of this conviction for one's own religious experience and tradition, he then argues for the rationality of generalizing this conviction to other traditions and forms of religious experience (i.e., they, too, can in principle mediate real contact with a higher reality). He further proposes—in light of the prima facie rough equality of moral and spiritual fruits of major religious traditions—the conditional rationality of the pluralist hypothesis that all the major traditions are in fact veridical and mediate real contact with a higher reality (i.e., conditional on the coherence and plausibility of the following phases and the theory as a whole).

What is perhaps most striking about these first steps is that both may be conceived as paralleling Hick's two original philosophical presuppositions. Thus, the revisionist conception of religions continues the Wittgensteinian emphasis on conceiving religions as cultural-linguistic systems composed of soteriologically oriented forms of religious life and practice and adds the more controversial idea that there is not only structural similarity among these culturally differentiated forms of life but also substantive identity or overlap inasmuch as the same soteriological goal and process is at issue, taking "different forms all over the world." Moreover, the basic religious conviction (methodological assumption of veridicality) appears to continue and to build on the other basic commitment to the ontological realism of religious language and belief, now expanding this presupposition into a rational conviction about the veridicality of religious experience and thought. Again, these are controversial moves on Hick's part, and both lie behind a recurrent worry cited in all the critical readings of Hick: namely, do these methodological moves not lead to distorted understandings of the goals and claims advanced by religious traditions? We will have occasion to return to this question below.

Ontological Postulate

From Hick's point of view, the pluralist hypothesis rationally requires the postulation of a divine noumenal reality underlying and unifying the diverse phenomenal religions through a common ultimate referent for their different and humanly limited conceptions of the Real.[6] As a corollary to this postulate, Hick construes the epistemological relation between the divine noumenon and the phenomenal religions as the divine noumenon (never experienced directly in itself) coming to consciousness (indirectly) in terms of culturally differentiated conceptual schemes (e.g., dualistic-personalistic and monistic-impersonalistic) generated at the interface between divine noumenon and different patterns of human consciousness.

It is worth noting even at this early point a number of features of this ontological postulate. First, it is a postulate that is rationally required if the pluralist hypothesis is to be held; therefore, the only reasons supporting the postulate at this point are internal. Second, this postulate makes an ontological claim; it says that there is a (single) divine noumenon that is the ultimate referent of the major religions. Third, this postulate makes an epistemological claim; it says that the noumenon cannot be directly experienced or known in itself, and it says that it can, at best, be only indirectly known (which means that any knowledge about it can only be indirect and inferential). And in light of the different types of religious conceptual schemes, it says that the divine noumenon comes to consciousness in terms of radically different concepts of personality and impersonality.

Epistemological Consequences

According to Hick, the epistemological corollary of the ontological postulate entails the relative insignificance of differences in religious conceptualization and belief among traditions, for these traditions are viewed as alternative soteriological frameworks in relation to the same ultimate reality and value.[7] Moreover, he argues for (1) the deconstruction of absolute claims to truth as pride-inspired tribal and ethnic preferences given the arbitrary stamp of divine approval and (2) skepticism over the possibility of settling in any conclusive or satisfactory way differences over historical and metaphysical claims. For these reasons Hick recommends adopting a tolerant agnosticism regarding differences in truth-claims among religions. This, however, is not to gainsay the in-principled cognitive significance of religious claims and beliefs, since the central elements of religious interpretive schemes are still eschatologically verifiable, according to Hick. Nonetheless, in this life he suggests that the phenomenal religions can only be assessed for their pragmatic adequacy—in terms of, for example, moral authenticity of founders, saints, and ideals, internal consistency and coherence of intellectual systems (e.g., theologies), and, most importantly, soteriological efficacy of whole systems conceived as frameworks of transformation. Applying these criteria to elements of the major faiths, Hick concludes that, so far as anyone can tell, the world's religions are roughly equal in their moral authenticity, intellectual impressiveness, and soteriological success. Therefore, from Hick's perspective, these religions are equally valid or veridical, supporting the pluralist hypothesis proposed as a conditional claim in the "first-steps" phase above.

Once again, we need to observe that Hick has developed a complex epistemological position that, in its two main aspects, continues and concludes the outworking of his initial philosophical presuppositions. The ontological realism presupposition undergirds both his justification for adopting tolerant agnosticism—for example, while religious historical and metaphysical claims are in principle settleable, says Hick, most are not conclusively adjudicable in practice—and his use of the notion of eschatological verification to pin down the continuing cognitive significance of religious beliefs. The Wittgenstein-ian orientation to the importance and primacy of religious practice and forms of life ap-pears to undergird Hick's attempt to develop a nascent epistemological pragmatism with respect to justifying and assessing religious systems. I believe that he sees these two episte-mological threads as ultimately compatible: (1) in this life, the only sort of truth and jus-tification we can attain with regard to religious beliefs and practices is that of pragmatic adequacy or authenticity; (2) nonetheless, it still remains possible that in the afterlife we will be able to see more exactly their ontological correspondence with reality; and (3) Hick seems to hold (not implausibly) that pragmatic adequacy or success is more likely than not to be an indication of ontological correspondence or truth.

It should be reasonably apparent from this reading that Hick's account of religious pluralism is composed of at least two different theoretical threads—cultural–linguistic and propositional–realist, respectively. Indeed, it is arguable that a number of others may be present as well.[8] The tendency to regard religious language and doctrine as metaphoric and mythic and to see all religions as expressions of a common core experi-ence or soteriological orientation is suggestive of what Lindbeck would call an experi-ential-expressive thread, while the final development of a pragmatic epistemology of religious belief is reminiscent of William James and suggestive of a pragmatic theory of religion.[9] And, of course, there is no denying the fact that Hick's ontological postulate reflects a Kantian thread. By itself the recognition of such diverse theoretical threads should give pause to anyone contemplating the development or acceptance of a critical reading constructed around only one of these threads.

Furthermore, in light of the manifest fact that at least two of these threads—cultural-linguistic and propositional-realist—carry through the whole development of Hick's theory, one should be reasonably wary of any critical reading that emphasizes only one of these at the expense of the other. Thus, I want to suggest that my reading of Hick is distinguished from the other readings I mentioned by the fact that it at the very least does justice to the complexity of Hick's theory. Clearly, for example, in view of what I have already said, his theory is not properly represented as "noncognitive"—to be sure there is a grammatical or seemingly antirealist thread, but we cannot overlook Hick's commitment to ontological realism, the cognitive significance of religious discourse via eschatological verification, and so on. By the same token, it seems somewhat misleading to label his theory "cognitivist" *tout court* simply because the view connoted by this seems to be at some odds with Hick's skepticism about resolving truth-claims in this life as well as with his focus on nonevidential reasons in the justification and assessment of religious belief and practices. And, again, to view his theory as simply a pragmatic inter-pretation of religious belief seems to do an injustice to the realist, ontological, and escha-tological elements in his account. We need, then, to examine Hick's theory apart from one-sided readings in order to be in a position to appreciate and assess the function, ef-fect, and significance of its multidimensional theoretical strands. We need now to iden-tify the principal critical issues or questions sighted in our reading of Hick's theory.

Each of the four phases of Hick's theory raises distinctive critical issues that have the potential of undermining the project as a whole. The first "presuppositional" phase, for example, seems composed of two very different—some would say incompatible—orientations to the epistemology of religious belief, the "grammatical" and the "realist."

This naturally generates the question of how these can be held together and coherently pursued in one theory. The second "methodological" phase introduces a fundamental premise of substantial overlap or identity of soteriological goals among diverse religions that immediately raises a question of hermeneutical adequacy: can such a premise do justice to the self-understandings of traditions that seemingly see themselves as believing quite different things about the universe and as pursuing quite different ends relative to these beliefs. Furthermore, one may wonder whether Hick is being sufficiently critical in his adoption and generalization of the methodological assumption of the veridicality of religious experience and thought. The third "postulate" phase seems bedeviled by a fundamental dilemma—how can an essentially inaccessible and unknowable postulated noumenon be made relevant to the phenomenal religions without somehow modifying its epistemic status? And the fourth epistemological phase, in simultaneously proposing a this-worldly agnosticism and pragmatism together with an other-worldly confirmability, generates not only an issue of conceptual coherence but also a concern that this approach may beg the question about the supposed correlativity of pragmatic fruits, on the one hand, and religious truth, on the other.

As I have already mentioned, Hick's theory has generated considerable critical response, much of it oriented to or at least touching on many of the issues I have just identified. Two outstanding recent critical evaluations of Hick's position—Netland and Corliss—warrant special attention because they represent two very persuasive readings of Hick's theory as an explicit contribution to the philosophy of religion and because, between them, in building on past critical efforts as well as Hick's response to these, they appear to address, in a sophisticated and coherent manner, many of the critical issues seemingly endemic to Hick's position.[10]

In what follows I want to examine and appraise Netland's and Corliss's handling of four critical issues in an effort to determine whether their arguments (and these issues) significantly undermine Hick's theory. The issues are possible hermeneutical inadequacy of the revisionist approach, possible fallacy of the generalization of veridicality, possible incoherence in the postulate of a divine noumenon, and possible epistemic inadequacy of Hick's pragmatic justification and assessment of religious belief. I will argue that most, if not all, of their criticisms are inconclusive against Hick and that his theory represents a plausible account of religious diversity. Let me now turn to the four areas of critical concern addressed by Netland and Corliss, beginning with the issue of hermeneutical adequacy.

Appraisal of Four Criticisms

1. Hermeneutical Adequacy of Hick's Revisionist Conception of Religion(s)

Hick begins the development of his theory by comparing and contrasting two views of religion and religious diversity—the standard view and an alternative revisionist view—both of which share the idea that religions are soteriological in aim, structure, and function but which diverge in interpreting the meaning of the diversity of religions.[11] The standard view conceives of religions as counterpoised rival systems of belief and practice whereby each system claims to have exclusive access to ultimate truth as well as the sole means of authentic salvation. The alternative revisionist view proposed and adopted by Hick, in contrast, sees religions as essentially related "kin" (rather than rival "strangers") that are concerned with the same vital process of moral and spiritual transformation (from ego- to reality-orientation) taking different forms in diverse cultural and historical settings. Particular religions, under this view, are working toward the same goal of human transformation in a mutually complementary rather than antagonistic way.

Now it is crucially important to realize that this revisionist conception entails a thesis much stronger than a more modest claim about a structural aim and pattern common to religions, for it incorporates the idea the same transformational process takes "different forms all over the world within the contexts of the different historical traditions."[12] This is a claim about substantive identity or overlap among diverse religious traditions, amounting to the adoption of "common core" or "unity" theory of religious pluralism, involving the claim of an underlying literal unity of some sort among all religions. The revisionist view, then, embodies a rather substantial thesis about the name of the world's religions, for it is, after all, a rather short step from claiming "the same transformational process" among different religions to claiming that these religions in fact refer in some important way to the "same ultimate reality."

It is not surprising to find critics challenging the propriety of this initial methodological move of Hick's theory, for with the revisionist conception Hick is taken considerably far in a particular theoretical direction—toward the transcendental unity of all religions. One immediate and pressing issue for these critics concerns precisely the hermeneutical adequacy of this move, especially considering the fact that its soteriological thesis seems to contradict the self-understanding of traditions about what they believe and practice.[13] And the issue is only made more exigent when one considers that, while many historians of religions might be willing to admit structural comparability in regard to cross-traditional soteriological aims, practices, and concepts, few seem willing to say that the data permit them to draw the conclusion of essential sameness or identity in soteriology cross traditionally. Indeed, most are likely to point to large differences in concept and practice that are in turn linked to equally large differences in meaning and reference. Thus, at the very outset of Hick's theory we need to record the serious—and some would say, decisive—reservation that it appears to overlook or discount what the religions say about themselves as well as what many historians of religions might say about how to understand properly religious beliefs and practices cross traditionally.

Perhaps the most explicit and pointed criticism of the hermeneutical adequacy of Hick's theory is that advanced by Netland.[14] Netland argues in a nutshell that Hick's theory is simply inadequate as a general second-order theory about religions precisely because it fails to take them on their own terms and reduces their central views and concepts (e.g., about soteriology) to understandings and terms unacceptable to the traditions themselves. Suggests Netland, a second-order theory such as Hick's must develop an account that can accommodate traditions' own orthodox understandings of doctrines, beliefs, and concepts without reinterpreting or reducing these (e.g., Incarnation) into other categories (e.g., mythological). With regard to the specific case at hand—soteriology—Netland claims that, in adopting "a lowest common denominator soteriology" (Netland's phrase for Hick's revisionist conception), Hick's theory is conceptually compelled to ignore or reinterpret the key soteriological concepts of various traditions in the form of minimizing their differences and claiming that they constitute one essential process (transition from ego to reality-orientation) taking place in different contexts. Indeed, he even goes so far as to suggest that Hick's "lowest common denominator soteriology" simply reduces all religious soteriologies to the terms of ordinary morality (i.e., transition from egoism to altruism). At the very least, then, it appears to be Netland's contention that Hick's revisionist approach to religious diversity is unable to accommodate adequately the various soteriological claims internal to traditions as these claims are understood within the traditions themselves. Hick's approach is, in short, hermeneutically deficient in its handling of first-order religious traditions and their complexity. I believe that this fairly represents one of Netland's major objections to Hick's revisionist conception, and I believe that Netland's objection, in turn, is a fair statement of a common critical reaction to Hick's initial methodological move.

Now, I want to suggest that this common reaction—often regarded as a decisive objection to Hick's theory—in fact suffers from a crucial ambiguity in its own formulation as well as from a crucial misunderstanding about the structure and development of Hick's theory. Let me first address the ambiguity before turning to the misunderstanding of Hick. The ambiguity is best gotten at by reflecting on a crucial distinction most ably drawn by Wayne Proudfoot in his recent book on the philosophy of religious experience.[15]

Proudfoot argues (correctly I think) that much work in this field suffers from a failure to note that "interpretation" may refer to one or the other of two different tasks that are often confused, collapsed, or elided one with the other: (1) identifying and describing a religious belief or practice in terms of the concepts and rules employed by the tradition or culture in which that belief or practice is imbedded; (2) explaining that belief or practice (already identified and described as in 1) in terms of some higher-order scheme, framework, or theory in the effort to arrive at the best explanation of the belief or practice at issue. As Proudfoot suggests, these two tasks are very different, though both are necessary for a full and adequate interpretative account of a religious belief or practice. The first task is primarily descriptive, involving the identification of a belief or practice under the description by which a subject (person) or culture identifies it. To describe such a religious phenomenon in terms unacceptable to the subject or culture would be to misidentify it altogether and to alter the object of inquiry: this is the fallacy of descriptive reduction. The second task, by contrast, typically involves offering an explanation of an already identified and described belief or practice—in terms or categories of an explanatory scheme or framework that are not those of, or necessarily acceptable to, the subject or culture: this is explanatory reduction, but it is not a fallacy. Explanatory reduction constitutes a normal explanatory procedure that sets a properly identified and described belief or practice (á la the first task) within a new context or framework (e.g., scientific or philosophical theory).

Though task 2 presupposes the achievement of task 1, they are distinct, and, suggests Proudfoot, the failure to distinguish between the two kinds of reduction (one a fallacy and the other not) results in the overly parochial and protective view that an explanatory account of a belief or practice must be restricted to the perspective and terms of the subject or culture. But this is precisely to confuse different levels or senses of interpretation (and interpretive adequacy) in such a way as to block genuine inquiry and attempts at explanation and theory from a perspective different from that of a subject or culture. This seems at best myopic and at worst a confused antiintellectualism. We now need to apply this clarification to Netland's critique of Hick's hermeneutical inadequacy.

We need first to ask whether Netland's criticism means to charge Hick with (1) descriptive inadequacy (reduction) at the level of identification and description of diverse soteriological beliefs and practices, or (2) explanatory inadequacy at the level of theoretical explication and account. If the charge is descriptive reduction (and if Netland is right to so charge), then Hick's theory may have a problem at the ground level, so to speak. If the charge is explanatory reduction (because of a supposed failure to adopt the categories of traditions as being truly explanatory and to use instead those of another theory or framework), then Netland's criticism itself may suffer from a problem of its own—namely, the undue imposition of an unreasonable explanatory or theoretic requirement. Let us consider each possibility, in turn, in connection with Hick's methodology.

It seems to me that, in proposing a revisionist conception of religious and religious diversity—which it will be the burden of his full theory to defend—Hick means to offer an explanatory hypothesis about how to account theoretically for the diversity of soteriological views and practices that are fully recognized by him to be quite different according to the viewpoints internal to the traditions themselves. Indeed, it is, from Hick's point of view, precisely the internal soteriological perspectives of religious traditions identified and understood in their own terms that generate the problem of the diversity of religions in the first place—for which he adopts the solution of the revisionist view. This implies, I think, that Hick must already have engaged in a prior step of identification and descriptive understanding from the viewpoints of the religious traditions themselves. Thus, if Netland's conclusion means to charge Hick with descriptive reduction, then this may be misguided since otherwise how is Hick so self-consciously aware of the diversity that needs to be explained and accounted for?

The possibility remains, of course, that Netland means to charge Hick with explanatory reduction, but this would seem myopic, for why should Hick at the level of theory and explanation be saddled with having to accept as adequate explanatory categories the conceptual schemes of the traditions themselves? Would this not simply generate competing explanatory accounts for which Hick (or someone else) would need to seek a higher-order explanation? At the level of explanation then, Hick seems perfectly within his rights as a scholar of (already identified and described) religious diversity to propose a theoretical-explanatory account that explains this diversity in terms of categories and concepts not fully acceptable to the traditions themselves (e.g., concepts of human transformation, common soteriological goal, contextual relativity, etc.). It is to be expected that a higher-order theoretical account would identify deeper (and perhaps common) explanatory factors that the more limited traditional perspectives would not have in view. On this reading, Hick simply takes (or assumes) first-order descriptions of soteriological processes and goals as the phenomena or data for which he now seeks an explanation in more comprehensive theoretical terms. That this might be seen as explanatory reduction is no objection at all.

As a consequence of the foregoing, I want to suggest that, on either interpretation of the charge of reductionism, Netland's criticism of Hick's theory as inappropriately reductionist seems to falter. I believe that Netland in fact simply fails to distinguish the two types of interpretive task—descriptive and explanatory—and then mistakenly conceives Hick's theoretical-explanatory account as being descriptively inaccurate. But this is a mistake, for why should we suppose that a theoretical-explanatory account must at that level simply replicate or be bound by traditional understandings and concepts? Netland writes, for example, "The traditional understanding of the Incarnation cannot be maintained on Hick's theory. Thus we are encouraged to reinterpret the Incarnation in mythological categories," or again, "The problem here is that Hick's theory cannot accommodate the Zen notion of satori as this is understood within the Zen tradition. Accordingly, Hick advocates a reinterpretation of satori . . . and this surely counts against his theory as a general theory."[16] Or yet again, "Can the great Pauline theme of justification, for example, . . . be reduced to transition from self-centeredness to Reality-centeredness?"[17] But the key question in all this is what Netland means by "adequately accounted for on Hick's analysis." Does he intend this in a descriptive-identification sense or an explanatory-theoretical sense? Netland does not say, but it does seem that the evidence he cites for a mistake on Hick's part involves claiming that Hick's theoretical-explanatory account is reductive. And one wants to say here: of course, the account is reductive, invoking nontraditional theoretical factors to explain in a systematic and comprehensive way what doctrines-as-they-are-understood-internally-to-traditions may really be all about. Is not this what a theory is supposed to do?

I think all of this justifies at least the claim that Netland's charge against Hick of hermeneutical inadequacy is inconclusive, though I am perfectly willing to concede that Hick himself could have been much clearer about the levels at which he works and which of two hats he is wearing when writing about religious pluralism. Sometimes, indeed, he speaks of writing as a Christian theologian to reinterpret in a first-order way the doctrine of the Incarnation because of the theory of religious pluralism he has developed in other places as a philosopher; knowing this about Hick sometimes encourages the confusion that Hick qua philosopher may be tampering reductively with the traditional understanding of doctrines.[18] But this is an illusion fostered by Hick's dual career. Qua philosopher, he accepts what traditions have to say about themselves (their doctrines and practices) and then asks, How can I qua philosopher account for this diversity, knowing what I do about philosophy and religious epistemology, and the like? The result of asking this question is a philosophical proposal that involves articulation and then elaboration, outworking, and defense of a revisionist conception of religions (contextual elaboration and differentiation of a process and goal held in common at the deepest level). If Hick really were to have committed the fallacy of descriptive reduction—thinking that all doctrinal schemes and practices obviously overlap, and so on—then I suggest Hick would have conducted his case in a different way, citing what he regarded as clear evidence of an essential core among religions and having no need to develop an argument of the sort that he does in fact develop. True descriptive reduction, I suggest, would be much more naive than Hick's evidently nonnaive argument, having no need to make methodological assumptions or to propose ontological postulates, and so forth. Hick is compelled to develop the elaborate defense that he does precisely because he is fully aware of diversity among traditions at the conceptual level of self-understanding.

2. Epistemic Adequacy of Hick's Basic Religious Conviction and Its Use

In initiating his theory, Hick adopts as a crucially important methodological assumption a "basic religious conviction" about the veridicality of religious experience—"religious thought and experience is not, as such, a matter of delusion and projection but mediates a real contact with a higher reality."[19] He is well aware of the pivotal role of this assumption within his theory, for he himself points out in responding to his critics that it has the effects of putting "out of bounds" the challenges of various forms of religious skepticism as well as coming close to entailing the key postulate of his theory.[20] Though he forthrightly states that "it is not the purpose of a philosophy of religious pluralism to provide the safeguard against atheism," Hick does at least refer to a line of argument in defense of his basic conviction, involving the appeal to a rational principle of credulity with respect to perceptual and more broadly experiential claims.[21]

It has been cogently argued by many philosophers (including Hick himself in *Why Believe in God?*) that it is rational to trust one's epistemic seeming experience so long as one holds one's credulity open to defeating conditions—for example, evidence of abnormal physiological factors, evidence of the absence or nonexistence of the supposed perceptual object, and so on—that such a principle seems necessary for acquiring knowledge of our environment, and that, aside from skeptical prejudice, there is no reason to exclude its use in religious contexts.[22] Hick is also quick to point out that, "if it is rational for the Christian to believe in God on the basis of his or her distinctively Christian experience, it must by the same argument be rational for the Muslim . . . for the Hindu and the Buddhist . . . on the basis of their own distinctive forms of experience."[23] That is, he argues that one must play fair with regard to the use of a principle of credulity in different religious and cultural contexts—if we regard it as reasonable to appeal to it for our entitlement in making epistemic claims on the basis of our experience, then by the same token it must be reasonable for others (even in other cultures and traditions) to appeal to it for a similar entitlement with regard to grounding their epistemic claims.

Netland contends that, at this point, Hick waffles between drawing one of two conclusions: (1) "Since the veridicality of religious experience in general cannot be ruled out a priori, then religious experience for any given tradition can in principle be regarded as veridical," and (2) "if it is shown to be reasonable to accept as veridical religious experience for a particular tradition, then the religious experience of the other great traditions must also be accepted as veridical."[24] And Netland is quick to point out that, while 1 is valid, 2 is not, for the simple reason that religious experience must be evaluated on a case-by-case basis to ascertain whether or not defeating conditions apply. Claim 1 is simply a fair generalization to all religions of a principle of credulity. Claim 2, by contrast, attempts to generalize a claim about actual veridicality to all traditions without taking into account the need to be epistemically responsible in using a principle of credulity.

Now, while Netland's distinction between claims 1 and 2 is certainly valid in itself, and while his objection to claim 2 as it stands is certainly correct, I believe that he is quite wrong in suggesting that Hick's "basic religious conviction" argument is ambiguous between claims 1 and 2 or that he even tries to advance claim 2 on the basis of simply "generalizing" a principle of credulity. My reason for saying this is quite simple: Hick does want to argue for something like claim 2—the equal veridicality of the major religious traditions—and in order to do this, he explicitly develops a whole theory of religious pluralism to support the contention. That is to say, Hick seems fully cognizant that the argument for claim 1 is insufficient to establish a version of claim 2; this is precisely why he leaves that argument and its conclusion (claim 1) behind in further proposing a pluralist hypothesis, for which he then goes on to develop a whole supporting framework of postulate, argument, and assessment of data that results finally in a pragmatic case for the equal authenticity (and hence veridicality) of the major traditions.

Hick is quite clear about the logic of his position when, after he has established the general in-principled applicability of a principle of credulity to religious experience, he goes on to suggest that this principle has its limits. He writes, "Treating one's own form of religious experience, then, as veridical . . . one then has to take account of the fact that there are other great streams of religious experience which take different forms."[25] And, asks Hick, What account is reasonable to develop here in light of the fact that these other traditions might well invoke a principle of credulity and from their points of view come to judge their forms of experience and their traditions as veridically as one judges one's own experience and tradition? How are we to adjudicate the challenge posed by this situation—what is the most reasonable response? Hick goes on to suggest three possible answers to this challenge, two of which he regards as flawed, with the third being the most reasonable, permitting us finally to hold that the major traditions are equally veridical.[26]

The first answer is that of exclusivism, which holds that only one's own form of religious experience is properly regarded as veridical, while all others are delusory. According to Hick, this exclusivist claim is unreasonably arbitrary. The second answer is that of inclusivism, which holds that religious experience in general is veridical, though this is most clear and effective in the case of one's own form of religious experience. According to Hick, the reasonability of this claim is belied by the fact of significant moral and spiritual transformations in other religious traditions. The argument here is that, assuming the premise of a strong correlation between veridicality and moral-spiritual fruits (actual transformation in people's lives), it is by no means clear that religious traditions differ greatly in either the quality of their fruits or, by implication, the degree of clarity of their veridicality. Finally, the third answer is that of pluralism, which holds that all forms of religious experience across traditions are properly regarded as being veridical (equally). And, according to Hick, this is the most reasonable position to adopt, for it avoids the flaws of the other two answers and is supported by a consistent line of reasoning as well as by evident facts. That is, assuming a strong correlation between veridicality and moral-spiritual fruits, this answer recognizes the equality of transformational fruits across traditions and, by implication, the equal authenticity or veridicality of these traditions.

Now it seems clear enough that, on the terms laid out by Hick, this third pluralist position can be regarded as reasonable only if there are good reasons to think that (1) there is a strong correlation between veridicality, on the one hand, and transformational moral and religious fruits, on the other, such that the latter fruits inductively support the former claim; and (2) the moral and spiritual fruits of the major traditions are equal. The premise represented by 1 needs support because for all we know these fruits can be had entirely apart from veridical religious experiences. The claim represented by 2 needs support not merely because it is not obviously true (and therefore requires convincing data) but also because the criteria for identifying and assessing moral and spiritual fruits are not self-evident (and therefore require articulation and defense). Since there is no reason at this point to accept the pluralist solution as the most reasonable response to Hick's challenge, we should expect Hick to develop a set of considerations bearing on the above premise and claim. And this I suggest is precisely the goal and burden of the remainder of his theory of religious pluralism. His theory is intended to provide us with a set of good reasons for accepting the pluralist hypothesis and its implications for equal veridicality. Thus, as I suggested in my original précis of Hick's theory, at this point Hick is proposing only the *conditional rationality* of the pluralist hypothesis that all the major religious traditions are in fact veridical and mediate real contact with a higher reality— that is to say, "conditional" on his subsequent adducement of good reasons.

It is precisely this "practical" turn in Hick's theory toward consideration of moral and spiritual authenticity that prompts Corliss's objection to Hick's basic religious conviction and its experience.[27] Whereas Netland challenges the way that Hick uses this conviction, Corliss objects to its use at all. He claims that Hick's basic conviction wrongly assumes that the primary cognitive content of religions is found in veridical religious experiences, and he claims further that Hick's contextual-linguistic thesis about such experience being shaped by traditional concepts and categories (imbedded in language games) undercuts the need for Hick's adopting such a conviction in the first place. From Corliss's perspective the cognitive content of religions resides in their views of life and the claims that they make, not in the experiences to which they give rise; to think otherwise illegitimately analogizes the role of religious experience in religions to the role of sense experience in dealing with the world around us. Therefore, Corliss would encourage Hick to put aside his basic religious conviction and concern for veridical religious experiences in order to focus exclusively on the validity of religious views of life.

There is something right about Corliss's complaint against Hick and also something wrong about it. Where Corliss goes wrong, I think, is in his flat-out rejection of any cognitive role for religious experience in religions analogous to the cognitive role of sense (e.g., perceptual) experience in dealing with the environment. It seems that the reason he gives for this rejection has to do with the fact that religious experiences are shaped and filtered by background concepts and categories. But this seems no less true of perceptual experiences, which anthropologists, psychologists, and linguists tell us are shaped and filtered by background conceptual and linguistic conditions. Furthermore, Corliss's rejection of a cognitive role for religious experiences appears to discount without clear and convincing reasons those cognitive practices internal to religious traditions involving adherents' appeals to religious experiences as a way to warrant their cognitive claims. Finally, it is not clear to me that Corliss has given any thought to a possible role for the principle of credulity (together with defeating conditions) in relation to religious experience; I wonder if the admission of such a principle might ease the need to draw a strong distinction between a cognitive role for perceptual experience and no cognitive role for religious experience at all.

What seems right about Corliss's complaint against Hick is this: Hick does in fact hold a conceptual-linguistic thesis about religious experience, and this does encourage us to wonder why he begins with an apparent methodological focus on the veridicality of religious experience.[28] And this puzzlement is heightened by Hick's own need to turn to other considerations (e.g., moral and spiritual fruits) as a way to assess issues of veridicality. Why not start with these other considerations in appraising background religious frameworks and views of life? Some of this puzzlement is dissipated, I think, by the realization that "religious experience" for Hick is a category intended by him to be equivalent to religious forms of life.[29] Thus, in speaking of veridical religious experience and thought, he is referring to the belief on the part of participants in religious forms of life (practices) that they are somehow in touch with, praying to, worshipping, and so forth, something that is real and not illusory. Hick does not mean "religious experience" to denote narrowly a religious sense percept. A second point to be made is that, in one sense, Hick agrees with Corliss—yes, it is important to assess the background religious framework for its cognitive content in religious experience—while at the same time disagreeing that this is somehow incompatible with an interest in the veridicality of religious experience and, of course, disagreeing that the focus ought to be truth-claims as contrasted with moral and spiritual fruits of religious practice (the latter represents another issue to which we will return). Indeed, we might ask, why cannot cognitive assessment have two foci (e.g., experience and belief), especially if these are seen to be conceptually related?

As in the case of Hick's "revisionist conception of religion," we are, I think, compelled to conclude that criticisms of his "basic religious conviction" are at best inconclusive (in the case of Corliss) or at worst simply wrong (in the case of Netland). Thus, it seems entirely legitimate for Hick to propose as the conclusion to the methodological phase of his argument a "pluralist hypothesis" about the deeper unity that may underlie the diversity of religions. We need now to consider what Hick has to say about the nature and implications of this hypothesis that is here only proposed as being conditionally rational and that will be the burden of his theory to defend more conclusively.

3. Coherence of Hick's Postulate of a Divine Noumenon

From Hick's perspective, the pluralist hypothesis can only make sense on the assumption of "a divine reality which is itself limitless, exceeding the scope of human conceptuality and language, but which is humanly thought and experienced in various conditioned and limited ways."[30] That is to say, in order to be coherently proposed and maintained, the pluralist hypothesis rationally requires the postulation of a divine noumenal reality (in itself infinite and unknowable) underlying and serving as the common ultimate referent of phenomenal religious systems, which in turn involve culturally shaped conceptualizations and experiences of the real. According to Hick, this postulation permits us to acknowledge in a consistent and coherent manner the diversity of forms of religious experience together with their mutual conditional veridicality—for though diverse they are all finally "about" (or better, "focused on") the same transcendent ultimate.

This postulation of a divine noumenon rests on an important distinction between the Real *an sich* and the Real-for-us that Hick sees as drawn by all religious traditions in their (structurally) common affirmations of a higher reality-in-itself exceeding human conceptualization and as lying beyond or behind the higher-reality-as-humanly-experienced-and-thought in their traditions. The fact that all the major traditions draw this distinction encourages Hick to propose the idea that the Real *an sich* is one cross-traditional reality in fact, though it is humanly experienced only in very limited culturally bound ways within the diverse religions. In other words, at the core of Hick's pluralist hypothesis is the postulated notion that the Real *an sich* of the different religions is one and the same reality in all cases and further that the Real-for-us (of each tradition) is the way that the tradition experiences and conceptualizes for itself the Real *an sich*. As Hick himself says, "this thought lies at the heart of the pluralist hypothesis," and it clearly constitutes a very substantive claim indeed.[31] It behooves us, therefore, to be clear about its conceptual content and logical function within his theory.

To begin with, we need to recognize that Hick's postulate has both ontological and epistemological dimensions—that is, it makes an ontological claim with an epistemological corollary. Ontologically speaking, Hick's postulate proposes that there is a Real *an sich* that is the unifying ground of the foci (Real-for-us) of the various traditions. This ground is the deeper source and object of all religious soteriologies and thus ontologically unifies them such that essentially the same process of moral and spiritual transformation is involved in all cases, for, in a significant sense, the process in each tradition has the same ultimate aim in the deepest sense. Epistemologically, Hick sees his Real *an sich* (divine noumenon) as the ground of religious experience and thought, making forms of religious experience across traditions veridical inasmuch as they all constitute our conditioned and limited access to the Real *an sich*. Hick elaborates on this epistemological dimension by suggesting, in conformity with his understanding of the conceptual-linguistic nature of religious experience, that the Real *an sich* impinges on culturally conditioned human consciousness, which for its part responds to and becomes aware of this impingement indirectly though the mediating lenses of culturally diverse conceptual schemes. Thus, the noumenon is not directly experienced or known but rather only indirectly encountered in terms of concepts, structures, and images "generated at the interface between the Real and different patterns of human consciousness."[32]

In this way, Hick manages to integrate the ontological and epistemological dimensions of his postulate: though the Real *an sich* is postulated as an ontological reality, it is known only through the mediating conceptual schemes of religious traditions that in turn are shaped by diverse cultural histories. Hick, of course, is well aware that conceptual schemes are very different—in fact, he identifies two clearly divergent types (personalist and impersonalist)—but he nonetheless holds that they all ultimately refer to the same divine noumenon or Real *an sich*. He explains how this can be conceived to be possible by developing an analogy to an application of the complementarity principle in physics: the personal and impersonal conceptual schemes of religion are to the divine noumenon in itself as the wave and particle conceptualizations of electromagnetic radiation are to light in itself.[33] In both cases, though the conceptualizations—personal/impersonal, wave/particle—are radically different, they still refer ultimately to the same logical subject (noumenon and light, respectively).

As might be expected, Hick's postulate of a divine noumenon has been the focus of considerable critical attention. Netland's discussion represents a particularly forceful and sustained critique of the postulate's coherence and its ability to succeed in the unifying and referential role cast for it by Hick.[34] The basic problem, according to Netland, resides precisely in Hick's distinction between the Real *an sich* and the Real-as-humanly-experienced and in the way he interprets their relation. Netland suggests that there are two possible interpretations of their relation, both of which are advanced by Hick in his writings. The first interpretation focuses on the element of continuity between the Real *an sich* and its various manifestations in phenomenal religious conceptions of the Real. In order for Hick to maintain that these latter conceptions are in fact manifestations or images of the divine noumenon, he must, suggests Netland, posit significant continuity (ontological and epistemological) between them—else why represent them as "manifestations or images" and why posit the divine noumenon as their unifying ontological ground and source? This continuity view, however, runs into a serious problem because of the great diversity—indeed seeming incompatibility—among conceptions or images of the divine (e.g., personal deity vs. impersonal principle or goal), yet it seems crucial to Hick's thesis that the Real *an sich* be ontologically and epistemological continuous with all conceptions. This seems to imply, however, that the noumenon must actually itself be (e.g.) both personal and nonpersonal at the same time, suggesting that it may suffer from an internal incoherence of some sort. The only way to avoid this consequence, suggests Netland, is to draw a distinction between the direct/penultimate referents of the phenomenal religious conceptions (e.g., "God" vs. "Nirvana") and their indirect/ultimate referents (e.g., Real *an sich*), which, of course, Hick regards as the same in all cases. But there is a problem here, according to Netland: given the great differences in the meanings of such phenomenal terms as "God," "Nirvana," and so on, it does not seem plausible to maintain that they all denote (ultimately) the same reality. What reason can be given for claiming that the ultimate referent of each is the same? The emphasis on continuity, then, from Netland's point of view runs smack up against the problem of radical phenomenal discontinuity of so-called manifestations or images with seemingly incompatible entailments that undermine the plausibility of claiming "same ultimate referent nonetheless." Netland suggests that the burden of proof is on Hick to come up with good reasons for "claiming that the ultimate referent of each is the same."

The second interpretation of the relation between the Real *an sich* and phenomenal religious conceptions focuses on their element of discontinuity. This interpretation, suggests Netland, highlights the strong Kantian implications of Hick's postulate of a divine noumenon that is never itself directly experienced, but rather "is posited in order to make sense of the fact of religious experience in general." Religious experience and thought, under this interpretation, is limited to culturally conditioned experience of phenomenal religious images and manifestations. But, argues Netland, this element of discontinuity, while avoiding the sort of problem addressed above in connection with the continuity view, raises problems of its own, stemming from the lack of knowledge of the divine noumenon. If this noumenon cannot be known in itself, then is it at all informative, asks Netland, to refer to phenomenal religious conceptions as images or manifestations of it? And, again, given the lack of knowledge about this Real *an sich*, on what grounds is it posited as a single divine reality rather than as a plurality of noumena? In short, suggests Netland, under this discontinuity view, the ontological status of the divine noumenon becomes very unclear in light of its epistemic obscurity. Indeed, Netland goes so far as to suggest that the reasons for postulating the existence of a divine noumenon are obscure: is it, he asks, anything more than an elaborate hypothesis developed to avoid concluding that perhaps all religions are not in touch with the same divine reality?

In a nutshell, then, Netland is arguing the following points against Hick's postulate of a divine noumenon. First, given the great differences—indeed, seeming incompatibilities—among phenomenal religious conceptions, it is not plausible for Hick to maintain that they all refer to the same ultimate reality. Furthermore, given the claim about the inaccessibility of this ultimate, it is not plausible for Hick to think that it can function adequately as a unifying referent for phenomenal religious conceptions. In the first case, the data of religious diversity suggest more plausibly the diversity of ultimate referents. In the second case, the epistemic gap between the noumenon and phenomenal religions undercuts the ability of the former to serve as unifying referent at all.

Now, despite the initial cogency of these criticisms, I believe their destructive force can be mitigated considerably by elements in Hick's position that Netland has either overlooked or discounted. The two principal ideas that Netland appears to miss are (1) the analogy that Hick draws between his postulate and the complementarity principle in physics and (2) the precise role that Hick casts for his postulate within the pluralist hypothesis and what this implies regarding the postulate's justification. The analogy with the complementarity principle addresses Netland's first point about compatibility and reference, while the postulate's role appears to address his second point about the destructiveness of the epistemic gap. Let me take each of these points in turn, beginning with the analogy.

Hick analogizes the ontological status and referential function of the divine noumenon (in relation to divergent phenomenal religious conceptions) to the ontological status and referential function of light (in relation to the divergent conceptions of wave and particle).[35] On the side of the analogical object, the analogy suggests that, when experimented on in different ways, light exhibits apparently divergent, contradictory behavioral properties, while at the same time in itself being such as to be capable of yielding these results or conceptualizations. On the side of the principal object, the analogy suggests that, when "experimented" on in different ways via the practices of different religious traditions, the divine noumenon exhibits apparently divergent, if not contradictory, qualities, while at the same time in itself being such as to be capable of yielding these results or conceptualizations. That is, the ontological status and nature of both light and divine noumenon are such that, under certain conditions, they exhibit what appear to be incompatible properties. Now for this force of the analogy: since the apparently incompatible properties in first case do not incline us to deny the plausibility of light's referential function in relation to these properties, so too, suggests Hick, the apparent incompatibilities in the second case ought not to undermine the plausibility of the divine noumenon's referential function in relation to these apparent incompatibilities. If in at least one important case—light—we accept the idea of one and the same referent for the incompatible conceptualizations of wave and particle, then it is not implausible to accept the idea in another case—divine noumenon—as well. It seems to me that Hick's analogy does in fact address the first of Netland's criticisms, mitigating its force or at least making its objection inconclusive.[36]

This analogy does not, however, address Netland's other concerns about Hick's postulate—that is, the positive justification for positing one ultimate referent and, further, the justification for thinking that such an inaccessible noumenon can in concept function referentially. Netland's concern about positive justification is met, I think, by emphasizing the "postulate" status and internal role of the divine noumenon within Hick's pluralist hypothesis. The "positive" reason justifying Hick's positing of the noumenon is that the postulate is rationally necessary for the internal consistency of the pluralist hypothesis, and this seems to be a strong enough justification at this point. Of course, we will want eventually to have reasons for adopting less conditionally the hypothesis as a whole, and when Hick undertakes to supply these reasons, then the justification for the postulate will also be stronger than internal rational necessity. But it seems a bit premature (and unfair) to require this fuller justification before accepting that the postulate is at least conditionally justified by its role within the pluralist hypothesis. And the latter is all that Hick means to claim in this phase of his theory: a divine noumenal reality is rationally needed to "complete" (so to speak) the pluralist hypothesis. That is, the divine noumenon as ultimate referent is, from Hick's point of view, the only way to reconcile religious diversity with conditional mutual veridicality.

But, at this point, Netland's remaining concern seems to rear its head—for he wants to know why Hick (or anyone) should think that such an epistemically inaccessible ultimate should be able conceptually to function as a referent for phenomenal religious conceptions. Does not the very lack of knowledge about this ultimate undermine its capacity to serve as a unifying referent in any serious sense? Despite the seeming cogency of this complaint, however, I think that Hick has answered it precisely by arguing that the postulate of a divine noumenon is both rationally necessary (for the hypothesis of mutual veridicality) and not implausible (by analogy with the principle of complementarity). Together, these two prongs of Hick's thinking about his postulate imply that an epistemically inaccessible noumenon can serve as a ultimate unifying referent. If Netland is requiring more reasons at this point, then he is requiring too much at this stage. What Hick is proposing in this phase is perfectly conceivable and coherent, and what he is proposing seems justified (internally) from the perspective of the pluralist hypothesis. Other and stronger reasons must, again, await Hick's defense of his hypothesis as a whole.[37]

It would not be amiss to mention that, unlike Netland, Corliss does apparently conceive of Hick's theory as referentially coherent in principle, though in arguing this he does think of himself as adding to or clarifying Hick's position. Thus, for example, in asking whether different divine phenomenal realities can be rooted in experience of the same ultimate, Corliss (also apparently unaware of Hick's complementarity analogy) argues that, inasmuch as value-contextualism is possible (e.g., same commitment to the importance of life underlying, in different contexts, strategies of nonviolence and proportionate use of force), so too is it possible for the same ultimate reality to underlie, in different contexts, diverse phenomenal conceptions of the divine embodying apparently different values.[38] This point seems to function logically very much like Hick's own complementarity analogy. And in asking whether it is consistent both to claim no knowledge of the noumenon itself and at the same time to claim that the One is beyond knowledge, Corliss (apparently discounting Hick's own representation of his position) answers that Hick needs to adopt the consistent approach of considering his theory an hypothesis for which knowledge is not attainable, but evidence and reasons appropriate.[39] But this is just what Hick does by conditionally proposing the pluralist hypothesis along with a postulate of a divine noumenon for which he later proposes to adduce evidence and reasons. This point on Corliss's part simply seems to recapitulate the logic of Hick's position.

4. Epistemic Adequacy of Hick's Justification for Adopting the Pluralist Hypothesis

In the final phase of the development of his theory, Hick proposes three mutually complementary lines of argument for adopting as valid the pluralist hypothesis (up to this point advanced only as a conditional claim).[40] The first line of argument advances a set of considerations supporting the adoption of an attitude of tolerant agnosticism in this life regarding differences and disagreements in belief among religious traditions. The second line of argument introduces the notion of afterlife verification in order to assure, nonetheless, the in-principled cognitivity of religious belief and discourse. And the third line of argument proposes and deploys a this-life pragmatic justification for the independent and equal veridicality of the diverse perceptions of and salvific routes to the Real as represented by the major faiths.

Hick initiates the first line of argument by drawing a distinction between the "goods" (salvation, liberation) conveyed by a religious system and the "claims" (salvation-claim, truth-claim) that it might make about these goods and related states of affairs.[41] According to Hick, the "goods" represent the valuable, essential, and primary content of religious traditions, while their "claims" and "doctrines" represent just so much secondary "packaging and labelling," though Hick concedes that these are nevertheless "essential" to transmitting the "vital" contents.[42] It seems clear that, in this weighting of goods over claims, Hick is reaffirming one of the logical consequences of his initial methodological preference for the revisionist conception of religion(s) as well as his Wittgensteinian perspective on the nature of religions.

In keeping with this methodological commitment, Hick then deconstructs those absolute claims often advanced by religions in the effort to assert their respective salvific superiority and truth over other traditions. Hick maintains that these claims simply represent in the context of religion an extension of the common social–psychological phenomenon of ethnic pride in one's heritage and tradition. Absolute claims, he suggests, are no more than instances of natural pride "elevated to the level of absolute truth and built into the belief system of a religious community," instances where, in short, "a natural human tribal preference . . . receives the stamp of divine approval."[43] Thus does Hick manage to introduce a note of skepticism about the truth value of claims to religious exclusivity.[44]

This modest skeptical point about religious belief is developed more extensively by Hick in his examination and assessment of differences in three principal types of beliefs advanced by religious traditions—historical, metaphysical, and ultimate.[45] In each case, Hick proposes reasons for being skeptical about whether differences in these beliefs can be conclusively settled in this life. Differences in historical belief among traditions, while in principle settleable by historical evidence, usually are not settled because of the paucity of data about many crucial founding events. Thus, Hick expresses considerable skepticism about whether many important differences in historical belief will ever be actually settled. Metaphysical differences, presumably settleable in principle by reference to actual states of affairs, tend to involve the interaction of conceptual, empirical, and ontological issues so complex that it is extremely difficult to resolve conclusively matters of their verification and truth. Again, Hick expresses much skepticism about the actual resolution in this life of such issues, suggesting that they will be debated until the end of human history. Finally, differences in ultimate belief, while presumably veridical in some important sense (compare Hick's basic religious conviction), nonetheless are embodied within complex and elusive mythic and metaphoric (rather than literal) formulations, making it difficult to settle conclusively which aspects of traditions might be veridical about the ultimate reality.

The upshot, then, of Hick's first line of argument is a rather skeptical view about the prospect of resolving in this life many disagreements in belief (at these various levels) among religious traditions. Thus, Hick recommends the adoption of an attitude of tolerant agnosticism regarding these differences in belief, suggesting—in conformity with his opening point about the priority of goods over claims—that while these might be of "philosophical importance as elements within respective theories about the universe they are not of great 'religious,' i.e., soteriological, importance."[46]

Despite his skepticism about settling differences in belief in this life, Hick nonetheless stalwartly defends in his second line of argument the in-principled cognitivity of religious belief. He does this by appealing to the notion of eschatological verification, which involves the concept of an ultimate afterlife situation capable of verifying (at long last) the truth of religious claims about the nature of reality.[47] Hick argues that such a situation—understood to include a transformed human existence involving a powerful sense of being in ultimate relation with an ultimate reality—could in principle confirm the truth of religious interpretations of the deep structure and process of the universe. Furthermore, suggests Hick, the very possibility of such future confirmation (or better, confirmability) means now that present religious accounts of the universe are factual in character, intending to claim that a given state of affairs (involving a transcendent reality) does in fact obtain. In effect, Hick conceives of eschatological verification as a post mortem experiential confirmation of religious convictions that are held now largely on the basis of faith and, further, as an expectation built into the structure of religious convictions having the logical function of making these convictions cognitive in principle.

As Hick himself observes, this notion is "not directly relevant to the assessment of the conflicting truth-claims of the various traditions" since subsequent eschatological confirmations (if any) are not available to us in the present.[48] Thus, from the vantage of those now living, Hick's appeal to eschatological verification amounts to a hypothesis unverifiable to us now but possibly verifiable to us post mortem (if there is an afterlife). And, maintains Hick, this implies that, despite a justified agnosticism about them in this life, religious beliefs are nonetheless in principle confirmable in another.

With the results of his first two lines of argument behind him, Hick is now faced with the difficult task of trying to provide justifying reasons for adopting the pluralist hypothesis as valid. In light of his argument for tolerant agnosticism regarding differences in religious beliefs, these reasons presumably cannot be evidential ones that somehow demonstrate conclusively the truth of the central claims of the diverse traditions. And it will hardly do for Hick to rely on his position of eschatological verification since that would only support the view that the pluralist hypothesis is cognitive in principle because it is eschatologically verifiable. Hick needs now to supply positive reasons for us to accept now, in this life, the actual validity of the pluralist hypothesis as contrasted with other possible hypotheses attempting to account for religious diversity. That is to say, the cogency of Hick's theory finally rests on his being able to cash out his earlier promissory note on supplying reasons for why his hypothesis is the stronger and more acceptable position.

Hick's third line of argument proposes that, in light of the soteriological aim and structure of religions, it may be most appropriate to develop a pragmatic justification and assessment of religious frameworks of belief and practice, focusing precisely on the issue of their effectiveness in accomplishing their avowed aim of transforming persons from ego-centeredness to Reality-centeredness.[49] He further proposes that the appropriate sorts of criteria for such appraisal and justification can be gleaned from the religious context itself—most particularly from the initial positive responses to great religious figures who founded new religious traditions. Suggests Hick, "human discriminative capacities must . . . have been at work, operating in accordance with at least implicit criteria" in the acceptance of these founders.[50] Furthermore, he continues, such criteria were (and are) presumably operative in subsequent phases of development of these traditions. What criteria exactly? Here Hick offers three sorts of related criteria, concerned, respectively, with the moral authenticity of the founder's teaching and personal character taken together as a unity; the combined intelligibility, plausibility, and attractiveness of the vision or reality he articulates; and, finally, the soteriological efficacy of his message and vision (i.e., capacity to evoke actual change in people in relation to the Real).

With these originary moral and spiritual pragmatic criteria identified, Hick then goes on to ascertain how they might be applied in the assessment and justification of religious–cultural phenomena. With regard to forms of religious experience as well as basic visions of reality (conceived as "maps" designed to lead people to the Real), he argues that the most appropriate question is whether they are, respectively, veridical and accurate and that this is best assessed by whether the total systems built up around them are soteriologically effective and actually put people in touch with the Real. With regard to the explicit interpretive schemes of religions (i.e., their theologies or philosophies), Hick argues that these may be rationally assessed in terms of their internal consistency and coherence as well as their adequacy to the root experiences and basic visions of their traditions. And with respect to the historical results or outworkings of religious soteriological systems, Hick argues that the most appropriate assessment is a moral one that focuses on the quality of the religions' actual and ideal fruits.

When he goes on to apply these criteria in assessing religious phenomena and traditions, Hick makes the following observations. First, to the extent that the interpretive schemes of different religions are compatible, they appear to be "equally massive and powerful systemizations of different basic visions."[51] Second, inasmuch as they involve transformation of the self composed of respect for persons and love of others, the ideal ways of life associated with the major traditions appear equally impressive from a moral point of view. Third, the historical records of the actual virtues and vices of the major traditions are so complex and diverse that it is not possible to render a defensible comparative judgment. Fourth, to the extent that we can ascertain soteriological efficacy in this life—in terms of, for example, whether people are made happier, lead more fulfilling lives, and are enabled to become better persons—it appears that the main historical streams of religious experience and life constitute equally impressive and successful soteriological frameworks for hundreds of millions for centuries. In light of all this, Hick concludes that, so far as we can tell, the major traditions are equally efficacious soteriologically and therefore possess equally valid (veridical) perceptions of the Real. Therefore, from Hick's perspective, the pragmatic assessment of religious traditions yields a pragmatic justification for accepting the pluralist hypothesis as valid.

Not surprisingly, the epistemic adequacy of Hick's justification for his pluralist hypothesis has been challenged on a number of grounds, most notably for its apparent denial of the significance of truth-claims in religion and for its seeming preference for the language of authenticity rather than truth in relation to the justification and assessment of religious beliefs and practices. Perhaps the two most vigorous criticisms along these lines have been those of Griffiths and Lewis and Byrne.[52] Griffiths and Lewis, for example, interpret Hick as explicitly developing a noncognitivist position on the nature and justification of religious belief, and they expend particular effort on challenging the hermeneutical adequacy of such a position in dealing with the beliefs and claims of diverse traditions. They argue against Hick that (1) since historically it is clear that religious spokesmen "really did think they were making claims about the nature of things," therefore, (2) any position that presupposes that the "creators and systematizers of religious worldviews were actually doing something other than what they thought they were doing" must be hermeneutically inadequate because (3) it fails to "take the tradition seriously on its own terms and . . . is almost certain to lead to a serious distortion of the tradition."[53]

This charge against Hick is not only unfounded but is also itself methodologically flawed. Clearly, from all that we have said about his position, Hick does not deny that religious spokesmen intend to make truth-claims about the nature of reality. Quite the reverse: he presupposes at the very outset of his study and reiterates throughout his position that they do intend to advance truth-claims. (And indeed, his own positions of tolerant agnosticism and eschatological verification entail the maintenance of an underlying commitment to the in-principled cognitivity of religious belief.) So, the charge against Hick appears unfounded. Furthermore, it appears to be methodologically flawed as well, inasmuch as it (like Netland's critique of Hick's claim about "same soteriological process") fails to take account of the distinction between descriptive reduction (a fallacy that is not committed by Hick) and explanatory reduction (which is no fallacy at all). Thus, for Hick to argue at the level of (second-order) theory an agnosticism about differences in (first-order) truth-claims among religious traditions appears to take adequate descriptive account of these latter claims—precisely in order to mount a higher claim about their lack of conclusive adjudicability, verification, and so on, in this life.

Byrne, while not necessarily agreeing with Griffiths and Lewis's interpretation of Hick as an explicit noncognitivist, argues nonetheless that Hick's position, in emphasizing notions of genuineness, authenticity, and practical appropriateness, and the like, borders on the abandonment of truth in religion. Byrne claims that Hick's "tolerant agnostic[ism] about different and even conflicting accounts which can all have an equal degree of truth akin to map projections of the earth" simply violates what he (Byrne) calls the "logic of truth," reducing cognitive appraisal to mere "terms of usefulness or clarity."[54] This criticism, however, seems quite inconclusive in light of its apparent failure to acknowledge an important turn in Hick's argument. Hick is clearly interested in epistemically relating his pragmatic assessment to claims about veridicality and truth: if, for example, a religious system proves to be soteriologically effective, then this, according to Hick, has some bearing on whether the system is veridical (i.e., whether its root religious experience is about something real and whether its basic vision actually corresponds to the way reality is structured). Such an interest indicates that Hick is inclined toward developing some sort of pragmatic epistemology in relation to the justification and assessment of religious belief and practice. And, if this is so, then Byrne cannot simply dismiss Hick's move here by asserting that it violates the "logic of truth" since it is precisely the nature of this truth that is at issue: is religious truth merely a matter of propositions that somehow correspond with reality (as Byrne seems to presuppose), or is it also a matter of personal being in relation to the ultimate (as Hick seems to propose)?

With the work of Corliss and Netland, the criticisms of the epistemic adequacy of Hick's position take a more sympathetic turn, for both appear to be fully aware of the cognitive intentions of Hick's theory, and, in the case of Corliss especially, there is considerable sensitivity to the way that Hick develops his justificatory position in light of the soteriological aim and structure of religions. This is not to suggest, however, that Hick's position somehow escapes unscathed. Quite the reverse, for Corliss expends considerable effort in trying the delineate the shortcomings of Hick's pragmatic approach to the justification of religious belief.

While he agrees with Hick that religions ought to be assessed in terms relating to their soteriological function, Corliss nevertheless sees Hick as having an overly narrow view of the criteria appropriate for assessing their fulfillment of this function—that is, pragmatic success in resolving individual unhappiness and advancing individual happiness.[55] According to Corliss, this perspective tends to discount the equally (if not more) important rational–moral appraisal of ends and ideals imbedded in traditions as well as their "spiritual hypotheticals" (complex combinations of moral-spiritual values and personal goods—for example, if one follows the Noble Eightfold Path, then he or she will resolve personal suffering and achieve Nirvana). From Corliss's perspective, religious views of life have validity to the extent that they embody or entail true or reasonable claims, and therefore the validity of such views is determined largely by the validity and reasonability of the value-claims and spiritual hypotheticals contained within them. This approach, suggests Corliss, permits a degree of agnosticism about the ultimate reality and yet permits the development of a rational faith filtered through a critique of moral-spiritual values and hypotheticals. By contrast, presumably, Hick's approach falls somewhat short of a "rational faith" precisely because, according to Corliss, it focuses only on some of the values pertinent to the soteriological process (i.e., those pertaining to personal happiness and fulfillment), while denying that others can also be assessed in a rational manner (moral–spiritual values, ideals, and hypotheticals).

The simple response to this critique of Hick's position is that it takes a rather limited view of what Hick intends to cover by the notion of pragmatic assessment or justification. From our reconstruction of Hick's arguments and proposals, it seems fairly clear that Hick includes rational–moral appraisal of values and ideals in what he intends by pragmatic assessment—how else to explain his criteria of moral authenticity and internal coherence as well as his concern with ideal ways of life and historical records of virtues and vices, in addition to soteriological efficacy of total religious systems? Furthermore, it seems fairly clear that what Hick means by soteriological efficacy includes a bit more than achievement of personal happiness or resolution of personal suffering since he appears to construe transformation of the self as a transition from egocentricity to Reality orientation involving respect and love for others. That is to say, Hick's notion of soteriological efficacy is properly conceived in large part as being moral and spiritual in nature, not narrowly hedonic and egoistic. Thus, I think that Hick can easily accommodate Corliss's criticism by simply arguing that it is another way to state his (Hick's) own understanding of pragmatic justification of religious belief and practice.

None of this quite addresses the deep epistemic issue raised by Byrne about Hick's view of knowledge and truth in religion. Though he fails to argue a counterposition against Hick's nascent pragmatic epistemology, Byrne's reaction does raise an important question about the adequacy of such an approach. Corliss, by contrast, while critical of what he (wrongly) perceives to be Hick's narrow concern with pragmatic success, nevertheless seems to accept without argument the adequacy of a (broadly) pragmatic approach to the nature of religious justification. So, despite the inconclusiveness of objections raised against Hick's pragmatic justification of his pluralist hypothesis, we still seem to be left with an important outstanding issue about the adequacy of his general underlying position on the epistemology of religious belief.

Nevertheless, I want now to contend that, despite appearances, Hick has in fact addressed this issue by developing a justificatory position resting on a two-tiered understanding of religious truth and a double-phased analysis of the epistemology of religious belief.[56] From Hick's point of view, religious truth is a complex epistemic category coordinating propositional truth with what he calls personalistic truth. Propositional truth refers to the correspondence between, on the one hand, a belief or claim purporting to describe reality (here including the Real) and, on the other, the reality itself. Personalistic truth refers to the "moral truthfulness of a person's life"—that is, the existential coherence between propositional beliefs and the sort of life and character developed in light of these beliefs.[57] For Hick, religious truth involves both propositional and personalistic truth such that the life a person leads coheres with beliefs or truth-claims that correspond to the way that reality is.

Now, corresponding to this analysis of religious truth and taking into account the arguments for tolerant agnosticism, Hick develops a two-phased epistemology of religious belief that undercuts any simple (strict) disjunction between a realist approach (Byrne) and a pragmatic approach (Corliss). On the one hand, he advances a notion of eschatological verification that not only sustains the cognitivity in principle of religious belief but also spells out (loosely, to be sure) a procedure for confirming in a conclusive way the propositional truth-claims associated with religious beliefs. On the other hand, he also advances a pragmatic justification for these beliefs inasmuch as they are associated with distinctive sorts of lives and self-development (oriented around human transformation), suggesting that beliefs thus justified are more likely than not to be in harmony with reality as it is. This latter point, of course, is hardly conclusive evidence for the propositional truth of religious beliefs; nonetheless, suggests Hick, pragmatic assessment (in the broad sense) of a set of religious beliefs may provide some indication—the best possible in this life—of their fuller correspondence with reality as it is. This, I believe, would be Hick's answer to both Byrne and Corliss: a proposal of two sorts of justificatory procedure—one for this life and a second for the afterlife—together with a wager about their correlation.[58]

Conclusion

Hick's theory of religious pluralism is a sustained attempt to account for the diversity of religions by combining elements from two views of and approaches to religious belief and practice: a Wittgensteinian-grammatical view, on the one hand, and a more traditional propositional-realist view, on the other. In this hybrid account, the diverse religions are conceptualized as cultural–linguistic grammars or idioms for engaging in soteriologically oriented forms of religious life that ultimately refer to one radically transcendent reality. From first to last, the various phases of the development of Hick's theory may be viewed as a grand attempt to mediate or synthesize these two views of religious belief. The methodological phase of the theory involves the adoption of precisely the two views in question, the revisionist conception of religions encapsulates a grammatical view of religions as cultural traditions, while the basic religious conviction incorporates the commitment to an ontologically real divine. The postulate phase puts those two philosophical commitments together by positing a radically transcendent ontological reality that can be encountered only indirectly through "grammatical" conceptual schemes or lenses. And the justification phase completes this integration by proposing a two-tiered epistemology of religious belief: a this-life pragmatic justification oriented to the authenticity of religious forms of life combined with an eschatological confirmability-in-principle of their implicit central truth-claims about the nature of reality. Thus does it seem that Hick's theory represents a deepening and extension of his initial philosophical presuppositions involving the simultaneous commitment to a grammatical view of religion as well as to an ontological realism about the meaning and reference of religious language.

It has been suggested by more than one philosopher that these two approaches to religious belief and to practice constitute rival epistemologies that show little, if any, common ground. Thus, it might be theorized that it would be difficult if not impossible to integrate them into one coherent theory or account. Stuart Brown, for example, in contrasting the views of a neo-Wittgensteinian theorist (Peter Winch) with the views of a traditional realist (Michael Durrant) has written of "the yawning gulf between the philosophical traditions from which Winch and Durrant write": "fundamentally different views about meaning . . .

imply[ing] further differences in the kind of theology they think possible."[59] Suggests Brown, the grammatical view "seems to yield a radically anti-metaphysical conception of religion" (i.e., theology as regulative grammar), while the traditional view "sees the loss of a metaphysical element . . . as the loss of something essential to religion." In view of such differences in orientation and implication, it is not surprising that many scholars understand these approaches as constituting rival and incompatible theories of religion. Even Hick himself notes the strong contrast between the standard conception of religions as rival and competing sets of propositional beliefs and the revisionist conception that he himself prefers. Nonetheless, he means for his pluralist theory to integrate these two approaches since each has, from his point of view, a contribution to make to the development of an adequate and unified theory of religious diversity. The grammatical view permits Hick to emphasize the elements of cultural conditioning and contextualization in working out his understanding of religious epistemology, while the realist view permits him to nonetheless hold together these diverse contexts at the deeper ontological level.

In view of these different theoretical strands in Hick's account of religious pluralism, it is perhaps not so surprising that critics have been able to interpret his project in radically different ways—for example, as akin to a neo-Wittgensteinian noncognitivism (Griffiths and Lewis) and as akin to traditional cognitivism (Netland). It is also not surprising that they would focus their critical attention on issues of meaning and reference and epistemology since these identify crucial points in Hick's theory where the successes or failures of his integrative effort would be most evident. Despite the initial theoretical implausibility of putting together elements from two such different views of religious language and belief, I believe that the success or failure of Hick's integrative effort needs to be assessed in light of the actual arguments and counterarguments about the theory rather than simply in terms of what one might, in the abstract, consider to be theoretically feasible. And, I suggest, when we look at the actual arguments pro and con the crucial points of theoretical tension in Hick's account, we will find that Hick's views fare pretty well and are not in any obvious way either incoherent or implausible. Indeed, as I have suggested in my review of the critical concerns raised by Netland and Corliss, major challenges to Hick's integrative effort can either be rebutted or at least be shown to be quite inconclusive. Therefore, I think we need to conclude on the basis of our critical scrutiny of Hick and his critics that Hick's theory of religious pluralism constitutes one coherent and not implausible account of the diversity of the world's religious traditions.

Notes

1. For example, John Hick "The Outcome: Dialogue into Truth," in *Truth and Dialogue in World Religions*, ed. John Hick (Philadelphia: Westminster, 1974), pp. 114–15, *God Has Many Names* (Philadelphia: Westminster, 1982), *Problems of Religious Pluralism* (New York: St. Martin's, 1985) (hereafter cited as *Problems*), *An Interpretation of Religion* (New Haven, Conn.: Yale University Press, 1989).

2. See Paul Griffiths and Delmas Lewis, "On Grading Religions, Seeking Truth, and Being Nice to People—A Reply to Professor Hick," *Religious Studies* 19 (1983): 75–80; Peter Byrne, "John Hick's Philosophy of World Religions," *Scottish Journal of Theology* 35 (1982):

289–301; George A. Netland, "Professor Hick on Religious Pluralism," *Religious Studies* **22** (1986): 249–61; Richard Corliss, "Redemption and the Divine Realities: A Study of Hick and an Alternative," *Religious Studies* **22** (1986): 235–48.

3. See Hick, *Problems,* Chapter 2.

4. See, e.g., Peter Winch, "Meaning and Religious Language," in *Reason and Religion,* ed. Stuart Brown (Ithaca, N.Y.: Cornell University Press, 1977), pp. 193–221.

5. See Hick, *Problems,* Chapters 3, 6, and 7.

6. *Ibid.*

7. *Ibid.,* Chapters 4, 5, and 6.

8. For this typology of theories of religion, see George Lindbeck, *The Nature of Doctrine* (Philadelphia: Westminster, 1984), Chapters 1 and 2.

9. See William James, *The Will to Believe and Other Essays in Popular Philosophy* (New York: Dover Library reprint, 1956), and *The Varieties of Religious Experience,* ed. John Smith (Cambridge, Mass.: Harvard University Press, 1985).

10. See Note 2.

11. See Hick, *Problems,* Chapter 3 (Note 1).

12. *Ibid.,* p. 29.

13. See the particularly trenchant comment by Griffiths and Lewis: "The goal at which religions direct their practitioners—tellingly described by Professor Hick as salvation/liberation (the use of "/" is usually a sign of a philosopher's rather uneasy attempt to combine two notions which really cannot be combined)—is single, universal, in all cases the same" (Griffith and Lewis, Note 2, p. 76).

14. Netland (Note 2), pp. 255–57.

15. See Wayne Proudfoot, *Religious Experience* (Berkeley and Los Angeles: University of California Press, 1985), Chapters 2 and 5.

16. Netland, p. 255.

17. *Ibid.,* p. 256.

18. See, e.g., Hick, *Problems,* Chapter 4.

19. *Ibid.,* pp. 102–3.

20. *Ibid.,* p. 106.

21. *Ibid.,* p. 103. Hick makes this point against Byrne's vigorous efforts to argue that Hick must deal more fully with the position of the rational skeptic, especially of the ilk of Feuerbach; see Byrne (Note 2), pp. 299–300. I agree wholeheartedly with Byrne on this score. Perhaps this is the place to remark on the great importance of Hick's basic religious conviction in preventing him from taking seriously the possibility of a completely projectionist account of religious diversity, i.e., the possibility that the conceptual schemes of cultural traditions might simply "constitute" the corresponding forms of religious experience entirely apart from any ultimate ontological reality. Though I do not discuss the issue in this article, I do believe that Hick needs to consider more fully and carefully the major alternatives to his theory of religious experience and thought purely as forms of projection and nothing more.

22. See, e.g., Richard Swinburne, *The Existence of God* (Oxford: Clarendon, 1979), Chapter 13; George I. Mavrodes, *Belief in God* (New York: Random House, 1970), Chapter 3; John Hick, "Mystical Experience as Cognition," reprinted in *Understanding Mysticism,* ed. Richard Woods (Garden City, N.J.: Doubleday, 1980), pp. 422–37 (see esp. pp. 433–36);

Michael Goulder and John Hick, *Why Believe in God?* (London: SCM, 1983), Chapter 2. Swinburne is particularly persuasive on the principle of credulity and its proper formulation. There are problems pertinent to the application of this principle that Hick does not consider. For example, Proudfoot has recently suggested that the noetic component of religious experience embeds or encodes a hypothesis about the perceptual object of the experience also being its cause, and this suggestion, if true, "ups the ante" with regard to critical evaluation of the truth of this hypothesis as contrasted with other possible explanations of the experience (e.g., projectionist accounts); see Proudfoot, Chapter 5.

23. Hick, *Problems* (Note 1), p. 103.

24. Netland (Note 2), p. 257, Note 1.

25. Hick, *Problems,* p. 37.

26. See esp. *ibid.,* Chapter 3.

27. Corliss (Note 2), p. 247.

28. See esp. Hick, *Problems,* Chapter 2.

29. Hick's opening move in his analysis of religious experience is to suggest that Wittgenstein was right to affirm the primacy of religious experience and practice over conventional religious organization and doctrine. Thus, according to Hick, students of religion must understand and investigate religious experience within the context of religious forms of life (experiential–dispositional–behavioral–linguistic "packages" of first-order religious life and practice) rather than theological doctrines and formal religious regulations. Hick goes on to apply Wittgenstein's discussion of the interpretive nature of perception to the religious context, suggesting in rough outline that religious experience is best understood as being aware of situations-in-the-world in terms of background systems of religious concepts associated with particular traditions and being disposed both to see these situations as (e.g.) manifesting divine presence and to act accordingly. In effect, the thesis is that religious experience must be understood as being shaped conceptually by background social–linguistic–contextual religious conditioning and learning. All religious experience is properly understood as experiencing-as, in which the experiencer is conditioned by his or her background religious language games and forms of life. For further elaboration, see *ibid.,* Chapter 2.

30. *Ibid.,* Chapters 3, 6, and 7; quote is from p. 104.

31. *Ibid.,* p. 40.

32. *Ibid.,* p. 32.

33. Hick develops his complementarity analogy in response to some criticisms made by Almond; see Philip Almond, "John Hick's Copernican Theology," *Theology* **86** (1983): 36–41.

34. Netland (Note 2), pp. 258–61.

35. Hick, *Problems* (Note 1), pp. 98–99.

36. In contrast, this analogy may seem less convincing for the simple reason that light is directly experienced and then indirectly conceptualized, while the divine noumenon is never directly experienced but only indirectly conceptualized and known. So, in the case of light, we can be confident that the apparently contradictory properties inhere in one reality. In the case of the divine noumenon, however, we cannot have the same degree of confidence, for it seems possible that at least two (and perhaps more) Realities *an sich* might be involved; and if so, then it would be improper to speak of the personal and impersonal as different faces of one Real *an sich.*

37. There are a couple of history-of-religions type of criticisms that occur to me but which I do not feel competent to pursue. The first is this: Do all religious traditions really mean to refer

to an ultimate ontological reality? Hick seems to claim this, but I wonder if it is true. Such a claim seems to fit best the theistic religions, but one wonders whether (e.g.) the goal-state of Nirvana is properly characterized as an ontologically ultimate Real *an sich*. To think of this transformed state of being—which looks past illusions, including those of a metaphysical variety—as an ontologically ultimate Real *an sich* seems to do some injustice to what Theravadin tradition (e.g.) is all about. And a recognition of the possible ill-fittingness between Hick's claim and some religious traditions suggests the possibility that his claim might well be theistically loaded and at best applicable only to those theistic traditions that are historically related (e.g., Judaism, Christianity, Islam). This suspicion of a theistic orientation or bias seems to gain some support from a second consideration: By what right does Hick claim an ultimate ontological unity rather than a plurality? This question presses the critical issue of why Hick prefers the claim of unity (oneness) when it seems that, logically speaking, it is possible to square religious diversity and equal veridicality by postulating a plurality of ontological ultimates, with each serving as the referent for a corresponding phenomenal religious system. Again, it seems possible that Hick's preference for an ontological unity might indicate a (mono)theistic loading.

38. Corliss (Note 2), pp. 245–46.

39. *Ibid.*, pp. 246–47.

40. See Hick, *Problems,* Chapters 3, 6, and 7.

41. *Ibid.,* Chapter 4.

42. *Ibid.,* p. 46.

43. *Ibid.,* p. 50.

44. In proposing this deconstructive account and introducing this note of skepticism about absolute claims, Hick seems perilously close to committing the genetic fallacy, i.e., the fallacy of thinking that a causal account of the genesis of a statement or belief settles the question as to its truth or falsity. Even if it were the case that a given absolute claim were to have arisen in the way Hick suggests, it seems to be another sort of question entirely as to whether the claim is true or false—the latter is an issue to be settled by an epistemic appraisal of the claim's presuppositions, the adequacy of evidence pertinent to its truth, the consistency of supporting arguments, etc. Hick seems to assume that his social–psychological account addresses these matters or somehow obviates the need to address them, but this is just not so. As it turns out, of course, Hick does offer a deeper and more extensive critique of the epistemology of religious beliefs; so there is no need to pursue this point any further.

45. See Hick, *Problems* (Note 1), Chapter 6.

46. *Ibid.*, pp. 93–94. Despite Hick's pessimism about our ability to find "conclusive" grounds for the acceptance or rejection of historical and metaphysical truth-claims, it is not clear that he is completely justified in his extreme pessimism. After all, some stable consensuses do seem to emerge on past historical events (e.g., about religious founders) and even on controversial metaphysical issues (e.g., the unlikelihood of a great chain of being). Thus, Hick's push toward an attitude of agnosticism may be somewhat premature. Nevertheless, I have to admit that it strikes me that Hick's attitude together with his subsequent pragmatism are steps in the right direction.

47. *Ibid.,* Chapter 8.

48. *Ibid.,* p. 125.

49. *Ibid.,* Chapter 5.

50. *Ibid.,* p. 74.

51. *Ibid.,* p. 81.

52. See Note 2.

53. Griffiths and Lewis (Note 2), pp. 78–79.

54. Byrne (Note 2), p. 296.

55. Corliss (Note 2), pp. 237–39, 248.

56. See esp. Hick, "The Outcome: Dialogue into Truth" (Note 1), pp. 140–55. For a helpful discussion and analysis of various views of religious truth, see Donald Wiebe, *Religion and Truth* (The Hague: Mouton, 1981), esp. Chapters 10–12. Wiebe refers briefly to Hick's view in connection with his (Wiebe's) critical appraisal of W. C. Smith's position (see pp. 213–14). See also Lindbeck's illuminating, "Excursus on Religion and Truth" in his *The Nature of Doctrine* (Note 8), pp. 63–69.

57. Hick, "The Outcome: Dialogue into Truth," p. 141.

58. My colleague Jock Reeder has suggested to me that Hick's epistemology may be fruitfully characterized as attempting to combine a pragmatist theory of the justification of religious belief with a correspondence theory of religious truth. Reeder goes on to ask whether Hick is a coherentist and pragmatist in this life while being a covert foundationalist in the next, or whether he is a thoroughgoing pragmatist in both this life and the next. The textual evidence bearing on this question is somewhat ambiguous, though I believe finally that Hick means to plumb for a thoroughgoing pragmatist epistemology. On the one hand, in developing his notion of eschatological verification, Hick speaks explicitly of the gradual and holistic confirmation of a religious (e.g., theistic) interpretation of the process of the universe, thereby suggesting a broadly coherentist and pragmatist account of such confirmation: "What we are seeking to verify is the truth of the theistic interpretation of the process of the universe . . . . Thus an eschatological situation which is to verify the truth of the theistic interpretation of the universe . . . will . . . have . . . the more limited task of confirming to the full that the history of the universe has led to an end-state in which the postulated divine purpose for humanity can be seen to be fulfilled" (Hick, *Problems,* Note 1, pp. 115–17). On the other hand, Hick also speaks occasionally of a maximal God-consciousness in the afterlife and of "living in continuous awareness of the divine presence" (*ibid.,* p. 117)—phrases that suggest shades of a more direct, experiential, and perhaps foundationalist understanding of the confirmation of religious belief. On balance, however, Hick appears to advance a coherentist and pragmatist interpretation of eschatological verification, for, from his point of view, this confirmation involves principally the "progressive awareness of humanity perfected" (*ibid.,* p. 119), and this understanding of confirmation appears to be an extension into the afterlife of Hick's earlier position: "an understanding of religious dogma and doctrines as not, for the most part, straightforward assertions of fact but as complex mixtures of the mythical, the symbolic, the philosophical, and the empirical. They are, therefore . . . to be judged . . . by the extent to which, as conceptual systems, they provide a framework within which the transformation of human existence from self-centredness to reality-centredness can take place" (*ibid.,* p. 207). For an illuminating discussion of recent changes in Hick's position on eschatological verification, see Myra B. Mackie, "Concerning 'Eschatological Verification Reconsidered,' " *Religious Studies* **23** (1987): 129–35.

59. Stuart Brown, "Religion and the Limits of Language," in his *Reason and Religion* (Note 4), pp. 233–55; the quotes in this paragraph are from pp. 240–41.

36. Atheism and Implicit Christianity

Karl Rahner

I

Implicit Christianity—it could also be termed 'anonymous Christianity'—is what we call the condition of a man who lives on the one hand in a state of grace and justification, and yet on the other hand has not come into contact with the explicit preaching of the Gospel and is consequently not in a position to call himself a 'Christian.'[1] Theologically there can be no doubt that there are such people, as we shall show later in more detail. It is in itself a question of secondary importance whether this particular state should be called 'implicit Christianity' or not. Yet if one attends to the implications of this phenomenon the question can be answered unreservedly in the affirmative.

In addition there is technical justification for the use of the concept. For everything which is explicit in the proclamation, the sacraments and institutions of Christianity is instrumental in securing the possession of the grace of justification (and maintaining it until the end as the foretaste, the initial instalment of eternal life), to such an extent that, as the 'pars potior' and goal of everything else which is 'Christian,' it may itself be called 'Christianity,' especially since this grace is the grace of *Christ*. Furthermore the concept of being 'implicit' is thoroughly common in theology: it even occurs in a related context in *fides implicita, votum (baptismi, Ecclesiae) implicitum* etc. However, we have no objection to anyone wishing to avoid the term 'implicit Christianity' for various reasons (e.g. the danger of misunderstanding). But he would be obliged to provide another term saying what is meant in just as clear and brief a manner. The same applies to the synonymous term 'anonymous Christianity,' which is distinguished from the other only by underlining the implications of this state as such *for other people*.

For the sake of full conceptual clarity we must emphasise this: By virtue of God's desire for universal salvation, the 'objective redemption' constituting a fundamental factor in every man's 'subjective' state of salvation, the 'supernatural *existentiale*' and the continual offer of the grace of God's supernatural saving activity, even the unbaptised person (in the state of original sin as well) is in a unique situation. Prior to any

Source: Karl Rahner, "Atheism and Implicit Christianity," in *Theological Investigations*, Vol. IX, trans. Graham Harrison (New York: The Seabury Press, 1976), 145–65.

existential attitude which he takes up, whether in faith and love or unbelief and sin, he is in a different position (and he himself is different too) from what would be the case if he were only the result of his 'nature' and his original sin. He can never be simply a 'natural' man and a sinner. By virtue of the grace of Christ (as possibility and obligation), which is at least a constant offer, he is always in a Christ-determined situation, whether he has accepted this grace or not.

Terminologically, however, it is better not to call this existentially (but not *existentiell*) 'Christian' position on the part of every man 'implicit' or 'anonymous' Christianity straight away. Otherwise we obscure the radical distinction between grace merely offered and grace existentially accepted in faith and love.

The basic thesis of this study is that even an atheist may possess this kind of 'implicit' Christianity.

This basic thesis is by no means self-evident. For it must be said that right up to most recent times official text-book theology has fairly unanimously supported the view (in spite of various theological qualifications) that it is impossible for a normal responsible human being to entertain a 'positive atheism' for any considerable time without becoming personally culpable.[2] Since in this context there is no sense in weakening this culpability as though it were only 'venial,' the official view involves a denial of the possibility of 'implicit Christianity' for any length of time in an adult atheist.

On the one hand one is obliged to appreciate the weight of the official view: in scripture God's knowability seems so clearly *given* and atheism seems to give evidence so definitely of being man's most terrible aberration, that it was only thought possible to understand it as a *sin* in which a man *freely* turns away in the *mysterium iniquitatis*, evilly suppressing the truth which everywhere impinges on him (Rom 1:18).

On the other hand it must be said that until now neither text-book theology nor scripture has been confronted with the experience of a world-wide and militant atheism, confident of its own self-evident nature and because of this it was possible to regard the earlier, ubiquitous, theistic 'common opinion' as something necessarily so, as an eternally valid quality of human nature. This was a mistake: it led to the official text-book view we mentioned being taken as self-evident.

Next, for the sake of brevity, it will be simplest if we have recourse to the doctrine of the Second Vatican Council in order to illustrate our basic thesis theologically. The texts concerned are Nos. 19–21 of the first chapter of the first part of *Gaudium et spes*, the fifth paragraph of No. 22 of the same chapter, No. 16 in Chapter 2 of *Lumen gentium* and finally—since what has been said about the polytheistic religions of mission lands also holds good in the case of atheism as the product of a different historical and sociological situation—No. 7 of the Decree on the Church's Missionary Activity.

It emerges from our definition of 'implicit' Christianity that the basic thesis can be suitably demonstrated in two stages:

1. According to Vatican II not every instance of positive atheism in a concrete human individual is to be regarded as the result and the expression of personal sin.
2. Such an atheist can be justified and receive salvation if he acts in accordance with his conscience.

II

1. In the first place, therefore, although it is relatively exhaustive in its treatment of atheism, the Council makes no reference to the traditional text-book view that positive atheism cannot be entertained for any considerable period of time by a fully developed person of normal intelligence without involving blame on his part.[3] Furthermore it is safe to say that the Council not only left this thesis[4] alone, but actually *assumed a contrary thesis*, i.e. that it is possible for a *normal adult to hold an explicit atheism for a long period of time*—even to his life's end—*without this implying moral blame* on the part of such an unbeliever. It is true, however, that this view is not taught explicitly: for example it is not pointed out that on the one hand we are faced with an explicit atheism, very widely extensive in society, characterised by a straightforward self-confidence, and on the other hand that in accordance with general Christian principles we do not have the right to declare these atheists to be living in a state of unequivocal and severe moral blame before God. The *absence* of the traditional view seems to be at the same time highly suggestive and most remarkable if one considers that, provided that it were assumed to be correct, the text-book answer would be *the* decisive statement concerning atheism. But in the description of atheism in Nos. 19–21 the traditionally held view appears to such a small extent; in No. 19 (third section) where the question of blame is touched on in half a sentence, there is reference to the evident truth that the holding of atheism is culpable *provided* that the person intentionally banishes God from him or intentionally and wilfully excludes religious questions from his consciousness. But by no means is it said that *every* concrete case of atheism in a man can only continue for a considerable period of time if he is wilfully trying to exclude God or the religious question in this way. When we come to demonstrate the second part of our basic thesis as the teaching of the Council it will be even clearer—it will be conclusive—that we are right to interpret the Council's silence thus. For if it is possible for an 'atheist' to be justified by grace, not every instance of atheism can be the result of the personal culpability of the atheist in question. It is an artificial and ultimately nonsensical excuse to say that atheism of this kind is always culpably induced, but can persist afterwards even if the guilt itself—which need not necessarily have consisted *formalissime* in the culpable reception of atheism as such—is cancelled by a moral change of heart: it does not dispose of the decisive issue, which is the possible coexistence of atheism and justification.

Later on we shall come to speak about the possibility of coexistence of a conceptually objectified atheism and a non-propositional and existentially realised theism. From this it will also be apparent that the Council's pronouncements in Nos. 19–21 concerning the unavoidability of the religious issue do not contradict what we have just said. Of course the Council's reticence with regard to the question of blame in atheism does not imply a trifling with the problem, for: 'the Church has already repudiated and cannot cease repudiating, sorrowfully but as firmly as possible, those poisonous doctrines and actions which contradict reason and the common experience of humanity, and dethrone man from his native excellence' (No. 21).[5] But after the Council, Catholic pastoral theology today will no longer be immediately under the impression, even when confronted with a committed atheist, that it is dealing with a fool or a knave; hence in a totally new way it will have to consider—with the Council (cf. No. 21)—what the *real* causes of modern atheism are, if it cannot be attributed simply to dullness of the mind or perversity of the heart. Without intending to give an exhaustive list or a deep analysis of such causes of atheism, the Council itself has indicated some of them. But in doing so it has not released Catholic theology, and Christian philosophy, pastoral theology and the teaching of religion from their task, a task which has not, as yet, been adequately tackled.

2. The second element in our basic thesis on atheism which is confirmed by the Council and which—judged by the accepted traditions of scholastic thought and religious practice—may cause offence is the conviction *that even an atheist* (holding the concepts and theory of atheism, as we shall explain in detail later) *is not excluded from attaining salvation, provided that he has not acted against his moral conscience as a result of his atheism.* We have already said that this proviso cannot be taken for granted, i.e. the atheist's blamelessness is thus not simply an immaterial hypothesis. This is observed by the Constitution on the Church *Lumen gentium* (No. 16): 'Nor does divine Providence deny the help necessary for salvation to those who, without blame on their part, have not yet arrived at an explicit knowledge of God, but who strive to live a good life, thanks to His grace.'[6] But for salvation both supernatural faith and the grace of justification are necessary. Technically speaking it cannot be here a question of those (entitatively natural or actually supernatural) graces which constitute an as yet remote preparation for justification and the consequent attainment of salvation which are mediated by (among other things) an explicit theism. For otherwise we would be merely stating the obvious, saying in effect that by the grace of God an atheist can become a theist and *thus* can be finally justified. Nor would this fit the context of the constitution, which is concerned with the different kinds of non-Catholics *in so far as* they are and actually *remain* non-Catholics. Thus No. 22 of the Pastoral Constitution says: 'All this'—the blessed Resurrection—'holds true not only for Christians, but for all men of good will in whose hearts grace works in an unseen way. For, since Christ died for all men, and since the ultimate vocation of man is in fact one, and divine, we ought to believe that the Holy Spirit in a manner known only to God offers to every man the possibility of being associated with this paschal mystery.' There is no reason to exclude atheists from this declaration. For it refers explicitly to No. 16 of the Constitution on the Church which concerns those who have not yet come to a conscious recognition of God. Moreover, mention of 'ways known only to God' is also made in the Decree on the Church's Missionary Activity (No. 7), where the 'heathen' who have not yet been reached by the Gospel are recognised as having a real possibility of supernatural faith and salvation even in their condition. But it would be arbitrary to wish to attribute a fundamentally much greater chance of salvation to a polytheistic heathen, who according to Paul is still 'without God' (Eph 2:12),[7] than to a modern atheist, whose 'personal' atheism is in the first place no less a product of his cultural situation.

With regard to all the texts quoted, as we have already said, it obviously cannot be a question of assuming at the outset that these atheists will become conceptually and theoretically *explicit* theists before death and *thus* saved. For in that case the texts would be merely repeating the platitude that an atheist can attain salvation when and in so far as he ceases to be one. Such an interpretation would deny any serious meaning to the texts; in producing them the Council would have been wasting its time.

III

Something really new has been said in these two elements of the Council's authoritative doctrine. If we consider the explicit statements of Scripture[8] and the traditional verdict on atheism, as well as the cautious reticence of Protestant theology with respect to the unbaptised person's possibility of salvation, we cannot say that this 'salvation optimism' as regards non-Christians (including atheists) is simply a theological truism for here we can see the development of something which really only began with Pius IX (*DS* 2865–2867) and led to the Holy Office's declaration of 8th August, 1949 (*DS* 3866–3873). Moreover this line of thought has really been developed *further* to the extent that, in a much clearer way than before, *atheists too* have been *explicitly included* in this 'salvation optimism.'

These declarations have rendered obsolete even the earlier, *moderately* optimistic interpretations of the situation of non-Christians and heathen and atheists too which were to be found in text-book theology. According to the latter, such people outside the jurisdiction of Christianity were recognised as capable of attaining a 'natural' salvation (similar to that which the text-books acknowledged in the case of children dying without being baptised) but excluded from a really *supernatural* salvation. The Decree on the Church's Missionary Activity (No. 7) expressly states that these people too, by the grace of God and in ways not known to us, can reach a real *saving* faith even without having accepted the explicit preaching of the Christian Gospel. And wherever the word 'salvation' occurs in the other texts we have quoted, what is meant is genuine supernatural salvation, more particularly since it is expressly declared that all men have only *one* vocation to salvation, and since the attainment of this salvation is understood as participation in Christ's Easter mystery.

Thus according to the teaching of Vatican II it is possible for an atheist to be living in the grace of justification, i.e. possessing what we have called 'implicit Christianity.' In this short investigation it cannot be our business to show how this conciliar doctrine is deduced from the genuinely original sources of revelation, nor how it is defended against the seemingly weighty objections which could be brought against it by Scripture and Tradition. The Council itself only gives a very brief and general justification for its approach. To a certain degree the Council makes its own case—the possibility of the unbaptised non-Christian's salvation without contact with the Gospel (thus including the atheist)—more difficult to defend by requiring a real supernatural faith even in such a case, i.e. not escaping the issue by saying that such a person attains supernatural salvation at the end of his life on the basis of a mere 'natural' morality.

In connection with the Council's teaching our basic thesis implies:

1. the thesis of God's will for the salvation of all men in Christ (he will is understood as 'infralapsarian'), and the availability of his grace, and the doctrine that there is only *one* supernatural goal for all men; and
2. the conviction that not every individual atheist can be regarded as a gravely culpable sinner.

The Council neither poses nor answers the question of how one arrives at the second part of this argument from a theological point of view. In this matter one can only say that on the one hand it rests on the theological conviction that one cannot and must not judge any man, but that each particular empirical state of affairs, ambivalent in itself, appeals to the judgment of God alone; and on the other hand that the modern historical situation of the previously nonexistent experience of a world-wide and growing atheism, whose culture and social forms are not directly conditioned by morality, makes it improbable that in each case atheism is the result of the incurring of personal guilt.

All the same, our basic thesis, confirmed as it is by the Council, has provided us with difficult theological problems. This is clear in the Council's statement that the 'ways' in which such non-Christians reach salvation and justification are 'known only to God.' Naturally a statement like this does not forbid further theological study of these 'ways,' but it shows that the Council was aware of a certain tension in what it said, even if this tension did not weaken its courage, in faith, to speak of this universal salvation optimism.

So far our observations on the possibility of implicit Christianity in an atheist have only served to set the task, not to give the answer we are looking for. We must now attempt to do this.

IV

In saying that according to the teaching of the Council an atheist does not automatically forfeit salvation, even if under certain circumstances he remains an atheist to his death, the question arises from the theological point of view as to whether in that case simply a 'good will' suffices to replace the knowledge about God and belief in God.

We have already seen that the Decree on the Church's Missionary Activity (No. 7) teaches the possibility of salvation for all men, and we have included atheists too in this category in so far as they are without blame. But the Decree expressly says that the people referred to attain salvation in so far as they come—by paths known only to God—to a saving *faith*.[9]

The question, therefore, is whether and how an atheist can demonstrate the preconditions under which this faith is at least conceivable. Here one cannot immediately refer to the minimum content of faith[10] which traditional theology, basing itself on the Epistle to the Hebrews (Heb 11:6),[11] declares to be sufficient under certain circumstances for a super-natural, saving faith. For this minimum content is precisely belief in the existence of God and in him as guarantor of the moral order. Put differently, the problem is that if belief is required as assent to the divine revelation, '*something*' must be believed. Even if we were to avoid the question as to how the atheist is to recognise this content as a revelation from God and not as the result of natural insight, the question remains just *what* this particular individual can embrace as an object of faith, in order for us to be able to talk about it being 'faith' at all.

In this connection the Council's texts which we have quoted always assume that the atheist in question is one who *acts in accordance with his conscience, seeks truth and fulfils the demands of his moral consciousness*; for to be considered free from blame and within the sphere of God's will for salvation, although he has not (yet) found God, he must act in line with the demands of his conscience. But is this 'content' of the atheist's awareness sufficient to provide an adequate object for *saving* faith? We must answer this question in several stages.

By reference to the doctrine of the Epistle to the Hebrews one is justified in answering *provisionally*: Yes, *provided that* this conscious content includes *at least implicitly* a knowledge about God, and moreover that this 'content' is affirmed by a free act elevated by grace in the manner of faith. Now this is in fact the case. It can be maintained as such, at least under certain epistemological conditions. The person who accepts a moral demand from his conscience as *absolutely* valid for him and embraces it as such in a free act of affirmation—no matter how unreflected—asserts the absolute being of God, whether he knows or conceptualises it or not, as the very reason why there can be such a thing as an *absolute moral demand at all*.

This preliminary answer needs a deeper grounding, and we shall attempt to do this in a more thorough treatment. Once we have assumed this kind of affirmation by the conscience of an absolute demand, it is not so important how far, in such an act, a man *is or is not consciously aware* of these presuppositions (both objective *and* subjective) which inform his concrete knowledge and action. It may even be that he is *not able* to reflect conceptually upon the subjective factors involved in his concrete spiritual action. Whenever a simple man in his everyday life acts sensibly and with insight, i.e. also logically, the ultimate principles of logic are not only found as the objective basis of his intelligent insight and action; he has also embraced them, they are his spiritual 'possession,' although as a simple man he would be probably quite incapable, even after instruction, of understanding the abstract principles of Aristotelian logic as such in its abstract formality.

This modest observation from everyday life can be heightened theoretically and applied to our question. In every one of its acts, human knowledge is to a certain extent *dipolar*: it implies a subjective knowledge of the knower himself and his act on the part of the subject as such, while at the same time this same knowledge has a known and conceptualised object which is its goal and with which it is concerned. In knowing about oneself and one's act one always knows *something*. The objective content of such an act can also be something which is known without reflection on the subjective side of the same act, i.e. when the subject, knowing itself subjectively, makes itself in addition the *object* of its judgment. But even in such a case the dipolarity, the difference between the subject present to itself and the known object, between knowing-ness and what is known, is not destroyed. Furthermore it is quite possible for such an act, the content of which the self-knowing subject of this act wishes to present to itself, to be inadequately or falsely interpreted by this selfsame subject, although on the subjective side what has been interpreted is present in its known reality. For instance, a man who performs an intellectual act knows 'subjectively' what an intellectual act is, because the subject with its intellectual act is present to itself in a real identity. In spite of this, however, a theoretical psychologist who is a sensist, denying in a materialist manner the subject's intellectuality, is *bona fide* capable of giving quite false theoretical explanations of his own intellectual act; i.e. what he experiences subjectively he may translate objectively falsely into objective concepts and statements.

Now in so far as every instance of intellectual knowledge and freedom on the part of the subject and his act is a 'transcendental experience', i.e. an experience of the intellect's unlimited rootedness in absolute Being, on the subjective side every instance of knowledge is a real, even if implicit (i.e. not necessarily objectified) knowledge of God, although we cannot show this in greater detail here. What we commonly call 'knowledge of God' is therefore not simply *the* knowledge of God, but already the objectified conceptual and propositional interpretation of what we constantly know of God subjectively and apart from reflection. Knowledge of God is certainly *a posteriori* to the extent, on the one hand, that even the subjective act—which by virtue of its transcendental nature always knows about God—is historically contingent; in order to be itself this subjective act always requires an 'objective' object, without which it cannot exist at all, but which it experiences *a posteriori*. Besides this, knowledge of God is also *a posteriori* in so far as the conceptual and propositional objectification of the transcendental experience first needs a vehicle to pass among the *a posteriori* given objects of knowledge of the world, in the way expounded in detail in the classical 'proofs of the existence of God.' On the other hand the knowledge of God is not *a posteriori* simply in the sense in which the knowledge of any external object is, e.g. the knowledge of the existence of Australia. It is true that there is no innate idea of God in the sense of an inborn conceptualised content, but nevertheless the conceptual and propositional knowledge of God is the objectification of that rootedness of the intellect in absolute Being which is always present to man's transcendental intellectuality; that rootedness which is a concomitant experience in every intellectual act, whether of knowledge or of freedom, irrespective of the particular object with which this act is concerned.

V

If we adopt these assumptions (which we have really only touched upon here) we can draw up a sort of table of the fundamental types of man's relationship with God. In doing so it must always be borne in mind that a conscious or known reality present to man's mind may exist in the mode of free acceptance or free rejection, since man is not merely a being who is intellectually knowing, but is also always a free being.

First possibility: God is present in man's transcendental nature and this fact is objectified in a suitably and correctly explicit and conceptual theism, and moreover is also freely accepted in the moral affirmation of faith (in the practice of living). In this case we have what constitutes simply correct theism, what we might call transcendental *and* categorial theism, accepted and affirmed by man's freedom in both these dimensions. In this way it represents in every respect a proper relationship between man and God such as we may assume in the case of a justified Christian.

Second possibility: Both transcendental and categorial theism are present, man knows of God in his transcendental experience and also his reflection upon the latter is correct, but in his moral freedom he rejects this knowledge, whether as a sinner, denying God, or going on to reject the God whom he has correctly 'objectified' conceptually in real free unbelief. This is the category in which the 'atheist' was thought of previously in religious and in specifically Christian matters. It was assumed that he had an objectified and more or less correct idea of God but rejected him in sin or freely turned away from him either in a merely practical 'godlessness' or in theoretical atheism as well.

Third possibility: The transcendental experience of God is present of necessity and is also freely accepted in a positive decision to be faithful to conscience,[12] but it is incorrectly objectified and interpreted. This inadequate, false (and under certain circumstances totally lacking) *idea of God* as such can be again the object of free acceptance or rejection in various ways, but we need not concern ourselves with that in any greater detail here. For instance, consider the case of a polytheist who, in the dimension of free reflection, freely 'believes' this polytheism or freely and 'atheistically' rejects it, without replacing it by a correctly conceived theism. In either case this third instance is the sort of atheism which is innocent in the sense of Vatican II. It is atheism on the plane of categorical reflection, co-existing in the subject with a freely affirmed transcendental theism. There can be such a thing as innocent atheism because of the difference between subjective transcendentality and categorial objectification in concepts and sentences, producing this coexistence of transcendental theism and categorial atheism. For the said 'difference' is necessarily present in every act of the mind. The components of this innocent atheism are: *on the one hand* the subject's continual transcendental dependence on God and the free acceptance of this dependence, especially in the moral act which respects absolutely the demands of conscience—i.e. a transcendental theism 'in the heart's depths'—and *on the other hand* the free rejection of the objectified concept of God, i.e. a categorial atheism in the forefront of conscious reflection, a rejection which cannot in itself be regarded as culpable.

Fourth possibility: The transcendental dependence on God is present; objectively it is interpreted falsely or insufficiently correctly in a categorial atheism, and this transcendental dependence on God is itself simultaneously denied in a free action by gravely sinful unfaithfulness to conscience or by an otherwise sinful, false interpretation of existence (as being 'totally absurd' or of no absolute significance, etc.). In this case the free denial does not refer merely to the categorial interpretation of man's transcendental nature, but to existence and thus to God himself. Here we have culpable transcendental atheism, which excludes the possibility of salvation as long as it persists.

By presenting these four basic types of man's relationship with God we do not wish to suggest that the table could not have been drawn up differently, especially as we ourselves have indicated further subordinate possibilities within this 'system.' Furthermore, by naïvely distinguishing the correct from the false conceptual objectification of man's necessary transcendental dependence on God we have made an over-simplification which does not correspond to concrete reality. For here there are naturally correct and less correct conceptualisations (e.g. an idea of God revealing partially false, pantheistic or polytheistic tendencies and blemishes). Indefinite transitions and fluid boundaries are also compatible with the exercise of freedom. So the system we have outlined is no more than a rough preliminary sketch. But it may be sufficient for our purposes all the same.

VI

Our whole concern here is to reach an insight into why there is in fact in man the possibility of innocent and of culpable atheism, and the knowledge of how on the one hand a man's innocent atheism by no means destroys every really fundamental relationship with

God, created by man's constant transcendental rootedness in God; and how on the other hand, in spite of this possibility, culpable atheism consists not necessarily merely in transgression in connection with any particular moral situation but in an *ultimate* 'No' to man's fundamental dependence *upon God himself*, i.e. in a free 'No' to God himself.

It must be further remembered that the categorial affirmation of God—as a theoretical and categorial action—is by no means a guarantee that the man concerned really seriously accepts his transcendental dependence on God at the very heart of his transcendental freedom of choice. Put simply, a man, even a 'Christian,' can accept God as objectified in knowledge and freedom, and can even declare that he is a 'theist' and think that he is keeping to God's moral norms, *and yet deny him* through immorality or unbelief in the depths of his heart. This is just as possible as the co-existence of a categorial atheism with a (freely affirmed) transcendental theism. So, too, categorial theism can coexist with a transcendental theism which is itself freely rejected, thus becoming freely adopted transcendentalatheism—in spite of the abiding experience of rootedness in God.

In the Pastoral Constitution the Council taught that there is also a culpable atheism. But it was not made clear enough how such an atheism is possible as an atheism really directed at God himself. The Council recognised the existence of innocent atheism, but without plainly showing how salvation and faith are reconcilable with it. The distinction we have indicated between transcendental and categorial atheism/theism provides a theoretical understanding of this teaching. Innocent atheism is always only categorial atheism, atheism on the plane of conceptual and propositional objectification, where it is ultimately immaterial whether this atheistic objectification as such is accepted or freely rejected by the person concerned, since this particular free act only involves the *categorial* object. On the other hand *transcendental* atheism (which is really possible) it always necessarily culpable, since God is always present to man in the dimension of man's transcendentality, and therefore can only be rejected by a free decision, not by knowledge as such. In this dimension the 'matter,' namely God, is necessarily correctly present, so that his rejection cannot be justified or thought to be justified on the grounds of an inadequate or falsely objectified concept of God in the dimension of categorial reflection.

VII

If what has been indicated here in very few and inadequate words is understood, pastoral insights emerge concerning the correct approach on the part of the person proclaiming theism or the Gospel. These insights might suitably serve to deepen and systematise the Council's necessarily very brief remarks on this approach. The preacher of the Gospel is never confronted with an atheist who has so far had simply nothing to do with God; the preacher's relationship to this particular listener is never like that of a geography teacher teaching a small boy for the first time that there is such a place as Australia and demonstrating the fact. Where free, responsible human beings are concerned, the preacher of the Gospel is confronted fundamentally with a man who already has a real experience of what is meant by God, but who for various reasons (either free from blame or—under certain circumstances—culpable) is not able correctly to interpret his own experience of

God in conscious reflection and consequently rejects the concept of God presented to him from elsewhere, as being either false or meaningless for him. To combat a categorial and conceptual atheism of this kind one must not remain solely on this particular plane as such; one must not only present proofs of the existence of God as if the latter were of the same structure and amenable to the same methods as the existence of an object which is merely accessible in purely *a posteriori* experience. If *this* were the case, under certain circumstances a man might be justified in rejecting the existence of such a God as being a matter of no interest and not worth bothering his head about.

Even if it is possible at all to speak to an atheist on the level of the 'proofs' so well known to us, to be successful today such a dialogue unavoidably presupposes that the atheist has been made aware of his own transcendental knowledge of God through a kind of 'mystagogy.' If he is really acquainted with unconditional faithfulness, absolute honesty, selfless surrender to the good of others and other fundamental human dispositions, then he knows something of God, even if this knowledge is not present to his conscious reflection. Of course, in a particular concrete instance, it can be very difficult to bring to the surface the theological implications of these fundamental dispositions and objectify them in conceptual form. In any particular case the attempt may simply fail. In itself that is no more strange than the fact that it is sometimes impossible to make formal logic clear to a person *in the mode of theoretical reflection* although he employs this very thing in his everyday affairs and has insight *into* the 'logic' of these affairs. In any case, however, the traditional 'proofs' can only be presented successfully to a person who is not already an explicit 'theist' provided that rational reflection is joined by this kind of 'mystagogy'. Depending on the case in question, this mystagogy must naturally also deal with the difficulties from which arise, according to the Council's Pastoral Constitution, the various forms of modern atheism; the protest against evil in the world, the supposed lack of any religious experience, the supposed threat to mankind in the idea of God, the strange ideas which people connect with the concept of God, etc.

Provided one understands what is meant by the transcendental theism we have described it is clear, furthermore, that according to genuine theism God is not present in our everyday experience like the other objects of our *a posteriori* experience. He is not an existent within the sphere of our experience but the precondition of our transcendental horizon. A theist or an apologete of theism must not proceed, therefore, as though God were—not of course an object directly present to our sense-experience, but—to all intents and purposes capable of being known rather like an electric current, which, not itself directly visible can be deduced from its effects.

Here we have a way in to an understanding of the phenomenon in atheism referred to by the Council itself when it says that certain atheists are held fast in a 'scientistic phenomenalism' and are unable to understand, so they say, what might be meant at all by the word 'God.' According to a proper understanding of the nature of the knowledge of God there can be no question of expanding and deepening the area of empirical experience by the *same* methods. What is required is rather to help man to appreciate that there is another mode of experience, a transcendental experience in intellectual knowledge and freedom, according to which what we mean by 'God' can be understood and known as real; and furthermore that what is meant by this transcendental experience, referential to God, is the precondition for every *a posteriori* experience whatsoever, whether in everyday matters or in science, even if it is not and cannot be the task of these *a posteriori* disciplines to reflect upon their own presuppositions.

The first Vatican Council expressly defined that God is incomprehensible (cf. *DS* 3001). No Christian doctrine of God and his knowability denies this. But the dogma is often forgotten in the practice of our apologetics of theism. For one cannot first of all know God—as one knows anything else according to its existence and nature—and then subsequently 'add on' the attribute of incomprehensibility. Both the proof of God's existence and the 'mystagogy' which is absolutely necessary if the former is to be successful must relate, from the very beginning, to the absolute mystery[13] which pervades and penetrates our whole existence; this mystery must be brought together with theoretical knowledge and the existential actualisation of life, and then one can say: This is what we mean when we speak of 'God.'

VIII

So far we have only taken the first of the steps (cf. V above) leading to a theological understanding of how an atheism which is not blameworthy can constitute 'implicit' Christianity. For what we have said up to now only serves to make it clear that a blameless categorical atheism can be a freely accepted, transcendental theism. But on its own this does not constitute the 'implicit' *Christianity* in which a man by grace accepts the self-imparting God in faith, hope and love.

In order to proceed further we must bear in mind that in the actual order of things the 'atheist's' transcendental, freely accepted theism, which here concerns us, is elevated by supernatural grace because of God's will for universal salvation, and man's essential transcendentality—at least in so far as it is freely accepted—finds its ultimate goal, by grace, in the God of Eternal Life. Although one must admit that the Council has expressed itself cautiously and somewhat indefinitely, it may certainly be said that as far as the texts we have quoted are concerned the Council professes no acquaintance with a merely 'natural' morality. Of course the latter does exist, but it is integrated into the concrete order of God's desire for mankind's supernatural salvation as a distinguishable, but not isolated, factor in a larger whole, of which God's offer of saving grace to all is also a part.[14]

In Catholic theology no-one can deny the possibility of justification and supernatural sanctification prior to Baptism (given the presence of supernatural faith, of which we shall say something in particular later, and an implicit *votum baptismi*). Thus there is in any case a divine offer of supernatural grace and the possibility of freely accepting it prior to Baptism, apart from the sacrament.[15] We have only to assume that this offer and the free acceptance of it (thus made possible) is *always* and *everywhere* present (on account of God's desire for universal salvation, not because of the natural goodness of a moral act) where a man freely accepts his own transcendentality—which includes an implicit, transcendental theism—by means of a moral decision in absolute faithfulness to his conscience, by means of 'righteousness of life' etc. We assume, therefore, that under these conditions there is *always* an occurrence of what Thomas calls *infusio et acceptatio gratiae.* In that case the concrete order of salvation together with the freely accepted transcendental theism which can even be found in an atheist, produces *implicit* Christianity.

The reason why traditional theology up to now for the most part has always counted on there being a phase of merely 'natural' morality in the course of a 'heathen's' life (and so too has been inclined to acknowledge only a 'natural' moral goodness—if any—even in the case of a bona fide atheist) is because on the one hand it is correctly assumed that justification is impossible without revealed faith, nor can a *fides virtualis* be a substitute for it, as for instance Straub suggested; and on the other hand it was thought impossible to imagine such a revealed faith in the case of a 'heathen,' let alone an atheist. The reference in the conciliar texts to the 'ways known only to God' witnesses above all to this difficulty, but also shows that the Council, particularly in the Decree concerning the Church's Missionary Activity, nevertheless has no doubt that this faith is possible even in the instances which are of interest here; moreover it does not restrict this possibility to cases of extraordinary, miraculous intervention on the part of God such as have been appealed to by previous text-book theology (private revelation, special illumination, etc.).

This obscure issue can be pursued further if one bears in mind, in *this* context as well, the well-known Thomist doctrine that every supernaturally elevated moral act on a man's part has, in connection with its essential elevation, a supernatural formal object which cannot be reached by any merely natural intellectual or moral act on his part, even if in both cases the material object, the objective, *a posteriori* content of the act, is the same.

If we assume this thesis, which Thomism has rightly regarded as fundamental to its 'system' and which can be held to be *at the very least* above reproach in theology, and apply it to our context, it gives us the possibility of revealed faith which we require for our cases: The communication of a supernatural formal object (in other words, the supernatural perspective within which, in a non-reflex but real manner, morality's material objectivity is grasped; the revealing of man's intellectual and spiritual trancendentality in its direct relation to God) is in a true sense 'revelation' already. It is constituted as such by the offer of saving grace itself (logically or temporally) prior to the *a posteriori* and historical communication of an objective content by means of historical revelation. The supernatural elevation in grace automatically involves revelation and the possibility of faith.[16]

Naturally *this* revelation is not simply identical with revelation as it is usually (and correctly) understood. It is obvious that much ought to be said about the relation of this 'transcendental' revelation (or rather, the transcendental *element* of revelation) to the categorial, historical, verbal revelation (or the categorial *element* of the *single* revelation). Certainly this relationship must not be thought of as if the transcendental element of revelation (constituted by grace) rendered the categorial element superfluous or threatened its meaningfulness.

But in the *first* place, if one considers that in any case this transcendental element is present in revelation and faith because the verbally objectified, categorial revelation can only be spoken in 'Pneuma' and heard in faith; and *secondly*, if one does not wish to have recourse to improbabilities (i.e. original or private revelation); and *thirdly*, if one still wishes to maintain the possibility of saving, supernatural faith and, in line with the Council, the existence of revelation for *all* men; then the only possibility left is to say that the elevation through grace of man's freely accepted transcendentality is in itself revelation, because it involves an *a priori* formal object of man's mind, not necessarily reflected in consciousness, which, *qua* formal object, cannot be reached by any natural intellectual ability but arises from God's self-communication in grace. It is a revelation without which a categorial, historical, verbal revelation—although it could constitute an utterance to do with God and 'about' him—could not be the 'Word of God' in its most proper sense.

These brief notes must suffice here to demonstrate how transcendental theism freely accepted on the part of a categorial atheist can be—or rather, actually *is*—revelation and the possibility of saving faith.[17] This is the case if it is assumed that this transcendentality of the mind, implying a theism, with its free acceptance, is elevated by grace. And we *may* assume this because of God's desire for universal salvation. Under these presuppositions the Council's optimism concerning salvation is theologically justified. Now a theism which is elevated through grace and which is freely accepted (by the grace supplied by the possibility of faith) is a justifying theism and hence an implicit Christianity. And this kind of existential transcendental theism (although not necessarily the object of reflection) is also possible in the case of a (categorial) blameless atheist, whose actions are good and arise from an absolute commitment; therefore *this* kind of atheist can be an implicit Christian.

In its Pastoral Constitution Vatican II most strongly emphasises that modern atheism requires new and most serious thought on the part of the Church and the preachers of the Gospel. This declaration must not remain a mere pious tag, a part of the inventory of courtesy used in dealing with an opponent. There really are questions which must be asked and answered *anew* if it is really intended to engage modern atheism in a real dialogue. These question do not merely concern the 'didactic' and 'pedagogical' methods best employed in speaking with today's atheists. They are questions to do with the *thing itself*. Thus the question in pastoral theology as to how to come to grips with modern atheism changes very quickly into the question as to what is actually meant by 'God,'[18] and how we theists and Christians come to have a direct approach to this incomprehensible mystery of our existence, which sustains us and at the same time constantly calls our whole being in question, a direct contact which cannot be reduced to the sociological phenomenon of Christians sharing common assumptions and talking among themselves about God, merely *thinking* they know *who* he is and *why* our life itself is meaningless without God.[19] In maintaining this one has uttered an ultimate truth about our life; but to really grasp it, life must first be *experienced* as meaningful, one must face the question whether one accepts this experienced meaning or not and know, in this experience and its acceptance, what is really meant by 'God.'[20]

Notes

1. cf. K. Rahner, 'Anonymous Christians,' *Theological Investigations* VI (London and Baltimore, 1969), pp. 390–398; further reference in Kl. Riesenhuber, 'Der anonyme Christ nach Karl Rahner,' *Zeitschrift für katholische Theologie* 86 (1964), pp. 286–303.

2. A more detailed treatment is given in K. Lehmann, 'Die Auseinandersetzung mit dem westlichen Atheismus und der pluralistischen Gesellschaft,' *Die Zukunft der Kirche*, ed. O. Mauer (Herder-Vienna, 1968).

3. In what follows the author is taking up some observations which have already appeared in *Concilium*: 'The Teaching of the Second Vatican Council on Atheism,' *Concilium* 3 (March 1967), pp. 5–13.

4. For its foundation and a more detailed interpretation cf. e.g. 'Patres Societatis Jesu facultatum theol. in Hispania professores,' *Sacrae Theologiae Summa* II (Madrid,[4] 1964), pp. 23–24 and notes 21–22.

5. For an authoritative condemnation of atheism previously cf. *Sacrae Theologiae Summa* II, p. 20, and K. Rahner, 'Atheismus (systematisch),' *LThK*[2] I, col. 985.

6. cf. the commentary on this text by A. Grillmeier, *Commentary on the documents of Vatican II*, ed. H. Vorgrimler (New York and London, 1967).

7. cf. H. Schlier's exegesis of this passage: *Der brief an die Epheser* (Düsseldorf,[4] 1963), p. 121.

8. cf. the concise synopsis in *LThK*[2] I, cols. 985–986. Many scriptural statements about the fate of unbelievers need to be understood more clearly than has been the case until now in Catholic exegetics, as eschatological, prophetic 'admonitions' in a very particular literary form.

9. See the study already quoted in note 6 and the further literature mentioned in it.

10. For the dogmatic side of this doctrine cf. *Sacrae Theologiae Summa* II, p. 804 (see note 5 above), with the differentiated views of Mitzka, Beraza, Pesch.

11. cf. especially the commentary by O. Michel, *Der Brief an die Hebräer* (Göttingen,[12] 1966), pp. 386–387; E. Grässer, *Der Glaube im Hebräerbrief* (Marburg, 1965), pp. 132 ff. *et passim*.

12. Whereby the consciously reflected object of this act of obedience to conscience is not explicitly God, but another moral object as envisaged by the conciliar texts quoted above, where the atheist is conceived as acting morally.

13. cf. K. Rahner, 'The concept of mystery in Catholic theology,' *theological Investigations* IV (London and Baltimore, 1966), pp. 36–73.

14. It would be arbitrary to wish to understand the 'grace' which is continually referred to in these texts with regard to the non-Christian or atheist merely as God's entitatively natural assistance towards the fulfilment of the natural moral law as such. For this theological issue cf. K. Rahner, *Theologie des Todes* (Freiburg,[5] 1965), pp. 79 ff.

15. For extra-sacramental justification cf. K. Rahner, 'The Word and the Eucharist,' *Theological Investigations* IV (London and Baltimore, 1966), pp. 253–286.

16. For this concept of revelation cf. K. Rahner/J. Ratzinger, *Revelation and Tradition* (Freiburg and London, 1966); K. Rahner, *Hörer des Wortes* (Munich,[2] 1963).

17. For a treatment in greater depth cf. the author's studies: 'Concerning the relationship between nature and grace,' *Theological Investigations* I (London and Baltimore, 1961), pp. 297–317; 'The Christian among unbelieving relations,' *Theological Investigations* III (London and Baltimore, 1967), pp. 355–372; 'Nature and Grace,' *Theological Investigations* IV (London and Baltimore, 1966), pp. 165–188; 'History of the world and salvation-history,' *Theological Investigations* V (London and Baltimore, 1966), pp. 97–114; 'Konziliare Lehre der Kirche und künftige Wirklichkeit christlichen Lebens,' *Schriften zur Theologie* VI (Einsiedeln, 1965), pp. 479–498.

18. For details in this issue cf, K. Rahner, 'Christian living formerly and today,' *Theological Investigations* VII (London and New York, 1971), pp. 3–24.

19. Cf. K. Lehmann's 'Some Ideas from Pastoral Theology on the Proclamation of the Christian Message to Non-believers Today,' *Concilium* 3 (March 1967), pp. 43–52.

20. cf. K. Rahner, 'The concept of mystery in Catholic theology,' *Theological Investigations* IV (London and Baltimore, 1966), pp. 36–73.

37. Theology and the World's Religious History

Wilfred Cantwell Smith

"A Universal Theology of Religion"

Professor Swidler, implicitly by organizing this conference, explicitly in its title and in his preconference paper, has set forth a vision of a new day dawning for the theological world. That vision is being seen by a minority of Christians; we are perhaps a small minority but a growing one. Some see it only dimly, or simply feel that it is, or ought to be, coming.

The important task is that the vision be articulated, and then refined and even corrected, by that even smaller minority who can clarify the vision and thereby facilitate the coming of that new day. My own sense is that this may prove more difficult, and meet more resistance, than Professor Swidler acknowledges. The arguments in favor, several of which he forcefully enunciates, are in danger of being opposed with vigor by those who think and feel in inherited and established ways, seemingly threatened by radical displacement. Whether a new style of Christian theology will prevail, I do not know. Our task at this conference is to delineate it and to proffer reasons for it. My own contribution to this corporate endeavor is to propose here a new basis for theological thinking, on the grounds that it promises to lead to truer, and as well to a more reverential, awareness. I am not unaware, however, that to suggest a different foundation for the theological task is indeed radical. "A Universal Theology of Religion," toward which this conference explicitly invites us to move, *is* a radical new idea. It can be attained, I am suggesting, by adopting a rather new starting point.

Nonetheless, what I proffer turns out to be more in line with earlier Christian outlooks than are more recent and now accepted ones. It is in some ways more continuous with the Church's past tradition than with—or than are some—current modes.

Source: Wilfred Cantwell Smith, "Theology and the World's Religious History," from *Toward a Universal Theology of Religion*, Leonard Swidler, editor (Maryknoll, N.Y.: Orbis Books, 1987), pages 51–72. Reprinted with the permission of the editor.

Theology: Speaking the Truth about God

Theology, several voices these days are telling us, is "talk about God." Further, the modern mood wishes us cheerily to "do theology," rather than in more traditional style to study it or to think about it. I myself hesitate about today's colloquializing that would reduce theology to "God talk."

First, there has been on earth virtually no people large or small that has not talked about God; yet relatively few have come up with theologies. When I say that peoples have spoken of God, of course I recognize that that is hasty. If they spoke some language other than English, then naturally they used some other term: more, or often less, closely equivalent to that English word. If they perceived the universe through some conceptual scheme other than the theist, then naturally they used some other concept, less or more closely counterpart. I happen to find quite fascinating the question of convergences and divergences among languages, and among the words within them that may be translated (but how loosely?—a teasing question) as "God"; and of convergences and divergences among worldviews; and in these last, of the concepts within them that play the role that the concept "God" plays in theist conceptualizations. (We have as yet no, or only barely incipient, translations among worldviews.) Also I take more seriously than do some the changes in meaning of a single term, as a language, and the society to whom it mediates the world, develop over time.

In Sanskrit, for instance, and therefore in Hindu apprehensions of the universe, there are two different words, one neuter, one masculine (*Brahman* and *Œsvara*, respectively) for the Godhead beyond God, the impersonal absolute, on the one hand, and on the other hand for the personal supreme God, to whom theists consciously devote themselves; and still another word for The Goddess. Again, in modern English there is a question as to whether God should be referred to as He, She, or It. Yet in so nearby a language as French, and therefore for the many Christians and Jews who think in it—and the same is true of Hebrew; and for Muslims, Arabic—there is no immediate distinction between "He" and "It" in speaking about God, or about anything else. In Persian or Chinese there is no distinction between "He" and "She." If we think of differences over time rather than over space, we might note that some of us now are more at ease with the concept "transcendence," in our day the term "God" having shifted for many to designating a particularist concept—that of theists—rather than a cosmic reference. In this paper, and otherwise, I still use the word "God." If there be readers who do not like or understand it (yet in the modern world we all have to understand each other's usage of terms of cosmic import, whether we like them or not), I would ask that such persons substitute for the term "God" in my presentation something like "transcendent reality," or everything that one recognizes as valuable, plus the transcendence and coherence of their value, or ultimate truth and beauty and goodness and various other such things.

In any case, the range of things that have been said about the divine, and the range of communities that have said them, are vast. In contrast, the range of theologies is fairly limited. The fact is that in past history here on earth, theology has been the prerogative of relatively few of the world's religious communities. Greece, India, and China are the three countries on earth that have produced philosophies, more or less simultaneously. Hindu religious thought has been more or less integrated with Indian philosophy;

Buddhist thought, greatly influenced by it, and by Chinese; and Christian theology is clearly a consequence historically of the contribution to the Church of Greek. In passing, one may observe that Islamic and Jewish theology have been strong or peripheral in their respective communities to the varying extent to which Muslim or Jewish thinkers have been influenced by Greek philosophy directly—participating in its on-going tradition; or in the Jewish case, have been influenced indirectly through Islamic and recently Christian thought. Christian theology has been influenced also indirectly, by Islamic and Jewish instances, especially in the salient case of the thirteenth century.

I distinguish, then, between theology, and mere talk about God. I do so not only because theology is systematic and rigorous, as is the philosophy with which it has been associated. A Ramanuja's theology can be distinguished from various exuberant Hindu mythologies and from village folklore, or an Aquinas's from, say, a Pacific cargo cult ideology, by its precision, comprehensive coherence, and self-critical sophistication. There is more to my point, however, than that theology is rational talk about God, important though that be; rational in the most rigorous sense of the term. Theology is as much more than talk about God as logic is more than talk in general. "Logic" has to do not with how people speak, simply, but how they should speak, rationally: the concept formulates Reason as the ideal for reasoning, to which actual reasoning by human beings approximates when it is functioning well. The Greek affirmation, after all, is that the universe is intelligible; put the other way round, that the human intellect is capable of apprehending the truth of the world; put mediatingly, that the universe is rational and that humankind (ho anthrōpos) is rational, that through his and her reason man participates in the ultimate order of things. To use more incarnationalist language: that Reason, the ultimate order of the universe, is to some degree finitely embodied in human beings.

Theology, if we may characterize it succinctly, and imperiously, is true talk about God. Again, the same point may be made by leaning on the Palestinian rather than on the Greek side of our double heritage: by emphasizing the first component of the concept "theology" rather than the second, stressing the first two syllables as well as the last two. If what we say of God is not true, then it is not of God that we are talking.

Theology is speaking the truth about God.

Admittedly, I am enough of a neo-Platonist that I would say as much of all human discourse—about anything whatever. To talk is, fundamentally, to speak the truth. This is why language is so awesome a matter; and, I suppose, why Trappists take a vow of silence. No doubt, people can tell lies; but that is to abuse the human capacity for speech. There is the old argument that counterfeit money is necessarily parasitic upon authentic. Similarly, there could be no lies, if talk were not inherently, and even normally, of truth. No doubt, less damnably, we can inadvertently be mistaken in what we think and therefore say. Yet if we speak what is not true, however well-meaningly, we have failed. All verbalized error is a misuse of speech.

To talk at all is to be under a formidable obligation to speak the truth.

If this seems too austere a doctrine in general, too little tolerant of whimsy and idle chatter, yet surely one will agree that frivolous talk about God is hardly acceptable; and is not theology. My point, simply—yet that "simply" is inapt—is this: that we must approach theology with reverence and with awe. To say something about God that is not the case, is to blaspheme!

How, then, dare any of us "do theology"? With trepidation, at best; and I, preferring to resist the novel terminology of that glib phrase, and thinking of theology as
"true talk about God," see even a Thomas Aquinas or a Calvin as attempting a theology, rather. This last way of speaking will enable us to recognize that all attempts at it
are inadequate; and yet will enable us to recognize too that some come off as less inadequate than do others. Perhaps especially, some attempts are less inadequate than are
others for our particular moment. It is this latter recognition that justifies our continuing at the endeavor—so that one proceeds *simul justus et peccator.*

This perspective, also, gives dignity to the erstwhile fashion of *studying* theology
before "doing" theology: becoming familiar with, and taking seriously, the least inadequate among the attempts of human beings in past circumstances, and reflecting upon
those, as our basis for our own endeavors to speak, however again inadequately, in and
for our new situation, the truth about God: endeavors to formulate the closest approximation to it towards which we are able, or are given the grace, to rise.

(That word "approximation," and the passing allusion to Plotinus—one could also
mention Ramanuja or the *Yogavisista;* some would allude to Hegel—must suffice for
the philosophic issue, not directly our topic today, of how one handles the question of
intellectual pluralism without falling into one or other of nihilism, or arbitrariness, or
logical contradiction. The less lively their sense of immanental transcendence, the more
troublesome some moderns seem to find this relativism issue.)

Trepidation is in order; or at least, will explain why I waited till my mid-sixties to
publish my first book with the word "theology" in the title. And even in that recent
work, the word "towards" is to be stressed, as well as "world." That work is a revision of
a lecture series that I agreed to give, agreed to tackle the subject, only after initially de-
clining, and then being pressed to do so. Similarly, it is with some hesitation that I take
this opportunity to place before you some ideas in the theological realm to which my
historical studies have gradually pushed me.

History of all Religion: True Basis for Theology

For I do have a couple of, I suppose, quite fundamental suggestions to submit to the
theological world—for criticism: one proposal, basically; but it ramifies. I am a student
of history; and have found myself with theological dimensions to the results to which
my historical awareness was leading. This was so already twenty-some years ago, with
my *Meaning and End of Religion;* and has become more conspicuous, perhaps, with my
recent trilogy (I call it so; the three volumes are formally quite distinct, but have converging theological impingement, explicit in the last). For I have come to feel—dare I
say: I have come to see—that the true historian and the true theologian are one and the
same. No doubt, I am a historian of *religion;* yet human history is essentially the history
of religion. And the history of religion, my studies have increasingly pushed me to
hold, is the one true basis for theology.

This, indeed, is my fundamental submission—in principle quite simple, although
it seem radical. (Doubtless it will appear more radical at first blush and from a distance

than it will prove, once understood.) Perhaps, since I take history seriously, we should rephrase my point thus: that in the next phase of world thought, the basis for theology must now be the history of religion. To speak truly about God means henceforth to interpret accurately the history of human religious life on earth.

Since my contention is that the true historian of religion and the authentic theologian are in the final analysis identical—that a true understanding of the history of religion, and theology, which means true theology, converge—therefore to fellow historians my presentation would take the form of showing that to improve our historical studies, we must perceive more fully and more exactly the transcendent component in human life across the centuries. It is part of the task of Religion departments in Arts faculties to enhance intellectual awareness by the academic, rational mind of the transcendent dimensions of human affairs. Since those dimensions are there, it is an intellectual error not to see them—as I argued in my Presidential Address to the American Academy of Religion this past winter. Yet this is an error that has often been made in Western academia since the Enlightenment. It is, frankly, preposterous to imagine that anyone insensitive to the presence of God can understand or interpret human history in any but drastically inadequate ways, given the extent to which human lives have been lived in that presence. Human beings have acted the way that they have acted, have been the persons that they have been, in the light of many other and finally less important, more mundane, reasons; but also, most of them quite consciously, also in the light of this. To fail to recognize the impingement of economic factors on human history would be obtuse; no less obtuse is to fail to recognize the impingement of transcendence.

I solicit your help in this enterprise: the theologian must enable the historian to be a better historian, and vice versa. If it be the case that secular historians are on the whole more dogmatic these days than are theologians—that the theological enterprise is more open to new ideas, however radical-seeming, provided that they be rationally persuasive, than are our secular academic friends, except perhaps among the young—then perhaps my task here in *this* group is the easier. In any case, it is today my task: to make plausible that the new foundation for theology must become the history of religion.

In favor of this position one argument could be that other bases are beginning, it would seem, to crumble. Some observers report themselves rather apalled at the disarray of much present-day theological activity. In the Christian case, neither the Bible nor the traditional doctrines of the Church, nor current philosophic movements, nor the latest social or intellectual fashions, seem sufficient to provide a stable basis for a theological construct firm enough to bear the weight that the culture at large, let alone the religiously committed themselves, would like to place upon it.

I myself do not find this particular argument appealing; a more positive, and more intrinsically theological, support for the new proposal is requisite. The positive pragmatic argument is, however, both interesting in itself, and corroboratingly significant.

That positive argument is this: that many of the outstanding theoretical problems of the day do seem to be resolved in the history-of-religion orientation. The Church does indeed sorely need, and an understanding of the worldwide history of religion can indeed provide, an intellectually strong, rationally coherent, empirically based, inductively argued, logically persuasive, transcendentally adequate, integrative theory to do justice to our faith and to our work: to what we know with our hearts and what we know with our minds, at their best.

In discussions on the reputed difference between Theology and what is called "Religious Studies," a remark has at times been heard to the effect that that difference is simple: to be in theology is to be close-minded, to be in the "academic" side is to be open-minded. What those who voice such a view presumably think of as a theologian is not someone endeavoring to ascertain what can truly be said about God, but someone who rather is defending or seeking to perpetuate what others have said (others in his or her own particular community). It is alas historically (and dolefully) the case that there have been of late people like that; but it is gratuitous to think of them as theologians. Apologists, perhaps; pitiable, certainly. No significant Christian (or for that matter Muslim or other) theologian of any stature over preceding centuries has ever been of that type. Theologians of repute have been men or women of high intelligence who have struggled to express in words the best understanding of the divine to which they could manage to rise, using the most promising data available to them and integrating those data sincerely with their own life experience and with whatever else they knew of the world. I am simply suggesting not only that what else we know is today of course new, but also that we can and must use a different and wider range of data: namely, those available to us from the whole history of humankind's religious and spiritual life. Our own group's certainly; but all other communities', too.

Any other starting-point for the journey of one's mind towards a true theology inevitably omits something. Most starting-points omit much. The history of religion omits nothing. More fully, mine is a double thesis: that the history of religion omits nothing germane to theology, and includes nothing not germane. This second point might seem obvious, in that nothing that exists is irrelevant to God, nor God to it; so that astronomy, economics, marine biology, a study of human wickedness, and all, deal with matters that pertain, less or more, to a proper human understanding of the divine. Yet the student of the history of religion subsumes all this, partly because all these other matters have impinged upon it, partly because the audience to whom the modern historian must make religious life intelligible knows about them, but also since insofar as any human being has discerned the relevance of any matter to an understanding of Ultimate Truth, that discernment has become part of the history of religion. That the history of religious communities other than Christian is irrelevant to theology, or at least to what is called Christian theology, is difficult for an intelligent sensitive person to hold today, but it has been held in the past (or: non-Muslim, to Islamic theology). It seems to me palpably false, yet it may require some attention, and we shall return to it.

Three Arguments for the Thesis

First, however, the contention that the history of religion omits nothing.

In the first place, let me make the perhaps not totally obvious point, that in "history of religion" I include—(may I add, "of course"?)—the history of the Christian Church, and of Christian thought. That history, that thought, are of course relevant for theology;

and they are not omitted. The situation that has arisen whereby the phrase "history of religion" or "comparative religion" connotes to some ears, or has denoted in some theological colleges and seminaries, everything but the Christian, is laughably anomalous—historically understandable, but rationally quite indefensible. What used to be called Church history is becoming or must become the Christian sector in the world history of religion.

Secondly, a critic might imagine that our thesis—that the grounds for an attempted theology must be neither less nor more than an understanding of the history of religion—must omit what God is *in se*, even if it include all God's relations to humankind. There are two answers to this objection. The first is the classical Christian, Buddhist, Hindu, Islamic, and other contention that this is true of all theological statements whatever. Thomas Aquinas and many another have affirmed that God *sicut est in se* is ultimately beyond the capacity of the human mind to apprehend, and of human language to convey. On this count, then, a theology attempted on a history-of-religion base would be no worse off than on any other. I do not rest my case there, however, cogent though this consideration seem. For I am much impressed by the capacity of the human mind to know that there is more to anything than it knows. History shows that we human beings are quite capable of postulating, and meaningfully using, self-transcending concepts, even though the mystery of this may have escaped some latter-day thinkers. Rather, my argument would take a form of insisting that the recognition of God as beyond our comprehension, if not our apprehension, is historically evidenced. It is an historical fact that the most intelligent human beings on earth who have attempted theology have with virtual unanimity averred that God transcends our intellectual grasp, and our theological precisioning. The fact that they have so averred is one of the salient data of the history of religion; and to understand it in its full import, and to take it seriously, are incumbent upon the historian who takes his or her history responsibly.

It is also the case that human history too cannot be fully understood. We shall be returning to this point. Every human being, ourselves and others, is beyond our full comprehension, let alone all human beings together in their and our course through time across this globe. History transcends our intellectual grasp, as does God. Yet ideally, if we could know the former fully, we should know the latter, at least as fully as is humanly conceivable. This last is, in fact, a tautology.

Thirdly, those who might be inclined to resist our thesis, that history is now the proper basis for any theological attempt, may feel so inclined because they discriminate between history and revelation, as sources of theological knowledge. The discrimination is vacuous, I reply. Not only is the concept of revelation demonstrably historical: a competent historian can trace its emergence and rise, its spread, its development, its many forms, its recent peregrinations, and its contemporary doldrums and re-invigorations—all this both within the Church and elsewhere. The historian can trace, too, the interrelations among Christian and other revelation concepts; interrelations rather subtly complex, it turns out. Beyond this, however, is the still more weighty fact, that apart from the concept of revelation, revelation itself, or revelations themselves, insofar as we use that term to interpret to ourselves what it conceptualizes, has or have occurred either within history or not at all. God has revealed Himself (Herself, Itself) in history, or else has not revealed Himself . . . at all. If the Qur'ān is the Word of God, it is the Word of God in human history. (Indeed it is not by studying the Qur'ān itself, but by studying religious history, that a non-Muslim comes to see that and how it has served God as His Word.)

I carry this point further than do many, contending that revelation must be recognized as a bilateral concept: there can be no revelation unless it be to somebody; and that means, to somebody at a particular time and place. Many have said, and say, that God has revealed Himself in Jesus Christ; this is at best a short-hand way of saying that He has revealed Himself in Christ to you or to me, in the twentieth century, and/or to St. Augustine in the fourth or fifth, and/or to a village grandmother in fourteenth-century Sweden, either every Sunday morning in church or throughout her life or whatever. To say that the Bhagavad Gītā is or is not a revelation of God is to say that God did or did not speak through it to M. K. Gandhi in India early this century, or to Ramanuja there in the twelfth. And so on. Moreover, only a person who has read and pondered Ramanuja's commentary on that work; or who knows Gandhi's life; or one who has read and pondered Ghazzali's writings set down in the conviction (which he himself, as an enormously intelligent and perceptive person, certainly had) that God spoke to him through the Qur'ān; or who has read and perceptively assessed a Christian's account, whether in words or in deeds, in response to her or his sense of knowing God in or through Jesus Christ—that is, only a sensitive historian—is in a position to have views worth considering, surely, on whether or not God has indeed revealed Himself here and there (or anywhere, or everywhere) through human history.

The question of revelation is an historical question. More specifically, it is a history-of-religion question.

Seeing Transcendence in History

Fundamentally, I am saying that I do not accept the dichotomy that would polarize history and transcendence. There is a transcendent dimension to human life—so far as I can see, there has always been, from palaeolithic times. Most human beings on earth over the centuries have been aware of this, and have lived their lives less or more vividly, less or more effectively, in terms of it. Leading thinkers among us, in all ages and climes, have articulated the awareness, in a vast variety of ways; and a certain number, on the whole among the most intellectually brilliant, have done so theologically. It is quite evident, as we now look back over the array of these, that whoever has done so has done so in ways pertinent to a particular time and place, and presumably this is quite right and proper. Yet it is also the case that the greatest among them have done so in a way that has in fact, historically, proven enduring; and various articulations have been preserved and cherished for centuries after, and even millennia, not in unvarying static rigidity but rather with dynamic force—although each generation has had to decide, consciously or otherwise, whether to preserve and to extrapolate an earlier articulation or to come up with a new one of its own, usually continuous with what went before, although at some times more starkly innovative than at others.

The history of religion is simply the process of humankind's double involvement in a mundane and simultaneously a transcendent environment. As for instance Rahner has insisted, virtually all human beings have lived with a mundane and a transcendent dimension to their lives. Whether the two environments, or the two dimensions, are radically different, are discontinuous, or constitute an unbroken continuum, or are in fact identical but differently perceived, or are the same perceived with less or more insight—these are questions to which there have been, historically, varying answers. My point at the moment is simply that it does not matter what answer you give to this question, so far as our present thesis is concerned. However you interpret the relation between time and eternity, both are related to the human (have been related to him and her). Human history is the locus of their intersection. Human awareness of God, of the infinite, of the absolute, human conceptions of the non-temporal, all take place within the flow of time. This is what the history of religion has been all about. Whether we see religion as human apprehension of transcendence, or the transcendent's, God's, apprehension of humankind, or any mixture of the two, the process of its on-going history includes all that there ever has been, is, or will be; or, to revert to my earlier wording, it omits nothing pertinent to theology.

It is sometimes said that certain types of Hindu, Buddhist, and Western mystics are not (*lege:* have not been) interested in history. One can even find such sentences as, "History is not important for him or her who experiences *satori.*" This is a short-hand way of saying that the range of history that interests such persons is exceptionally narrow: namely, perhaps only the moment during which the experience of *satori* occurs. My own observation is that virtually all human beings on their way through time are aware however dimly of what some call the timeless; even if for a few, at certain moments, that dimness gives way to overwhelming clarity. The curve plotting the conscious participation of men and women on earth in what a certain vocabulary distinguishes as the time-bound and the timeless may be asymptotic at the two extremes to zero and one hundred per cent of either, with most of us falling somewhere in between, each with our ups and downs. Yet however that may be, it all happens within the historical process. This is another way of saying that history, for other kinds of creature—rocks and grasshoppers—may (as some think) be totally within time; but for human beings—man being what he and she are—history is the on-going process of human involvement in what my vocabulary verbalizes as the mundane and the transcendent.

It will be evident to you by now that my idea of history is larger and deeper—is, if you like, more theological—than is some people's. And indeed the reason why one has to advocate the thesis that the history of religion is the right basis for theology, and to expect this view's acceptance presently rather than finding it already established as obvious, has much to do with the current inadequacies of prevalent concepts of history—as much as it does with the current narrowness of inherited concepts of theology. Once again, the recent bifurcation is understandable in historical perspective, even if it not be defensible in logic.

Let me elucidate a little further what I intend by "history of religion." First, I like to discriminate between history and historiography. I know that the Western term "history" originally—etymologically, and historically—designated the account of what had happened, and only later what did in fact happen, the actual course of events. The term is therefore now ambiguous: the history of England is long and complicated, whereas a

History of England may be short and simple and weigh two pounds. Nonetheless we now have no other word for the former, that course of events; and I deem it important not only to distinguish the two in our thinking but also to keep remembering that the report of what has taken place is and must be subordinate to a prior reality, of what has indeed taken place. One could call that reality "objective" in the sense that it is what it is independently of our awareness or ignorance of it. One could call it transcendent, for the same reason and since it always transcends our grasp: all our ideas about it and our knowledge of it only approximate to the reality itself. Until recently, the approximation was very remote indeed, especially for world history, and in minute fraction; and still today, it is still very superficial, although its range has become in principle total.

For me, then, the phrase "history of religion" names not an academic discipline, as it does for instance at the University of Chicago. Rather, it refers to a many-thousand-year-old process, the actual course of human religious and spiritual life: a process variegated, world-wide, intertwined to some degree with virtually all human affairs, and involving virtually all persons, regularly at their most central and most profound. The historiography of religion is an intellectual study, relatively recent and predominantly Western; the history of religion, in contrast, is a dynamic reality of which the intellectual, the recent, and the Western are each relatively small segments.

Second: "history" means not only the past. History is process, which includes also the present, and presumably will include some future or other. The future of our galaxy, and even of much of our solar system, are predictable with considerable precision. The future sector of human history is radically problematic, as we all know; and even of that portion of the solar system that man can modify by his and her doings. History is a long-range on-going process, in which we participate, for good or ill, in the current relatively brief phase. Similarly, to be a theologian is to participate in the current phase of the long-range process of human attempts to speak the truth about God, about the universe.

Naturalistic Fallacy

I have spoken of current misconceptions in our recent Western understanding of history. Salient is the naturalistic fallacy. This is an interpretation of human affairs that imposes a naturalistic ceiling on human history, and legislates it for historiography—insisting that historians *qua* historians must not step beyond the rigid boundaries of that particular ideology. One might expect secularists to feel this way, even though one might permit oneself some surprise in finding how dogmatic a position it prevalently is and how fiercely held; also, how derivative, from a dubious metaphysics. Yet the disappointing matter is that many Christians and Jews have also become victims of it; most readily of course in that area where it does most harm, the history of religion, thought of as the history of other people's religion. Christians entered the modern world suffering from the fallacy that they alone were in God's grace, were saved, so that as they began to look out on the rest of the world they joined with the atheists and secularists in the West in opining that all other religious histories were fictitious nonsense. The more pious the Christian and the more positivistic the secularist, the more heartily they agreed that the history of Hindu, Buddhist, Islamic traditions is a this-worldly construct and aberration. The Western academic discipline that called itself "History of

Religion" is only beginning to recover from this absurdity. It has largely dropped the aberration idea, no doubt. Yet it is told that it is not allowed to drop the this-worldly-construct notion, or it will be academically illegitimate.

To approach the study of history with *a priori* rigidities is crippling—whether they be naturalistic dogmas or theological ones. A good historian is one who is perceptive and open, to find things however unexpected among however unfamiliar ages or groups, and who then reports what he or she finds; who understands what he or she observes, and makes it intelligible to others. To be a good historian one must be able to learn from history—since there is always more there than one brings to it. Whether or not one must understand a fair bit about science before one takes up the task of being an historian of science, surely it is evident that if one becomes a true historian of science, one will end up understanding it. It is possible to argue that one must be reasonably sensitive to music before setting up as an historian of music, or to the transcendent dimensions of human life before setting up as an historian of religion; yet in any case it would seem incontrovertible that the history of either music or of religion includes all that until now has been significant in the two realms. (More accurately, let us say one-and-a-half realms?) Therefore in the course of studying, one becomes sensitive to, appreciative of, what has been going on. Otherwise, one fails as an historian.

My recent book on World Theology includes the following sentence. It occurs in the course of a discussion pressing the point that what used to be called "Buddhism," rather than being a given abstract entity that some people "have," has been rather a living movement in process, with a diversified history, constituted of the lives of historical persons; they do not "have" it but participate in it, in its on-going development, and our task is to understand them, and their participation. The sentence reads: "Living life religiously—for Buddhists as for all human beings, even if in the Buddhist case it be a little more obvious—has been a complex interaction among four things:

(i) the accumulating religious tradition that, in one or another particular limited form, each inherited;
(ii) the particular personality—with its own potentialities and its own quirks—that each brought to it;
(iii) the particular environment—new every morning—in which each happened to live (this and the first above include the community in which each participated); and
(iv) the transcendent reality to which the tradition pointed, and in relation to which the life was lived."

It is the fourth point that is the crux: "the transcendent reality to which the tradition pointed, and in relation to which the life was lived."

I cite this here, in order to remark that when I used a preliminary draft of this material in seminars at Harvard, both theological students from the Divinity School and history-of-religion doctoral students from the Arts Faculty joined to protest that I could not say that. At least, I could not say it as an historian, they insisted. (The passage comes in a presentation of the historical section of the work.) "That is not an historical judgment; it is a theological judgment" was the chorus. It seemed to them obvious that if it were theological, it could not be historical. In the face of their continued resistance, over two or three years, I did not alter the statement, but I have added to the printed version an additional sentence following it: "Without the fourth component here, human history cannot be rendered intelligible." It is precisely *qua* historian that I make the statement. Anyone who does not understand this truth about Buddhist life has misunderstood human history.

Mind you, I did not start my studies with the conviction that other communities' lives were lived in God's grace. I have come to this recognition only slowly, as I got to know the people and carefully studied their history.

It is sometimes remarked that a Westerner, or a Christian, or a modern, that a member of any given culture, always interprets another culture from within his or her own perspective. My response is that of course that is so at first, but is less so in the end. Gradually, as I have learned more, I have come to recognize the power and wealth and profundity of Asian religious life, in all its variety, just as over the years I have come to appreciate more deeply the power and wealth and profundity (and diversity) of the history of Christian religion.

There is a deal of discussion these days in academic quarters about methodologies, preconceptions, and the like. I yield to no one in observing (historically) that conceptual presuppositions color what one observes and how one interprets it. Indeed, I have noticed that a certain complex of presuppositions (which I happen not to share) underlies the present-day emphasis on methodology, and underlies even the concept methodology itself. (Ultimately, methodology, I am beginning to think, is a modern form of atheism.) Rather than engaging, especially here, in debates on those issues, however, I would rather insist that the true scholar, whatever the convictions with which he or she begins the work, must be open in the course of study to modifying those previous convictions. Especially one may argue that that historian of religion is of little worth, to put it mildly, who does not modify—quite radically—underlying convictions, however tacit, in the course of coming to understand other cultures, other centuries, other visions. It is interesting to speculate on whether, on the whole, Christians are better at this than are secularists, in the history-of-religion field. However that may be, I would wager that any modern Western scholar who emerges from say twenty years of study of Asian religious life with either his secular or his Christian doctrines unenlarged, is a woefully poor historian.

"Studying History Backwards" Fallacy

We turn next to a "studying history backwards" outlook, as I have called it: that Western academic propensity that must be rectified or at least supplemented before we can truly understand anything historical, and especially the religious. It has to do with what might uncharitably be called a stunted antiquarianism, which does little justice to the on-going process of human history with, of course, its forward-moving direction. I recently did an article elaborating this point, on the true understanding of the Qur'ān as scripture, a non-reductionist historical understanding. Let me illustrate the point here, however, briefly, in—rather—the Biblical case. The same point would apply in questions of Christology, ecclesiology, and any other; to the Gita; or to new questions such as the femininity of God. In the Biblical case also a decade back I published an article on an historical understanding of the Bible, as a recognition of its on-going role in

Christian life over the two millennia that begin, not end, with the first century A.D., and that are still in process. Some of you may remember that piece. In any case, I find some present-day theologians speaking of the difficulty that they face, or that the Church faces, in attempting to bridge the radical gap between two cultures, that of the ancient world in which the Bible was composed, and our own, so starkly different. They see the task of making the Bible "relevant" to our day as a formidable one, because of what they feel to be the drastic gap between its world and ours. This results from adopting a view of the Bible from a position of recent scholarship that calls itself historical, but for which the nineteen-century gap between Jesus and us is effectively empty. As you see, I call this antiquarianism, not history. It is one particular nineteenth-century kind of historicism, which it is time for our much better understanding today to leave behind. If one perceives the Bible (or for that matter, Christ) in the on-going life of the Church with anything approaching historical fidelity, which carries them steadily and step by step from the first century in Palestine through each succeeding century to just the other day, here, and indeed into today, then our business is simply to put "historical criticism" in proper perspective, as a recent step in an on-going process, and our task becomes not that of bridging a yawning gap between the first century and this, but rather of constructing the next phase in a continuing process—in the on-going historical development of Christian understanding of scripture (or of Christ).

Instead of a yawning gap between the first century and the twentieth, the gap becomes simply that between, for instance, my mother and myself. Her world-view was that of a highly intelligent, educated, warm-hearted traditionalist—you might say, fundamentalist. Or one may say that the gap is that between my childhood and my maturity; although to construct this next phase we must of course bring to bear upon its construction all the resources of our current knowledge. This last includes both our modern awareness of nineteen intervening centuries of the life of the Bible as scripture, and of the preceding millennium or two as the environment out of which that Bible first arose, and also now our modern awareness of other scriptures, our enhanced historical knowledge of the development of the concept scripture on earth, the varying roles that it has played, and the light that this throws upon the human mind and spirit—and the capacity of the Word to mediate between the human spirit and God, and *vice versa:* in theological terms, God's activity in using scripture, in varying forms and varying cultures and varying ways, to enter historically into the life of humankind. One of my most enriching recent experiences has been a post-doctoral seminar at Harvard on Scripture and its role in human history. Are prose, poetry, and scripture three important ways in which humankind uses the gift of language?

Dichotomizing Fallacy

Let us turn next to a third fallacy, as I have called them; namely, that of dichotomizing. This has already surfaced in passing.

Some will protest that this kind of thinking is all very well, but what about the distinction between the descriptive and the normative? It was Hume, I guess, who contended that one can never pass from an "is" to an "ought"; and it is important to understand historically the prevalence in recent Western intellectuality of an outlook that, even when it may not go all the way with Hume on that particular point, nonetheless acquiesces in a sense of two distinct, even disparate, realms. At a static philosophic level, the question may be tricky; but my own view is that this outlook has distorted our awareness of history, and that a true understanding of human affairs in their development over time both enables and requires a healing of this doleful breach. I have already averred that human life is lived in both realms, if two realms they be. The locus of the relation between what is and what ought to be is, and always has been, man; and the study of his and her history—especially religious history—is a study of that interrelation.

This is not merely to say that an historical awareness is an awareness of the mutual impingement, interaction, if not convergence, of "is" and "ought"—although that is certainly included. In addition, however, there is the surely manifest point that if my Christian heritage tells me that I should see the face of Christ in every man and woman, does not this mean that I should indeed do so only if and insofar as it is in fact truly there? Similarly, if the Buddhist aspirant is taught that ultimately *saṃsāra* is *nirvāṇa*, then a full understanding of human history should not only comprehend what this thesis meant to those who promulgated it and those who heard and received and pondered and structured their lives less or more in terms of it, but should include, which finally is the same thing, an understanding of the universe that would make clear what it was not only in their environment and inner life but in ours, today, that made and makes that thesis persuasive. Whatever the conceptualities that those Buddhists concocted, and that we must understand, after all the universe that they were observing is also our universe; and the humanity that they talked of, we share.

Indeed, if history and theology were to be polarized, on which side would one put the history of theology—including present-day theology?

Or, the same question put in other terms: does the statement that *saṃāra* is *nirvāṇa* tell us something about *nirvāṇa,* but nothing about *saṃsāra?*

Once again, however, the Western error on this descriptive/normative disjunction is something that the historian can understand, and therein overcome. For it has arisen from the fact that our recent thinking about what "is" has been drawn chiefly from science, not from history: it arises from our attending to the material world, and neglecting the human. Once we subordinate science to history, as a rational mind soon again must, these problems tend to evaporate. As I shall urge presently, science itself too becomes clearer.

A failure to see this, plagues those who have become victims of the subject/object dichotomy also in their orientation to persons, not only to things—so that many moderns think of history as the history of "them," those other people: over there, or long ago. But we too are within history. The historian's chief task is to help all to see that we too participate in history, this entrancing on-going process—and that they too did, those whom one mistook as *others*. The crux (I choose that word wittingly) is to recognize history as the history of *us*, human beings. Once that corner is turned, the problems indeed evaporate.

And if you say, does true critical intellectuality not require a certain distancing of the reflective mind from what it contemplates, I counter happily by saying that one of the richest rewards that my study of world history has given me has been my ability intellectually to distance myself from current Western culture, in which so many of my friends and especially my critics are still, alas, imprisoned.

Modern Western thought should surely contribute to our understanding of the universe and of ourselves; but equally surely, should not constitute it—just as our heritage of Christian thought should, and should not.

Either I am wrong in seeing Christ's face in all human persons, or the historian is wrong who does not. Of course, the image is poetic, but that does not affect the facts of the situation—only the way they are expressed in words. Similarly I fail as an historian if I fail to see those aspects of our common universe that Gandhi saw and articulated in Bhagavad-Gītā terms, or that the most intelligent and perceptive among Buddhists have seen and reported in Buddhist terms. Of course the world historian must forge new vocabulary in order to communicate to a public audience what the various religious communities among us have seen and have thus far articulated in terms that are today private in the sense that only those within one's own restricted circle of discourse could understand. Yet insofar as there is any truth in what Hindus have seen, these are not truths "in Hinduism": they are truths in the universe, to which Hindus in this case happen to have called attention. There are no *Christian* truths—the phrase is an absurdity, almost a blasphemy. An historian of religion who has not understood and has not made understandable such truth as Christians have discerned or been vouchsafed, is no historian. Similarly for Jewish or Confucian, Zarathustrian or Muslim, matters. The historian of religion is that scholar whose aspiration (grandiose, no doubt; but to understand human history is indeed a grandiose endeavor)—that scholar whose aspiration is to apprehend, and to render intellectually apprehensible, what human beings on earth have reported or found to be transcendently true. The theologian, equally grandiosely (and I stress that "equally"), is that thinker whose aspiration is to apprehend, and to make intellectually apprehensible, the truth about God: the transcendently true. It is the same task. Insofar as in the past the two have conceived their task differently, is it not that that ceiling above which historians once wrongly supposed that they could not or need not go was artificially imposed, and indeed was imaginary, while the several grounds on which the various and disparate private theologians attempted to build towards the goal were less solidly reliable?

The Muslim theologian, who in olden times thought that the Qur'ān as Word of God provided an adequate starting point, or the Christian theologian who thought that Christ as that Word did, have been replaced in our day by their respective sectarian successors who do not know quite what to make of each other, nor quite what to make of those erstwhile starting points in the light of each other or of modern knowledge generally; whereas the comparative historian of religion's task is to understand and to make rationally intelligible to modern intellects the historical fact of both Words in a global coherence. Once we recognize, as today we can and must, that God has spoken to men and women and children, historically, both through the Qur'ān and through Christ, in differing times and places, differing languages, differing moods and modes, the historian's task becomes recognizably theological, and the theologian's, recognizably historical.

The Church, we used to say, is a divine-human complex; and so, nowadays we can go on to say, is the Islamic community, and the Buddhist and the rest. All human history is a divine-human complex in motion; a fact most noticeably discernible in its religious dimension. The task of the historian of religion is to tell the truth about that reality, that *Heilsgeschichte*; the task of the theologian is to tell the truth about God.

In the past I have found that views such as I am endeavoring to set forth are resisted—perhaps I should say, rather: my vocabulary is resisted—by, for instance, sensitive Jews or Muslims (the two chief groups that have shared with us Christians the massive exclusivistic strand in human religious orientation) who do so because of that very polarity, even dichotomy, between the sense of history and the sense of God's presence. The Passover, for Jews, or the *Laylat al Qadr*, for Muslims—the annual ritual celebrations enlivening in on-going history the continuing sense of God's presence and of His having acted for their particular community—are felt as transcending the mundane. (Christians say the same of the eucharist, for example.) In modern jargon, this is sometimes formulated by saying that these occasions are felt as transcending history (or as enabling the participants to transcend history). The point here is that this sort of ritual and celebration expresses an orientation to the historical process, and to the relation of its past to its present, that the modern mind-set has lost. Contemporary ideology, with its straining after objectivity and objectification, has objectified also the past and distanced us from it, separating us from continuity and intimacy with it. The more normal human attitude has been, nurtured through rituals of this kind, to "re-appropriate one's past," as modern writers using their own inapt terms sometimes put it, but anyway enabling participants in the ceremonies to participate thus in their "past" yet on-going history, to recognize that it participates in their lives, that the historical process transcends us but that we by participating in it participate in transcendence and that transcendence—God—participates in us. Of course the Passover enables Jews, and *Laylat al Qadr* enables Muslims, to transcend the mundane. But to misread this by saying, rather, that they thereby transcend history is to fail to recognize that human history is precisely the arena, the process, in which human beings live simultaneously in the mundane and the transcendent: in God and world, in time and eternity, or however one wishes to put it. (They have done so in varying proportions, of course, as well as in various forms.) Jews, Christians, and Muslims share a sense of a clear divine dimension to their "past" history, but share also the unhappy distinction of exclusivistic orientations; and have been almost as slow as are secularists in recognizing the fact that human history has normally been like that—all human history. To suggest that *our* religious life, *our* experience, *our* knowing, transcends history is to have what I would call a both intellectually and spiritually untenable sense either of human history, what it has been and is, or else of the history of other groups than one's own. I rather, far from denying the experience of those communities in those precious moments, and far even from denying its validity, am affirming both; while adding that it is insensitive not to recognize that something comparable has been true of most human history in most centuries.

The Sabbath, say Jews, "is a taste of eternity in time." I agree; and I teach my students that to fail to see this is to mis-read the human scene. Therefore I cannot agree with an esteemed Jewish thinker whom I recently heard say that these things "are in time but not really in history." To propose such a dichotomy is to be victim of the false naturalistic view both of history and of the human; the secularists' unwillingness or incapacity to see human history as indeed that divine-human complex in motion.

Similarly I have heard it said that at moments of ceremonial observance "the flow of time is interrupted by the intrusion of the divine into the historical." Is it not blasphemy to say that God's presence is an interruption? It is the secular aridity of modern life, with its obtuseness to transcendence and its blinkered view of day-to-day life, that constitutes the interruption of genuinely human history—impoverishing history and making us less than human. Secularism has taught that religion is an addendum, an aberration; but it is wrong. Secularism is the aberration, both historically and logically. Religion has not conferred color and significance on essentially bleak and meaningless human lives, as the sympathetic secularists would have it; rather, what we call the world's religious traditions have at their best simply enabled humanity to open its eyes to the divine color and significance that are there and are our true environment—or to change the metaphor, have enabled us to hear at least an echo of the music of the spheres.

A Word About Truth

I close with just a word about truth as such; for on this matter also the historical dimension of the matter has in our day become salient.

One of the fundamental problems in this realm has to do with that persistently teasing fact that philosophy in recent times has become distracted by a pre-occupation with science. For a time, this took the form of supposing that science was the avenue to truth—not merely *an* avenue, but the sole significant one. Presently, however, it went further, to the point where the concept of truth itself has tended to become defined in relation to science; particularly the notion of a true statement (statements, you may recall, I have come to deem the misplaced locus of truth), and the notion of objective truth (which I am beginning to find a contradiction in terms). Western theology, itself dazzled by science directly (were we not all?) and also influenced by philosophy's dazzlement by it, has in part fallen prey to these philosophic fallacies.

My concern at the moment is simply to press the thesis that, at least so far as the human is concerned (as over against objects and things), a study of history brings us closer to the truth than does science. The historical and the scientific outlooks were the two great intellectual achievements of the nineteenth century and of the first half of this. My contention is that of the two, the historical is the greater, and the truer; and that this is especially so, indeed overwhelmingly so, in the case of human affairs. My thesis in this realm I have recently summarized in the aphorism that history can comprehend science, but science cannot comprehend history.

Within the next generation or so, I would predict, philosophers will come round to wrestling with history primarily, putting science in at best second place. (This is because humanity is more important than things; and the truth about humanity is of a higher order than the truth about things.) Anyway, so far as theology is concerned, although for a century it was perhaps inescapable, and even proper, that theologians should concern themselves first and foremost with the challenge from science, that era is now effectively over. Today, and for the coming century, the primary challenge, on the one hand, and the primary potential support, on the other, come and will come from a study of history. The support will be primarily from a study of the history of religion. Just as to say that God is creator of the world, must today mean that God has created the kind of world that scientists (and not only poets) make known to us, so to say that God is active in human history means that God has been and continues active in the history that primarily the historian of religion studies. I should like to think that theologians might lead the way here for philosophers, rather than again being led.

In any case, it is significant that even with regard to science itself, it is the new attention to the history of science that is now raising the most interesting philosophic questions—not least, the question of truth. Awareness of the history of science is making much more understandable what science itself is, as Kuhn has shown.

One illustration which I have thought up has to do with Copernicus, and his heliostatic theory. (Sometimes his view is called heliocentric, but this is not quite accurate: in order to conform to his precise measurements, he located the sun at a short distance from the center.) Anyway, as everyone knows, for the earlier view that the earth stands still while the sun revolves around it, and elaborately the planets, he substituted the new conception that the sun, rather, stands still, close to the center of things, with the earth and planets circling about it. Indeed, on this innovating vision the modern scientific movement has by some been seen to be based. We now know, however, that in fact the sun does not stand still: it is much more vagrant than he ever thought the earth to be. And it is no nearer the center of the physical universe than is our own planet. On these matters, we may see that he was wrong. Yet obviously he had a point!

Are we then to say that modern science is founded on an insight that is true, expressed in statements that are false?

To an historian of religion, that is entrancing. It is, however, too glib; and in my recent publications I have wrestled at length with this issue. Let me here simply suggest three positions for which a student of history must have a concept of truth capacious enough to make room: Copernicus's in the fifteenth century that the sun stands still; Christians' over many centuries that Jesus Christ is the Son of God; Muslims' over somewhat fewer centuries that Jesus Christ is not the Son of God. An inability to accommodate all three in one's notion of truth would be an inability to interpret history authentically, may we not say—and an inability to understand what truth is. It would also suggest an inability to understand what language is.

Christian Theology—or, Theology

One final point, and I close. It is to make explicit what was implicit in my opening: that theology ideally is the truth about God. Throughout I have spoken of "theology," never of "Christian theology." Indeed, the phrase "Christian theology," once one stops to reflect about it, is a contradiction in terms. At the very least, it is un-Christian, in any serious meaning of the word. This suggestion, which I have elsewhere adumbrated, may strike you as novel, unexpected, and even bizarre. Historically, however, it is the phrase "Christian theology" that, rather, is recent, odd, and finally untenable. It is virtually unknown before the nineteenth and rare before the twentieth century.

Into the history of the concept "Christian" I obviously cannot go here, though I am entranced by it and have pondered a little its present-day radical ambiguity, between on the one hand a transcendent or metaphysical meaning, signifying "pertaining to Christ," and on the other a mundane, almost positivistic meaning, signifying, pertaining to the earthly community of (perhaps nominal) Christians, as over against or parallel to Jews, Buddhists, Hindus, and the like—terms that seldom, and in some cases never, had a transcendent reference in English (or any) usage. On the whole this second, mundane sense for "Christian" (and indeed for the others) has arisen only in the nineteenth, and become prevalent in the twentieth, centuries; but it nowadays predominates. Specifically as qualifying the concept "theology," it is virtually unknown before modern times. When St. Thomas Aquinas wrote a book that he called *Summa Theologiae* (not *Summa Christianae Theologiae*), he was illustrating as well as carrying forward the main tradition of the Church; and I feel that I need hardly apologize if I urge with some insistence that we return today to that main stream. The attempt to theologize is intimidating, as I have stressed, and trepidation is indeed in order; but let us not evade the challenge by settling for anything less than the aspiration, at least, to speak the truth about God. There may be a Christian attempt at theology; and indeed there should be. An attempt at Christian theology, on the other hand, is too narrow a goal; and in the end, is self-contradictory.

The concept "Christian theology," and counterparts such as "Christian faith," were un-thought-out and unsuccessful parts of the Church's first endeavor to deal with religious plurality, beginning last century. Before that time, Christians had been right in aspiring to theology, *simpliciter,* wrong in imagining that outside the Church there is and can be no significant or adequate knowledge of God. As my *Faith and Belief* attempts to document, those Christians were right in affirming that faith is one, wrong in imagining that it occurs in no form other than the Christian. The first book ever on "Christian faith" was Schleiermacher's in the nineteenth century; and even he did not mean by it what his English readers in the twentieth hear him as saying, in the now demonstrated mistranslation of his title as *"The" Christian Faith.* Since the Church began to discover where it was wrong, it has unfortunately withdrawn also from where it had been right, into a kind of frightened ghetto. My *Faith and Belief,* in addition to documenting the past situation on "faith," attempts to contribute towards forging a new conception adequate to our modern situation. My present plea is that the same sort of task needs tackling in the whole of theology.

Conclusion

The history of religion, I have claimed, omits nothing pertinent to theology, and includes nothing irrelevant.

Included in that history, of course, are not only the greatest truths that anyone, Christian or other, has ever known or seen or felt or sensed, about God, the world, our neighbors, or ourselves, but also, of course, much that is grotesque, stupid, wicked, and perverse. God's best efforts to give Himself/Herself/Itself, through the sacraments, Christian or other, through His/Her/Its Son, through the Bhagavad Gītā, through the

Torah, and to participate in our lives, to save us in this or that century, on this or that continent, have often been but meagerly successful, at best, God knows—and we should know it too. To study history—that is, to have one's intellect participate in broad reaches of the life of humankind over time and space—is to know more fully the grandeur and the pathos of man in his and her relation to God. If theology be the truth about God, surely part of that truth is that God is confronted with the recalcitrance, ineptitude, obtuseness, of us human beings. One cannot speak the truth about God without incorporating something of God's relation to us human beings as history has shown and shows us sorely to be. The history of religion at its best shows in careful detail the highest human potential for an awareness, including intellectual awareness, of God—decisive for theology; and at its worst, the actual relation of God to man, also no small component for theology, surely.

But our time is up. An hour was too short a span to develop the view that the attempt to discern and to report the truth about human history, especially religious history, requires theology; and that the attempt to theologize requires a grounding in awareness of that history.

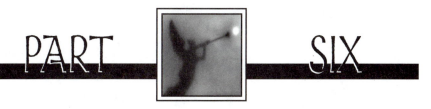

PART SIX

The Experience of the Divine

Over the centuries, mystics have claimed knowledge of God through direct religious experience. Although not apparently available to all, such experience seems to offer an avenue to God analogous to ordinary sense perception of other objects. William James, in his discussion of mysticism from his Varieties of Religious Experience *(1901–2), examines the accounts of both eastern and western mystics. He concludes that such experiences may be genuine and certainly can be authoritative for those who undergo them, but he acknowledges that they cannot possess any persuasive authority for others. Thomas Merton (1961) describes his own religious experiences and provides, thereby, a first-hand account of such direct apprehensions of the Divine. In the articles that follow, William Alston (1982) argues that religious experience corresponds, in many ways, with the paradigm of sense perception and that the differences between the two can largely be explained by the nature of the object being experienced. Wayne Proudfoot (1982), and Richard Gale (1960) offer more critical assessments of the epistemic nature and value of such mystical accounts, and they argue that these experiences can support only psychological and not existential claims.*

38. Mysticism

WILLIAM JAMES

Over and over again in these lectures I have raised points and left them open and un-finished until we should have come to the subject of Mysticism. Some of you, I fear, may have smiled as you noted my reiterated postponements. But now the hour has come when mysticism must be faced in good earnest, and those broken threads wound up to-gether. One may say truly, I think, that personal religious experience has its root and cen-tre in mystical states of consciousness; so for us, who in these lectures are treating personal experience as the exclusive subject of our study, such states of consciousness ought to form the vital chapter from which the other chapters get their light. Whether my treat-ment of mystical states will shed more light or darkness, I do not know, for my own con-stitution shuts me out from their enjoyment almost entirely, and I can speak of them only at second hand. But though forced to look upon the subject so externally, I will be as ob-jective and receptive as I can; and I think I shall at least succeed in convincing you of the reality of the states in question, and of the paramount importance of their function.

First of all, then, I ask, What does the expression 'mystical states of consciousness' mean? How do we part off mystical states from other states?

The words 'mysticism' and 'mystical' are often used as terms of mere reproach, to throw at any opinion which we regard as vague and vast and sentimental, and without a base in either facts or logic. For some writers a 'mystic' is any person who believes in thought-transference, or spirit-return. Employed in this way the word has little value: there are too many less ambiguous synonyms. So, to keep it useful by restricting it, I will do what I did in the case of the word 'religion,' and simply propose to you four marks which, when an experience has them, may justify us in calling it mystical for the purpose of the present lectures. In this way we shall save verbal disputation, and the re-criminations that generally go therewith.

1. *Ineffability.*—The handiest of the marks by which I classify a state of mind as mystical is negative. The subject of it immediately says that it defies expression, that no adequate report of its contents can be given in words. It follows from this that its quality must be directly experienced; it cannot be imparted or transferred to others. In this pe-culiarity mystical states are more like states of feeling than like states of intellect. No one can make clear to another who has never had a certain feeling, in what the quality or worth of it consists. One must have musical ears to know the value of a symphony; one must have been in love one's self to understand a lover's state of mind. Lacking the heart

Source: William James, *The Varieties of Religious Experience* (New York: Longman, Green & Co., 1902). Foot-notes omitted.

or ear, we cannot interpret the musician or the lover justly, and are even likely to consider him weak-minded or absurd. The mystic finds that most of us accord to his experiences an equally incompetent treatment.

2. *Noetic quality.*—Although so similar to states of feeling, mystical states seem to those who experience them to be also states of knowledge. They are states of insight into depths of truth unplumbed by the discursive intellect. They are illuminations, revelations, full of significance and importance, all inarticulate though they remain; and as a rule they carry with them a curious sense of authority for after-time.

These two characters will entitle any state to be called mystical, in the sense in which I use the word. Two other qualities are less sharply marked, but are usually found. These are:—

3. *Transiency.*—Mystical states cannot be sustained for long. Except in rare instances, half an hour, or at most an hour or two, seems to be the limit beyond which they fade into the light of common day. Often, when faded, their quality can but imperfectly be reproduced in memory; but when they recur it is recognized; and from one recurrence to another it is susceptible of continuous development in what is felt as inner richness and importance.

4. *Passivity.*—Although the oncoming of mystical states may be facilitated by preliminary voluntary operations, as by fixing the attention, or going through certain bodily performances, or in other ways which manuals of mysticism prescribe; yet when the characteristic sort of consciousness once has set in, the mystic feels as if his own will were in abeyance, and indeed sometimes as if he were grasped and held by a superior power. This latter peculiarity connects mystical states with certain definite phenomena of secondary or alternative personality, such as prophetic speech, automatic writing, or the mediumistic trance. When these latter conditions are well pronounced, however, there may be no recollection whatever of the phenomenon, and it may have no significance for the subject's usual inner life, to which, as it were, it makes a mere interruption. Mystical states, strictly so called, are never merely interruptive. Some memory of their content always remains, and a profound sense of their importance. They modify the inner life of the subject between the times of their recurrence. Sharp divisions in this region are, however, difficult to make, and we find all sorts of gradations and mixtures.

These four characteristics are sufficient to mark out a group of states of consciousness peculiar enough to deserve a special name and to call for careful study. Let it then be called the mystical group.

Our next step should be to gain acquaintance with some typical examples. Professional mystics at the height of their development have often elaborately organized experiences and a philosophy based thereupon. But you remember what I said in my first lecture: phenomena are best understood when placed within their series, studied in their germ and in their over-ripe decay, and compared with their exaggerated and degenerated kindred. The range of mystical experience is very wide, much too wide for us to cover in the time at our disposal. Yet the method of serial study is so essential for interpretation that if we really wish to reach conclusions we must use it. I will begin, therefore, with phenomena which claim no special religious significance, and end with those of which the religious pretensions are extreme.

The simplest rudiment of mystical experience would seem to be that deepened sense of the significance of a maxim or formula which occasionally sweeps over one. "I've heard that said all my life," we exclaim, "but I never realized its full meaning until now." "When a fellow-monk," said Luther, "one day repeated the words of the Creed: 'I believe in the forgiveness of sins,' I saw the Scripture in an entirely new light; and straightway I felt as if I were born anew. It was as if I had found the door of paradise thrown wide open." This sense of deeper significance is not confined to rational propositions. Single words, and conjunctions of words, effects of light on land and sea, odors and musical sounds, all bring it when the mind is tuned aright. Most of us can remember the strangely moving power of passages in certain poems read when we were young, irrational doorways as they were through which the mystery of fact, the wildness and the pang of life, stole into our hearts and thrilled them. The words have now perhaps become mere polished surfaces for us; but lyric poetry and music are alive and significant only in proportion as they fetch these vague vistas of a life continuous with our own, beckoning and inviting, yet ever eluding our pursuit. We are alive or dead to the eternal inner message of the arts according as we have kept or lost this mystical susceptibility.

A more pronounced step forward on the mystical ladder is found in an extremely frequent phenomenon, that sudden feeling, namely, which sometimes sweeps over us, of having 'been here before,' as if at some indefinite past time, in just this place, with just these people, we were already saying just these things. As Tennyson writes:

> "Moreover, something is or seems,
> That touches me with mystic gleams,
> Like glimpses of forgotten dreams—
>
> "Of something felt, like something here;
> Of something done, I know not where;
> Such as no language may declare."

Sir James Crichton-Browne has given the technical name of 'dreamy states' to these sudden invasions of vaguely reminiscent consciousness. They bring a sense of mystery and of the metaphysical duality of things, and the feeling of an enlargement of perception which seems imminent but which never completes itself. In Dr. Crichton-Browne's opinion they connect themselves with the perplexed and scared disturbances of self-consciousness which occasionally precede epileptic attacks. I think that this learned alienist takes a rather absurdly alarmist view of an intrinsically insignificant phenomenon. He follows it along the downward ladder, to insanity; our path pursues the upward ladder chiefly. The divergence shows how important it is to neglect no part of a phenomenon's connections, for we make it appear admirable or dreadful according to the context by which we set it off.

Somewhat deeper plunges into mystical consciousness are met with in yet other dreamy states. Such feelings as these which Charles Kingsley describes are surely far from being uncommon, especially in youth:—

"When I walk the fields, I am oppressed now and then with an innate feeling that everything I see has a meaning, if I could but understand it. And this feeling of being surrounded with truths which I cannot grasp amounts to indescribable awe sometimes. . . . Have you not felt that your real soul was imperceptible to your mental vision, except in a few hallowed moments?"

A much more extreme state of mystical consciousness is described by J. A. Symonds; and probably more persons than we suspect could give parallels to it from their own experience.

"Suddenly," writes Symonds, "at church, or in company, or when I was reading, and always, I think, when my muscles were at rest, I felt the approach of the mood. Irresistibly it took possession of my mind and will, lasted what seemed an eternity, and disappeared in a series of rapid sensations which resembled the awakening from anæsthetic influence. One reason why I disliked this kind of trance was that I could not describe it to myself. I cannot even now find words to render it intelligible. It consisted in a gradual but swiftly progressive obliteration of space, time, sensation, and the multitudinous factors of experience which seem to qualify what we are pleased to call our Self. In proportion as these conditions of ordinary consciousness were subtracted, the sense of an underlying or essential consciousness acquired intensity. At last nothing remained but a pure, absolute, abstract Self. The universe became without form and void of content. But Self persisted, formidable in its vivid keenness, feeling the most poignant doubt about reality, ready, as it seemed, to find existence break as breaks a bubble round about it. And what then? The apprehension of a coming dissolution, the grim conviction that this state was the last state of the conscious Self, the sense that I had followed the last thread of being to the verge of the abyss, and had arrived at demonstration of eternal Maya or illusion, stirred or seemed to stir me up again. The return to ordinary conditions of sentient existence began by my first recovering the power of touch, and then by the gradual though rapid influx of familiar impressions and diurnal interests. At last I felt myself once more a human being; and though the riddle of what is meant by life remained unsolved, I was thankful for this return from the abyss—this deliverance from so awful an initiation into the mysteries of skepticism.

"This trance recurred with diminishing frequency until I reached the age of twenty-eight. It served to impress upon my growing nature the phantasmal unreality of all the circumstances which contribute to a merely phenomenal consciousness. Often have I asked myself with anguish, on waking from that formless state of denuded, keenly sentient being, Which is the unreality?—the trance of fiery, vacant, apprehensive, skeptical Self from which I issue, or these surrounding phenomena and habits which veil that inner Self and build a self of flesh-and-blood conventionality? Again, are men the factors of some dream, the dream-like unsubstantiality of which they comprehend at such eventful moments? What would happen if the final stage of the trance were reached?". . .

Certain aspects of nature seem to have a peculiar power of awakening such mystical moods. Most of the striking cases which I have collected have occurred out of doors. Literature has commemorated this fact in many passages of great beauty—this extract, for example, from Amiel's Journal Intime:—

"Shall I ever again have any of those prodigious reveries which sometimes came to me in former days? One day, in youth, at sunrise, sitting in the ruins of the castle of Faucigny; and again in the mountains, under the noonday sun, above Lavey, lying at the foot of a tree and visited by three butterflies; once more at night upon the shingly shore of the Northern Ocean, my back upon the sand and my vision ranging through the milky way;—such grand and spacious, immortal, cosmogonic reveries, when one reaches to the stars, when one owns the infinite! Moments divine, ecstatic hours; in which our thought flies from world to world, pierces the great enigma, breathes with a respiration broad, tranquil, and deep as the respiration of the ocean, serene and limitless as the blue firmament; . . . instants of irresistible intuition in which one feels one's self great as the universe, and calm as a god. . . . What hours, what memories! The vestiges they leave behind are enough to fill us with belief and enthusiasm, as if they were visits of the Holy Ghost."

Here is a similar record from the memoirs of that interesting German idealist, Malwida von Meysenbug:—

"I was alone upon the seashore as all these thoughts flowed over me, liberating and reconciling; and now again, as once before in distant days in the Alps of Dauphiné, I was impelled to kneel down, this time before the illimitable ocean, symbol of the Infinite. I felt that I prayed as I had never prayed before, and knew now what prayer really is: to return from the solitude of individuation into the consciousness of unity with all that is, to kneel down as one that passes away, and to rise up as one imperishable. Earth, heaven, and sea resounded as in one vast world-encircling harmony. It was as if the chorus of all the great who had ever lived were about me. I felt myself one with them, and it appeared as if I heard their greeting: 'Thou too belongest to the company of those who overcome.' "

The well-known passage from Walt Whitman is a classical expression of this sporadic type of mystical experience.

> "I believe in you, my Soul . . .
> Loaf with me on the grass, loose the stop from your throat; . . .
> Only the lull I like, the hum of your valved voice.
> I mind how once we lay, such a transparent summer morning.
> Swiftly arose and spread around me the peace and knowledge that
>   pass all the argument of the earth,
> And I know that the hand of God is the promise of my own,
> And I know that the spirit of God is the brother of my own,
> And that all the men ever born are also my brothers and the
>   women my sisters and lovers,
> And that a kelson of the creation is love." . . .

We have now seen enough of this cosmic or mystic consciousness, as it comes sporadically. We must next pass to its methodical cultivation as an element of the religious life. Hindus, Buddhists, Mohammedans, and Christians all have cultivated it methodically.

In India, training in mystical insight has been known from time immemorial under the name of yoga. Yoga means the experimental union of the individual with the divine. It is based on persevering exercise; and the diet, posture, breathing, intellectual concentration, and moral discipline vary slightly in the different systems which teach it. The yogi, or disciple, who has by these means overcome the obscurations of his lower nature sufficiently, enters into the condition termed *samâdhi*, "comes face to face with facts which no instinct or reason can ever know." He learns—

"That the mind itself has a higher state of existence, beyond reason, a superconscious state, and that when the mind gets to that higher state, then this knowledge beyond reasoning comes. . . . All the different steps in yoga are intended to bring us scientifically to the superconscious state or samâdhi. . . . Just as unconscious work is beneath consciousness, so there is another work which is above consciousness, and which, also, is not accompanied with the feeling of egoism. . . . There is no feeling of *I*, and yet the mind works, desireless, free from restlessness, objectless, bodiless. Then the Truth shines in its full effulgence, and we know ourselves—for Samâdhi lies potential in us all—for what we truly are, free, immortal, omnipotent, loosed from the finite, and its contrasts of good and evil altogether, and identical with the Atman or Universal Soul."

The Vedantists say that one may stumble into superconsciousness sporadically, without the previous discipline, but it is then impure. Their test of its purity, like our test of religion's value, is empirical: its fruits must be good for life. When a man comes out of Samâdhi, they assure us that he remains "enlightened, a sage, a prophet, a saint, his whole character changed, his life changed, illumined."

The Buddhists use the word 'samâdhi' as well as the Hindus; but 'dhyâna' is their special word for higher states of contemplation. There seem to be four stages recognized in dhyâna. The first stage comes through concentration of the mind upon one point. It excludes desire, but not discernment or judgment: it is still intellectual. In the second stage the intellectual functions drop off, and the satisfied sense of unity remains. In the third stage the satisfaction departs, and indifference begins, along with memory and self-consciousness. In the fourth stage the indifference, memory, and self-consciousness are perfected. [Just what 'memory' and 'self-consciousness' mean in this connection is doubtful. They cannot be the faculties familiar to us in the lower life.] Higher stages still of contemplation are mentioned—a region where there exists nothing, and where the meditator says: "There exists absolutely nothing," and stops. Then he reaches another region where he says: "There are neither ideas nor absence of ideas," and stops again. Then another region where, "having reached the end of both idea and perception, he stops finally." This would seem to be, not yet Nirvâna, but as close an approach to it as this life affords.

In the Mohammedan world the Sufi sect and various dervish bodies are the possessors of the mystical tradition. The Sufis have existed in Persia from the earliest times, and as their pantheism is so at variance with the hot and rigid monotheism of the Arab mind, it has been suggested that Sufism must have been inoculated into Islam by Hindu influences. We Christians know little of Sufism, for its secrets are disclosed only to those initiated. To give its existence a certain liveliness in your minds, I will quote a Moslem document, and pass away from the subject.

Al-Ghazzali, a Persian philosopher and theologian, who flourished in the eleventh century, and ranks as one of the greatest doctors of the Moslem church, has left us one of the few autobiographies to be found outside of Christian literature. Strange that a species of book so abundant among ourselves should be so little represented elsewhere—the absence of strictly personal confessions is the chief difficulty to the purely literary student who would like to become acquainted with the inwardness of religions other than the Christian.

M. Schmölders has translated a part of Al-Ghazzali's autobiography into French:—

"The Science of the Sufis," says the Moslem author, "aims at detaching the heart from all that is not God, and at giving to it for sole occupation the meditation of the divine being. Theory being more easy for me than practice, I read [certain books] until I understood all that can be learned by study and hearsay. Then I recognized that what pertains most exclusively to their method is just what no study can grasp, but only transport, ecstasy, and the transformation of the soul. How great, for example, is the difference between knowing the definitions of health, of satiety, with their causes and conditions, and being really healthy or filled. How different to know in what drunkenness consists,—as being a state occasioned by a vapor that rises from the stomach,—and *being* drunk effectively. Without doubt, the drunken man knows neither the definition of drunkenness nor what makes it interesting for science. Being drunk, he knows nothing; whilst the physician, although not drunk, knows well in what drunkenness consists, and what are its predisposing conditions. Similarly there is a difference between knowing the nature of abstinence, and *being* abstinent or having one's soul detached from the world.—Thus I had learned what words could teach of Sufism, but what was left could be learned neither by study nor through the ears, but solely by giving one's self up to ecstasy and leading a pious life.

"Reflecting on my situation, I found myself tied down by a multitude of bonds— temptations on every side. Considering my teaching, I found it was impure before God. I saw myself struggling with all my might to achieve glory and to spread my name. [Here follows an account of his six months' hesitation to break away from the conditions of his life at Bagdad, at the end of which he fell ill with a paralysis of the tongue.] Then, feeling my own weakness, and having entirely given up my own will, I repaired to God like a man in distress who has no more resources. He answered, as he answers the wretch who invokes him. My heart no longer felt any difficulty in renouncing glory, wealth, and my children. So I quitted Bagdad, and reserving from my fortune only what was indispensable for my subsistence, I distributed the rest. I went to Syria, where I remained about two years, with no other occupation than living in retreat and solitude, conquering my desires, combating my passions, training myself to purify my soul, to make my character perfect, to prepare my heart for meditating on God—all according to the methods of the Sufis, as I had read of them.

"This retreat only increased my desire to live in solitude, and to complete the purification of my heart and fit it for meditation. But the vicissitudes of the times, the affairs of the family, the need of subsistence, changed in some respects my primitive resolve, and interfered with my plans for a purely solitary life. I had never yet found myself completely in ecstasy, save in a few single hours; nevertheless, I kept the hope of attaining this state. Every time that the accidents led me astray, I sought to return; and in this situation I spent ten years. During this solitary state things were revealed to me which it is impossible either to describe or to point out. I recognized for certain that the Sufis are assuredly walking in the path of God. Both in their acts and in their inaction, whether internal or external, they are illumined by the light which proceeds from the prophetic source. The first condition for a Sufi is to purge his heart entirely of all that is not God. The next key of the contemplative life consists in the humble prayers which escape from the fervent soul, and in the meditations on God in which the heart is swallowed up entirely. But in reality this is only the beginning of the Sufi life, the end of Sufism being total absorption in God. The intuitions and all that precede are, so to speak, only the threshold for those who enter. From the beginning, revelations take place in so flagrant a shape that the Sufis see before them, whilst wide awake, the angels and the souls of the prophets. They hear their voices and obtain their favors. Then the transport rises from the perception of forms and figures to a degree which escapes all expression, and which no man may seek to give an account of without his words involving sin.

"Whoever has had no experience of the transport knows of the true nature of prophetism nothing but the name. He may meanwhile be sure of its existence, both by experience and by what he hears the Sufis say. As there are men endowed only with the sensitive faculty who reject what is offered them in the way of objects of the pure understanding, so there are intellectual men who reject and avoid the things perceived by the prophetic faculty. A blind man can understand nothing of colors save what he has learned by narration and hearsay. Yet God has brought prophetism near to men in giving them all a state analogous to it in its principal characters. This state is sleep. If you were to tell a man who was himself without experience of such a phenomenon that there are people who at times swoon away so as to resemble dead men, and who [in dreams] yet perceive things that are hidden, he would deny it [and give his reasons]. Nevertheless, his arguments would be refuted by actual experience. Wherefore, just as the understanding is a stage of human life in which an eye opens to discern various intellectual objects uncomprehended by sensation; just so in the prophetic the sight is illumined by a light which uncovers hidden things and objects which the intellect fails to reach. The chief properties of prophetism are perceptible only during the transport, by those who embrace the Sufi life. The prophet is endowed with qualities to which you possess nothing analogous, and which consequently you cannot possibly understand. How should you know their true nature, since one knows only what one can comprehend? But the transport which one attains by the method of the Sufis is like an immediate perception, as if one touched the objects with one's hand."

This incommunicableness of the transport is the keynote of all mysticism. Mystical truth exists for the individual who has the transport, but for no one else. In this, as I have said, it resembles the knowledge given to us in sensations more than that given by conceptual thought. Thought, with its remoteness and abstractness, has often enough in the history of philosophy been contrasted unfavorably with sensation. It is a commonplace of metaphysics that God's knowledge cannot be discursive but must be intuitive, that is, must be constructed more after the pattern of what in ourselves is called immediate feeling, than after that of proposition and judgment. But *our* immediate feelings have no content but what the five senses supply; and we have seen and shall see again that mystics may emphatically deny that the senses play any part in the very highest type of knowledge which their transports yield.

In the Christian church there have always been mystics. Although many of them have been viewed with suspicion, some have gained favor in the eyes of the authorities. The experiences of these have been treated as precedents, and a codified system of mystical theology has been based upon them, in which everything legitimate finds its place. The basis of the system is 'orison' or meditation, the methodical elevation of the soul towards God. Through the practice of orison the higher levels of mystical experience may be attained. It is odd that Protestantism, especially evangelical Protestantism, should seemingly have abandoned everything methodical in this line. Apart from what prayer may lead to, Protestant mystical experience appears to have been almost exclusively sporadic. It has been left to our mind-curers to reintroduce methodical meditation into our religious life.

The first thing to be aimed at in orison is the mind's detachment from outer sensations, for these interfere with its concentration upon ideal things. Such manuals as Saint Ignatius's Spiritual Exercises recommend the disciple to expel sensation by a graduated series of efforts to imagine holy scenes. The acme of this kind of discipline would be a semi-hallucinatory mono-ideism—an imaginary figure of Christ, for example, coming fully to occupy the mind. Sensorial images of this sort, whether literal or symbolic, play an enormous part in mysticism. But in certain cases imagery may fall away entirely, and in the very highest raptures it tends to do so. The state of consciousness becomes then insusceptible of any verbal description. Mystical teachers are unanimous as to this. Saint John of the Cross, for instance, one of the best of them, thus describes the condition called the 'union of love,' which, he says, is reached by 'dark contemplation.' In this the Deity compenetrates the soul, but in such a hidden way that the soul—

> "finds no terms, no means, no comparison whereby to render the sublimity of the wisdom and the delicacy of the spiritual feeling with which she is filled. . . . We receive this mystical knowledge of God clothed in none of the kinds of images, in none of the sensible representations, which our mind makes use of in other circumstances. Accordingly in this knowledge, since the senses and the imagination are not employed, we get neither form nor impression, nor can we give any account or furnish any likeness, although the mysterious and sweet-tasting wisdom comes home so clearly to the inmost parts of our soul. Fancy a man seeing a certain kind of thing for the first time in his life. He can understand it, use and enjoy it, but he cannot apply a name to it, nor communicate any idea of it, even though all the while it be a mere thing of sense. How much greater will be his powerlessness when it goes beyond the senses! This is the peculiarity of the divine language. The more infused, intimate, spiritual, and supersensible it is, the more does it exceed the senses, both inner and outer, and impose silence upon them. . . . The soul then feels as if placed in a vast and profound solitude, to which no created thing has access, in an immense and boundless desert, desert the more delicious the more solitary it is. There, in this abyss of wisdom, the soul grows by what it drinks in from the well-springs of the comprehension of love, . . . and recognizes, however sublime and learned may be the terms we employ, how utterly vile, insignificant, and improper they are, when we seek to discourse of divine things by their means."

I cannot pretend to detail to you the sundry stages of the Christian mystical life. Our time would not suffice, for one thing; and moreover, I confess that the subdivisions and names which we find in the Catholic books seem to me to represent nothing objectively distinct. So many men, so many minds: I imagine that these experiences can be as infinitely varied as are the idiosyncrasies of individuals.

The cognitive aspects of them, their value in the way of revelation, is what we are directly concerned with, and it is easy to show by citation how strong an impression they leave of being revelations of new depths of truth. Saint Teresa is the expert of experts in describing such conditions, so I will turn immediately to what she says of one of the highest of them, the 'orison of union.'

> "In the orison of union," says Saint Teresa, "the soul is fully awake as regards God, but wholly asleep as regards things of this world and in respect of herself. During the short time the union lasts, she is as it were deprived of every feeling, and even if she would, she could not think of any single thing. Thus she needs to employ no artifice in order to arrest the use of her understanding: it remains so stricken with inactivity that she neither knows what she loves, nor in what manner she loves, nor what she wills. In short, she is utterly dead to the things of the world and lives solely in God. . . . I do not even know whether in this state she has enough life left to breathe. It seems to me she has not; or at least that if she does

breathe, she is unaware of it. Her intellect would fain understand something of what is going on within her, but it has so little force now that it can act in no way whatsoever. So a person who falls into a deep faint appears as if dead. . . .

"Thus does God, when he raises a soul to union with himself, suspend the natural action of all her faculties. She neither sees, hears, nor understands, so long as she is united with God. But this time is always short, and it seems even shorter than it is. God establishes himself in the interior of this soul in such a way, that when she returns to herself, it is wholly impossible for her to doubt that she has been in God, and God in her. This truth remains so strongly impressed on her that, even though many years should pass without the condition returning, she can neither forget the favor she received, nor doubt of its reality. If you, nevertheless, ask how it is possible that the soul can see and understand that she has been in God, since during the union she has neither sight nor understanding, I reply that she does not see it then, but that she sees it clearly later, after she has returned to herself, not by any vision, but by a certitude which abides with her and which God alone can give her. I knew a person who was ignorant of the truth that God's mode of being in everything must be either by presence, by power, or by essence, but who, after having received the grace of which I am speaking, believed this truth in the most unshakable manner. So much so that, having consulted a half-learned man who was as ignorant on this point as she had been before she was enlightened, when he replied that God is in us only by 'grace,' she disbelieved his reply, so sure she was of the true answer; and when she came to ask wiser doctors, they confirmed her in her belief, which much consoled her. . . .

"But how, you will repeat, *can* one have such certainty in respect to what one does not see? This question, I am powerless to answer. These are secrets of God's omnipotence which it does not appertain to me to penetrate. All that I know is that I tell the truth; and I shall never believe that any soul who does not possess this certainty has ever been really united to God."

The kinds of truth communicable in mystical ways, whether these be sensible or supersensible, are various. Some of them relate to this world,—visions of the future, the reading of hearts, the sudden understanding of texts, the knowledge of distant events, for example; but the most important revelations are theological or metaphysical.

"Saint Ignatius confessed one day to Father Laynez that a single hour of meditation at Manresa had taught him more truths about heavenly things than all the teachings of all the doctors put together could have taught him. . . . One day in orison, on the steps of the choir of the Dominican church, he saw in a distinct manner the plan of divine wisdom in the creation of the world. On another occasion, during a procession, his spirit was ravished in God, and it was given him to contemplate, in a form and images fitted to the weak understanding of a dweller on the earth, the deep mystery of the holy Trinity. This last vision flooded his heart with such sweetness, that the mere memory of it in after times made him shed abundant tears."

Similarly with Saint Teresa. "One day, being in orison," she writes, "it was granted me to perceive in one instant how all things are seen and contained in God. I did not perceive them in their proper form, and nevertheless the view I had of them was of a sovereign clearness, and has remained vividly impressed upon my soul. It is one of the most signal of all the graces which the Lord has granted me. . . . The view was so subtle and delicate that the understanding cannot grasp it."

She goes on to tell how it was as if the Deity were an enormous and sovereignly limpid diamond, in which all our actions were contained in such a way that their full sinfulness appeared evident as never before. On another day, she relates, while she was reciting the Athanasian Creed,—

> "Our Lord made me comprehend in what way it is that one God can be in three Persons. He made me see it so clearly that I remained as extremely surprised as I was comforted, . . . and now, when I think of the holy Trinity, or hear It spoken of, I understand how the three adorable Persons form only one God and I experience an unspeakable happiness."

On still another occasion, it was given to Saint Teresa to see and understand in what wise the Mother of God had been assumed into her place in Heaven.

The deliciousness of some of these states seems to be beyond anything known in ordinary consciousness. It evidently involves organic sensibilities, for it is spoken of as something too extreme to be borne, and as verging on bodily pain. But it is too subtle and piercing a delight for ordinary words to denote. God's touches, the wounds of his spear, references to ebriety and to nuptial union have to figure in the phraseology by which it is shadowed forth. Intellect and senses both swoon away in these highest states of ecstasy. "If our understanding comprehends," says Saint Teresa, "it is in a mode which remains unknown to it, and it can understand nothing of what it comprehends. For my own part, I do not believe that it does comprehend, because, as I said, it does not understand itself to do so. I confess that it is all a mystery in which I am lost." In the condition called *raptus* or ravishment by theologians, breathing and circulation are so depressed that it is a question among the doctors whether the soul be or be not temporarily dissevered from the body. One must read Saint Teresa's descriptions and the very exact distinctions which she makes, to persuade one's self that one is dealing, not with imaginary experiences, but with phenomena which, however rare, follow perfectly definite psychological types.

To the medical mind these ecstasies signify nothing but suggested and imitated hypnoid states, on an intellectual basis of superstition, and a corporeal one of degeneration and hysteria. Undoubtedly these pathological conditions have existed in many and possibly in all the cases, but that fact tells us nothing about the value for knowledge of the consciousness which they induce. To pass a spiritual judgment upon these states, we must not content ourselves with superficial medical talk, but inquire into their fruits for life.

Their fruits appear to have been various. Stupefaction, for one thing, seems not to have been altogether absent as a result. You may remember the helplessness in the kitchen and schoolroom of poor Margaret Mary Alacoque. Many other ecstatics would have perished but for the care taken of them by admiring followers. The 'otherworldliness' encouraged by the mystical consciousness makes this over-abstraction from practical life peculiarly liable to befall mystics in whom the character is naturally passive and the intellect feeble; but in natively strong minds and characters we find quite opposite results. The great Spanish mystics, who carried the habit of ecstasy as far as it has often been carried, appear for the most part to have shown indomitable spirit and energy, and all the more so for the trances in which they indulged.

Saint Ignatius was a mystic, but his mysticism made him assuredly one of the most powerfully practical human engines that ever lived. Saint John of the Cross, writing of the intuitions and 'touches' by which God reaches the substance of the soul, tells us that—

"They enrich it marvelously. A single one of them may be sufficient to abolish at a stroke certain imperfections of which the soul during its whole life had vainly tried to rid itself, and to leave it adorned with virtues and loaded with supernatural gifts. A single one of these intoxicating consolations may reward it for all the labors undergone in its life—even were they numberless. Invested with an invincible courage, filled with an impassioned desire to suffer for its God, the soul then is seized with a strange torment—that of not being allowed to suffer enough."

Saint Teresa is as emphatic, and much more detailed. You may perhaps remember a passage I quoted from her in my first lecture. There are many similar pages in her autobiography. Where in literature is a more evidently veracious account of the formation of a new centre of spiritual energy than is given in her description of the effects of certain ecstasies which in departing leave the soul upon a higher level of emotional excitement?

"Often, infirm and wrought upon with dreadful pains before the ecstasy, the soul emerges from it full of health and admirably disposed for action . . . as if God had willed that the body itself, already obedient to the soul's desires, should share in the soul's happiness. . . . The soul after such a favor is animated with a degree of courage so great that if at that moment its body should be torn to pieces for the cause of God, it would feel nothing but the liveliest comfort. Then it is that promises and heroic resolutions spring up in profusion in us, soaring desires, horror of the world, and the clear perception of our proper nothingness. . . . What empire is comparable to that of a soul who, from this sublime summit to which God has raised her, sees all the things of earth beneath her feet, and is captivated by no one of them? How ashamed she is of her former attachments! How amazed at her blindness! What lively pity she feels for those whom she recognizes still shrouded in the darkness! . . . She groans at having ever been sensitive to points of honor, at the illusion that made her ever see as honor what the world calls by that name. Now she sees in this name nothing more than an immense lie of which the world remains a victim. She discovers, in the new light from above, that in genuine honor there is nothing spurious, that to be faithful to this honor is to give our respect to what deserves to be respected really, and to consider as nothing, or as less than nothing, whatsoever perishes and is not agreeable to God. . . . She laughs when she sees grave persons, persons of orison, caring for points of honor for which she now feels profoundest contempt. It is suitable to the dignity of their rank to act thus, they pretend, and it makes them more useful to others. But she knows that in despising the dignity of their rank for the pure love of God they would do more good in a single day than they would effect in ten years by preserving it. . . . She laughs at herself that there should ever have been a time in her life when she made any case of money, when she ever desired it. . . . Oh! if human beings might only agree together to regard it as so much useless mud, what harmony would then reign in the world! With what friendship we would all treat each other if our interest in honor and in money could but disappear from earth! For my own part, I feel as if it would be a remedy for all our ills."

Mystical conditions may, therefore, render the soul more energetic in the lines which their inspiration favors. But this could be reckoned an advantage only in case the inspiration were a true one. If the inspiration were erroneous, the energy would be all the more mistaken and misbegotten. So we stand once more before that problem of truth which confronted us at the end of the lectures on saintliness. You will remember that we turned to mysticism precisely to get some light on truth. Do mystical states establish the truth of those theological affections in which the saintly life has its root?

In spite of their repudiation of articulate self-description, mystical states in general assert a pretty distinct theoretic drift. It is possible to give the outcome of the majority of them in terms that point in definite philosophical directions. One of these directions is optimism, and the other is monism. We pass into mystical states from out of ordinary consciousness as from a less into a more, as from a smallness into a vastness, and at the same time as from an unrest to a rest. We feel them as reconciling, unifying states. They appeal to the yes-function more than to the no-function in us. In them the unlimited absorbs the limits and peacefully closes the account. Their very denial of every adjective you may propose as applicable to the ultimate truth,—He, the Self, the Atman, is to be described by 'No! no!' only, say the Upanishads—though it seems on the surface to be a no-function, is a denial made on behalf of a deeper yes. Whoso calls the Absolute anything in particular, or says that it is *this*, seems implicitly to shut it off from being *that*—it is as if he lessened it. So we deny the 'this,' negating the negation which it seems to us to imply, in the interests of the higher affirmative attitude by which we are possessed. The fountain-head of Christian mysticism is Dionysius the Areopagite. He describes the absolute truth by negatives exclusively.

> "The cause of all things is neither soul nor intellect; nor has it imagination, opinion, or reason, or intelligence; nor is it reason or intelligence; nor is it spoken or thought. It is neither number, nor order, nor magnitude, nor littleness, nor equality, nor inequality, nor similarity, nor dissimilarity. It neither stands, nor moves, nor rests. . . . It is neither essence, nor eternity, nor time. Even intellectual contact does not belong to it. It is neither science nor truth. It is not even royalty or wisdom; not one; not unity; not divinity or goodness; nor even spirit as we know it," etc., *ad libitum*.

But these qualifications are denied by Dionysius, not because the truth falls short of them, but because it so infinitely excels them. It is above them. It is *super*-lucent, *super*-splendent, *super*-essential, *super*-sublime, *super* everything that can be named. Like Hegel in his logic, mystics journey towards the positive pole of truth only by the 'Methode der Absoluten Negativität.'

Thus come the paradoxical expressions that so abound in mystical writings. As when Eckhart tells of the still desert of the Godhead, "where never was seen difference, neither Father, Son, nor Holy Ghost, where there is no one at home, yet where the spark of the soul is more at peace than in itself." As when Boehme writes of the Primal Love, that "it may fitly be compared to Nothing, for it is deeper than any Thing, and is as nothing with respect to all things, forasmuch as it is not comprehensible by any of them. And because it is nothing respectively, it is therefore free from all things, and is that only good, which a man cannot express or utter what it is, there being nothing to which it may be compared, to express it by." Or as when Angelus Silesius sings:—

> "Gott ist ein lauter Nichts, ihn rührt kein Nun noch Hier;
> Je mehr du nach ihm greiffst, je mehr entwind er dir."

To this dialectical use, by the intellect, of negation as a mode of passage towards a higher kind of affirmation, there is correlated the subtlest of moral counterparts in the sphere of the personal will. Since denial of the finite self and its wants, since asceticism of some sort, is found in religious experience to be the only doorway to the larger and more blessed life, this moral mystery intertwines and combines with the intellectual mystery in all mystical writings.

> "Love," continues Behmen, is Nothing, for "when thou art gone forth wholly from the Creature and from that which is visible, and art become Nothing to all that is Nature and Creature, then thou art in that eternal One, which is God himself, and then thou shalt feel within thee the highest virtue of Love. . . . The treasure of treasures for the soul is where she goeth out of the Somewhat into that Nothing out of which all things may be made. The soul here saith, *I have nothing*, for I am utterly stripped and naked; *I can do nothing*, for I have no manner of power, but am as water poured out; *I am nothing*, for all that I am is no more than an image of Being, and only God is to me I AM; and so, sitting down in my own Nothingness, I give glory to the eternal Being, and *will nothing* of myself, that so God may will all in me, being unto me my God and all things."

In Paul's language, I live, yet not I, but Christ liveth in me. Only when I become as nothing can God enter in and no difference between his life and mine remain outstanding.

This overcoming of all the usual barriers between the individual and the Absolute is the great mystic achievement. In mystic states we both become one with the Absolute and we become aware of our oneness. This is the everlasting and triumphant mystical tradition, hardly altered by differences of clime or creed. In Hinduism, in Neoplatonism, in Sufism, in Christian mysticism, in Whitmanism, we find the same recurring note, so that there is about mystical utterances an eternal unanimity which ought to make a critic stop and think, and which brings it about that the mystical classics have, as has been said, neither birthday nor native land. Perpetually telling of the unity of man with God, their speech antedates languages, and they do not grow old.

'That art Thou!' say the Upanishads, and the Vedantists add: 'Not a part, not a mode of That, but identically That, that absolute Spirit of the World.' "As pure water poured into pure water remains the same, thus, O Gautama, is the Self of a thinker who knows. Water in water, fire in fire, ether in ether, no one can distinguish them; likewise a man whose mind has entered into the Self." "'Every man,' says the Sufi Gulshan-Râz, 'whose heart is no longer shaken by any doubt, knows with certainty that there is no being save only One. . . . In his divine majesty the *me*, the *we*, the *thou*, are not found, for in the One there can be no distinction. Every being who is annulled and entirely separated from himself, hears resound outside of him this voice and this echo: *I am God:* he has an eternal way of existing, and is no longer subject to death.' " In the vision of God, says Plotinus, "what sees is not our reason, but something prior and superior to our reason. . . . He who thus sees does not properly see, does not distinguish or imagine two things. He changes, he ceases to be himself, preserves nothing of himself. Absorbed in God, he makes but one with him, like a centre of a circle coinciding with another centre." "Here," writes Suso, "the spirit dies, and yet is all alive in the marvels of the Godhead . . . and is lost in the stillness of the glorious dazzling obscurity and of the naked simple unity. It is in this modeless *where* that the highest bliss is to be found." "Ich bin so gross als Gott," sings Angelus Silesius again, "Er ist als ich so klein; Er kann nicht über mich, ich unter ihm nicht sein."

In mystical literature such self-contradictory phrases as 'dazzling obscurity,' 'whispering silence,' 'teeming desert,' are continually met with. They prove that not conceptual speech, but music rather, is the element through which we are best spoken to by mystical truth. Many mystical scriptures are indeed little more than musical compositions.

> "He who would hear the voice of Nada, 'the Soundless Sound,' and comprehend it, he has to learn the nature of Dhâranâ. . . . When to himself his form appears unreal, as do on waking all the forms he sees in dreams; when he has ceased to hear the many, he may discern the ONE—the inner sound which kills the outer. . . . For then the soul will hear, and will remember. And then to the inner ear will speak THE VOICE OF THE SILENCE. . . . And now thy *Self* is lost in SELF, *thyself* unto THYSELF, merged in that SELF from which thou first didst radiate. . . . Behold! thou hast become the Light, thou hast become the Sound, thou art thy Master and thy God. Thou art THYSELF the object of thy search: the VOICE unbroken, that resounds throughout eternities, exempt from change, from sin exempt, the seven sounds in one, the VOICE OF THE SILENCE. *Om tat Sat.*"

These words, if they do not awaken laughter as you receive them, probably stir chords within you which music and language touch in common. Music gives us ontological messages which non-musical criticism is unable to contradict, though it may laugh at our foolishness in minding them. There is a verge of the mind which these things haunt; and whispers therefrom mingle with the operations of our understanding, even as the waters of the infinite ocean send their waves to break among the pebbles that lie upon our shores.

> "Here begins the sea that ends not till the world's end. Where we
>   stand,
> Could we know the next high sea-mark set beyond these waves that
>   gleam,
> We should know what never man hath known, nor eye of man
>   hath scanned. . . .
> Ah, but here man's heart leaps, yearning towards the gloom with
>   venturous glee,
> From the shore that hath no shore beyond it, set in all the sea."

That doctrine, for example, that eternity is timeless, that our 'immortality,' if we live in the eternal, is not so much future as already now and here, which we find so often expressed to-day in certain philosophic circles, finds its support in a 'hear, hear!' or an 'amen,' which floats up from that mysteriously deeper level. We recognize the passwords to the mystical region as we hear them, but we cannot use them ourselves; it alone has the keeping of 'the password primeval.'

I have now sketched with extreme brevity and insufficiency, but as fairly as I am able in the time allowed, the general traits of the mystic range of consciousness. *It is on the whole pantheistic and optimistic, or at least the opposite of pessimistic. It is anti-naturalistic, and harmonizes best with twice-bornness and so-called other-worldly states of mind.*

My next task is to inquire whether we can invoke it as authoritative. Does it furnish any *warrant for the truth* of the twice-bornness and supernaturality and pantheism which it favors? I must give my answer to this question as concisely as I can.

In brief my answer is this,—and I will divide it into three parts:—

(1) Mystical states, when well developed, usually are, and have the right to be, absolutely authoritative over the individuals to whom they come.

(2) No authority emanates from them which should make it a duty for those who stand outside of them to accept their revelations uncritically.

(3) They break down the authority of the non-mystical or rationalistic consciousness, based upon the understanding and the senses alone. They show it to be only one kind of consciousness. They open out the possibility of other orders of truth, in which, so far as anything in us vitally responds to them, we may freely continue to have faith.

I will take up these points one by one.

1.

As a matter of psychological fact, mystical states of a well-pronounced and emphatic sort *are* usually authoritative over those who have them. They have been 'there,' and know. It is vain for rationalism to grumble about this. If the mystical truth that comes to a man proves to be a force that he can live by, what mandate have we of the majority to order him to live in another way? We can throw him into prison or a madhouse, but we cannot change his mind—we commonly attach it only the more stubbornly to its beliefs. It mocks our utmost efforts, as a matter of fact, and in point of logic it absolutely escapes our jurisdiction. Our own more 'rational' beliefs are based on evidence exactly similar in nature to that which mystics quote for theirs. Our senses, namely, have assured us of certain states of fact; but mystical experiences are as direct perceptions of fact for those who have them as any sensations ever were for us. The records show that even though the five senses be in abeyance in them, they are absolutely sensational in their epistemological quality, if I may be pardoned the barbarous expression,—that is, they are face to face presentations of what seems immediately to exist.

The mystic is, in short, *invulnerable*, and must be left, whether we relish it or not, in undisturbed enjoyment of his creed. Faith, says Tolstoy, is that by which men live. And faith-state and mystic state are practically convertible terms.

2.

But I now proceed to add that mystics have no right to claim that we ought to accept the deliverance of their peculiar experiences, if we are ourselves outsiders and feel no private call thereto. The utmost they can ever ask of us in this life is to admit that they establish a presumption. They form a consensus and have an unequivocal outcome;

and it would be odd, mystics might say, if such a unanimous type of experience should prove to be altogether wrong. At bottom, however, this would only be an appeal to numbers, like the appeal of rationalism the other way; and the appeal to numbers has no logical force. If we acknowledge it, it is for 'suggestive,' not for logical reasons: we follow the majority because to do so suits our life.

But even this presumption from the unanimity of mystics is far from being strong. In characterizing mystic states as pantheistic, optimistic, etc., I am afraid I over-simplified the truth. I did so for expository reasons, and to keep the closer to the classic mystical tradition. The classic religious mysticism, it now must be confessed, is only a 'privileged case.' It is an *extract*, kept true to type by the selection of the fittest specimens and their preservation in 'schools.' It is carved out from a much larger mass; and if we take the larger mass as seriously as religious mysticism has historically taken itself, we find that the supposed unanimity largely disappears. To begin with, even religious mysticism itself, the kind that accumulates traditions and makes schools, is much less unanimous than I have allowed. It has been both ascetic and antinomianly self-indulgent within the Christian church. It is dualistic in Sankhya, and monistic in Vedanta philosophy. I called it pantheistic; but the great Spanish mystics are anything but pantheists. They are with few exceptions non-metaphysical minds, for whom 'the category of personality' is absolute. The 'union' of man with God is for them much more like an occasional miracle than like an original identity. How different again, apart from the happiness common to all, is the mysticism of Walt Whitman, Edward Carpenter, Richard Jefferies, and other naturalistic pantheists, from the more distinctively Christian sort. The fact is that the mystical feeling of enlargement, union, and emancipation has no specific intellectual content whatever of its own. It is capable of forming matrimonial alliances with material furnished by the most diverse philosophies and theologies, provided only they can find a place in their framework for its peculiar emotional mood. We have no right, therefore, to invoke its prestige as distinctively in favor of any special belief, such as that in absolute idealism, or in the absolute monistic identity, or in the absolute goodness, of the world. It is only relatively in favor of all these things— it passes out of common human consciousness in the direction in which they lie.

So much for religious mysticism proper. But more remains to be told, for religious mysticism is only one half of mysticism. The other half has no accumulated traditions except those which the text-books on insanity supply. Open any one of these, and you will find abundant cases in which 'mystical ideas' are cited as characteristic symptoms of enfeebled or deluded states of mind. In delusional insanity, paranoia, as they sometimes call it, we may have a *diabolical* mysticism, a sort of religious mysticism turned upside down. The same sense of ineffable importance in the smallest events, the same texts and words coming with new meanings, the same voices and visions and leadings and missions, the same controlling by extraneous powers; only this time the emotion is pessimistic: instead of consolations we have desolations; the meanings are dreadful; and the powers are enemies to life. It is evident that from the point of view of their psychological mechanism, the classic mysticism and these lower mysticisms spring from the same mental level, from that great subliminal or trans-marginal region of which science is beginning to admit the existence, but of which so little is really known. That region contains every kind of matter:

'seraph and snake' abide there side by side. To come from thence is no infallible credential. What comes must be sifted and tested, and run the gauntlet of confrontation with the total context of experience, just like what comes from the outer world of sense. Its value must be ascertained by empirical methods, so long as we are not mystics ourselves.

Once more, then, I repeat that non-mystics are under no obligation to acknowledge in mystical states a superior authority conferred on them by their intrinsic nature.

3.

Yet, I repeat once more, the existence of mystical states absolutely overthrows the pretension of non-mystical states to be the sole and ultimate dictators of what we may believe. As a rule, mystical states merely add a supersensuous meaning to the ordinary outward data of consciousness. They are excitements like the emotions of love or ambition, gifts to our spirit by means of which facts already objectively before us fall into a new expressiveness and make a new connection with our active life. They do not contradict these facts as such, or deny anything that our senses have immediately seized. It is the rationalistic critic rather who plays the part of denier in the controversy, and his denials have no strength, for there never can be a state of facts to which new meaning may not truthfully be added, provided the mind ascend to a more enveloping point of view. It must always remain an open question whether mystical states may not possibly be such superior points of view, windows through which the mind looks out upon a more extensive and inclusive world. The difference of the views seen from the different mystical windows need not prevent us from entertaining this supposition. The wider world would in that case prove to have a mixed constitution like that of this world, that is all. It would have its celestial and its infernal regions, its tempting and its saving moments, its valid experiences and its counterfeit ones, just as our world has them; but it would be a wider world all the same. We should have to use its experiences by selecting and subordinating and substituting just as is our custom in this ordinary naturalistic world; we should be liable to error just as we are now; yet the counting in of that wider world of meanings, and the serious dealing with it, might, in spite of all the perplexity, be indispensable stages in our approach to the final fullness of the truth.

In this shape, I think, we have to leave the subject. Mystical states indeed wield no authority due simply to their being mystical states. But the higher ones among them point in directions to which the religious sentiments even of non-mystical men incline. They tell of the supremacy of the ideal, of vastness, of union, of safety, and of rest. They offer us *hypotheses,* hypotheses which we may voluntarily ignore, but which as thinkers we cannot possibly upset. The supernaturalism and optimism to which they would persuade us may, interpreted in one way or another, be after all the truest of insights into the meaning of this life.

"Oh, the little more, and how much it is; and the little less, and what worlds away!" It may be that possibility and permission of this sort are all that the religious consciousness requires to live on. In my last lecture I shall have to try to persuade you that this is the case. Meanwhile, however, I am sure that for many of my readers this diet is too slender. If supernaturalism and inner union with the divine are true, you think, then not so much permission, as compulsion to believe, ought to be found. Philosophy has always professed to prove religious truth by coercive argument; and the construction of philosophies of this kind has always been one favorite function of the religious life, if we use this term in the large historic sense. But religious philosophy is an enormous subject, and in my next lecture I can only give that brief glance at it which my limits will allow.

◼

39. Contemplation

Thomas Merton

What Is Contemplation?

Contemplation is the highest expression of man's intellectual and spiritual life. It is that life itself, fully awake, fully active, fully aware that it is alive. It is spiritual wonder. It is spontaneous awe at the sacredness of life, of being. It is gratitude for life, for awareness and for being. It is a vivid realization of the fact that life and being in us proceed from an invisible, transcendent and infinitely abundant Source. Contemplation is, above all, awareness of the reality of that Source. It *knows* the Source, obscurely, inexplicably, but with a certitude that goes both beyond reason and beyond simple faith. For contemplation is a kind of spiritual vision to which both reason and faith aspire, by their very nature, because without it they must always remain incomplete. Yet contemplation is not vision because it sees "without seeing" and knows "without knowing." It is a more profound depth of faith, a knowledge too deep to be grasped in images, in words or even in clear concepts. It can be suggested by words, by symbols, but in the very moment of trying to indicate what it knows the contemplative mind takes back what it has said, and denies what it has affirmed. For in contemplation we know by "unknowing." Or, better, we know *beyond* all knowing or "unknowing."

Poetry, music and art have something in common with the contemplative experience. But contemplation is beyond aesthetic intuition, beyond art, beyond poetry. Indeed, it is also beyond philosophy, beyond speculative theology. It resumes, transcends and fulfills them all, and yet at the same time it seems, in a certain way, to supersede and to deny

---

Source: Thomas Merton, from *New Seeds of Contemplation,* © 1961 by The Abbey of Gethsemani, Inc. Reprinted by permission of New Directions Publishing Corp.

them all. Contemplation is always beyond our own knowledge, beyond our own light, beyond systems, beyond explanations, beyond discourse, beyond dialogue, beyond our own self. To enter into the realm of contemplation one must in a certain sense die: but this death is in fact the entrance into a higher life. It is a death for the sake of life, which leaves behind all that we can know or treasure as life, as thought, as experience, as joy, as being.

And so contemplation seems to supersede and to discard every other form of intuition and experience—whether in art, in philosophy, in theology, in liturgy or in ordinary levels of love and of belief. This rejection is of course only apparent. Contemplation is and must be compatible with all these things, for it is their highest fulfillment. But in the actual experience of contemplation all other experiences are momentarily lost. They "die" to be born again on a higher level of life.

In other words, then, contemplation reaches out to the knowledge and even to the experience of the transcendent and inexpressible God. It knows God by seeming to touch Him. Or rather it knows Him as if it had been invisibly touched by Him.... Touched by Him Who has no hands, but Who is pure Reality and the source of all that is real! Hence contemplation is a sudden gift of awareness, an awakening to the Real within all that is real. A vivid awareness of infinite Being at the roots of our own limited being. An awareness of our contingent reality as received, as a present from God, as a free gift of love. This is the existential contact of which we speak when we use the metaphor of being "touched by God."

Contemplation is also the response to a call: a call from Him Who has no voice, and yet Who speaks in everything that is, and Who, most of all, speaks in the depths of our own being: for we ourselves are words of His. But we are words that are meant to respond to Him, to answer to Him, to echo Him, and even in some way to contain Him and signify Him. Contemplation is this echo. It is a deep resonance in the inmost center of our spirit in which our very life loses its separate voice and re-sounds with the majesty and the mercy of the Hidden and Living One. He answers Himself in us and this answer is divine life, divine creativity, making all things new. We ourselves become His echo and His answer. It is as if in creating us God asked a question, and in awakening us to contemplation He answered the question, so that the contemplative is at the same time, question and answer.

The life of contemplation implies two levels of awareness: first, awareness of the question, and second, awareness of the answer. Though these are two distinct and enormously different levels, yet they are in fact an awareness of the same thing. The question is, itself, the answer. And we ourselves are both. But we cannot know this until we have moved into the second kind of awareness. We awaken, not to find an answer absolutely distinct from the question, but to realize that the question is its own answer. And all is summed up in one awareness—not a proposition, but an experience: "I AM."

The contemplation of which I speak here is not philosophical. It is not the static awareness of metaphysical essences apprehended as spiritual objects, unchanging and eternal. It is not the contemplation of abstract ideas. It is the religious apprehension of God, through my life in God, or through "sonship" as the New Testament says. "For whoever are led by the Spirit of God, they are the sons of God. . . . The Spirit Himself gives testimony to our own spirit that we are the sons of God." "To as many as received

Him He gave the power to become the sons of God. . . ." And so the contemplation of which I speak is a religious and transcendent gift. It is not something to which we can attain alone, by intellectual effort, by perfecting our natural powers. It is not a kind of self-hypnosis, resulting from concentration on our own inner spiritual being. It is not the fruit of our own efforts. It is the gift of God Who, in His mercy, completes the hidden and mysterious work of creation in us by enlightening our minds and hearts, by awakening in us the awareness that we are words spoken in His One Word, and that Creating Spirit (*Creator Spiritus*) dwells in us, and we in Him. That we are "in Christ" and that Christ lives in us. That the natural life in us has been completed, elevated, transformed and fulfilled in Christ by the Holy Spirit. Contemplation is the awareness and realization, even in some sense *experience,* of what each Christian obscurely believes: "It is now no longer I that live but Christ lives in me."

Hence contemplation is more than a consideration of abstract truths about God, more even than affective meditation on the things we believe. It is awakening, enlightenment and the amazing intuitive grasp by which love gains certitude of God's creative and dynamic intervention in our daily life. Hence contemplation does not simply "find" a clear idea of God and confine Him within the limits of that idea, and hold Him there as a prisoner to Whom it can always return. On the contrary, contemplation is carried away by Him into His own realm, His own mystery and His own freedom. It is a pure and a virginal knowledge, poor in concepts, poorer still in reasoning, but able, by its very poverty and purity, to follow the Word "wherever He may go."

What Contemplation Is Not

The only way to get rid of misconceptions about contemplation is to experience it. One who does not actually know, in his own life, the nature of this breakthrough and this awakening to a new level of reality cannot help being misled by most of the things that are said about it. For contemplation cannot be taught. It cannot even be clearly explained. It can only be hinted at, suggested, pointed to, symbolized. The more objectively and scientifically one tries to analyze it, the more he empties it of its real content, for this experience is beyond the reach of verbalization and of rationalization. Nothing is more repellent than a pseudo-scientific definition of the contemplative experience. One reason for this is that he who attempts such a definition is tempted to procede psychologically, and there is really no adequate *psychology* of contemplation. To describe "reactions" and "feelings" is to situate contemplation where it is not to be found, in the superficial consciousness where it can be observed by reflection. But this reflection and this consciousness are precisely part of that external self which "dies" and is cast aside like a soiled garment in the genuine awakening of the contemplative.

Contemplation is not and cannot be a function of this external self. There is an irreducible opposition between the deep transcendent self that awakens only in contemplation, and the superficial, external self which we commonly identify with the first person singular. We must remember that this superficial "I" is not our real self. It is our "individuality" and our "empirical self" but it is not truly the hidden and mysterious person in whom we subsist before the eyes of God. The "I" that works in the world, thinks about itself, observes its own reactions and talks about itself is not the true "I" that has been united to God in Christ. It is at best the vesture, the mask, the disguise of that mysterious and unknown "self" whom most of us never discover until we are dead.* Our external, superficial self is not eternal, not spiritual. Far from it. This self is doomed to disappear as completely as smoke from a chimney. It is utterly frail and evanescent. Contemplation is precisely the awareness that this "I" is really "not I" and the awakening of the unknown "I" that is beyond observation and reflection and is incapable of commenting upon itself. It cannot even say "I" with the assurance and the impertinence of the other one, for its very nature is to be hidden, unnamed, unidentified in the society where men talk about themselves and about one another. In such a world the true "I" remains both inarticulate and invisible, because it has altogether too much to say—not one word of which is about itself.

Nothing could be more alien to contemplation than the *cogito ergo sum* of Descartes. "I think, therefore I am." This is the declaration of an alienated being, in exile from his own spiritual depths, compelled to seek some comfort in a *proof for his own existence*(!) based on the observation that he "thinks." If his thought is necessary as a medium through which he arrives at the concept of his existence, then he is in fact only moving further away from his true being. He is reducing himself to a concept. He is making it impossible for himself to experience, directly and immediately, the mystery of his own being. At the same time, by also reducing God to a concept, he makes it impossible for himself to have any intuition of the divine reality which is inexpressible. He arrives at his own being as if it were an objective reality, that is to say he strives to become aware of himself as he would of some "thing" alien to himself. And he proves that the "thing" exists. He convinces himself: "I am therefore some *thing*." And then he goes on to convince himself that God, the infinite, the transcendent, is also a "thing," an "object," like other finite and limited objects of our thought!

Contemplation, on the contrary, is the experiential grasp of reality as *subjective*, not so much "mine" (which would signify "belonging to the external self") but "myself" in existential mystery. Contemplation does not arrive at reality after a process of deduction, but by an intuitive awakening in which our free and personal reality becomes fully alive to its own existential depths, which open out into the mystery of God.

For the contemplative there is no *cogito* ("I think") and no *ergo* ("therefore") but only *SUM*, I AM. Not in the sense of a futile assertion of our individuality as ultimately real, but in the humble realization of our mysterious being as persons in whom God dwells, with infinite sweetness and inalienable power.

Obviously contemplation is not just the affair of a passive and quiet temperament. It is not mere inertia, a tendency to inactivity, to psychic peace. The contemplative is not merely a man who likes to sit and think, still less one who sits around with a vacant stare. Contemplation is much more than thoughtfulness or a taste for reflection. Certainly, a thoughtful and reflective disposition is nothing to be despised in our world of inanity and automatism—and it can very well dispose a man for contemplation.

---

*"Hell" can be described as a perpetual alienation from our true being, our true self, which is in God.

Contemplation is not prayerfulness, or a tendency to find peace and satisfaction in liturgical rites. These, too, are a great good, and they are almost necessary preparations for contemplative experience. They can never, of themselves, constitute that experience. Contemplative intuition has nothing to do with temperament. Though it sometimes happens that a man of quiet temperament becomes a contemplative, it may also happen that the very passivity of his character keeps him from suffering the inner struggle and the crisis through which one generally comes to a deeper spiritual awakening.

On the other hand, it can happen that an active and passionate man awakens to contemplation, and perhaps suddenly, without too much struggle. But it must be said, as a rule, that certain active types are not disposed to contemplation and never come to it except with great difficulty. Indeed, they ought perhaps not even to think about it or seek it, because in doing so they will tend to strain themselves and injure themselves by absurd efforts that cannot possibly make any sense or have any useful purpose. Such people, being given to imagination, passion and active conquest, exhaust themselves in trying to attain contemplation as if it were some kind of an object, like a material fortune, or a political office, or a professorship, or a prelacy. But contemplation can never be the object of calculated ambition. It is not something we plan to obtain with our practical reason, but the living water of the spirit that we thirst for, like a hunted deer thirsting after a river in the wilderness.

It is not we who choose to awaken ourselves, but God Who chooses to awaken us.

Contemplation is not trance or ecstasy, nor the hearing of sudden unutterable words, nor the imagination of lights. It is not the emotional fire and sweetness that come with religious exaltation. It is not enthusiasm, the sense of being "seized" by an elemental force and swept into liberation by mystical frenzy. These things may seem to be in some way like a contemplative awakening in so far as they suspend the ordinary awareness and control exercised by our empirical self. But they are not the work of the "deep self," only of the emotions, of the somatic unconscious. They are a flooding up of the dionysian forces of the "id." Such manifestations can of course accompany a deep and genuine religious experience, but they are not what I am talking about here as contemplation.

Nor is contemplation the gift of prophecy, nor does it imply the ability to read the secrets of mens' hearts. These things can sometimes go along with contemplation but they are not essential to it, and it would be erroneous to confuse them with it.

There are many other escapes from the empirical, external self, which might seem to be, but are not, contemplation. For instance, the experience of being seized and taken out of oneself by collective enthusiasm, in a totalitarian parade: the self-righteous upsurge of party loyalty that blots out conscience and absolves every criminal tendency in the name of Class, Nation, Party, Race or Sect. The danger and the attraction of these false mystiques of Nation and of Class is precisely that they seduce and pretend to satisfy those who are no longer aware of any deep or genuine spiritual need. The false mysticism of the Mass Society captivates men who are so alienated from themselves and from God that they are no longer capable of genuine spiritual experience. Yet it is precisely these ersatz forms of enthusiasm that are "opium" for the people, deadening their awareness of their deepest and most personal needs, alienating them from their true selves, putting conscience and personality to sleep and turning free, reasonable men into passive instruments of the power politician.

Let no one hope to find in contemplation an escape from conflict, from anguish or from doubt. On the contrary, the deep, inexpressible certitude of the contemplative experience awakens a tragic anguish and opens many questions in the depths of the heart like wounds that cannot stop bleeding. For every gain in deep certitude there is a corresponding growth of superficial "doubt." This doubt is by no means opposed to genuine faith, but it mercilessly examines and questions the spurious "faith" of everyday life, the human faith which is nothing but the passive acceptance of conventional opinion. This false "faith" which is what we often live by and which we even come to confuse with our "religion" is subjected to inexorable questioning. This torment is a kind of trial by fire in which we are compelled, by the very light of invisible truth which has reached us in the dark ray of contemplation, to examine, to doubt and finally to reject all the prejudices and conventions that we have hitherto accepted as if they were dogmas. Hence is it clear that genuine contemplation is incompatible with complacency and with smug acceptance of prejudiced opinions. It is not mere passive acquiescence in the *status quo,* as some would like to believe—for this would reduce it to the level of spiritual anesthesia. Contemplation is no pain-killer. What a holocaust takes place in this steady burning to ashes of old worn-out words, clichés, slogans, rationalizations! The worst of it is that even apparently *holy* conceptions are consumed along with all the rest. It is a terrible breaking and burning of idols, a purification of the sanctuary, so that no graven thing may occupy the place that God has commanded to be left empty: the center, the existential altar which simply "is."

In the end the contemplative suffers the anguish of realizing that he *no longer knows what God is.* He may or may not mercifully realize that, after all, this is a great gain, because "God is not a *what,*" not a "thing." That is precisely one of the essential characteristics of contemplative experience. It sees that there is no "what" that can be called God. There is "no such thing" as God because God is neither a "what" nor a "thing" but a pure "*Who.*"* He is the "Thou" before whom our inmost "I" springs into awareness. He is the I Am before whom with our own most personal and inalienable voice we echo "I am."

Seeds of Contemplation

Every moment and every event of every man's life on earth plants something in his soul. For just as the wind carries thousands of winged seeds, so each moment brings with it germs of spiritual vitality that come to rest imperceptibly in the minds and wills of men. Most of these unnumbered seeds perish and are lost, because men are not

---

*This should not be taken to mean that man has no valid concept of the divine nature. Yet in contemplation abstract notions of the divine essence no longer play an important part since they are replaced by a concrete intuition, based on love, of God as a *Person,* an object of love, not a "nature" or a "thing" which would be the object of study or of possessive desire.

prepared to receive them: for such seeds as these cannot spring up anywhere except in the good soil of freedom, spontaneity and love.

This is no new idea. Christ in the parable of the sower long ago told us that "The seed is the word of God." We often think this applies only to the word of the Gospel as formally preached in churches on Sundays (if indeed it is preached in churches any more!). But every expression of the will of God is in some sense a "word" of God and therefore a "seed" of new life. The ever-changing reality in the midst of which we live should awaken us to the possibility of an uninterrupted dialogue with God. By this I do not mean continuous "talk," or a frivolously conversational form of affective prayer which is sometimes cultivated in convents, but a dialogue of love and of choice. A dialogue of deep wills.

In all the situations of life the "will of God" comes to us not merely as an external dictate of impersonal law but above all as an interior invitation of personal love. Too often the conventional conception of "God's will" as a sphinx-like and arbitrary force bearing down upon us with implacable hostility, leads men to lose faith in a God they cannot find it possible to love. Such a view of the divine will drives human weakness to despair and one wonders if it is not, itself, often the expression of a despair too intolerable to be admitted to conscious consideration. These arbitrary "dictates" of a domineering and insensible Father are more often seeds of hatred than of love. If that is our concept of the will of God, we cannot possibly seek the obscure and intimate mystery of the encounter that takes place in contemplation. We will desire only to fly as far as possible from Him and hide from His Face forever. So much depends on our idea of God! Yet no idea of Him, however pure and perfect, is adequate to express Him as He really is. Our idea of God tells us more about ourselves than about Him.

We must learn to realize that the love of God seeks us in every situation, and seeks our good. His inscrutable love seeks our awakening. True, since this awakening implies a kind of death to our exterior self, we will dread His coming in proportion as we are identified with this exterior self and attached to it. But when we understand the dialectic of life and death we will learn to take the risks implied by faith, to make the choices that deliver us from our routine self and open to us the door of a new being, a new reality.

The mind that is the prisoner of conventional ideas, and the will that is the captive of its own desire cannot accept the seeds of an unfamiliar truth and a supernatural desire. For how can I receive the seeds of freedom if I am in love with slavery and how can I cherish the desire of God if I am filled with another and an opposite desire? God cannot plant His liberty in me because I am a prisoner and I do not even desire to be free. I love my captivity and I imprison myself in the desire for the things that I hate, and I have hardened my heart against true love. I must learn therefore to let go of the familiar and the usual and consent to what is new and unknown to me. I must learn to "leave myself" in order to find myself by yielding to the love of God. If I were looking for God, every event and every moment would sow, in my will, grains of His life that would spring up one day in a tremendous harvest.

For it is God's love that warms me in the sun and God's love that sends the cold rain. It is God's love that feeds me in the bread I eat and God that feeds me also by hunger and fasting. It is the love of God that sends the winter days when I am cold and sick, and the hot summer when I labor and my clothes are full of sweat: but it is God

Who breathes on me with light winds off the river and in the breezes out of the wood. His love spreads the shade of the sycamore over my head and sends the water-boy along the edge of the wheat field with a bucket from the spring, while the laborers are resting and the mules stand under the tree.

It is God's love that speaks to me in the birds and streams; but also behind the clamor of the city God speaks to me in His judgments, and all these things are seeds sent to me from His will.

If these seeds would take root in my liberty, and if His will would grow from my freedom, I would become the love that He is, and my harvest would be His glory and my own joy.

And I would grow together with thousands and millions of other freedoms into the gold of one huge field praising God, loaded with increase, loaded with wheat. If in all things I consider only the heat and the cold, the food or the hunger, the sickness or labor, the beauty or pleasure, the success and failure or the material good or evil my works have won for my own will, I will find only emptiness and not happiness. I shall not be fed, I shall not be full. For my food is the will of Him Who made me and Who made all things in order to give Himself to me through them.

My chief care should not be to find pleasure or success, health or life or money or rest or even things like virtue and wisdom—still less their opposites, pain, failure, sickness, death. But in all that happens, my one desire and my one joy should be to know: "Here is the thing that God has willed for me. In this His love is found, and in accepting this I can give back His love to Him and give myself with it to Him. For in giving myself I shall find Him and He is life everlasting."

By consenting to His will with joy and doing it with gladness I have His love in my heart, because my will is now the same as His love and I am on the way to becoming what He is, Who is Love. And by accepting all things from Him I receive His joy into my soul, not because things are what they are but because God is Who He is, and His love has willed my joy in them all.

How am I to know the will of God? Even where there is no other more explicit claim on my obedience, such as a legitimate command, the very nature of each situation usually bears written into itself some indication of God's will. For whatever is demanded by truth, by justice, by mercy, or by love must surely be taken to be willed by God. To consent to His will is, then, to consent to be true, or to speak truth, or at least to seek it. To obey Him is to respond to His will expressed in the need of another person, or at least to respect the rights of others. For the right of another man is the expression of God's love and God's will. In demanding that I respect the rights of another God is not merely asking me to conform to some abstract, arbitrary law: He is enabling me to share, as His son, in His own care for my brother. No man who ignores the rights and needs of others can hope to walk in the light of contemplation, because his way has turned aside from truth, from compassion and therefore from God.

The requirements of a work to be done can be understood as the will of God. If I am supposed to hoe a garden or make a table, then I will be obeying God if I am true to the task I am performing. To do the work carefully and well, with love and respect for the nature of my task and with due attention to its purpose, is to unite myself to God's will in my work. In this way I become His instrument. He works through me. When I act as His instrument my labor cannot become an obstacle to contemplation, even though it may temporarily so occupy my mind that I cannot engage in it while I am actually doing my job. Yet my work itself will purify and pacify my mind and dispose me for contemplation.

Unnatural, frantic, anxious work, work done under pressure of greed or fear or any other inordinate passion, cannot properly speaking be dedicated to God, because God never wills such work directly. He may permit that through no fault of our own we may have to work madly and distractedly, due to our sins, and to the sins of the society in which we live. In that case we must tolerate it and make the best of what we cannot avoid. But let us not be blind to the distinction between sound, healthy work and unnatural toil.

In any case, we should always seek to conform to the *logos* or truth of the duty before us, the work to be done, or our own God-given nature. Contemplative obedience and abandonment to the will of God can never mean a cultivated indifference to the natural values implanted by Him in human life and work. Insensitivity must not be confused with detachment. The contemplative must certainly be detached, but he can never allow himself to become insensible to true human values, whether in society, in other men or in himself. If he does so, then his contemplation stands condemned as vitiated in its very root.

---

40. Religious Experience and Religious Belief

William P. Alston

I

Can religious experience provide any ground or basis for religious belief? Can it serve to justify religious belief, or make it rational? This paper will differ from many others in the literature by virtue of looking at this question in the light of basic epistemological issues. Throughout we will be comparing the epistemology of religious experience with the epistemology of sense experience.

Source: William P. Alston, "Religious Experience and Religious Belief," *NOÛS,* Vol. 16 (1982), pages 3–12.

We must distinguish between experience directly, and indirectly, justifying a belief. It indirectly justifies belief B_1 when it justifies some other beliefs, which in turn justify B_1. Thus I have learned indirectly from experience that Beaujolais wine is fruity, because I have learned from experience that this, that, and the other bottle of Beaujolais is fruity, and these propositions support the generalization. Experience will directly justify a belief when the justification does not go through other beliefs in this way. Thus, if I am justified, just by virtue of having the visual experience I am now having, in taking what I am experiencing to be a typewriter situated directly in front of me, then the belief that there is a typewriter directly in front of me is directly justified by that experience.

We find claims to both direct and indirect justification of religious beliefs by religious experience. Where someone believes that her new way of relating herself to the world after her conversion is to be explained by the Holy Spirit imparting supernatural graces to her, she supposes her belief *that the Holy Spirit imparts graces to her* to be indirectly justified by her experience. What she directly learns from experience is that she sees and reacts to things differently; this is then taken as a reason for supposing that the Holy Spirit is imparting graces to her. When, on the other hand, someone takes himself to be experiencing the presence of God, he thinks that his experience justifies him in supposing that God is *what* he is experiencing. Thus, he supposes himself to be directly justified by his experience in believing God to be present to him.

In this paper I will confine myself to the question of whether religious experience can provide direct justification for religious belief. This has implications for the class of experiences we shall be considering. In the widest sense 'religious experience' ranges over any experiences one has in connection with one's religious life, including any joys, fears, or longings one has in a religious context. But here I am concerned with experiences that could be taken to *directly* justify religious beliefs, i.e. experiences that give rise to a religious belief and that the subject takes to involve a direct awareness of what the religious belief is about. To further focus the discussion, let's confine ourselves to beliefs to the effect that God, as conceived in theistic religions, is doing something that is directed to the subject of the experience—that God is speaking to him, strengthening him, enlightening him, giving him courage, guiding him, sustaining him in being, or just being present to him. Call these "*M*-beliefs" ('*M*' for 'manifestation').

Note that our question concerns what might be termed a general "epistemic practice," the accepting of *M*-beliefs on the basis of experience, rather than some particular belief of that sort. I hold that practices, or habits, of belief formation are the primary subject of justification and that particular beliefs are justified only by issuing from a practice (or the activation of a habit) that is justified. The following discussion of concepts of justification will provide grounds for that judgment.

Whether *M*-beliefs can be directly justified by experience depends, *inter alia,* on what it is to be justified in a belief. So let us take a look at that.

First, the justification about which we are asking is an "epistemic" rather than a "moral" or "prudential" justification. Suppose one should hold that the practice in question is justified because it makes us feel good. Even if this is true in a sense, it has no bearing on epistemic justification. But why not? What makes a justification *epistemic*? Epistemic justification, as the name implies, has something to do with knowledge, or, more broadly, with the aim at attaining truth and avoiding falsity. At a first approximation, I am justified in believing that p when, from the point of view of that aim, there is something O.K., all right, to be approved, about that fact that I believe that p. But when we come to spell this out further, we find that a fundamental distinction must be drawn between two different ways of being in an epistemically commendable position.

On the one hand there is what we may call a "normative" concept of epistemic justification (J_n), "normative" because it has to do with how we stand *vis-a-vis* norms that specify our intellectual obligations, obligations that attach to one *qua* cognitive subject, *qua* truth-seeker. Stated most generally, J_n consists in one's not having violated one's intellectual obligations. We have to say "not having violated" rather than "having fulfilled" because in all normative spheres, *being justified* is a negative status; it amounts to one's behavior not being in violation of the norms. If belief is under direct voluntary control, we may think of intellectual obligations as attaching directly to believing. Thus one might be obliged to refrain from believing in the absence of adequate evidence. But if, as it seems to me, belief is not, in general, under voluntary control, obligations cannot attach directly to believing. However, I do have voluntary control over moves that can influence a particular belief formation, e.g., looking for more evidence, and moves that can affect my general belief forming habits or tendencies e.g., training myself to be more critical of testimony. If we think of intellectual obligations as attaching to activities that are designed to influence belief formation, we may say that a certain epistemic practice is normatively justified provided it is not the case that the practitioner would not have engaged in it had he satisfied intellectual obligations to engage in activities designed to inhibit it. In other words, the practice is justified if and only if the practitioner did not fail to satisfy an obligation to inhibit it.

However epistemologists also frequently use the term 'justified' in such a way that it has to do not with how the subject stands *vis-a-vis* obligations, but rather with the strength of her epistemic position in believing that p, with how likely it is that a belief of that sort acquired or held in that way is true. To say that a practice is justified in this, as I shall say, "evaluative" sense (J_e), is to say that beliefs acquired in accordance with that practice, in the sorts of circumstances in which human beings typically find themselves; are generally true. Thus we might say that a practice is J_e if and only if it is reliable.

One further complication in the notion of J_n remains to be canvassed. What is our highest reasonable aspiration for being J_n in accepting a belief on the basis of experience? Being J_n no matter what else is the case? A brief consideration of sense perception would suggest a negative answer. I may be justified in believing that there is a tree in front of me by virtue of the fact that I am currently having a certain kind of sense experience, but this will be true only in "favorable circumstances." If I am confronted with a complicated arrangement of mirrors, I may not be justified in believing that there is an oak tree in front of me, even though it looks for all the world as if there is. Again, it may look for all the world as if water is running uphill, but the general improbability of this greatly diminishes the justification the corresponding belief receives from that experience.

What this shows is that the justification provided by one's experience is only defeasibly so. It is inherently liable to be overridden, diminished, or cancelled by stronger considerations to the contrary. Thus the justification of beliefs about the physical environment that is provided by sense experience is a defeasible or, as we might say, *prima facie* justification. By virtue of having the experience, the subject is in a position such that she will be adequately justified in the belief *unless* there are strong enough reasons to the contrary.

It would seem that direct experiential justification for *M*-beliefs, is also, at most, *prima facie*. Beliefs about the nature and ways of God are often used to override *M*-beliefs, particularly beliefs concerning communications from God. If I report that God told me to kill all phenomenologists, fellow Christians will, no doubt, dismiss the report on the grounds that God would not give me any such injunction as that. I shall take it that both sensory experience and religious experience provide, at most, *prima facie* justification.

One implication of this stand is that a particular experiential epistemic practice will have to include some way of identifying defeaters. Different theistic religions, even different branches of the same religion, will differ in this regard, e.g., with respect to what sacred books, what traditions, what doctrines are taken to provide defeaters. We also find difference of this kind in perceptual practice. For example, with the progress of science new defeaters are added to the repertoire. Epistemic practices can, of course, be individuated with varying degrees of detail. To fix our thoughts with regard to the central problem of this paper let's think of a "Christian epistemic practice" (*CP*) that takes its defeaters from the Bible, the classic creeds, and certain elements of tradition. There will be differences between subsegments of the community of practitioners so defined, but there will be enough commonality to make it a useful construct. My foil to *CP*, the practice of forming beliefs about the physical environment on the basis of sense-experience, I shall call "perceptual practice" (*PP*).

Actually it will prove most convenient to think of each of our practices as involving not only the formation of beliefs on the basis of experience, but also the retention of these beliefs in memory, the formation of rationally self-evident beliefs, and various kinds of reasoning on the basis of all this. *CP* will be the richer complex, since it will include the formation of perceptual beliefs in the usual way, while *PP* will not be thought of as including the distinctive experiential practice of *CP*.

One final preliminary note. J_n is relative to a particular person's situation. If practice P_1 is quite unreliable, I may still be J_n in engaging in it either because I have no way of realizing its unreliability or because I am unable to disengage myself: while you, suffering from neither of these disabilities, are not J_n. When we ask whether a given practice is J_n, we shall be thinking about some normal, reasonably well informed contemporary member of our society.

II

Let's make use of all this in tackling the question as to whether one can be justified in *CP* and in *PP*. Beginning with J_n, we will first have to determine more precisely what one's intellectual obligations are *vis-a-vis* epistemic practices. Since our basic cognitive aim is to come into possession of as much truth as possible and to avoid false beliefs, it would seem that one's basic intellectual obligation vis-a-vis practices of belief formation would be to do what one can (or, at least, do as much as could reasonably be expected of one) to see to it that these practices are as *reliable* as possible. But this still leaves us with an option between a stronger and a weaker view as to this obligation. According to the stronger demand one is obliged to refrain (or try to refrain) from engaging in a practice unless one has adequate reasons for supposing it to be reliable. In the absence of sufficient reasons for considering the practice reliable, it is not justified. Practices are guilty until proved innocent. While on the more latitudinarian view one is justified in engaging in a practice provided one does not have sufficient reasons for regarding it to be unreliable. Practices are innocent until proved guilty. Let's take J_{ns} as an abbreviation for 'justified in the normative sense on the stronger requirement,' and 'J_{nw}' as an abbreviation for 'justified in the normative sense on the weaker requirement.'

Now consider whether Mr. Everyman is J_{nw} in engaging in *PP*. It would seem so. Except for those who, like Parmenides and Bradley, have argued that there are ineradicable inconsistencies in the conceptual scheme involved in *PP*, philosophers have not supposed that we can show that sense perception is not a reliable guide to our immediate surroundings. Sceptics about *PP* have generally confined themselves to arguing that we can't show that perception is reliable; i.e., they have argued that *PP* is not J_{ns}. I shall assume without further ado that *PP* is J_{nw}.

J_{ns} and J_e can be considered together. Although a practice may actually be reliable without my having adequate reasons for supposing so, and vice versa, still in considering whether a given practice is reliable, we will be seeking to determine whether there are adequate reasons for supposing it reliable, that is whether Everyman *could* be possessed of such reasons. And if we hold, as we shall, that there are no such reasons, the question of whether they are possessed by one or another subject does not arise.

I believe that there are no adequate noncircular reasons for the reliability of *PP* but I will not be able to argue that point here. If I had a general argument I would unveil it, but, so far as I can see, this thesis is susceptible only of inductive support, by unmasking each pretender in turn. And since this issue has been in the forefront of the Western philosophical consciousness for several centuries, there have been many pretenders. I do not have time even for criticism of a few representative samples. Instead I will simply assume that *PP* is not J_{ns}, and then consider what bearing this widely shared view has on the epistemic status of *CP*.

If J_{nw} is the most we can have for perceptual practice, then if *CP* is also J_{nw} it will be in at least as strong an epistemic position as the former. (I shall assume without argument that *CP* can no more be noncircularly shown to be reliable than can *PP*.) And *CP* will be J_{nw} for *S*, provided *S* has no significant reasons for regarding it as unreliable. Are there any such reasons? What might they be? Well, for one thing, the practice might yield a system that is ineradically internally inconsistent. (I am not speaking of isolated and remediable inconsistencies that continually pop up in every area of thought and experience.) For another, it might yield results that come into ineradicable conflict with the results of other practices to which we are more firmly committed. Perhaps some fundamentalist Christians are engaged in an epistemic practice that can be ruled out on such grounds as these. But I shall take it as obvious that one can objectify certain stretches of one's experience, or indeed the whole of one's experience, in Christian terms without running into such difficulties.

III

One may grant everything I have said up to this point and still feel reluctant to allow that CP is J_{nw}. CP does differ from PP in important ways, and it may be thought that some of these differences will affect their relative epistemic status. The following features of PP, which it does not share with CP, have been thought to have this kind of bearing.

1. Within PP there are standard ways of checking the accuracy of any particular perceptual belief.
2. By engaging in PP we can discover regularities in the behavior of the objects putatively observed, and on this basis we can, to a certain extent, effectively predict the course of events.
3. Capacity for PP, and practice of it, is found universally among normal adult human beings.
4. All normal adult human beings, whatever their culture, use basically the same conceptual scheme in objectifying their sense experience.

If CP includes PP as a proper part, as I ruled on above, how can it lack these features? What I mean is that there is no analogue of these features for that distinctive part of CP by virtue of which it goes beyond PP. The extra element of CP does not enable us to discover extra regularities, e.g., in the behavior of God, or increase our predictive powers. M-beliefs are not subject to interpersonal check in the same way as perceptual beliefs. The practice of forming M-beliefs on the basis of experience is not engaged in by all normal adults. And so on.

Before coming to grips with the alleged epistemic bearing of these differences, I want to make two preliminary points. (1) We have to engage in PP to determine that this practice has features 1.–4., and that CP lacks them. Apart from observation, we have no way of knowing that, e.g., while all cultures agree in their way of cognizing the physical environment they differ in their ways of cognizing the divine, or that PP puts us in a position to predict while CP doesn't. It might be thought that this is loading the dice in favor of my opponent. If we are to use PP, rather than some neutral source, to determine what features it has, shouldn't the same courtesy of self-assessment be accorded CP? Why should it be judged on the basis of what we learn about it from another practice, while that other practice is allowed to grade itself? To be sure, this is a serious issue only if answers to these questions are forthcoming from CP that differ from those we arrive at by engaging in PP. Fortunately, I can avoid getting involved in these issues by ruling that what I am interested in here is how CP looks from the standpoint of PP. The person I am primarily concerned to address is one who, like all the rest of us, engages in PP, and who, like all of us except for a few outlandish philosophers, regards it as justified. My aim is to show this person that, on his own grounds, CP enjoys basically the same epistemic status as PP. Hence it is consonant with my purposes to allow PP to determine the facts of the matter with respect to both practices. (2) I could quibble over whether the contrast is as sharp as is alleged. Questions can be raised about both sides of the putative divide. On the PP side, is it really true that all cultures have objectified sense experience in the same way? Many anthropologists have thought not. And what about the idea that all normal adult human beings engage in the same perceptual practice? Aren't we loading the dice by taking participation in what we regard as standard perceptual practice as our basic criterion for normality? On the *CP* side, is it really the case that this practice reveals no regularities to us, or only that they are very different from regularities in the physical world? What about the point that God is faithful to His promises? Or that the pure in heart will see God? However, I believe that when all legitimate quibbles have been duly registered there will still be very significant differences between the two practices in these respects. So rather than contesting the factual allegations, I will concentrate on the *de jure* issue as to what bearing these differences have on epistemic status.

How could the lack of 1.–4. prevent *CP* from being J_{nw}? Only by providing an adequate ground for a judgment of unreliability. And why suppose that? Of course, the lack of these features implies that we lack certain reasons we might conceivably have had for regarding CP as reliable. If we could ascertain that *PP* has those features, without using *PP* to do so, that would provide us with strong reasons for judging *PP* to be reliable. And the parallel possibility is lacking for *CP*. This shows that we cannot have certain reasons for taking *CP* to be reliable, but it doesn't follow that we have reasons for unreliability. That would follow only if we could also premise that a practice is reliable only if (as well as if) it has 1.–4. And why suppose that?

My position is that it is a kind of parochialism that makes the lack of 1.–4. appear to betoken untrustworthiness. The reality *CP* claims to put us in touch with is conceived to be vastly different from the physical environment. Why should the sorts of procedures required to put us in effective cognitive touch with this reality not be equally different? Why suppose that the distinctive features of *PP* set an appropriate standard for the cognitive approach to God? I shall sketch out a possible state of affairs in which *CP* is quite trustworthy while lacking 1.–4., and then suggest that we have no reason to suppose that this state of affairs does not obtain.

Suppose, then, that

(A) God is too different from created beings, too "wholly other," for us to be able to grasp any regularities in His behavior.

Suppose further that

(B) for the same reason we can only attain the faintest, sketchiest, and most insecure grasp of what God is like.

Finally, suppose that

(C) God has decreed that a human being will be aware of His presence in any clear and unmistakable fashion only when certain special and difficult conditions are satisfied.

If all this is the case, then it is the reverse of surprising that *CP* should lack 1.–4, even if it does involve a genuine experience of God. It would lack 1.–2. because of (A). It is quite understandable that it should lack 4. because of (B). If our cognitive powers are not fitted to frame an adequate conception of God, it is not at all surprising that there should be wide variation in attempts to do so. This is what typically happens in science when investigators are grappling with a phenomenon no one really understands. A variety of models, analogues, metaphors, hypotheses, hunches are propounded, and it is impossible to secure universal agreement. 3. is missing because of (C). If very difficult conditions are set it is not surprising that few are chosen. Now it is compatible with (A)–(C) that

(D) religious experience should, in general, constitute a genuine awareness of the divine.

and that

(E) although any particular articulation of such an experience might be mistaken to a greater or lesser extent, indeed even though all such articulations might miss the mark to some extent, still such judgments will, for the most part, contain some measure of truth; they, or many of them, will constitute a useful approximation of the truth;

and that

(F) God's designs contain provision for correction and refinement, for increasing the accuracy of the beliefs derived from religious experience. Perhaps as one grows in the spiritual life one's spiritual sight becomes more accurate and more discriminating; perhaps some special revelation is vouchsafed under certain conditions; and there are many other conceivable possibilities.

If something like all this were the case then *CP* would be trustworthy even though it lacks features 1.–4. This is a conceivable way in which *CP* would constitute a road to the truth, while differing from PP in respects 1.–4. Therefore unless we have adequate reason for supposing that no such combination of circumstances obtains, we are not warranted in taking the lack of 1.–4. to be an adequate reason for a judgment of untrustworthiness.

Moreover it is not just that A.–C. constitute a bare possibility. In the practice of *CP* we seem to learn that this is the way things are. As for (A) and (B) it is the common teaching of all the higher religions that God is of a radically different order of being from finite substances and, therefore, that we cannot expect to attain the grasp of His nature and His doings that we have of worldly objects. As for (C), it is a basic theme in Christianity, and in other religions as well, that one finds God within one's experience, to any considerable degree, only as one progresses in the spiritual life. God is not available for voyeurs. Awareness of God, and understanding of His nature and His will for us, is not a purely cognitive achievement; it requires the involvement of the whole person; it takes a practical commitment and a practice of the life of the spirit, as well as the exercise of cognitive faculties.

Of course these results that we are using to defend *CP* are derived from that same practice. But in view of the fact that the favorable features of *PP,* 1.–4., are themselves ascertained by engaging in *PP,* our opponent is hardly in a position to fault us on this score. However I have not forgotten that I announced it as my aim to show that even one who engaged only in *PP* should recognize that *CP* is J_{nw}. For this purpose, I ignore what we learn in *CP* and revert to the point that my opponent has no basis for ruling out the conjoint state of affairs A.–F., hence has no basis for taking the lack of 1.–4. to show *CP* to be untrustworthy, and hence has no reason for denying that *CP* is J_{nw}.

I conclude that *CP* has basically the same epistemic status as *PP* and that no one who subscribes to the latter is in any position to cavil at the former.

---

41. Religious Experience and Religious Belief

Wayne Proudfoot

Reductionism has become a derogatory epithet in the history and philosophy of religion. Scholars whose work is in other respects quite diverse have concurred in advocating approaches to the study of religion which are oriented around campaigns against reductionism. These campaigns are often linked to a defense of the autonomy of the study of religion. The distinctive subject matter of that study, it is argued, requires a distinctive method. In particular, religious experience cannot properly be studied by a method that reduces it to a cluster of phenomena that can be explained in historical, psychological, or sociological terms. Although it is difficult to establish exactly what is meant by the term, the label "reductionist" is deemed sufficient to warrant dismissal of any account of religious phenomena.

Questions have been raised about this wholesale rejection of reductive accounts and about the theological motivations that sometimes underlie it, but the issues in the discussion have not been sufficiently clarified.[1] Penner and Yonan (1972), for example, take the problem to be crucial for the study of religion, survey the meaning of *reduction* in empiricist philosophy of science, and deplore the negative connotations that have become attached to the term. But they admit that they have found the issue difficult. They show no appreciation of why the attack on reductionism has such an appeal, and thus they are unable to elucidate the discussion. The warnings against reductionism derive from a genuine insight, but that insight is often misconstrued to serve an apologetic purpose. I shall try to

Source: Wayne Proudfoot, "Religious Experiences as Interpretive Accounts," in *Religious Experience* (Berkeley: University of California Press, 1985), 199–227.

clarify the confusion surrounding the term *reduction* as it is applied to accounts of religious experience and to distinguish between the insight and the misapplications that result in protective strategies. A recent essay in the philosophy of religion devoted to the exposure and critique of reductionism will serve to illustrate those misapplications and strategies.

The Problem

One of the most influential critics of reductionism in the study of religion has been Mircea Eliade. He has argued that the task of the historian of religion is a distinctive one and has contrasted it with what he takes to be the reductionist methods of the social sciences (Eliade, 1969: 1–53). According to Eliade, a historical or sociological approach fails to grasp the meaning of religious phenomena. Like the literary critic interpreting a text, the historian of religion must attempt to understand religious data "on their own plane of reference." He or she should adopt a hermeneutic method. Just as literary works cannot be reduced to their origins, religious phenomena ought not to be reduced to their social, psychological, or historical origins or functions. Eliade (1969: 6) contends that "a religious datum reveals its deeper meaning when it is considered on its plane of reference, and not when it is reduced to one of its secondary aspects or its contexts." He cites Durkheim and Freud as examples of those who have adopted reductionist methods for the study of religion.

Two points are worthy of note: (1) Eliade thinks that what is lost by reductive approaches is the *meaning* of religious phenomena. He praises van der Leeuw for respecting the peculiar intentionality of religious data and thus the irreducibility of religious representations (Eliade, 1969: 35); (2) his examples of reductionist approaches are drawn almost exclusively from history and the social sciences. Theories that purport to account for religious phenomena in terms of their origins or the functions they serve in a particular social context are *ipso facto* reductionist.

Eliade holds further that religious data represent the expression of religious experiences. Religion is "first of all, an experience *sui generis,* incited by man's encounter with the sacred" (Eliade, 1969: 25). In order to understand religious data on their own plane of reference, the scholar must "'relive' a multitude of existential situations" (Eliade, 1969: 10). Only through such a procedure can the meaning of the data be grasped. To reduce those data to their origins or social functions is to fail to understand them as expressions of religious experience. That understanding can come only from acquaintance. Since Eliade regards religious experience as experience of the sacred, he can summarize his antireductionist position by reference to "the irreducibility of the sacred."[2]

Religious experience is the experience of something. It is intentional in that it cannot be described without reference to a grammatical object. Just as fear is always fear of something, and a perceptual act can only be described by reference to its object, a religious experience must be identified under a certain description, and that description must include a reference to the object of the experience. Eliade employs the term *sacred* to characterize the object of all religious experience. The notorious obscurity of that term need not concern us here, nor need we accept the suggestion that all religious experiences have the same object. The point is that when Eliade refers to the irreducibility of the sacred, he is claiming that it is the intentional object of the religious experience which must not be reduced. To do so is to lose the experience, or to attend to something else altogether.

This point is well taken. If someone is afraid of a bear, his fear cannot be accurately described without mentioning the bear. This remains true regardless of whether or not the bear actually exists outside his mind. He may mistakenly perceive a fallen tree trunk on the trail ahead of him as a bear, but his fear is properly described as fear of a bear. To describe it as fear of a log would be to misidentify his emotion and reduce it to something other than it is. In identifying the experience, emotion, or practice of another, I must restrict myself to concepts and beliefs that have informed his experience. I cannot ascribe to him concepts he would not recognize or beliefs he would not acknowledge.[3] Though historical evidence might turn up to show that Socrates was dying of cancer, no evidence could show that he was afraid of dying of cancer. No such fear could be ascribed to him because he didn't possess the concept of cancer which is presupposed by that emotion.

Consider two examples cited by William James. The first is an experience reported by Stephen Bradley which took place some years before the one considered in chapter three.

> I thought I saw the Saviour, by faith, in human shape, for about one second in the room, with arms extended, appearing to say to me, Come. The next day I rejoiced with trembling; soon after my happiness was so great that I said that I wanted to die; this world had no place in my affections, as I knew of, and every day appeared to me as the Sabbath. I had an ardent desire that all mankind might feel as I did; I wanted to have them all love God supremely. (James, 1902: 189–190)

The second is from Mrs. Jonathan Edwards.

> Part of the night I lay awake, sometimes asleep, and sometimes between sleeping and waking. But all night I continued in a constant, clear, and lively sense of the heavenly sweetness of Christ's excellent love, of his nearness to me, and of my dearness to him. I seemed to myself to perceive a glow of divine love come down from the heart of Christ in heaven into my heart in a constant stream, like a stream or pencil of sweet light. At the same time my heart and soul all flowed out in love to Christ, so that there seemed to be a constant flowing and reflowing of heavenly love, and I appeared to myself to float or swim, in these bright, sweet beams, like the motes swimming in the beams of the sun, or the streams of his light which come in at the window. (James, 1902: 276)

Bradley tells of a vision in human shape, and Edwards reports a lively sense of Christ's love, which seemed to glow like a stream or pencil of light. Each of these experiences can only be properly described by reference to Christ and to Christian beliefs. One might try to separate the description of the core experience from its interpretation and to argue that only the interpretation is specifically Christian. But if the references to the Savior, the Sabbath, and God are eliminated from Bradley's report, we are left with something other than his experience. After deleting references to Christian concepts, we have a vision of a human shape with arms extended saying, "Come." Is this any less informed by Christian beliefs and doctrines than was the original experience? Surely the vision of a person with outstretched arms is not some universal archetype onto which

Bradley has added an interpretation in Christian terms.[4] Nor can his experience of comfort and salvation be abstracted from his Christian beliefs. Sarah Edwards's experience is not a vision, but it would be inaccurate to describe it exclusively in general terms and to characterize it only as a lively sense of sweetness, accompanied by the sensation of floating in streams of bright light. Her report cannot be purged of references to Christ and Christian beliefs and still remain an accurate description of the experience.

An emotion, practice, or experience must be described in terms that can plausibly be attributed to the subject on the basis of the available evidence. The subject's self-ascription is normative for describing the experience. This is a kind of first-person privilege that has nothing at all to do with immediate intuitive access to mental states versus mediated inferential reasoning. It is strictly a matter of intentionality. It is like the distinction between the words of a speaker and those of one who reports what he says. The speaker's meaning, and his choice of words to express that meaning, are normative for the reporter. The latter may choose to paraphrase or elaborate, but the words uttered by the speaker are authoritative for determining the message. Where it is the subject's experience which is the object of study, that experience must be identified under a description that can plausibly be attributed to him. In the cases cited above, the subject's own words constitute the description. If, however, an observer or analyst describes the experience of another, he must formulate it in terms that would be familiar to, incorporating beliefs that would be acknowledged by, the subject. If challenged, he must offer reasons in support of his ascription of those concepts and beliefs to the subject. He is not responsible for reasons offered in support of those beliefs.

The explanation the analyst offers of that same experience is another matter altogether. It need not be couched in terms familiar or acceptable to the subject. It must be an explanation of the experience as identified under the subject's description, but the subject's approval of the explanation is not required. Bradley's experience might be explained in terms of the conflicts of early adolescence and that of Sarah Edwards as a consequence of her life with Mr. Edwards. No reference need be made to God or Christ in the construction of these explanations. If the explanation is challenged, the one who proposed it is responsible for providing reasons to support it and for showing how it accounts for the evidence better than any of its rivals does.

Schachter's subjects experienced anger or euphoria. An accurate description of the experience of a subject in the anger condition would require that it be described as anger and that the anger be specified by reference to its object. The subject was angry at the experimenters for subjecting him to insulting questions. The ascription of this anger to the subject assumes he does in fact find the questions insulting and he holds the experimenters responsible for them. He also explains the arousal he feels by reference to the experimenter's insults. Schachter and his colleagues, however, explain the anger in terms of which the subject is ignorant. They explain it in terms of the physiological effects of epinephrine and their manipulation of the cognitive cues in the experimental setting. The subject's explanation of his arousal must be cited in a description of his experience, but it need not figure in the explanation of the experience which Schachter and his colleagues adopt.

In the study of religion considerable confusion has resulted from the failure to distinguish the requisite conditions for the identification of an experience under a certain description from those for explaining the experience. The analyst must cite, but need not endorse, the concepts, beliefs, and judgments that enter into the subject's identification of his experience. He must be prepared to give reasons for his ascription of those beliefs and judgments to the subject, but he need not defend the beliefs and judgments themselves. If he proposes an explanatory hypothesis to account for the experience, he need not restrict himself to the subject's concepts and beliefs, but he must be prepared to give reasons in support of his explanation.

Descriptive and Explanatory Reduction

We are now in a position to distinguish two different kinds of reduction. *Descriptive reduction* is the failure to identify an emotion, practice, or experience under the description by which the subject identifies it. This is indeed unacceptable. To describe an experience in nonreligious terms when the subject himself describes it in religious terms is to misidentify the experience, or to attend to another experience altogether. To describe Bradley's experience as simply a vision of a human shape, and that of Mrs. Edwards as a lively warm sense that seemed to glow like a pencil of light, is to lose the identifying characteristics of those experiences. To describe the experience of a mystic by reference only to alpha waves, altered heart rate, and changes in bodily temperature is to misdescribe it. To characterize the experience of a Hindu mystic in terms drawn from the Christian tradition is to misidentify it. In each of these instances, the subject's identifying experience has been reduced to something other than that experienced by the subject. This might properly be called reductionism. In any case, it precludes an accurate identification of the subject's experience.

Explanatory reduction consists in offering an explanation of an experience in terms that are not those of the subject and that might not meet with his approval. This is perfectly justifiable and is, in fact, normal procedure. The explanandum is set in a new context, whether that be one of covering laws and initial conditions, narrative structure, or some other explanatory model. The terms of the explanation need not be familiar or acceptable to the subject. Historians offer explanations of past events by employing such concepts as socialization, ideology, means of production, and feudal economy. Seldom can these concepts properly be ascribed to the people whose behavior is the object of the historian's study. But that poses no problem. The explanation stands or falls according to how well it can account for all the available evidence.

Failure to distinguish between these two kinds of reduction leads to the claim that any account of religious emotions, practices, or experience must be restricted to the perspective of the subject and must employ only terms, beliefs, and judgments that would meet with his approval. This claim derives its plausibility from examples of descriptive reduction but is then extended to preclude explanatory reduction. When so extended, it becomes a protective strategy. The subject's identifying description becomes normative for purposes of explanation, and inquiry is blocked to insure that the subject's own explanation of his experience is not contested. On this view, to entertain naturalistic explanations of the experiences of Bradley and Edwards is reductionist because these explanations conflict with the convictions of the subjects that their experiences were the result of divine activity in their lives.

Many of the warnings against reductionism in the study of religion conflate descriptive and explanatory reduction. Eliade exhorts the historian of religion to understand religious data on their own plane of reference and contrasts this understanding with the reductive accounts offered by social scientists.[5] Wilfred Cantwell Smith (1976: 152; 1981: 97) contends that a necessary requirement of the validity of any statement about a religion is that it be acknowledged and accepted by adherents of that religious tradition. This is appropriate if addressed to the problem of providing identifying descriptions of experiences in different traditions, but it is inappropriate if extended to include all statements about religion.

For some years Smith has waged a campaign against the use of the term *religion* in the study of what he calls faith and the historical traditions (Smith, 1964, 1979). In criticizing this use of the term, he brings forth abundant evidence to show that it is of rather recent and parochial origin. According to his research, there is no concept in most of the world's cultures and traditions which can accurately be translated by our term *religion.* In other words, there is no evidence to support the ascription of that concept to people outside the modern West. From this evidence Smith concludes that the term ought to be avoided by scholars of the faiths of mankind. Even if the results of his philological researches were granted, however, there would be no more reason to reject *religion* than to reject *culture* and *economy.* The fact that it cannot accurately be ascribed to people in many societies does not require that it be excluded from the accounts we give of those societies. Smith's conclusion follows from his evidence only with the addition of the premise that any account of the religious life, including explanatory accounts, must be couched in terms that are familiar and acceptable to participants in that life. Smith accepts this premise and regards it as a requirement of the comparative study of religion, but we have seen that explanatory accounts are not subject to this restriction.

Protective Strategies

The neglect or refusal to distinguish between descriptive and explanatory reduction constitutes the core of an apologetic strategy. Recognition of the requirement that religious experience and belief must be identified under the description employed by the subject is used to argue that all accounts of religious experience must be acceptable to the subject. This accords with the assumption that in order to understand religious experience one must participate in that experience or reproduce it in oneself.

Smith (1976: 146) explicitly formulates the rule that "no statement about a religion is valid unless it can be acknowledged by that religion's believers." He contends that in order to understand the Qur'an as a religious document, one must approach it in the same spirit as a Muslim would (Smith, 1976: 31). One must read it as if he already believed it to be the word of God. We ought not to study Muslim, Buddhist, or Jewish beliefs and practices but must learn to see the world through Muslim, Buddhist, or Jewish eyes. Understanding requires the scholar to share in the experience or the way of life of a particular tradition and to elicit or reproduce the same in his readers. Eliade describes the task of understanding as a hermeneutic one and exhorts the historian of religion to "relive" the existential situation of those whom he studies.

This requirement gains its appeal from the consideration that a religious experience, belief, or practice must be identified under the description employed by the subject; but it exhibits confusion when it is extended to preclude explanatory hypotheses that differ from those of the subject. In order to understand Astor's experience of a miracle, I must ascribe to him the belief that the event cannot be exhaustively explained in naturalistic terms, but I need not endorse that belief. After accurately citing Astor's description of the event, including his explanation of what he saw, I may go on to propose a competing explanation both of the event and of Astor's perception. To require that any explanation of a religious experience be one that would be endorsed by the subject is to block inquiry into the character of that experience.

A recent work by D. Z. Phillips, entitled *Religion Without Explanation,* provides a clear illustration of the confusion of the concepts of descriptive and explanatory reduction in the service of an apologetic or protective strategy. Phillips argues that any attempt to explain religious experience, belief, or practice is reductive and is for that reason to be rejected. He devotes the first half of his book to a brief survey of what he takes to be reductionist accounts of religion and the second half to an elucidation of religious phenomena which avoids reductionism. Frazer, Tylor, Marett, Freud, Feuerbach, and Durkheim are all labeled conscious reductionists because they attempt to explain religious phenomena in nonreligious terms. Those who assume that religious beliefs and doctrines purport to refer to some object or to describe matters of fact are said to be unconscious reductionists because they construe religious statements as referential rather than expressive. Phillips criticizes both types of reductionists for their failure to accept religious beliefs "at face value." His comments show, however, that he misconstrues both the theories he criticizes and the religious beliefs he is attempting to elucidate. Since the key to his misconstructions lies in a confusion between descriptive and explanatory reduction, they provide a convenient illustration of the importance of this distinction. The confusion can be seen in his criticism of the approaches of Durkheim and Freud and in his misinterpretation of the intentional character of religious experience and belief.

Phillips characterizes Durkheim's theory of religion as follows:

> When one does go below the religious symbol to the reality it represents, one finds it is society itself. Religion is in fact the worship of society. This is an extremely odd claim and it is not at all easy to understand why anyone should want to make it. (Phillips, 1976: 90)

As an identifying description of primitive worship, this is indeed an odd claim, and it is not one that Durkheim makes. The Australian people of whom he wrote did not identify their practice as the worship of society. The intentional object of their worship or respect was not society but their totemic representations and the animals or vegetables that served as totems for the clans. Given the respect, fear, and authority elicited by these sacred totems, Durkheim set out to offer a hypothesis to explain their force. He argued that the totems were imbued with the power of the social order. The authority of the totems over members of the clans required an explanation in terms of some source or power that could plausibly elicit such fear and respect. The Arunta "worshipped" the totems, but Durkheim hypothesized that the authority of those objects over the clan members was to be explained by reference to the authority of the social order over the individual. One might disagree with Durkheim's hypothesis, but Phillips's dismissal is based on a misunderstanding. He assesses Durkheim's explanatory hypothesis as if it were meant as an identifying description, and he finds it extremely odd. But it was not intended as such a description.

Phillips makes a similar error when he criticizes as reductionist Durkheim's comment that from the fact that a religious experience occurs "it does not follow that the reality which is its foundation conforms objectively to the idea which believers have of it" (Phillips, 1976: 94; Durkheim, 1965: 465). Durkheim is here drawing the required distinction between identification and explanation. The subject's identification of his experience in religious terms makes it a religious experience and is normative for describing that experience. But the subject's explanation may not be the correct one; it may be that the correct explanation requires no reference to religious realities. Astor's perception of what he saw at Lourdes as anomalous with respect to the natural order and consequently demanding a religious explanation constitutes for him a miracle experience, but his perception and its embedded judgment about the proper explanation of the event may be inaccurate.

The same confusion is exhibited in Phillips's remarks on Freud. He correctly notes that a person's beliefs, motives, and emotions must be described in a manner that is intelligible within that person's way of life. A contemporary concept of freedom, or a desire for that freedom, cannot accurately be ascribed to a person in the ancient world. Freud (1950: 27–28) juxtaposes a Maori taboo with an obsessional prohibition experienced by one of his patients. Phillips objects to the comparison between a ritual practice and obsessive behavior.

> Freud does not offer an account of the situations in terms of reasons which have their life within the activities of the tribe. Freud says that it is a waste of time to listen to the reasons of the tribesmen. Notice that he is ruling out their references to the sacred as a possible satisfactory account of their activities. (Phillips, 1976: 61)

Freud does not say that it is a waste of time to listen to the reasons of the tribesmen. That would be uncharacteristic. One of the most important lessons Freud has taught us is to listen carefully to everything, even and especially to what appears to be trivial and unimportant. Close attention is necessary in order to identify accurately the beliefs, intentions, and emotions that are to be ascribed to an individual. But he has also taught us to listen skeptically. One needn't accept the reasons offered by the subject. In the passage to which Phillips alludes, Freud says that we cannot expect the tribesmen to give us the real reason (*die wirkliche Motivierung*) for their prohibitions or the origin of their taboo because psychoanalytic theory would lead us to expect that the real motivation is unconscious (Freud, 1950: 31). The explanation he offers for the practice differs from that of the tribesmen. Whether by choice or by accident, Phillips employs the ambiguous phrase "satisfactory account" in his criticism of Freud for not accepting the Maori reference to the sacred as a satisfactory account of their activities. This phrase is ambiguous with respect to the distinction between description and explanation. If the Maori did make such a reference, it would be necessary to cite that in any adequate description of the Maori practice, but Freud is under no obligation to explain the practice in terms of the sacred.[6]

Phillips construes Freud's theory of religion not as an explanatory hypothesis but as an alternative description of religious emotions and practices. He contends that despite the fact that Freud intended to offer an explanation, he was actually proposing a description of religious emotions and practices which competes with the description employed by the subjects.

> But why can't we say that what we have here is things being looked at from the aspect of the sexual? By looking at things in this way, their aspect changes too. (Phillips, 1976: 69)

Following a suggestion made by Wittgenstein, Phillips claims that Freud's interpretation of emotions and practices in the light of his mythology of the sexual charms people away from the religious alternative but is of no use in elucidating that alternative. But a psychoanalytic explanation is not meant to be an accurate identifying description of a practice from the subject's perspective. Like Durkheim, Freud sought an explanation of the power religious concepts and ritual practices exert over people's lives. Such an explanation must invoke a force or interest that could conceivably have that kind of impact. Sexuality, like the authority of the social order, is a sufficiently powerful force to serve as a plausible explanation, especially in the light of Freud's demonstration of the pervasiveness and strength of libidinal drives.

This misconstruction of Freud's theory of religion as an alternative description of religious phenomena permits Phillips to dismiss it as irrelevant to the study of those phenomena. Freud did not offer his psychoanalytic account as an accurate representation of the Maori way of viewing the world, nor did Durkheim claim that the Arunta worshipped society. The Maori practices are governed by their concepts, and the Arunta respect and fear totems and totemic spirits. The power of the social order and the pervasive force of the sexual may enter into the explanation of those practices, but not into their identification. One is free to take exception to the theories of religion offered by Durkheim and Freud, but Phillips's dismissal is based on a misrepresentation of their status.

The characterizations of religious belief offered by Phillips are as inadequate as his accounts of the theories of others. The problem arises from his attempt to attribute to believers the neutrality appropriate for the scholar describing religious beliefs. His concern to show that religious beliefs and practices do not presuppose explanatory hypotheses that might conflict with those of science leads him to deny that they entail any assertions at all. They are expressive attitudes and activities. The theories of Durkheim and Freud are explicitly reductionist, but the real problem in the philosophy of religion, according to Phillips, stems from the unconscious reductionists, particularly from those who hold that religious beliefs refer and that they sometimes make claims about the world. He contends that religious language is not referential but expressive. It expresses religious practices and forms of life.

> If we mean by reductionism an attempt to reduce the significance of religious belief to something other than it is, then reductionism consists in the attempt, however sophisticated, to say that religious pictures must refer to some object; that they must describe matters of fact. That is the real reductionism which distorts the character of religious beliefs. (Phillips, 1976: 150)

The meaning of Phillips's title now becomes clear. Not only is any attempt to explain religious phenomena *ipso facto* reductionist but any construal of religious beliefs as themselves assuming explanations is similarly reductive. By precluding explanatory hypotheses about religious phenomena, and by refusing to permit the assessment of religious beliefs as hypotheses, Phillips has adopted an effective apologetic strategy. Conflict between religious beliefs or practices and our theoretical commitments is precluded from the outset.

Like all attempts to block inquiry, this one has its costs. In these terms Phillips cannot accurately account for actual examples of religious belief. For instance, he criticizes E. B. Tylor for attempting to explain beliefs in souls or spirits rather than taking them "at face value." But by taking beliefs at face value Phillips does not seem to mean taking them literally. He says that talk about souls entails neither opinions, hypotheses, theories, nor explanations.

> Talk about the soul is a way of talking about people, a way of talking which, perhaps, is not so familiar as it used to be. What is important to note for our present purposes, however, is that such talk is not based on opinion or on any kind of conjecture about some odd substance inside the body called the soul. Yet, when we listen to Tylor speaking of primitive conceptions of the soul, he speaks of such a substance. He speaks as if the question of whether people have souls is a hypothetical question, an assumption, and in his view one which is empirically false and without foundation. (Phillips, 1976: 39)

Despite his call for beliefs to be elucidated by close attention to details and to their contexts, Phillips does not offer any evidence for his claim. Talk about the soul has probably meant many things in different contexts, and it is highly unlikely that hypotheses about an immaterial substance have not been among those meanings. By taking the belief at face value, Phillips appears to mean construing it in such a way as to preclude its falsity.

Ironically, despite Phillips's contention that religious beliefs are expressive of the attitudes and practices of the religious life and consequently can neither support nor conflict with any theories, his practice suggests that any belief that appears to conflict with our mundane and scientific views requires reinterpretation. Elucidation of religious beliefs is thus dependent on our ordinary and scientific beliefs. Religious beliefs are always to be construed in such a way that they accord with the beliefs we hold to be true. This is clearly a protective strategy. Quine (1960: 59) argues for what he calls "the principle of charity." We ought so to assign meanings to the sentences of an alien language that we ascribe to the speakers of that language beliefs that, in the main, accord with our own. At some point it becomes more plausible to assume we have mistranslated than to ascribe to other speakers beliefs that seem widely off the mark. If our translation leads us to ascribe to the speaker such sentences as "The sunlight is usually brighter at night than in the daytime" or "No one can throw a stone farther than the distance measured by ten paces," then we ought to consider revising the translation to accord with the beliefs that we know to be true and that we ascribe to the speaker. But Phillips is arguing that whenever our understanding of religious doctrines leads to a conflict between those doctrines and what we know or believe to be true about the world, we must reconstrue those doctrines in order to preclude that conflict. This is charity with a vengeance.

In order to give an account of religious belief from the perspective of the believer and to maintain his thesis about religious language, Phillips must elucidate the reality of God or the religious object in a way that requires no reference outside itself and that entails no claim. He tries to do this by exploiting the intentionality of emotion and belief and an ambiguity in our use of the term *real.* The objects of our experiences, emotions, and beliefs are real by the very fact that they inform those states, and therefore the experiences, emotions, and beliefs cannot be identified without mention of those objects. If a person believes in ghosts, those ghosts are real for him. Insofar as they affect that person's thoughts and actions, they are real *tout court.* A significant part of the world (i.e., that part including the subject's beliefs, experiences, emotions, and actions) cannot be described without reference to those ghosts. In this sense, the ghost of Hamlet's father, Hamlet himself, and unicorns are all real. Brentano, who revived the scholastic doctrine of intentionality and introduced it into the modern discussion, characterized the status of such objects as one of "intentional inexistence" (Brentano, 1874: 115–118). Hamlet is real, though Hamlet does not exist. Phillips ignores this distinction between reality and existence and claims that the reality of an intentional object is the reality a believer ascribes to God.

Phillips introduces an example to make this point. He quotes a comment by Peter Winch on a passage from Simone Weil. Weil said that the longing of a bereaved person for one who has died is not imaginary. The absence of the dead one is very real and is itself a manner of appearing. Winch comments that the dead person is real precisely as the object of the other's longing, since mention of that object is essential for describing the world.

> It is important to what Simone Weil is saying that longing is intentional. I long *for* something or someone. In other words my longing itself, which is undoubtedly something real, cannot be grasped except as a longing for that person. So mention of her is essential to describing the reality of the world as it is for me; she has *not* become something unreal, imaginary, because mention of her is indispensable to describing the world as it is. Her absence is, henceforth, "her way of appearing"; she makes a difference to the world by virtue of her absence.[7]

The deceased is real as an object of the longing of the beloved. Phillips concludes from this that the reality of God and of other objects of religious belief and practice need only be intentional reality and that the question of the existence of such objects outside of those beliefs and practices need never arise. But the reality of God for the theist is not adequately captured by the concept of intentional inexistence, or by the reality of the remembered loved one or Hamlet. The scholar describing the beliefs and practices of another can and must accord intentional reality to the objects of those beliefs and practices, but he must not attribute his indifference with respect to the existence of those objects to the subjects themselves.

I can long for something that does not exist and that is real only as the object of my longing. A person might entertain the concept of God, long nostalgically for the God of his childhood, or wish that there were a Savior to relieve him of his burdens. God and the Savior would be real as objects that must be cited in order to describe accurately his mental states, but they would not be real in the same sense that they were for Bradley and Sarah Edwards. James can be indifferent with respect to the existence and efficacy of the objects of the experiences of those whose reports he has collected, but the subjects of those experiences are not indifferent to their existence. James must cite the Christian belief in God and a Savior to characterize Bradley's experience; he need not endorse it. Phillips erroneously attributes to the subject of an experience or belief an indifference with regard to the existence of the object of that experience or belief which is an appropriate stance for the analyst. If accurate, this move would protect religious beliefs from the results of inquiry, but it does not adequately capture the role of those beliefs in the religious life.

The characterization of reductionism as "an attempt to reduce the significance of religious belief to something other than it is" is crucial to Phillips's apologetic program. It is ambiguous with respect to the distinction between descriptive and explanatory reduction. Phillips characterizes what must be reduced, not as the identifying description of a religious belief, but as the *significance* of that belief. One might identify the experiences of Bradley and Edwards in their own terms and then proceed to offer a natural explanation of those experiences. According to Phillips, such an explanation would reduce the significance of those experiences and would consequently be reductionist. In fact, it would be an example of explanatory but not descriptive reduction. The term *significance* is ambiguous in this context, as is Eliade's use of the term *meaning* for that which is to be preserved. Phillips elicits assent by producing examples of descriptive reduction and then criticizes those who have proposed reductive explanations. This equivocation constitutes his protective strategy.

Force

In order to elucidate an experience, one must identify it under a description that can be ascribed to the subject of that experience. But when the analyst has given an identifying description of the experience, and has cited the relevant concepts and beliefs while withholding his endorsement of those beliefs, has he really captured the force of the experience? Some would argue that he has not, that to describe the experience of Astor, Bradley, or Edwards in such a way as to understand its force, one must have recourse to the kind of acquaintance or participation called for by Schleiermacher and Otto. A commitment by the analyst to a nonreligious explanation is said to preclude appreciation of the authority of the experience for the subject.

In his remarks on Frazer's *The Golden Bough*, Wittgenstein (1979: 1–9) suggests that the story Frazer tells about the King of the Wood at Nemi is impressive in a way that his proposed explanation of the practice of killing the king is not. Wittgenstein concludes that the satisfaction we seek cannot come from any kind of explanation but only from a description that draws connections between our practices and those of the people whom we are trying to understand. The proper identifying description satisfies where the explanation does not. It is implausible to suggest that such gripping practices rest on mistaken perceptions or theories about the world.

> Even the idea of trying to explain the practice—say the killing of the priest-king—seems to me wrong-headed. All that Frazer does is to make this practice plausible to people who think as he does. It is very queer that all these practices are finally presented, so to speak, as stupid actions.
>
> But it never does become plausible that people do all this out of sheer stupidity . . .
>
> I think one reason why the attempt to find an explanation is wrong is that we have only to put together in the right way what we *know*, without adding anything, and the satisfaction we are trying to get from the explanation comes of itself . . .

We can only *describe* and say, human life is like that. . . .

Compared with the impression that what is described here makes on us, the explanation is too uncertain. (Wittgenstein, 1979: 1–3)

The practices themselves are deeper and more gripping than any theories or explanations either we or the practitioners might associate with them.

This is an important point. An explanation must satisfy in that it must account for the force of the experience. It is not necessary for the analyst to share the experience, however, to understand its force. It is the account which must satisfy, and an account can satisfy if it makes clear why the experience has the power it has for the subject. Knowing that my partner takes the log on the trail ahead to be a bear is sufficient for me to understand why it has a dramatic effect on his emotions and behavior. I have elucidated his fear by identifying the object of that fear as he perceives it, and I can see how the fear was occasioned. I can understand his fear without sharing his perception.

The appeal to the force of the experience can be used to serve a protective strategy. Phillips argues that religious beliefs are irreducible in the sense that they cannot be explained in nonreligious terms. The impressive character of any religious belief or practice eludes all attempts at explanation.

One may be interested in investigating the consequences of various religious beliefs for other social movements and institutions, or the historical development of religious beliefs. Yet, such investigations would not be an investigation into the impressiveness of the beliefs. The impressiveness may be elucidated—we have seen how symbol may be placed alongside symbol—but it cannot be explained. (Phillips, 1976: 151)

Force or impressiveness is not defined independently but is said to be that which is lost whenever an attempt is made to explain religious phenomena. This remark suggests that what is really distinctive about religious phenomena is their resistance to explanation, or their anomalous status with respect to all natural explanations. No attempt to explain them can be permitted without losing their distinctively religious character. The impressiveness of religious phenomena is identified as that which is lost whenever explanations are proposed for those phenomena.

The rejection of any kind of explanation is presented by Phillips as a plea for neutrality with respect to the truth of religious beliefs and a rejection of reductionism of all kinds. In fact, however, it is not a neutral position at all but conceals a substantial commitment. The function of Phillips's remarks is similar to that of Otto's instructions to his readers.[8] If the experience can be explained, it is not religious. Like *numinous* and *miracle,* the *impressiveness* of religious beliefs, as Phillips uses the term, includes in the rules for its proper application the condition that it will be anomalous with respect to any proposed explanation.

The protective strategy Phillips and others adopt is similar in an important respect to the position of Schleiermacher and Otto and serves similar apologetic concerns. Both seek to restrict accounts of religious experience and belief to the perspective of the subject. Schleiermacher holds that piety is a form of immediate self-consciousness which is independent of concepts and beliefs and consequently can only be understood by acquaintance. One must experience it in oneself in order to describe it. Any nonreligious explanation must be ruled out as inadequate to the feeling as the subject experiences it (CF 32.2). Phillips recognizes that religious experience is constituted by concepts and beliefs, and he urges attention to the grammar of those concepts. He argues that the rules of that grammar must govern any account of the experience. If questions are raised about the validity of beliefs assumed by the subject in his identification of the experience, one has imported issues from outside the religious form of life and *ipso facto* shown that one does not understand that life. Both positions assume that religious experience and belief can be understood and assessed only from the inside. Both are then able to say that religious beliefs can never come into conflict with scientific or other nonreligious beliefs. If the possibility of such conflict is entertained, that is evidence that one has not understood the expressive character of religious language. In one case, that language expresses a moment of feeling which is allegedly independent of beliefs and practices; in the other case, it expresses a form of life that is constituted by concepts and practices that can be understood only in terms of the grammatical rules by which they are governed. In both instances, accounts are restricted to those that accord with the perspective of the believer.

When the question of how to account for the force of the experience is not employed in a protective strategy, it is a legitimate one. It is likely that no general account can be given which is adequate to capture the force or impressiveness of different kinds of experience. Let us briefly consider two kinds of experience, ordinary perception and the power of a work of art. Both can be gripping and forceful, though in different ways. The authority of perception consists in what we have called, following James, its noetic quality. In chapter five we saw that this quality is best accounted for by the assumption of a causal connection between the perceptual experience and that which is perceived. I will withdraw my claim to have seen a tree if I learn that my visual image of the tree can be traced to some irrelevant cause and that I would have had the same image even if the tree had not been there. The force of my experience of climbing Mount Rainier, as compared with merely imagining the climb, derives from the judgments I make about the connections between myself, the mountain, and the rest of the world. My judgment about how the image in my mind is caused affects the experience, making it more vivid and gripping than if I believe I am just entertaining the possibility of the climb.

Hume thought that belief in a proposition was to be distinguished from merely entertaining that proposition by the greater vivacity of the impression. He illustrates this by comparing the experiences of one who reads a book believing it to be true and another who takes it to be fiction.

> If one person sits down to read a book as a romance, and another as a true history, they plainly receive the same ideas, and in the same order; nor does the incredulity of the one, and the belief of the other hinder them from putting the very same sense upon their author. His words produce the same ideas in both; tho' his testimony has not the same influence on them. The latter has a more lively conception of the incidents. He enters deeper into the concerns of the persons: represents to himself their actions, and characters, and friendships, and enmities: He even goes so far as to form a notion of their features, and air, and person. While the former, who gives no credit to the testimony of the author, has a more faint and languid conception of all these particulars; and except on account of the style and ingenuity of the composition, can receive little entertainment from it. (Hume, 1965: 97–98)

Hume is wrong on two counts. It is not a matter of common experience that what is taken to be true is more vivid and lively than what is thought to be fiction. Often novels, plays, and films move us more dramatically than do newspapers or history texts. We do experience something we take to be true in a manner that differs from our experience of something we consider fictional, but that difference is not accurately described by reference to the vivacity of the conception. It is a matter of the connections that we believe hold between what we are reading and the world in which we live. If I read in the paper that a portion of the west-side highway has been closed for repairs, I will alter my route when leaving the city. The murder in a mystery novel may be more vividly portrayed than the murder that took place last night on my block and about which I am now reading in the morning paper, but the latter may have a force and effect upon my emotions and behavior which the novel lacks.

The force of the experience is due to judgments and assumptions about the relation of this experience to the rest of my life and to the world in which I live. Those judgments and assumptions are constitutive of the experience. Wittgenstein and Phillips are correct in calling attention to the fact that the force of the experience is a matter of subtle connections between our concepts and the practices that inform our lives, but they are incorrect in claiming that these connections never involve explanations. The difference between my skiing down a slope and my entertaining the possibility of skiing down the slope is not only a matter of logical or conceptual connection. If I take it to be an accurate perception of what is happening to me now because it stands in a certain causal relation to the slope, the snow, and the terrain I am speeding past, the experience will differ considerably from one in which I am entertaining the possibility of that run, either eagerly or with some trepidation, as I ride up the chair lift. The relevant connections are conceptual, but they include conceptions of causes.

Despite Hume's claim to the contrary, novels, paintings, rites, and other works of art move us deeply even when we are aware that they are fictions. Many different theories have been proposed to account for the force of our experience of art, and it is not possible to examine them here. Wollheim (1974: 84–100; 1979) has suggested that the power of a painting, a musical composition, or a ceremony derives from its having been constructed so as to invite the projection and externalization of complex mental states. A work of art succeeds to the extent that it does not foster denial or romanticization but enables a person to experience his or her own inner states with honesty and precision, and so aids in the process of self-discovery. Wolterstorff (1980) has proposed that art is best understood as the creation of possible worlds other than the actual one. Fictional characters are denizens of those worlds, and the power of the work derives from the possibilities presented by those alternatives. In either case, a work of art shows something that is true of ourselves and opens up new possibilities, and it can achieve both functions while we recognize it to be a fiction.

Of the two kinds of force we have considered, the noetic quality of religious experience in theistic traditions is closer to the force of ordinary perception than it is to the power of fiction. To experience God or his providential activity is not, from the subject's point of view, to entertain a possible world in which there is a God and he governs events in the world, nor is it to entertain a concept that permits one to externalize certain hopes and fears by projecting them onto another plane. One might suspect that the proper explanation of religious belief and experience would be found along these lines, but it is not the account that would be given by the believer. The experience has a noetic quality for the subject and is taken to reveal something about the world beyond the individual self. In this way, it is similar to the experience of actually skiing down the slope, as contrasted with that of thinking about skiing down the slope.

Schleiermacher claims to offer an account of piety which is neutral with respect to explanations and beliefs about the world. But causal claims are included in the criteria for identifying either the sense and taste for the infinite or the feeling of absolute dependence. Otto builds an explanatory commitment into his allegedly phenomenological description by his statement that if the experience can be explained in natural terms it is not a numinous experience. Edwards stresses the sensible quality of the new sense of the heart, but that quality and his attention to the fruits of religious affections are significant chiefly as symptoms by which one can discern whether or not the affections have been produced by the Holy Spirit. James writes of a "More" that is operative in the universe outside the self. In each of these instances, despite protests to the contrary, a reference to the causal explanation of the experience is employed to discriminate it from others.

The force of religious experience is best accounted for by the fact that the criteria for identifying an experience as religious include reference to an explanatory claim. The experience is perceived by the subject as eluding explanation solely in terms of his own mental states but as having been produced in such a way that it supports his beliefs about the world, beliefs that are distinctive of the tradition within which it is being characterized as religious. The experience provides support for and confirmation of those beliefs.

Evidence for the hypothesis that the identification of an experience as religious includes an embedded causal claim is of two kinds. First, the descriptions of religious experience which purport to be neutral with regard to beliefs and explanations include disguised explanatory commitments. Second, critics of reductionist approaches claim that the distinctive character of religious experience and belief is lost when the attempt is made to explain them. This shows that what is distinctive about religious belief and practice for these critics is that they are not amenable to nonreligious explanations. These criticisms provide support for the claim that the distinguishing mark of the religious is, after all, a matter of explanation.

Explaining Religious Experience

The term *experience* is ambiguous. When I inquire about what a person has experienced at a certain moment, my question is ambiguous between two meanings: (1) how it seemed to that person at that time; and (2) the best explanation that can be given of the experience. This ambiguity is present in our ordinary talk about perception. I may have been frightened by the bear that I saw up ahead on the trail. My friend points out to me that it is not a bear but a log, and my fear subsides. What did I really see up ahead? By one interpretation of the word *see*, I saw a bear. That is the way I apprehended it, and that apprehension accounts for my fear and behavioral response. By another interpretation, what I really saw was a log, and I took it for a bear. I was wrong about what I experienced, and now that I can explain what happened I can correct my mistake.

This distinction is similar to, but differs from, Chisholm's distinction between the comparative and epistemic uses of "appear" words. It differs because Chisholm suggests that the comparative use, the description of how it appears to the subject, is a report of an immediate experience that is independent of interpretation or other beliefs. No such unmediated experience is possible. The distinction drawn here is between one interpretation, which presupposes a particular explanation of the experience, and another interpretation, also assuming an explanation, which is adopted by another person or by the same person at a later time. The perception of the object ahead as a bear was one explanation, and that was replaced by a better explanation when more information became available. That better explanation led to a reinterpretation of the experience.

It is important to note that both senses of *experience* assume explanations. It is not the case that explanation enters only into the second sense. The first, the description of his or her experience as assumed by the subject at the time of the experience, presupposes an explanation. If the distinguishing mark of the religious is that it is assumed to elude natural explanation, then the labeling of the experience as religious by the subject includes the belief that it cannot be exhaustively explained in naturalistic terms. The attempts of scholars as diverse as Eliade and Phillips to preclude issues of explanation from entering into accounts of religious experience and belief are undercut by the recognition that explanatory commitments are assumed in the identification of an experience as religious.

The distinction we have drawn between descriptive and explanatory reduction is tailored to meet this ambiguity. Descriptive reduction is inappropriate because the experience must be identified under a description that can be ascribed to the subject at the time of the experience. The experience must be described with reference to its intentional object. In the example given above, my fright was the result of noticing a bear ahead of me. The fact that the analyst must attempt to formulate a description of the experience which captures the way it was apprehended by the subject does not mean that no explanation is incorporated into the subject's description, nor does it mean that the analyst is not engaged in an inference toward the best explanation in his attempt to arrive at that formulation.

The identification of an experience under a description that can be ascribed to the subject is required before any explanation of the experience can be proposed. Every explanation assumes a description of that which is to be explained. One cannot explain phenomena as such but only phenomena under a description (Danto: 1975: 218–232). An event, action, emotion, or experience can be identified only under a certain description, and reference must be made to that description in any explanation that is offered. If the relevant description is not acknowledged, it will be tacitly assumed. The analyst's choice of the appropriate description of an experience or action is not entirely independent of the explanation he goes on to offer. If a practice is completely baffling to me under a certain description, and would be recognizable as a practice common to the culture in which it is ensconced if the description were altered slightly, then I will be tempted to alter it and to ascribe the discrepancy to defects in my observation or in the reports from which I am working. If the evidence for the original description is compelling, I must accept the anomaly and search further for an explanation; if it is weak, I may adjust the description in the interest of overall plausibility. This is the proper point at which to invoke Quine's principle of charity. I want my total account, with its descriptive and explanatory components, to be the most plausible of the available alternatives. I adjust each until I reach a reflective equilibrium.

The recognition that religious experience is constituted by concepts and beliefs permits an optimism with respect to the descriptive task which would not otherwise be possible. There is no reason, in principle, to despair about the possibility of understanding the experience of persons and communities that are historically and culturally remote from the interpreter. The difficulty is not posed by an unbridgeable gap between an experience that can only be known by acquaintance and the concepts in which that experience is expressed. Because the concepts and beliefs are constitutive of the experience, careful study of the concepts available in a particular culture, the rules that govern them, and the practices that are informed by them will provide access to the variety of experiences available to persons in that culture. Though it may be difficult to reconstruct, the evidence required for understanding the experience is public evidence about linguistic forms and practices. We attempt to formulate a description of the experience from the perspective of the subject, but the evidence is, in principle, accessible to us.

This conception of religious experience also shows that the variety of that experience is much greater and richer than has been suggested by those who claim that a single experience of the numinous or sacred, or a few such types, underlie all the diverse reports in different traditions. Just as the experiences of nirvana and devekuth differ because they are informed by different concepts and beliefs, so the often rather subtle doctrinal differences between religious communities, or subgroups of the same community, will give rise to different experiences. Kierkegaard was able to distinguish rather precisely several different forms of despair by examining the concepts that enter into those forms. A wide variety of conversion experiences or experiences of religious awe or wonder can be distinguished in the same manner. The catalogue of varieties can never be completed.

If explanation is as central to the study of religious experience as this account suggests, then why has it not been recognized as such? Why is the explanatory component so often disguised or ignored in favor of appeals to a sense or a consciousness that is contrasted with belief? There are two motivations for this procedure: phenomenological accuracy and a protective strategy adopted for apologetic purposes. The first arises from the fact that those who report religious experiences typically take them to be independent of and more fundamental than beliefs or theories. The sense of the infinite or the consciousness of finitude is not apprehended as a theoretical commitment but as an inchoate sense that provides a practical orientation. It seems to the subject to be inaccurate to classify it with inference, inquiry, and hypothesis. Since an understanding of the experience requires that it be identified under a description that accords with that of the subject, it is tempting to assimilate it to the case of sensations, and to assume that sensations are independent of practices and beliefs. For these reasons, phenomenological accuracy appears to some to require that the experience be described so as to make it independent of beliefs.

The appeal to a sense or consciousness that is allegedly innocent of explanatory commitments has an apologetic advantage. If such an appeal could be made, it would be unaffected by any developments in science or other kinds of inquiry. It would, as Schleiermacher said, leave one's physics and psychology unaffected. Religious belief and practice could be seen as derived from this independent experience, and the difficult questions that have been raised for religion by changes in our other beliefs could be circumvented. Rather than seeing the experience as constituted by the beliefs, one could view the beliefs as expressive of the experience. The direction of derivation would be reversed, and that would serve the task of apologetics. If it did not provide a way of justifying religious beliefs and practices, it would at least protect them from the criticism that they conflict with ordinary and scientific beliefs.

As we have seen, the protective strategy used by those who argue that religious experience is independent of concepts and beliefs is parallel to that adopted by those who claim it is permeated by concepts but independent of referential or explanatory commitments. In both cases, accounts of religious experience are restricted to those that would be endorsed by the person having the experience, and consequently the possibility of those accounts conflicting with the claims of the believer is precluded. Whether one describes an allegedly prelinguistic affective experience or confines oneself to elucidating the grammar of a particular religious practice or experience, the result cannot possibly come into conflict with any beliefs or explanations from outside the religious perspective.

A consequence of such strategies is that language that appears to be descriptive may be intended to evoke or reproduce the experience that is purportedly described. Schleiermacher is explicit about his assumption that direct acquaintance is required for understanding the sense of the infinite; thus he sees the need to elicit that sense in his readers. Rhetorical language is carefully constructed, and the speech or essay becomes an edifying discourse, of which Schleiermacher's *On Religion* is a prime example. He regards his evocative language as a catalyst that directs the reader's attention to a sense that is already present but has not been nurtured. In fact, however, the language may be not merely catalytic but constitutive of the experience. If the reader follows Schleiermacher's instruction to attend to the moment before the rise of consciousness and to recognize the unity intuited there, he or she may discover that unity. That discovery ought not, however, to be cited as evidence for the unity of the world or of the infinite. An experience that has been evoked by carefully chosen rhetoric and by assuming a cultural tradition informed by theism cannot be taken as evidence for a unity that is independent of our concepts and beliefs.

Descriptions of doubt, anxiety, or faith in existentialist literature are often employed in a similar way. Kierkegaard displays dazzling literary and analytic skills in the service of edification. His analyses are often designed to elicit experiences and affections in his reader. Just as the spiritual director and the skilled revivalist preacher know how to evoke certain emotions and attitudes, an author can employ rhetorical skills to elicit affections in a reader. That ability presupposes a considerable amount of analysis. Kierkegaard's writings contain very subtle analyses of despair, faith, and doubt. As Aristotle knew, one can often learn more about emotions and attitudes from the orator or poet than from anyone else. Unlike Aristotle's *Rhetoric*, however, Schleiermacher's *On Religion* and most of Kierkegaard's pseudonymous works are written in a rhetorical style intended to elicit that which is being described. Much of the literature in the history and phenomenology of religion can also be viewed in this light. Such terms as *numinous, holy,* and *sacred* are presented as descriptive or analytical tools but in conjunction with warnings against reductionism, they function to preclude explanation and evoke a sense of mystery or awe. They are used to persuade the reader that the distinguishing mark of the religious is some quality that eludes description and analysis in nonreligious terms. Otto's use of *numinous* is an example of how one can employ the term to create a sense of mystery and present it as analysis. Such approaches to the study of religion are offered as neutral descriptions, but they assume not only a theory of religion but also religious theory.

We have distinguished the tasks of description and explanation and have argued that explanation is central both to religious experience and to its study. What kind of explanation, then, might we expect to construct for religious experience? An experience or an event can be explained only when it is identified under a description. And we have concluded that the distinguishing mark of religious experience is the subject's belief that the experience can only be accounted for in religious terms. It is this belief, and the subject's identification of his or her experience under a particular description, which makes it religious. If the concepts and beliefs under which the subject identifies his or her experience determine whether or not it is a religious experience, then we need to explain why the subject employs those particular concepts and beliefs. We must explain why the subject was confronted with this particular set of alternative ways of understanding his experience and why he employed the one he did. In general, what we want is a historical or cultural explanation.

This holds both for discrete, datable religious experiences, of the sort on which James concentrates, and for the identification of an underlying and pervasive religious moment in experience. Why did Stephen Bradley identify his accelerated heart rate as the work of the Holy Spirit? What caused Astor to regard what he saw as a miracle whereas Bingham remained skeptical? Why did Schleiermacher apprehend the moment that precedes thought as a sense of the infinite and discern a feeling of absolute dependence which accompanies all consciousness of the polarity of self and world? For Bradley, we would need to know something about Methodist revivalism in early nineteenth-century New England, about the particular meeting he attended earlier in the evening, and about the events in his life up to that moment. To explain Astor's beliefs about what he saw it would be necessary to acquaint oneself with Roman Catholic teachings on miracles, the significance of the shrine at Lourdes, and the details of Astor's background. To explain Schleiermacher's sense of the infinite, his feeling of absolute dependence, and his apprehension of all events as miracles one would need to know more about his early years among the Moravians, his study of Spinoza, and the circle of friends in Berlin for whom he wrote *On Religion*. Each of these instances requires acquaintance with the Christian tradition and with the particular forms of that tradition which shaped the person and his experience.

For experiences sought in highly manipulative settings, as in meditative traditions where the training is carefully prescribed and a person is guided by a spiritual director in the interpretation of the states of mind and body achieved by the regimen, explanations of the sort suggested by Schachter's experiment seem clearly relevant. The novice learns to make attributions that accord with the tradition, and he engages self-consciously in manipulations to attain states that confirm those attributions. For seemingly more spontaneous but still relatively discrete and datable experiences in less contrived settings, one would still look to explain the experience by accounting for why the subject makes these particular attributions. Just as Schachter's experiment sheds light on the experience of emotions in natural settings, attention to the meditative traditions may provide insight into the allegedly natural, spontaneous examples of religious experience. The phenomenologist of religion has often claimed that elaborately contrived ritualistic settings are expressions of the pervasive sense of the sacred or the infinite in human experience, but it seems more likely that the supposedly natural and spontaneous experiences are derived from beliefs and practices in much the same way that an experience is produced in the more disciplined traditions of meditative practice. How did Schleiermacher and others come to think that the sense of the infinite or the sense of finitude was independent of and prior to the beliefs and practices of a culture shaped by theism? His identification of what he takes to be a universal moment in human experience seems clearly to reflect the concept of God as Creator and Governor derived from the Hebrew Bible and the traditions it formed. The consciousness Schleiermacher accurately describes may, upon investigation, turn out to be the product of prior religious beliefs and practices.

Inquiry may demonstrate that some sense or intuition that appears to be independent of beliefs and practices is actually an artifact that developed under particular historical circumstances. Elizabeth Anscombe (1958: 1–19) calls attention to the fact that some of the central concepts of modern moral philosophy, including the distinctively moral uses of *ought* and *right,* have no parallel in Aristotle or in other classical authors. Contemporary moral philosophers debate Hume's claim that one cannot derive ought from is, or Moore's discussion of the naturalistic fallacy, as if they were trying to clarify concepts that are invariant across periods and cultures and that are crucial for moral experience everywhere. Why, then, does that sense of *ought* seem so alien to the moral reasoning we find in Aristotle? Anscombe points out that between Aristotle and Hume our language and practice was shaped by theism, particularly by Christianity. She suggests that the modern concept of moral obligation is not an intuition that is independent of culture and belief, but that it derives from a law conception of ethics, and that that conception assumes belief in a divine lawgiver.

> Naturally it is not possible to have such a conception unless you believe in God as a lawgiver; like Jews, Stoics, and Christians. But if such a conception is dominant for many centuries, and then is given up, it is a natural result that the concepts of "obligation," of being bound or required as by a law, should remain though they had lost their root; and if the word "ought" has become invested in certain contexts with the sense of "obligation," it too will remain to be spoken with special emphasis and a special feeling in these contexts. (Anscombe, 1958: 6)

The concept of ought, and the related sense of obligation, have survived outside of the conceptual framework that produced them and made them intelligible. The moral sentiments Hume describes and maps so well are artifacts that were formed by earlier beliefs and practices.

It seems quite likely that the feeling of absolute dependence and Otto's sense of the numinous are legacies of belief in the God of the Hebrew Bible and Christian tradition and of the practices informed by that belief. These experiences now appear to be autonomous and independent of that belief and that tradition. At a time in which belief in a transcendent Creator and associated metaphysical doctrines have been rejected by many, the habits of interpretation informed by those beliefs remain firmly entrenched in cultural patterns of thought, action, and feeling. Belief in God as Creator once provided the justifying context for these affections and practices. Now the direction of justification is reversed, and attempts are made to defend the beliefs by appeal to the affective experiences and practices. The sense of finitude, the feeling of absolute dependence, the practice of worship, and the grammar that governs the use of the word *God* are appealed to in order to justify the traditional religious statements without which this sense, feeling, practice, and grammar would not be intelligible.

These are only some suggestions of the kind of explanation that might be offered of religious experience. While one might venture a hypothesis to account for Bradley's accelerated heart rate or the recovery that Astor witnessed, that approach will not yield an explanation of their experiences. What must be explained is why they understood what happened to them or what they witnessed in religious terms. This requires a mapping of the concepts and beliefs that were available to them, the commitments they brought to the experience, and the contextual conditions that might have supported their identification of their experiences in religious terms. Interest in explanations is not an alien element that is illegitimately introduced into the study of religious experience. Those who identify their experiences in religious terms are seeking the best explanations for what is happening to them. The analyst should work to understand those explanations and discover why they are adopted.

Notes

1. See John Y. Fenton, "Reductionism in the Study of Religion," *Soundings* 53 (1970), 61–76; and Hans H. Penner and Edward Yonan, "Is a Science of Religion Possible?" *Journal of Religion* 52 (1972), 107–33. (In his original text, Wayne Proudfoot used the author/date system of endnoting. To provide a fuller citation for the reader, the editor has amplified the notes as necessary.)

2. "To try to grasp the essence of such a phenomenon by means of physiology, sociology, economics, linguistics, art, or any other study is false; it misses the unique and irreducible element in it—the element of the sacred." Mircea Eliade, *Patterns in Comparative Religion,* trans. R. Sheed (New York: Meridian, 1966), xiii.

3. The ascription of unconscious beliefs or desires presents special problems. For a good discussion, see Arthur W. Collins, "Unconscious Belief," *Journal of Philosophy* 66 (1969), 667–80. Even in these cases, the beliefs and desires must be described in terms that the subject would understand and that could plausibly be attributed to him or her.

4. Eliade assumes the existence of archetypal patterns that are given different interpretations in different cultures. See Eliade, *Patterns in Comparative Religion.* The identification of such patterns is highly arbitrary, however, and encourages the scholar to ignore the contextual details of religious experience.

5. Explanatory reduction is permissible, but descriptive reduction is not. However, Eliade *(Patterns in Comparative Religion)* decries explanatory reduction, while his practice of treating symbols and rites as universal archetypes abstracted from their social cultural contexts amounts to descriptive reduction. This is precisely the wrong combination.

6. It is unlikely that the Maori employed the concept of the sacred. Sigmund Freud quotes James Frazer, *The Golden Bough,* 3d ed., Part II, "Taboo and Perils of the Soul" (London: Macmillan, 1911), 136. Frazer drew his information from R. Taylor, *Te Ika a Maui* (London, 1870), which I have not been able to find. I suspect that *sacred* is a term added by either Taylor or Frazer.

7. Peter Winch, "Knowledge and Practice," an unpublished essay on Simone Weil, quoted by D. Z. Phillips in his *Religion Without Explanation* (Oxford: Basil Blackwell, 1976), 125–26.

8. See chapter 3.

———————————————————— ■ ————————————————————

42. Mysticism and Philosophy

RICHARD M. GALE

This paper will be an attempt to deal with the key problems which mysticism poses for philosophy, these being the alleged ineffability of mystical experiences, the relation between the so-called eternal and temporal orders of being and the objectivity of mystical experiences. We will use Professor Walter Stace's *Time and Eternity* as a springboard for our own critical analysis of these problems.

1. Alleged Ineffability of Mystical Experiences

Basic to Professor Stace's thesis is his claim that mystical experiences, unlike all other types of experience, are completely ineffable, or non-conceptualizable. From this it follows that nothing revealed through mystical experience could possibly be either proved or disproved by anything known through the intellect, which is the process of understanding objects by means of concepts. His discussion, however, is marred by a failure to state clearly in exactly what sense mystical experiences are ineffable. I believe that a careful reading of the book will reveal that four different criteria or senses of ineffability

Source: Richard M. Gale, "Mysticism and Philosophy," *The Journal of Philosophy* 57 no. 14 (July 7, 1960), 471–81. Reprinted by permission of *The Journal of Philosophy* and the author.

are appealed to. It will be necessary to discuss each one of these four senses separately to determine, first, whether mystical experiences are ineffable in any of these senses, and, second, if they are ineffable in any sense, whether this sense is trivial, i.e., one which would apply equally well to certain non-mystical experiences.

(1) *Within the mystical experience there is an undifferentiated unity, affording no foothold for any concept.* During the mystical experience, as viewed phenomenologically from the standpoint of the experient, there is a dissolution of the dualism between subject and object as well as a unification of what was originally a multiplicity of objects. For this reason mystical experiences are ineffable.

In opposition to this it can be maintained that mystics as a matter of fact *do* manage to conceptualize their mystical experiences when they are outside them. By applying concepts such as "the undifferentiated unity," "the dissolution of the personal ego," "non-temporal and non-spatial," "the sense of peace and sacredness," etc. to their experiences they succeed in distinguishing mystical from non-mystical experiences.

Professor Stace's counter to this would be that *within* the mystical experience the mystic cannot conceptualize his experience because the use of any concept presupposes a multiplicity of objects as well as the subject-object dualism, and this is just what is wiped out during the experience. In claiming that mystical experiences are ineffable because they cannot be conceptualized by the mystic *while he is within* the experience, Professor Stace seems to be appealing to the following criterion of ineffability: *An experience is ineffable if a proposition describing this experience cannot be either formulated, consciously considered, or verified by the experient during the time that he is actually having the experience.* I will attempt to show that this sense of ineffability is trivial because many non-mystical experiences would equally well qualify as candidates for the title of ineffable.

We would all agree that the experience of wrestling with an alligator is conceptualizable. However, the proposition, "Tarzan is wrestling with an alligator," could not possibly be either formulated, consciously considered, or verified by Tarzan while he is actually having the experience described by the proposition. Similarly, and for slightly different practical reasons, Schnabel is not capable of formulating or verifying the proposition, "Schnabel is concentrating *solely* on interpreting Beethoven's 14th Sonata," while he is actually engaged in performing the sonata; for if he were to attempt to verify this proposition while he was performing the Sonata he would automatically render it false, because that would mean that he could not possibly be concentrating *solely* on interpreting the Sonata.

Because an experience, whether of the mystical or the Tarzan-Schnabel type, is not conceptualizable by the experient while he is having the experience, it does not follow that a third person cannot describe the experience at the very moment the experient is having his experience, or that the experient himself cannot conceptualize his experience after the experience is over.

Professor Stace's answer to this argument would be that there still is a significant difference between mystical experiences and the Schnabel-Tarzan type of experiences, for only in the former is there a complete dissolution of the personal ego. Whether the mystic actually experiences the dissolution of his own ego is open to some doubts, for if this were so how would it be possible for the mystic to remember that *he* had had such an experience? In what sense could it be said to be *his* experience? How can someone experience the dissolution of his ego? But if we waive these difficulties and grant Professor Stace his point that there actually is such a dissolution of the personal ego, this would have no logical relevance to the claim that mystical experiences are ineffable in some unique sense. It would show only that there are different practical reasons why the mystic cannot conceptualize his experience when inside the experience than why Tarzan and Schnabel cannot.

(2) *Mystical experiences are unique, being totally different from all other types of experience.* Mystics themselves claim that they cannot find adequate words to describe their experiences. They have not been able to invent a new language in which their experiences would no longer be ineffable.

However, against this, it can be said that many mystics have been autobiographical mystics. Such mystics manage to communicate the nature of their experience not only to fellow mystics but to many non-mystics as well. When we read the descriptions of mystical experience given by an Eckhart or a Suzuki we seem to know what they are talking about. If we should be soaking in a hot bath one night and suddenly have an experience in which our personal ego was dissolved by melting into an infinite ocean which was an undifferentiated unity and which furthermore gave us a sense of peace and sacredness far transcending anything previously experienced, we would leap to our feet saying with great excitement, "Why that Eckhart wasn't just pulling our leg! There really are such experiences and I just had one!"

There is something woefully inconsistent in Professor Stace's saying, in one breath, that mystical experiences are ineffable—that no concepts can be used to describe them—and, in the next breath, that there is unanimity among the mystics—that all mystics describe their experiences in pretty much the same way. If one of these claims is true then the other must be false.[1] Also, if mystical experiences were as ineffable as mystics claim they are, then what sense could we make of their claim that their experiences are in principle verifiable if the proper steps are taken? What kind of an experience would serve as a confirming instance?

To say that mystical experiences are ineffable in the sense of not being adequately described by language is to make a trivial claim. No concepts can completely describe any direct experience; they can never serve as substitutes for such experiences. My concept of a loud, deafening noise is not itself a loud, deafening noise. Our experience of yellow is just as unique and ineffable as a mystical experience; we cannot define the color yellow in terms of anything more simple or basic. But this does not mean that we cannot conceptualize our direct experience of yellow and communicate with others about it. If the experience of the color yellow were unique, and accessible to only one person in the universe, then it would be impossible for this person to communicate with others about this experience. What is presupposed in communicating propositions about simple color experiences as well as mystical experiences is an experiential awareness on the part of the addressee of the experience referred to by the proposition.

I believe that the real reason for the mystic's claiming some sort of unique ineffability for his experience is to be found in the inestimable significance and value which the experience has for him. It seems that the more highly we prize some experience the more we shun applying concepts to it. Like the composer who shuns writing program notes for his symphony because he fears, and rightly so, that eventually the reading of the program notes will take the place of the direct listening experience of the music, the mystic is afraid that the concepts by which he describes his experience will become surrogates for the experience itself. Both men are telling us by their refusal to conceptualize their experience that it is the direct experience itself which counts and that language is a very poor substitute.

(3) *Propositions describing mystical experiences contain self-contradictions.*[2] Professor Stace finds the basic paradox of the Divine in the contradiction between the positive and negative conceptions of the Divine. "The latter denies all predicates of Him, even that of existence; whereas, the former says that He is the fullness of Being, the ultimate reality" (p. 34).

It seems to me that this alleged contradiction between the positive and negative conceptions of the Divine rests on the equivocation of the term "exist." When in the negative conception of the Divine the mystic denies that God *exists*, he means, by "exist," "to be a fact in a spatio-temporal order"; whereas, when from the positive conception of the Divine he claims that God *exists* or *Is*, he means now, by "exist," "to be an eternal or timeless Being," which is supposedly apprehended through mystical experiences. If we distinguish between these two different meanings of "exist" the alleged contradiction between the positive and negative conception of the Divine disappears.

This still does not explain away many seemingly self-contradictory statements made by mystics. They refer to their experience as being at once passive and active, personal and impersonal, full and empty, containing a multiplicity of objects and still being a Oneness without parts, etc. What I will try to show is that such statements are not literal self-contradictions because the law of contradiction does not apply to them. The function of mystical statements is not the cognitive one of literally describing facts in space and time, but rather that of evoking in the addressee certain feelings and emotions in the same way that esthetic language does. In the following discussion we will consider *only* propositions having some sort of empirical meaning, i.e., propositions referring to something which is a content of a direct experience. Mystical propositions, while not having existential import in the strictest sense since they do not refer to facts in space and time, still come under the heading of propositions having empirical meaning, since, as we tried to prove, they do have experiential import.

Now in regard to propositions having empirical meaning we can say that one proposition contradicts another proposition only if we first know the time factor of the two propositions.[3] The law of contradiction has application only to those empirical propositions in which the time factor can be specified. For this reason *we can never say that two mystical propositions are contradictories because the time factor of the two propositions can never be specified.* The reason why the time factor of a mystical proposition can never be specified is that such a proposition refers to an experience which is, as the mystic himself claims, phenomenologically atemporal, containing within itself no change and therefore no relations of before and after. Therefore when we read in the *Isa Upanishad*, "It (the Self) stirs and it stirs not," we cannot say that such a proposition is a self-contradiction because the mystic can never tell us whether it stirs and also stirs not *at one and the same moment of time.* He cannot supply us with this information because his experience is atemporal.

The conclusion to be drawn from this analysis is that mystical propositions cannot be said to be literally self-contradictory.[4] The law of contradiction is a rule of discourse applying *only* to propositions having a cognitive function, i.e., propositions referring to events locatable in some definite region of space and time. The propositions of the mystics are alogical. They do not violate the law of contradiction—it simply does not apply to them. Professor Stace would agree with the end result of this analysis if not with the means by which it is achieved; for he has said that the function of mystical propositions is not cognitive, but rather that of *evoking* within us a certain type of experience (p. 120). But the evocative function of language is not unique to mystical symbolism; it is equally true of the esthetic use of language, so that we would not have shown that mystical experiences were ineffable in some unique sense. In describing my listening experience of the second movement of Beethoven's 7th Symphony I might say that it is the most tragic and yet the most joyous music I ever heard. If someone should then ask, "Do you mean at the same moment of time?," I would not know how to answer, for, as in the case of mystical propositions, I would not be able to specify the time factor. By describing the movement as being both tragic and joyous I am referring to an emotional quality which permeates the *entire* movement, and the function of my language is to evoke in the addressee an emotional experience of a similar type to the one I had when I listened to the movement.

(4) *Propositions describing mystical experiences contradict propositions describing non-mystical experiences.* This is unquestionably the case, for mystical propositions claim that space, time, and multiplicity are unreal; whereas propositions describing non-mystical experiences deny this. But it does not follow that mystical propositions are empirically meaningless, and consequently that mystical experiences are ineffable. We can understand the empirical meaning of each one of a pair of contradictory propositions; it is only the conjunction of these two contradictory propositions into a single proposition which becomes empirically meaningless. If our analysis has been correct, we understand what sort of experiences are being referred to by mystical propositions, and the fact that such propositions contradict propositions referring to non-mystical experiences does not render mystical experiences ineffable any more than it renders non-mystical experiences ineffable. Because mystical experiences are so different from the ordinary run-of-the-mill experiences, the mystic feels that these experiences are mysterious and paradoxical.

2. Relation of the Eternal to the Temporal Order of Being

During the mystical experience the mystic experiences only one order of being, the so-called eternal order. Within his experience there is no opposition between the eternal and temporal since the temporal world then simply does not exist for him; therefore, there is no contradiction for him to be puzzled over or to try and explain away. But most of the mystic's life is lived outside of the mystical moment, and it is then that he feels the contradiction between his mystical and non-mystical experiences. He may then even attempt to reconcile intellectually these two seemingly diametrically opposed realms of being, and so become involved in contradictions.

Professor Stace's answer to the seeming contradiction between the eternal and temporal order of being takes the form of an *exclusive* disjunction: *Either* we take our stand *outside* the mystical experience, as the naturalist does, in which case mystical experiences are purely subjective feelings and emotions; *or* we take our stand *inside* the mystical experience, in which case the natural world of space, time, and multiplicity is unreal or illusory. These two possible standpoints or perspectives are disjuncts in an exclusive disjunction, which means that *we cannot take both of these standpoints at the same time.* We must affirm one of these disjuncts and so deny the other.

However, in his theory of intersection Professor Stace makes this disjunction *inclusive.* The eternal and natural order intersect at each point of space and time. We know of such an intersection through the experience of the mystic. The mystic lives in both orders and at the moment of his mystical experience the two orders intersect. The point at which his experience takes place can be considered as a moment of time if viewed from the naturalistic standpoint, or it can be seen from within as the eternal Now-moment. "It is one and the same human consciousness which experiences both the temporal or natural and the eternal and infinite order which is disclosed in mystical illumination. Thus this identity of eternity with a temporal moment is an actual experienced fact, and this fact is what is metaphorically represented by the image of intersection" (p. 82).

Professor Stace's claim that the "identity of eternity with a temporal moment is an actual experienced fact" is ambiguous. It could mean: (1) that one and the same person has mystical experiences and *at other times* has experiences of a non-mystical variety; and (2) that the mystic experiences in the mystical experience the intersection of the two orders. In the case of (1) there is no direct experience of the intersection of the two orders; herein we are still left with an exclusive disjunction between the naturalistic and mystic standpoints. In the case of (2) the intersection is the content of a single direct intuitive experience.

I believe that the first interpretation is the only defensible one. It is certainly the case that one and the same person can have both mystical and non-mystical experiences, but it is not true that a person can have an experience which is *at once both* mystical and non-mystical. As the mystic himself has proclaimed, a person cannot at the same time experience both the eternal and the temporal; by definition it follows that if a person is having a mystical experience he cannot at the same time be having a non-mystical experience. Therefore it is not possible for a person to have a single direct experience in which the temporal and timeless realms of being intersect because for this to happen he would have to have an experience which was at once both mystical and non-mystical, and by definition this is impossible. The intersection of the eternal and the temporal is arrived at through an intellectual interpretation, and can never be the content of any direct experience.

In his theory of intersection, Professor Stace uses at the same time the language of both mystic and naturalist, and in this way attempts to escape the confines of his own exclusive disjunction. By saying that *at a moment in time* a mystic experiences the *eternal* he is employing at the same time the language of both mystic and naturalist, and thereby makes his disjunction inclusive by *adopting both standpoints at the same time.* But insofar as we use the language of the naturalist we must describe the mystical experience as a subjective psychological event taking place at some moment of time, and insofar as we adopt the mystical standpoint we must describe the experience as union with the eternal or infinite and so deny that there is a temporal order. From the latter standpoint there is no *moment in time* at which the experience takes place.

3. Objectivity of Mystical Experience

It may appear that we have been begging the question up to now by referring to mystical experiences as subjective psychological experiences when viewed from the naturalistic standpoint. Some mystics would argue that the same criterion by which we judge a sense experience to be veridical or objective can be used to prove the objectivity of a mystical experience. This is the argument: The criterion for objectivity in sense experience is unanimity or agreement among observers; since there is unanimity among mystics it follows by analogy with the criterion for objectivity in sense experience that mystical experiences are objective. The fact that very few persons have had mystical experiences is not evidence against the objectivity of such experiences; for a mystical proposition, like any non-mystical one, is really a hypothetical statement saying what experiences a person will have *if* certain verifying procedures are followed. However, in the case of propositions about sense experience we can specify exactly what operations must be performed by the verifier; whereas, in the case of mystical propositions, it is far more difficult to do this. The proper steps to be taken by one who wishes to verify a mystical proposition may include living an ascetic life for twenty years—staying out of bars, not watching television, doing breathing exercises, etc. If after following the "mystic way" for twenty years this poor chap still does not have a mystical experience there is the tendency for the mystic to beg the question by definition by saying that this only proves that this person has not taken the proper steps. In this case part of the very definition of what constitutes the proper steps is the stipulation that the verifier must have a mystical experience.

Waiving this difficulty and also granting the claim for unanimity among the mystics, we can still point to a basic flaw in this argument which is due to the fact that the criterion for objectivity which is appealed to is inadequate even in the realm of sense experience. Mere unanimity or agreement among observers is not a sufficient condition for objectivity. *Everybody* who presses his finger on his eyeball will see double, *everybody* who stands at a certain spot in the desert will see the mirage, etc. The true criterion for objectivity is the Kantian one: An experience is objective if its contents can be placed in a spatio-temporal order with other experiences in accordance with scientific laws. The objectivity of a sense experience means the verifiability of further possible sense experiences which are inferred from this experience in accordance with known scientific laws. In accordance with this criterion we would say that our sense experience of seeing things double when we press our finger on our eyeball is subjective—a mere illusion—because the inferences we make from this sense experience to other possible sense experiences do not hold. When we reach out to touch the two objects which we saw we find only one. There is, then, a rupture in the temporal continuity of our experience.

In accordance with this new criterion for objectivity we must classify mystical experiences as subjective because they represent a break in the temporal continuity of our experience. What we have in the case of mystical experience is a moment of eternity, i.e., phenomenological atemporality, suddenly appearing in the midst of a temporal sequence of events. When the mystic reports that during his experience all change and multiplicity were obliterated, we must, from the naturalistic standpoint, tell him that he was "seeing things." Because we cannot fit the content of mystical experiences into a temporal order with other experiences in accordance with scientific laws, we must call these experiences subjective.

Since Professor Stace defines God or the Eternal ostensively in terms of the content of the mystical experience itself, he is not claiming that a mystical experience is evidence for the existence of some Being or Reality which transcends the experience. By God we mean the mystical experience and *nothing more.* If we accept Professor Stace's ostensive definition of God in terms of the mystical experience itself, and if we grant the fact that there are mystical experiences, then it follows that God, *in his sense,* must exist. All of this is perfectly compatible with our classification of mystical experiences as subjective psychological experiences from the naturalistic standpoint. We cannot add to such psychological facts any existence claim; an existence claim cannot follow either deductively or inductively from a psychological claim. Since mystical experiences do not point beyond themselves to other facts they are irrefutable. We cannot dispute the claim of the mystic because, from the naturalistic standpoint, he is not making an existence claim—he is making only a psychological claim.

Professor Stace argues that each mystic experiences the same reality or Oneness. He states that since the mystic is identical with the One or God during his experience, his experience is identical with all other mystical experiences, whether of himself or of others, and this moment of time is identical with all other moments of time. "And hence there is, from within, no relation at all between one mystical experience and another and therefore no likeness or unlikeness" (p. 84). Professor Stace is writing here from the eternal standpoint; from this standpoint there is no problem of the identity of one mystical experience with another or of one moment of time with another simply because there are no other mystical experiences or moments of time. There is only the undifferentiated unity. But from the naturalistic standpoint it is not true that the moment of one mystical experience is identical with the moment of every other mystical experience. Two or more mystical experiences can be alike as two peas in a pod as far as the phenomenological content of the experiences are concerned, but they can still be distinguished from each other by the experient's position in space and time. The fact that two mystical experiences are phenomenologically identical is no more evidence for the objective existence of the content of these experiences than is the fact that two dreams are phenomenologically identical evidence for the objective existence of the content of the dreams.

What we are left with, then, is an exclusive disjunction between the mystical and naturalistic standpoint. There is no way of getting rid of the contradiction between the claim of the mystic and the naturalist. Such a dispute is not resolvable by any empirical means; for the very criterion for objectivity in terms of temporal continuity is made from the naturalistic standpoint, and so the mystic would accuse us of begging the question from the outset. The question, "Which is the *true* reality, the one revealed to us in mystical experiences or the one revealed to us in our non-mystical experiences?" is really a value question and cannot be settled by any logical means. What a man takes to be the *really* real is a value judgment expressive of what experiences have the greatest significance for him.

Notes

1. I believe that Professor Stace, in accordance with his latest formulation of the empirical theory of meaning, put forth in "Some Misinterpretations of Empiricism" (*Mind*, 1958), would be forced to attribute empirical meaning to mystical propositions. There he states that a word or sentence has empirical meaning if it refers to some specific but unanalyzable experiential datum or if it is amenable to a process of analysis, the end-terms of which will be such experiential data.

2. Paul Henle, in his excellent article, "Mysticism and Semantics" (*Philosophy and Phenomenological Research*, 1949), claims that the mystic is not entitled to claim that his mystical utterances are ineffable in regard to all symbolism, possible as well as actual. In principle we cannot know that any utterance is ineffable in any possible symbol system; for, in order to know that a certain utterance is ineffable, we should have to find a new symbolism for expressing what is now ineffable.

3. In formulating the law of contradiction Aristotle wrote, "The same attribute cannot *at the same time* belong and not belong to the same subject in the same respect" (*Metaphysics*, 1005b, 17).

4. Professor Stace writes: "The Ultimate can be neither self-consistent nor self-contradictory, for both of these are logical categories. It is neither logical nor illogical, but alogical" (p. 153). This is in complete concordance with the conclusion reached in this paper. However, Professor Stace's claim that the Ultimate is alogical is obviously inconsistent with his assertion that there is a logical contradiction between the negative and positive conceptions of the Ultimate or Divine.